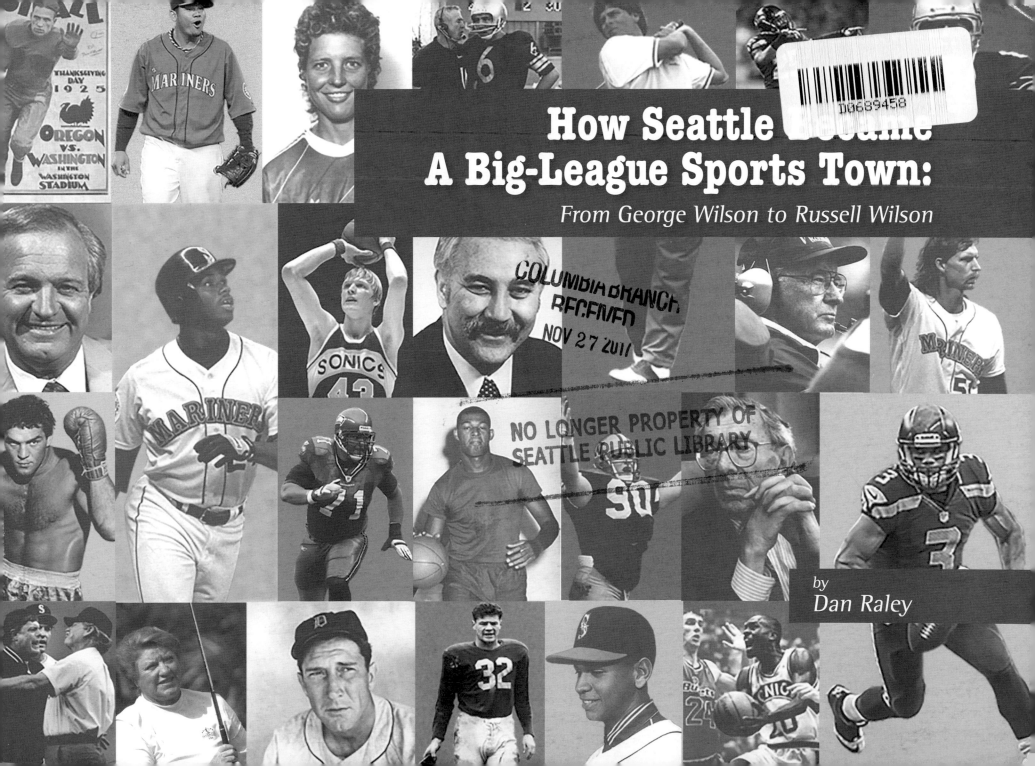

How Seattle Became A Big-League Sports Town:

From George Wilson to Russell Wilson

by
Dan Raley

Publisher & Editor: Jeff Shelley

Book Design & Layout: Anni Shelley

Copy Editor: Nick Rousso

Printed in the United States of America by Consolidated Press (Seattle, WA)

Published by:

Fairgreens Publishing, LLC
Seattle, Washington

For book inquiries, call: 206 522 6981 or 425 830 7670
Email: fairgreens@seanet.com
For more information, visit www.fairgreenspublishing.com.

ISBN: 978-0-578-15905-8

This book is dedicated to the memory
of my late grandfather James Roland Barron.
He introduced me to
University of Washington football.
He gave me total access to Husky Stadium.
He made me a lifelong sports fan.
Thanks for everything, JR.

Table of Contents

Seductive Seventies - A Decade Of Seattle Thrills, Chills And Frills 143

Eighties and Nineties - Temptation And Redemption 207

The New Millennium - Seattle Suffers Before It Turns Super 257

Acknowledgements

Twelve years ago, Jeff Shelley envisioned this book. He called me and said as much, insisting that Seattle's complete sports history needed to be told in an entertaining storytelling fashion - and that I was the guy to do it.

Admittedly, I wasn't always so sure, but Jeff doggedly kept after me. We did another book together and I wrote two others, and Jeff reminded me throughout that this one needed to be done, too. My beloved newspaper, the *Seattle Post-Intelligencer*, ceased operations and I moved to the South to work for the *Atlanta Journal-Constitution*, and even long distance Jeff still talked about this book. I appreciate my friend's vision and persistence.

Then there's Dave Eskenazi. He talked me into writing my first book, *Pitchers of Beer*. He has backed me in every one of my book projects, including this one. Without hesitation, he has generously shared his vast Seattle sporting knowledge and unbelievable vault of local sports photos with me. I would not be an author if not for my friend, Dave.

Behind the scenes is Anni Shelley, Jeff's wife. She greatly impressed me with her organization and design in our previous book collaboration, *Tideflats to Tomorrow: The History of Seattle's SoDo*. She's done it again with this book. She makes my words look good. She makes me look good.

Others who deserve credit for making this book happen are former *Seattle P-I* colleagues Art Thiel, Bill Knight, J Michael Kenyon, Josh Trujillo, David McCumber, Casey McNerthney, Jim Moore and Nick Rousso; friends Greg Fry, Eric Sallee, Dave DePartee, Frank McDonald and the late Bob Houbregs, plus a host of female family members: Nancy, Dani, Kayla and Kathy Jo Raley, and Jenni Creveling. I'd also like to thank the Mariners, Seahawks, University of Washington, Seattle University and Emerald Downs publicity staffs for their help. I'd thank the Sonics if they were still around. ❖

Dan Raley

Foreword

By Art Thiel

If you are a reader who thinks this book requires a minimum age of 50 or so to appreciate it, you are a silly person. Put the book/tablet down and move on.

For those under 30, new to town, don't know many outside your work station and don't quite get why 700,000 people stood in downtown Seattle for hours on a 15-degree day to blow kisses at large men in slow-moving jitneys, this book is for you. That's because in 10 or 15 years, you will become the political, business, social and cultural leaders of this mossy, misty metro, so you better get to know it.

Start here. With this book. It's fun. And wise. It allows you to graduate to the gnarlier matters of civic history, as in how people in Seattle can't get from here to there without at least a brief detour through traffic hell, although the detour more recently has become a destination.

Until the recent magnum success of the Seahawks, the sports profile of Seattle and Washington was mostly wretched. From a standpoint of won-loss records and championships won, that was relatively true. But a look past the bleakness reveals a vivid sports landscape of majestic achievers of national and international renown, hilarious schemes by dubious promoters, and complex men and women who knew success and failure, often several times over.

The cool thing is that the people here are described honestly, independent of the vanity or profit needs of the sports, schools and media outlets who want to make a buck off sanitized versions of our sports heroes.

Dan Raley would have it no other way. He enjoys sports, playing, watching, describing. But he enjoys just a little more the telling of a good, honest story. Those chronicled here have shaped the Seattle sports narrative, mostly for good and some for ill, often with controversy and not a little regret.

To those new to the area or the topic, the real stories will be as surprising as they are compelling, and worthy to know in order to appreciate what is now. Raley has lived among them and searched deep for those who preceded him.

Raley grew up in Seattle with many of the people chronicled here, worked alongside many more as a journalist, and now as a senior eminence, can reflect upon the feats, deeds and missteps of a century with the learned eye of a historian and the compassion of a pal.

Raley and I were around town for the final days of Royal Brougham, the legendary *Seattle Post-Intelligencer* sports editor and columnist, who began his career as a reporter on the combustible Seattle waterfront before World War I (that's one, not two) and died watching the Seahawks in the Kingdome.

Brougham had a pet name for Seattle: "Dad Yesler's little sawmill town." Even Brougham was too young to remember Henry Yesler's wood-products start-up at the city's 1852 founding. But Brougham knew the value of metaphorical connection to the civic roots: You can't know where you are until you know where you've been.

Raley shares Brougham's understanding. Fortunately, he's a helluva lot better writer.

Now, as big data does for the economy and profile what a big saw once did, legions of new workers come from around the world to Amazon, Microsoft and other tech companies to create Seattle's latest boom.

In their spare time, they have become part of the "12s," the seismic disturbers who follow the Seahawks. They make Sounders FC one of the world's most well-supported soccer clubs. They pay for and shake new Husky Stadium, college football's most spectacular place, and celebrate the return to baseball contention of the Seattle Mariners, as well as the return of big-time pro golf with the U.S. Open at Tacoma's Chambers Bay in June 2015.

The newcomers to Seattle sports can now catch up with long-timers in one place. Here. Raley artfully conveys what was, so they can savor what is. ❖

Publisher's Note

You never know about elite athletes. They may have the most talent in the world. But being the humans that they are can quickly be brought to earth.

That can happen because of injury, personal failings, fatal missteps, or by short-sighted team leaders who didn't recognize what they had.

Then there are those otherworldly performers who transcend everything, fully realizing their nonpareil abilities into fame and fortune.

No one knows the vagaries of these people better than Dan Raley, who showed he was an all-star when he worked the *Seattle P-I* sports beat for 30 years.

There is something about his keen eye for research and style, which were allowed to flourish at a newspaper that wisely gave him the column inches necessary to tell a story. I was personally smitten with his "Where Are They Now" installments.

When we became friends back in the last century, I, somewhat offhandedly, said to Dan, "When you want to compile these into a book I'd love to publish it."

So here we are, one of the Emerald City's foremost sportswriters doing what he does best, all in one remarkable compendium. And that's looking deeply into the foibles of Seattle's athletic headliners you've read about for decades.

Seattle is one hell of a sports town. Here is its history by its lead chronicler.

Jeff Shelley

PS: I'd like to thank my wife, Anni, who designed this book. This beautiful woman didn't have an affinity for sports when we first met over 30 years ago. Funny how things have worked out. ❖

Introduction

Seattle christened itself as a big-league town on Oct. 20, 1967, when an announced crowd of 4,473 — fewer than a third of capacity — showed up at the Seattle Center Coliseum for the Seattle SuperSonics' first home game in franchise history. People sat back and watched the local pro team lose 121-114 to the San Diego Rockets in an unappetizing Friday night match-up of National Basketball Association expansion franchises.

There were no headliners on either roster, just recycled players. The game didn't spur a big rush to the ticket window. The occupied seats didn't come close to matching the advertised attendance for the landmark event either. For the sake of first impressions, the meager Coliseum head count was purposely inflated.

"Walter Kennedy, the NBA commissioner, was there and he said, 'I knew this wouldn't work,' " recalled Dick Vertlieb, then a Sonics front-office executive. "There were only 2,800 there and I said to myself, 'We can't have it under 3,000.' I pumped the attendance. It was the first and only time I fibbed."

The big-league beginning for the city was so inauspicious that three enterprising north-end Seattle boys snuck in that night without paying — and I was one of them. Coliseum personnel, dressed in garish burnt-orange jackets, stared straight down and systematically tore tickets apart in a robotic

and detached manner while ushering people through narrow partition openings, providing ample opportunity for my friends, Scott Keeney and Mick Rehn, and I to become sly gate-crashers. We had done this before at Seattle University basketball games in the same arena, giving us a trial run and the courage to try it again. One by one, we shadowed other fans through the different

Seattle P-I writers played against members of the Sonics' 1979 NBA title team in a charity basketball tournament outside the Kingdome: Left to right are Sonics' Joe Haslett, the P-I's Art Thiel, the Sonics' Fred Brown and Jack Sikma, the P-I's Dan Raley and Tim Egan, the Sonics' John Johnson and the P-I's Duff Wilson.

entry points, stepping when they stepped, and hoping the ticket-takers wouldn't look up, or some cop from the upper concourse wouldn't look down, and spot this ruse.

We were aspiring basketball players, Laurelhurst Park Department teammates in fact, and eager to rub up against the real thing. We had our pick of Coliseum seats. We plopped down in some of the most expensive and no one bothered us as we hung out just a few rows from the court. No one sat anywhere around us in the near-empty arena. No one asked to see the ticket stubs we didn't have.

On the house, we soaked up this newfound NBA atmosphere as long as we could, gathering outside the locker rooms after the game and chatting up Super-Sonics and Rockets players alike when they walked out the door freshly showered. On a game program, possibly the only expense for our group on that opening night, I collected autographs from several obscure and accommodating players, among them Al Tucker, Bud Olsen and Henry Finkel. On closer inspection, their basketball profiles weren't nearly enough for me to warrant hanging onto that keepsake souvenir as an adult and I sold it to a Seattle trading card shop. On the premise of full disclosure, we next called my mom to come pick us up in her car.

Sports became my passion because of adventurous nights like this. Sports were a diversion, too, a way for me to cope with the death of both of my parents by the time I was 16. I played every sport I could. I followed every Seattle team religiously. I had great access. For a decade I was given a stadium pass by my grandfather Jim Barron, one of

Husky Stadium's game-day operations supervisors, allowing me to run errands for him and go anywhere on Saturdays. After a UW alumni-varsity spring game, for example, I stood mesmerized next to Ben Davidson in the locker room as part of an attentive group that listened to his nonstop wisecracks while this giant and popular TV pitch man pulled off his football armor.

It wasn't all that surprising then that I became a *Seattle Post-Intelligencer* sportswriter for three decades. I was able to interact with nearly every one of Seattle's sporting legends and rebels in some manner. On the job for the *P-I*, I hung out with Hugh McElhenny alongside his backyard pool in suburban Las Vegas while he chain-smoked and I listened to him come clean about the free stuff he had received as a University of Washington football player. In the same Nevada city, I sat in the living room of a cancer-weakened Vertlieb, even as death was certain, and heard the former Sonics and Mariners executive tell of his front-office shenanigans. I also admitted to Vertlieb that I owed him the price of an opening-night Sonics ticket.

I sat in Elgin Baylor's Los Angeles Clippers office at the Staples Center for a couple of hours and replayed his Seattle University basketball career with him, more than four decades after I approached Baylor as a shy 12-year-old for an autograph, with my mother in tow, at a near-empty Osborn and Ulland sporting goods store in downtown Seattle. Ken Griffey Jr. usually ran from me in the clubhouse when I wanted him to answer a Mariners-related question, but he swung a bat over my head and generally wouldn't leave me alone when I tried to ignore him.

I went to Roosevelt High School with a couple of UW football coach Jim Owens' daughters. I met Max Soriano, the former Pilots' owner, more than three decades after I played high school baseball with his son, Larry. I laced

Don James addresses, from left, reporters Don Borst of the Morning News Tribune, Dick Rockne of the Seattle Times, Gary Larson of the Everett Herald and Dan Raley of the Seattle Post-Intelligencer.

up as a prep basketball player alongside future NBA player James Edwards, later reminding him where I fit in among his most memorable teammates: Michael Jordan, Kareem Abdul-Jabbar, Isiah Thomas and me.

I twice played in pickup basketball games with "Downtown" Freddie Brown, for charity at the Kingdome and for fun at Oregon's McArthur Court, and I took part in that same charity game and a round of golf with former Sonics center Jack Sikma. I got to know former Sonics forward Spencer Haywood as a scholarly looking and relaxed middle-age man rather than that flashy and sometimes self-centered young player. As a young Alaska sports editor, I was asked to interview a Seahawks wide receiver named Steve Largent, who at the time was an NFL unknown and centerpiece of an off-season publicity tour. I caught up with him 25 years later in Tulsa when Largent made an unsuccessful run for Oklahoma governor.

I drove through the streets of Shreveport, La., with Don James as a passenger in my tiny rental car after

the legendary UW football coach was left behind at a local high school and an Independence Bowl practice; sadly, I attended his memorial service, too. My kidneys were jumbled after bouncing around in a beat-up sports utility vehicle when Huskies All-America defensive tackle Steve Emtman took me on an impromptu tour of his 2,000-acre family farm in Cheney.

I was giving down-and-out former UW football player Spider Gaines a ride when he impulsively asked me to pull over and buy him a six-pack of beer, which I regrettably did; years later, I picked him up from a seedy-looking drug and alcohol rehabilitation center in the shadows of Seattle-Tacoma International Airport. I sat opposite former UW running back Donnie Moore and watched him cry for two days at a Riverside, Calif., hotel as he recited an overly promising college football career needlessly sacrificed.

In his living room with a Mariners game blaring, I listened to former UW football player George Jugum tell me how he had killed a teenager decades earlier, not feeling any remorse coming from him. I sat in a bar and had beers a couple of times with former Huskies quarterback Sonny Sixkiller, someone I considered my ultimate sports idol as a kid, though I didn't burden him with that revelation until much later.

I let Herman Sarkowsky, the former Seahawks owner, take me to lunch at the Rainier Club and I watched other people fawn all over one of Seattle's richest men. I sat and made peace with golfer Fred Couples in the Augusta National clubhouse in Georgia at his invitation two years before he won the Masters and a couple of years after I had made him angry with a harsh story detailing his then-puckish behavior. Johnny O'Brien, former Seattle U All-America basketball player, big-league ballplayer and Kingdome administrator, sat me down on his front porch and generously talked to me for hours about his and his twin brother's athletic careers.

On the night the Sonics won the 1979 NBA championship on the East Coast, I hung from a lamp post outside the J&M Cafe in Seattle's Pioneer Square and raised a celebratory glass or two of beer inside with a couple of friends. I was a *P-I* sportswriter who worked the 1992 Rose Bowl that capped the UW's national championship run on a gloriously sunny day in Pasadena. Fourteen years later, I was elbow to elbow with hundreds of reporters covering the Seahawks' 2006 Super Bowl XL in snow-covered Detroit. My newspaper ceased operations and I was out of the business by the time the Seahawks won Super Bowl XLVIII in 2014.

I can tell you that the city has a sporting past that stretches more than 12 decades, and that some of it is glorious, some not so much, but it is one well worth preserving. Seattle collectively has trotted out teams at the highest pro levels for nearly a half-century now, and I've been lucky enough to witness it all. On the following pages are dozens of selected people — either imported or exported — who are the city's most successful, influential, entertaining or controversial sports figures.

Amateur or pro, good or bad, demonstrating unblemished complexions or saddled with hideous warts, they form a comprehensive timeline: They've made Seattle a big-league town. ❖

Dan Raley

Bob Houbregs and Mike McCutchen, starters from the UW's 1953 Final Four team, share a moment with Dan Raley at Alaska Airlines Arena.

Roaring Twenties to World War II

Seattle suffers as much as anyone through the Great Depression, hosting one of the country's bigger "Hooverville" encampments along the waterfront, yet establishes itself as a trusted aiplane-maker on a large scale during World War II, producing 12,000 B-17 bombers.

Likewise, the city experiences great sporting growing pains, building Husky Stadium for football in 1920 and Clarence "Hec" Edmundson Pavilion for basketball in 1927 while watching Dugdale Park, its baseball fortress, burn to the ground in 1932.

GEORGE WILSON

Seattle's First Superstar

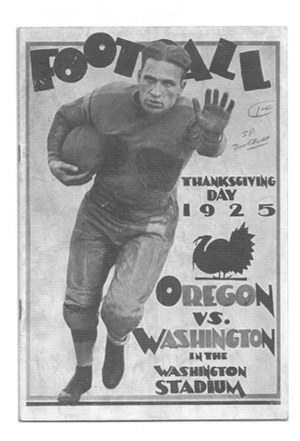

George Wilson slammed into Red Grange, pro football's first great player, rocked him backward and left the man called "the Galloping Ghost" crumpled on the ground, sending 70,000 wildly entertained fans into a frenzy at Los Angeles Memorial Coliseum.

A former University of Washington football player, Wilson was a noted tough guy who lost his leather helmet during this fierce collision. Even without his protective headgear, he was still lurching toward Grange with a crazed look, his rigid body language suggesting he couldn't wait to deliver another unsettling blow.

In a hastily arranged American Football League game on Jan. 16, 1926 — one showcasing these running backs as ticket-selling headliners and treated like an early-day Super Bowl — Wilson, in the ruddy blue and gray colors of the Los Angeles Tigers, outplayed if not manhandled Grange, who was wearing a chocolate-brown Chicago Bears uniform.

Wilson was coming off a Rose Bowl appearance against Alabama two weeks earlier and had moved across town in California's largest city to this more raucous football setting. He had stepped into a far bigger media spotlight. He was surrounded by twice as many fans. He didn't disappoint any of them either. After all, he had turned a legend into a rag doll in an instant.

With moments such as these — and the crushing hit on Grange was photographed and reprinted on a program cover for a future barnstorming game — Wilson established himself as Seattle's first athletic superstar of any kind. He was the city's first college All-America selection and its original National Football League player. For turning into a Roaring 20s sensation, the rugged Huskies halfback also represented a true sporting milestone for his college town: Wilson was the definitive starting point for Seattle's serious-minded athletic history — no apologies to unbeaten UW football coach Gil Dobie (58-0-3 in 1908-16) or the 1917 Stanley Cup-champion Seattle Metropolitans hockey team, with each winning in relative obscurity — because Wilson gave his isolated Puget Sound seaport its first real taste of the national spotlight.

> Wilson established himself as Seattle's first athletic superstar of any kind. He was the city's first college All-America selection and its original National Football League player.

Born in rural Arkansas and raised in Washington, Wilson was a gifted yet crude and complicated man. He led his Everett High School teams to a 24-0-2 record, which included victories in schoolboy national championship games over teams from Salt Lake City and Cleveland. Wilson and his brother Abe moved from Everett to the UW, sharing in powerhouse teams at each level. George carried the Huskies to their first Rose Bowl in 1924, a 14-14 tie against Navy, and that aforementioned Pasadena match-up against Alabama, a difficult 20-19 defeat.

The son of a saw filer who worked in different Snohomish County mills, Wilson was boisterous and extroverted, and he answered to a host of nicknames, one of which was the "Bone-crusher," yet another "the Purple Tornado" from his college days, and later "Wildcat" as a pro football player.

"He was a real extrovert, very outgoing kind of guy and loud," nephew Don Wilson said. "He was a really big guy and I was awed."

There was an unrefined side to him, as well. The sexually promiscuous Wilson contracted syphilis while in Alaska working a summer cannery job, according to his relatives. He was left with an illness that so poisoned him as a college senior he repeatedly was forced to run under whatever football grandstands were nearby that season and vomit violently.

Wilson, who lived at 4710 University Way N.E. while in college, was a compact 5-foot-10, 185-pound package of full-fledged football fury. In 1925, he went airborne and knocked Stanford halfback Ernie Nevers unconscious with a piercing fourth-and-two tackle on the Huskies 18-yard line, preserving a 13-7 victory in Seattle.

His reputation was further enhanced in the Rose Bowl against Alabama when he rushed for 134 yards on 15 carries while running mostly off tackle, and he threw two touchdowns passes, all while missing the third quarter after taking a jolting hit combined with the reported lingering aftereffects of pneumonia, which might have been a concocted explanation for his syphilis.

"George was a football machine," said Harold Paton, a fellow UW running back, shortly before his 1991 car-accident death in Wenatchee. "He played every second of it as hard as he could. I admired his stiff arm as much as anything else."

Yet in the worst way, Wilson tried to resist the second Rose Bowl appearance. He was anxious to move on and turn pro, and he led a Huskies' vote against playing Alabama. Everyone ultimately took the long train ride down the coast to Los Angeles, but not until school officials supposedly promised several players a monetary incentive.

Ten years after losing to the Crimson Tide, Wilson told an *Oakland Tribune* writer that the UW offered him $10,500 to play in the Rose Bowl, a counter-proposal to the $3,500 per game he was promised if he immediately appeared in three pro outings against Grange at the end of the college regular season.

"Officials of the university approached me and assured me that if I would forget the professional offer, they would take care of me with an agreed sum from the gate receipts," Wilson said. "I never got it, but it was my own fault. I have learned since I should have collected first and played afterward."

For this confessional, he was castigated publicly by the Seattle press corps, UW officials and former teammates. He told family members that he and several Huskies had received $150 each from pro sports agent C.C. Pyle in exchange for a firm guarantee that everyone would play in the Rose Bowl.

Seattle Post-Intelligencer columnist Royal Brougham couldn't hold back his disdain for Wilson because of the bartering involved. "The most popular athlete of his generation, he threw away his brilliant opportunities and, against the advice of his friends, became a tramp athlete," Brougham wrote.

George Wilson wrestled following his football career.

Pyle, who founded the short-lived AFL in 1926 to run counter to the newly-created NFL, had pressing marketing concerns. After first trying to get Wilson to skip the bowl game, the promoter concluded it was more beneficial to have the UW player go up against Alabama and properly display his talents for the series of exhibitions against Grange.

Two days following the Rose Bowl, Wilson signed a contract that paid him $5,000 per game to appear in pro football exhibitions in Los Angeles and San Francisco. The instant cash was welcome, but he expressed another reason for playing in those contests. "No, I don't need the money badly," Wilson told the *Los Angeles Times*. "I turned professional in order to meet Grange on the gridiron."

Before the largest crowd to watch a sporting event at the L.A. Coliseum to that point, Wilson's Tigers were beaten 17-7. Grange outscored him two touchdowns to one, but the former UW player nearly doubled Grange's rushing yardage total, 137-75, besides pulling the fans out of their seats with his vicious kickoff tackle. A headline in the *L.A. Times* concluded this much: "Grange outshone by Wilson."

Exhibition games were arranged in Portland and Seattle and Wilson received $1,000 paydays in the smaller markets. The running back next spent a full season with the newly-created Los Angeles Wildcats, a barnstorming team that played only on the road.

While coming and going from California, Wilson appeared in the film "One Minute to Play," which featured Grange, but the former UW player was discouraged from pursuing an acting career. His snarly appearance was deemed unfit for the camera. "He had a screen test and evidently Uncle George didn't photograph well for them," said George Keplinger, another nephew.

> "Ever since my father gave me a football for a Christmas present and someone yelled 'down,' which caused my falling on the gift and blasting it, I have packed a football under my arm."

Wilson spent three seasons with the Providence Steam Roller and won an NFL championship in 1928. While on the East Coast, the running back felt the need to explain his pro football ambitions to the UW fans back home.

"I have been asked by many people why I am playing professional football and I can best answer that query by telling them what my ambition has been since I wore rompers and believed in Santa Claus," Wilson wrote in the UW's *Columns* magazine. "Ever since my father gave me a football for a Christmas present and someone yelled 'down,' which caused my falling on the gift and blasting it, I have packed a football under my arm."

The Great Depression curtailed Wilson's football ambitions. Once the financial markets crashed in 1929 there wasn't enough money in the pro game to keep him on the field; he had received perhaps $125 per game with Providence. He turned to the more lucrative pro-wrestling circuit and went on European and Australian tours until that money dried up, too.

Wilson was married for three years to Kathreen Flyzik, an Everett woman and fellow UW student who accused him of cruelty and a failure to support her, and she eventually sought a divorce.

Using his fame as leverage, Wilson always had some get-rich scheme in mind, whether it was holding shares of mining stock in Montana or coming up with a plan to farm oysters in San Francisco. He worked as an oil rigger in Texas before he settled in as a Bay Area longshoreman.

Wilson spent his final years living alone in a hotel at 640 Eddy St. in San Francisco, surrendering to a seedy existence in the city's red-light district. He was a lonely old man no longer athletic or intimidating, rather a heavy drinker and smoker, when his unhealthy lifestyle caught up with him.

On Dec. 27, 1963, Wilson was found dead on the waterfront. He had suffered a massive heart attack and collapsed while measuring cargo alone on San Francisco's Pier 15 for the State Steamship Company. He was 62.

Wilson died just days before he was to drive to Pasadena for the upcoming Rose Bowl game between Washington and Illinois, Red Grange's school. The old halfbacks would have been reunited once more. But like a lot of things in Wilson's world, it didn't happen. Glory was fleeting for Seattle's first superstar.

"I think he had so much adulation put on him for so long it didn't do him a lot of good," said Keplinger, his nephew. "Uncle George had a lot of possibilities that were never fulfilled." ❖

On one side of the quarter-inch-thick 1932 Olympic gold medal was the daunting image of a young woman dressed in robes, holding up a crown of olive branches with her left hand. She hovered above an ancient sporting arena, forever frozen in a triumphant pose. Helene Madison emerged from the Los Angeles Games that summer with three of these precious medallions dangling around her neck. Upon closer inspection, it wouldn't have been farfetched at all to suggest that the metallic heroine was Madison.

Fame came suddenly to the 19-year-old swimmer, branding her as Seattle's first female sports superstar and its first athlete — man or woman — to command international attention and emerge as a world champion. If only briefly, she was an American sporting institution. Unfortunately, she wasn't all that different from Seattle's original sports headliner, George Wilson, gaining widespread acclaim in a hurry yet flaming out just as quickly.

Madison was a tall and sleek water-bound wonder from Lincoln High School who, over three years, broke 117 U.S. or world records, at one point holding top times in 16 different events from 100 yards to 1,600 meters. She first drew attention to herself in Los Angeles in January 1930 by beating world-record holder Josephine McKimm in her first high-profile race. Two months later, Madison won eight races and set as many world records in Miami at the AAU women's swimming championships. With her trips paid by the Washington Athletic Club, she established world records in 14 consecutive races.

In 1931, Madison, 18, was chosen as the first *Associated Press* Female Athlete of the Year, opposite the male winner, Major League Baseball player Pepper Martin. She next put a global spotlight on Seattle that wasn't there before.

HELENE MADISON

Sister To The Fish

At the L.A. Games, the 5-foot-10, 150-pound Madison continually took bows on a big stage, first dazzling everyone with an Olympic-record victory in the 100-meter freestyle and supplying Seattle with its first gold medalist. With her long, almost violent strokes, she swam the event in 1 minute, 8.8 seconds — five seconds faster than the previous record. She finished four feet ahead of her nearest competitor. She was still two-tenths of a second shy of her own world record.

Legendary sportswriter Damon Runyon was so impressed by Madison's commanding opening performance, the journalist described the Seattle swimmer in an Olympics dispatch as the "sister to the fish." Madison anchored a winning U.S. 400-meter relay effort for a second gold medal. She completed her Olympic triple crown with more gold and a world record in the 400-meter freestyle, rushing through the water

She wasn't all that different from Seattle's original sports headliner, George Wilson, gaining widespread acclaim in a hurry yet flaming out just as quickly.

in 5:28.5 to beat Lenore Kight of Homestead, Pa. The attention showered on Madison multiplied with each victory lap. "She breaks a world record as you would break an egg," *New York Journal* editor Arthur Brisbane wrote.

Swimming in the Great Depression, Madison was out to distance herself from poverty surroundings. She was treated to a fancy dinner in Los Angeles by Brisbane, who was anxious to meet this new American sporting darling. After claiming her third gold medal, Madison was taken to the Coconut Grove nightclub, where she danced with actor Clark Gable. She was the luncheon guest for a dozen Fox Studio executives, all eager to exploit her newfound fame.

After impulsively agreeing to appear in a Mack Sennett-directed Hollywood film titled "Help, Help Helene," and thus forfeiting her amateur standing — a career move that would haunt her — Madison was accompanied, if not chaperoned, by *Seattle Post-Intelligencer* sports editor Royal Brougham for a weekend of mingling with

celebrities at the Hearst Castle in San Simeon, Calif. She played tennis and gave everyone a close-up look at her powerful swimming strokes in the ornate estate's Grecian outdoor pool.

"Something drove me," Madison told the *Post-Intelligencer*. "I came up from Bagley Grade School and Lincoln High School and Seattle a nobody. And I always had a feeling that everybody I raced against was trying to make me a nobody again. Maybe that's why I never lost a race — I was always afraid that I would."

Once back in Seattle, Madison stepped off a United Airlines prop plane at Boeing Field and was met by 4,000 fans. She received the keys to a new car, a Buick. Beginning at Yesler Way, she was escorted up 2nd Avenue for a downtown tickertape parade, traveling through an adoring human gauntlet estimated at 200,000. People screamed, police sirens wailed and planes flew low overhead. The *Post-Intelligencer* described the scene as the "greatest homecoming since the World War boys came back in 1919."

Madison was rushed to a banquet dinner attended by 1,000 dignitaries. Reaching her parents' Green Lake home at 1132 N. 76th St. late that night, she encountered still another 5,000 people waiting outside to catch a glimpse of her.

Yet all of this attention disappeared overnight. Her film debut, largely a swimming exercise, was a bust. She could no longer swim competitively because of her cinematic contract. After abandoning her athletic career for those anticipated but elusive riches, she was

left to sell hotdogs at a Green Lake concession stand in the middle of the city while the 1936 Olympics played out in Germany. While handing over the confectionary treats, the once-unbeatable swimmer muttered out loud that she should have been basking in the European spotlight.

Madison failed at acting, nightclub singing and a series of jobs. She failed at marriage three times. She had a daughter and they never got along. She failed at being anyone other than a teenager repeatedly winning swimming races. Life soon became as unbearable for her as it once was intoxicating and exciting.

> Madison failed at acting, nightclub singing and a series of jobs. She failed at marriage three times. She had a daughter and they never got along. She failed at being anyone other than a teenager repeatedly winning swimming races.

She grew bitter and sat alone in her modest Green Lake basement apartment at 6612 Sunnyside Ave. N., just her, a Siamese cat and a parakeet, staring at her room filled with 87 medals, trophies and other gilded remembrances. She fell from the limelight to obscurity.

Madison wasn't forgotten by her hometown; it just felt that way in her staid adult existence. Swimming

Top 10 Seattle Olympians

1. Helene Madison, swimming
   (3 gold)

2. Apollo Ohno, speed skating
   (2 gold, 2 silver, 4 bronze)

3. Charlie Greene, track
   (gold, silver)

4. 1936 UW eight-man crew, rowing (gold)

5. Jack Medica, swimming
   (gold, 2 silver)

6. Anna Mickelson, rowing
   (gold, silver)

7. Ralph Bishop, basketball
   (gold)

8. Debbie Armstrong, skiing
   (gold)

9. Michelle Akers, soccer
   (gold)

10. Bill Buchan, sailing
    (gold)

pools at the Washington Athletic Club and in north Seattle were named in her honor and she was inducted into the International Swimming Hall of Fame.

Yet once reaching middle age, Madison was a sullen, chain-smoking nurse working at the Seattle Convalescent Center, no longer a picture of Olympic fitness and glory. Soon she needed her own around-the-clock medical care. Terminal cancer ravaged her throat, diabetes took its toll and depression set in. She was so beaten down she openly contemplated suicide.

Brougham, one of her few close friends and her former Hearst Castle envoy, was asked to intercede. He encouraged Madison to find a finishing kick. The journalist made her situation as public as he could with a front-page newspaper story that detailed her harsh fall from grace.

In 1968, Brougham passionately wrote what was described back in his office as "the $10,000 column."

His account of Madison's failing health, dwindling money and spiraling attitude was so vivid that letters of concern with donations attached came rushing in. This was enough to ease the pain, to convince the swimmer to let nature take its course and get her needed medical attention.

Madison was so touched by this round of public affection she bounced back from her depressive depths. She had surgery at Virginia Mason Hospital and lived another two years in relative peace. Cancer claimed her on Nov. 27, 1970. She was 57.

Well after she was gone, one of Madison's Olympic gold medals was acquired by David Eskenazi, a Seattle man who kept this ancient treasure safely locked away with his other valuables. He didn't mind getting it out and showing it off to an interested guest. He knew that Madison was once every bit as impressive as that finely encrypted gold medallion. ❖

ROYAL BROUGHAM

Seattle's Media Giant

Royal Brougham was the Seattle newspaper story that wouldn't end. He was 84 and still working. He was tireless and still typing. Retirement was never a remote consideration. His pension would go untouched.

The seven-decade career as the *Seattle Post-Intelligencer* sports columnist, one-time sports editor and iconic civic figure didn't conclude until he wandered through the Kingdome press box, nibbling on free food while chatting up colleagues during the second half of a Seattle-Denver NFL game and suddenly collapsed from a heart attack on Oct. 29, 1978.

Felled was a man who made it his calling to become close friends with the nation's most visible sports personalities, promote his hometown at every turn and serve as a human welcome mat. Even as the life drained out of him at the Kingdome, as his heartbeats became numbered, Brougham was rearranging his social calendar. While gently lifted onto a stretcher, he fretted that a friend, a dinner date, would be stood up, waiting for him after the game. He asked then-*Post-Intelligencer* sports editor John Owen to find this person and pass along his regrets.

On a plunging ride to a waiting Medic I ambulance unit on the ground level, though in grave condition, though with matters far more pressing, Brougham tugged on the elevator operator's pant leg. It was one last question from someone who had asked a million of them: "What's the score?"

Eight hours later, Brougham was pronounced dead at Swedish Hospital. Gone was Seattle's most influential sports journalist, though at times he was far more carnival barker and circus ringleader than hardened newsman. Gone was a man who came into full media power in the 1930s, developing a carefully cultivated profile while crisscrossing the country in search of stories when transportation was limited and pedestrian. Brougham preceded and outdistanced Georg N. Meyers of the *Seattle Times*, Emmett Watson of the *P-I* and *Times*, Owen of the *P-I*, and, in more modern times, the *P-I's* Art Thiel and the *Times'* Steve Kelley, all attention-getting columnists with wide followings, in terms of holding public sway.

Attending the biggest sporting events of his day, Brougham befriended such legendary athletes as Babe Ruth, Jack Dempsey, Jesse Owens and Babe Didrikson Zaharias, enticing each icon to come to the Northwest and attend his various charity functions.

President Franklin Roosevelt invited Brougham to dinner, not at the White House, but at his private home in Hyde Park, N.Y. Brougham reciprocated by taking Roosevelt's third son, John, to the 1935 Max Baer-James Braddock heavyweight fight that he covered in New York.

At the 1936 Summer Olympics in Germany, Brougham boldly approached a heavily guarded

> Gone was Seattle's most influential sports journalist, though at times he was far more carnival barker and circus ringleader than hardened newsman.

Adolf Hitler, a move that easily could have gotten him shot or imprisoned but simply resulted in him being turned away. Evangelist Billy Graham always called on Brougham whenever he was in Seattle. William Randolph Hearst made Brougham a regular guest at the Hearst Castle.

Brougham was short, absentminded and impulsive, but people were naturally drawn to him, if not amused by his antics. "He was such a jolly little elf, you had a hard time not liking him," said former ABC sports broadcaster Keith Jackson, who began his TV career in Seattle and considered Brougham a mentor.

Brougham didn't drink alcohol, unusual for the fast company he kept, Babe Ruth in particular. He remembered faces but rarely names, calling most people "fellah" or "girlie." He drove like a mad man, often pointing his Cadillac in the wrong direction down Seattle's one-way streets and collecting his fair share of dents and scratches. "He was Mr. Magoo," granddaughter Cathi Soriano said, comparing him to a cartoon character. His desk was always full of crumpled-up, uncashed paychecks. His generosity was widespread and secretive.

"I was still hearing stories, 25 years after his death, about guys he helped on the QT over the decades," said J Michael Kenyon, former *P-I* sportswriter and one of Royal's beneficiaries. "It must be a phenomenal number, and included a great many near-hoodlums and gangsters, Brougham always seeming to have a special place in his heart for ruffians. If someone were to tell me he'd given away tens of thousands, in the manner of a few hundred here, a few hundred there, a thousand here, I wouldn't be surprised."

In 1910, Brougham was this waifish teen, recently fired for now unknown reasons by the Fuzzy Wuzzy Rug Company, when he frantically ran through Seattle's downtown

Royal Brougham was friends with boxer Jack Dempsey.

streets and dodged the maze of streetcars, unwilling to wait for one to take him to his next destination.

He had spied a *Post-Intelligencer* advertisement seeking a copy aide, in a sense an errand boy who was eager to please, which was a job description that fit him perfectly. Brougham was in such a hurry to reach the newspaper offices he didn't notice the line in the want ad that said don't apply until 2 p.m. It was his fate and good fortune.

He was just 16 and ready to abandon his classes at Franklin High School, and his eagerness was rewarded.

He was hired by the newspaper before the other candidates had a chance, setting in motion a 68-year journalism career that turned him into a tireless caretaker of all things Seattle.

Brougham stuck his nose in everything, to the point that Seattle Pacific College named its basketball gymnasium after him. He always used his column, of which he wrote an estimated 12,000, to advance the fortunes of his hometown, especially its athletic teams.

To honor the city's sports heroes, he organized his own sports banquet in 1938 that remains active today. He created Little League baseball in Seattle. He established Golden Gloves boxing in the city. He pushed hard for pro sports teams and a domed stadium to house them. He even arranged for the Harlem Globetrotters to play Seattle University's basketball team at the University of Washington, publicizing the 1952 exhibition game well in advance of asking the latter school for permission.

"He has done more good than any other in the sporting fraternity, and I say that from the bottom of my heart," Dempsey said at a 1946 dinner honoring Brougham.

The great Ruth visited Seattle on three separate occasions for fundraising activities, all at Brougham's invitation on behalf of the *Post-Intelligencer*. Proof of their friendship was preserved in photos and correspondence connecting the two men, including a letter kept safely locked away by Cathi Soriano. It was postmarked April 27, 1944, four years before the slugger's death.

In it, the Bambino extolled Brougham's concentrated efforts to collect $150,000 to purchase athletic equipment for military base use during World War II, to encourage the troops during those unsettling times. Ruth's unsolicited message was as follows:

Dear Royal,

Several of the New York baseball writers have told me about what you are doing for the boys in uniform. I've been around these camps a lot and know that baseball and other sports mean a lot to them and I want to congratulate you on your campaign. Incidentally, I often think of the wonderful time I had in Seattle with you, years ago, when we had that record-breaking crowd at your ballpark one Sunday afternoon. I don't think there is a city in the United States with a greater bunch of baseball fans than Seattle — and I know they're helping you send those balls and bats and gloves to the boys.

With old-time regards I am sincerely yours,
Babe Ruth

Brougham was never shy when he had something to say. He used his written word to personally challenge the Secretary of the Interior over the neglect of Mount Rainier, Cleveland Indians executives who pondered whether to move their baseball team to Seattle and black activist Harry Edwards when he called for a boycott of UW athletic teams in response to the school's questionable racial practices. Further showing his altruistic side, Brougham publicly gave away most of a $300,000 windfall he inherited from former *P-I* sports editor Portus Baxter.

He was funny and impulsive. He spotted me at a boys' basketball state tournament game in Everett, a college student wearing a ridiculous maroon blazer that said *Skagit Valley Herald* on it, and he remarked how his paper had never given him a coat like that. He was either envious or devious, but it was hard to tell.

Brougham kept working, even as he lost his bearings: At the 1978 Rose Bowl, 10 months before he died, he climbed onto the wrong bus and rode some 30 miles out of his way, forcing his colleagues in Seattle to frantically search for him. To the end, he often wrote his column at his Magnolia home at 2633 42nd Ave. W. and had a cab deliver the hard copy to the *P-I*.

He lived long enough to see his city receive and operate pro franchises in each of the three major sports, with these teams alternately playing their games in the pro stadium he had long championed, though the Kingdome was eventually torn down and replaced by Safeco Field and Century Link Field more than two decades after he was gone.

Brougham still turned up in the middle of Seattle's frantic modern-day athletic activity: The street that traverses between the new sporting palaces, formerly South Connecticut, was renamed in his honor, Royal Brougham Way. He would have approved of this gesture. He liked being in the middle of the action.

A few weeks before his 1978 death, Brougham was paid tribute at a Washington Athletic Club banquet in his honor. At the outset of the festivities, several telegrams were read praising the columnist's long newspaper career.

Only a few snickering colleagues back at the *Post-Intelligencer* knew that these salutations were written by the man himself in the office earlier that day and sent over to Western Union. The resourceful Brougham made sure he was properly lionized, playing up his role as the city's unmatched sports promoter all the way to the end. ❖

Top 10 Seattle Columnists

1. Royal Brougham, P-I
2. Georg N. Meyers, Times
3. Art Thiel, P-I
4. John Owen, P-I
5. Emmett Watson, P-I, Times
6. Steve Kelley, Times
7. George Varnell, Times
8. Steve Rudman, P-I
9. John McGrath, Tribune
10. Jim Moore, P-I

Don Hume's life was filled with mystery. Disappearing for months on end, he often didn't tell anyone where he was until well after the fact. To contact him, you had to send a message a month in advance. His address sometimes was nothing more than a Seattle-area mail drop. Home to Hume was a world with no bounds: He counted Russia, Chile, Tibet, Borneo and Japan among his many faraway destinations – and Germany.

Never married, Hume regularly turned up for University of Washington rowing reunions, sometimes clutching a bottle of champagne in each hand, and for holiday gatherings at his brother Dale's home, armed with exotic trinkets to give to his three nephews. But everything else about his itinerary was the great unknown.

"We used to kid in our family that he might have been in the CIA," said Tim Hume, one of those nephews.

Hume was no covert spy. He worked in oil and gas exploration for long periods in fairly obscure locations globally. His previous life, however, was easily explained. He was one of Seattle's greatest oarsmen, more importantly the difference between victory and defeat in what turned into a coming-of-age achievement for the city early in its sporting history – the UW crew's resounding gold-medal conquest in the 1936 Berlin Olympics before Der Fuhrer himself, Adolf Hitler.

It was such a watershed moment that six and a half decades later the *Seattle Post-Intelligencer* determined the outcome was the city's sporting event of the century, even greater than the Sonics' 1979 NBA title or the Huskies' 1992 football national co-championship. A bestselling book by Daniel James Brown, *The Boys in the Boat*, came next in 2013 to detail this unique story, with a Hollywood film involving Kenneth Branagh not far behind.

Leave it to Hume to have his whereabouts in doubt on Germany's choppy Lake Grunau, too. On Aug. 14,

DON HUME

Captain Of The Ship

1936, under dark and gloomy skies with a vicious crosswind making conditions extra challenging, the UW boat was the last to leave the starting line from the outermost lane six, unable to properly decipher the French command given by a Belgian official. Hume and the others, rowing in the wooden Husky Clipper, fell so far behind that a medal of any kind initially seemed hopeless.

He was one of Seattle's greatest oarsmen, more importantly the difference between victory and defeat in what turned into a coming-of-age achievement for the city early in its sporting history – the UW crew's resounding gold-medal conquest in the 1936 Berlin Olympics before Der Fuhrer himself, Adolf Hitler.

Don Hume, second from left, and his UW rowers were 1936 Olympic gold-medal winners in Germany.

Hume was sick to the point he was bed-ridden much of his time in Europe, able to do little more than loosen up between races. He was nearly replaced as the pace-setting stroke, though UW coach Al Ulbrickson Sr. was quick to tell reporters that the Huskies couldn't win without him. Hume had a chest cold that turned into walking pneumonia. Normally a robust 172 pounds, he lost 14 of them while dealing with his month-long illness. Worse yet, Hume was accused by coxswain Bob Moch of momentarily passing out during the 2,000-meter Olympics finals — something he vigorously denied to the day he died.

With the race at a critical stage, Moch claimed he repeatedly asked Hume to increase the stroke rate from the normal 35, but he received no response whatsoever, even with his megaphone a foot away from the stroke. Moch was so concerned by this he considered desperate means midstream: He was seconds away from turning the boat over to No. 7 oarsman Joe Rantz.

"Don had absolutely no expression on his face," Moch said. "His eyes were closed. His jaw was open and slack. I was yelling at him every five or six yards to get the stroke up. I don't think he heard me. I think he was just rowing on instinct. I don't think he was there."

Rantz, the emergency alternative, confirmed as much about the Hume disconnect, saying, "Everybody in our boat knew Don was in trouble. He was so weak he just didn't understand. He was dazed, like he had been hit over the head."

Hume offered a far different take on this precarious situation, suggesting he was lucid all along and

Adolf Hiter presides over the Olympic rowing finals.

only lost in a competitive zone. He insisted that Moch had come up with a story that was only embellished thereafter. At a UW rowing reunion decades later, Hume even wisecracked that he couldn't possibly have his photo taken with Moch and the others at that moment because he was about to pass out.

"There was a piece of tape in the boat and I always looked at it and concentrated on it," Hume said, explaining his limited response to the coxswain. "The story gets more and more exaggerated as the years go on."

Regardless, Hume responded and the Huskies received an immediate surge of power when they needed it most, raising their stroke rate to 40, matching their highest level in practice. With 200 meters remaining, they pushed it to a near-breaking-point 44 and heroically shot past everyone at the end, beating the Italians by eight feet and leaving the

Hume and his UW teammates, in the top boat, closed fast to win a gold medal.

Germans in third place. Hume collapsed in the shell as it made its way to shore, as did No. 3 rower Gordon Adam, who also was ill. All of the UW rowers were so spent they couldn't get out of their seats right away.

"Hume surfaced," said Jim McMillin, the No. 5 oarsman. "He looked at me and said, 'I was not out of it, I didn't pass out.' He's going to deny it no matter what. He came to, and when he came to, we just flew."

The Huskies had zipped past a floating grandstand, one so close the rowers felt they could practically reach out and touch the Germans hanging over the edge. It was deafeningly loud, with fans chanting "Deutsch" and "Land" as German oars lifted in and out of the water, requiring Moch to rattle dowels on the side of the shell to communicate with his oarsmen at the end. Adrenaline was on overdrive for everyone.

UW rowers had craned their necks to see Hitler during opening ceremonies, though they were unwilling to stand at attention in his presence. The German leader watched the race from the boathouse balcony, turning away in disgust when the Huskies won. Hitler had a brief exchange with his Seattle visitors at dock-side, but only to fulfill ceremonial requirements and nothing more.

"He came down and presented us with a large olive wreath, and we all got individual ones, too," McMillin said. "As I remember, he wasn't too happy about giving it to us. We weren't the 'master race.' "

Morris said this of his glimpse of Hitler, "He was pretty fat. He was pretty chunky. He hadn't missed many meals."

Over 6 minutes, 25.4 seconds, the time it took for them to go from last place to first, Hume and his fellow UW rowers became Seattle sporting legends. Athletically and socially, it was quite a feat. Whereas the other Olympic crews in Germany consisted of blue-

Surviving members of the 1936 gold-medal-winning UW crew reunite in 1999. Pictured from left to right are Joe Rantz, Roger Morris, Bob Moch, Don Hume and Jim McMillin.

bloods, soldiers and police officers, the Huskies were the sons of farmers, fishermen and loggers, all children of the Depression.

They had survived ponderous UW tryouts that topped out at 250 rowing candidates and were lopped to 40 that filled up five boats. They were good together,

smooth and powerful, with Hume a human rudder of sorts. This Olympic feat made them lifelong friends and got them inducted into the Helms Rowing Hall of Fame in 1971.

Fourth-seat oarsman John White, No. 2 Charles Day, bow Roger Morris and McMillin were Seattle-raised, while No. 6 George "Shorty" Hunt grew up in Puyallup, Rantz in Sequim and Moch in Montesano. Hume was born in Olympia but moved to Anacortes and became a high school football, basketball and track star while his father moved from mill to mill in search of post-Depression work.

Finding his athletic calling, Hume came across a discarded rowboat and refurbished it, touring the nearby San Juan Islands and Bellingham Bay. He rowed from Anacortes back to Olympia, a grueling 100-mile trip over a number of days, just to show that he could do it. At the UW, he was singled out as a gifted and tireless rower, outperforming two upperclassmen to earn the stroke seat in the 1936 varsity 8 boat. He didn't lose a race until his final outing in 1938, the setback coming at the Intercollegiate Rowing Association finals.

White and Day were the most fun and outgoing to be around of these elite Huskies rowers. Moch could be bossy — as all coxswains are prone to be. At 6-foot-7, McMillin was the tallest and also the oldest. Hunt was gregarious and the strongest. Rantz and Adam were quiet and serious-minded. Morris was even less communicative and constantly ribbed about it during workouts, told by teammates to wake up though he always came ready to row. Hume fit somewhere in the middle of this wide range of personalities.

Three rowers, Hume included, were nearly ruled academically ineligible prior to leaving for the 1936 IRAs, but everyone would eventually graduate. Hume, Rantz, Hunt, McMillin, White, Morris and Adam received UW engineering degrees while Moch became a lawyer and Day a physician. McMillin and Moch also served as college rowing coaches, both for MIT. Day, a lifelong smoker despite his medical expertise, was the first to die in 1962, a gruesome victim of his steady cigarette habit; he had one lung removed and

the other turn cancerous. Morris was the last to pass away in 2009.

Hume traveled and worked until he died from complications of a stroke suffered at age 86 on Sept. 16, 2001, not long after the 9/11 attacks. He tested his physical limits to the end, describing to Morris in a letter how he had suffered frostbite to his hands and feet at an Arctic exploration camp.

"That guy has done more world traveling than anyone you can name," Rantz said shortly before Hume's death. "He is always opening up a forest reserve or coal mine, doing research. He's always gone. He's always on the road somewhere. I don't think he lives anywhere."

> Athletically and socially, it was quite a feat. Whereas the other Olympic crews in Germany consisted of bluebloods, soldiers and police officers, the Huskies were the sons of farmers, fishermen and loggers, all children of the Depression.

The year before his death, Hume sent a letter to me at the *Seattle Post-Intelligencer* postmarked from Tuktoyaktuk, Northwest Territories, complimenting a story I had written detailing the 1936 gold-medal race, which had been mailed to Hume by five of his friends. A few months earlier, I met with the vibrant and

mustachioed Hume, plus McMillin, Morris, Rantz and Moch, on a cold winter night at a Woodinville retirement home to oversee a photo session. Hume expressed a desire more than once to get together and sit and talk sports with me — someone whose father, Bill Raley, was a 1943 UW rower. Sadly, that time never came.

While he circled the globe in his private manner, Hume left his precious Olympic gold medal and other rowing memorabilia on display at his brother's home in Olympia. The only tradeoff was that he would check in with his relatives from time to time in person, which were always memorable visits.

"Don lived the life he wanted," Tim Hume said. "He would always come around every Christmas for a night or two and when he did it was the highlight of the year. You never really knew what he was doing or where he was going, but he always had great stories."

The best one, of course, was about a bunch of determined Seattle rowers winning in Germany against all odds. ❖

People were drawn
to the most epic
pre-World War II sporting
event of any kind
held in Seattle and the most
glorious prize fight arranged in
any era, and it was won
by Hostak, the city's very
own Cinderella Man.

Catching a break from Hitler-filled headlines and increasing world unrest, Seattle couldn't resist a pro boxing match that featured a working-class hero against a reigning champion. Fight fans came out in record numbers. The electricity surrounding this epic event could have powered the city for weeks.

On July 26, 1938, a paid crowd of 30,102 filled up well-worn Civic Stadium, anxious to see hometown challenger Al Hostak slug it out with world middle-weight title-holder Freddie Steele under the stars and in front of them.

People were drawn to the most epic pre-World War II sporting event of any kind held in Seattle and the most glorious prize fight arranged in any era, and it was won by Hostak, the city's very own Cinderella Man and its first boxer to reach for national accolades. Comedians Jack Benny and Bob Hope sat ringside. Former heavyweight champion Jack Dempsey was inside the ring, flown in from New York to referee the match. Philadelphia mobster Frank "Blinky" Palermo and several associates were easy to identify among the overflow gathering.

AL HOSTAK
Seattle's Knockout Punch

"The Mafia was there in force," said Dick Francisco, a witness to the proceedings and later a Northwest boxing trainer. "They had a whole section."

Francisco was one reason the estimated crowd count was closer to 35,000 — he didn't pay to get in. He was a cocky, 15-year-old kid who lived in the surrounding lower Queen Anne neighborhood and felt a sense of entitlement in the Great Depression aftermath with this frenzied boxing activity on his home turf. Tickets were priced at $5.75, $3.45, $2.30 and $1.15, but none of that made any difference to Francisco. He was going inside to see Hostak and Steele, and he wasn't handing over any cash to get there.

To protect the gate, young National Guard soldiers patrolled inside, carrying long sticks and rattling the outer fences with them whenever people got too close. That didn't discourage Francisco any. He mocked one of the guys in uniform, challenging the guardsman to personally show him how tough he was, and they passed each other going over the metal fence in different directions.

Once inside, Francisco quickly disappeared into the crowd. As it turned out, it was important to find a good vantage point before the 10 p.m. main event began because the fight was over in a minute and 43 seconds.

Alice Brougham, Royal's daughter, sits with Al Hostak in 1938.

"Somebody dropped something and reached between the seats to pick it up, and it seems to me it was Bob Hope," Francisco said. "When he sat up, Freddie Steele was knocked out, laying on the mat, and Al Hostak was in a neutral corner."

Hostak, just 22 and a Cleveland High School dropout, had come from the hardscrabble Georgetown community, growing up in a house at 501 S. Lucille St. Six years earlier, he had splurged and bought a ticket that he couldn't really afford in order to watch the same Freddie Steele fight Cerefino Garcia. An aspiring boxer, Hostak thought he might learn something that night. He jumped out of his seat and cheered when Steele delivered a lusty knockout punch.

As he moved through the boxing ranks and built his own reputation, Hostak visualized Steele's decisive blow. Hostak wanted that moment of glory all to himself on a big stage. To say that Steele never knew what hit him in that 1938 bout would be erroneous — it was a studious copycat.

On a cool, summer night, the much-anticipated fight began with the champion coming out aggressively and throwing the first punches, but leaving himself wide open for serious punishment. Hostak, nicknamed "the Savage Slav," hit Steele in the heart and heard a loud grunt. Steele dropped his hands. Hostak toppled him altogether with a ferocious left hook to the chin that landed flush. The crowd erupted.

"It was a great punch," Francisco said. "It hit Steele on the button. If he didn't go down after that, Al should have started running and got out of the ring. School was out."

Hostak later said he didn't remember anything following that direct hit. His adrenaline took over and obscured the action thereafter. He knocked down Steele three times before Dempsey stepped in and mercifully

> "It was a great punch," Francisco said. "It hit Steele on the button. If he didn't go down after that, Al should have started running and got out of the ring. School was out."

stopped the match and declared a new champion. The upset was clear in terms of the disparity of the fight payout to the combatants: Hostak received a check for $8,503.13, Steele $30,000.

"That night I could have fought Joe Louis," Hostak said. "It was just the way I felt, that I could hit any man in the world. That night, I made it work."

Hostak returned to Georgetown the triumphant hero. Beer flowed and wild partying lasted well into the night. A rematch was never considered. Steele, who hailed from nearby Tacoma, won all except one of his previous 41 fights, but he was so shaken by this sudden defeat he retired on the spot. Steele came back three years later and fought once more, before getting out of boxing for good with an 84-5-5 record and turning his attention to acting roles in small-scale films. Steele was 72 when he died in 1984.

Just days after the 1938 fight, Hostak received bitter disappointment that stunted his career. The National Boxing Association, representing 37 states, recognized him as the middleweight champion, but the New York Boxing Commission, deemed the sport's ultimate authority, coldly snubbed him.

Fred Apostoli, who considered the Hostak-Steele fight important enough to warrant his ringside presence in Seattle, was designated as the new title-holder. It made no difference that Steele earlier had beaten Apostoli, making the transfer of power to Hostak a natural outcome. New Yorkers were miffed after failing to host the fight on the East Coast and now they had to be appeased. Their boxing decisions could be fairly one-sided for obvious reasons.

"The middleweight division was controlled by the Mafia," Francisco said. "That wasn't hearsay; that was fact. You didn't fight anybody unless they wanted you to. They knew if you should win or lose."

The *New York Journal-American* saw through this charade. The newspaper published a cartoon that ridiculed the boxing commission and its treatment of Hostak. A figure representing the commission was shown holding up the hand of a boxer who resembled a buffoon; yet another character, depicting the public, was portrayed defiantly waving a hand and walking off, suggesting that everyone knew who the real champ was and the fix was in.

Hostak's career lost serious momentum. He broke his hand and lost to Solly Krieger. He beat Krieger in a rematch, but lost to Tony Zale twice. Although known as one of boxing's fiercest punchers, Hostak never came close to another title.

"When I fought Steele, my fists were so fast," Hostak said. "These other fights, I couldn't get them to go. All those guys who beat me weren't as good as Steele. They beat me because of my bitterness. It was, 'Why the hell fight anyone if they wouldn't recognize me?' I didn't care. I was just out there to make a few bucks."

Hostak retired in 1949 with a 64-9-11 record. Forty-eight years later, he was chosen as a World Boxing Hall of Fame inductee, a proud and overdue moment for him. He attended the event in Los Angeles with one of his sons, Phil Hostak.

He was an alert and robust man well into his 80s, living alone in his White Center family home at 10436 21st Ave. S.W., one that he oddly filled to the ceiling with records and tapes from thrift-shop excursions, all of which I witnessed on a visit. This intense hoarding might have been a reflexive Depression-era action.

He moved to a suburban Issaquah convalescent center once he demonstrated the earliest signs of Alzheimer's disease and eventually was unable to recognize family members or fellow boxers. Hostak was 90 when he died on Aug. 13, 2006, nearly seven decades after his spotlight moment. His time of death was 1:43 p.m. – numbers that mirrored the length of his Steele fight.

There was never another Seattle boxing match that put anywhere near as many people in the seats as Hostak and Steele did. Hometown heavyweight Boone Kirkman fought highly regarded Ken Norton at the Seattle Center Coliseum in 1974 in front of 11,039 – fewer than a third of the Hostak bout. The hype was similar in 1957 at Sicks' Stadium for a Floyd Patterson-Pete Rademacher heavyweight title bout, a unique match-up that featured the reigning champion against the Olympic gold-medal winner who was a Northwest native making his pro debut. But their fight attendance was 16,961 – less than half of what the middleweights drew.

Hostak's victory was a milestone event for Seattle, and Dick Francisco knew this all along. Although unwilling to purchase a ticket in 1938 on the way in, while eluding those menacing National Guard soldiers guarding the perimeter, Francisco picked up a discarded stub off the ground on his way out.

Francisco had the ticket framed and hung it on a wall at his home in Whidbey Island, forever reminding him of Al Hostak's dominance and Seattle's most memorable fight night. ❖

> There was never another
> Seattle boxing match that
> put anywhere near as many
> people in the seats as
> Hostak and Steele did.

JEFF HEATH

Seattle's Big-League Mouth

Swinging from the left side, Jeff Heath could hit a baseball as well and as far as anyone. If only he could have kept his mouth shut, his impulsiveness under wraps. Heath was Seattle's gift to the big leagues, the city's first homegrown talent to make it big at the top level. He also was its first certifiable sporting showboat, if not malcontent. Everywhere he went, this sturdy man with the Jay Leno jaw, linebacker shoulders and general lack of grace brought wanted and unwanted attention to himself.

After graduating from Seattle's Garfield High School in 1934, Heath earned a roster spot with the Cleveland Indians within two summers. By 1939, he had baseball's full attention by hitting a career-best .343, just six percentage points behind Boston's Jimmie Foxx, the American League batting champion.

In 1941, Heath became the answer to a baseball trivia question: Who was the first A.L. player to collect

> Heath was Seattle's gift to the big leagues, the city's first homegrown talent to make it big at the top level. He also was its first certifiable sporting showboat, if not malcontent.

at least 20 doubles, triples and home runs in a season? Heath supplied 32, 20 and 24, respectively. His .340 batting average that year was exceeded only by the benchmark .406 heroics of Boston's Ted Williams, and it dwarfed Heath's .219 average from the season before, one held down by bad knees and bad luck.

"It just seemed like that whenever I came to the plate there were a hundred guys out there and everybody had a glove, so I increased my average by 121 points in one season," Heath told the *Seattle Post-Intelligencer.* "It makes me mad when I look at my record; so inconsistent. The great ballplayers have that good season every year."

The Canadian-born Heath was never content. From 1938 to 1944, he was a spring-training holdout, demanding healthy pay increases. He always threatened to quit the game, once suggesting he would rather keep his war-time job as a Seattle-Tacoma Shipyard warehouseman than go back to Ohio and play baseball. If his disenchantment wasn't enough, he had to supply the needle, as well: "Cleveland is a swell baseball town and I've got lots of friends there, but this Indians' park is lousy."

Heath emerged from Seattle as this cocky and ultra-confident young man, an all-city selection for Garfield High in baseball and football, and someone surrounded by pioneering black men. As a schoolboy fullback, Heath teamed with end Homer Harris, who became the first African-American captain for a Big Ten football team while playing for Iowa; halfback Charley Russell, one of the University of Washington's earliest black football players; and halfback Sammy Bruce, who died in World War II on a bombing mission as a Tuskegee airman.

Heath, who turned down a scholarship offer to play football and baseball for the University of Washington,

Jeff Heath was a controversial player for the Cleveland Indians.

twice led the A.L. in triples, legging out 18 in 1938 and those aforementioned 20 in 1941. He was an All-Star selection in 1941 and 1943.

At the same time, he was regarded as a rampant trouble-maker. National baseball writers such as Shirley Povich of the *Washington Post* questioned Heath's egotistical actions in print and labeled him "a problem child," and the outfielder offered no rebuttal, only supporting evidence.

In 1939, Heath fouled out in the ninth inning of a game and punched a mouthy fan who had run to a railing in the stands, leaned out and heckled him – at a home game in Cleveland. "The guy had been riding us all afternoon," the ballplayer said, explaining away his tawdry behavior. The day before, Heath tossed his bat into the box seats after striking out, again at home. In 1940, he led a successful revolt to oust Indians manager Ossie Vitt, a move that prompted local fans to describe Heath and his teammates as "the Cleveland crybabies" and opposing fans to wave diapers at them.

The Indians finally had enough of Heath's antics and traded him to the Washington Senators for centerfielder George Case before the 1946 season. Heath didn't last long in the nation's capital either. He continually harassed light-hitting teammate Sherry Robertson, unaware his target was related to franchise owner Clark Griffith.

Heath was traded at midseason to the St. Louis Browns and had his ill-mannered moments there, too. Heath, according to Joe Posnanski's book *The Soul of Baseball*, became so upset when teammate Willard Brown used his bat without asking to hit an inside-the-park home run, he broke it so the other player couldn't swing it again.

In 1948, Heath was shipped to the Boston Braves and enjoyed a career renaissance, helping his final big-league team clinch a World Series berth. He batted .319 and collected 20 homers and 76 RBI.

Heath couldn't fully enjoy himself in Boston. During the final week of the season, with postseason play locked up, he broke his ankle in a grotesque manner while sliding home and getting tagged out by Brooklyn Dodgers catcher Roy Campanella. Alert photographers captured images of Heath's ankle completely twisted around and his face contorted in pain. Without him, the Braves lost the World Series to his old Cleveland Indians team in six games. Heath was quick to point out that his absence was the difference.

> He often showed up drunk at the *Post-Intelligencer* sports department offices, mouthing off about something that bugged him. He became the Rainiers' color TV analyst, a risky assignment for an unbridled, outspoken man.

In 1949, Heath made a Braves comeback that lasted just 36 games; his weakened ankle brought his off-season release. In 1950, he played another 57 games for his hometown Rainiers, batted just .245 for the minor-league team and finally pulled the plug on his pro baseball career.

Heath was home but that didn't mean all was calm in his world. He often showed up drunk at the *Post-Intelligencer* sports department offices, mouthing off about something that bugged him. He became the Rainiers' color TV analyst, a risky assignment for an unbridled, outspoken man. He had some Dizzy Dean in him, repeatedly tripping over his sentences and words in a homespun manner, which seemed to endear him to Seattle fans.

He still took batting practice regularly with the Rainiers, entertaining them with his spot-on imitation of a hung-over Babe Ruth trying to bat. With a meat-packing company sponsoring the broadcast, he gorged on hotdogs night after night, offering his personal endorsement.

In his third season in the booth in 1956, Heath got into big trouble with his employers when he blurted out an expletive on the air — "Take that, you lousy bastard!" — once a Portland Beavers pitcher he didn't like served up a Rainiers' home run ball. In a subsequent telecast, he had to apologize to his younger viewers for swearing, another comical TV moment.

A few days later, Heath engaged in a fierce argument with KTVW station manager Bob Veneman, shoving the other man out of the broadcast booth and down a flight of stairs in full view of Sicks' Stadium fans. "Jeff was a piece of work," said Bill Sears, the Rainiers' publicity director. Heath's contract wasn't renewed for the following season, but that didn't keep him out of the headlines.

In 1957, Heath was arrested, booked into jail for disorderly conduct and released on a $250 bond. Police said the family man had pushed his way into Geraldine Eystad's Fremont home at 908 N. 46th St. She told officers that she was Heath's mistress. Eystad claimed she had attempted to break off their relationship and was struck by the man in anger. A month later, the *Post-Intelligencer* reported that Eystad had dropped all charges; she apparently wanted no part of the publicity that would surround a trial involving the former ballplayer.

At the end of that summer, Heath was back in the news once more. He was 43 when he suffered the first in a series of heart attacks while serving as a celebrity participant in the city's annual Seafair Parade. He recovered and tried to stay out of the public spotlight.

When the *Post-Intelligencer* contacted him a decade later, asking to do a story updating his activities, Heath curtly told the reporter, "If anybody wants to know what happened to me, let them call me." The morning paper took him at his wise-guy word: It unapologetically published his home number (284-9597) for everyone to read and dial.

On Dec. 9, 1975, the former ballplayer, ex-broadcaster and career hell-raiser was just 60 when he ate dinner at former big-leaguer Mike Budnick's home, walked five blocks to his Queen Anne house and collapsed from a fatal heart attack. Seattle's first MLB headliner and offbeat sports character was tagged out one last time, though probably not without an argument. ❖

> Steele was a trailblazer, joining the combined Steagles team (Steelers and Eagles) that was credited with helping keep pro football together once the outbreak of World War II threatened a league collapse. He was Seattle's most successful war-time sports figure.

Ernie Steele wore a leather helmet with no facemask and high-top shoes with long cleats. He looked like everyone else who played college and pro football during the 1930s and 1940s. It was a bland sporting era in which athletes were strongly encouraged to blend in rather than stick out in any manner, and even jersey numbers were considered a radical measure.

Yet people could always tell who Steele was once he took off running: No one was faster and no one could catch him. Not his NFL teammates. Not his University of Washington teammates. Not even the great Jackie Robinson.

The gift of speed was something Steele, a two-way back and kick-return specialist, realized at an early age when he grew up in south Seattle. He easily covered 100 yards inside 10 seconds. He ran from home to the neighborhood store four blocks away to buy milk and he had his mother time him on those trips.

He used his fleet feet to his advantage whenever possible, once brazenly telling a principal at Southern Heights Elementary School who wanted to discipline him with a paddle, "If you can catch me, you can hit me."

The speedy Steele wasn't Seattle's first NFL player — George Wilson carried that distinction, though Wilson's involvement lasted just three seasons because of Depression-era fallout — but Steele was the city's first to enjoy a lengthy and well-decorated pro football career. Steele was a trailblazer, joining the combined Steagles team (Steelers and Eagles) that was credited with helping keep pro football together once the outbreak of World War II threatened a league collapse. He was Seattle's most successful war-time sports figure.

His speed took him from Highline High School, where he was a highly-decorated athlete in football, basketball and track, to Washington, where his World War II-era football teams couldn't catch a break. In his three varsity seasons, Steele's Huskies finished 4-5, 7-2 and 5-4 — and all but two of the losses were decided by a touchdown or less. A Rose Bowl opportunity was squandered during his junior year in 1940 with a 20-10 defeat at Stanford. He still demonstrated how incredibly fast he was against Washington State that season, returning a kickoff 87 yards and a punt 83 yards for touchdowns.

The Huskies had plenty of backfield speed in Dean McAdams, Jack Stackpool and Steele, but UW coach

ERNIE STEELE
HALFBACK

Jimmy Phelan apparently didn't know how to use it to his advantage.

"The reason we lost all those games is we didn't play the T-formation," Steele said. "We had the Notre Dame shift and all that crap. Phelan was just so stubborn and he knew it all. He kept us from going to the Rose Bowl with his formations."

Still the 6-foot, 180-pound Steele flourished at Husky Stadium, providing a formidable running, receiving and passing threat at left halfback. He led the Pacific Coast Conference in punt returns and was named second-team All-American as a junior, and he ranked in the top 10 nationally in returns over his final two seasons.

Steele's exceptional acceleration easily landed him an NFL job in 1942 after he was drafted in the 10th round by the Pittsburgh Steelers and promptly traded to the Philadelphia Eagles. Reporting to training camp on the edge of Lake Erie, he was among 100 eager players looking for Eagles' roster spots and asked to line up on a field and run the 100-yard dash.

"I ran away from everybody," said Steele, initially paid $350 per game. "I was the fastest of all 100. That's how I made the ball club. From then on I always made the club."

In his first NFL game for Philly, he returned a punt 89 yards for six points against the Chicago Cardinals. The following season for the war-time Steagles, he took an interception 91 yards for a score against the New York Giants.

Nicknamed "Hoot" because he had owl-like dark circles under his eyes, Steele played seven seasons, mostly as a defensive back, earning All-Pro honors in 1943. He had a well-rounded NFL career: 19 touchdowns, 1,337 yards rushing (5.2 per carry), 31 receptions for 520 yards, 94 punt and kickoff returns

for 1,652 yards, 24 interceptions for 404 yards and 12 fumble recoveries.

In each of his final two seasons, he played in the NFL championship game in inclement December weather, both times against the Chicago Cardinals. His team lost 28-21 on an ice-covered field in Chicago in 1947 and won 7-0 in deep snow in Philadelphia a year later. On the final play of his career in the 1948 title game, Steele made a game-saving interception on his 15-yard line.

Steele, who was given a belt buckle and ring to commemorate the NFL title-game appearances, easily could have played a couple more pro seasons. However, he got only as far as Montana while driving to training camp in 1949 before turning his car around and heading back to Seattle. His family and a budding restaurant business needed him.

For 46 years, he operated Ernie Steele's, a popular corner bar on Capitol Hill at 300 Broadway E. It was dark and smoky inside and had its regulars, giving it a "Cheers" atmosphere. For 65 years, he was married to his wife, Jo. Steele was 88 when he died on Oct. 16, 2006.

Nobody ever beat him in a football footrace. That included earlier college games in Seattle and Los Angeles against Robinson, a swift and elusive UCLA running back better known as the man who broke Major League Baseball's color line in 1947. "He was fast but I could run away from him," Steele said.

Robinson, who had 9.8-second speed in the 100-yard dash, played in Husky Stadium just once, against a Steele-led team, and he was spectacular. On Oct. 7, 1939, the legendary athlete gathered in a perfectly spiraling punt from

the UW's McAdams at the east end, a ball kicked high enough to allow the coverage to properly surround him. With a half-dozen players closing in, this exquisite player for UCLA lazily veered to his left, away from the sideline. It was all a clever, baiting ploy.

As anxious defenders reached for him, Robinson made a sharp cut to the right and exploded up the field through flailing arms. He didn't stop running until repeatedly crisscrossing the field before tiring and permitting McAdams, the last man, to get the angle on him and bump him. That interrupted Robinson's considerable momentum long enough to allow the Huskies' Bill Marx to make a saving tackle on the UW 5. Robinson officially covered 63 yards in an improvised manner that might have been double that because of the cutbacks.

> "I met him on the field and I met him off the field," Steele said. "We talked. It was, 'Good game,' and everything. He was a helluva guy and a helluva player. We never looked at it any other way. Color didn't mean a damn thing."

Robinson set up a tying touchdown that came on the next play and shifted things to the Bruins, who emerged from Seattle that day with a 14-7 victory. Steele provided Washington's only score on a first-quarter, four-yard run. Robinson's lightning bolt of a return was all anyone talked about after the stadium emptied.

"He reversed the field at least five times," said Walt Milroy, a UW student and Huskies baseball player who was among the 15,017 who witnessed Robinson's greatness firsthand. "They didn't tackle him; he just collapsed. It was the most exciting run I've ever seen."

The Huskies didn't have any black players on the field that day, and Steele didn't have a black teammate in college or the NFL, but he was hardly standoffish or unfriendly toward Robinson. UCLA's headline-making athlete was so magical Steele was eager to exchange greetings with him. When it came to race relations, Steele embraced them easier than most people at the time and he sought out Robinson at Husky Stadium.

"I met him on the field and I met him off the field," Steele said. "We talked. It was, 'Good game,' and everything. He was a helluva guy and a helluva player. We never looked at it any other way. Color didn't mean a damn thing."

Speed made Steele and Robinson football contemporaries, respectful opponents, fellow speed merchants and, above all, color-blind. ❖

CHUCK GILMUR

Seattle's First NBA Player

Chuck Gilmur didn't have an entourage surrounding him or reside in a sprawling mansion in a gated community. He didn't have 10 cars parked in and around his driveway, wear layers of gold chains draped around his neck or answer to a know-it-all sports agent. He didn't have an explosive crossover step, money 3-point stroke or wide assortment of rim-shaking dunks either.

Gilmur's athletic calling card was this: He was Seattle's first NBA player. He was the city's pro hoops pioneer, the first to lace it up around the country and get paid for it, and the first to lock elbows with the best. Nearly two dozen homegrown players have made it to basketball's highest level, and it all started with Gilmur.

Three years after playing his final basketball game for the University of Washington, Gilmur returned home from World War II military service with his body intact and opportunity beckoning. After serving as a sergeant for the Eighth Armored Infantry and getting shipped to Europe, he re-enrolled in school for the 1946 summer quarter. He was told a man wanted to meet him on campus.

Chuck Taylor of Converse basketball sneaker fame, but representing other interests on this trip, posed the following question to Gilmur: Would he consider playing for the newly formed Basketball Association of America during the 1946-47 season, specifically for the Chicago Stags?

The attraction to Gilmur was his height. He was a shade under 6-foot-4 and represented one of the taller amateur players available from this far more compact basketball generation. He was a big man, though by modern pro standards not very big at all. He had a readymade niche awaiting him in the BAA based on his inches alone.

"I was the league's second-tallest player – and Gary Payton was taller than I am," said Gilmur, reaching for modern-day perspective.

Basketball and the laidback Gilmur were initially an unlikely pairing. As a senior at Seattle's Lincoln High School, he was a guard who sat on the bench, feeling lucky to be there. He admittedly wasn't a very good player. He was a deep reserve who needed 32 minutes of playing time just to letter for the Lynx; he received 33 and barely made it. He lived at 4006 Latona Ave. N.E., several blocks from the UW and what seemed a million miles from college basketball success.

Yet once with the Huskies, he grew three inches and packed on 30 pounds, going from basketball misfit to a well-utilized player for coach Hec Edmundson. Gilmur started three seasons and became an all-conference selection. He was strong and aggressive, and led the league in personal fouls. He was a big reason the UW came up with its first NCAA Tournament berth during the 1942-43 season.

> He was Seattle's first NBA player. He was the city's pro hoops pioneer, the first to lace it up around the country and get paid for it, and the first to lock elbows with the best.

"If there was ever a walk-on, it was me," Gilmur said. "I hadn't anticipated that. I think I kind of grew into myself. I was certainly a clumsy senior in high school."

Gilmur wasn't exactly sure what he was getting into, but he signed with the Stags for a league-minimum $4,500 salary. He played three seasons for the start-up BAA and another two when the league evolved into the NBA. He was a pro basketball trailblazer on many fronts: Gilmur played in the original BAA league championship semifinals, which the Stags won in six games over the Washington Capitols; and he appeared in the first BAA championship finals, which the Stags lost in five games to the Philadelphia Warriors. He was a postseason standout even in a losing effort, earning sufficient job security in the process.

Gilmur never scored much as a pro player, averaging just 5.8 points over those five seasons, though he rang up a career-best 21 points in a game against the Boston Celtics. His Chicago coach, Harold Olsen, described Gilmur as the league's most improved player, citing his aggressiveness around the basket.

Gilmur's college nickname was "Elbows," and there was no reason to change it in the pros. In his second season with the Stags, he set a league record by committing 251 personal fouls and was now labeled throughout the BAA as "the bad man of basketball."

Allen Sawyer, a forward who teamed up with Gilmur for the Capitols, viewed him this way: "He was hard-working and he rebounded and he was strong. I can't remember him shooting."

In addressing his physical playing style, the soft-spoken Gilmur conceded, "I had an awful lot of elbows. Ninety percent of my scoring probably came on offensive rebounds. It kept me on the team."

Gilmur played at a time when pro basketball was scrambling to survive among all the other post-World War II sports offerings, if not struggling to generate its own fan base. Most BAA teams played in sports arenas operated by men who owned hockey teams. Pro basketball was little more than a way to fill playing dates between the better-attended games on the ice.

Travel was hardly glamorous, less so for the Chicago Stags than any other team. Olsen, the Stags coach, hated to fly and wouldn't do it unless there was no alternative. As a result, Gilmur and his teammates rode trains to their games 90 percent of the time, which meant they were always more fatigued than their opponents.

Gilmur played those first three seasons in a uniform that had a little deer emblem sewn on the front and became his lone trading card image. A memorable outing was his appearance in the preliminary game of a Chicago doubleheader in front of 20,000 people who were more anxious to see the match-up between the Harlem Globetrotters and a Minneapolis Lakers team featuring 6-10 center George Mikan.

The NBA was created for the 1949-50 season and it combined with the BAA, supplying 17 teams, just as Gilmur's stint with the Stags ended. He was traded straight up for Washington's 6-8 Clarence "Kleggie" Hermsen. The NBA, however, had grown far too rapidly in its maiden season. Attendance lagged for the Capitols. Thirty-five games into Gilmur's second season with Washington, the franchise disbanded. It was the end of his pro basketball career, too.

A chronically swollen knee limited him to 16 games during the 1950-51 season and it wasn't going to get any better. His only previous health setback was a broken tooth, requiring a dental bridge. The weakened knee was not easily repairable. Gilmur retired from pro basketball on the spot.

"They would treat me for three days and the knee would go down," Gilmur said. "I'd play and it would swell up. There was no chance I could go anywhere with that knee, so I went home."

Always the hoop pioneer, Gilmur stuck around just long enough during that final season to take part in the first NBA game that involved an African-American player, in this case Earl Lloyd. Gilmur and Lloyd were Capitols teammates and fellow forwards. In a landmark outing on Oct. 31, 1950, Gilmur went scoreless as a starter and Lloyd had six points in his first appearance as a reserve in Washington's 78-70 loss at home to the Rochester Royals.

"We both had the distinction of playing in the first game that one of the black kids played," Sawyer said. "There were three in the league in 1951. I had come from UCLA and played for John Wooden and we had more of a flow of various people, so it wasn't quite as different for us as it was in the East."

Gilmur became an unassuming teacher and basketball coach in Tacoma. His Lincoln and Mount Tahoma high school students had no idea this genial man was once a pro basketball player known for his rough play.

He watched in wonder as NBA salaries took off and the game changed dramatically in style over later decades. He never envisioned any of this when he helped launch the league. He understood the modern upgrades that pro basketball required, just not the nonstop contact now permitted, though trading elbows was always his calling card.

Gilmur, who was 88 when he died in Tacoma on Jan. 14, 2011, surrounded by family members, kept tabs on the NBA on TV in his final years but only in small doses. "I don't sit and watch the entirety," he explained. "I just like to watch the last five minutes."

He witnessed more of the NBA, up close and at a distance, than anyone else from Seattle. ❖

Fabulous Fifties

Seattle jumpstarts the commercial jet age with the rollout of the 707, making Boeing the global leader; operates a state-run ferry system across Puget Sound, the largest anywhere in the country; and introduces the Dick's Drive-in hamburger chain, which remains a popular city-wide staple.

The city enjoys an unmistakable sporting golden era, sending two teams to the Final Four, supplying two college basketball players of the year, providing three first-team All-American quarterbacks and serving up one of the most dominant University of Washington football teams in history.

HUGH MCELHENNY

The Ultimate Free Pass

The University of Washington had to have football player Hugh McElhenny at any cost. This directive came from the highest administrative level on campus, from school president Raymond B. Allen, and few people knew of this illicit arrangement. Long-time alumni donors threatened to withhold $35 million in general contributions – foremost delaying medical school funding – if something wasn't done about a lackluster Huskies football program and McElhenny wasn't part of the solution. Allen couldn't let that happen.

The school pushed limits wherever it could to secure this marquee player from Los Angeles. McElhenny wasn't even academically eligible to enroll in classes at the UW when he showed up in Seattle. It didn't matter to Allen, a man who ran the university in a controlling fashion. The president proved an effective lead blocker in getting this football savant into school.

"McElhenny didn't meet standards, the admissions people asked to see his academic records, and Allen refused to provide those records," said Donald Wollett, a UW athletic faculty representative privy to the back-room dealings. "Allen said they were sequestered and that made the records department mad. The president reached down to sequester those records. That was an indication of how deep the corruption was – it went all the way to the president."

McElhenny easily became Seattle's most pampered and improperly financed athlete, leading the city down a far less innocent sporting path as it entered the progressive 1950s and grew impatient for success. Colleges everywhere were caught up in the clandestine practice of purchasing talented players to restore football programs slow to recover from the disruption of World War II. The UW jumped all the way in with McElhenny.

For three years, the checkbook was always open for this game-breaking player who went from Los Angeles' Washington High School to USC to Compton Junior College before landing with the Huskies. The joke passed around Seattle for decades was that McElhenny got paid more to play for the UW than he did to put on an NFL uniform. It was funny and true. He laughed and winked along with everyone – and got away with it.

"I think everybody knew," an unapologetic McElhenny said. "There was a lot of that stuff going on around the country. [All-America halfback] Charlie Trippi told me he got pieces of Texaco gas stations to go to Georgia, and he was still getting checks. Alabama said if I came down there I wouldn't have to play my senior year of high school. They offered cash and free lodging. Everybody was trying to build their programs back up."

> McElhenny easily became Seattle's most pampered and improperly financed athlete, leading the city down a far less innocent sporting path as it entered the progressive 1950s and grew impatient for success.

The brewery executive allowed McElhenny to live in his home when the football player was temporarily separated from his wife Peggy because of his coed indiscretions. Larsen bought McElhenny a Ford convertible. And in a contrived ceremony, with his 5-year-old daughter Lynn watching from an upper staircase with profound curiosity, Larsen diligently peeled off bill after bill from a large wad of cash and handed them over to the exciting running back after each outing.

"It was being done, Hugh was careful about it and we had to be quiet about it," Larsen's wife, Dottie, said of the favors provided. "My husband felt it was his civic duty."

McElhenny became a source of community pride in Seattle for being this shifty running back who left fans breathless once he tucked a ball under his arm and took off. Best of all, he was pilfered from the backyard of the annoyingly superior USC, which had struck its own improper deal with McElhenny.

He first agreed to play football and run track for the Trojans, but didn't have a necessary foreign language credit and was academically ineligible when he showed up there, too. No presidential waiver was offered in this instance. Waiting to get into his hometown university, he was supposed to receive $65 per month extra for the nonsensical chore of watering the grass around the Trojan horse statue three times a week. When the school didn't pay up as promised for three consecutive months, McElhenny walked away from USC and went on a nationwide car trip with a friend.

After spending a season at Compton, McElhenny agreed to play for the UW, but had second thoughts after considering the muddy field he would have to trudge through at times. He finally relented and was given a sweet deal, one brokered by school supporters

Hugh McElhenny was a hard player to bring down in 1950.

An uninterrupted Saturday night ritual during football season was McElhenny's visit to Les Larsen's Montlake home at 2142 E. Hamlin St., a few blocks south of the stadium, where 50 to 75 of Seattle's leading citizens gathered for big parties in the basement after every Husky home game. Everyone always anxiously awaited the running back's arrival. Larsen was the Rainier

Brewery vice president and sales manager, the right-arm man for brewery owner Emil Sick, who parked his car on the front lawn for these fall get-togethers. Larsen also was McElhenny's designated benefactor, something not permitted in the intercollegiate handbook but a role strongly encouraged in Seattle's social circles.

and the player's father, Hugh Sr., a Los Angeles vending machine distributor.

Among the extras provided, the school paid for the following: a Palm Springs honeymoon for McElhenny and his new bride; air travel to Seattle for the couple, with athletic director Harvey Cassill and football coach Howie Odell waiting for them at the airport; a Camlin Hotel room and meals, all put on a tab; apartment furnishings, delivered by others; a $300 monthly stipend, on top of the permissible $75 scholarship check; that aforementioned car, which might have been one of many; and other cash advances that weren't limited to his game-day reward.

UW boosters Paul Schwegeler and Al McCoy were the point men in getting McElhenny to Seattle. McCoy was entrusted to pack up McElhenny's car with the player's personal belongings and drive it up the coast. Peggy McElhenny was provided with a permissible job at Washington Physician Services, working directly for Wendell Broyles, who doubled as the Huskies public-address announcer (full disclosure, she shared the same office with my grandfather, James Barron, a WPS sales manager). Cassill and Odell personally drove the couple from Seattle-Tacoma International Airport to

In 1950, Husky Stadium was expanded in grand fashion, erecting its first upper deck on the south side largely because of the running back's presence. Alums referred to the revamped stadium as "the house that Hugh built."

their downtown hotel, officially condoning the improper activity at two more levels of university authority.

The UW running back readily admitted that he let the adulation and favors go to his head, and that his relationship with his wife suffered at times, which was verified by others.

"It was a sad life for Peggy," Dottie Larsen said. "He didn't acknowledge their marriage then. He was very popular. He was overwhelmed by all the attention. They kept it quiet, but he had other girlfriends. They got over it."

As far as the Huskies were concerned, the man nicknamed "Hurryin' Hugh" and later "The King" was worth every illegal penny. He was a fullback used as a breakaway runner and could go the distance at any time. In his second UW game in 1949, he raced 96 yards for a touchdown against Minnesota on a kickoff return. He provided a 91-yard punt return against Kansas State. He had a conference-record, 100-yard punt runback in 1951 against USC, faking out the touted Frank Gifford at the end of the run.

McElhenny finished his UW career with 10 touchdowns from 50 yards or more and became the school's all-time rushing leader with 2,499 yards. In 1950, Husky Stadium was expanded in grand fashion, erecting its first upper deck on the south side largely because of the running back's presence. Alums referred to the revamped stadium as "the house that Hugh built."

Money, however, couldn't buy total happiness for the Huskies and their loyal, well-heeled followers. The program didn't climb back on its feet, at least for long. With McElhenny on the roster, the Huskies actually lost one more game than they won, finishing 3-7, 8-2 and 3-6-1 (14-15-1), and never reached the Rose Bowl.

McElhenny did his part individually, earning first-team *Associated Press* All-America honors as a senior

Once in the NFL, McElhenny enjoyed a Pro Football Hall of Fame career and even greater popularity.

in 1951 and finished eighth in the Heisman Trophy balloting. People worshipped this player with rugged looks, wavy hair and laidback demeanor. McElhenny used to double-park his chartreuse 1948 Dodge coupe outside his UW fraternity house and arrive to find what he thought were parking tickets left on the windshield. Upon closer inspection, they were notes written by admiring police officers on citations that offered words of encouragement such as "Go get 'em, Hugh!" or "Score one for me this weekend!"

McElhenny often skipped class, which got him into trouble with Huskies coach Howie Odell, and he twice was forced to take summer school to stay eligible for football. Economics classes gave him the most trouble. Bill Knight, later a *Seattle Post-Intelligencer* sports editor, shared a classroom with the football player, in concept. "The difference was he came to class disguised as an empty chair," Knight said.

Thirty-two credits short of graduating, McElhenny found out the university was willing to go only so far in giving him preferential treatment. After his final UW football season in 1951, McElhenny returned for winter quarter classes and discovered the school had erased him from its enrollment records, so he left.

McElhenny pocketed more improper inducements than anyone else at the UW. As a senior, his total financial package was worth $10,000, which was $3,000 more than his original NFL salary as the 49ers' first-round draft choice and the eighth player taken overall.

"What they did with me was illegal," McElhenny said. "I know it was illegal for me to receive cash, and every month I received cash. I know it was illegal to receive clothing, and I got clothing all the time from stores. I got a check every month, and it was never signed by the same person, so we never really knew who it was coming from. They invested in me every year. Peg and I made more in college than I made in pro ball. When I look back, it was funny. I was a movie star up there. The people made you feel that way. It got to my head. I don't know if I took advantage of it or didn't take advantage of it enough."

Top 10 Seattle Athletes

1. Ken Griffey Jr., Mariners
2. Elgin Baylor, Seattle U
3. Hugh McElhenny, UW
4. Walter Jones, Seahawks
5. George Wilson, UW
6. Jack Sikma, Sonics
7. Steve Emtman, UW
8. Richard Sherman, Seahawks
9. Gary Payton, Sonics
10. Kevin Durant, Sonics

Once in the NFL, McElhenny enjoyed a Pro Football Hall of Fame career and even greater popularity. He had such a devoted nationwide following that a New Jersey man christened Steve McIlhenny at birth had his last name legally changed to match the spelling of his football hero's without telling family members until well after the fact.

"As I married and had a family my children became aware of this name change and we all kind of laughed about it, although my father still hasn't forgiven me," the now Steve McElhenny said.

McElhenny was an even better pro player than collegian, named NFL Rookie of the Year and All-Pro in his sensational debut season. Playing 13 years for pay that was within the rules, he finished with career totals of 5,281 yards rushing, 3,247 receiving and 2,841 in returns, scoring 60 times.

He had far more fame and fortune on the field than off. He invested in a California grocery market venture that went bankrupt. He returned to Seattle and lobbied unsuccessfully on behalf of Minnesota businessman Wayne Field to obtain an NFL franchise in his college town. He asked to become the Seattle Seahawks general manager candidate and never got a call back. He nearly died and was paralyzed for a year after contracting a rare nerve disorder, Guillain-Barre Syndrome, forcing him to move to the warmer Las Vegas climate to recover.

Yet McElhenny never had to answer for all of the favors and money he received in Seattle. He was romanticized for his actions as someone who beat the system. Five years after McElhenny left, similar college crimes by others brought down the entire UW athletic department and put it on probation and disbanded the then-Pacific Coast Conference. McElhenny remained smug about his involvement.

Johnny O'Brien, the former Seattle University All-America basketball player and a McElhenny contemporary, was forever humored by the following cocky exchange he had with the well-compensated Husky running back: "When we were in college, he once said to me, 'You get paid by the basket, don't you? I get paid by the yard.' " ❖

DON HEINRICH

Seattle's All-American Boy

Heinrich rarely went missing in action. He twice was selected first-team *Associated Press* All-America at football's glamour position, becoming Seattle's most decorated college player.

Don Heinrich and Hugh McElhenny met on the field on the first day of 1949 spring football practice at the University of Washington and formed an inseparable bond. Heinrich was a sophomore quarterback with a notable swagger, a big-name recruit from the nearby Navy town of Bremerton, and McElhenny was the flashy new fullback, a junior-college transfer and even bigger name from Los Angeles. They took to each other immediately.

"I was just kind of there and I wasn't sure if the guys were going to accept me or not, coming from California as this big hotshot," McElhenny said. "I guess my concern was being one of the guys. He was the local hero. He made me feel welcome."

They shared the huddle, the Huskies' offense and conquests and disappointments. There was no clash of egos. They had each other's back. This was never more apparent than when Heinrich suffered a shoulder separation in practice two weeks before the 1951 opener against Montana and was lost for what would have been their senior and final season together.

They had experienced a Rose Bowl near-miss and were anxious to make another run. Instead, Heinrich was a patient at Seattle's Providence Hospital, recovering from surgery with his throwing arm sticking out awkwardly after it was put into a cast when McElhenny made one of his more supportive visits.

The quarterback was restless and needed a diversion. The fullback had a creative solution.

"We went out the window and down the fire escape, and we went to a little tavern a block away," McElhenny said. "An hour later, two nuns came walking in and got Heinrich and took him back to the hospital."

Heinrich rarely went missing in action. He twice was selected first-team *Associated Press* All-America at football's glamour position, becoming Seattle's most decorated college player. He heads up an impressive list of local quarterbacks that includes Bob Schloredt, Warren Moon, Billy Joe Hobert, Mark Brunell and Marques Tuiasosopo, all Rose Bowl offensive MVP honorees; plus Jack Thompson, Marc Wilson and Jake Locker, all first-round NFL draft picks; pro football-bound Chris Chandler, Brock Huard, Damon Huard, Hugh Millen, Steve Pelluer and the fabled Sonny Sixkiller.

A junior in 1950, Heinrich led the country in passing, completing 60 percent by hitting on 134 of 221 throws, good for 1,846 yards and 14 touchdowns. He edged Kentucky's Babe Parilli for first-team *AP* honors.

Heinrich threw a pinpoint pass that often left a distinctive reddish mark on his target. George Black, an

> Heinrich played at a time when the nation's top players were showered with improper benefits from school boosters.

end who caught a then-school-record, 80-yard scoring pass from the hard-throwing quarterback against Stanford, had more of those battle scars than anyone.

"I'd end up where I had a post pattern, where I planted and pushed back, and the ball hit me near the shoulder pads, knocking them up, and I'd end up after the game with four or five red spots on my chest," Black said. "With the long stuff, you could put up one hand and the ball would just float into it. I would have been another water boy if it wasn't for Heinrich."

All that separated Heinrich and his teammates from a 10-0 season and a Rose Bowl trip in 1950 were tough, close losses to Illinois (20-13) and California (14-7). Settling for lesser rewards, the Huskies accommodated their big-time passer in the final game that season, allowing rival Washington State to score late in order to get the ball back and give Heinrich a chance to break the national completions record, which he did by throwing a pass to McElhenny that unexpectedly went for a touchdown.

Heinrich and McElhenny were ready to make amends for missing out on the elusive Pasadena trip when they approached their third season together. The quarterback, however, took a needless blow to his shoulder from a deep sub on a rollout play during a fall scrimmage, sending Heinrich to the hospital and the offending and scorned reserve to points unknown, leaving everyone outwardly frustrated and angry.

"It was one of those things," Heinrich told reporters. "I was tackled high. I've been tackled that way before and I don't hurt easily. But I landed on my shoulder this time and my shoulder went numb. It didn't hurt, but I knew I'd had it."

McElhenny was less forgiving, even decades later, over what was lost on the overzealous play. His league contender overnight was relegated to a 3-6-1 season even while the fullback became a first-team *AP* All-America selection himself.

"I don't know who the kid was, but it was a dummy scrimmage and that was so stupid," McElhenny said. "It was dumb. It wasn't even a tackling situation. God damn, Heinrich was the difference in us going to the Rose Bowl in 1951. Heinie had that extra spark that a winner has. I knew if he would have been with us we would have gone to the Rose Bowl."

With McElhenny now in the NFL, Heinrich returned for his final college season in 1952, led the nation in passing again and repeated as first-team *AP* All-America while leading the Huskies to a respectable 7-3 season. He finished with career passing marks of 335 completions in 610 attempts for 4,392 yards and 33 TDs. He ended up ninth in the Heisman Trophy balloting.

"He was the best college quarterback of the 1950s," McElhenny said. "He was a pretty calm guy, but he was tough as nails. He was mentally and physically tough. He didn't yell or scream. It seemed like his mind was always into the game. He'd throw you out of the game if you were not doing what you were supposed to."

Heinrich, super-confident to the point it bordered on arrogance, played at a time when the nation's top players were showered with improper benefits from school boosters. He was not exempt from the practice. He asked to become part of it. As a Northwest recruit

Don Heinrich
Washington Quarterback

he had to make his personal needs known, which ran contrary to the special treatment an outsider such as McElhenny received without solicitation.

"Heinie complained to me that he wanted an automobile, so I took him to Torchy Torrance's office," said McElhenny, referring to an alumni team supporter who oversaw an improper players' slush fund. "Next thing I know, he had a blue '41 Chevy. Everybody was for the Huskies in those days."

Heinrich, same as McElhenny, didn't turn to school for an education. Those two players were there only for football and all of the trappings that came with being UW stars intent on playing in the NFL.

"He was quite a guy but I never understood him, because he was brilliant but he didn't go to class," said Black, who later became a Moses Lake dentist. "He did just enough to sneak by."

The UW quarterback, who lived at 4826 Terrace Dr. N.E., played six of his eight pro seasons for the New York Giants, appearing in three NFL championship games. He was a journeyman player at best at the next level. In a unique arrangement, he actually started and played the first two series of the infamous 1958 title game won by the Baltimore Colts in the league's first sudden-death overtime before giving way to Charley Conerly, which made Heinrich a reliever in reverse order.

Heinrich moved to coaching and served as an assistant for five NFL teams, made an unsuccessful bid to become the Seattle Seahawks' first head coach, and turned to broadcasting. Teaming with Barry Tompkins, Heinrich was refreshingly blunt and critical as a UW radio analyst, though it was too much for loyal fans to bear. He published a popular football magazine that carried his name and operated a summer football camp, both ventures based in Seattle. He had a son, Kyle, who played safety for the Huskies and played in the 1978 Rose Bowl.

On Feb. 29, 1992, Heinrich was 62 when he died of pancreatic cancer at his home in Saratoga, Calif. As his health slipped away, the quarterback and his Huskies fullback huddled on the phone, even when a two-way conversation was no longer possible.

"I talked to him every day the last six weeks of his life," McElhenny said. "The last week his wife said he can't talk anymore, just say hi to him."

There was no more heading for the fire escape, no sneaking off to a tavern this time, no ordering up cold ones. It was just two old All-America players staying loyal to the end. ❖

FRED HUTCHINSON
Seattle's First Big-League Boss

Fred Hutchinson was summoned from the Detroit Tigers' bullpen for a midseason relief appearance, a move that surprised people throughout Major League Baseball. The Seattle man was handed a lineup card, not a ball. The pitcher was asked to salvage a season, not rescue an inning. On July 5, 1952, on the day following the nation's annual fireworks display, Hutchinson — appropriately a man known for his explosive manner as a player — was installed as the Tigers' 14th manager.

This grim-faced person known as Hutch had no prior managing experience at any level of baseball. He was five weeks shy of his 33rd birthday. He was a year removed from making his only All-Star Game appearance and was putting the finishing touches on a 95-71 career pitching record in the big leagues. He was not mentioned in press accounts as a logical successor when it became clear Detroit manager Red Rolfe was going to lose his job.

The Tigers, however, saw a natural leader in Hutchinson while handing him a job previously held by Hall of Fame inductees Ty Cobb and Mickey Cochrane. Hutch was effective in contract

> This unconventional move turned Hutchinson into the only homegrown big-league manager culled from the sandlots of Seattle, a city generally light in supplying professional sports leaders.

negotiations as the Detroit players' representative and as the A.L. players' rep, and the feeling was he could carry that influence onto the field.

"You had to be around the man," said the late Ron Santo, a Hall of Fame third baseman for the Cubs and White Sox and a Seattle native. "He exuded energy and charisma. You felt good about being around him. He was just a winner. He reminded me a lot of Leo Durocher. Durocher was not liked but he was highly respected. Fred was liked and highly respected."

This unconventional move turned Hutchinson into the only homegrown big-league manager culled from the sandlots of Seattle, a city generally light in supplying professional sports leaders. George Irvine (Detroit Pistons, Indiana Pacers) and Quin Snyder (Utah Jazz) are the only locally produced NBA coaches. Don Coryell (St. Louis Cardinals, San Diego Chargers), Dennis Erickson (Seattle Seahawks, San Francisco 49ers) and Jim Mora Jr. (Atlanta Falcons, Seattle Seahawks) are the only NFL coaches pulled from the area.

Hutchinson managed for 12 seasons in the big leagues, also directing the St. Louis Cardinals and Cincinnati Reds. He learned what it was like to be fired, his Cardinals' dismissal coming a season after he was named N.L. Manager of the Year. He experienced the baseball ultimate, guiding the Reds to the 1961 World Series against the New York Yankees and Roger Maris

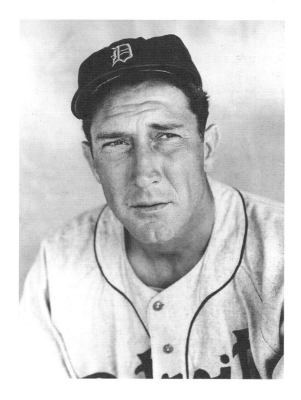

Boxer Al Hostak gets a Hutchinson autograph in 1938.

the Detroit leader, beating the St. Louis Browns 5-0 on the way to compiling a 830-827 managerial record. He walked away from a franchise that employed him for 11 seasons in different capacities when the Detroit front office wouldn't give him more input on personnel matters and offered him a one-year contract extension instead of two.

He stuck around as the Tigers manager long enough to endear himself to everyone with his volcanic temper, which was usually directed at the umpires. He was witty and funny, too. After getting tossed out of a game by umpire Bill McKinley, Hutch served up an unforgettable post-game comment to reporters, alluding to an assassinated president, when he remarked, "You can say for me that they shot the wrong McKinley."

Hutch, who grew up in Rainier Beach at 6102 S. Keppler St., returned home and managed his old team, the Triple-A Rainiers, to the 1955 Pacific Coast League pennant, before St. Louis brought him back for another big-league dugout stint the following season as a replacement for the fired Harry "The Hat" Walker.

Hutch's Cardinals teams went 76-78, 87-67 and 69-75. He alternately was loved and jeered once back in the Midwest, and he received his most identifiable and endearing nickname, "The Big Bear," from former big-league catcher and St. Louis radio broadcaster Joe Garagiola for his serious, if not perpetually stone-faced, demeanor.

"I used to call him that because of the way he conducted himself," Garagiola said. "He looked at you like a big old bear. He came at you, looking at you with those eyes. He was rugged and tough, but could be so gentle. I'd always tell him, 'You're happy inside, you just never tell your face.' "

Infielder-pitcher Johnny O'Brien, previously a Seattle University All-America basketball player, was traded

He turned over his pennant-contending Cincinnati team to coach Dick Sisler, another former Rainiers manager, on Aug. 13, 1964. He formally resigned on Oct. 19. He died in Florida, surrounded by family members, on Nov. 12. He was 45.

from the Pittsburgh Pirates to the Cardinals midway through the 1958 season. He already knew Hutchinson from home, but had never played for him. O'Brien caught on quick to the routine.

After a Cardinals relief pitcher blew a big lead and the game in the ninth inning in San Francisco, O'Brien noticed how all of the St. Louis players cleared out in a hurry. Walking up the tunnel from the dugout to the clubhouse, O'Brien witnessed Hutch scream uncontrollably at the umpires and break every overhead light bulb, showering the defenseless arbiters with glass. "The umpires were yelling, 'Now, now, Hutch, take it easy!' " O'Brien said.

As a player and a manager, Hutchinson never turned his smoldering mood on another player. He made it a rule to wait a day before speaking with an offending underling. He locked himself in his office or hotel room and broke furniture, windows and doors.

At different managerial stops, he had a punching bag installed to release his frustration. Umpires suffered his wrath without fail, but never his players. After all, the Hutchinson silent treatment could be far more

coming off his 61-homer regular season. And Hutch went from the majors' least-known manager to sadly the most recognizable as he hung on as long as he could before dying from terminal lung cancer shortly after the 1964 season ended.

Gene Freese, who played third base for Hutchinson in St. Louis and Cincinnati, forever admired this tough-minded man. "He was like Billy Martin; he didn't take nothing from nobody," Freese said. "He ran a team the way it should be run — he put confidence in you and he always kept it there."

Hutch was a player-manager for two of his three seasons in charge of the Tigers, though he pitched only three times in the dual role. He won his first game as devastating to someone than a string of harsh words.

"He got the best out of your ability by not saying anything, but just looking at you," Santo said. "That's respect and it's very unique."

After Hutchinson was fired in St. Louis before the 1958 season ended, the Triple-A Rainiers brought him home to manage again and talked of making him the general manager, if not a part-owner. Hutch stayed in Seattle for a half-season, until Cincinnati summoned him back to the big leagues as a replacement for the fired Mayo Smith, becoming the fourth Reds manager in less than a year.

Hutch compiled records of 39-35 (half-season), 67-87, 93-61, 98-64, 86-76 and 60-49 (two-thirds of a season). He gave the Reds their first National League pennant in 22 years, though they lost in five World Series games to the Yankees.

He was a fearless man, unafraid to mix it up, and he could handle himself. On a road trip to San Francisco, Hutchinson went out to dinner alone and returned to the clubhouse wearing sunglasses, covering up two black eyes. He'd been caught off-guard and was mugged by a group of men on the street. He wasn't done with them.

"Somebody jumped him while he was out having dinner and it took two or three of them to get him," Freese said. "Our third-base coach, Reggie Otero, said, 'Some guys attacked my manager and he knows who they are.' Two nights later, Hutch came in with a smile on his face. Reggie said he had got them all."

Hutchinson, however, could not beat lung cancer despite trying everything. Before the 1964 baseball season began, the lifelong smoker discovered a lump below his right collarbone that was malignant and the cancer soon spread throughout his body. He kept his Reds managerial job while traveling back and forth

Fred Hutchinson managed the Cincinnati Reds.

to Seattle for radiation treatments in a hyperbaric chamber. "It was almost like a year-long death watch," O'Brien said.

Hutch received hundreds of letters from sympathetic baseball fans. He was hospitalized at midseason, forced to miss road trips to Milwaukee and St. Louis. He withered away in front of everyone as the season played out, losing 25 pounds from spring training to July 25.

He turned over his pennant-contending Cincinnati team to coach Dick Sisler, another former Rainiers manager, on Aug. 13, 1964. He formally resigned on Oct. 19. He died in Florida, surrounded by family members, on Nov. 12. He was 45.

Hutchinson's brother, Bill, a surgeon, went on a crusade against cancer, motivated by his sibling's death. He helped found the Fred Hutchinson Cancer Research Center, an internationally known medical facility that rose like an outfield fence alongside the city's Lake Union shoreline. He resolutely reminded other baseball players what had killed his brother.

"I was a smoker and I smoked when I played up there," said Ed Sukla, a former Seattle Angels and big-league relief pitcher. "Bill Hutchinson walked into the clubhouse and said, 'Hey Ed, when are you going to stop smoking?' I said, 'I kind of like it.' He said, 'I'll take you to a cancer ward and show you guys in the prime of their life who are suffering — they have holes in their tongues.' I quit smoking that year. I've never had a cigarette since."

Hutchinson posthumously was named *Sport* magazine's Man of the Year. Cincinnati retired Hutch's No. 1 jersey, forever honoring the fallen leader. He was a conscientious baseball man to the end.

Five weeks from his death, Hutch watched the Philadelphia Phillies blow a big lead and let the 1964 N.L. pennant slip away, and he put in a consoling phone call to Phils manager Gene Mauch, who later shared that tidbit with the *Post-Intelligencer*.

"Imagine that, he was asking if *he* could help me," Mauch marveled. ❖

HARRY "THE KID" MATTHEWS

The Cold War Boxer

Harry Matthews cried when he came home from school. In 1931, he was 9 and inconsolable after a classmate picked on him and knocked him around in Boise, Idaho. Matthews' tough-guy father, a blacksmith who doubled as a city councilman, came up with an impatient but spine-building solution: He made the boy take boxing lessons.

This worked out better than anyone could have imagined because it brought young Harry a lifetime vocation, a catchy nickname and cult-figure status built on carefully orchestrated fight-game propaganda. By the time he was 14, Matthews had his first professional fight. In the ring at such a young age, he became forever known as "The Kid." He wouldn't stop punching until he became Seattle's first boxer groomed for a heavyweight championship bout and the first fighter from the city to put it all on the line in New York City.

Matthews fought for 12 years in Idaho, turning into a hard-hitting man who answered to his youthful moniker. He gravitated to Seattle in 1949 to make more money and build a bigger fight following. He aligned himself with boxing manager Jack Hurley, a colorful character who had deep connections in the fight game and always had his hand out.

The negotiations between Matthews and Hurley became Northwest sporting legend, though the provisions of their business arrangement were enough to make The Kid cry again. Settling on a fee, Hurley said he wanted half of everything Matthews made. The boxer balked, insisting that no other fight manager got that amount.

"How much are you making now?" Hurley retorted.

"Nothing," was the boxer's response.

"Well, 50 percent of nothing is nothing," Hurley huffed. "Fifty percent of what you'll get is 50 percent better than what you've got now."

> By the time he was 14, Matthews had his first professional fight. In the ring at such a young age, he became forever known as "The Kid."

They shook hands and were partners. They were invested in each other. They had seven good years together.

Matthews compiled an 87-7-7 pro record with 61 knockouts, fighting from 1937 to 1956. He competed in the middleweight, light heavyweight and heavyweight divisions, though never topping 180 pounds. Among his most notable victories were 10-round decisions over middleweight title-holder and Seattle native Al Hostak, lightweight title contender Bob Murphy and one-time heavyweight champion Ezzard Charles.

Without much prompting, Seattle adopted The Kid. He kept the city entertained at all times. Every time Matthews broke a sweat it turned up in the headlines. There were newspaper photos of him posing with

Boxer Harry "The Kid" Matthews shares a moment with his daughter Connie, 2.

dignitaries or holding up a newborn daughter. Nothing he did escaped the outside world. "Mrs. Kid Matthews, who filed for divorce a week ago, called it off and returned to Harry's corner," Emmett Watson wrote in his *Seattle Post-Intelligencer* column.

Matthews, who lived in West Seattle at 2211 S.W. Myrtle St., was a natural for the limelight, given his appearance combined with his popular endeavor and the international climate — that of an articulate and ruggedly handsome fighter taking on all challengers during the Cold War era.

"He didn't fit the concept of a fighter, of pug-ugly," said Bill Sears, a publicist for several Seattle teams. "He was a real gentleman. Of all the fighters we had around here, he probably was the one who captured the imagination of everyone more than anyone else."

They practically had no choice. Hurley was a boxing promoter so adept at swaying public opinion he had outraged congressmen investigating the fight game when a title bout for The Kid wasn't arranged quickly enough to suit the boxing manager. Matthews was a good boxer, but Hurley carefully built him into something bigger than life, often spewing his fun-loving histrionics from cluttered living quarters at the Washington Athletic Club or the Olympic Hotel.

There were no apologies either when Hurley's fighter crashed hard to the canvas on July 28, 1952, at Yankee Stadium in New York, knocked out in the second round by the great Rocky Marciano. "He went amateur on me," Hurley said afterward. Others weren't quite so sure the cantankerous trainer didn't sacrifice Matthews for a big payday by making him more of a finesse fighter than bawdy brawler.

"Jack Hurley was for Jack Hurley," said the late Pat McMurtry, another heavyweight who fought out of Seattle. "He wanted me badly. I didn't care for him. His

training. He was undersized. He faced an East Coast media highly skeptical of his chances.

Matthews also faced one of boxing's great ones in Marciano, who was 41-0, a year from becoming world champ and three years from finishing as the only undefeated heavyweight title-holder in history (49-0). Yet Matthews fought in New York the year before and beat Murphy with a unanimous 10-round decision, leading to title-fight discussions. The Kid had gone through 55 bouts undefeated earlier in his career. It wasn't nearly enough against Marciano.

Under the lights and media glare, The Kid gamely won the first round, though he missed with a half-dozen punches. Marciano had seen enough. Two minutes and four seconds into the second round, he landed two sharp left hooks and Matthews landed on the canvas, not sure where he was and unable to regain his feet. The fight was over just like that. There were no tears from this whipping, just great disappointment.

The blows were enough to knock all the momentum out of Matthews' career. In 1951 alone, he had 15 bouts. After losing to Marciano, he fought only 13 more times over the next five years. "He handled it pretty well," daughter Connie O'Keeffe said. "He always said it was one of those things."

Five years later, Marciano visited Seattle for a guest appearance at a local Golden Gloves tournament. The champ made a point of contacting Matthews and visiting his former opponent at his home. Marciano

hadn't been in the ring long with The Kid, but it was enough to form a favorable opinion.

"I like this guy," Marciano said. "Back in New York, before our fight, he just minded his business and didn't tell everybody what he was going to do. Then after I beat him he didn't pop off or alibi. He just packed his bags and went home. There was something about the guy I liked and I'm glad I got to be friends with him."

Giving up boxing in 1957, Matthews became a King County sheriff's deputy, owned and operated the Bell Pine Tavern in Seattle, and had his own rental equipment and welding business in Everett. He also was a novice inventor, creating a winch device that could parallel park a car and a motorized cart he could ride behind the bar and deliver drinks, though he never tried to commercialize these efforts.

Matthews lived in Everett until 1999 when he began to suffer from dementia. A live-in housekeeper took advantage of the former boxer, allegedly stealing $15,000, a cellular phone and assorted boxing memorabilia, and coercing Matthews into purchasing a car for her. In his debilitated state, he couldn't fight back.

O'Keeffe, one of the boxer's three daughters, interceded and moved her father to her California home and then to an assisted-care facility, where he died of a heart failure on March 11, 2002. Matthews was 80. He was brought back to the Northwest for burial, to the region that revered him, to a place where he would always remain The Kid. ❖

biggest mistake was he changed Matthews' style. I'd rather fight a person who tried to swap punches instead of some slick boxer. My phone rang once and it was Matthews. What I said to him was what I was supposed to say, 'Stay away from Hurley. He's a bandit. He takes all the money. He was a known thief.' "

The Marciano fight was Matthews' one chance at ultimate glory and Seattle was giddy over this moment, which was another chance for it to collectively puff out its chest and attempt to become a big-league city. The *Post-Intelligencer* ran a story every day for nearly a month leading up to the bout and sent sports editor-columnist Royal Brougham by train to cover the event.

Washington's U.S. senators, Warren Magnuson and Harry Cain, were ringside and seated among the 20,000 people who turned out at Yankee Stadium. There were obvious distractions to overcome. Matthews' second of three wives had just given birth to a daughter and he arrived in New York later than planned for his pre-fight

William Henry Harrison "Tippy" Dye was the new University of Washington basketball coach in the fall of 1950, a man with deep Ohio roots and an appreciation for presidential history. Dye was christened after the country's ninth president, William Henry Harrison, who served as an Indiana governor and Ohio senator before campaigning for the Oval Office using the popular slogan, "Tippecanoe and Tyler, too."

Dye, barely 5-foot-8, had no catchy phrases to offer his next team. Instead, he laid out an executive order that was fairly blunt and straightforward: Players would dress a certain way, act a certain way and play a certain way, and, if they did this, he promised they would be successful. By Dye's third season he had them in the Final Four, the Huskies' only appearance in program history. He became the first Seattle coach to take one of the city's highest-profile teams – football, basketball or baseball – and put it in a national championship setting.

Dye was a noticeable upgrade over his predecessor, Art McLarney, whose career path took him from Roosevelt High School's state championship team to UW assistant coach to a convenient replacement for

> By Dye's third season he had them in the Final Four, the Huskies' only appearance in program history. He became the first Seattle coach to take one of the city's highest-profile teams – football, basketball or baseball – and put it in a national championship setting.

the legendary Clarence "Hec" Edmundson. The latter was 61 when he was forced into retirement against his wishes after 27 years on the job. McLarney coached the Huskies to an NCAA Tournament berth in the first of his three seasons in 1947-48, but he drank too much and ultimately had to go, too.

"McLarney was the nicest guy, but he had an alcohol problem," said Bob Jorgensen, a former UW basketball player. "He hated flying. We wanted to fly to Kansas City for the NCAA regionals, instead of the train. Nobody wanted to take the train. We got off the bus at the airport and McLarney was gone for 30 minutes and he came back snockered. He had to be carried onto the plane. He was singing songs."

Dye turned up in Seattle as a surprising hire because it meant he had to leave Ohio State, his alma mater. He coached the Buckeyes to the NCAA Tournament and Big Ten championship, and their finest season to that point, 22-4. He distinguished himself like no other OSU athlete by earning nine letters in three sports. He quarterbacked the Buckeyes football team to three consecutive victories over Michigan and scored several times as a punt returner. He was twice named all-conference in basketball and was a second-team All-America selection as a senior.

Pro sports beckoned the multitalented Dye, who was pursued by the New York Giants in football and

St. Louis Cardinals in baseball, but those offers didn't hold his interest. "I didn't want to play either one," Dye said. "I wanted to play basketball, but they didn't have a pro sport yet."

Dye became the UW basketball coach for two reasons: 1) The school was willing to pay him $12,500 per year, a sizeable raise over his Ohio State salary of $7,500; and 2) he expected to become an athletic director and figured he needed to know as many influential people in as many places as he could to make that happen, including the West.

"We were all excited for the opportunity," UW center Bob Houbregs said. "Everybody accepted it because it had been a loose operation before."

Dye didn't have to overhaul the Huskies program, just put the pieces together in an orderly fashion, beginning with Houbregs, who became the 1953 College Player of the Year. He coached for nine seasons, compiling a 156-91 record. While his most successful UW team was 28-3 and finished third in the country in 1953, Dye considered his 1952 team, one that went 25-6 games and failed to reach the postseason, his most talented group. "We had more scoring in '52 with [Frank] Guiness at forward," Dye said. "We had a better bench."

As good as Dye was, the national championship eluded his Huskies because of a clever coaching ploy formulated on the opposing bench in the Final Four semifinals. On March 17, 1953, Phog Allen instructed his Kansas players to jump in front of Houbregs whenever he crossed mid-court on offense, a strategy that fouled out the big man early in the second half and led to a crushing 79-53 outcome.

The blowout was uncharacteristic for these Houbregs-led teams, which lost just 14 other games during the big man's career, no others by more than

Tippy Dye sits next to center Bruno Boin in 1957.

11 points and most by five points or less. To his credit, Dye got his team reassembled and routed LSU 88-69 the next night in the consolation game.

"I built it around Houbregs, naturally, just getting the ball to him; it was very simple, there was nothing to it," Dye said. "We didn't get much help [against Kansas]. We don't like to say a thing about it, but, yes, we had a good enough team to win it all."

Dye coached six more seasons at Washington and even fielded one of the nation's tallest teams at the time, in 1959. He built those Huskies around 6-9 center Bruno Boin and 6-7 forward Doug Smart, but backcourt shortcomings limited the team to an 18-8 season.

Dye, who lived at 4113 55th Ave. N.E., resigned at the UW to become an athletic director for the next 15 years at, in order, Wichita State, Nebraska and Northwestern. He pursued the same job with the Huskies, but the school passed him over in 1956 and hired George Briggs, a California assistant athletic director, to clean up an athletic program mired in a football-related scandal.

Harvey Cassill, the UW AD who hired Dye, told the coach that he was next in line for the job, but Cassill was fired over the football improprieties, taking that promise with him. "I wanted to be the director here," Dye said. "Unfortunately, I didn't make it. I knew I could do it."

It was time for the former Buckeye to move on and return to the Midwest. Others saw the man's obvious disappointment in not becoming the top UW athletic administrator. "I think he lost his focus a little because he was looking to become an athletic director," Houbregs said.

In 1962, Dye was hired by Nebraska and was credited with turning that school into a football powerhouse by immediately installing Bob Devaney as the coach. Dye also improved the Cornhuskers' basketball program by hiring Joe Cipriano, a UW starting guard for his 1953 Final Four team, from Idaho to become his coach. Dye retired at Northwestern in 1974.

Dye returned to Seattle for a 2008 basketball reunion at Edmundson Pavilion. Forward Mike McCutchen and Houbregs were the only living starters from the Final Four team. Two of Dye's Huskies coaching successors, Marv Harshman and Lorenzo Romar, were among those who visited him. Harshman, who was 90 at the time and three years younger than Dye, quipped, "If I could be as young and springy as you I'd be all right."

Dye, who was 97 when he died on April 11, 2012, sat at a table and was plugged into a sound system so he could hear everyone speak. Five decades later, the UW's most successful basketball coach still had that great name and a presidential aura about him, not to mention everyone's respect and attention. He had left an undeniable impact.

Each exchange was heartfelt. Houbregs thanked his coach for making him the player he was. Dye reminded him that he had a lot of natural talent. One by one, former Huskies' players approached Dye that day, eager to gain his attention, retired men turning into college kids again. ❖

Bob Houbregs launched his shot from deep in the corner, the top of the key, blanketed by defenders, wherever and whenever he wanted. He was granted a freedom not unusual for a high scoring basketball player. Yet Houbregs separated himself from all others with this offensive green light: The graceful University of Washington center tossed in a sweeping hook from outrageously long distances and he did it with uncanny accuracy.

Houbregs didn't invent the hook shot; he just customized it in a way that was near impossible to replicate. UCLA center Lew Alcindor, after he converted to Islam, became Kareem Abdul-Jabbar and moved to the NBA, perfected what became known as the skyhook, or half-hook, always used up close. Clyde Lovelette, a Kansas All-America center and Houbregs' contemporary, was the first big man to serve up a more conventional hook shot with great frequency. But Lovelette never went beyond the foul line with his one-handed offerings.

The UW's lanky 6-foot-7 Houbregs regularly prowled the perimeter and catapulted them from what later became 3-point range. It was an intricate basketball ballet. He should have received four points for each make, considering the degree of difficulty involved, but they were still worth just two. He became Seattle's most unique basketball player of any generation.

The UW's lanky 6-foot-7 Houbregs regularly prowled the perimeter and catapulted them from what later became 3-point range. It was an intricate basketball ballet.

BOB HOUBREGS
The Ultimate Captain Hook

"In my sophomore year I didn't take it past 12 feet," said Houbregs, nicknamed "Hooks" by Seattle sportswriters. "Later on, as they double-teamed me, I came out a little higher and higher. Thank goodness, I kept making them. It's embarrassing to think I went out that far. I don't know why I did it. It wasn't a good shot. I wasn't in good position if I missed."

Only the defenders had reason to be red-faced or apologetic. Crowds packed arenas up and down the West Coast to watch Houbregs entertain them like no other college player of his era. He was named the 1953 Helms Foundation Player of the Year and he used his amazing hook shot to average 25.6 points per game that season, sending the Huskies to a 28-3 record and a Final Four appearance.

His patented offensive move was all finesse and rhythm. Houbregs cleared his hips and did a perfect pirouette away from defenders before softly unleashing the ball in front of his face with a full extension of his arm and watching it swish through.

Houbregs was a sophomore when he and teammates Doug McClary and Lee Wade were asked to try the hook by new Huskies coach Tippy Dye, who had taught it to his Ohio State center at his previous stop. McClary and Wade didn't take to it, but Houbregs was a natural.

Bob Houbregs and his 1957 Topps basketball card.

He shot it with both hands, initially more left-handed than right, before Dye urged him to concentrate on one hand as a junior, and he chose his right one. He shot 200 hooks during each practice, fed by Dye until the coach tired and then by a manager until the drill was done.

Houbregs always aimed for the net and never banked in his shots, and for good reason: As a kid hanging out at Seattle's Mercer Playfield, he learned how to shoot using only a rim attached to a pole with no backboard.

"I took to the hook immediately and I had success with it; it was a big shot for me," Houbregs said. "The idea was to get away from the defense a little bit. I extended it farther than probably I should have in my senior year because we were playing different defenses. It just came easy to me. It was the swing. Once I got into rhythm, I could shoot any distance."

Houbregs scored 30 points or more in 10 games as a senior. He came up with a school-record 49 points against Idaho at midseason, breaking Jack Nichols' previous school mark by 10 points. He scored 45 points against Seattle University and one of the nation's top point-producers in Johnny O'Brien in the NCAA tournament. He had 42 against Louisiana State, out-scoring the equally offensive-minded and NBA-bound Bob Pettit by six points in his final college outing at the Final Four.

"Bob had a hook shot that copied me," Lovelette insisted. "Not too many people used the hook shot in our era. George Mikan and Bob Kurland might have used it a little more, too. Bob had more of a laid-out, lazy hook, sort of a straight-arm type of hook, and he would step away when he shot it. Myself, I would just spin either right or left and toss it up. I can't remember Bob shooting other shots. That's what was different between us."

Seattle U's O'Brien disagreed strongly, saying, "Houbregs didn't copy anyone. He started low. He had superb hand control. It came off his fingertips. Bob had tender hands."

California coach Pete Newell, widely known for his expertise with big men, was even more emphatic about the UW player when he told the *Seattle Post-Intelligencer*, "Bob Houbregs changed the game of basketball with his hook shot."

Houbregs turned up in Seattle as the Canadian-born son of a well-traveled, minor-league hockey player who brought his family to the city after joining the Seattle Eskimos, and he was raised in lower Queen Anne at 600 4th Ave. N. He gave the skating game a try but didn't like it, and found a sport that better suited him at Queen Anne High, earning a college basketball scholarship.

When Houbregs was a UW sophomore in 1950-51, he averaged 13.6 points per game and started at center for a 24-6 Huskies team that made it to the second round of the NCAA Tournament, beating Texas A&M 62-40 before losing to Oklahoma A&M 61-57.

As a junior, Houbregs averaged 18.6 ppg and was a second-team All-America choice. Yet his 25-6 UW team failed to reach the NCAA tourney, losing two of three games in the Pacific Coast Conference playoffs to a John Wooden-coached UCLA team, an outcome that was doubly disappointing because the Final Four was held in Seattle that year. A Lovelette-led Kansas team won the NCAA championship at Edmundson Pavilion, but Houbregs was not there to see it.

"I sold programs outside, that's all I did," Houbregs said. "I didn't want to go in. My heart was still broken."

A year later, Houbregs and the Huskies returned to the NCAA Tournament and were favored to win it all when they advanced to the 1953 Final Four in Kansas City. In the semifinals, however, Kansas players were instructed to step in front of Houbregs once he crossed the midcourt line and phantom offensive fouls were called on the big man until he drew his fifth early in the second half. Houbregs finished with 18 points, all in the opening half, and watched helplessly from the bench as a close game turned into a 79-53 defeat without him, the worst of his college career.

"I thought we were the best team there, I really did, I still do," Houbregs said of a Final Four won by Indiana. "It was a shame we weren't able to prove it."

Houbregs played at a time when an athletic slush fund headed up by booster Roscoe "Torchy" Torrance was in place for the Huskies, though mostly for football players. The nation's best basketball player was loosely involved. "They helped out one guy on the basketball team and I won't name him," Houbregs said. "The only thing I ever got was a suit to wear because I didn't have one. I got it from Littlers [clothing store]. I assume it was from Torchy."

He spent five NBA seasons in five cities after getting drafted in the first round, traded and having a franchise disappear. He wasn't quite the same scorer as a pro, averaging a pro-best 11 points per game for two Fort Wayne teams that advanced to the NBA finals. He had a high game of 30 twice.

Houbregs' NBA career came to a sudden end after he ran into a basket support, severely injuring his back. Doctor advised him to retire. Keeping his hand in the game, he sold basketball shoes and became a Converse executive. He returned to the pros and served a four-year stint as Seattle SuperSonics general manager that ended with his resignation in 1973, a situation he handled gracefully.

The big man, who was 82 when he died on May 28, 2014, gravitated to Edmundson Pavilion and watched UW games beneath a blanket-sized purple banner hanging from the rafters that carried his name and number (25). Houbregs was the only basketball player at the school to have his jersey retired until Brandon Roy (3) joined him 56 years later. The hook shot, however, faded from prominence in favor of the jump shot, more out of ignorance than anything else.

"I don't think many coaches these days know much about the hook shot," Houbregs said. "I wish they'd bring it back, at least a short hook shot. It worked for me." ❖

Top 10 UW Basketball Players

1. Brandon Roy, G
2. Bob Houbregs, C
3. Christian Welp, C
4. Nate Robinson, G
5. Steve Hawes, C
6. James Edwards, C
7. Isaiah Thomas, G
8. Jack Nichols, C
9. Chuck Gilmur, C
10. Detlef Schrempf, F

JOHNNY & EDDIE O'BRIEN

Basketball Bookends

Begrudgingly, the Catholic priest and the rest of the city welcomed the lookalike little guys from Jersey, not at all certain they would amount to much, yet in the end astounded by what they did. The O'Briens became Seattle's most prominent set of athletic twins.

Johnny and Eddie O'Brien at Seattle University.

As Johnny and Eddie O'Brien prepared to board a Northwest Airlines flight to Seattle in 1949, their grandmother cried and cried. She was concerned for the safety of the twins from South Amboy, N.J., who were headed to an unfamiliar and supposedly unrefined place three time zones away. "She still thought there were Indians out there," said Jim O'Brien, yet another sibling.

Grandma's airport consternation was understandable because the brothers actually had agreed to become Chieftains. She was not the only one connected to this trip who was misled, whether innocently or not.

Seattle University basketball coach Al Brightman, who enticed the O'Briens west with athletic scholarships, somehow failed to mention an important detail while seeking upper-campus approval: Johnny stood just 5-foot-9, Eddie a half-inch shorter. This omission was discovered in an uncomfortable manner when the brothers were introduced to Father Albert Lemieux, the university president. That first campus meeting didn't go well.

"He said, 'You're not the O'Brien twins,' and he walked away," Eddie O'Brien said. "Brightman had told a little white lie, that we were 6-3 or 6-4."

Begrudgingly, the Catholic priest and the rest of the city welcomed the lookalike little guys from Jersey, not at all certain they would amount to much, yet in the

end astounded by what they did. The O'Briens became Seattle's most prominent set of athletic twins, heading up a list that includes Jim and Lou Whittaker, mountain climbers from West Seattle; Jon and Jerry Knoll, starting University of Washington offensive tackles from Ballard; Lodrick and Rodrick Stewart, Rainier Beach basketball guards who played together for USC before Rodrick transferred to Kansas; and pairs skaters Karol and Peter Kennedy, silver medalists at the 1952 Oslo Olympics who grew up in Queen Anne.

None of the others were as visible or as romanticized as the O'Briens. The brothers were responsible for transforming a small-college basketball program into a national power, a reputation firmly cemented when Seattle U played a competitive game against the Harlem Globetrotters and pulled a huge upset. They ran opponents dizzy during their 1951-53 college career, propelling the Chieftains into the National Catholic, NCAA and National Invitational tournaments for the first time, winning 90 of 107 games and elevating the school to Division 1 status.

They made Seattle U such a popular college basketball destination that future NBA players Elgin Baylor, Eddie Miles, John Tresvant and Tom Workman, among others, followed them there, with Baylor leading a Chieftains team to the NCAA Final Four. "Ed and I helped get it started," Johnny O'Brien said, "and Baylor put the cap on it."

One brother was a point guard and the other, amazingly, a center. Although dwarfed in the post, Johnny O'Brien was the first NCAA player to score 1,000 points or more in a season (1,051) when he averaged 28.4 points per game as a junior in 1952. He finished with 2,733 points in his career. He had amazing quickness. He had excellent touch. And he was hardly a one-man show for the Chieftains.

By the time they were seniors in 1953, Johnny was a first-team All-America selection for the *Associated Press* and *United Press International*, Eddie a *UPI* third-teamer. In their final collegiate season together, Johnny averaged 28.6, Eddie 16.6.

"The notoriety was shared together," Johnny O'Brien said. "I was perfectly aware that without Ed in there I wouldn't have been able to accomplish a lot of what I did. Ed was a good enough scorer. We both realized that."

That was evident when the twins made a triumphant return to the East Coast as seniors. At Madison Square Garden, Eddie scored a career-best 33 points and Johnny added 29 as the Chieftains won a wild one with New York University, 102-101, marking the first time two college teams had broken the 100-point barrier in the same game.

At Boston Garden, Johnny struck for 41 points and Eddie contributed 21 in Seattle U's 99-86 victory over Boston College. At Philadelphia's Convention Hall, Johnny came up with 26 points and Eddie supplied 22

in the Chiefs' 90-77 victory over St. Joseph's. East Coast sportswriters couldn't dig deep enough for superlatives to describe the puny pair. "The Shrimps from Seattle have done it again," wrote David Eisenberg of the *New York Journal-American*.

The O'Briens, whose father Edward ironically was nicknamed "The Chief," previously couldn't convince anyone back East that they had any basketball skills. In South Amboy, they were cut as sophomores and juniors at St. Mary's High School. During that second year, however, they were pulled from the stands and asked to play against the varsity team when snow postponed the scheduled game. The O'Briens' makeshift group won and the twins were handed jerseys on the spot. As seniors, they led St. Mary's to a state title. It still wasn't enough to land two college basketball scholarships.

Columbia offered them one scholarship to split. To obtain their pro baseball rights, the Brooklyn Dodgers offered to pay their tuition and books at St. John's — but not room and board — in exchange for a handshake deal. Iona and Mount St. Mary's passed on them. The brothers thought they were headed to Seton Hall, making it to the final cut of a 100-player tryout before they were chased off. "No one would take us," Eddie O'Brien said. "Height was the No. 1 reason."

The O'Briens, who were offered minor-league baseball contracts by 14 of the 16 MLB franchises, stayed out of school for a year but continued to play at the semipro level, advancing to the National Baseball Congress tournament in Wichita, Kansas. They went up against a Mount Vernon Milkmaids team that featured Brightman, who dabbled as a first baseman when he wasn't coaching basketball. The game went 19 innings. The O'Briens scored big before the final out.

"In the 12th, I got on first and Brightman asks, 'How are your grades?' " Eddie O'Brien said. "I told

him, 'I can't talk to you now, I just got the steal sign,' and I stole second. That was it. A week later, we got scholarship offers in a telegram."

The twins were so good they could dunk, though they didn't do it in games, unwilling to show up opponents. The O'Briens offered a set offensive formula that worked well enough to leave it alone — Eddie to Johnny, over and over.

With the ball in his hands, Johnny O'Brien kept defenders guessing at all times. On three different trips down the floor he might use three different shots: A right-handed hook, left-handed hook and fall-away jump shot. It was Brightman's idea to put him in the post, using the logic that bigger players couldn't run or jump with Johnny, though defenders repeatedly tried to intimidate him. He was left with seven broken noses and three sets of teeth. He just took the substantial abuse and played on.

Eddie and Johnny flank coach Al Brightman.

Johnny O'Brien scored in double figures in all of his Seattle U games except one: Sick with the flu against St. Martin's as a senior, he scored nine points in the first half and, against his objections, was taken to Seattle's Providence Hospital for fluids at halftime. He didn't return to the gym. "I felt I could have played in the second half, but I wasn't the coach of the team," he said.

Johnny O'Brien scored 20 points or more in 76 of his 107 career games, 30 points or more in 24 games, and 40 or more on seven occasions, and he broke 50 once, coming up with a career-high 51 at Gonzaga as a senior. He had a huge following.

"He had more moves than anybody I've seen," said Rod Belcher, a former KING-TV sportscaster and Humboldt State basketball player. "It was still the greatest thrill I've had in basketball — watching that little son of a bitch play the big man's game."

Eddie O'Brien shared in all of it, authoritatively running the offense and offering subtle differences. He was more of a set shooter while his brother offered jumpers and hooks. Eddie shot with two hands; Johnny typically launched the ball with one hand. Eddie wore No. 3, one digit lower than Johnny. While his sibling usually led the Chieftains in scoring, Eddie took care of other needs, such as 21 assists against St. Martin's.

Yet Eddie O'Brien could influence a big game with points when needed. At Oregon as a senior, he stunned a sellout crowd of 8,200 at McArthur Court when he dropped in a 25-foot set shot with two seconds left to give Seattle U an 81-79 victory.

"Brightman's instructions to us were whoever has the ball with two seconds left takes the shot and let's get out of here," Johnny O'Brien said. "With two seconds left, Ed had the ball and a set shot. I started walking up the floor. I knew it was in."

The O'Briens were resourceful in many ways. They lived on campus in Veterans Hall, paying $30 per month to stay in a place that catered mostly to Korean War veterans, and no longer exists. Everybody used hot plates, which caused building fuses to blow all the time, and people often were forced to eat and study by candlelight.

Father Lemieux, with the twins' height discrepancy no longer an issue for him, was appalled when he visited and found them sitting at a card table, eating Campbell's soup, grilled-cheese sandwiches and two-day-old donuts, standard fare for them. The priest made sure they were given cafeteria privileges.

The twins' most amazing feat came in 1952 when a midseason game was arranged between the Chieftains and the Harlem Globetrotters at the University of Washington's Hec Edmundson Pavilion. It was one of three U.S. Olympic Team fund-raisers involving the popular touring team. Seattle U won 84-81 in a serious game played before a sellout crowd of 12,500, which included celebrity trumpeter Louis Armstrong, who played "Baby, It's Cold Outside," and actress Joan Caulfield. This was the Globetrotters' first loss in their storied history.

Johnny O'Brien scored 43 points over the guard of the legendary Goose Tatum. Eddie O'Brien sank a midcourt shot before the halftime buzzer. Everyone except the visitors went away happy. "I find that it cost me considerable to get O'Brien-ized," Globetrotters owner Abe Saperstein said memorably after the game.

The O'Briens bypassed the NBA. They were drafted by the Milwaukee Hawks but turned to baseball instead, as infielders and relief pitchers, going where the money was. Scouts closely followed their Seattle U baseball careers, which mimicked each other: In their final college season as juniors, Johnny led the Chieftains

with a .4324 batting average, barely edging Eddie's .4323. Each accepted a reported $25,000 signing bonus from the Pittsburgh Pirates and went straight to the big leagues, becoming its first set of twins to play on the same team in the same game. They were encouraged to sign with Pittsburgh by entertainer Bing Crosby, one of the owners, and put under contract by Branch Rickey, best known as the GM who brought Jackie Robinson to the big leagues and broke the color line.

The brothers were teammates for five seasons with the Pirates, interrupted by a 21-month Army call-up for each. They were together until Johnny was traded to the St. Louis Cardinals during the 1958 season. Johnny hung on one more year with the Milwaukee Braves before both were finished with the big leagues.

Johnny, who moved to a Green Lake home at 2405 N. 75th St., ventured into Seattle politics as county commissioner and served as the top Kingdome administrator. Eddie became Seattle U's athletic director and baseball coach for two decades, plus he spent another season in the big leagues as the Seattle Pilots bullpen coach to collect his pension. He was living at 552 Alder St. in Edmonds when he died on Feb. 20, 2014, the morning after attending a Seattle U basketball game, while suffering from Parkinson's disease. He was 83. He received an emotional eulogy from his brother at a huge funeral service in downtown Seattle.

The New Jersey siblings chose to ignore their detractors and not let their confidence waver, no matter how big the slight over their obvious lack of height. Everybody, they learned, came around and warmed to them.

"Father Lemieux later told us, 'You guys can't believe how little you looked,' " Eddie O'Brien said. ❖

GUYLE FIELDER
Seattle's Ice Man

Guyle Fielder retired to Arizona, where the temperature often exceeds 100 degrees and seems an unlikely place for a man who made his living on the ice. Yet little about this talented hockey player's existence ever made sense. The man known as "Golden Guyle" was considered pro hockey's greatest minor league player and an offensive genius on skates.

Fielder belonged in the National Hockey League, yet his impatience and limited opportunities largely confined him to the Northwest, making him Seattle's greatest rink presence and minor-league player in any sport. He spent 15 dazzling seasons in the city, nine of them as the Western Hockey League scoring champion, during his 22-year pro career. He turned up in Seattle in 1953 and stayed so long he played for the Bombers, Americans and Totems. He was the first skater anywhere in pro hockey to accumulate 100 points in a season, totaling 122 for the 1956-57 Seattle Americans. Fielder became one of four hockey players to surpass 2,000 career points at any level, joined only by NHL mainstays Gordie Howe, Wayne Gretzky and Mark Messier.

"It's totally mind-boggling to me he couldn't play in the NHL and not be a great player in the NHL," said the

> **Fielder belonged in the National Hockey League, yet his impatience and limited opportunities largely confined him to the Northwest, making him Seattle's greatest rink presence and minor-league player in any sport.**

late Bill McFarland, Fielder's Seattle hockey teammate and coach, and former World Hockey Association and WHL president. "He was sort of Gretzky before Gretzky."

While Fielder never backed away from the net, he always had a certain reticence in promoting himself. Against his wishes, the Guyle Fielder Trophy — which annually recognized the WHL leading scorer — is positioned in the front entryway of Fielder's home in Mesa. His second wife, Georgia, put it there. She practically had to body-check the former center to have her way.

The trophy, which is five feet tall and mounted on a wood frame, was given to Fielder when the league folded in 1974. His spouse wanted it on display.

"It's probably one of our worst arguments," Georgia Fielder said. "He's so humble he thought people would think he's a showoff. It's still sitting there. Now Fielder, we're not putting it on eBay."

If only Georgia Fielder were calling the shots when the Idaho-born and Saskatchewan-raised player was launching his hockey career. He did it the hard way. Fielder was just 9 when he was taught the game in Canada and right away learned how to flip-pass the puck but not get out of the way of it. He caught one in the mouth and broke his two front teeth, giving him lifetime caps.

Fielder was a puck-handling magician, preferring to devilishly play keep-away with defenders in frustrated

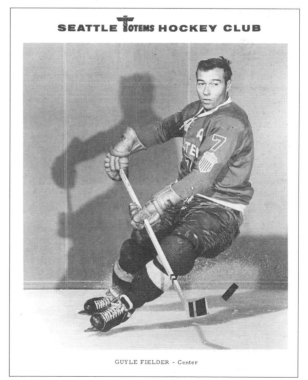

SEATTLE TOTEMS HOCKEY CLUB

GUYLE FIELDER - Center

Guyle Fielder featured in a Totems' publicity photo.

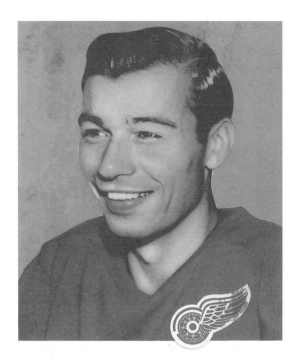

pursuit rather than move the puck around to everyone else, which ran counter to the way the NHL offensively played the game. He never thought he was a good enough shooter, though his stats said otherwise.

"I was told for years to shoot the puck, but I didn't have a very good shot," Fielder said. "If I was in front of the crease I could get the puck in the back of the net."

With just six NHL teams in operation, Fielder couldn't emulate his greatness at the sport's highest level. He briefly auditioned with half of them, the Chicago Blackhawks, Detroit Red Wings and Boston Bruins.

He went to the Red Wings after his groundbreaking 100-point season with the Seattle Americans. He played on the first line with the offensive-minded Howe and Jim Wilson, providing one too many playmakers. They didn't mesh early on and Fielder was moved to the second line and then the bench. He asked to be sent back to Seattle, but Detroit general manager Jack Adams gave Fielder a $500 raise to mollify him, boosting his salary to $8,000. Fielder asked to go back to Seattle a second time and the request was granted.

"I was 27 and some people don't mature until an older age, and that's what happened to me," Fielder said. "I didn't realize the opportunity I had in Detroit and how good it was. Maybe if I had stuck around and worked my way back, I might have got my chance."

In Seattle, Fielder was a 13-time WHL all-star, counting first- and second-team selections; a six-time league most valuable player, including divisional and playoff honors; and a member of three Totems championship teams, appearing in the finals six times. He played in 1,487 regular-season games in the minor leagues, producing 438 goals and 1,491 assists, and in another 110 playoff games, coming up with 25 goals and 83 assists, totaling 2,037 career points.

The NHL missed out on a great hockey talent, though Fielder had reservations he would have been as offensively proficient had he stuck around. "I kind of doubt I could do it on that level, but I would have liked to had more time to see that style," he allowed. "It never happened. But I wasn't going to sit around."

Fielder was a clever left-hander with finesse moves, someone who would rather set up a goal than score one, yet another reason his rich talents went overlooked. Before a WHL game in Vancouver, however, he read a Canadian newspaper account that dismissed his scoring prowess. He went out that night and collected all of the goals in a 4-3 victory against a reputable and NHL-bound goaltender in Lorne "Gump" Worsley.

> "I was 27
> and some people
> don't mature until an older age,
> and that's what happened
> to me," Fielder said.

"It said, 'Fielder never scores; he just passes off to his wingers all the time. You don't have to worry about him,' " Fielder said. "I went out and got all four goals."

Fielder, who lived in Richmond Beach at 19827 19th Ave. N.W., was so beloved by Seattle hockey fans that some of them named their sons after him. One person christened in this manner was Guyle Wilson, who become a London businessman and kept a Totems puck on his desk at work.

"We had some great teams in Seattle, but we had a couple of coaches who weren't that great and we didn't make the playoffs enough," Fielder said. "I was successful because we had good teams and good players to play with. They treated my family well in Seattle. My folks lived there. I stuck around as long as I could. I didn't know any better."

In 1969, Fielder retired from the Totems over a contract squabble. But the WHL expansionist Salt Lake Golden Eagles lured him back with a hefty $20,000 contract and he played four more seasons.

He left the game for good with the Portland Buckaroos in 1973.

Fielder was 39 when he went to Utah because he needed to come up with $10,000 for a business venture and didn't know how to raise it otherwise; he was paid half of his contract in cash up front and received the rest throughout the season.

Out of hockey, Fielder worked behind a pari-mutuel window, alternating between a Phoenix horse track and a Portland dog track, before he finally moved to the desert year-round. In his home, he kept hockey sticks stacked in a corner, a green Totems' jersey No. 7 framed in a case, team photos, plaques and autographed photos from daredevil Evel Knievel and NHL legend Bobby Hull. Hockey was good to him and he took advantage.

"I had no mentors; I just had this lady luck back then," Fielder said. "I just loved to play. I almost would have played for nothing. I was very lucky. I also liked to think I was smarter than all of those dudes."

In 2002, Fielder's wife convinced him to travel to Toronto and visit the Hockey Hall of Fame. They drove cross-country in a motor home accompanied by Fielder's sister and brother-in-law, spending a

"I had no mentors; I just had this lady luck back then," Fielder said. "I just loved to play. I almost would have played for nothing. I was very lucky. I also liked to think I was smarter than all of those dudes."

month on the road and covering 10,000 miles. They visited Niagara Falls. They stopped to see old hockey connections, foremost among them former Totems teammate Pat Quinn, who enjoyed long-running NHL success as a player and coach.

Once at the Hall of Fame, they checked out a display specifically devoted to Fielder, one that held a life-sized photo, jersey, trophy and plaque. "The light over it was out," noted Fielder, ever the perfectionist. That was odd, too, because whenever he was on the ice, the light usually came on. ❖

10 Totems to the NHL

1. Guyle Fielder (Detroit, Boston, Chicago)
2. *Pat Quinn (Atlanta, Vancouver, Toronto)
3. Noel Picard (St. Louis, Atlanta, Montreal)
4. *Bill Dineen (Detroit, Chicago)
5. John Hanna (N.Y. Rangers, Philadelphia)
6. *Emile Francis (N.Y. Rangers, Chicago)
7. Don Ward (Boston, Chicago)
8. *Keith Allen (Detroit)
9. *Marc Boileau (Detroit)
10. Bobby Schmautz (Chicago, Van., Boston, Edm., Colo.)

* Quinn, Dineen, Francis, Allen & Boileau also were NHL coaches

KEITH JACKSON

The Big-League Voice

Keith Jackson practically climbed out of the box that delivered the first TV set to Seattle. He was new and different, too. With a camera pointed at him, Jackson provided journalistic brashness at a time when a less-confrontational on-air approach was the norm for this new medium.

He was a KOMO TV and radio presence during 1954-64, anchoring the nightly news and cutting his sporting vocal cords as a play-by-play announcer for University of Washington football, Seattle University basketball and Triple-A Seattle Rainiers baseball. This sent him to a much bigger stage.

Jackson was the first national sports broadcaster to emerge from Seattle, becoming a legendary figure while calling college football games for ABC. Among those following him from the Northwest to the TV big leagues were John Clayton, Kenny Mayne, Linda Cohn and Ed Cunningham, each turning up as a familiar

> Jackson was the first national sports broadcaster to emerge from Seattle, becoming a legendary figure while calling college football games for ABC.

face for sports cable giant ESPN. This city was the launching pad.

"It's where you started," Jackson said of Seattle. "It was the first big job."

Jackson took great pride in turning annoying when a tough story dictated it. He had no problem showing his overbearing side, even with station clients. "The University of Washington said, 'You can't come in here with a television camera,' and I said, 'Throw me out,' and they did," he recalled.

The Georgia native wanted access to closed administrative hearings in 1955 dealing with a UW football slush-fund scandal. Jackson was denied entry. He reminded school officials that his station held Huskies broadcast rights and suggested rather strongly there was more to this relationship than puff coverage. Again he was rebuffed. Jackson and the station took their argument to the state Supreme Court. The broadcaster was blunt when it came to his reporter rights, "I said, 'Horse[bleep], I'm a legitimate newsman.' " Closed doors were forced open.

"Keith was so damn good," said Herb Robinson, a fellow KOMO broadcaster. "He was very precise. He also had that fantastic temper. He would get so mad. I remember coming back to the newsroom and him saying, "God damn it, we're never going to mention the University of Washington again.' There was always some hassle."

Jackson arrived in Seattle as an enterprising Washington State College graduate and transplanted Southerner who had served in the Marines. In 1952, he called his first football game over campus radio station KWSC in Pullman, describing Stanford's 14-13 victory over his alma mater. "The Cougar quarterback fumbled the damn snap for the extra point," he said, still doing commentary and disgusted at the outcome.

When the WSC football team was on the road, Jackson pulled Western Union reports and recreated the action, a broadcasting necessity at the time and a chance to test his creativity. For his first basketball game he had to deal with the lights going out at halftime, leaving him to improvise. "I didn't have the foggiest idea what to do," Jackson said. "I just told stories."

Jackson was a natural for this line of work. His family back in the South could have predicted it, but his relatives didn't always understand it. "I was a fantasy kid, a dreamer," Jackson said. "My grandma once told my mama, 'The kid is crazy, walking around the cornfields, talking to himself.' I was calling ballgames."

He had two broadcasting offers when he left Pullman: He could work for WSB in Atlanta for $69.50 per week or in Lewiston, Idaho, for $82.50. He accepted the heftier Northwest offer. He hadn't cashed too many paychecks before KOMO beckoned him to Seattle. He drove around his new city in a small Chevrolet, wore a crewcut and impressed everyone with his supreme confidence and relentless style.

"He was different from the other reporters," said Howard Ramaley, a KOMO cameraman. "He impressed me with his knowledge and his ability to handle almost any situation. No one got the best of Keith."

Actually that wasn't always the case. Seattle turned into a competitive broadcast market and Jackson, as this earnest kid straight out of college, had dues to pay early on. KING's Rod Belcher, another no-nonsense broadcaster, and Jackson were heady competitors in pursuit of viewers and listeners and awards.

"Not to blow my own horn, but for three straight years when we were going head to head I was voted the state's top sportscaster," Belcher said of their rivalry.

Jackson anchored KOMO's nightly newscasts.

"I have the damn plaques to prove it. I think Keith was kind of pissed off at that."

Covering sports was not a full-time job back then. Jackson did the news, too. He kept a rigorous schedule, often arriving at the station in the morning, or whenever a story broke, and anchoring the 6 p.m., 10:30 p.m. and 11 p.m. newscasts.

"You put in 16-hour days and that was ordinary and you didn't think about it," he said. "You were young

and strong and not thinking about it. We went in and worked until we dropped."

The networks noticed Jackson's ability right away. In 1958, ABC made him a job offer that he turned down. The money wasn't right. Plus, he wasn't done with Seattle. That summer, Jackson and Ramaley traveled to Great Britain and Russia, accompanying the UW's eight-man rowing team that was denied the right to race for Intercollegiate Rowing Association championships because of the aforementioned football slush fund. Every team in the athletic department, regardless of guilt or innocence, was penalized. To temper the inequitable treatment, crew races for the Huskies were arranged against London's and Moscow's best.

Jackson saw opportunity for himself, as well. He was bent on doing the first live foreign radio broadcast on Russian soil. There were countless logistical problems. Asked for a credential he didn't have, Jackson pulled out his Seattle police media card and did some fast talking to gain access to the reservoir race site. The Huskies won a historic race in Russia and Jackson's description was heard back in Seattle.

"I could tell that story in such a way that it was as good as Mark Spitz and seven gold medals," Jackson said, comparing the UW crew to the Olympic swimmer. "It was as good as Eric Heiden and five medals. It was as good as two successive Super Bowls. It was a glorious thing. I'll never forget it because it told me about the fiber of society after people had said to hell with you. It remains one of my highlights."

He was a relentless newsman, though not always a perfect one. Jackson signed off a Gold Cup hydroplane race on Lake Washington by declaring a wrong winner and the station went to a movie. Before long Jackson was back on the air, interrupting the film and sheepishly getting the outcome right.

Jackson was a UW football radio broadcaster.

He was the voice of UW football, his broadcast time highlighted by the 1961 Rose Bowl team. A typical call for him at Husky Stadium, such as when Don McKeta caught a game-winning TD pass against Oregon, went like this, "It's a touchdown! It's a touchdown! It's a touchdown! Holy Mackerel!"

Yet at no time in Seattle did he utter his trademark game observation "Whoa Nellie." He first heard his expressive grandfather use that phrase, but it wasn't until he left for ABC and Los Angeles and a local

broadcaster bellowed those words that he decided to make them his own, too. A network job demanded a customized approach.

"I turned down a very good offer in 1958," Jackson said. "I wasn't sure in '58 that I was ready to leave. In '64, I had to leave. I had to find out."

Jackson was worthy of the big time. He pulled choice assignments from the beginning, calling the Winter and Summer Olympic Games, Monday Night Football and the NBA and Major League Baseball before settling in almost exclusively as ABC's chief college football presence for four decades. He often returned to Husky Stadium to call games and reminisce about his broadcast beginnings.

His fading name still adorns the beat-up metal mailbox at 18130 60th Ave. N.E. at a Kenmore house overlooking Lake Washington, forever keeping him connected to the city, if not providing an unusual sporting artifact. Seattle forever remains Jackson's audition, his first take, his test audience. ❖

George Bayer was never confused with Jack Nicklaus or Arnold Palmer, his golf contemporaries. Bayer won just four PGA Tour events. Yet he carved out a unique place in the fairway sport that made everyone envious: People claimed Bayer was the longest hitter in tour history. They likened him to John Daly without the personal drama, neon golf clothes and souped-up drivers.

Bayer played on the tour in 1955-73 and was an agreeable guy with a big body who strode up to the tee without much fanfare and let loose with fearsome power. The former University of Washington football player could crush a golf ball so far people half expected the powerful Bremerton native to tee one up in his waterfront hometown and sail it across Puget Sound on the fly.

Bayer was a long-drive contest waiting to happen whenever he stepped on the course, making him Seattle's biggest athletic novelty act. *The Guinness Book*

> Bayer was a long-drive contest waiting to happen whenever he stepped on the course, making him Seattle's biggest athletic novelty act. *The Guinness Book of World Records* credited him with launching a ball a record 436 yards in an official PGA Tour event, a drive since exceeded by others using modern equipment.

GEORGE BAYER

The Big Stick

of World Records credited him with launching a ball a record 436 yards in an official PGA Tour event, a drive since exceeded by others using modern equipment. For his longest drive anywhere, Bayer leaned into a tee shot on a par-5 hole at a sun-baked Lakes Golf Club in Sydney, Australia, and, with a slight breeze behind him, drove it over a hill 315 out, got a huge downhill kick and ended up inside 50 feet of the green. The hole measured 586 yards.

"What was it like when he hit it? That's a simple answer: A-W-E," said Tacoma's Ken Still, who played with Bayer on the PGA and Champions tours. "When have you ever seen a guy hit it over 300 yards with a persimmon driver? And he hit it 350. How far could he hit it with a metal driver and today's ball? It might be 400-plus."

Bayer was called the Babe Ruth and Paul Bunyan of golf. He combined his ample 6-foot-5, 250-pound frame with innate power to become a PGA Tour sideshow. He was another Hale Irwin, someone who went from accomplished college football player to a golfer worthy of the game's highest level.

With Bayer, his ball never came out of orbit. At the 1953 Las Vegas Invitational, a non-tour event back then, his tee shot hit a spectator standing greenside on the second bounce — 476 yards away.

"Big George could knock the living snot out of the ball," golf legend Sam Snead told the *Washington Times*. "I once saw Bayer drive a ball through the green on a 430-yard hole, and that was 40 years ago before the age of metal woods, graphite shafts and the modern golf ball. If he was out there with [modern] equipment, I bet he'd average near 350 yards off the tee. He was such a big man; it was all muscle left over from his football days."

Bayer was one of five brothers who grew up in a house that bordered Kitsap Golf and Country Club. He started playing when he was 7 and caddied, but golf didn't consume him. Leaving Bremerton High School, he joined the Navy for three years and served in World War II, and then enrolled at the UW.

An all-around athlete, he became a two-way lineman for the post-war Huskies football team, lettering for four consecutive seasons and serving as a game captain. Among his UW teammates were Don Coryell, Don Heinrich, Hugh McElhenny and Arnie Weinmeister. Bayer, who lived at 311B 2nd Ave. N., was good enough that he played in the East-West Shrine Game in San Francisco and was drafted in the 20th round (252nd overall) by the NFL's Washington Redskins. His football career, however, brought mixed reviews.

"I don't think, in my opinion, that George made much of an impact on our offense; now on defense, that might have been different," McElhenny said. "He was our giant, our big guy. He was so much bigger than anyone else. The others were around 200 to 210 pounds on the offensive line. He was a quiet, laidback guy and wasn't very talkative. He was kind of aloof. He didn't say much on the football field; he just did his job."

No records exist to prove that Bayer appeared in a regular-season NFL game, but he always insisted that the paperwork was incomplete and he briefly pulled duty as a Redskins reserve player in 1950. He injured a knee and quit following a squabble with owner George Preston Marshall. Bayer later played for the Brooklyn Brooks and Richmond Arrows of the minor-league American Football League.

When his football pursuits ended, Bayer retreated to Los Angeles and worked in a Ford auto dealership. He started playing golf again because the other salesmen did. With his ability to knock a golf ball out of sight as his calling card, he received countless offers to play in celebrity tournaments. The big guy, who wore his hair in a trademark crewcut, joined entertainers Bob Hope, Danny Kaye and Gary Cooper, plus Supreme Court Justice Hugo Black, on the golf course just so they could marvel over his rockets. Hope encouraged him to turn pro.

Seattle's first full-time PGA Tour player, Bayer polished his game to the point he played for 19 years, collecting career earnings of $188,868. He was more than just a long-ball hitter. He won the 1957 Canadian Open, 1958 Mayfair Inn Open, 1958 Havana International and 1960 St. Petersburg Open. In the Cuban event, he had a double-eagle after holing a shot from 240 yards out and defeated Snead in a one-hole playoff.

The power was on at all times. Bayer regularly destroyed MacGregor golf balls after only a few

Bayer regularly destroyed MacGregor golf balls after only a few prodigious swings and he had to replace them, usually needing four per round.

prodigious swings and he had to replace them, usually needing four per round. That's what people expected from him.

"Every golfer wants to be known as a good player, not a freak," Bayer said in 1959. "It got a little tiresome, watching some fellow jump over a fence to see where my drive went and then never seeing any other part of my game. But you get used to it."

While galleries flocked to see Bayer pulverize the ball, he was entertaining in other ways, too, on the occasions he let his temper unwind. He tried to withdraw from a tournament once in Kentucky and was refused; playing angry, Bayer took a 17 on a hole, drew a $200 fine and was handed three months probation from PGA Tour officials.

At the 1960 Masters, Bayer and Jack Fleck were so disgruntled over slow play they decided to show what could be done with a little hustle in the final round. They brazenly rushed through 18 holes in an hour and 52 minutes. Bayer shot 72, Fleck 74.

Bayer also spent nearly a full decade on the Champions Tour, often returning home for the GTE Northwest Classic at Seattle's Inglewood and Sahalee country clubs, before hip and knee replacements effectively curtailed his game.

On March 16, 2003, Bayer died of an aneurysm at home in Palm Desert, Calif., stricken while dining with his wife Mary Ann and former PGA and Champions tour player Bob Goalby. Bayer was 77. A funeral service was held in Palm Springs and he was memorialized in his hometown of Bremerton.

Bayer was the guy who hit a golf ball longer than anyone — and that meant any generation, anywhere, any time. His length off the tee was so rare that every one of his peers would have given anything to experience it just for a day, round or shot. ❖

John Cherberg was a natural politician, always campaigning, forever endearing himself to the people of Seattle. He was an able glad-hander who could work a room and impress everyone with his charm, and he was tough and strong-willed when necessary. He served for 32 years as Washington's lieutenant governor, answering to five governors. "Cowboy Johnny" just wasn't any good at kissing babies, such as the kind who wore shoulder pads and helmets.

While Cherberg's legacy remains tied to his political success, his profound failure as a University of Washington football coach was a close second. He lasted three seasons. Yet he was on the job long enough to help bring down the football program, the entire Huskies athletic department and the Pacific Coast Conference.

> Caught in the middle of an ugly 1955 player revolt, Cherberg got even with the mutinous bunch: He went on KING-TV, with the small screen still a new broadcast medium, to explain his firing by the school administration and he stunned everyone by publicly exposing an alumni slush fund headed by loyal booster Torchy Torrance.

JOHN CHERBERG
The Payback Coach

Caught in the middle of an ugly 1955 player revolt, Cherberg got even with the mutinous bunch: He went on KING-TV, with the small screen still a new broadcast medium, to explain his firing by the school administration and he stunned everyone by publicly exposing an alumni slush fund headed by loyal booster Torchy Torrance. Cherberg pulled the wraps off this well-entrenched payoff system that benefited UW players: If the coach was going down, everyone was going with him. He was the man in the center of the Seattle's first serious athletic scandal. The city has never had a more vindictive sports figure.

Now the player payments weren't Cherberg's idea, and he actually might have done college football a huge service by helping speed the clean-up. His actions clearly interrupted the game's standard way of doing business back then — which was compensating players in excess of prescribed scholarship amounts through secretive booster funds — and USC, UCLA and California soon joined the UW as guilty parties.

However, Cherberg's overriding pettiness and failure to connect with his players made the situation far more untidy than needed, and the Huskies ultimately were held up for national ridicule as model cheaters. *Sports Illustrated*, in its second year of existence, did one of its first investigative pieces on the UW's disturbing downfall.

UW football coach John Cherberg, left, greets UCLA's Red Sanders before a game.

"Cherberg was an extremely poor football coach," said Huskies receiver Corky Lewis, who became a Yakima doctor. "He didn't have the background or the talent to take that job. The pressure seemed to get to him. He was technically a poor football coach and he couldn't manage the players."

In 1953, Husky football fans hailed the promotion of Cherberg from freshman coach to head coach because of his local connection. He was one of them. Although Florida-born, he was raised primarily in Seattle, growing up in a Magnolia house at 3055 21st W. He was a quarterback and running back for Queen Anne High and the UW. Replacing the fired Howie Odell, who was canned following a 7-3 season, Cherberg was the first former Huskies player put in charge of the football program.

He also had that catchy nickname, "Cowboy Johnny," given to him by *San Francisco Examiner* sports editor Prescott Sullivan. In 1932, Sullivan saw Cherberg use his galloping running style to race 88 yards on a punt return for a touchdown in an 18-13 victory over the then-Stanford Indians – it was a cowboy against Indians.

The good feelings for Cherberg as the football coach began to erode after 3-6-1 and 2-8 seasons, and his job fell into serious jeopardy when his players rebelled in 1955. The Huskies found the coach strange and abusive. His edicts left them genuinely puzzled. They couldn't whistle or chew grass in his presence, cross their legs while seated on the bench, take more than one dessert at the training table under his watchful gaze, or walk on a different side of a post.

Cherberg was old school in approach, superstitious to a fault and blunt beyond reason. He had his ways of doing things and some were painful. Lewis wore a jockstrap and nothing more when Cherberg approached him in the locker room before a game.

Are you mad, the coach demanded to know in an animated tone.

"I said, 'I don't have to be mad. I'm always ready to play a good game for you,' " Lewis said. "He said, 'No, I want you mad!' He stomped on my foot with his cleats. My foot was so swollen during the game, I wasn't sure I could play."

The Huskies coach often couldn't make up his mind, sending a player into the game and repeatedly calling him back to the sideline. He fetched a cup of water and, in maddening order, drank it, spit into the 40-yard sideline cone and threw the paper cup away at the 50-yard line, and players watched and shook their heads at this ritual.

"Cherberg was so paranoid," said UW quarterback Steve Roake, who became a Pan American Airlines pilot. "What really disturbed me was he would tear down a player in front of the other players. He berated [quarterback] Sandy Lederman in front of everyone. You just got embarrassed for him."

UW halfback Dean Derby, who later played for the Pittsburgh Steelers and Minnesota Vikings, said this about his coach, "He was really a weirdo. It was terrible. Everything was about luck."

Cherberg's football empire came unraveled in 1955, in a season that started out promisingly enough. The Huskies dominated Minnesota 30-0 in Minneapolis. They won a 7-0 thriller from USC at home on a storybook, hook-and-ladder pass play from Roake to Jim Houston to Lewis that covered 80 yards in the closing moments. They were 4-0, ranked 12th in the nation and harbored realistic Rose Bowl dreams.

Two things got everyone in the mood for a football mutiny: The Huskies stopped winning and the head coach turned deeply jealous of an assistant coach. Cherberg's team went more than a month without a

victory, dropping close one after close one, the most agonizing a 19-17 road defeat to fourth-ranked UCLA on a last-second field goal.

Jim "Suds" Sutherland was Cherberg's other sticking point. Sutherland was an assistant hired away from California and pining for a head-coaching job, and not afraid to show it. A faction of players sensed the rebel in Sutherland and rallied behind him.

Before their final game against Washington State, players approached Torrance at his Grosvenor House apartment complex downtown to air their complaints about Cherberg. They decided that night to push for the removal of the UW coach and replace him with Sutherland.

Yet Cherberg was wise to the rebellion. Four days after beating the Cougars 27-7 and finishing with a 5-4-1 record, he dismissed Sutherland. The players' meeting and resulting vote to oust the head coach were made public. Thirty Huskies in opposition to Cherberg were identified by name in the *Seattle Post-Intelligencer*.

Unnerved by the wide-ranging turmoil within the football team, UW regents met and concluded that Cherberg could keep his job if he could get his players under control. Five weeks later, on Jan. 28, 1956, they decided this wasn't possible after all and fired the man. Cherberg next revealed the player payoffs.

The Greater Washington Advertising Fund was exposed as the source of the Huskies' extra benefits. Torrance, a short, personable UW alumnus who considered it his calling to make life easier for the athletes, enlisted 70 to 75 of the city's more influential businessmen to open their wallets and upgrade the Huskies. He was convinced there was no better way to compete with the California schools, which had their own well-tended booster organizations. These alumni groups were almost as competitive as their teams.

"Somebody from USC came up to the Northwest and was told we had a slush fund with $28,000 in it," said lineman Paul Wallrof, who became a Puget Sound football coach. "The USC guy said, 'We spill that much booze at our alumni association.' "

Roake, a highly recruited athlete from Chicago, visited Michigan, Illinois and Washington, and was tempted with extra benefits at each school. After joining the Huskies, he became one of their higher-paid players, receiving $250 each month on top of the $75 scholarship stipend. Carl Williams of Rhodes Department Store was his designated benefactor. "We were all getting a little something," Roake said.

The Huskies secured the services of Ed Sheron, a big lineman from Montana, in a recruiting battle with Notre Dame, Michigan, SMU and Minnesota. He was paid $100 extra per month. He received free shoes from retailer Lloyd Nordstrom and occasional cash from jeweler Paul Friedlander. "I was supposed to get a car," Sheron said. "It was on order when the whole thing broke."

Once league investigators sifted through Torrance's operation, they determined that 27 Huskies had received $65 on average more than the scholarship limit. At least those were the people willing to admit to accepting booster payments. Players had to make restitution or sit out the first five games or last five games of the 1956 season. Four UW players accepted temporary suspensions.

One who didn't cop to anything was Derby. The Walla Walla product received $50 a month extra in 1955. New UW football coach Darrell Royal advised him to tread carefully with probing league officials. "He said, 'Dean, I'm not going to tell you to lie but if you tell the truth you're not going to play football next year,' " Derby said.

10 Notable Sports Firings

1. John Cherberg (UW coach)
2. John Castellani (SU coach)
3. Rick Neuheisel (UW coach)
4. Jim Mora Jr. (Seahawks)
5. Bob Hopkins (Sonics)
6. Marv Harshman (UW coach)
7. Chuck Knox (Seahawks)
8. Dick Vertlieb (Sonics, Mariners)
9. Jack Patera (Seahawks)
10. Bob Blackburn (broadcaster)

Derby told investigators any extra money he had came from his father-in-law. He continued to receive an added $100 per month from a clothing company the following year — even after the penalties were meted out. "My job, once a month, was to go down there and pick up my check," Derby said. "I don't look at that proudly, frankly."

George Briggs was the Huskies' new athletic director, entrusted with replacing the fired Harvey Cassill and restoring order. The UW athletic program was socked with a two-year probation that affected every sport at the school and a $52,000 fine — then the stiffest punishment in league history. Briggs' first move was to hire Royal away from Mississippi State and the SEC, a league that didn't always play by the rules either.

"He let me know when he hired me that there wouldn't be any rule-breaking," said Royal, who left after one season for Texas.

While the Huskies put things back together, the PCC broke up, with sportswriters bringing a black wreath to a final solemn meeting in Portland. The California schools were guilty as charged in paying players extra, but balked at the harsh penalties and wanted out. The Huskies regrouped with their rivals in a new league, the Athletic Association of Western Universities, and gradually expanded into the Pacific-8, Pac-10 and Pac-12 conferences.

Cherberg, who was 81 when he died on April 8, 1992, rebounded nicely from his turbulent period with UW football. Within a year of his ouster, he was elected as lieutenant governor, a job he kept for more than three decades. From Olympia to Seattle, people knew who he was.

Helped by all of that negative slush-fund publicity and public squabbling, Cowboy Johnny was a loveable martyr and, with all of his quirks and strong-armed tactics, he was readymade for politics. ❖

BILL MUNCEY

Seattle's Lead Roostertail

Hydroplanes became instantly popular in Seattle when the calendar turned to 1950, their roaring engines and geyser-like roostertails drawing thousands of giddy race fans to Lake Washington. People showed up in their yachts and pleasure cruisers, tying them to a log boom for a close-up view and a weekend party, or they came by land and camped out along the shoreline, which was equally festive.

It was an aquatic Woodstock, nothing but fun and hydro music. The boat races soon were part of Seafair, the city's annual summer celebration and the crowd count for the event eventually reached an estimated 500,000.

There was just one problem with all of this frenzied activity: The hulking thunderboats, even with their colorful names and paint jobs, were hard to distinguish at times as they bunched up around the turns and lurched together through the continuous lake spray. Hydro racing needed a rock star, a front man. Swashbuckling, full-throttle driver Bill Muncey became that guy, turning into Seattle's greatest and most popular motor sports athlete and helping make hydro racing a city institution.

In 1955, Muncey arrived from the Midwest and stood out as this human rocket hurtling through liquid space. With his ruggedly handsome looks and natural charisma, the Detroit native resembled the equally dashing Arnold Palmer of the golf world. If Arnie had

his army, Muncey answered to a Northwest navy. Both men competed in a fearless, aggressive manner in their sports, and Muncey's gung-ho style won him a huge following throughout the city.

"I was a big fan of Muncey," said Billy North, a devoted Seattle hydro fan as a kid and later a big-league baseball player, "because he had guts."

Muncey gave Seattle its much-needed hydro hero and fans always knew where this man was whenever he pulled out of Stan Sayres Pits and roared onto the course. He had an explosive foot on the pedal and aggressive mindset in his open cockpit, running hell-bent for the inside lane at the start of each heat, unconcerned if he got in anyone's way. All of his moves were calculated.

"Bill Muncey was like a grand chess master who could figure 20 or 25 moves in advance," said Bob Senior, a Seattle hydro enthusiast. "At the five-minute gun, he knew where all his competitors were and would be, as the clock ticked down, and he would beat every one of them over the line with a flying start."

Muncey won a record 62 races, including eight Gold Cups, and claimed seven national-point titles while driving the *Miss Thriftway*, the *Miss Century 21*, the

> Swashbuckling, full-throttle driver Bill Muncey became that guy, turning into Seattle's greatest and most popular motor sports athlete and helping make hydro racing a city institution.

Notre Dame, the *Miss U.S.* and the *Atlas Van Lines*. He was dubbed "Mr. Unlimited" and referred to as "the Babe Ruth of boat racing."

The son of a wealthy Michigan auto dealer, Muncey left home to create his own identity and did so while boosting the profile of his fledgling water sport. Seattle welcomed him enthusiastically and let him mix with everyone, on and off the dock. He had his own local radio show, spinning modern jazz records. An accomplished musician with a saxophone, he played with the Seattle Symphony. He even ran for lieutenant governor — and lost.

Muncey, who lived at 9056 E. Shorewood Drive on Mercer Island, could be dashing and impulsive, too. Divorced, he met Fran Norman from Puyallup and two weeks later they talked of getting married. Muncey and Norman sought advice from Pat O'Day, the well-known KJR radio personality, Seafair TV race broadcaster and one-time owner of the *Miss KYXX* hydro. To his credit, O'Day, who was big on outlandish, on-air promotions and probably not the best choice for a marriage counselor, had the couple draw up pros and cons on a legal pad regarding the proposed nuptials.

"When all the questioning was complete, when I had explained to Fran all the obstacles I could see, when Fran said none of them frightened her for a minute, and when Bill mirrored her points of view, I said, 'OK, here's the list, you're both all right with potential problems, you're big kids, you want to do this right now and I can't think of any reason, other than traditions, that you shouldn't, so go get married,'" O'Day recounted. "That next Wednesday they did."

While the hydro victories piled up, Muncey's setbacks were equally riveting. In 1957, he flipped the *Miss Thriftway* in front of the judges' stand in Indiana while traveling 175 mph and was catapulted 100 feet out of

Bill Muncey, shown in 1959, was a media favorite.

his boat. On Lake Washington in 1958, Muncey threw up his hands in despair when he lost a rudder and all steering control while rounding the south turn and he dove out of his hydro right before it struck a 40-foot Coast Guard cutter with such great force that it sunk both boats.

He injured both kidneys and tore his abdominal wall in other mishaps. He banged up his legs and shoulders. Twice he was given up for dead after emergency rescuers found no pulse. "I think about dying a lot and I don't want to die," Muncey said.

Yet he kept racing and winning, surviving dry spells and the aging process, while making concessions to his health. On doctor's orders, he moved to San Diego and the warmer California climate in 1971 to give his chronically aching back a break, pulling up stakes in Seattle after 16 years, though he regularly returned to the city that adored him and kept racing and winning.

While Muncey seemed ageless and unbeatable and was considering retirement, he went from heroic to tragic figure in a faraway place. In 1981, Muncey turned up in Acapulco to run a season-ending championship race that seemed far more contrived than a serious venture because of the Mexican resort setting. It didn't resemble the sport's more traditional sites in the Northwest and Midwest.

The only media member present was the *Seattle Post-Intelligencer's* John Engstrom, who combined a vacation with a writing assignment because it was paid for by a hydro community desperate for coverage. A sparse crowd was on hand. The weather was unbearably hot. The pit area was empty rather than its usual bustling center of activity. Against this backdrop Muncey was still his usual accommodating self.

"I remember Muncey being gracious and available between races," said Engstrom, who died in 2014. "I chatted with him more than once as we stood in the shade of the palm trees."

On Oct. 18, 1981, on a lagoon north of the city, Muncey was just a few weeks shy of his 53rd birthday when he came charging through the second turn of the first lap in the final heat. He was in front of everyone when his powder-blue and white *Atlas Van Lines* boat lifted out of the water and blew over backward in a violent manner. Muncey broke his neck on impact.

He had no pulse and his pupils were dilated when rescuers loaded him into a boat that transported him to a waiting ambulance. He was carted to a Mexican naval hospital and to yet another hospital where he was pronounced dead, four hours following the accident.

In this dangerous sport, 13 others previously were killed, including Seattle drivers Rex Manchester and Ron Musson and Florida racer Don Wilson in 1966 on the Potomac River in a haunting race in Washington, D.C.

Muncey always seemed lucky and sturdy enough to survive any type of mishap, and now he was gone, too. The popular driver knew the risks he faced. The day before his death, Muncey eerily foreshadowed what was to come when he told fellow driver Ron Armstrong the following: "I don't eat the day before or the day of a race because they can't operate on you if you've eaten too much food recently. I just want them to operate right away, glue me back together. Leave me unconscious, but do it right away while I can't feel the pain."

He also wore an older racing headgear, one that resembled a football helmet and wasn't nearly as protective as the others then in use, simply because it was his favorite. However, doctors said the impact was so severe the type of equipment wouldn't have mattered. A somber scene came the day following the accident when an *Atlas Van Lines* crew member walked slowly through an Acapulco hotel, clutching Muncey's battered helmet.

"Muncey is the one I thought would never die in competition," said Bill Knight, a *Post-Intelligencer* hydro writer for a dozen years. "I thought he was too smart to make the mistake that could be fatal."

The sport didn't pack up once Muncey was dead, but it lost considerable momentum.

The sport didn't pack up once Muncey was dead, but it lost considerable momentum, a situation made worse a year later when veteran driver Dean Chenoweth, Muncey's replacement as the hydro circuit headliner, was killed on the Columbia River in Kennewick.

Unlimited hydro officials decided canopies should be installed over each cockpit, a move some drivers initially resisted because it increased their chances of drowning if not suffering serious injury while banging up against the new lids. However, once this safety feature was introduced, the hydroplane sport didn't suffer another death in competition for 18 years before one came in San Diego — in a race ironically christened the Bill Muncey Cup.

Seattle-area drivers Chip Hanauer and Steve Reynolds built huge followings in the post-Muncey years. Yet Reynolds, whose looks and engaging personality reminded people a lot of Muncey, was left with a permanent brain injury from a 1987 blow-over accident in a canopy boat that forced him out of the sport.

Hanauer grew up in the Seattle suburbs as a Muncey fan and was chosen by the man's widow as the next *Atlas Van Lines* driver, and he enjoyed widespread success and popularity. In 1999, however, Hanauer walked away from the sport.

The driver wouldn't say publicly why he was leaving, but Hanauer retired because he was either unwilling to break Muncey's records or concerned he would meet the same fate, or both. Even in death, Muncey dictated the course of the hydro world. ❖

10 Who Died on the Job

1. Bill Muncey (hydro crash)
2. Ila Ray Hadley (jet crash)
3. Ray Hadley Jr. (jet crash)
4. Fred Hutchinson (cancer)
5. Scott Fischer (mountain climbing)
6. Dean Chenoweth (hydro crash)
7. Jack Lelivelt (heart attack)
8. Rex Manchester (hydro crash)
9. Dennis Johnson (heart attack)
10. Ron Musson (hydro crash)

RUTH JESSEN
The Glamour Golfer

Blonde, beautiful and vivacious Ruth Jessen easily could have been a movie star rather than one of the pioneers of the LPGA Tour. She drove a Cadillac and always made a big entrance, especially when traveling from one side of the country to the other and stopping to visit relatives along the way. Her luxury car often was packed with practically everything she owned.

On one occasion it was stuffed with 50 blouses, 40 pairs of shorts, 20 sweaters, 20 cocktail dresses, 20 pairs of slacks, 20 pairs of golf shoes, four sets of golf clubs, four fishing rods and three dozen golf gloves.

"She was the richest and most famous person I knew," said Steve Jessen, a cousin who lived in Billings, Mont.

Ruth Jessen was Seattle's most glamorous big-league athlete, plus the first from the city to play on the LPGA Tour and just the second local woman, following Olympic swimmer Helene Madison, to embrace the national spotlight.

Growing up in modest surroundings in north Seattle, Jessen's mother was a district circulation manager for the *Seattle Post-Intelligencer*, which meant the younger Jessen was rousted out of bed at 1 a.m. to help make doorstep deliveries. Soon the morning newspaper was writing all about Jessen's captivating activities during the daylight hours — that of a naturally gifted golfer making things happen in a hurry.

> ## Ruth Jessen was Seattle's most glamorous big-league athlete, plus the first from the city to play on the LPGA Tour.

At 19, Jessen was the youngest member of the relatively new 25-player LPGA Tour. Three years later in 1959, she won for the first time. By 1964, she was a headliner, capturing five tournaments that season and finishing second on five other occasions, including losing the U.S. Open in a playoff to Mickey Wright. Jessen, who won 11 times in her career, did everything except stay healthy and become a Hall of Fame inductee.

"I was putting very well, that was the biggest thing," said Jessen, known for her unorthodox straddle stance on the greens, setting her feet as much as four feet apart. "The wider I got, the better I putted. It was like doing the splits. It was like getting down and reading the green when I did it, because I could really see the line."

Jessen, however, couldn't envision what would happen to her health. She lost feeling in her left arm because of nerve damage, possibly caused by years of hitting off mats. She suffered a neck injury when a concession tent pole collapsed on her during a freak windstorm in Massachusetts, losing feeling in her arm again. At 32, she was diagnosed with uterine cancer. She underwent 14 surgeries.

The last of her LPGA victories came in 1971 at the Sears Women's World Classic in Port St. Lucie, Fla., an outcome so inspirational to the pro golf world that she was given the Ben Hogan Award signifying her as the comeback golfer of the year.

Ruth Jessen and Anne Quast were competitors.

Ruth Jessen is shown here in 2006, a year before her death.

"I figured I got to play 10 years of the 20 I was out there," said Jessen, who finished with $158,816 in career earnings. "Every time I had surgery, it took a year to get over it."

When healthy, Jessen had all of the magical shots. She grew up at 11034 30th Ave. N.E., a half-block from Meadowbrook Golf Course, where she picked raspberries, hunted for golf balls and got in her first rounds with a driver, 7-iron and putter. At Roosevelt

High School, the principal let her out of class early if she agreed to play golf with some of his buddies. She held her own in the "golden era" of Northwest women's golf, competing against the likes of JoAnne Gunderson, Ann Quast, Peggy Conley and Pat Lesser (Gunderson, Quast and Lesser were all U.S. Women's Amateur champions).

Jessen briefly attended Seattle University and played in the fifth spot on the men's golf team, offering compassion whenever she showed up the opposite sex, which was often. "I always felt bad for the guys when I out-hit them because other guys would razz them," Jessen said.

She turned pro shortly after competing alongside LPGA star Patty Berg in a nine-hole golf exhibition and clinic held at Jackson Park. "When I got to play with Patty, I just knew I could play [on the tour]," Jessen said confidently. "Patty wanted to try my driver because I was out-hitting her. When I was 14, I could just kill it."

Jessen's presence likewise was a huge motivator for Gunderson, later Carner, who was two years younger and bound for the LPGA and a Hall of Fame career. JoAnne decided right then and there she had to have Jessen's length.

"When I was 14, she flew it by me like 20 to 25 yards and I went home and I said, 'I know I'm as strong as her and as agile,' " Carner said. "But I couldn't figure out why she was hitting it longer. I thought about it two days and realized she hit it higher than me. I spent the next few days trying to hit it higher. The next time we played, I hit it 20-25 yards past her."

Riding in a black Ford initially, Jessen made her entrance onto the LPGA Tour accompanied by her mother and sister, and she played in three California tournaments. She was much bolder the next year, driving by herself across the country. "My sister

Jessen's presence likewise was a huge motivator for Gunderson, later Carner, who was two years younger and bound for the LPGA and a Hall of Fame career.

couldn't believe it, that my parents let this girl go by herself back East," Jessen said. "I just remember being in Florida over the holidays and being homesick, but I got over it."

In 1959, Jessen won for the first time in Tampa, pocketing $1,100. A dozen years later she received a $10,000 winner's check in Port St. Lucie, the money jump demonstrating how much the LPGA Tour had grown. She was an established player. "I brought my scoring down," she said. "I managed myself better. Some never learn that."

She also changed to her unconventional wide putting stance at the suggestion of player Marlene Hagge's husband, Bob, a golf course designer, and watched the ball start to drop in the cup at an amazing rate. She lost the U.S. Open by two strokes to Wright, who enjoyed a Hall of Fame career and was her nemesis but a big fan. "She told me, 'If I could putt as well as you I'd win every time,' " Jessen said. A week after the Open loss, Jessen beat Wright by three strokes in a Michigan tournament.

Beyond her control were bizarre mishaps that seemed to gravitate to her. Playing outside of Detroit, she was crossing a bridge on the back nine when it collapsed. Luckily, no one was killed, though there were injuries. People dove into the water to make sure no one was trapped below the surface. On another trip to Michigan, Jessen noticed the sky suddenly turn dark and a fellow golfer yelled, "Hit the ground!" A swarm of bees passed overhead. "It was like watching something on TV," Jessen said.

That stuff was more scary than painful. Her luck turned worse in 1965 when Jessen and her caddie were buying Cokes at a concession stand during another Massachusetts tournament when a gust of wind uprooted the tent and a falling pole struck the golfer in her neck. She suffered a disk injury and lost feeling in her left arm. Depression soon set in as her game was derailed. Jessen could never get healthy enough again to win big. In 1968, she was dating an East Coast doctor when she complained of back pain. He told her to see a Seattle gynecologist, who diagnosed uterine cancer.

When she wasn't in pain, Jessen had a fun-loving existence on the LPGA Tour. The players caravanned by car to events, with Berg usually riding in the lead car. A Ping Pong paddle stuck out a window meant everyone had to pull over at the next stop.

Fellow golfer Norma Shook was an hour overdue in joining the caravan one night; she had a flat tire and knocked out a man who stopped to help her and tried to assault her. On another occasion, Hagge was put in jail after she was caught going 120 mph in her Oldsmobile down a West Texas highway; the others had to wire bail money to her. Carol Mann wore pajamas and a raincoat when she crossed a median to reach a drive-through restaurant in Pensacola, Fla., got into an argument with a police officer after she was pulled over and was jailed. She called the tournament director to come bail her out and wasn't released until 3 a.m. "We called her 'The Fugitive,' " Jessen said.

Jessen also became friends with the great Babe Didrikson, an all-around athlete who played briefly on the LPGA Tour before she died from colon cancer. The women were the same size and Didrikson handed over a lot of her clothes to Jessen, who kept them as keepsakes, complete with laundry tags signifying the original owner.

As personable and attractive as Jessen was, she never married. She retired to Arizona and gave golf lessons. She visited Seattle periodically and stayed with relatives during the summers and considered moving back to her hometown. She seemed lonely at the end, dying on Sept. 21, 2007, a week after she suffered a stroke at her desert home. She was 69. One thing was clear: The nation's highways wouldn't be nearly as fun to navigate without this adventuresome woman and her jam-packed Cadillac. ❖

> Jessen also became friends with the great Babe Didrikson, an all-around athlete who played briefly on the LPGA Tour before she died from colon cancer. The women were the same size and Didrikson handed over a lot of her clothes to Jessen, who kept them as keepsakes.

ELGIN BAYLOR

Seattle's Michael Jordan

Elgin Baylor was a newcomer to Seattle, a transfer for the Seattle University basketball team, an unknown to all but those who coaxed him to the city. To become eligible to play for the Chieftains, he had to sit out the 1955-56 season per NCAA mandate. To give him a basketball outlet, arrangements were made for Baylor to join an elite AAU team, Westside Ford, sponsored by West Seattle car dealer and staunch Seattle U supporter Ralph Malone and run by former Chieftains All-America player Johnny O'Brien. To create a roster spot, the phone conversation between Malone and O'Brien went back and forth like this:

"I've got a new player for you."

"No, you don't. I've got 11 players."

"Let him work out. His name is Elgin Baylor."

"Who the hell is Elgin Baylor?!"

O'Brien found out soon enough when Baylor walked into the gym and threw down a two-handed dunk with ease. The smooth swingman proceeded to tear up the local circuit, drawing huge crowds to the games and creating his own basketball buzz across town well in advance of his local college career. He was the first coming of Michael Jordan, and he became Seattle's most revolutionary athlete in any sport.

Baylor was widely considered the man who invented basketball hang time. With technique based on levitation and improvisational principles, he changed how the college game was played and he later did the same in the NBA. His creativity was a well-kept secret until he turned up in a red-and-white Chieftains jersey with the trademark short sleeves. Soon, everybody knew about this graceful 6-foot-5 player.

"I think he was one of the four best players who ever played the game," said Bob Houbregs, former Sonics general manager, lumping Baylor with Bill Russell, Oscar Robertson and Jordan.

Baylor scored 40 points in his first Seattle U game. He led the nation in rebounding (20.3 per game) in his first season. He finished second in the nation in scoring (32.5) behind Cincinnati's Robertson, in his second season. Baylor had consecutive games of 60, 43, 42, 46 and 47 points. He came up with a 51-point, 37-rebound game against the Marv Harshman-coached Pacific Lutheran. Baylor scored 20 points over the final eight minutes against Portland to rescue his team from a 19-point deficit. In half of his 54 SU games, he piled up 30 points or more.

Baylor was named the Helms Foundation College Player of the Year and a first-team *Associated Press* All-America selection in 1958, and he put Seattle U in the NCAA championship game that year against Kentucky.

> The smooth swingman proceeded to tear up the local circuit, drawing huge crowds to the games and creating his own basketball buzz across town well in advance of his local college career.

"I probably surprised myself," Baylor said, "that I was better than I thought."

The Washington, D.C., native played the 1954-55 season for the College of Idaho, a nondescript NAIA school later renamed Albertson College. He accepted a football scholarship, but joined the basketball team once on campus and averaged 31.3 ppg as a Coyotes freshman. Al Lightner, an Oregon-based college basketball referee who doubled as the *Salem Statesman* sports editor, tipped off Seattle U officials to this prodigious talent. Lightner said Baylor was the best player he had ever seen and the Chieftains moved quickly on the lead.

Malone called Baylor and invited him to visit the Seattle U campus and look over the city. The car dealer arranged for him to fly to Seattle aboard a four-seat Piper Cub, accompanied by Malone's brother-in-law. Baylor was scared to death on the trip north; it was his first airplane ride. He hadn't seriously considered leaving Idaho, but he willingly allowed himself to be pirated away.

"I was curious about the talent level and how good they were and if I was good enough to play at that level; I didn't know," Baylor said. "They wanted me to go out there and work out. Obviously, I did OK."

Baylor, whose first name came from an expensive watch favored by his father, learned the game on the playgrounds of the nation's capital. He emerged as a can't-miss player from Springarn High School, one of the city's five black schools. Yet most college recruiters didn't know him because of the rigid segregation practices in place.

Baylor accepted a college football scholarship, though he played the contact sport only on the sandlots, because a friend from home, Warren Williams, was a College of Idaho football player and arranged for Baylor to join him. Baylor's only basketball scholarship offer came from Virginia Union, an all-black school.

When Seattle U reached out to him, Baylor already knew a lot about the basketball program and needed no primer. He read about O'Brien in a magazine and was fascinated by the 5-9 former post player. The scenic city and its friendly atmosphere were strong selling points, too.

"I had really never been anywhere else but Virginia and Maryland," Baylor said. "Seattle was beautiful with all the mountains and snow. I met some really nice people. I liked it."

Once on Seattle U's campus, Baylor lived with teammate Francis Saunders in Room 331 of Xavier Hall at 1110 E. Spring St. He worked a job and drove a beat-up blue Ford supplied to him by Malone, who might have bent the rules more than people knew at the time. "Put it this way, if Baylor needed anything they took care of him," former Seattle U publicist Bill Sears said.

Baylor was arrested while driving that old car way too fast down Seattle's Aurora Avenue. He and Bill Wright, an AAU basketball teammate and the first black golfer to win a United States Golf Association title, the 1959 U.S. Amateur Public Links, were accused of racing each other, booked into jail and released on $100 bonds before appearing before a judge.

"Wright was stopped and I could have kept going, but I stopped, too," Baylor said. "They said Wright was going 85 miles per hour and I said, 'Your honor, there's no way my car could go 85 miles per hour, and, if it could, I would pay the fine right now.' The judge laughed and told us to be careful after that."

Elgin Baylor, shown against Pacific Lutheran in 1958, was widely considered the player who invented "hang time."

Seattle U players were surprised by Baylor's unselfishness and shyness. He had physical gifts without the superstar attitude. He took plenty of shots but he was a team player.

"Baylor was a little strange, if not withdrawn most of the time," Sears said. "He was very shy. He didn't talk much. He was just a guy who had trouble articulating and was always a little defensive. But he sure could play."

Baylor was always twitching on the court, as if he had a built-in head fake, which seemed to greatly throw off defenders. Teammates made sure to get him the ball whenever it appeared. Baylor's condition was never addressed publicly, but his roommate claimed he knew what it was. "People didn't say anything, but he had Tourette Syndrome," Saunders insisted.

In his first season, Baylor led the Chieftains to a 22-3 record, which included an 18-game win streak, and his team finished No. 5 in the final *Associated Press* poll. He was the nation's third-leading scorer at 29.7 ppg and a second-team *AP* All-America pick.

School officials decided that Seattle U would try to win the NIT rather than wait for an NCAA bid that season, a move that backfired on them. Unable to deal with a full-court press, the top-seeded Chieftains lost in the first round to St. Bonaventure 85-68 at New York's Madison Square Garden.

A year later, while dealing with a much tougher schedule, the Chieftains were the nation's 18th-ranked team when they accepted an NCAA invitation and nearly ran the table with a 23-6 team. They beat Wyoming in their postseason opener, USF on Baylor's extra-long buzzer shot, California in overtime and top-seeded Kansas State in a blowout to advance to the title game.

Against USF, Baylor connected on a 35-foot jump shot as the horn sounded to provide a resounding 69-67 upset at San Francisco's Cow Palace, fluidly rising up and shooting the ball as if he were 15 feet away. The play was designed for Baylor to win the game and he dribbled and considered his options before rifling home a shot that came from halfway between the midcourt line and the top of the key.

"I was watching the clock and I started counting down in my head," Baylor said. "They set up their defense not to let me drive. In the Cow Palace, against USF, I thought, 'If I'm going to go to the basket and I got fouled, am I going to get the call?'"

The postseason was all smiles for Baylor and his teammates until they took their flight from Chicago to Louisville and the Final Four on a prop plane that was no match for a Southern storm.

"We flew between two tornadoes," SU point guard Jim Harney said. "The plane was pitching all over the place. Elgin had a horrible fear of flying. I don't know if he picked it up on that airplane ride. We were sideways in the air at times. I was sitting next to him. We talked about how frightening it was. It was horribly frightening."

In the Final Four semis, Baylor had 23 points and 22 rebounds to help the Chieftains pull a stunning 73-51 upset of tourney favorite Kansas State, but he didn't survive the game intact. Baylor collided with Wildcats forward Bob Boozer, an NBA-bound player, and injured his ribs.

"It was nothing malicious," Baylor said. "A guy called switch, I went up for a shot and Boozer turned around, and, wham, his elbow hit me right here [left side]. It was the worst pain I ever felt. I remember going up and Boozer just turned. It was really an accident. He even apologized. We got to be friends. I knew Boozer. He wasn't a dirty player at all."

On March 22, 1958, Baylor was nowhere near full strength when he faced Kentucky in the title game. He also was in game-long foul trouble, drawing three personals in the first 10 minutes. He was taped up, barely able to breathe and run the floor, and was held to 20 points, 12 under his average. The Wildcats got hot and got off easy, overcoming an 11-point deficit to pull out an 84-72 victory.

"You knew about him from the newspapers," Kentucky's Adrian Smith said of Baylor, the Final Four MVP. "He was a great player. They just prepared you at Kentucky to go out and play against your opponent, no matter who it was. Seattle was probably favored for that game because of him. Maybe we weren't supposed to beat Seattle, yet we did."

Appearing on TV on Sunday night's *Ed Sullivan Show*, Baylor announced he would return for another college season, but he changed his mind once the Chieftains got mixed up in a recruiting scandal. Drafted No. 1 overall by the Minneapolis Lakers, Baylor demonstrated right away there was no need for him to play another college season.

He spent 14 seasons with the same Lakers franchise, which moved from Minnesota to California, and he was even more spectacular as a pro player than a collegian. He averaged 27.4 during a Hall of Fame career — and an unstoppable 38.2, 31.8 and 34.0 over consecutive seasons — before degenerative knee problems forced him to quit playing. He influenced players in countless ways. "I used to wear my hair like Elgin Baylor," Seattle SuperSonics forward Spencer Haywood confided.

Baylor worked as the New Orleans Jazz coach, a TV broadcaster and as the embattled Los Angeles Clippers general manager before he was forced out of the latter job. He bristled at people who dishonored him at the end, suggesting he had hung around the pro game too long. A certain Northwest city gladly would have held onto him longer and let him dictate his terms of departure.

"In Seattle, that was the beginning," Baylor said. ❖

JOHN CASTELLANI

The Greediest Coach

John Castellani needed just two seasons as a head basketball coach to reach the 1958 Final Four championship game. Swept up in all the attention and celebrity that came with it, the 32-year-old Castellani made one reckless decision to throw it all away.

He was an overnight sensation for Seattle University when he rode the superlative talents of swingman Elgin Baylor to a national runner-up finish against Kentucky in Louisville. Trying to keep the Chieftains' dynasty going, the fast-talking, sharp-dressing coach became an instant outcast after breaking NCAA rules in the process. He got greedy and paid for it.

Castellani's was the greatest rise and fall for any coach in Seattle's sports history, though more than four decades later University of Washington football coach Rick Neuheisel proved an able challenger, winning a Rose Bowl in his second season before he was fired for a betting scandal following his fourth.

Castellani was caught providing airfare to a neutral meeting spot and offering monthly cash incentives to a pair of coveted recruits, 6-foot-6 forward Ben Warley and 7-foot center George Finley, who played for Tennessee A&I State (renamed Tennessee State). Warley later spent several seasons in the ABA and NBA, and Finley was drafted by the Detroit Pistons but never made it as a pro player.

They hailed from Washington, D.C., which was Baylor's hometown, and Castellani consulted his All-America player about adding them to his roster.

> ## Castellani's was the greatest rise and fall for any coach in Seattle's sports history.

"I think at the time Castellani obviously made a mistake," Baylor said. "I remember him asking me about it, and I said, 'I don't think you should do it.' "

The 1958 NCAA championship game was barely a month old when the program was rocked by the scandal. On April 22, 1958, Castellani was fired after the Chieftains were slapped with a two-year postseason ban for those recruiting improprieties. He publicly accepted all guilt.

Castellani created something special in a hurry and felt pressure to keep it going. With Warley and Finley in Chieftains uniforms, he was convinced the limelight would never leave his basketball team. "I probably crossed the line," Castellani said. "They were slipping away from me. I get those two guys and it's all over. We're in the Final Four for the next three or four years."

Charlie Brown, a starting guard for Seattle U's Final Four team, knew all of the sordid details. Brown had a brother who played for Tennessee A&I State and coach John McClendon, and he said McClendon did everything he could to keep his team from being raided.

"Ben Warley was the guy Castellani was trying to get and I guess Warley was going to take my position," Brown said. "McClendon got Castellani on a recording. Everything Castellani said was on tape. It's really ironic that we did not get the death penalty, other than two years. That was the demise. We could have been good. I don't know if Castellani realized what he had."

Castellani with, from left, Lloyd Murphy, Jim Harney, Elgin Baylor, Bob Miller, Thornton Humphries and Dick Stricklin from his 1956-57 team.

Castellani was shoved out the door of college basketball. He turned the Chieftains over to Vince Cazzetta, his assistant coach and childhood buddy from New Britain, Conn. He pursued other jobs, such as Creighton, but his rules-breaking track record kept him unemployed for the next 12 months until he briefly coached Baylor and the Lakers. Soon Castellani was out of basketball and seeking a law career.

Castellani was on the coaching fast track when he came to Seattle U for the 1956-57 season from Notre Dame, where he was the Fighting Irish freshmen and assistant coach for five years. He was eager to move up after missing out on head-coaching opportunities at Providence and Toledo. He was 29, Catholic, passionate and considered a top-notch recruiter when he was

interviewed in South Bend, Ind. He accepted the Chieftains position without first visiting Seattle.

The Seattle U job came open after the previous coach, the popular Al Brightman, was forced to resign for postseason misconduct: He came drunk to a 1956 NCAA Tournament game against UCLA in Corvallis and caused the school great embarrassment when he leaped off the bench and verbally assaulted legendary Bruins coach John Wooden on the sideline during the Chieftains' 94-70 loss. Reverend Robert Rebhahn, the Seattle U athletic director, had to pull the coach away, but not before Brightman swore at Wooden and bumped up against him. Brightman was angry after losing the night before to a so-so Utah team and got plastered at a hotel bar. He showed up at Gill Coliseum barely able to walk and his night went downhill from there.

"How he made it to that game I don't know," SU point guard Jim Harney said. "Brightman had Wooden by his lapels and that was the end of him. He lost his job that night – and he had Baylor coming in."

Castellani, who lived at 805 Spring St., supposedly was hired without knowledge that Baylor was sitting out as a transfer and waiting for him. Addressing reporters upon his Northwest arrival, the brash Castellani insisted he knew all about this player. He was winging it, telling the assembled media that he was eager to meet this "L.G. Bailey."

Of Baylor's presence, Castellani conceded the following, "They kind of hid him from me. They didn't want me taking the job just because of Elgin. I had not heard of him. Years ago, in the '50s, there was a very limited communication. There weren't any scouts, not like there are now, but I was easily converted to Baylor-ism."

The short, fiery coach and the abundantly talented yet reserved player advanced to the NIT and NCAA

tournaments and created nonstop college basketball excitement in Seattle, winning 45 of 54 games.

"I liked John very much," Baylor said. "He was funny. We used to have fun with John. He was entertaining, always upbeat, never down."

In his second season, Castellani got off to a slow start when the Chieftains lost four of their first eight games, and the coach was twice hung in effigy in downtown Seattle. He was able to right things in a big way, winning 19 of 20 games, and landed in the NCAA championship game opposite coaching giant Adolph Rupp of Kentucky.

Unfortunately for the Seattle U leader, the game was played just 90 minutes from the UK campus and Castellani's integrated team was coolly welcomed by the all-white crowd of 18,803. Worse yet, Baylor was nursing a broken rib suffered in a rousing 73-51 semifinal upset of tourney favorite Kansas State.

Wildcats coach Fred "Tex" Winter, who a decade later ended up in Seattle as the University of Washington coach, didn't take the loss well. "After the Kansas State game, Tex didn't shake my hand," Castellani said. "He was supposed to win it and he got trounced before every coach in the country."

For Saturday night's title game, college basketball's leading coaches sat in long rows of seats set aside for them close to the floor. When Seattle U came out, the Kentucky band started playing "Sweet Georgia Brown," which was the Harlem Globetrotters theme song and a show of disrespect for the integrated Chieftains. Racial slurs were loudly heard among this mostly Southern audience.

"I convinced a friend to drive to Louisville for the Final Four and we arrived that Friday night before the tip-off of the Kentucky-Temple game," said Pat Gogerty, a Seattle U student and later a Seattle public-relations firm owner. "We were in for a culture shock in the form of open racism."

The Chieftains basketball team had to find another Louisville hotel once it arrived in the city because the one set aside wouldn't allow blacks as guests. Rupp was overheard in a hotel elevator making derogatory remarks about blacks and Jews. "There were 18,000 at the game and not an African-American in the crowd," Castellani said.

Castellani's team led Kentucky by 11 points in the first half. The Chieftains were still on top 60-58 with seven minutes left to play. Title hopes diminished as Baylor struggled to breathe at times and played with four fouls most of the second half; Seattle U tried to compensate with radical means.

"I made a mistake and we used a zone, and they killed us," Castellani said. "Because Elgin had four fouls, we didn't want him to foul out. We put him in the back of the zone."

Seattle U lost 84-72, knowing it easily could have won it all. In the locker room, Castellani was in tears, banging on lockers, after coming so close to an NCAA championship and having it slip away. He refused to return to the floor and retrieve the runner-up trophy, sending publicist Bill Sears in his place. While the final outcome was disappointing, the Chieftains' basketball future appeared promising. Baylor said he might return for his senior season, though he was eligible to turn pro because he sat out as a transfer and his class was graduating. Castellani's player-tampering snuffed out those dreams.

He offered $200 and $90 monthly stipends to Warley and Finley to come to Seattle U. He flew one of them to Washington, D.C., for a secret meeting, and offered free flights for both of them to visit Seattle. Finley actually made a Seattle connection a decade

later, signing a contract with the NBA's SuperSonics only to jump to the ABA's Anaheim Amigos before playing a game in the Northwest.

Castellani resigned two hours after the NCAA levied its two-year postseason ban on the Chieftains. He talked his way into another basketball job, as coach of the Lakers and Baylor, but he was fired at midseason, let go after his NBA team stumbled to an 11-25 record during its final season in Minneapolis.

He relocated to Milwaukee, a place he enjoyed recruiting on behalf of Notre Dame, and he enrolled in Marquette's law school. He became a bankruptcy and trust attorney, and started his own firm. He returned to Seattle only for Final Four basketball games, visiting the city when it hosted three of the showcase events at the Kingdome.

Castellani watched basketball from a distance, attending Marquette and Milwaukee Bucks games and often sitting courtside with Senator Herb Kohl, owner of the NBA franchise. He had moved on following one of the briefest and strangest coaching careers in Seattle, one mixed with extraordinary success and failure, highlighted by that night in the NCAA championship game.

"I always said we had the best team, we just didn't have the best coach," Castellani said. "I had coached 60 games; Rupp had coached 600." ❖

Castellani in his later years.

JIM OWENS

Seattle's Platoon Leader

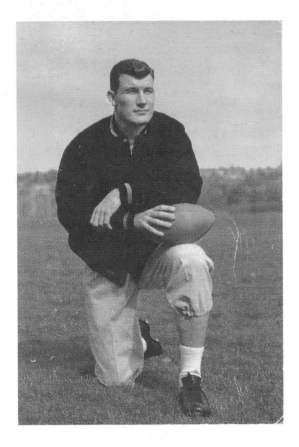

He was young Jim, big Jim and bad Jim. As the University of Washington football coach, Jim Owens was eyed cautiously when he took the job because of his youth and later worshipped like a god for consecutive New Year's Day successes, and finally hung in effigy at the end, his career soaring and dropping as if caught in a swirl of wind blowing in off Lake Washington.

Owens physically filled up Husky Stadium like no other man in charge of the place, his sturdy 6-foot-4, 225-pound frame and rugged looks helping offset the fact he was just 29 (for appearances' sake, school officials said the coach was 30) when he arrived to direct Seattle's most beloved sports team.

In his third and fourth seasons, Owens startled everyone by leading the Huskies to Rose Bowl victories in 1960 and 1961 — the first for the school after four winless Pasadena trips — and he was credited with reinvigorating and restoring West Coast football after it had been decimated by slush-fund scandals that ended the Pacific Coast Conference. He gave Seattle benchmark sporting success previously unattainable. Yet later on, as the losses piled up in bunches, the Oklahoma native was an easy target for mounting critics, assailed for racially insensitive practices and deemed as outdated as he was once the latest thing in college football. He walked away in 1974, resigning as a tested and tired man after 18 demanding seasons.

Owens startled everyone by leading the Huskies to Rose Bowl victories in 1960 and 1961 – the first for the school after four winless Pasadena trips – and he was credited with reinvigorating and restoring West Coast football after it had been decimated by slush-fund scandals that ended the Pacific Coast Conference.

No Seattle coach has experienced such extreme highs and lows in terms of public opinion.

There were people who would tell you that Owens was a man above reproach and of the highest moral character, and that he actually walked on water from his lakefront Laurelhurst home to his coaching offices and Husky Stadium. Others stubbornly insist that he had more faults and racial biases than were readily acknowledged by those who employed him, and that he would have needed a life preserver had he tried the mythical walk across the inlet separating his house at 3007 Webster Point Road N.E. and the football facilities.

The Huskies coach actually fell somewhere in between. He was neither saint nor abject sinner. He was a demanding and militaristic leader who was blindsided by radical societal change and didn't properly respond. He physically challenged players in not-so-subtle terms, sometimes joining drills and occasionally manhandling someone after a blown assignment.

Owens was hired in 1957 as a replacement for Darrell Royal, who was first entrusted with cleaning up the UW mess once the practice of illegally paying players was uncovered. Royal came to the Huskies from Mississippi State and departed after one season for Texas. Owens and Royal knew each other well; they were teammates during the Oklahoma Sooners' long-running football dynasty.

Owens was a Texas A&M assistant for Paul "Bear" Bryant and was selected as the Huskies coach only after Nebraska's Pete Elliott had rejected an offer and taken a job at California. With reporters continually checking Seattle hotels, both Owens and Elliott stayed at the Laurelhurst home of Huskies athletic director George Briggs while interviewing.

"I had a list of prominent names and high on the list was Owens," Briggs said. "I called three people and offered them the job, not thinking they would take it. It was Bear Bryant, Bud Wilkinson and Duffy Daugherty. I thought they would recommend someone. All three mentioned Owens. I wanted to keep the same kind of program going, with mental and physical toughness and hardnosed football. His name had come up the year before but I wasn't interested at the time."

Ready to move up, Owens was interviewed by a handful of other schools trying to fill coaching openings. He never blanched at putting things back together at Washington under trying circumstances after Royal left him with a 5-5 team.

"I knew they were in trouble, but usually when you get a job the program is down, the coaches haven't won and there have been problems," Owens said. "We knew we had to work at it to get it back on a normal plane."

There was nothing casual about his approach. As one of Bryant's most trusted lieutenants, Owens was on the staff when 1954 Texas A&M players were subjected to inhumane training practices in searing heat made legendary decades later when depicted in the TV movie "Junction Boys."

For that first year at the UW Owens instituted his own rigid standards during spring and fall practices. Conditioning and toughness were stressed above all else. Players were encouraged to challenge others ahead of them almost daily for their positions. Things could get bloody and demoralizing. A weeding-out process took place, eliminating the weak-hearted.

Jim Owens' staff, from left to right: Dave Phillips, Don White, Bob Schloredt, Tom Tipps, Owens, Chesty Walker, Ed Peasley, Don McKeta and Bob Monroe.

During an August practice in 1957, with the temperature hovering close to 90 degrees, Owens ran his players through stop-and-start sprints for two hours after they had stumbled through a lackluster 90-minute scrimmage. No one was permitted any drinking water. Former Huskies running back Carver Gayton claims to have lost 15 pounds that day. Several players passed out. Six reportedly were taken to the hospital.

This particular UW torture session was referred to as the "Death March." The coach said there was a point to all of this madness, adding that the previous A&M outcome wasn't as bad as depicted on film.

"I didn't see the movie," Owens said. "I heard some comments about it, but it was too Hollywood for me. A lot of things were exaggerated in it. We still had it tough. Like Army Rangers and Navy SEALS in the service, you have those same kinds of drills. Conditioning is about 20-percent physical and 80-percent psychological. Services have units that are specialized and then you have the rest of the soldiers. You have one group that can take it to the limit."

With single-platoon football, Owens needed just 11 strong-minded players he could depend on. He found them during his second season in Seattle. The Huskies finished just 3-7 in 1958, but they lost four games by five points or less, including a begrudging 12-7 defeat at Ohio State. They left enough bruises on the opposition to know they were making progress.

Owens and his players, who were nicknamed the "Purple Gang," became folk heroes when they won 20 of 22 games over the next two years. Even the losses, 22-15 to USC and 15-14 to Navy, both at home, were near-misses. Each season was capped in magnificent fashion at the Rose Bowl with the Huskies embarrassing favored Wisconsin 44-8 and stuffing No. 1-ranked Minnesota 17-7.

The UW enjoyed everything except ultimate rewards at the time. *The Associated Press* and *United Press*

International polls were decided well before the bowls were played, though the Helms Athletic Foundation, a less recognized entity, later pegged the Huskies as national champions.

"They didn't make us No. 1; we were second to Minnesota, which we beat, which graveled everyone," Owens said of the wire-service rankings. "We felt we were No. 1. We beat No. 1."

Washington's elevated status under Owens' stern leadership didn't go unnoticed. Over the next year, Texas A&M, Southern Methodist and Houston each tried to pry the coach loose from the UW, and his previous employer in College Station was the most persistent. Under an assumed name, Owens flew to Los Angeles and met with a pair of A&M alums to hear them out. The UW's reflexive five-year contract extension of $25,000 per year, a sizable raise over his original $15,000 annual payout, and the added title of athletic director kept the coach in Seattle.

The love affair wouldn't last in Seattle. Owens took the Huskies to another Rose Bowl, losing 17-7 to Illinois in 1964. However, the program dipped significantly after two-platoon football was introduced to the college game in 1966.

Players rebelled at Owens' tough-guy tactics rather than embraced them. At one practice, the Huskies coach, unhappy with the play of starting offensive tackle Bob Richardson, treated the veteran lineman in a manner that stunned the other players.

"We were doing a perfection drill on the lower field, where you have to do it perfect or start over," Huskies receiver Steve Sanford said. "Owens started yelling. Then he picked up Richardson and threw him over his head to the ground. There was stuff like that. Players today would be calling lawyers."

The talent level dipped as African-American players were urged to bypass Seattle and a prejudiced coaching staff. The midseason dismissal in 1966 of black running back Donnie Moore, allegedly for drinking beer in a tavern while accompanied by two dozen white teammates, only seemed to reaffirm the racial inequities in place at Washington.

"I went into Jim Owens' office as a captain on the team and I challenged him about the way black players were being treated," said defensive tackle Steve Thompson, who later played for the New York Jets and was a minister. "I made the comment, 'If things didn't change, our program would never be the same. We would never go back to the glory years if they didn't change,' and they didn't."

The Huskies bottomed out in 1969, finishing 1-9 amid racial upheaval. Four black players were suspended for their refusal to give Owens an on-field loyalty oath, with three later reinstated. None of the blacks on the team traveled to a game at UCLA, a blowout loss. Charges of racism became widespread against the coach.

Although these problems were never resolved to everyone's satisfaction, with more blacks quitting the team in subsequent seasons, Owens survived and righted the program in an unlikely manner — he relied on a superlative athlete from another minority race. Owens won 22 of 32 games primarily using a Native American quarterback, Sonny Sixkiller, who had a powerful arm rare for a man of any ethnicity.

Once Sixkiller used up his eligibility, however, the Huskies suffered through two more lackluster seasons and the coach gave up his job under intense outside pressure. Owens somberly announced his resignation at the team banquet, three days after winning his final game in 1974, 24-17 over Washington State in the Apple Cup.

"Looking back I think we should have tried to have more specialty players," Owens said, referring to two-platoon needs. "We still wanted to have the best athletes we possibly could find and use that ability, but we probably didn't stress specialized players enough. It was pretty hard to judge those players in high school. It wasn't effective for us."

The former Huskies coach, who was 82 when he died on June 6, 2009, kept his distance from the football program he once ruled for nearly three decades. He pursued business interests, moved to Texas and Montana, and returned only for the occasional low-key visit. He dealt with a brain tumor.

Yet in 2003 Owens was brought back for the unveiling of a huge, bronze statue of him in a classic pose, kneeling just outside the stadium. It was a trip that required him to return to the field and make a halftime appearance at a Washington-USC football game. Old wounds were reopened that weekend. The once undiplomatic coach again was loudly assailed for his past racial practices. He held a private meeting with a handful of former black players. He sat through an awkward news conference that he requested at the Washington Athletic Club and still denied that he had stacked players at positions by race.

Once on the Husky Stadium field he had roamed and ruled with an iron fist, Owens, now a fragile old man rather than the imposing sideline presence, accepted one more brush with glory while trying to ease the tension around him. With microphone in hand, he thanked the UW fans for remembering him and then, for several long and agonizing minutes, the old coach apologized to anyone he might have offended. ❖

Ron Santo was a poor Italian-American kid from Rainier Valley whose need for employment was always a high priority and standard fare for someone from his 1950s working-class neighborhood known as "Garlic Gulch."

For four consecutive summers Santo threw himself into menial jobs at nearby Sicks' Stadium, tending to the general needs of the Triple-A Seattle Rainiers baseball team. He raked the infield and watered the grass. He delivered hotdogs during games to the beat writers seated in the press box, and picked up the players' dirty clubhouse laundry. He pulled batboy duty early on. On a daily basis he polished the baseball shoes that belonged to highly regarded Rainiers centerfielder Vada Pinson, who wasn't much older than him.

"He didn't like them dirty," Santo said. "He always loved them shined."

From those eager-to-please baseball beginnings Santo became the first of two Seattle clubhouse attendants to make it to the Major League level as a

> Santo became the first of two Seattle clubhouse attendants to make it to the Major League level as a player. From Franklin High, he turned himself into a superlative third baseman for 15 seasons with the Chicago Cubs and Chicago White Sox.

player. From Franklin High, he turned himself into a superlative third baseman for 15 seasons with the Chicago Cubs and Chicago White Sox. Three decades later, Tom Lampkin from Blanchet High went from picking up and folding towels in the Seattle Mariners locker room to a journeyman catcher for 13 seasons for six big-league teams, including those Mariners.

Without living long enough to see it, Santo moved up the baseball ranks as far as he could go: On Dec. 5, 2011, he posthumously was voted into the Baseball Hall of Fame, his selection following his death by 12 months and installing him as Seattle's only home-grown ballplayer to be enshrined in Cooperstown, N.Y. No one in the city has gone from more humble baseball beginnings to greater reward.

Few of those Rainiers were aware that Santo was a high-grade athlete himself and soon to be better than all of them. He could play anything: Quarterback, point guard, third base. He moved easily from season to season. At Franklin High, he was an all-city selection in three sports, three times in baseball. The hard part for him was choosing one athletic endeavor over the other.

Football was a possibility. At a time when Seattle's schoolboy teams were rushing-oriented, Santo was the league's leading passer, completing 45 of 91 attempts for 550 yards and six touchdowns. He had such a powerful right arm the University of Washington was

among those offering him an athletic scholarship. "I was definitely thinking about football," Santo said. "I loved football, loved playing quarterback and safety."

Basketball sort of ruled itself out. Santo was an accomplished ballhandler and defender who had decent quickness, but he didn't shoot well or much. "He was a big guy, a pretty stocky guy," said Keith Kingsbury, who played against Santo and was later Edmonds Community College's basketball coach.

That left baseball. Santo's springs at Franklin High and summers at Sicks' Stadium helped pull him firmly in that direction. Santo, who lived just north of the ballpark at 2310 25th Ave. S., was good and everyone knew it, too. He batted a wieldy .512 as a Quakers senior in 1958.

"Ron Santo just had it," said Jim Gyselman, a Franklin classmate and son of former Rainiers third baseman Dick Gyselman. "He waved a magic wand. He hit line drives, doubles, home runs. He never struck out. It was unbelievable. He always had a tremendous inner confidence. It wasn't conceit, it was just there. He was so good. It was that simple."

Santo always played up a level in baseball. American Legion instead of Babe Ruth. Semipro when he should have been in Legion ball. He gave himself a strict deadline to make things happen as a Major League player.

"I just loved baseball more than any other sport," Santo said. "I just said to myself during my senior year that I was going to give baseball four years. There were 16 big-league teams and every one of them had about 20 minor-league teams and I had heard of players spending six to seven years in the minors. I was going to give it four years."

Without an amateur draft back then, every team in the majors made a bid for Santo. The Cincinnati Reds, in a working agreement with the Rainiers, asked him to take batting practice before their annual exhibition game at Sicks' Stadium and offered him the highest signing bonus, $75,000. The New York Yankees, Milwaukee Braves and St. Louis Cardinals each sat him down and tried to sign him when he graduated from Franklin.

Santo ruled out the Reds because he would have had to come back through Seattle to reach the big leagues and he wanted to avoid the local pressure sure to squeeze him. "I didn't want to play in my hometown, that was it," he said.

He came to trust Dave Kosher, a Seattle-based Cubs scout and a man physically handicapped. Chicago felt right all along, particularly after Santo had a long talk with his stepfather, John Constantino, a Boeing worker and replacement for his alcoholic birth father, Louis Santo, who walked out of the house when Santo was 6 and never come back.

"My dad said, 'Look, how do you feel about this? You can take the highest offer and be set for life. What do you want to do?'" Santo said of Constantino. "I said, 'You know, Dad, there's something about Chicago and the Cubs and Wrigley Field.' To me, money was not the criteria; getting to the big leagues was. It paid off. In a year I was in the big leagues. I had just one season in the minors."

Although on a baseball fast track, Santo faced significant challenges. Shortly after signing a contract

Ron Santo, at left, confers with City-State Game teammates in 1958.

and accepting a $25,000 bonus, he was diagnosed with diabetes. For a month, he made daily trips to Seattle's Providence Hospital to learn how to manage it. He decided against taking insulin, choosing to play in the minor leagues without it.

He played through this medical hardship, not feeling its full fury until he was a much older man, when diabetes forced him to have both legs amputated and heart trouble set in. For the longest time, baseball kept him healthy.

"I knew I had a gift," Santo said. "Even when I signed, I remember my Dad telling me, 'Now be a professional and know how good you are. You're going to find out that players are as good as you are in pro ball.' When I got to the rookie camp, I saw it. He even said to me, 'You're probably going to want to come home.' I never felt that way."

Santo, who married his Franklin High School sweetheart, Sandy, made his debut on June 2, 1960, in a doubleheader sweep over the Pittsburgh Pirates, a team that won the World Series that year. He went 3-for-7 and drove in five runs in the two games. He was in the big leagues to stay.

> "I just loved baseball more than any other sport," Santo said. "I just said to myself during my senior year that I was going to give baseball four years."

He spent the next decade and a half as a popular and productive third baseman for the Cubs and White Sox. He was an All-Star Game selection nine times. He was a Gold Glove recipient five times. He slugged 342 home runs. It got him into the Hall of Fame.

Santo, who was 70 when he died on Dec. 3, 2010, from complications of bladder cancer and pneumonia, regularly visited his hometown after first making it in

the big leagues. In 1961, he came back for the *Seattle Post-Intelligencer* sports banquet as a top candidate for the newspaper's Man of the Year award. Always the competitor, he was irked when he finished as runner up to amateur golf champion Anne Sander.

"I was up for the Rookie of the Year award, I'm in the big leagues at 20 and wanted by all 16 major-league teams and that did not make sense to me," Santo said of the banquet snub. "I always felt Seattle was more of a minor-league city."

Santo set deep roots in bustling Chicago. He became a fixture for the Cubs similar to Ernie Banks, Ferguson Jenkins and Billy Williams. He was one of seven players to have his jersey number retired (10), receiving a banner hanging on the left-field foul pole at Wrigley Field. He made business deals there, opening up a chain of pizza places. He became a beloved Cubs' radio announcer.

For tragic reasons that devastated him, Santo lost all interest in his Northwest birthplace. On March 18, 1973, his stepfather and mother, Vivian, were traveling by car from Seattle to watch him in spring training in Scottsdale, Ariz., when they were killed in a horrific traffic accident. The couple was driving on Interstate 40, east of Barstow, Calif., when a truck and another car collided head-on, and the truck rolled into the Constantinos' vehicle and crushed it. Santo's deep-rooted connection to his hometown died with his parents that day.

"I hate to say this, but there was nothing back in Seattle for me after that," Santo said. ❖

10 Homegrown MLB Players

1. Tim Lincecum, P
2. Ron Santo, 3B
3. Earl Averill, CF
4. Jeff Heath, LF
5. John Olerud, 1B
6. Bill North, CF
7. Fred Hutchinson, P
8. Floyd Bannister, P
9. Sammy White, C
10. Travis Snider, RF

ANNE SANDER
The Cover Girl

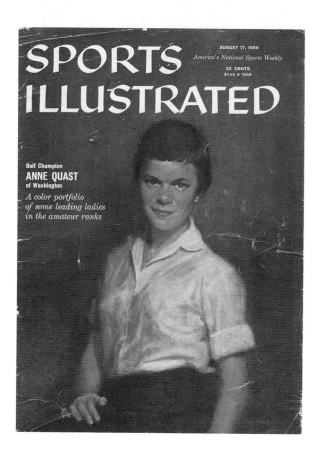

SPORTS ILLUSTRATED
America's National Sports Weekly
AUGUST 17, 1959
25 CENTS
$7.50 A YEAR

Golf Champion
ANNE QUAST
of Washington

A color portfolio
of some leading ladies
in the amateur ranks

Anne Sander played golf with the pros, but she never wanted to be one of them. She maintained her amateur standing to preserve her home life, limit her travel and stay out of the sporting spotlight.

However, on Aug. 17, 1959, there she was, staring out at America from the cover of *Sports Illustrated*. Against a brown magazine backdrop, she wore a blue blouse, sparkling necklace and smug expression. On glossy paper, she was golf royalty for all to see.

This was a painting rather than a photo. Artist Daniel Schwartz convinced Sander, who was the then-unmarried Anne Quast, 21, and a Stanford student, to show up for 10 consecutive days, an hour at a time, at Ricky's Motel in Palo Alto, Calif., to capture her likeness. It was her reward for winning the first of her three U.S. Women's Amateurs, which represented the first of her eight national and international championships.

"I was just kind of in awe," Sander said. "To sit for my portrait, I thought it was unbelievable."

Not only was she one of the first women anywhere to appear on the cover of the then five-year-old *SI*, Sander was Seattle's first athlete of any kind to receive this journalistic honor, something rarely bestowed on the city's great ones early on. She preceded University of Washington quarterbacks Bob Schloredt and Sonny Sixkiller, Huskies point guard Isaiah Thomas, the Sonics'

Gary Payton, Gus Williams, Jack Sikma, Paul Westphal and Marvin Webster, the Mariners' Ken Griffey Jr., Alex Rodriguez, Randy Johnson, Bret Boone, Jay Buhner and Robinson Cano, and the Seahawks' Matt Hasselbeck, Shaun Alexander, Russell Wilson and others.

Sander was so taken by her newfound fame that she went to a Bay Area newsstand and bought out all of the copies. Unbeknownst to her, the magazine cover came with a legendary jinx — and she paid for it as much as anyone.

Always a complicated, fussy woman, Sander resisted the ever-pressing temptation to join the LPGA Tour to become a dutiful wife and homemaker, but she never could make it work, marrying and divorcing four times. She made unwanted history by winning four championships under four different last names (Quast, Decker, Welts and Sander), something that embarrassed her to the point she stopped playing at one point.

Golf was where she kept things simple, using an enviable putting stroke and short game to offset her shortness off the tee. She won her second U.S. Women's

Not only was she one of the first women anywhere to appear on the cover of the then five-year-old *SI*, Sander was Seattle's first athlete of any kind to receive this journalistic honor, something rarely bestowed on the city's great ones early on.

Amateur in Tacoma in 1961 by a record 14-and-13 margin over Tish Preuss that still stands. She captured four U.S. Senior Women's Amateurs, plus the Ladies British Open Amateur.

Sander, who lived and learned the game at Marysville's Cedarcrest Golf Course that her parents owned, moved to Seattle to attend the Bush School and University of Washington. Her golfing prowess, simultaneous with JoAnne Gunderson's, brought national attention to her adopted hometown in the 1950s that was starved for it.

With each amateur conquest, Sander was asked if it was now time for her to join the pros, and she resisted each opportunity. While somewhat of a mechanical golfer, she was highly proficient, described by different authorities as golf's greatest overall women's golfer, its greatest woman putter, its female Ben Hogan.

The pros didn't scare her. Sander finished second to Patty Berg in the 1957 Titleholders Championship and was among the leaders throughout the 1973 U.S. Women's Open before finishing fourth. Others such as *Sports Illustrated's* John Garrity were left to guess what kind of LPGA Tour player she would have been had she given in.

"Sander's self-deprecating wit; her quick, intelligent speech; and her bold body language (she sometimes grabs her stomach and staggers when she laughs) would surely have won over the fans and the media, while her accuracy and consistency would have been well-suited to medal play," Garrity wrote in *SI*.

All along Sander, who lived at 1207 Parkside Drive E. in Broadmoor among several Seattle residences, juggled her limited golf pursuits with her revolving romantic relationships, though she didn't give in to all offers. Arnold Palmer found that out.

Anne Sander was part of golf golden era with JoAnne Carner, Pat Harbottle, Ruth Jessen and Edean Ihlanfeldt.

Sander was invited to play with Palmer in a pro-am event leading up to the PGA Tour's 1962 Seattle Open. At Broadmoor Golf Club, she was part of a VIP foursome filled out by Palmer's agent Mark McCormack and comedian Bob Hope. As they made their way around Broadmoor, a majority of the 5,500 course spectators surrounded them from hole to hole in a festive manner.

It was great fun for Sander. It also was a lot of pressure, even in a non-tournament setting. Palmer was

this flamboyant person, the next big thing in the sports world at the time and someone gloriously nicknamed "The King." Sander was excited, if not a little intimidated, to play golf with him.

Palmer was his usual dashing self in a sweater, dark shirt and slacks as he toured the golf course and showed off his bold and precise shot-making ability. Hope, who wore a bucket hat, white sweater and perpetual big grin, was as funny as advertised,

Palmer and McCormack asked Sander to have dinner that night at a downtown Seattle hotel restaurant. After an elegant meal, the men laid out a business proposition for Sander

offering nonstop wisecracks for anyone within earshot. McCormack, from the International Management Group, an agency that he and Palmer started together, hung in the background, shadowing his biggest client and staying out of everyone's way. They were nice enough to Sander as they walked the course together.

Palmer and McCormack asked Sander to have dinner that night at a downtown Seattle hotel restaurant. It was innocent enough. After an elegant meal, the men laid out a business proposition for Sander. They wanted her to work in a public-relations capacity for them at IMG. She later learned they had planned to pay her $50,000, which was a lot of money in those days.

As Sander sat and listened to the offer, she suddenly felt what she thought was a hand brush her leg under the table. This made Sander jump.

She was too surprised to say anything. She moved away in a subtle yet purposeful manner.

On the elevator ride down, Sander said Palmer asked her to have dinner alone with him the following night. She said no thank you, that she was busy, or something to that effect. She was flustered by the extra attention.

"Arnie is such a flirt," said Judy Bell, a fellow player and future USGA president. "Does Anne agree that he's a flirt? I can believe that happened, though. I can believe that whole thing. God knows what happened there."

Sander said she told only her parents about the dinner meeting and her interaction with the King, whose photo hung from a wall at the family's Cedarcrest Golf Course. Palmer's offer of employment didn't go very far with her either.

"I never considered taking that job," Sander wisecracked. "It might have involved more than public relations."

Had she been willing to share this story back in 1963, it could have led to another *Sports Illustrated* cover. ❖

Pat Harbottle and Anne Quast accept trophies at the 1956 Western Open.

Everybody was talking, chattering, yelling in her backswing. The only way she could see the flight of the golf ball was if she played toward the moon and happened to catch the silhouette. Other than that, she only knew where it went by the sound and feel of the shot at impact. For JoAnne Carner, this was her raw introduction to golf, a sporting adventure she totally embraced.

She was one of 10 or 12 neighborhood kids, mostly boys, who teed it up at night at the nine-hole Juanita Golf Course that ran alongside Lake Washington, fanning out over the fairways well after all the paying customers had finished and gone home. They constantly goaded and made each other better.

"Most things never bothered me on the golf course because of the way I was brought up playing," Carner said.

She was JoAnne Gunderson back then and just 10 when she started hanging around the Juanita course. Her older sisters and brother worked there, selling snacks, and watering everything. The Gunderson family lived in Kirkland, just a mile and a half from

> Carner figured it out and became Seattle's greatest woman golfer, and more. She remains one of the most storied players in the history of the game, amateur or pro, man or woman, landing her in the LPGA and World Golf halls of fame.

JOANNE CARNER
Seattle's Big Mama

the course at 10828 108th Ave. N.E. The unwritten rule was everyone who worked at the golf club was expected to play. Waiting for her brother to walk her home, Carner started swinging a golf club. The early reviews were not favorable.

"What did my brother say? 'You will never learn this game; you don't know how to hold a club,' " she recounted.

He could not have been more wrong. Carner figured it out and became Seattle's greatest woman golfer, and more. She remains one of the most storied players in the history of the game, amateur or pro, man or woman, landing her in the LPGA and World Golf halls of fame. She won the U.S. Junior Girls championship in 1956. She captured U.S. Women's Amateur championships in 1957, 1960, 1962, 1966 and 1968. She claimed a pair of U.S. Women's Open titles in 1971 and 1976, beating Kathy Whitworth by seven strokes and Sandra Palmer in a playoff, respectively. She won 43 times on the LPGA Tour. Apparently her grip was just fine.

"I'd never seen anyone who had so much potential as JoAnne," said Judy Bell, an amateur golfing contemporary and the USGA's first woman president. "She oozed with raw talent."

The Juanita course disappeared long ago, after it was neglected and overtaken by weeds, and it

The then-Anne Quast and JoAnne Gunderson were rivals, beginning in their teens.

eventually became an expensive waterfront property turned into a park. So close to the lake, drainage was always a problem. Yet the place stayed dry enough to make a highly accomplished golfer out of Carner, ultimately producing a wisecracking woman who could hit the ball as far as the men and compete with virtually anyone.

"I played terrible and, all of a sudden, it came around," Carner said. "I would mimic the men players and their swings. The women had this little raise-up and dip-down to their swings and weren't supposed to hit it long. I thought that was rather boring."

For free rounds, Carner collected dead geraniums and honeysuckles from the flowerbeds surrounding the Juanita clubhouse. For free lessons, she shagged range balls. By 14, Carner was a serious player, shooting 1-over par at Tacoma's Fircrest Golf Club despite hitting a shot out-of-bounds and three-putting three times. Her 25 handicap was no longer believable.

Anything athletic this 5-foot-7 strawberry-blonde girl tried, such as swimming, bowling and even baseball, she was highly proficient. As a Lake Washington High School senior, Carner was urged by a friend to play tennis and they went undefeated as doubles partners. Carner took her golf game to Seattle's Sand Point Country Club and studied under head golf pro John Hoetmer in preparation for high-level play.

Carner was 16 when she entered her first national tournament, 17 when she

In 1969, Carner was the last woman amateur player to capture an LPGA event, Burdine's Invitational in Miami, an outcome that encouraged her to turn pro at age 30.

finished as U.S. Amateur runner-up and 18 when she won that elite event. She realized she was pretty good after that first national championship victory in 1957 when a huge parade through Kirkland was held in her honor and the *Seattle Post-Intelligencer* selected her as the city's Man of the Year. Her high school presented her with a letterman's sweater even though it didn't have girls' teams. Carner was the first woman to receive a full college golf scholarship, accepting one from Arizona State.

During the summer months Carner played in national tournaments but had to be creative. She was raised in a family of limited means. Her father, Gustav, was a carpenter put on the Sand Point Country Club payroll simply to help pay for her golf trips. She cut costs further by staying at the home of a Tennessee golf friend, Judy Eller, and using it as a hub to reach events on that side of the country. Eller nicknamed her "the Great Gundy."

In 1969, Carner was the last woman amateur player to capture an LPGA event, Burdine's Invitational in Miami, an outcome that encouraged her to turn pro at age 30. A year later, Carner was named LPGA Tour Rookie of the Year. She finished as LPGA Player of the Year three times and was the tour's top money-winner three times, with those achievements overlapping in 1982. She was entertaining to watch, especially during crunch time.

In 1971, she wrapped up her first U.S. Open victory in Erie, Pa., by booming her tee shot 310 yards on the 17th hole and unloading another drive 295 yards on the 18th. Both times Carner pitched onto the green while challenger Mary Mills had to approach with a 4-wood shot, an unsettling disparity.

"I think it was just growing up with the boys," Carner said. "They all wanted to hit it long and I started doing it the same way. To me, it was more fun. In match play, if you could hit the first drive long and straight, you scared half of your opponents and won it on the first tee."

She won her other U.S. Open in 1976 in Spring-field, PA. The player who lost to her, Palmer, was so impressed by this she gave the Northwest golfer yet another classic nickname: "Big Mama."

Carner played with supreme confidence, not unlike Babe Ruth. She was a chain-smoker, too, something she did to steady her nerves while she played. Her humor could be downright crude, and her acerbic comments drew comparisons to comedic actress Shelly Winters. She loved talking to her opponents and the fans, who felt she had the best attitude of anyone on the course.

In three decades on the LPGA Tour, she had only one outcome that really upset her for slipping out of her hands. Chasing after her third U.S. Open victory in 1987, she lost in a playoff to Laura Davies by three-putting after hitting two exemplary shots to reach the green.

"I really had no fear," Carner said. "I learned all the recovery shots. If I hit a bad shot, it never bothered me. I just hit the next shot. I would think about the next shot coming up. On the pro tour, they don't do that. The great ones do. The others walk down the fairway doing backswings instead of thinking about the next shot."

Carner lived in Palm Beach, Fla., sometimes wondering why after hurricanes repeatedly battered the place. Her husband of 36 years, Don, died in 2000. He served as her business manager and coach, and they were quite a sight together, traveling from LPGA Tour event to event in an Airstream trailer. When she wasn't golfing, she and Don entertained themselves by fishing in the Atlantic Ocean for mahi-mahi or yellowtail snapper from their 42-foot boat.

In 1985, Carner won for the 43rd and final time on the LPGA Tour, doing it close to home in the Safeco Classic at Kent's Meridian Valley Country Club. In 2003, at 64, she became the oldest LPGA player to make the cut in a tournament. In 2005, she appeared in her final event and retired after breaking her wrist — 20 years following her World Golf Hall of Fame induction. She wasn't done playing, though.

She joined the LPGA Legends Tour for senior women players and in her mid-70s was still entering tournaments around the country as its oldest competitor. She even found her way back to the Seattle area for a couple of events.

> She joined the LPGA Legends Tour for senior women's players and in her mid-70s was still entering tournaments around the country as its oldest competitor. She even found her way back to the Seattle area for a couple of events.

Carner also taught women and girls how to play the game at her JoAnne Carner Golf Academy for Ladies in Florida. Everyone had a chance to learn from a legend. With her students, Carner might have considered turning out the lights and yelling in their backswings. It worked for her. ❖

10 Locals to LPGA Tour

1. JoAnne Carner (ASU)
2. Ruth Jessen (SU)
3. Jo Ann Washam (WSU)
4. Jimin Kang (ASU)
5. Louise Friberg (UW)
6. Paige Mackenzie (UW)
7. Robin Walton (UW)
8. Jing Yan (UW)
9. Dodie Mazzuca (UW)
10. SooBin Kim (UW)

A Sixties Upgrade

A true Seattle icon, the Space Needle, sprouts out of the landscape, and later is joined by Interstate 5 bisecting the city, the Evergreen Point Bridge connecting it to the suburbs and Jimi Hendrix tying the Northwest to Woodstock and the global music scene.

The Huskies capture the Rose Bowl for the first time, actually winning consecutive Pasadena trips in impressive fashion, and then the pros arrive in a flurry, with the NBA's Seattle SuperSonics followed into the city by Major League Baseball's Seattle Pilots, who didn't stay long.

BOB SCHLOREDT

Seattle's Blind Spot

The older boy set up a Coca-Cola bottle, stuck a firecracker inside, placed a rock on top and lit the fuse. He repeated this activity over and over. Seven-year-old Bob Schloredt and his friends in Moorcraft, a small, ordinary Wyoming town an hour's drive from the North Dakota border, stood off to the side and watched the steady demolition. Unfortunately, they weren't far enough away to be safe from the jagged debris. Their summer fun in 1947 turned to horror when Schloredt, son of a grade-school principal and basketball coach, was struck in the left eye by a piece of flying glass.

Schloredt's parents rushed him to the nearest hospital, 30 miles up the road in Gillette, and then to a bigger emergency room, another agonizing 100 miles away in Sheridan. Each time, doctors offered the same prognosis: There was nothing they could do to save the vision in the kid's pierced eye. "They just sewed it up," Schloredt said.

Thereafter he could see only out of his right eye. Yet both ears worked just fine. His feet and hands were fully functional, too. Most of all, his competitive spirit remained intact. He never heard anyone offer him sympathy nor did he consider himself any less capable than anyone else, especially on athletic fields, and it showed.

Partially blind, Schloredt relied on sheer will rather than perfect eyesight to turn himself into a first-team

Associated Press All-America quarterback for the University of Washington, a two-time Rose Bowl Most Valuable Player, and the most riveting figure on the Huskies' talent-laden roster.

His football heroics made him Seattle's most inspirational hard-luck sports story – that of a quarterback overcoming a physical disability that should have kept him from the spotlight but, instead, helped catapult him into it. Largely because of Schloredt, the city entered the 1960s embracing its first championship of national significance in any of the three major sports, and then a year later did it again.

After his family left Wyoming and moved to Oregon, to the suburbs south of Portland, Schloredt emerged as an all-conference player in football, basketball and baseball as a senior for the Gresham Union High School Gophers. He felt no different than anyone else, except in a positive manner.

"I had not thought at all that I was handicapped in any shape or form," he said. "I'd make adjustments in football and baseball. I did have a hard time hitting a

> His football heroics made him Seattle's most inspirational hard-luck sports story – that of a quarterback overcoming a physical disability that should have kept him from the spotlight but, instead, helped catapult him into it.

curveball breaking away from me, though." Schloredt's instinctive quarterbacking prowess led to league championships and scholarship offers. He visited UCLA and USC, and Alabama called. He juggled recruiting pitches from Oregon and Washington, ultimately uncertain how he would say no to one of these Northwest schools that he now favored. The Ducks tried their best to entice him to Eugene, encouraging him to come and play both football and basketball.

Yet this was the 1950s and Schloredt wasn't required to sign any college paperwork in advance, so he took his time in making up his mind. By the rules in place, he actually was permitted to show up at a school, turn out for the football team for a few days and leave if he wanted, and go elsewhere with no penalties assessed.

Without much fanfare, he arrived in Seattle, liked it and stayed. There was plenty of incentive to play for the Huskies. "My dad was a coach and somebody made the comment to him that if I went to Washington there would be five quarterbacks ahead of me," Schloredt recalled. "My dad said, 'They'll have a damn good team then.' "

On the UW freshman team and as a sophomore, Schloredt endeared himself to the coaching staff as a tough, competitive player, though offering nothing outwardly special in his football skill set. He could hit people, run the ball and punt it a long way, but his passing was considered suspect.

In his first varsity season in 1958 for a 3-7 Huskies team, he started one game as an emergency fill-in at fullback and another at quarterback. Otherwise, Schloredt backed up Bob Hivner, a California native who possessed a decidedly better throwing arm. No one anticipated what came next from the guy with one good eye.

On the eve of the 1959 season, Schloredt, with an improved passing touch, won the starting quarterback job outright. Hivner officially dropped from the competition by breaking his thumb days before the first game. What followed were 16 months of absolute football magic for Schloredt.

Bob Schloredt jokingly wears an eye patch.

Handed the quarterback reins, Schloredt was sensational. A clever rollout threat, he ran for 10 touchdowns and passed for five more in 1959. He led the Huskies to a stunning 10-1 season, capped by the UW playing in the Rose Bowl for the first time in 16 years.

Directing the Huskies to their first Rose Bowl victory in school history, Schloredt ran for a touchdown and passed for another as his underdog team demolished Big Ten champion Wisconsin 44-8 on a warm afternoon in Pasadena, shocking the college football world and turning Seattle euphoric. Schloredt and teammate George Fleming, a prolific halfback, kicker and punt returner, were selected as the game's co-Most Valuable Players.

Limited vision put no limits on Schloredt. He saw what he needed to see. He made all the necessary adjustments. "I swiveled my head a lot," he said. "I was never lazy about checking the area where I was throwing the ball. I never felt I was doing anything different than anyone else."

From a reserve player the year before, Schloredt was singled out as the nation's top quarterback. He was named to the 1959 *Associated Press* All-America first team, picked ahead of Southern Methodist's Don Meredith, Georgia's Fran Tarkenton and UCLA's Billy Kilmer, all prolific quarterbacks and later accomplished NFL players.

Schloredt still had his senior year to play and, in 1960, he was touted as a leading Heisman Trophy candidate, featured on the cover of *Sports Illustrated* and known everywhere as this feel-good story from the Northwest for overcoming his handicap. Another setback, however, slowed his fast-track success.

Four and a half games into his senior season, Schloredt, also a defensive back during this time of one-platoon football, broke his collarbone while making an open-field tackle against UCLA. This was gloomy front-page news. He was out for the rest of the regular season.

Somehow the Huskies advanced to the Rose Bowl without him, again losing just once in 11 outings, the only blemish a one-point defeat to an Orange Bowl-bound Navy team that was decided in the closing seconds and involved a healthy Schloredt.

The UW needed its starting quarterback for a second tour of Pasadena: the Huskies faced Minnesota, the nation's top-ranked team. Schloredt was inserted for the third offensive series of a scoreless game, replacing Hivner, and he ran and passed for touchdowns again in a much closer New Year's Day battle. Beating the Gophers 17-7, the newly healed quarterback was named MVP without having to share the award this time, becoming the Rose Bowl's first two-time recipient.

Schloredt was full of football heroics but not pro football opportunities. He was not drafted by the NFL, though the Chicago Bears considered signing him as a free agent. The Dallas Texans didn't pick him until the 27th round of the AFL draft. His bad eye had finally gotten in the way. "They thought because of the eye injury I couldn't be a drop-back passer," he said ruefully.

Schloredt turned to the CFL and spent two seasons north of the border with the B.C. Lions. He passed on a third year when he was encouraged to come home and become an assistant coach on Jim Owens' UW staff. Schloredt was unsuccessful in bids for the head coaching jobs at Hawaii and Oregon. He served as an assistant coach for the WFL's Hawaii Hawaiians only to have the pro franchise fold up at midseason.

Settling into a Shoreline home at 1827 N. 167th St., Schloredt held a series of regular jobs, among them working for a chocolate company and doing building inspections, while remaining close to the UW football program.

It was traumatic when that Coke bottle exploded in Wyoming and curtailed Schloredt's vision in his left eye for good. Yet he never had any trouble looking back on his life and counting the good things that came his way on the football field. In that regard, his vision never left him.

"I got a hell of a lot more than I expected," Schloredt said. ❖

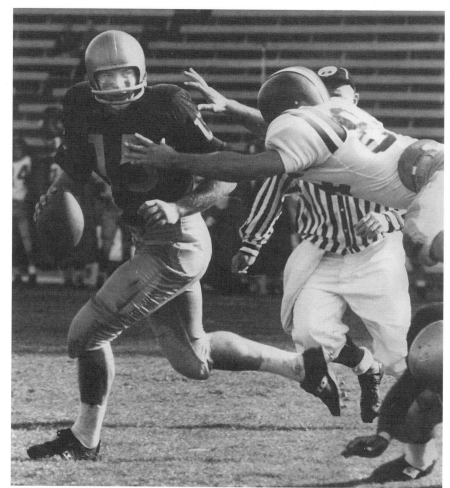

The mobile Bob Schloredt was a tough man to tackle.

GEORGE FLEMING

Seattle's Rose Bowl Ticket

George Fleming was born in the same Parkland Hospital in Dallas in which President John F. Kennedy died, which might help explain Fleming's eventual political ambitions. Yet before he sat in a legislative chamber and rendered any decisions, Fleming had other business to complete. Even though he lived in a city that offered the Cotton Bowl, his dream was to play in the Rose Bowl.

As a Texas teenager he watched the New Year's Day football game every year on TV. He was enamored with the bright colors. He loved the pageantry. He pictured himself in the middle of it.

An all-state quarterback, Fleming decided he would do whatever it took to become involved in the Rose Bowl. His best college bets, he figured, were joining a team such as Ohio State, UCLA or USC, all regular Jan. 1 qualifiers. He contacted an aunt in Los Angeles who worked for a UCLA alumnus and a meeting hastily was arranged with the coaching staff.

"They said, 'Tell him to bring his scrapbooks,' " Fleming recalled. "They were impressed. They were interested."

Fleming had a 3.3 grade average, but it wasn't enough to get him into school on the first try – UCLA

> **Fleming got his bearings, found his way to Seattle and became the city's first highly accomplished African-American football player.**

wanted out-of-state students to carry 3.5 – so the Bruins coaching staff stashed him at East Los Angeles College, where his teammates included a tall, rangy lineman named Ben Davidson. Used at running back, Fleming injured his knee and missed several games for the two-year school, but he was still a second-team, all-conference selection. The Bruins, whose backfield was built around future NFL quarterback Billy Kilmer, suddenly stopped coming around.

"I said, 'Coach, what's the problem?' " Fleming recalled. "He said, 'UCLA thinks you're injury-prone.' "

Catching him on the rebound, a new Washington Huskies coaching staff headed by Jim Owens offered him a scholarship. Yet the young Texan was unfamiliar with the school and its geographic location and Fleming hesitated before accepting the offer. "The University of Washington, where's that? Up in Alaska? You've got to be kidding," he said at the time.

Fleming got his bearings, found his way to Seattle and became the city's first highly accomplished African-American football player, but not without more reservations that nearly drove him away from the UW program. He second-guessed his decision, finding far more challenges than he envisioned. As the losses piled up in 1958 for a 3-6-1 team, a trip to the Rose Bowl didn't seem feasible any time soon.

> "In the heat of the battle,
> they used the 'N' word,"
> Fleming said.
> "Whether it was
> racism or not,
> Owens wasn't used to
> the black athlete."

Black players were stacked at positions. Negative racial overtones were interspersed throughout the program, as was an underlying current of discord.

"There were four or five African-Americans and all of us played left half, and I asked Chesty Walker, 'What's going on here?'" Fleming said, referring to the Huskies' offensive coordinator and a fellow Texan. "He said, 'Black guys are better runners from left half.'"

Fleming was left incredulous the day that Walker, someone whom he otherwise admired, said he was going to take his boat out on nearby Lake Washington and go "nigger fishing." Fleming also heard Huskies defensive coordinator Tom Tipps in the middle of practice heatedly tell a black player, "You run around like a nigger on Sunday." All of this racist condemnation seemed to be condoned by Owens, whose coaching staff possessed strong Southern roots throughout, and Fleming was deeply insulted.

"In the heat of the battle, they used the 'N' word," Fleming said. "Whether it was racism or not, Owens wasn't used to the black athlete. There were things I could see that were wrong and I was close to leaving the University of Washington. Finally a bunch of us got together and told the captain, 'You have to go talk to the man and tell him this is unacceptable.'

George Fleming was 1959 UW standout.

"The next year we began to see some changes. They began to treat us like human beings. They knew in 1959 if they didn't start winning, they'd be gone."

Winning was the cure for a lot of ills. From that dismal first season, the Huskies won 10 of 11 games in 1959, which could only mean one thing for Fleming: He got to play in his coveted Rose Bowl. And he not only ran onto that field in Pasadena, he owned it all day long. With a large contingent of relatives and friends watching from the stands, Fleming had an unforgettable day.

He returned a first-quarter punt 53 yards for an instant touchdown. He set up a second-quarter score with a 55-yard punt runback. He caught a fourth-quarter pass from Bob Schloredt and raced for a 65-yard gain, leading to a fifth and final Huskies' TD in a stunning 44-8 rout of the Wisconsin Badgers. He also kicked a field goal and five extra points.

From that New Year's beat-down, Fleming and Schloredt were named co-Most Valuable Players of the game, though the left halfback easily could have been singled out alone for his explosive postseason performance. Making two players, one white and one black, share the honor almost seemed racially cautious, but it didn't matter much to Fleming.

"It was total joy," he said. "I was just so happy. We had won the game. They said I was going to be MVP. It was a dream come true."

Then it happened again. Twelve months later, Fleming and another once-beaten Huskies team captured the 1961 Rose Bowl by upending the No. 1-ranked Minnesota Gophers 17-7. Although held in check by a rugged Big Ten defense, Fleming kicked a record 44-yard field goal.

By now, he had experienced far more of Pasadena than he could have hoped for. He also received overdue respect from a remorseful UCLA football coach Bill Barnes during the regular season.

"I think we made a mistake," Barnes told reporters. "If we would have had Fleming, we would have gone to the Rose Bowl, not Washington.'"

Fleming finished his UW career with 588 yards rushing, 383 receiving, eight touchdowns, 55 kicking conversions and 11 field goals, modest numbers in some categories because he too frequently had to share that left-halfback position with talented newcomer Charlie Mitchell rather than play beside him.

Turning briefly to the pros, Fleming spent a season with the AFL's Oakland Raiders, kicking a league-record 54-yard field goal; two years with the CFL's Winnipeg Blue Bombers, booting a league-record 55-yard field goal; and two years kicking for the semipro Seattle Ramblers. Lingering pelvic and back injuries, caused by a low blow from an opposing linebacker, made him switch careers.

Urged to enter local politics by others, Fleming was a distinguished leader, serving two years in the state House of Representatives followed by 20 in the Senate. He was the state's first African-American to become a senator. He pushed through legislation benefiting minorities, women and the elderly, counting the state passage of a Martin Luther King holiday among his most satisfying accomplishments.

> **Fleming finished his UW career with 588 yards rushing, 383 receiving, eight touchdowns, 55 kicking conversions and 11 field goals.**

While he inevitably walked away from football, Fleming, who lived in Leschi at 1100 S. Lake Washington Blvd., never turned his back on the Rose Bowl. He continued to watch his favorite game each year, sometimes in person, bringing back the remembrances.

Among his keepsakes, he received silver cups from the Helms Athletic Foundation and Touchdown Club of Columbus saluting his efforts during those Rose Bowl-bound seasons. He had a watch from the 1960 game tucked away in a drawer. He wore a diamond ring commemorating the 1961 contest. Mostly, he pinched himself repeatedly, making sure that this all really took place, that he actually played in the Rose Bowl, and not just once, but twice.

"I was saying to myself: "Did this really happen?'" Fleming said. ❖

BEN DAVIDSON

Seattle's Super Villain

Davidson used to bring down quarterbacks and the house. He delivered punches and punch lines. He had people running for cover or doubled over in laughter. In or out of uniform, he had great timing. Seattle has never produced a more theatrical or TV-ready athlete.

Ben Davidson was this cleverly invented football villain with a handlebar mustache and wild gleam in his eye, a memorable character who could have been pulled from a comic book or pro wrestling ring. While he went somewhat unnoticed as a reserve University of Washington football player, he became an Oakland Raiders icon. His profile was expanded once his huge frame filled out and TV discovered his comedic talent.

Davidson used to bring down quarterbacks and the house. He delivered punches and punch lines. He had people running for cover or doubled over in laughter. In or out of uniform, he had great timing. Seattle has never produced a more theatrical or TV-ready athlete. "Big Ben" could keep a room full of people spellbound when he recounted his football career that took him from Los Angeles to Seattle and ultimately back to California.

He didn't play the game in high school. He didn't pull on a uniform until 1957, when Davidson attended two-year East Los Angeles College in his old neighborhood. He was the son of a Los Angeles police officer and wasn't exactly sure what to do on the football field until an opponent rudely clipped him from behind, and Davidson reacted in a manner he said easily could have got him arrested by his father.

"I reached into his helmet and there was his head, his face and right under my thumb I felt something

like an eye socket," Davidson said in his fierce, gravelly voice. "I gouged his eye a little. He screamed and ran off the field. That's when the light bulb went on in my head and I said, 'I can do this.' I think that's when I became a Raider."

Actually, Oakland was still three years from landing a pro football franchise and using the silver helmets that sported the black decal of a man wearing an eye patch. Davidson joined the Huskies first and did more sitting than playing for a pair of victorious Rose Bowl teams. During two seasons in Seattle, he rotated between the second and third units. He started just two UW games, one assignment earned in practice and another as an injury fill-in.

He was tall and skinny back then, barely resembling the 6-foot-8, 280-pound behemoth and four-time Pro Bowl player he would become with the Raiders, with the exception of temperament.

"I remember the Huskies playing Utah and having a big lead in the fourth quarter, and Ben went in to substitute," said Richard Pelto, a *Seattle Times* photographer who worked close to the action. "The following play, the Utah tackle waved at the sideline and the referee, yelling loudly, 'This guy' — and he was pointing at Ben — 'slugged me!' Ben looked especially innocent when he ran off the field. He was definitely in training for being a Raider."

Leaving JC ball, Davidson had considered Arizona, Fresno State and San Jose State before settling on the Huskies. Growing up in smoggy L.A., he had just one question for UW recruiters: How's the air up there? Their answer was "fresh," which was all he wanted to hear. "I said, 'That's it, I'm out of here,' " Davidson said. "They forgot to mention one thing: There was fresh air because it rained every day!"

Even as a substitute player for the UW, he was an All-Coast honorable-mention pick as a senior. The Huskies advanced to the Rose Bowl each year he was in Seattle, and Davidson played just one minute in each postseason game. In his first season, he started the opener against Colorado, didn't play well and was relegated to reserve duty thereafter. He still didn't feel slighted or overlooked by Jim Owens' Huskies coaching staff.

"I never looked at it that way," Davidson said. "I didn't play high school football, so I had a late start. I was young, too. I came out of high school when I was just 16, out of college when I was 20."

Somebody noticed the potential lurking inside the huge frame because Davidson was drafted higher than any of his fellow Huskies, going in the fourth round to the NFL's New York Giants. Based on potential, Davidson was selected for the College All-Star team that annually played against the reigning NFL championship team in Chicago. He remembers riding around that city on the el train

with another physically imposing pro prospect, 6-9, 300-pound Ernie Ladd. "People thought killers were on the loose in the subway," Davidson wisecracked.

The pros still weren't sure what they had. He was traded by the Giants during training camp and spent his rookie season with the Green Bay Packers. He was waived and played the next two years for the Washington Redskins. After he was cut again, the Raiders claimed him. The Bay Area franchise and Southern California native were meant for each other. Davidson was an extroverted personality joining an already unruly cast of characters. For the second of his eight seasons in Oakland, he showed up with a handlebar mustache when facial hair was frowned upon around the league, but those whiskers were here to stay. From 1965 on, Davidson never played without the foliage. It fit his image, which was coarse and unrestrained.

"We played the Eagles and we decided to see how many Eagles we could leave lying on the field," Davidson said, describing his pro career in a rapid-fire monologue. "We rushed the passer and the other guys gang-tackled the quarterback before I got there and I figured I'd drill him anyway. We hurt a lot of quarterbacks and it was good. I once gave the peace sign to [Giants coach] Allie Sherman. He was pretty upset; he only gave half of it back to me."

Otis Sistrunk, a fellow Raiders defensive lineman and frightening enough himself that former NFL player turned broadcaster Alex Karras once quipped that Sistrunk hailed from "the University of Mars," said this of Davidson, "He scared me the way he talked."

Davidson's football timing was always perfect. With the Packers, he appeared in the 1961 NFL championship game. For the Raiders, he started at defensive end in Super Bowl II in 1968. Against Joe

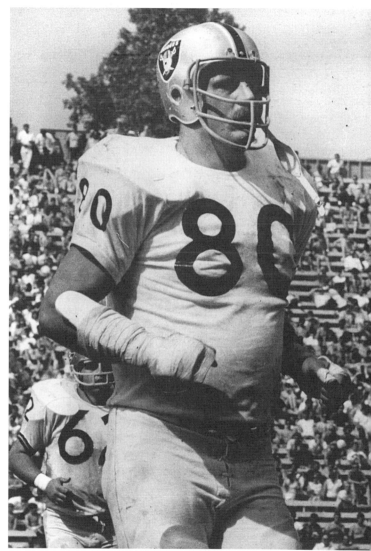

Ben Davidson was an intimidating Oakland Raiders player.

Namath, the defensive lineman was credited with breaking the cheekbone of the cocky and high-profile New York Jets quarterback — when Oakland teammate Ike Lassiter was responsible — and Davidson's reputation took off.

Namath publicly complained that the Raiders were a bunch of cheap-shot artists before playing them and he got leveled for it. Yet all anyone remembered from that rough-and-tumble game was a classic photo taken by *Life Magazine* of Davidson throwing a forearm and knocking the helmet off of the Jets quarterback, a visually compelling yet far less lethal play. "Isaac did it but I got all the publicity," Davidson said.

The TV and movie cameras couldn't resist Big Ben and his huge and unique appearance. Once his football career ended with the WFL's Portland Storm in 1974, he made his cinematic debut in the movie "M*A*S*H." He appeared in another film, "Conan the Barbarian." He turned up on countless TV shows, among them "Charlie's Angels," "Fantasy Island," "Dukes of Hazzard," "Happy Days" and "CHiPs."

Davidson's greatest exposure, however, came as a popular character on those long-running Miller Lite beer commercials, which favored several pro athletes in a chorus of humorous situations. He made 27 of the well-received TV spots. "Tastes great, less filling," became a steady part of his vernacular.

He identified so strongly with the popular beverage that corporate outings were encouraged and he turned these into another post-football job that mushroomed. He traveled to every state except Delaware and a long line of countries pitching his favorite beer.

Davidson, who owned a home at 23722 107th Ave. S.W. on Vashon Island, was 72 when he died from prostate cancer on July 2, 2012. He had walked away from football with a sense of humor and his body fairly intact. He had wisely used his renegade Oakland image as a protective shield.

"Playing for the Raiders was pretty safe," Davidson said with a sly smile. "People knew if they did something to you, something might happen to them." ❖

Top 10 Post-Sports Job

1. Ben Davidson (actor)
2. John Cherberg (lt. governor)
3. Junior Coffey (horse trainer)
4. Harvey Blanks (actor)
5. George Fleming (senator)
6. Steve Largent (congressman)
7. Jim Bouton (author)
8. Boone Kirkman (truck driver)
9. Dewey Soriano (ship pilot)
10. George Wilson (longshoreman)

Eddie Miles had 50 solid college basketball scholarship offers. The 6-foot-4 guard from Arkansas possessed unlimited shooting range and could score practically anywhere at any time, and recruiters in 1959 were willing to push aside long-standing discriminatory practices in an effort to put a uniform on him.

Miles' largely Midwest suitors included Kansas, Illinois, Iowa State, Michigan, Michigan State, Minnesota, Oklahoma State and Wisconsin. Arkansas offered to make him the school's first black player. The Razorbacks and the others, though, never had a chance.

While all were tempting, none of these basketball programs had anything close to what Seattle University offered: Elgin Baylor. He was the Chieftains' most famous basketball alumnus and Miles was a huge fan. The school put the two of them together on the phone and a deal was easily struck to bring Miles to the Northwest, where he became the city's best pure shooter in its college basketball history.

"I was a hero-worshipper of Baylor," Miles said. "I always idolized Elgin. I started following him after reading a magazine article about him when I was a

> While all were tempting, none of these basketball programs had anything close to what Seattle University offered: Elgin Baylor. He was the Chieftains' most famous basketball alumnus and Miles was a huge fan.

EDDIE MILES
The Man With The Golden Arm

little boy. I don't know why I started liking him. He called and talked to me. You know how that was."

Seattle U landed a player from North Little Rock who mesmerized people with his advanced basketball ability. In four varsity seasons at all-black Scipio A. Jones High School, he averaged 18, 25, 30 and 32 points per game, with a high outing of 55. He developed his deft touch in a most unusual manner: Jones High coach A.B. Calvin wouldn't let his players use a basketball when working on shooting; they had to practice shadow shooting. They didn't see any misses that way, didn't get bent out of shape when the ball wasn't dropping. They just worked on developing a smooth stroke.

Miles led the Dragons to four state titles and a runner-up finish in the now-defunct black high school national tournament, which annually invited African-American teams from 20 states to Tennessee A&I State in Nashville. Curtis Jackson, a Seattle U scout, made it a point to attend these events and wave at Miles after each game.

Miles was everything as advertised once reaching Seattle. The points kept coming in bunches. Beginning in 1961, Miles averaged 20, 22.2 and 25.7 points per game for the Chieftains, ranking him seventh in the nation as a senior. He finished as the school's second-highest career scorer with 1,874 points, 71 more than Baylor (in two seasons) and exceeded only by Johnny O'Brien's 2,733. Miles also finished with Seattle U's third-best career scoring average at 23.1 points per game, surpassed only by Baylor's 31.1 and O'Brien's 25.8. It almost didn't happen. Baylor or no Baylor, Miles wasn't sure the damp Northwest climate was right for him once he sampled it. "When I first came, I was totally homesick," he said. "I made a promise to myself that I was leaving. I wasn't used to seeing all that rain. But when spring came, it was beautiful. I thought, 'Man, this is nice.' If it hadn't stopped raining, I wouldn't have stuck it out."

Miles never became close friends with Baylor because of their age difference, but he spent a glorious summer in 1962 playing pickup ball on campus alongside his hero when the Los Angeles Lakers superstar was required to fulfill a military commitment at nearby Fort Lewis in Tacoma. "Every weekend he would come up and play in the gym and we'd all have fun," Miles said.

Miles was allowed to freelance and shoot at will by Chieftains coach Vince Cazzetta. The guard played decent defense and could drive to the basket, but his outside jumper was what everyone wanted to see. Range was no issue, with Miles often launching shots from 25 feet at a time when no 3-point line existed.

This sweet-shooting guard had no match when it came to catchy nicknames. Miles became the Chieftains' most marketable player by far when he was handed a different promotional tag each season, with the final label his most memorable.

As a sophomore, Miles was christened by Seattle U publicist Bill Sears as "The Arkansas Traveler" for obvious geographic reasons. As a junior, with the World's Fair in full swing across town, Miles was tagged with the somewhat corny "The Space-Age All-American." Sears made up for that lapse the following season, coming up with something that sounded like it came

straight from a James Bond movie and it stuck: "The Man with the Golden Arm."

Explaining his creative inspiration for the slogan, Sears said Miles' capable right arm could send a basketball through the hoop all night long. The Chieftains publicist considered the guard a highly unique player. "He was the greatest outside shooter I ever saw," Sears said. "We had some fun with him. I had a press book done with his arm in gold. I was able to get a cutout of him full-sized, with him dribbling, on the sides of Seattle Metro buses. He could handle the notoriety and everything."

Miles, a third-team *Associated Press* and *United Press International* All-America choice as a senior, played for teams that went 18-8, 18-9 and 21-6. The Chieftains qualified each year for the 24- or 25-team NCAA Tournament. The postseason, however, was never kind to Miles. He and his teammates suffered a harsh first-round defeat every year, losing to Arizona State 72-70 on a last-second shot, Oregon State 69-65 in overtime and Oregon State 70-66, with each game played at a different site in the state of Oregon.

Arizona State overcame an 11-point halftime deficit and Miles' 24 points to win on Gary Hahn's 15-foot shot as the final buzzer sounded in Portland. In 1962, Oregon State, which hosted the Far West Regional in Corvallis, beat the Chieftains in OT despite Miles' 26 points on 10-for-14 shooting. In Miles' final collegiate game in Eugene, he connected on 11 of 19 shots for 28 points, but it wasn't enough to prevent another four-point defeat to the Beavers, who were led by 7-footer Mel Counts' 30 points. "Maybe we depended too much on Eddie Miles," Seattle U teammate John Tresvant said.

The pros wanted to do the same. Miles was the fourth player selected overall in the 1963 NBA draft by the Detroit Pistons. After an aborted attempt to turn him into a playmaker, he averaged 19.6, 17.6 and 18.5 points in successive seasons while starting the All-Star Game in 1966.

SU pocket schedule featured Eddie Miles.

He played nine seasons in the NBA, later joining the Baltimore Bullets and New York Knicks, before his career ended prematurely because of an Achilles tendon injury. He figured that mishap cost him four or five seasons.

"It should have been better," Miles said of his pro career. "When I got to camp, the coach [Charles Wolf] said they were looking for a passer. He said he didn't want me to shoot it. The assistant coach said, 'That man is too good of a shooter to not shoot.' The coach didn't play me that much at first. I destroyed his guards in practice."

Miles hurt his heel by coming down on a teammate's foot in a game in San Francisco. The Pistons team physician told him to play on and the pain would go away. Miles found he couldn't stop or cut properly. Not nearly as effective, he was traded by the Pistons after six seasons to Baltimore.

In a game in Detroit, Miles allowed the Bullets trainer to give him an injection and he went out and scored 30 on his old team, but that was one of his final shining moments. By 1972, he was out of the NBA after a season with the Knicks.

Miles returned to Seattle and was a Chieftains' assistant coach in 1978-1980 until the school downsized the program from Division I to NAIA, citing a lack of interest and too many minor scandals. He lived at 7902 S. 112th St. in Edmonds and raised a family, with one of his sons demonstrating a similar long-range shooting ability. Troy Miles played for O'Dea High School and Nevada and Idaho State, and attended CBA tryout camps before an Achilles injury did him in, too. Eddie and Troy later coached south Seattle's Tyee High School team together.

In 2009, Miles joined Baylor and other former Chieftains players for an emotional occasion. They watched as Seattle U, after a near 30-year absence and now answering to the more politically correct Redhawks, returned to Division I.

Miles was reunited with his idol and his beloved basketball program was made whole again. While his team was identified as something different now, he still answered to the best nickname, if only part of it.

"People just call me 'Arm' now," Miles said. ❖

Top 10 Seattle U Basketball Players

1. Elgin Baylor, F
2. Johnny O'Brien, C
3. Eddie Miles, G
4. Eddie O'Brien, G
5. Tom Workman, F
6. John Tresvant, F
7. Charlie Williams, G
8. Jawann Oldham, C
9. Frank Oleynick, G
10. Clint Richardson, G

In 2009, Miles joined Baylor and other former Chieftains players for an emotional occasion. They watched as Seattle U, after a near 30-year absence and now answering to the more politically correct Redhawks, returned to Division I.

JOHN TRESVANT

Seattle's Leading Rebounder

John Tresvant was forgotten in time. As he welcomed his 2002 induction to Seattle University's Hall of Fame, the former Chieftains center had grabbed the most rebounds in a Division I college basketball game by any player for nearly 50 years, and no one outside of campus knew it. His 40-rebound effort against Montana on Feb. 8, 1963, at the Seattle Center Arena was regularly listed in Seattle U game programs, but it wasn't found in the NCAA record book.

Forty would have left Tresvant tied for fourth place all-time with Connecticut's Art Quimby, who had that amount against Boston in 1955. Tresvant would have trailed only William and Mary's Bill Chambers, who latched onto 51 against Virginia in 1953; Marshall's Charlie Stack, who had 43 against Morris Harvey in 1953; and Holy Cross' Tommy Heinsohn, who pulled down 42 against Boston College in 1955.

Against Montana, Tresvant came up with a rebound every minute. He finished with three rebounds more than the previous school record held by Elgin Baylor, whose total likewise wasn't recognized by the NCAA.

With or without national confirmation, Tresvant's rebound total proved to be the most unique individual statistical performance registered by a Seattle athlete, especially in basketball, where rebounds have always been a lot harder to come by than points. And, according to Tresvant, 40 was an inaccurate count.

With or without national confirmation, Tresvant's rebound total proved to be the most unique individual statistical performance registered by a Seattle athlete, especially in basketball, where rebounds have always been a lot harder to come by than points. And, according to Tresvant, 40 was an inaccurate count.

"Actually, I had 44," said Tresvant, who, if correct, would have had the second-highest rebound total ever recorded in a college game. "I know I got more when I went back over the game. The guy keeping the stats told me later he didn't mark them all down."

There were logical reasons for Tresvant's record-setting performance being overlooked by the NCAA. He came up with his total during his junior season in a 100-63 victory over Montana in a game fraught with emotion and expected to be overly physical. Everyone was greatly distracted. Two days before the Grizzlies game, popular Chieftains coach Vince Cazzetta was fired after losing a running battle with athletic director Eddie O'Brien, resulting in O'Brien being hung in effigy by Seattle U students.

A few weeks earlier, the Chieftains and the same Montana team had brawled in Missoula. People were prepared to count punches, not rebounds, in the rematch. "We were really hot for that game because we had got into a big fight over there," Tresvant said of the road game. "A guy kept elbowing me, and my team-mate Greg Vermillion punched him in the face, the police came and it really got out of hand."

Tresvant was a fundamentally sound rebounder, taught how to properly block out and clear out after picking up basketball late. He grew up in Washington, D.C., and attended Springarn High School, the same place that produced Baylor, yet Tresvant was cut from the basketball team. He played football and baseball instead. Once out of Springarn, he was 17 when he joined the Air Force, was stationed at Paine Field north of Seattle and busied himself repairing aircraft radar units.

In the process, he grew several inches, started playing AAU basketball for Renton's Puhich Cleaners and was impressive enough to warrant a Chieftains scholarship offer. He didn't shoot or dribble that well at first, but he could rebound with anyone. He was a raw talent. Seattle U was so interested a school official wrote to a congress-man asking for Tresvant's early military release.

"Joe Puhich kind of liked the way I played and recruited me for Seattle U," Tresvant said. "I guess I learned how to be physical in the Air Force. The thing I could do really well was rebound."

An all-around player for the Chieftains, Tresvant averaged 17.9 points and 14 rebounds per game as a senior, and 12.6 points and 11.1 rebounds during his career. Typical of his ability, he had 35 points and 17 rebounds in 108-88 victory over Gonzaga in his final regular-season game. He came up with 20 points and 20 rebounds in the 1964 NCAA Tournament, a tough 95-90 loss to a UCLA team that went on and finished 30-0 and claimed the school's first national championship. His all-out approach was no different in practice either.

"Someone took a long jump shot and Tres took off running from the wing to follow up with a dunk," teammate Peller Phillips said. "He actually hit his head on the rim and cut a gash above his eyebrow. We all laughed and nicknamed him 'Jungle Jim.' "

From that scrawny high school kid, Tresvant grew into a solid 6-foot-8, 250-pound player who spent nine seasons with six NBA teams, averaging 9.2 points and 6.3 rebounds per outing, with high pro games of 36 points and 18 rebounds. He played for the Baltimore Bullets, Cincinnati Royals, Detroit Pistons, Los Angeles Lakers, St. Louis Hawks and Seattle SuperSonics. He appeared in the 1970 NBA Finals with the Lakers and 1971 NBA Finals with the Bullets, losing both times.

His career ended after he tore up his right knee in a collision with Atlanta Hawks 7-foot center Tom Payne during an exhibition game. He eventually needed two knee-replacement surgeries. "I probably would have played three or four more years at least if that hadn't happened," Tresvant said. "I was happy to get drafted by the pros. I had the hard-work ethic to keep me in there for nine years. I'm glad I was able to stay so long."

When pro basketball ended for him, Tresvant returned to the Seattle area and became a Snohomish middle-school industrial arts teacher. While he never advertised his basketball background, students found out and were so impressed to have a former NBA guy running their classroom they went out and ordered his basketball trading cards on eBay and brought them in to be signed. It wasn't hard for him to come back to the Northwest, moving into a suburban Snohomish home at 14814 61st Dr. S.E. "Seattle had more retired basketball players than anywhere else," he said.

The well-rounded man liked to dabble and tinker in his spare time. He grew flowers and vegetables, opened a smoked-foods business and built things in

John Tresvant played for six NBA teams, including Seattle.

his garage. He also maintained an unwavering interest in rebounding. He was coaching the Centennial Middle School girls' team when he designed a rebounding machine, frustrated because his players wouldn't jump and showed no inclination to want to jump.

His career ended
after he tore up
his right knee in a collision
with Atlanta Hawks
7-foot center Tom Payne
during an exhibition game.
He eventually needed two
knee-replacement surgeries.

"Take all the teams that win on a consistent basis, from high school to college to the pros, and they control the boards," Tresvant said. "The Spurs controlled the boards when they won the NBA title, so did the Pistons and the Miami Heat when they won. Anyone can score 30 points and lose. Not everyone can rebound."

His invention, the TRES, or Total Rebounder Exercise System, was a mobile, miniature basket adjustable in height with a lever, a contraption that came with a basketball hanging from a cord and a $3,000 price tag. It was easily folded up and stored in a car or closet. The University of Washington women's basketball team bought one. He also offered 10 rebounding drills to anyone who was interested. He wasn't teaching anything new to anyone, just dusting off a lost art form.

Sadly, the once robust Tresvant was 68 when he suffered a debilitating stroke that paralyzed him over much of the left side of his body, affected his speech and forced him to use a cane to remain mobile. He was faced with a far more difficult rebound situation, but he courageously pressed on, accepting invitations to Seattle U Hall of Fame dinners and other events.

While his body betrayed him, Tresvant at least was able to witness the NCAA right a grievous basketball wrong on his behalf. He was always rebounding. In 2004, his 40-rebound game was recognized and added to the basketball record book by the college governing body, as were Baylor's 37 boards. Tresvant never forgot how Seattle U fans had chanted for him to return late in the Montana game and break Baylor's rebound record. Now everyone would know.

The NCAA record-keepers were sympathetic and accommodating when I pointed out the Seattle U omissions, asking only to see old newspaper clippings to verify the astounding rebound totals. Long overdue, Tresvant finally was recognized as one of college basketball's four best single-game rebounders. Since 1955, no one else in a Division I college game has grabbed as many as 40 rebounds.

"I'm not a person to talk about myself much; I get embarrassed about that," Tresvant said. "They didn't have to induct me into the Hall of Fame. They had to talk me into accepting it. I didn't think anybody would remember what I did or who I was. But I guess I could rebound, though nobody believed it. It's in the record book." ❖

On May 1, 1963, the hearty Seattle man became the first American mountain climber to stand atop 29,028-foot Mount Everest, the highest point on Earth and glorious only in concept, and he fulfilled a task that forever cast him as the greatest alpine figure in his heavily mountaineering-influenced hometown.

JIM WHITTAKER

The Mountain Man

The top of the world wasn't glamorous. Jim Whittaker practically had to crawl the last leg to get there. The temperature was a brisk 35 degrees below zero, wind was howling and snow was blowing. Whittaker couldn't see much at all.

On May 1, 1963, the hearty Seattle man became the first American mountain climber to stand atop 29,028-foot Mount Everest, the highest point on Earth and glorious only in concept, and he fulfilled a task that forever cast him as the greatest alpine figure in his heavily mountaineering-influenced hometown.

Whittaker likened Everest to straddling the roof of a single-story house that sloped off treacherously, saying, "Basically, you were as close as you can get to heaven and still touch Earth, and it was not very heavenly."

Whittaker and Nawang Gombu, a Nepalese Sherpa, found this trek exhilarating if not overwhelming. They

were the 10th and 11th people to visit this dangerous and imposing lookout. They stayed just 20 minutes. They dropped their packs and took photographs. Whittaker pounded a three-foot-long aluminum stake that held an American flag into the ice. They looked for any sign of British climbers George Mallory and Andrew Irvine, who had failed to return from an Everest expedition four decades earlier, and found none. They caught a brief glimpse of Nepal but couldn't see Tibet.

It was a tense 20 minutes on top and it was time to go. Whittaker wore a red Eddie Bauer down parka over an orange parka shell, down pants over wool long underwear and Sherman boots that had three layers of leather, and he carried a yellow pack. He had shaved to give his oxygen mask a tight fit.

Yet he was frostbitten and temporarily blind in one eye, his goggles failing to properly shield him on one side from the crystalline gusts. He was thirsty but his water bottle was frozen, because he had absentmindedly placed it in an unprotected pocket of his backpack. Both climbers were out of bottled oxygen.

"I felt like a fragile human being," said Whittaker, then 34, and otherwise a strapping 6-foot-5, 205-pound man who possessed ample determination and enough athleticism to pull off this difficult task.

After pausing long enough to pick up a loose rock, a keepsake that was later set in gold and made into a ring by a Seattle jeweler, Whittaker started down the mountain with his mountaineering companion. They understood this would be the toughest part of the landmark climb.

They were fatigued but fully aware that Everest never got tired. They hadn't gone far when a huge section of cornice, a ledge-like overhang, broke off sharply and sailed out of sight. Gone in an instant was half of the track they had used in their ascent. The drop was 10,000 feet of sheer mountain wall into Tibet.

"If we had been over a little more to one side, if we had moved over just a foot, we would have gone with it," Whittaker pointed out. "Maybe we were numbed by the lack of oxygen, but we were not concerned. A couple of days later, I thought about it and said to Gombu, 'My gosh, we almost went over!' "

Twenty minutes on top changed Whittaker's life forever. He had spent a grueling three months above 18,000 feet, including 35 days above 23,500 feet. He returned home an American hero, treated that summer to a festive parade through downtown Seattle and summoned to the White House to receive a gold medal from President John F. Kennedy.

Whittaker was put on the cover of *Life Magazine*. He wrote a book titled *Life on the Edge*. His accomplishments would turn his hometown into a mountain-climbing Mecca. People everywhere wanted Whittaker to run for political office, to hear him speak about his high-altitude adventure, and to put their lives in danger on the tallest mountain in the world and do what he did.

Seated with Secretary of Defense Robert McNamara, NBC-TV newscaster Tom Brokaw and JFK, and having

a drink in the nation's capital, Whittaker was saluted by the president in the following manner, "Here's a toast to Jim Whittaker, the first American to climb Mount Everest – and we didn't have to have a chimpanzee do it first."

Whittaker and his twin brother, Lou, were hand-picked to join the 1963 Everest expedition headed up by American Norman Dyrenfurth and sponsored by the National Geographic Society. The latter was bent on making the U.S. a serious player in the race to one of the most treacherous places anywhere on the planet after British, Swiss and Chinese teams had turned in successful climbs.

The brothers, who graduated from West Seattle High and Seattle University, grew up at 9802 44th Ave. S.W., south of the Fauntleroy ferry dock. At an early age, they formed an instant bond with 14,411-foot Mount Rainier – yet not even half as tall as Everest – and earned a widespread reputation as climbers, rescuers and guides, which led to this opportunity.

> There wasn't any shortage of courage either. Approaching on a southeastern route, Whittaker and Gombu scaled the top of Everest on a day when everyone else on the mountain stayed put, discouraged by high winds up to 50 miles per hour.

"It's a wonderful mountain," Whittaker said of Mount Rainier. "It's got everything, the whole works, glaciers, ice falls and storms. A bunch of good climbers guided there and got their start on that mountain."

At a cost of $400,000, 19 climbers, 37 Sherpas and 907 porters spent four months involved in the Everest mission. In the end, Lou Whittaker was not among them. He couldn't break away from the responsibilities of his sporting goods business, leaving his brother to fend for himself.

Jim Whittaker, employed by Recreational Equipment Incorporated (REI), gradually worked his way to the front of the backpacking line and into position to make climbing history.

"That's just how it unfolded," said Tom Hornbein, a member of the American climbing party who three weeks later successfully reached the summit with three others, using a different route up the west side of the mountain. "He was a very strong climber, honest, ingenious. His feelings were right up front. There wasn't any hidden agenda or anything."

There wasn't any shortage of courage either. Approaching on a southeastern route, Whittaker and Gombu scaled the top of Everest on a day when everyone else on the mountain stayed put, discouraged by high winds up to 50 miles per hour. The two climbers weren't given much of a chance to make it. Two others accompanying them, including Dyrenfurth, who had hoped to film the completion of the climb, turned back after spending an hour in the wicked alpine elements.

From their camp at 27,300 feet, Whittaker and his guide left at 6 a.m. and needed seven hours to finish the ascent. They had pushed forward days earlier in the adventure, even after fellow climber Jake Breitenbach was struck and killed by a falling ice wall, forcing the others to step over the fallen climber's body to continue up the mountain. They pushed on after others had suffered altitude sickness and pulmonary edema. They were running on empty.

"I lost 35 pounds," Whittaker said. "I was working real hard and it was, hopefully, I'll get to the top of the mountain before I wear out. We had bad weather but we had to go. It was my only chance. I knew I would never get another one."

They returned to camp just before dark at 6 p.m. They came down with all their fingers and toes intact, a claim others who followed them to the top wouldn't make. They made history and no one immediately knew it back home in this era of crude international communications. News that two unidentified people had climbed their way to the top of Mount Everest reached the U.S. a day later.

Yet it took another six days before Whittaker was confirmed as the first American to sample this dangerous place, spending the most exciting 20 minutes of his life standing on top of the world.

"People have asked me, 'Why do you climb?' " Whittaker said. "It's wonderful. It's fun, damn it. You look out over everything. You test yourself and you don't have to do it with drugs or Russian roulette. You can test yourself with nature, and nature is always fair."

Mount Everest, so ruthless and deadly with other people, permitted Whittaker to become Seattle's biggest rock star. ❖

Climber Jim Whittaker trained on Mount Rainer.

PHIL SHINNICK & BRIAN STERNBERG

The Track Tragedies

Phil Shinnick

Brian Sternberg

Phil Shinnick and Brian Sternberg were gifted University of Washington track and field athletes who, for perhaps a few hours, together were the world's best at what they did. For some unknown reason they were punished for this.

At the Modesto Relays on May 25, 1963, they challenged each other to set world records in their respective events, the long jump and pole vault. They were sophomores in need of inspiration, dissatisfied with performances at the AAWU championships earlier that day and determined to become Olympians the following year in Tokyo. There was light banter and a friendly wager.

Just after 7 p.m. in sweltering central California heat, with the temperatures still hitting 85 degrees, Shinnick took off down the runway. Moments before, Sternberg had tossed grass into the air, checking for wind and giving his friend the OK to proceed. Shinnick came up with the jump of his life – 27 feet, four inches – beating Russian Igor Ter-Ovanesyan's world record by three-quarters of an inch and shattering his personal best by nearly two feet. Sternberg was one of the first to greet the Spokane native as he climbed out of the sand.

Less than an hour later and just 30 feet away, with the sky illuminated by a full moon, Sternberg used his new-age fiberglass pole to hurtle himself into uncharted vaulting territory – 16-7. The Seattle-raised vaulter's effort was three-quarters of an inch better than the world record held by American John Pennel, who

Together they became Seattle's unluckiest athletes, Shinnick robbed of his glory and Sternberg his health.

had just wrestled the top mark away from Sternberg. Shinnick was among the purple-shirted envoy offering excited congratulations.

Shinnick's glee wouldn't last the night, Sternberg's the summer. "The very best and very worst thing happened to me in the same day," Shinnick said.

Together they became Seattle's unluckiest athletes, Shinnick robbed of his glory and Sternberg his health. To no fault of the UW long jumper, meet officials working inside the Modesto Junior College stadium failed to use a wind gauge on Shinnick's record-beating leap and negated it as a new world mark. Sternberg's vaulting record would stand and he increased it by an inch at another California meet. Yet five weeks after his Modesto breakthrough, while working out on a trampoline on campus in the UW's Edmundson Pavilion in preparation for a trip to Russia, the Huskies' vaulter lost nearly everything else.

Performing a "double-back somersault with a twist," something the Seattle native had done hundreds of times, Sternberg landed hard on his neck and his life changed forever. He was left a quadriplegic with a bleak prognosis for survival.

For decades, Shinnick, a fearless advocate for any number of social and political causes, pushed fervently to have his long jump record recognized, unwilling to let go, to the point of being a huge pest, if nothing else for the principle involved.

Sternberg, his pole vault accomplishments intact, bravely dealt with a world much more unfair, demonstrating a quieter but firmer resolve to catch his next breath. Together in Modesto, they were the best on the planet, if ever so briefly. Apart, their magic faded away.

"When he hurt himself, I lost my bearings," said Shinnick, a New York doctor who specializes in Chinese-based medicines, including acupuncture. "It was

For decades,
Shinnick pushed fervently
to have his long jump
record recognized,
unwilling to let go.

devastating to me. It was not right. I didn't have my vision. My buddy was gone. We were superb athletes. He was the only one who could push me to do great things. If Brian and I had stayed together, we would have destroyed the world records."

Sternberg's spinal cord was badly bruised, not severed, but the injury two days before the Fourth of July was so severe the original outlook was bleak. He was working out with another Huskies gymnast, Bob Hall, when he landed wrong. There was no feeling in his arms or legs. Sternberg asked Hall not to move him. "Brian was given a very poor prognosis," his mother, Helen, said. "They said with his condition he probably would have five years to live. But he's a fighter."

In old photographs, Sternberg could have passed for one. He had a sharply defined frame, a body-builder look, thick muscles everywhere. "He was in fantastic shape, with huge deltoids and biceps," Shinnick said. "He was just ripped."

Following the injury, a middle-aged Sternberg spent most days in a first-floor room at his family's Queen Anne home at 500 W. Barrett St., one that afforded him a panoramic view of the city, including Edmundson Pavilion, the site of his fateful trampoline mishap. He required full-time nursing care.

Photos and drawings of the vaulter froze him in time and covered a wall of the house, as did a first-place

Russian medal, sent to him in a thoughtful gesture after he canceled that trip because of the accident. Framed letters from President John F. Kennedy, his wife Jacqueline Kennedy and his brother Bobby Kennedy were cherished keepsakes and served as vivid reminders of Sternberg's 1960s athletic prominence.

"It greatly disappointed me that you could not join your teammates on the United States Track Team this summer, but it is heartening to know that you are making progress in your recovery," President Kennedy wrote in a note dated one month after Sternberg was paralyzed and three months before the nation's leader was assassinated in Dallas.

While Sternberg dealt with ensuing illnesses, including two bouts of pneumonia and accompanying high fever, he lost some memory. He didn't have the lung capacity to engage in extended conversation either. Visitors were permitted mostly a visual glimpse of his world.

Of surviving his horrific injury and incapacitated state, the injured vaulter said softly, "I never really thought about that kind of thing. You do the best you can. You still have fun. That's all I was doing [when he was hurt]. I never strove for a record or anything."

In 1996, Sternberg experienced an upgrade in his condition. He underwent radical surgery in Germany, performed by Dr. Harry Goldsmith, an American. Scar tissue was removed from the damaged spinal cord and stomach lining was loosened and wrapped around it, forming a natural adhesive in hope that this would stimulate circulation. The procedure permitted Sternberg to breathe deeper, speak louder, remain upright for longer periods, improve muscle definition and generally feel better. "There was extreme irritation on his spinal column," his mother said. "His pain has gone from a 10 to a two."

Sternberg retained a considerable zest for life until his death at age 69 from heart and lung failure on May 23, 2013. He dutifully kept up on the vaulting world, one that had no choice but to move on without him. The world record increased to 20-2½ feet, set by French vaulter Renaud Lavillenie in 2014. "I don't know how far I would have gone," Sternberg said wistfully.

Blunt and opinionated since college, Shinnick never shied from protest, no matter how unpopular. He was anti-war, anti-racism, anti-nuclear, pro-Soviet, pro-Chinese, pro-Contra. He was labeled a subversive, called a Communist, put on the FBI watch list and imprisoned for two months in a federal facility in Allenwood, Pa., for an alleged but never proven connection to Patty Hearst's kidnapping by the Symbionese Liberation Army, a radical group. He was a crusader for a smoke-free environment decades before anyone else thought of it. "Everything I got in trouble for, it happened," he said. "But nobody cares anymore."

Shinnick, who lived at 700 E. Olive St., gave of himself, worked tirelessly on behalf of others and asked for nothing in return except in one instance: They took his world record from him, for no discernible reason that he could see, and he wanted it back.

"For years, I used to introduce myself as a world-record holder," said Shinnick, a 1964 Olympian who did not make it to the finals. "If I was to accept this, I would deny myself. It's justice and it's also a torment."

It's not that he was on a one-man crusade either. In the days immediately following the record foul-up, leading track officials spoke out in support of the UW long jumper. Sure, there was no wind gauge. There wasn't any jump-aiding gale either.

"There is no reason in the world why it shouldn't be recognized," Dr. Hilmer Lodge, director of the Mount San Antonio Relays and a witness, told the *Seattle Post-Intelligencer* in 1963. "I was right there and can testify there was hardly any wind."

Olympic gold-medalist hammer thrower Harold Connolly and gold-medalist long jumper Ralph Boston, both world record-holders several times over in their day, pleaded Shinnick's case to Craig Masback, USATF chief executive officer. Connolly and Boston were in Modesto in '63.

"He had the one great performance in his life, where everything was right, he was right and the conditions were right, and he should get credit for it," Connolly said. "Somebody didn't go through the right steps. But nobody knows what goes on in that back room when they look at all the paperwork."

After 40 years of fierce protest, Shinnick finally got a measure of satisfaction: His Modesto long jump was recognized as a one-time American record by USA track officials in 2003. However, the IAAF, which governs track globally, continued to ignore him. In all that time, the world record had grown two feet longer, 29-4½, set by American Mike Powell in 1991.

Shinnick surmised that the final resistance to confirmation of his world record was simply money: A track record-holder typically receives $100,000 or more for such a noteworthy achievement. Either way, Shinnick was pleased that the American delegation had changed its stance. The facts, not money, had always motivated him.

"The key is I feel pretty good about the whole affair and the truth to me is as important as to what happened," he said. ❖

Top 10 Track Athletes

1. Charlie Greene, sprinter
2. Brian Sternberg, pole vaulter
3. Phil Shinnick, long jumper
4. Doris Heritage, long-distance runner
5. Jim Lea, sprinter
6. Patty Van Wolvelaere, hurdler
7. Herman Brix, shot putter
8. Steve Anderson, hurdler
9. Hec Edmundson, middle-distance runner
10. Spider Gaines, hurdler

Junior Coffey's feet hurt all the time. Once he joined the University of Washington football team, he experienced nonstop podiatric pain, something that wasn't a problem before. The running back from Texas was convinced it was the ill-fitting football shoes the Huskies forced him to wear and he was helpless to do anything about it.

He pulled on size 12 in high school; for unexplained reasons, he was forced to jam his feet into size 10½ for the UW. Whenever he said anything about the discrepancy, the equipment room people at this highly regimented program only looked at him warily as if he were a wise guy or trouble-maker.

"I'd turn the shoes in and they would stretch them out and give them right back to me," Coffey said. "You couldn't say anything or they'd think you were rebellious."

The 6-foot-2, 215-pound Coffey was possibly Seattle's most misunderstood athlete and underutilized talent. His time at the UW in 1962-1964 turned out to be one of the more mind-boggling developments of the Jim Owens coaching era, stifled by subtle racial bias and those confounding shoes and corresponding foot injuries.

Even with his aching feet scrunched together, Coffey had moments of brilliance for the Huskies, especially early on. As a sophomore, he led the Athletic Association

> ## The 6-foot-2, 215-pound Coffey was possibly Seattle's most misunderstood athlete and underutilized talent.

JUNIOR COFFEY
Seattle's Caffeine Rush

of the Western Universities (a precursor to the Pacific-8 Conference) in rushing, averaging nearly six yards a carry – and did it as a reserve player, starting just one game that season.

Long-legged and powerful, he scored eight touchdowns and was something to see, a fullback with breakaway ability streaking to the end zone from 57 yards out against California and 43 yards away against Oregon State – with each of his scores coming as a backup.

"I was one of the first guys to get the crowd's attention because of my running style and you could hear the crowd yelling, 'Put in Coffey!' " the imported back said. "With Jim Owens, it was the Washington Huskies and no one was bigger than them. When I started to do well he sort of put the rings on that."

Had he been given the freedom to totally unleash his talents and keep his health, there's no telling what the can't-miss fullback, or the Huskies, would have done. With his catchy first and last names he was meant to be a college football standout, though people thought he made it up.

"When I went to the University of Washington, they wanted to know what my real name was; they said, 'Junior's not your name,' " Coffey said. "I said, 'It's on my birth certificate and that's what my mom put on it. I'm not changing it. It's unusual. You will remember it.' "

When healthy, Junior Coffey was a tough UW runner.

Husky Stadium fans loudly called out on Saturday afternoons for him to play more. Bob Monroe, Washington's starting fullback, told Coffey that he should be playing more. Owens thought otherwise, supposedly convinced that having a star system would negatively affect his college football program, especially if that headliner was black.

When he wasn't corralled by the rigid UW system, Coffey was hemmed in by those never-ending injuries.

As a junior in 1963, he suffered three stress fractures in his feet, greatly restricting his play during a Rose Bowl season. He broke his right foot during spring practice and once again on the eve of the season opener, then splintered his left one during bowl practice. He sat out the first four games of the season, three of them losses, for the 6-5 Huskies.

He played only briefly on New Year's Day against Illinois, a 17-7 defeat for the Huskies. Team followers were convinced the outcome would have been different had the fullback been more available against an Illini defense headed up by linebacker Dick Butkus.

Coffey, who lived in the Central District at 512 32nd Ave., was healthy enough and the fullback starter when his UW senior season began in 1964, but again his momentum was muffled by the bizarre. He rushed for 100 yards or more in three of the first five games. He next was branded a malcontent and put on the bench.

After a full scrimmage that followed a difficult loss to Oregon, Washington players were ordered to run off the field by the coaches. Coffey walked, unable to trot after suffering a serious hip-pointer injury during the workout. He lost the starting job to Jeff Jordan for the final five games because of his supposed abstinence. "I went to see Owens to try and get a meeting," Coffey said. "I wasn't received. Everybody thought I was a rebel but I did everything the coaches asked of me."

Admittedly, he kept his distance from the Huskies in later years because of these misadventures before reconnecting with the program in 2008. His disgusted outlook changed over time.

"Really I've had a rosy life, even with all these adversities," Coffey said. "It taught me a lot. What I learned is you stand up for yourself, no matter what consequences. I didn't do that before. If I'd come in and said, 'Coach, I can't wear these shoes,' things could

have been different. When I played professionally I never had a problem with my feet. I never had any regrets, but I definitely felt the man in charge had his own hang-ups."

Coffey arrived at the UW from Dimmitt, Texas, a football-crazed town of 5,000 in the Lone Star State's Panhandle. It was true "Friday Night Lights" at the 2A level with a pioneering twist for him: He was the school's first black athlete.

He was discriminated against by restaurants that refused to serve him alongside his Dimmitt High Bobcats teammates and by opposing players who crassly taunted him. A versatile athlete, he played tight end, taking direct pitchouts from that offensive position, and got into a stance at defensive tackle.

The Huskies knew about Coffey because he had dominated a 3A Phillips High School team once coached by Chesty Walker, who left to become a Washington assistant coach. Walker showed up at Dimmitt one day and asked Coffey to join him in Seattle.

The Southwest Conference didn't integrate until 1967, so Coffey had to leave his home state to play college football. He picked the Huskies over Illinois, Kansas, Missouri and Minnesota. Coffey was treated to an Olympic Hotel dinner by Dr. Alexander Grinstein, his recruiting host, and it proved both unnerving and persuasive. Coffey was hesitant to go inside the fancy downtown Seattle restaurant, afraid he would be turned away and embarrassed just like in Texas. Grinstein, a team booster, assured him nothing like that would happen and nothing did.

Coffey excused himself from the table midway through the meal and called his aunt, Maudie Sanders, from the hotel and told her they would be moving to Seattle soon. She wanted to know why. "You'll see when you get here," he told her. "We're free here."

His eventual UW football constraints ran counter to that dinner outing, but Coffey never second-guessed his college choice. He finished his career with 1,648 yards rushing, which included seven 100-yard games, and scored 16 times, chalking up numbers that could have been so much better. The rigidity of the program toughened him up for pro football and he was thankful for that.

Coffey played one season for the Green Bay Packers and legendary coach Vince Lombardi, and won an NFL championship; he went to the Atlanta Falcons in the expansion draft, and twice led the team in rushing over three seasons; and played his final season for the New York Giants. He had 2,037 career rushing yards and scored 15 times as a pro.

After a knee injury curtailed his NFL career, Coffey turned to horseracing and made it his new passion. He worked at Renton's Longacres track, the predecessor to Auburn's Emerald Downs, on a cleanup crew for a college job and was drawn to the environment. He remembers laying down a $5 wager and winning $78. "I said, 'How easy is this?' " he recalled.

Coffey figured if he could get in shape to play pro football, he could condition horses to win races. He started out with three horses, bought some equipment, and won a few races early on. He won seven races with claiming horse Alice's Heart, and people allowed him to keep the filly and flourish rather than rightfully collect her.

At his peak involvement, Coffey's section of the Emerald Downs barn area was 16 horse stalls, each brightly decorated with a black and red bib sporting a football helmet logo and the initials J.C., mixing his former profession with his current one. As the veteran horse trainer walked through the barn area of the suburban track, frisky thoroughbreds poked their heads out and playfully strained to get Coffey's attention.

These were Coffey's athletes and he was their coach. He rubbed their noses, whispered into their ears and readjusted hanging hay bales. He even laid down beside them when they were ill, reassured them and caringly nursed them back to health. He was cognizant of their needs and determined to provide them with every opportunity to succeed, something that didn't always happen when he was a breakaway runner headed for the pros.

Coffey trained 10 to 11 thoroughbreds a year and was always looking for a once-in-a-lifetime find that would carry him to major races and enhance his reputation. Owners trusted him. The horses responded to him.

Best of all, when Coffey made his way around the Emerald Downs race track, his shoes fit and his feet didn't hurt. ❖

Coffey figured
if he could get in shape
to play pro football,
he could condition horses
to win races. He started out
with three horses,
bought some equipment,
and won a few races early on.

PELLER PHILLIPS

The Shakedown Victim

Peller Phillips and Leo Casale met in a California gym. One was a black kid from Detroit, the other a white guy from Chicago. Two time zones from home, they were enrolled at Coalinga Junior College, 50 miles southwest of Fresno, where they had come to play basketball. Phillips was the star of the team, averaging 26.1 points per game during his second and final season. Casale had washed out as a player and had his athletic meal card revoked.

Every day, they played one-on-one basketball games in the Coalinga gym. And every day, Phillips delivered food to his hungry and appreciative companion, sneaking it out of the school cafeteria. It was a curious relationship, one built only on pick-up-game sweat and smuggled sandwiches.

"I always kind of looked at it that he was never a close friend, but I knew him and we enjoyed playing basketball together and I helped him out," Phillips said.

Phillips transferred to Seattle University and, naively, let Casale use their old connection to re-enter his world. Disastrous consequences resulted. The two were singled out as the central figures in the worst kind of college basketball scandal: Shocking the city, Phillips was arrested by FBI agents on Feb. 17, 1965, picked up on campus with fellow starting guard Charlie Williams and accused of shaving points in a home game against Idaho, while Casale and another man, Joseph Polito, were taken away in handcuffs in Chicago.

Phillips was charged with bribery conspiracy and expelled from school with Williams and SU backup center L.J. Wheeler – and, almost totally unnoticed, he was later exonerated of everything. Yet great damage was done to the game, school and him, turning Phillips into Seattle's most victimized athlete.

"I couldn't watch or play basketball for years," Phillips said. "I felt really, really bad for the school, coaches and fans that it occurred. What could you do? I had to figure out what to do with the rest of my life. At the time, it was so disturbing to go through. I just withdrew from basketball and didn't want to play anymore."

Phillips might have been guilty of nothing more than failing to turn away an old acquaintance, unaware underworld connections were involved and his basketball career would be sacrificed. In his second season with Seattle U, the 5-foot-10 guard was in Chicago, preparing to meet DePaul, when Casale called him at his hotel and casually asked about the outcome of the upcoming game. Phillips assured him the Chieftains would win. They lost 91-77.

> Phillips was charged
> with bribery conspiracy and
> expelled from school with
> Williams and SU backup center
> L.J. Wheeler – and,
> almost totally unnoticed,
> he was later exonerated
> of everything.

Following the game, Casale invited Phillips and a couple of other Chieftains to a nightclub he managed. He mentioned how his friends had lost a lot of money on the DePaul game and they needed a chance to win it back. No promises were made by the Seattle U players to rectify this and no pressure was put on them to do something.

A month later, Casale impulsively called Phillips at his Seattle apartment and asked him for information about a home game against Idaho. There was no point-shaving request at this point; Casale wanted only insider information. The point spread was 17½ and the Chieftains won 89-72. Three weeks later, Casale showed up at the team's Spokane hotel the night before Seattle U played its rematch against Idaho 80 miles away in Moscow. The Chicago man's persistence and presence now turned people nervous. He didn't hold back this time. He bluntly asked if anyone could influence the point spread. He made vague references to an under-world reliance on him. His actions would destroy three basketball careers and land him in prison.

"I said, 'We don't do anything to control the game or any game,'" said Phillips, who was married and expecting his first child. "I really feared for my life. He said he could be physically harmed and so could I, and that they knew where I lived. Leo told me these were pretty bad people."

Casale, acknowledging his overbearing ways, left $130 on the hotel bed in Spokane and said, "I've put you through all this and you've been good to me. Take this money and buy your wife a dress and, when the baby is born, buy it some food." Phillips refused the cash and then accepted it, giving $50 to Wheeler, a back-up Chieftains center, and pocketing the rest.

Williams, an All-America guard candidate, 20.3-point scorer and pro prospect, was only privy to

Following the game, Casale invited Phillips and a couple of other Chieftains to a nightclub he managed. He mentioned how his friends had lost a lot of money on the DePaul game and they needed a chance to win it back.

the conversation with Casale, but he suggested that his teammates refrain from informing Seattle U coach Bob Boyd of the situation to avoid a backlash, and everyone paid for it anyway.

"I don't think I had the level of sophistication to deal with that or know what I was getting into," Phillips recalled. "I didn't think to go to the coach and tell him about it. I was hoping it would go away."

"He was an altruistic guy and a great athlete, and he did nothing in that process to deserve anything," Casale said. "I've always put it on my back that he was harmed the way he was."

FBI agents followed Casale, who was acting on behalf of four Chicago Mafia families, to the Northwest. Arrests were made within a week. Agents interviewed all Seattle U players. A federal case was pursued, the first nationally under a new statute that tried to indict players involved and not just gamblers. This was a reaction to previous point-shaving scandals that came through New York and reached all the way to elite programs such as Kentucky, leaving deep scars on college basketball.

After the initial bold headlines, the federal case was dropped against the Seattle U players. By watching game film, investigators determined that Phillips and Williams hardly played in the second half against Idaho and couldn't have influenced the outcome. The players still were tossed off a 19-7 team that had three games remaining on the schedule and watched as Seattle U's legitimate NCAA Tournament hopes died with news of the point-shaving scandal.

"Zealous prosecutors wanted to have that case and they should have done their research before accusing us," Phillips said. "They realized we were just innocent kids caught up in something we didn't do."

Casale was punished for his actions. He was convicted and served time in several prisons, among them McNeil Island (Wash.), Lompoc (Calif.), La Tuna (Texas), Leavenworth (Kan.) and Sandstone (Minn.). Polito also was imprisoned but he twice became a government witness in the case and it might have cost him his life. In 1967, Polito was gunned down and killed, presumably for his cooperation.

During his court proceedings, the brash Casale approached Phillips one more time on the second level of a Seattle parking garage. The Chicago man, always in need of a favor, asked him to change his upcoming federal court testimony. Phillips declined, telling Casale he wasn't going to commit perjury.

In 2009, Casale loosely admitted to me that he and his father had underworld ties. "I tried to get out of it but what took me out of it got me right back into it," said Casale, who managed the Action A-Go-Go Lounge. "You don't operate a nightclub in Chicago without mob influence, plus the fact I'm Italian. I know every wise guy in town. I'm connected in a sense. Do I do what they did? No. Some people might consider it a colorful life and some might consider it a tragedy."

> "Zealous prosecutors wanted to have that case and they should have done their research before accusing us," Phillips said. "They realized we were just innocent kids caught up in something we didn't do."

Casale insisted the Seattle U players were never in any physical danger. The threat of potential bodily harm passed along to Phillips was nothing more than desperate manipulation on the Chicago man's part to try and get the players to respond to his point-shaving requests. Casale said he satisfied his associates by serving his sentence and keeping his mouth shut.

"I went to jail and took the heat off all those creeps," he said. "All of the problems as a result of that incident stayed in Chicago. Peller was never in jeopardy. I was never going to let that happen."

The biggest loser in the scandal was the player who had only a loose connection to it: Williams. His worst crime was he admitted knowing about the bribe and didn't report it. Even though Williams was criminally exonerated, he was banned from playing in the NBA. In 1967, Williams signed a free-agent contract with his hometown Seattle SuperSonics after turning in an impressive rookie camp showing, but the league wouldn't recognize the deal. An NBA rule at the time stated that anyone expelled from school for something other than scholastic reasons was ineligible to play in the league.

Williams, the son of a minister, was forced to turn to the ABA and he became one of the new league's better players, leading the Pittsburgh Pipers to the 1968 league championship while scoring 35 points in the deciding game. He took up residence in Cleveland, got involved in the steel industry and resisted all future requests to talk about the Seattle U scandal.

Wheeler, a Maryland native who transferred to Seattle U from a California junior college, became a heavyweight boxer in the Northwest and a pool shark. He died not long after his athletic career ended.

A fourth Seattle U player, forward Elzie Johnson, was aware of the bribe attempt but denied any knowledge when questioned, saving him from ruin.

"I was a freshman and Charlie, L.J. and Elzie knew about the bribe attempt and didn't tell anybody," Chieftains guard Steve Looney said. "They went on and won the game. Nothing should have happened. They shouldn't have talked to the FBI. The FBI came to the school and told all of them, 'Interview and nothing is going to happen.' Three of them told the truth. Elzie lied and stayed in school."

In 1969, Phillips was offered $10,000 to join the Harlem Globetrotters and turned it down, figuring it would disrupt his family life. He briefly considered playing in the ABA, same as Williams. He became a mortgage broker and school teacher. He raised four athletic- minded children, and three of them received college track scholarships. Six years after leaving in disgrace, he returned to Seattle U and earned his bachelor's degree.

Ten years after the incident, Phillips entered a restaurant and was spotted by then-Seattle U athletic director Eddie O'Brien and others who invited him to sit with them and have a drink. Thereafter, the school regularly invited him back for alumni dinners and special functions. All was forgiven on both sides.

In 2009, Phillips' story was retold by me the day before the *Seattle Post-Intelligencer* ceased operations. His junior college, renamed West Hills Coalinga College, was so moved it reconnected with him and voted Phillips into the school's athletic hall of fame. HBO's "Real Sports with Bryant Gumbel" called and expressed interest in doing its own story.

Phillips lived at 5222 26th Ave. S. when he died from congestive heart failure on Feb. 18, 2013. He was 72. No mention of any scandal was made when people crowded into a quaint Mount Baker-area church eulogized and mourned him. Hs wife, Deena Fuller, later said all of the positive attention had given him closure regarding his basketball past. He no longer felt shame.

"I never had a person say anything to me in a negative way," Phillips said before his death. "Everyone who talked to me was more sympathetic. They thought I got a bad deal out of the whole situation. I'm at peace with it now." ❖

A 6-foot-7, 230-pound junior forward who later played in the NBA and ABA, the tough-minded and always cocky Workman was the central figure in an unforgettable Seattle sports history lesson.

TOM WORKMAN
Seattle's History Lesson

Tom Workman grabbed the ball off the opening tip and headed to the basket, faked once and went up for a shot. He was sent crashing hard to the floor. He was shown no mercy. The college basketball game between Seattle University and unbeaten Texas Western was 10 seconds old and this was how it would play out on March 5, 1966, at the Seattle Center Coliseum. It was rough and unapologetic.

A crowd of 11,557 watched the home team and the Miners wage an intense, physical battle that ended in a memorable upset. Workman and the Chieftains were up to the task, demonstrating considerable grit in pulling out a 74-72 victory.

A 6-foot-7, 230-pound junior forward who later played in the NBA and ABA, the tough-minded and always cocky Workman was the central figure in an unforgettable Seattle sports history lesson, responsible for providing the ending and temporary overthrow of a culturally unique basketball kingdom.

Workman supplied the game's deciding points while surviving the brutal give-and-take inside. He was knocked to the court three times over the game's first 10 minutes. He remembers only the first blow, one

administered by Texas Western's powerful center David "Big Daddy" Lattin.

"I went up and Lattin grabbed me by the head, by the eyes, and jerked me to the floor," Workman said. "It was a nasty start."

Texas Western, renamed Texas-El Paso a year later, had a Division I team as diverse as any other, starting five African-American players and rotating seven in and out of games. This group used quickness, toughness and frightening athleticism to unsettle opponents and make a landmark run through the college game.

Two weeks after stumbling in Seattle, the Miners upset No. 1-ranked Kentucky 72-65 in the NCAA title game in College Park, Md., capping a 28-1 season marred only by that loss to the Chieftains and becoming the first predominantly black team to claim the championship. The game of college basketball changed overnight with this progressive Texas team showing up lily-white Kentucky and its admitted segregationist coach, Adolph Rupp, at the Final Four.

Back in the Northwest, Seattle U players – both black and white – clustered around TV sets and witnessed the sporting renaissance, content in knowing that they were the only ones that season who didn't roll over in the face of the imposing Miners. Workman was the leader of a Chieftains team nearly as skilled and diverse but lacking the season-long chemistry of Texas

Western. Throughout his career, he brought a surly approach to each game and showed he could take a pounding. The Miners' NCAA championship breakthrough pleased him no end.

"We all watched that game and it was over before it got started," recalled Workman, who became a Portland bar owner and college basketball referee. "It was the intimidation factor. I remember David Lattin and Nevil Shed rejecting shots and you could see the Kentucky players looking around and wondering who was going to come out of nowhere next? We were never intimidated. We traveled and played enough teams of diversity. Our roster was half black and half white. It was no big deal to us."

In an earlier game held at Idaho, Workman demonstrated rather emphatically where his loyalties fell. After hearing one too many racist taunts directed at his African-American teammates, the big forward backpedaled up the floor with both arms raised and his middle fingers extended in a threatening fashion at the offending student section.

Workman, who grew up in Greenwood at 610 N.W. 81st St., was one of Seattle's most heavily recruited basketball players in several years after leading Blanchet High to the 1962 state championship and an unbeaten season. He rejected a scholarship offer from a much more conservative University of Washington basketball program and was recruited by Notre Dame, Stanford, Santa Clara, Oregon and Oregon State. He became a highly productive player for SU, averaging 19.2 points and 8.4 rebounds per game over his career.

The Chieftains and Texas Western players were well acquainted. The schools regularly played a home-and-home series and their 1966 meeting in Seattle was the most competitive encounter. As both teams closed out the regular season that night, the Chieftains weren't going to the postseason, having underachieved with a 15-10 record to that point, with one of those defeats coming to the Miners in El Paso 76-64 in January.

Texas Western, with a perfect 23-0 record, provided a welcome bulls-eye. A festive crowd filled up the Coliseum. Dressed in colorful orange sweats, the Miners put on a memorable show during warm-ups alone. Willie Worsley, an extra-springy 5-6 guard, got the crowd excited by dunking several times. Fans screamed throughout the tense Saturday night match-up.

Once Workman picked himself up off the ground after Lattin's initial greeting, the teams hung close to each other to the final buzzer. They traded the lead 19 times. Workman and Lattin already had pounded on each other for a season and a half so they knew what to expect and could almost predict what was coming that night.

"He was always very difficult for me to play against but I enjoyed the challenge," said Lattin, who became a Houston liquor distribution executive after his own NBA and ABA career ended.

The action was particularly frantic over the game's final three minutes and 11 seconds. The Chieftains' Jim LaCour completed a three-point play for a 72-68 lead, but Lattin responded with two free throws. After a Seattle U. turnover, the Miners' Willie Cager hit two free throws to tie the game at 72-72 with 1:53 left. It stayed that way until 55 seconds remained, when Workman, who led all scorers with 23 points, got free for a 20-foot jumper from the top of the key and swished through the game-winner.

"I was like a 24-hour supermarket – I was always open," Workman said in his typical brash fashion. "And I never passed up a shot if I was open."

The closing seconds were decidedly inartistic: Texas Western's Cager and the Chieftains' Steve Looney

Tom Workman was the eighth pick in the 1967 NBA draft.

missed free throws, and Cager hit the underside of the basket with a close-in shot. With five seconds remaining, the Chieftains' Plummer Lott had a free throw bounce off. Cager's midcourt heave was short at the buzzer.

Fans rushed the court and engulfed Workman and the home team, and the Chieftains cut down the nets. In shock at finally being beaten, the Miners headed for the locker room but didn't stay long or use the showers. The visitors put on their brightly colored orange sweats and wandered aimlessly through the exiting crowd in the Coliseum concourse area, all of them pausing patiently to sign autographs on a program for a newfound young fan, which was me.

The Miners got over the loss fairly quickly, though. Texas Western had to play its first NCAA Tournament game against Oklahoma City two nights later in Wichita, Kan. "We probably thought we were bullet-proof at the time because we hadn't lost," Lattin said of the Seattle U game. "We didn't do what we needed to do. It made me more serious. The best team won that night."

The Miners' huge center sat on a jet that left the Northwest behind the following day, looking over the stat sheet, wondering what little thing he could have done to prevent the setback. He noted that he had missed three free throws against the Chieftains. He didn't miss another in five postseason games. The loss might have been beneficial for Big Daddy and his teammates, making them more hardened and focused with everything on the line. The Miners swept through the NCAAs, beating, in order, Oklahoma City 89-74, Cincinnati 78-76 in overtime, Kansas 81-80 in double overtime, Utah 85-78 and Kentucky in the champion-ship game.

A year later, newly rechristened UTEP and Seattle U split their regular-season games again, with the Chieftains winning 69-56 at the Coliseum before a record 14,252 fans. Workman and Lattin were seniors now. Their teams next met in the first round of the NCAA tourney in Fort Collins, Colo., with the Miners

Workman was the eighth pick overall in the first round of the 1967 NBA draft by the St. Louis Hawks.

advancing with a 62-54 victory after Workman injured an ankle halfway through the game and he was done as a collegian.

"Fred Carr, who was a goon coming off the bench and later played linebacker for the Packers, cut me on a fast break and I tore up my ankle," he said.

Workman was the eighth pick overall in the first round of the 1967 NBA draft by the St. Louis Hawks. Lattin went two players later to the San Francisco Warriors. They were still shadowing each other at every turn. Both wound up their careers in the ABA. A chronic knee injury ended Workman's pro aspirations by 1971 after he had played for the Hawks, Baltimore Bullets, Detroit Pistons, Los Angeles and Utah Stars, and Denver Rockets. Lattin was finished by 1973. Their glory days were relegated to the college ranks.

Years later Workman and Lattin encountered each other while walking through the Houston airport and they chatted amiably. There were no elbows thrown, no whistles blown, no fouls called. There might have been a joke or two about their ferocious old times inserted into the conversation. Mostly it was just two old warriors showing each other ultimate respect after all the bruises had healed and their cherished college basketball victories had stood the test of time. ❖

DONNIE MOORE

The Sacrificial Lamb

Donnie Moore had huge thighs and ridiculously thick calves. A bull-like, 5-foot-8 and 210 pounds, he was a once-in-a-lifetime running back, the kind of football player that college teams coveted and cheated in every way imaginable to obtain. Moore was timed in the 40-yard dash just once, running 4.45 seconds in full pads, and insisted he was faster than that. He claimed to have bench-pressed 500 pounds, without being pushed for a maximum lift. He left people in awe or knocked out cold.

Incredibly, the University of Washington landed and tossed him aside, turning Moore into Seattle's biggest waste of elite athletic talent. Decades later, former Huskies teammates would describe the Tacoma native as another Emmitt Smith, only bigger. Moore likened himself to Earl Campbell, only smaller, a comparison shared with the man who got rid of Moore.

"Donnie was a little quicker than Campbell and almost as strong," said Jim Owens, who coached Moore at the UW and coached against Texas' Campbell, a Heisman Trophy winner and Pro Football Hall of Fame selection. "I think their speed was comparable."

Ohio State coach Woody Hayes had his own barometer. On Oct. 1, 1966, on a rainy afternoon in Columbus, Ohio, Moore carried the ball 30 times for 221 yards and scored twice in a 38-22 victory over Hayes' Buckeyes before a stunned gathering of 80,241 at the Horseshoe, with the back explaining the outcome in this manner, "We got down and dirty in the trenches. Then we broke their spirits."

Moore didn't lose a yard all day. Running between the tackles, he went for 20 the first time he touched the ball, 21 the third time and 47 and a touchdown the last time. He gained more yards at Ohio State than any other opposing back before him. He was hailed as the *Associated Press* and *Sports Illustrated* national back of the week.

"They unloaded that good back on us," a disconsolate Hayes told reporters. "They think he's another Mike Garrett [USC's Heisman Trophy winner], and they're probably right. He has excellent balance and great strength. He's real strong and has good speed. We had quite a few good hits at him and he just ran away."

Unfortunately, Moore would learn what it felt like to be on the receiving end of unbearable punishment, too. Three weeks after the Ohio State game, the NCAA's seventh-leading rusher at the time, a guy who wore No. 40 because he deeply admired Gale Sayers, was dismissed from the UW football team.

His stated crime was drinking beer in a north Seattle tavern. He had no recourse or appeal. He had his scholarship taken from him and he was cast away.

> Incredibly, the University of Washington landed and tossed him aside, turning Moore into Seattle's biggest waste of elite athletic talent.

A yard-gobbling runner and potential superstar who offered glimpses of the incredible, he was jettisoned for matters that today still seem trivial. "What happened to me was nowhere near fair or equitable," Moore said.

Just like that, 15 games into his collegiate career with at least 15 more to go, Moore was discarded, taking with him all sorts of intriguing possibilities. Had the talented back returned for his senior season in 1967, his former teammates lamented, the UW would have advanced to the Rose Bowl that year, not USC and O.J. Simpson. "If it hadn't happened, he would have been the greatest running back in the history of the University of Washington," former Huskies quarterback Jerry Kaloper said.

Considering all the energy the Huskies expended in pursuing Moore, cutting him loose made no sense at all. Moore was such a highly regarded prospect from Tacoma's Lincoln High School, one of the nation's top-four schoolboys according to a 1963 magazine list, the Huskies started recruiting him as a ninth-grader. A UW alumnus was assigned to stay in close contact with the family at all times. According to Moore, who was the youngest of seven children raised by a single mother, summer jobs were provided to him, family members and friends. In three seasons at Lincoln, Moore was a prep record-breaker, rushing for 2,353 yards, and trying to stop him was a weighty prospect. "He was a man among boys and I was a boy trying to tackle him," said Dennis Erickson, an Everett High School opponent and later an NFL and college coach.

Moore had considerable personal baggage the UW overlooked. He was a father by 15, the father of three when he left high school. With him off playing college football, the mother of Moore's children, Mary Mazanares, filed a paternity suit, which was settled out of court with the school somehow financially involved.

Moore said details of any past arrangements remained hazy but conceded, "By the time I was 17, I had entered into a formal agreement that if I went and played pro football, I would pay them back for any expenses back then."

UW football teammates gravitated to him. He was personable. They could see he was a great player. Not only that, he was as tough, if not tougher, than anyone else on the team. At practice, Bill Sprinkle, a fearless Huskies defensive back from Montana, and Moore collided with such ferocity both were knocked unconscious on the play.

Yet Moore, like many of his teammates, had to sample the Seattle nightlife. Only as a football player, he had to be discreet, and that was tough for the running back. As one of the few black players on the team, and the one who proudly wore his letterman's jacket wherever he went, he stuck out in a crowd.

His college football career came to an end because someone saw him at the Little Red Hen, a popular tavern near Woodland Park Zoo, and told Owens. The place was a Husky hangout. Players drank there. Players worked there. Even a graduate assistant coach supposedly had a job there. Owens warned that anyone spotted sipping a cold one in public would be banished from the team, no exceptions. Still, they went.

Two nights before the Ohio State game, defensive end Jeff Huget organized a late-night encounter. He was accompanied by defensive back Dave Dillon, offensive end Greg Peters, quarterback Tom Sparlin — and Moore. "It was, 'Hey, come on, let's go out,' " Huget said. "The fifth guy was Donnie."

Moore said 12 or 13 starters were in the tavern. This seemingly tame adventure somehow went unpunished until the Huskies thumped Ohio State and then lost bitterly to USC 17-14 and California 24-20. Moore showed

Donnie Moore breaks tackles against Ohio State in Seattle in 1965, a year before he was suspended.

up for a Wednesday practice readying for Oregon but was told to report straight to Owens' office. The head coach tersely informed the player he had been spotted in the tavern, a drink in hand, before the Ohio State game. Moore was suspended for the rest of the season.

Teammates went to Owens to protest Moore's removal but were refused an audience with the coach. Players privately questioned why the running back was sacrificed over a beer outing, especially when no one else was.

"He was no different than any other player," said Huskies defensive end Steve Thompson, who played in the NFL with renowned late-night partier Joe Namath. "If he had been a white player, he would have been talked to. It hurt the team. It hurt him for life."

Two former UW players said they heard Moore's troubles might have involved the improper usage of a credit card, which the running back denied. Another player heard Moore was joyriding in a car and wrecked it, which the back also denied. Yet another player mentioned that the previously settled paternity suit might have come back to haunt Moore, again not true.

There was no mystery to this unpleasant situation, according to the retired UW coach. "It was a training violation, that's all it was," said Owens before he died in 2009. "It was a tough decision. It was a case where if I was going to have those standards, I had to enforce them."

As for the other UW players who went unpunished, Owens said he didn't know about those indiscretions. Players said an underachieving 6-4 UW team, one capable of beating Ohio State on the road and third-ranked UCLA at home but handed upset losses by lesser teams in Air Force, Oregon State and California, thus falling out of Rose Bowl contention early in the season, forced the coach to make a drastic move. "I

think Owens just had enough," Sprinkle said. "He had to send a message. We were in the bars every week and maybe Owens wanted to put a stop to that."

The Ohio State game would be Moore's signature moment, an individual road performance unparalleled in program history. By halftime, he had run for 114 of his 221 yards against the Buckeyes. He also suffered a right hip pointer and severely sprained ankle. He was a mess. The training staff had a couple of solutions. Moore received an injection in his leg and was handed a green pill. He took half of what he described as "an upper," or amphetamine. He went out and ran for another 107 yards.

Moore was humiliated by his fall from grace but had little time to rue his suspension or even consider transfer options. Two months after the UW let him go he was drafted into the Army. He had signed with the CFL's British Columbia Lions, but his pro football aspirations had to wait. He was in boot camp in Missouri by March and later stationed in Louisiana.

Moore was an energetic soldier, leading by example, doing one-handed pushups and using camaraderie stuff he had learned from Huskies drills. He made sergeant in 11 months. His plan was to serve two years and resume his football career. A mandatory physical for his military release turned up something strange — little white patches near his collarbone. On X-rays the spots looked like cancer. He had exploratory surgery. He was diagnosed with sarcoidosis, an autoimmune disease that primarily affects the lungs and can kill. The disease robbed him of his football prowess.

After a three-year absence from football, he reported to the Canadian team, played in four exhibition games and was cut; he had trouble hanging onto the ball. And when he could get a good grip on it, Moore discovered he was two steps slower than before. He played part

of a season with the Seattle Rangers, a minor-league team, and went to an off-season training camp with the Los Angeles Rams, but the football magic was gone.

The late George Allen liked Moore's old-school attitude, was impressed by the supposed 500-pound bench press and signed him to an NFL contract. When it came time to report to the Rams, Moore was hit with the first of three sarcoidosis episodes that landed him in the hospital, made him consider his mortality and required a tough decision. "I gave up football," he said wistfully.

Moore eventually went back to Washington and obtained his degree in 1974, though taking great care to keep his distance from the football program. His cousin, Ahmad Rashad (Bobby Moore), refused to play for the Huskies because of the way his relative was treated. Moore got married, had more kids, worked a number of well-paying jobs and made his home in Riverside, Calif.

In 2003, Moore surprised everyone when he showed up unannounced to watch a Huskies pre-season football practice in Olympia. Keith Gilbertson, the Huskies coach and a high school contemporary of Moore's, stopped everything, gathered his players around and enthusiastically introduced them to one of the Huskies' great ones.

A few years later, Moore showed up for a players' reunion at Husky Stadium and wept openly as he mixed with ex-teammates and other notable UW players.

"He was crying he was so happy to be there," said quarterback Sonny Sixkiller, one of the Huskies' most famous players. "He was absolutely happy to be there. I told him, of anyone, he was the guy I wanted to meet." ❖

The car raced down East Madison Street with Seattle police giving chase, traveling at speeds estimated at 120 miles per hour before it lost control and plowed into a pair of parked vehicles. Officers shouldn't have been too surprised that Charlie Greene, an elusive teenager on this September night in 1965, was behind the wheel. Within three years, he would become the world's fastest man.

Greene's powerful legs carried him from the Northwest to the University of Nebraska and multiple NCAA championships, sprint records and Olympic medals, and he did it with a flourish. Setting himself apart with style, he was the first elite sprinter to wear sunglasses while competing. He shared the world record in the 100 meters – 9.9 seconds – with fellow Americans Jim Hines and Ronnie Ray Smith, and he was the favorite coming into that event at the 1968 Mexico City Olympics.

The fact that Greene hailed from such a weather-challenged climate turned him into even more of a track and field curiosity. "They would ask, 'Does it rain in Seattle?' " the sprinter said. "I'd say, 'I don't know. I used to run in between the raindrops. I could practice and never get wet.' "

Greene grew up in the Central District at 825 23rd Ave., just a few blocks from Garfield High School. He was raised by a single mother, Bertha Johnson, who

> Greene became the fastest man produced in Seattle and the city's most prominent track athlete of any era, yet Greene would run from his hometown.

insisted he attend private O'Dea High School because they were Catholic. He always knew he was a fast runner but didn't realize the importance of his talent until he went out for track as a freshman and started beating everybody.

"All of a sudden running became an important part of my life," he said. "Running actually took over my life. It's what I did best. Being a sprinter was like being a thoroughbred."

Greene won the 100-meter dash at the state meet as an O'Dea junior, the 100 and 200 as a senior. He didn't receive widespread attention until after graduation, when he was the last of eight sprinters invited to the 1963 Golden West Invitational near Sacramento. He won the 100, becoming the nation's No. 1-ranked schoolboy. He accepted a track scholarship from Nebraska at his mother's insistence, forsaking offers from a host of other colleges, among them Arizona State, San Jose State and Washington.

Greene became the fastest man produced in Seattle and the city's most prominent track athlete of any era – attracting more international and national attention than locally acclaimed Brian Sternberg, Phil Shinnick, Doris Heritage, Jim Lea and Patty Van Wolvelaere – yet Greene would run from his hometown.

"My mother wouldn't let me go to the University of Washington because the racial climate there was not good,"

he said. "I didn't know that. My mother, in networking and talking to others, found that out. Three years later, it exploded in the football program with Jim Owens."

In his first season at Nebraska, Greene was considered the world's second-fastest sprinter, giving way only to Bob Hayes. A leg injury during the Olympic trials prevented Greene from going to the Tokyo Games in 1964, but that was just a temporary setback. He won three consecutive collegiate titles in both the 60- and 100-meter dashes. He surprised everyone back home. "I was much faster than I thought and much faster than anyone in Seattle thought," Greene said.

In his second summer home from college he was caught joyriding at night through the Central District and unwisely tried to outrun police. He lost them once but the chase ended abruptly when he hit a parked vehicle, spun out and slammed into another parked car in the 1000th block of 25th Avenue.

Greene, then 19, couldn't explain his actions to the officers responding to the scene, outside of temporarily acting like a knucklehead. He was arrested, taken downtown to jail and later released on a $166 bond.

"I didn't have anything to do," he said. "That's when I found out when you go away to college and come back home, people forget about you and your place is lost. I realized then I needed to stay in Nebraska because every time I came home I got into some junk."

Back in the Midwest, Greene was on better behavior as he turned his full attention to the 1968 Olympics. He had a chance at ultimate glory. The smooth and stylistic sprinter held the label as the world's fastest man that year and wanted to reaffirm it on a big stage. It wouldn't happen.

In Mexico City, Greene easily won two Olympic heats before he finished a disheartening third behind Hines and Lennox Miller in the 100 final and accepted the bronze medal. Hines, the gold medalist, had never beaten him until right before the games. Miller, who took silver, had never beaten him at all.

All eight sprinters in the final heat were bunched at 50 meters. As Greene's normally smooth glide turned labored and awkward, he grabbed at his thigh once he crossed the finish line and he was lucky to finish third, sinking to his knees on the track. Pressed at the time, the Seattle native dismissed the injury as a cramp. Four decades later, Greene revealed he had pulled a hamstring muscle at the 70-meter mark.

"If you tell people you didn't win because you got injured, it's sour grapes," Greene said. "Everybody knew when we had to race. Everybody knew we had to do the best we could. That's part of running if you can't keep your legs together. It's tough luck."

Before the gun sounded for the 100 final, Greene was feeling patriotic, if not ready to finish off a dominant year. He was left only with a consolation prize.

"The fact I got third did not make me happy but, as I said to Jimmy before we ran, 'One of us must win this 100 meters; America must have the fastest sprinter,'" Greene said.

A day later, he had his gold, straining through the first leg of the 400-meter relay to share in victory with Mel Pender, Smith and Hines. He never considered pulling himself from the competition, even as gimpy as he was. "I was in bad shape but I knew I was better injured than someone else at full speed," Greene said.

Three months later, he married a *Philadelphia Inquirer* reporter he met on a blind date in Mexico City, someone who was sent there to write Olympics stories and came away with a romantic one. Five months after the Games, he entered the Army ROTC program and became a career military officer. He made another run at the Olympics in 1972 but couldn't get through the trials and was done.

"One day as a sprinter, you're faster than other people; the next day, you're not," he said. "It happens just like that. It's not a complicated process."

Greene regularly reunited with 30 fellow Olympians at a track and field clinic outside of Oakland. He often hung out with Hines. The competition now entailed who got in the best digs, not who had what medal hanging around his neck.

Luckily, it didn't rain that much in California, because Greene was the first to admit he wasn't as young, or as fast, as he used to be, though he had become a much better, and slower, driver. ❖

DORIS HERITAGE
Seattle's High-Mileage Model

Doris Heritage ran to Sunday church service, her teaching and coaching jobs, home from airline flights, in the Olympics, all over Seattle and all over the world, everywhere she could. By loose estimates, she logged more than 20,000 miles on foot, a personal odometer that started turning over nonstop when she was a grade-schooler and self-professed tomboy growing up in Gig Harbor. That was enough to cross the U.S. nearly seven times.

She ran under different names. She ran with short hair and long. She ran wearing nerdy eyeglasses. She ran until her left hip gave out after more than 50 years of steady pounding. And even then, Heritage ran until the very last minute she could.

Check-in time was 6 a.m. for her 2004 hip-replacement surgery at Seattle's Swedish Medical Center. At 4:30 a.m., Heritage prepped for the medical procedure by going on a final five-mile run, accompanied by four supportive friends. They toured Alki Point in the June darkness, starting and finishing on the road leading to Heritage's hillside home. They ran through Schmitz

> At her doctors' urging, this small, slender person – the world's greatest female distance runner in her prime and Seattle's most accomplished woman track athlete – gave up her lifetime passion when her left hip couldn't handle any more pounding.

Park, around the West Seattle High School track, on a neighborhood loop.

"That was the last time," Heritage said. "I felt so blessed these people would want to come do that with me."

At her doctors' urging, this small, slender person – the world's greatest female distance runner in her prime and Seattle's most accomplished woman track athlete – gave up her lifetime passion when her left hip couldn't handle any more pounding.

In 2008, Heritage, then 65, took the running disconnect yet another step, retiring after four decades of coaching track and cross country at her alma mater, Seattle Pacific University.

It had all started so innocently at her home on the other side of Puget Sound. "I always liked getting up early and feeding the chickens and rabbits, and then running down the beach," she said, not letting arthritic feet slow her. The former Doris Severtson enrolled at Seattle Pacific thinking she was a long jumper and wouldn't stay at the school long. Falcons men's track and field coach Ken Foreman convinced her she was a distance runner with unlimited potential, and, except for a couple of junior high school teaching jobs, she never strayed far from the college. Running consumed her to hypnotizing levels.

Known as Doris Brown after marrying a Seattle Pacific classmate, she held every woman's world record from the 440-yard dash to the mile at one point. She won the first five women's world cross-country championships, collecting the first one in Wales. She won 14 national titles. She qualified for the 1968 and 1972 Olympics. She left her footprints all over Seattle.

From residences in Shoreline and West Seattle, she ran to work, ran with her athletes during their afternoon workouts and ran home. The commuting alone often was 12 miles each way at times, or just shy of a marathon every day. On Sundays, she ran from her home to the First Free Methodist church on the Seattle Pacific campus, stopping only to change clothes in her athletic department office before attending services.

Heritage switched jobs as a junior high school physical education teacher, from Kellogg to Butler, because her first principal gave an ultimatum about her running. "He told me I had to be a runner or a teacher 'because people see you in a meet on TV and they're never going to vote for the levy,' " she recalled.

She often ran with one of her two Dobermans alongside for company. She named the first one Lasse Viren, after the Finnish male runner and four-time Olympic gold medalist, and the other Zola Budd, after the South African female runner who competed barefoot and set world records. "Lasse could do all the running I did and all the running the team did," she said of her pets. "Zola Budd would eat hamburgers and wasn't quite as trim."

Heritage was so into her sport that she got off flights at Seattle-Tacoma International Airport, changed into her running clothes, placed her street clothes in a locker and ran home, then drove back to the airport in her car and retrieved her belongings. "Some of the students' parents probably wondered about me if they were watching what I was doing," she said.

Taking laps around Green Lake, Heritage encountered men who weren't eager to share the recreational space with a serious-minded female runner; they threw balls at her or pushed her in the lake. Yet there were enough familiar faces to keep her coming back. "I knew every runner," she said. "If I saw a runner, I knew them. I met real interesting people who were runners."

She was married to her second husband, Ralph Heritage, at Lower Woodland Park. A biathlon served as the reception. On her 5-foot-3 frame, her weight never ventured outside 105 to 111 pounds once she become an adult. Her body fat nearly doubled with aging – everyone should have this problem – increasing from 5.5 percent to 10. "I've always been fit," Heritage said. "I've always had good heredity."

If there was a void in her running career, it was an Olympic medal. In 1960, she finished second in the 800 meters at the U.S. trials and just one American advanced. Four years later, she finished fourth in the same event, again one spot shy of making it. Heritage finally secured a berth at the 1968 Olympics in Mexico City, holding the top 800 time in the world and coming off her best year of competition. She stumbled during the race and finished fifth.

"I had reason to believe I would get a medal but I wasn't used to running with bodies all around me," she said. "Coming off the last turn, I had a collision. It wasn't a good time to have that happen."

Heritage qualified in the 1,500 meters, a new women's event and a longer race better suited for her talents, at the 1972 Olympics in Munich. She suffered even worse luck. Marching onto the track for her event, she didn't see a movable curb sticking out, one used to extend the high jump pit that was not properly restored to a closed position, and she stepped on it. "I tore my peroneal tendon and broke five bones in my foot," she said.

Heritage later became a coach in distance running at Seattle Pacific University.

Heritage recovered and ran for three more decades. She returned to the Olympic Games as a distance coach and liaison. She was inducted into the USATF and the national distance halls of fame.

As she pushed away from SPU, Heritage was forced to walk or ride a bike for exercise. It wasn't the same. She once envisioned retirement as a way to run more, not less, and had to cope with that life change. She had endured injuries before – including seven foot surgeries – but the hip replacement was unrelenting in requiring a new routine.

"I really miss running," Heritage said. "Running is a lifestyle. It's a stress reliever, not just a way to stay fit. I feel like not running has aged me considerably." ❖

The Seattle SuperSonics expansion team and its general manager Dick Vertlieb were new to the NBA and expected to take their lumps. Yet once their debut 1967-68 season was over, the Sonics had beaten everyone – the 76ers with Wilt Chamberlain, the Lakers with Jerry West and Elgin Baylor, even the Celtics with Bill Russell – with the exception of the Hawks. They lost eight times in as many tries to the St. Louis entry that first year, exasperating Vertlieb no end.

The front-office executive decided that extra-creative measures were necessary to reverse things on the Hawks' first trip to Seattle the following season: Vertlieb stationed an exceptionally attractive woman in a short skirt in a front-row seat directly across from the Hawks bench.

She was a head-turner from the beginning and even more so when she kept crossing her legs during the game. A newspaper photo would show opposing players standing in a huddle and everyone looking away from their coach. On Vertlieb's orders, the woman pulled a game-long Sharon Stone stunt from the film "Basic Instinct" that would come years later on the big

> Vertlieb, who was 78 when he died on Dec. 5, 2008, remains Seattle's most unique and improvisational sports executive, putting his fingerprints all over each one of the city's pro franchises and doing it in unconventional ways.

DICK VERTLIEB
The Most Front-Office Fun

screen – she wasn't wearing any underwear and she was more than willing to make that omission clear to her target audience at the Seattle Center Coliseum.

The Hawks, now based in Atlanta, were distracted by this incessant teasing and overly revealing spectator. For Vertlieb, it was mission accomplished: On their ninth try, the Sonics finally beat the Hawks 123-112. "I did it for just one team – Atlanta," the exec chortled.

Vertlieb, who was 78 when he died on Dec. 5, 2008, remains Seattle's most unique and improvisational sports executive, putting his fingerprints all over each one of the city's pro franchises and doing it in unconventional ways. He was GM for the SuperSonics and Seattle Mariners and a key player in securing Seattle Seahawks and Seattle Sounders franchises, even owning a small piece of the then-NASL team. He hired broadcaster Dave Niehaus and traded for guard Lenny Wilkens.

The Sonics general manager wasn't done with the Hawks in that 1968-69 season either. He wanted more payback. For another game in Seattle, Vertlieb arranged for a different woman to show up at the hotel room of Atlanta player-coach Richie Guerin and, put it this way, keep him busy all afternoon. The guard was selected by the Sonics in the expansion draft but Guerin maneuvered his way out of it by announcing his retirement, rescinding it and getting the teams to cut a deal to keep his playing rights with the Hawks.

Vertlieb didn't forget this arrangement during Seattle's first year in the league, holding a mock ceremony in which Guerin's number was retired before a game. As for the latest woman, the Sonics' front-office executive wanted the visiting coach to know what he was missing in terms of local hospitality.

"I had a very nice friend from a small town bring over a bottle of champagne and get Guerin loaded and . . ." said the impish GM, noting that the targeted player seemed lethargic and played very little that night.

If he had another breath in him, Vertlieb would have insisted that he lived four months too long — because he outlived his beloved Sonics by that much. He couldn't contain his disgust when a change in team ownership, from Starbucks CEO Howard Schultz to a group headed by Oklahoma City businessman Clay Bennett, sealed the eventual shift of his franchise to the Midwest. "Oh God, Schultz, you asshole, I hope you choke on your coffee," Vertlieb said with great rancor.

In 1966, Vertlieb was a bored Hollywood stockbroker and a diehard Los Angeles Lakers fan when he read in the paper how Eugene Klein and Sam Schulman, owners of the nation's second-largest group of movie theaters, purchased the San Diego Chargers and jumped into the pro sports world almost overnight. He impulsively dialed the first guy's number.

For years, Vertlieb, the son of one of Los Angeles' leading bookmakers, a USC graduate and perpetual daydreamer, had second-guessed the inner workings of his favorite team, the Lakers, telling anyone who would listen at the brokerage firm of Merrill, Lynch, Pierce, Fenner and Smith that he could do better.

For months, he plotted ways to put his brilliance with numbers and brashness with people to work in an expanding NBA. Vertlieb explained to Klein how his close friend, Don Richman, a USC fraternity brother,

was well-acquainted with NBA commissioner, Walter Kennedy. The two of them had served as college sports publicists, Richman at his alma mater and Kennedy at Notre Dame.

Vertlieb brazenly informed Klein that he was plugged into this upwardly mobile league and the Pacific Northwest, an untapped frontier for the sports-entertainment dollar that was the likeliest target for new business. It was something to invest in. It was the ultimate stock tip.

"I said, 'Portland or Seattle? I would support Seattle because they're used to paying high prices, to going to New York and going to shows. What do you want? It's impossible to lose money in basketball. If you would like to join a club more exclusive than the U.S. Senate, than you will give us your signature,' " Vertlieb recalled.

Klein and Schulman provided their business reputations but no cash to get things in motion. Their available funds were tied up in the NFL. Vertlieb and his buddy had to charm their way through the rest of the deal and come up with $1 million in guaranteed, first-year operating expenses. They secured a TV-radio contract from Atlantic Richfield Oil Co. and a loan from People's Bank to pay for the franchise.

With creative bookkeeping, they were ready for the opening tip. The owners had to be pleased with this enterprise. After a public stock offering was made available, Klein and Schulman pocketed millions. The risk was zero.

Vertlieb and Richman were such an interchangeable pair they flipped a coin to see how they would divvy up the jobs of general manager and business manager. Vertlieb eventually held both posts. They named the team the SuperSonics, paying homage to the local airplane industry, and settled on green and gold colors, representing trees and the Alaska Gold Rush.

The general manager could be flamboyant, demonstrating his quirkiness for the Sonics fan base to see. He liked to mix with people, not hide from them. He sat a few rows up for Coliseum home games, surrounded by paying customers, always smoking a big cigar. He took his basketball seriously, sometimes as a personal affront. He forced others to scramble out of his way or double over laughing.

One night while incensed over an official's call that favored the visiting Hawks, Vertlieb threw down his stogie and kicked it. He watched in horror as the burning cigar landed in the back of a women's coat. Vertlieb retrieved the cigar, threw it down again and tried another drop kick. This time he lost his footing and tumbled down the arena steps. He wasn't hurt, just humiliated. He didn't get up. He called for a stretcher. "I heard Jack Curran, our trainer, say, 'Oh my God, Dick's had a heart attack,' " Vertlieb said. "I was so embarrassed I just let them carry me out of there."

On another night, the Baltimore Bullets and Sonics brawled at the Coliseum and Vertlieb unwisely ran into the middle of it. After bruising Bullets forward Bob Ferry and often-annoying Sonics guard Walt Hazzard started the tiff, teammate Tom Meschery came to the aid of Hazzard by tackling Ferry. Sonics coach Al Bianchi took an elbow to the face and received a cut over his eye as he tried to separate Meschery and Ferry. Bullets forward Gus Johnson, one of the game's noted tough guys, went for Bianchi, unable to resist taking a shot at an opposing coach. Vertlieb stepped in to rescue Bianchi from further injury and he now had Johnson's full attention.

"He saw a GM's face," Vertlieb said. "All his life he wanted a shot at a GM. He was going to knock all my teeth out, break my nose and leave me a wreck."

Vertlieb was saved when Sonics enforcer Dorie Murrey picked up Johnson and tossed him hard into the front-row seats, leaving Johnson incredulous. They were friends. "I couldn't let you kill the man," Murrey told Johnson.

If Vertlieb had a little outlaw in him, there was good reason. He was the son of Jack Burke, a man who changed his name to protect his family and ran bookmaking numbers for high-profile mobsters such as Lucky Luciano and Bugsy Siegal. Burke became the manager of the Flamingo Hotel in Las Vegas at the request of Gus Greenbaum, another Mafiaso type. "He always said, 'I don't want to dirty you up,' " Vertlieb said. "I would have never got into sports if people knew who my father worked for." At 10, Vertlieb watched Burke board a train for Vacaville, Calif., to serve an 18-month prison sentence.

Vertlieb ran with a much safer, if not entertaining, crowd. After graduating from USC with a business degree, he shared a rental home with aspiring actors Martin Milner and David Janssen. They were fun-loving bachelors. Milner used to entertain a striking young woman with dark hair and piercing eyes, or at least everyone assumed she was a woman. One night, an eavesdropping Vertlieb heard Milner's angry voice echo through the air vent connecting their rooms: "What do you mean you're only 17?! Get the [bleep] out of here!" With that, Natalie Wood, who was headed for considerable screen time herself, walked out the door.

Vertlieb survived just two and a half seasons with the Sonics, outlasting Klein and Richman but not Schulman. Owners Klein and Schulman had a blow-up and parted ways. Klein gave up his NBA interest in exchange for Schulman's NFL share. Richman preferred a California lifestyle and resigned. Vertlieb continually irritated Schulman by making personnel moves without his consent.

The last straw was his hiring of Meschery as an assistant coach. That prompted a 1 a.m. phone call from a screaming Schulman, waking Vertlieb at home. Vertlieb was fired before he could get out of bed. He left the Sonics behind and four years later won an NBA championship with the San Francisco Warriors.

In 1977, Vertlieb, who in the interim had helped negotiate deals bringing the Seahawks and Sounders to Seattle, was hired as general manager to head up the Mariners expansion baseball franchise. He had big plans for the team. He wanted to name it the Hustlers or Professionals. He wanted to dress the players in black uniforms. No one listened. A nautical theme was preferred and, for the next two decades, long after he was gone, the team best resembled a sinking ship.

He kept things fun in his office with a barber chair and pool table. He was always upbeat, constantly uttering his favorite word, "Sen-saaaaay-shun-aaaaaal!" He was fired early in his second season after locking horns once more with his bosses and replaced by Lou Gorman, his director of baseball operations.

"Everybody drinks whiskey in professional sports, lots of whiskey," Vertlieb said. "The Seahawks ended up with a coach [Jack Patera] who drank too much. The Mariners ended up with a manager [Darrell Johnson] who drank too much. The owners of the Mariners drank too much. They always had an open bar with the Seahawks. It was always the whiskey talking."

Vertlieb, who lived at 6280 W. Mercer Way on Mercer Island, also was the Indiana Pacers general manager, helped run Seattle's Goodwill Games, worked as a sports agent, fled to Europe and moved back to Las Vegas basically to die, suffering from stomach cancer among other ailments. In his final years, he was holed up in a modest home on the outskirts of that overheated Nevada city, living with his son and sitting

in an air-conditioned room while watching his body deteriorate. He was outrageous to the end, calling and informing me, "I'm sitting here naked talking to you."

The former sports executive asked that his ashes be spread in Hood Canal outside of Seattle, a city that gave him more joy than aggravation. It was a place where some of its basketball fans didn't always wear underwear, and it hired and fired him, and then hired and fired him again. Still, the city and this man shared an unbreakable bond.

"When the world comes to an end," Vertlieb liked to say, "Seattle will still have a year to go." ❖

Dick Vertlieb in his later years.

J MICHAEL KENYON

The Press Box Peacock

The car went over a dune and landed in San Diego Bay with a splash. J Michael Kenyon was behind the wheel. He was just 23, a *Seattle Post-Intelligencer* reporter in his first year of covering the Seattle SuperSonics, and out of control. He climbed out into four feet of surf.

He hadn't made it through NBA training camp and was out drinking with members of the San Diego Chargers football team. He came to as he went airborne. He waded back to shore, abandoning the submerged car, which was a loaner.

Of the dozens of sportswriters who have come through Seattle and sized up its athletic teams in print, some demonstrating heavyweight journalism skills and personalities that would take them to national TV opportunities, such as the *P-I's* Bill Plaschke and the *Morning News Tribune's* John Clayton, and a boorish few guided by overbearing egos or a lack of ethics, such as the *P-I's* Harold Torbergson, Kenyon was the most outlandish and unforgettable.

He entered the local sports world as Michael Glover and left it as J Michael Kenyon for no other reason than to impress a woman. He was driven by newspaper deadlines but few other boundaries. He constantly tested the limits of his professional and personal lives. He often became a better story than the one he was writing.

He changed jobs, wives and watering holes so frequently it was hard to keep track of him. He was

lovable and despicable, all in one. He was talented and self destructive. He was the city's own Hunter S. Thompson, the sports edition.

"Not everybody gets to drive a car into the Pacific Ocean, but the kind of people I was around made it all sort of interesting," Kenyon said. "The guy who arranged for me to have the car had some perfectly good advice when I called, still dripping wet, and asked, 'What should I do?' 'Run away,' he said. 'You may as will learn right now there is no problem too big in life that you can't run away from.'

"For a good many years, I maintained that as my credo."

Kenyon, who grew up in Lake City at 1532 N.E. 97th St., was pulled into journalism after reading and rereading 10 years worth of *Post-Intelligencer* sports sections stacked in the attic for him by his father, a postman and huge sports fan. He became a copy boy at the *Seattle Times* and was dazzled by all of the newsroom characters and wanted to be one of them. He attended Roosevelt High School and the University of Washington, joining the college newspaper *The Daily* but rarely attending a class. He enlisted in the Army rather than explain to his parents how he had squandered his college tuition, and this led to writing assignments in and out of the military service.

Of the dozens of sportswriters who have come through Seattle and sized up its athletic teams in print, Kenyon was the most outlandish and unforgettable.

Kenyon came to the *Post-Intelligencer* in 1965 – two years before there were SuperSonics – in an appropriate manner. The aforementioned Torbergson was caught in an FBI sting feeding horse-racing information to a local bookmaker and he was fired. Federal agents used a hidden camera at the paper to make their case against Torbergson, who pulled horse scratch reports from an old wire teletype machine in a hallway and delivered them to the gambler.

Looking for a replacement, *P-I* sports editor John Owen read Kenyon's stories in the *Yakima Morning Herald*, his post-Army landing spot, and was so impressed he hired him. Thus began an on-again, off-again relationship of 15 years between the newspaper and the young sports-writing prodigy. "John Owen gave me more chances than I may have deserved," Kenyon said. "[Columnist] Royal Brougham, aware of my proclivities to drink and wild living, was always trying to tame me."

Personal histrionics aside, Kenyon was a talented journalist who could write interesting stuff and make insider connections, and he was on hand for multiple Seattle sports milestones. On Oct. 13, 1967, the then-Michael Glover sat courtside for Seattle's first official big-league event, the SuperSonics' season-opening 144-116 loss to the San Francisco Warriors on the road. The first paragraph of his first game story went like this: "The long thin form of Al Tucker lay sprawled on a bench in the Seattle dressing room, his nose bleeding. And that was before the game even started."

On the long plane rides across the country, he was encouraged to join in mysterious card games called "Boo-Ray" with Sonics starting guards Walt Hazzard and Rod Thorn and reserve forwards Bud Olsen and Henry Akin, regularly handing over his paychecks to them. He also lost a considerable amount of money while playing gin rummy with radio broadcaster Bob Blackburn.

"That ended, once and for all, one night late at the

> ## Personal histrionics aside, Kenyon was a talented journalist who could write interesting stuff and make insider connections, and he was on hand for multiple Seattle sports milestones.

Detroit Sheraton Cadillac hotel, where, several hundred dollars down, I tore up the deck and hurled the pieces out a window into a swirling snowstorm," he said. "And I had to work, free, as Bob's statistician, out on the road, for almost the rest of the NBA season to pay off what I owed."

Halfway through that first season, he left the first of his five marriages for a woman he met in a Baltimore bar, an ex-dancer. He quit the *P-I* for the *Baltimore Sun*. At her suggestion, he also changed his name; she thought Michael Glover sounded too boring.

His new identity didn't take a lot of creativity. Driving down Highway 99 through suburban Seattle, he spotted the Kenyon Printing Co. and saw his new surname. He added a 'J' to the front end, had everything typeset at the *P-I* to see how it looked in print and enlisted Bill McFarland, the Seattle Totems hockey coach and a lawyer, to legally change his name. The relationship lasted just six months, but the new moniker was permanent.

In 1975, Kenyon was back at the *P-I* as a features editor and encouraged to put his meandering ways on the record in a sports-page story entitled: "Confessions of

J Michael Kenyon was born Michael Glover.

a Basketball Reporter: He Dunked Too Many Shots." He was depicted in a cartoon sitting in a bar with a smiling woman, presumably that ill-fated Baltimore acquaintance, with each holding a drink and a cigarette.

On April 6, 1977, Kenyon was seated in the press box for the Mariners' first game in franchise history, covering a 7-0 loss to the California before a sold-out crowd of 57,762 at the Kingdome. All along, he was the life of the party. He got to know various coaches and managers well because they liked to hang out in bars and chase women, too. They shared information with him. He entertained them to the point it got painful.

"Once I'd developed the habit of doing drunken, front somersaults off the countertops of bars, well, my playmates couldn't get enough of that," Kenyon said.

In 1980, Kenyon went on the air at KVI with one of Seattle's first sports radio talk shows, preceded only by KIRO's Wayne Cody, whose approach was more self-promoting showman than sporting expert. Kenyon mixed astute observations with an amazing recall of sports trivia. Daredevil Evel Knievel was a regular guest on his show, in one stretch doing four phone interviews from four different hospitals. Legendary football player Red Grange was so impressed with Kenyon's knowledge of him, he said, "I like the way you talk, J Michael, I like the way you talk."

Jobs always proved complicated for him, though. Kenyon worked four different times at the *P-I* through 1980. He quit in a huff or got fired at several places. He once left the *P-I* after having a story killed, announcing his departure on a KVI drive-time radio show accompanied by sound effects. He abruptly got up and walked out for good in the middle of his own KING radio show over a manager's meddling. He was fired from the *Daily Breeze* in Torrance, Calif., for running a full-page photo collage of Richard Nixon topped by the

headline, "Would you buy a used car from him now?" He wrote his final newspaper piece at Tacoma's *Morning News Tribune* in 1990 before he was let go.

He fuzzily remembers trying to shimmy under a limbo bar with Chubby Checker. Working for the *Hollywood Citizen-News*, he dated one of the original Dean Martin Golddiggers, who worked during the day as one of his reporters. He became a boxing promoter for former big-league pitcher Dean Chance. As an auto-racing promoter, he squired porn star Linda Lovelace around Seattle for a week. Everywhere he went, it was an adventure.

Kenyon's devil-may-care lifestyle finally caught up with him once he became an older man. The party was over. He developed congestive heart failure and throat cancer and it was a race to see how long he could last. He moved to the southern Oregon coast with his fifth wife, Joan, where he could stare out at the Pacific Ocean and go in peace. This was a far cry from his earliest sportswriting days, when he splashed down in the Pacific and wasn't quite sure how he got there.

"I can only imagine what I might have been able to accomplish had I not tried to bed and marry every comely female on the planet, let alone the million or so bucks I tossed away on whiskey, cigarettes and cheap motel rooms along the way," Kenyon conceded. ❖

Top 10 Seattle Sportswriters

1. Bill Plaschke, *P-I*
2. Emmett Watson, *P-I*
3. Art Thiel, *P-I*
4. J Michael Kenyon, *P-I*
5. Tom Farrey, *Times*
6. Jim Caple, *P-I*
7. John Clayton, *Tribune*
8. Hy Zimmerman, *Times*
9. Gil Lyons, *Times*
10. Bud Withers, *P-I*, *Times*

After three days of negotiations in Florida, a deal was struck. Both sides agreed to the sale price of $13.5 million, enough to buy an American Football League franchise and a Washington, D.C., building in the same transaction. Handshakes were exchanged. In February 1969, the Miami Dolphins now belonged to a Seattle ownership group headed up by businessman Walter Schoenfeld, a man who had every intention of moving this pro football team to the Northwest.

The Seattle Dolphins had a nice sound to it, though a name more like the Seattle Salmon or Seattle Halibut, or even an early version of the Seattle Seahawks, would have better suited the Puget Sound's colder aquatic corridor. While attorneys drew up the papers, Schoenfeld and the others headed out to play Miami's challenging Blue Monster Course at Doral Golf Resort and Spa.

Schoenfeld had sat at the negotiating table with another Seattle man in future Delta Airlines chief executive officer Jerry Grinstein, who was Sen. Warren Magnuson's administrative assistant at the time. They bartered for the team with Dolphins majority owner William "Bud" Keland, who made his fortune as a Wisconsin cattle rancher and land developer.

> Schoenfeld didn't have to let go legally, but he did, leaving him as the Seattle's most hard-luck pro sports owner, saddled with the city's biggest near-miss.

WALTER SCHOENFELD

Seattle's Dolphin Daydream

In operation three seasons, Miami's NFL franchise was a big-money loser, failing to build much of a fan base at the Orange Bowl. In 1968, fewer than 30,000 fans showed up for each home game and the team lost $800,000. Keland, a 70-percent owner, badly wanted out. Schoenfeld had helped Seattle roll out its first pro franchise the year before, retaining a significant ownership piece and front-office position with the NBA's Seattle SuperSonics, and he was eager to add another team to the city.

As they teed it up on the Blue Monster, Schoenfeld was told by his associates to let Keland win so not to upset him. Unknowingly, Keland had decided on the same approach with his guest from Seattle. Once this overly friendly golf round was over, these men sat down again and signed the franchise-sale paperwork.

"We were all laughing that we were going to bring Mercury Morris to Seattle and he would have to learn to play in the rain," said Schoenfeld, referring to a drafted running back who would become a Miami mainstay. "We went to bed thinking we owned the Dolphins. It was done."

Plans were made to ask the University of Washington, Schoenfeld's alma mater, if the Dolphins could use Husky Stadium as a temporary home field, which was considered a given. "With the senators [Henry "Scoop" Jackson and Magnuson] behind it, I don't think we would have had a problem with that," Schoenfeld said. "It's a state institution. If not, we would have built our own stadium, though certainly not in today's grandiose way."

A press announcement of the sale was withheld until NFL commissioner Pete Rozelle could be consulted. The AFL and NFL recently had agreed to merge into one league, hence Rozelle's necessary intervention. This is where everything started to unravel. Keland, who purchased his share of the team from entertainer Danny Thomas, was at constant odds with Dolphins minority owner Joe Robbie, and Keland pushed the deal ahead without consulting the latter. Robbie supposedly failed to meet a deadline required to retain his voting rights in general partnership matters, or so Keland was convinced.

Robbie now held up a $1 million note owed him by his partners and threatened to sue everyone involved if the league recognized the sale to the Seattle interests and the Dolphins were uprooted from the Sunshine State.

In a conference call to discuss the agreement, Rozelle asked Schoenfeld to void the sale. He promised to give Seattle strong consideration when the next expansion franchise became available if trouble could be averted. A reluctant Schoenfeld complied with the request, convincing himself the NFL commissioner was working in good faith and not needlessly giving in to Robbie's threats.

Schoenfeld didn't have to let go legally, but he did, leaving him as the Seattle's most hard-luck pro sports owner, saddled with the city's biggest near-miss. With the Miami franchise, he could have totally rearranged the local sporting landscape and been a major player rather than a behind-the-scenes guy.

"We had signed a contract," Schoenfeld said. "We actually owned the team for about 18 hours. This Dolphin thing was extremely disappointing. It was really distressing."

At an NFL owners meeting later that year, Robbie hedged on the truth when asked directly about a possible Northwest interest in his franchise and if any negotiations had taken place. "We know of Seattle people interested in pro football, but we have not had any discussions with any of them," said Robbie, who had put together a group to buy out Keland's majority interest.

Schoenfeld was a Broadway High and UW graduate who grew up on Capitol Hill at 1107 Federal Ave. E. He was raised in a blue-blood Seattle family of wily investors and extraordinary endurance – his father, Max, built a clothing-manufacturing empire and lived to be 108. Walter made his money by launching Brittania Sportswear, a company that was the first to match blue jeans with coordinating jackets, shirts and sweaters, before selling to Levi Strauss. Almost as a hobby, he pursued pro sports teams for his hometown.

He was the first local investor approached by California owners Sam Schulman and Eugene Klein to join their Sonics ownership lineup, becoming vice president and director for the expansion team from 1968-79. He and Schulman were part of a group that pursued a Seattle NFL expansion franchise in 1973, losing out to a group headed up by Herman Sarkowsky and the Nordstrom family, who created the Seahawks.

Schoenfeld also was part of two different Seattle Mariners ownership groups after participating in a near-miss attempt to purchase the Chicago White Sox from owner Bill Veeck and move them to Seattle in 1974. "We got down to the final strokes and almost bought them," Schoenfeld said of the White Sox. "We had agreed on a price. We went back to sign a deal. We had complete agreement with Veeck. But in baseball, there are so many agreed-upon deals that never get made."

In 1977, Schoenfeld became one of the Mariners' six original owners, joining Hollywood entertainer Danny Kaye, radio station mogul Les Smith, and businessmen Jim Stillwell, Stan Golub and Jim Walsh. He was accustomed to strange dealings when it came to swapping franchise ownership rights, none stranger than Canadian Nelson Skalbania's attempt to buy the Mariners from him and the others. "We had four meetings and they said, 'OK, we have a deal,' and they walked out the door and we never heard from them again," Schoenfeld said.

The six original Mariners owners eventually broke even after selling their chronically bad baseball team to California businessman George Argyros in 1981.

Meantime, the Dolphins under Robbie's total control established a stronghold in Miami after their dalliance with overnight Seattle ownership, winning consecutive Super Bowls in 1972 and 1973, and the franchise became immovable.

Schoenfeld was involved in Seattle's biggest block-buster sports transaction never completed. He was as responsible as anyone for bringing pro football to Seattle, though he didn't share in the end result.

It was intriguing to envision how the original deal might have altered the local sporting scene had it played out. There might have been earlier championships and Super Bowl trips to savor with the Seattle Dolphins on hand.

"Mercury Morris would have looked good up here," Schoenfeld said wistfully. ❖

DEWEY SORIANO & MAX SORIANO

Seattle's Brothers Grim

Max Soriano, left, and his brother Dewey were baseball players before owners of the ill-fated Seattle Pilots.

Dewey Soriano was the jowly and extroverted brother, either the life of the party or an overbearing man. Max Soriano was the handsome yet reticent one, always private and detached. Together these polar opposites with shared bloodlines and civic passion talked the American League into awarding a Major League Baseball franchise to Seattle. Unfortunately, their powers of persuasion, coupled with an underfunded financial commitment, went no further than that.

The Soriano brothers' beleaguered Seattle Pilots baseball team stuck around for a solitary season, long enough to lose 98 of 162 games, use 53 players, fire a cartoonish manager and shut down operations after 27 months of calamity, becoming the oddball pro sports footnote.

For all the excitement the Sorianos created in their hometown, they left the city deeply wounded and embarrassed by their bold enterprise. They set a disturbing precedent for big-league failure: No pro sports owners in Seattle, or anywhere else in modern-day sports annals, have gone belly up any quicker. The city felt like a loser. As the purveyors of the Pilots, the brothers took a huge risk in trying to operate their Major League team in a remodeled Pacific Coast League ballpark. They were warned not to do it. They couldn't help themselves.

"With 20-20 hindsight we could have waited until we got a stadium built or gave this one a bigger facelift, but we wanted to go forward," Max Soriano said of Sicks' Stadium. "[A.L. president] Joe Cronin said, 'This is a minor-league stadium and you're going to have a tough time drawing crowds.' He knew. We were hard-nosed or dumb or something."

The big-league baseball disconnect was apparent from the first pitch at Sicks' Stadium. For the home opener on April 11, 1969, outfield hammering was heard all the way to home plate, often drowning out the crackling sounds of batting practice and rhythmic thumping of those playing catch. Construction workers were still installing leftfield bleacher seats with the first pitch approaching. Fans entering that newly-built section incredibly were asked to stand in line and wait for something to become available.

One man ripped his pants on the hastily assembled bleachers and complained so loudly to the Pilots that

> For all the excitement the Sorianos created in their hometown, they left the city deeply wounded and embarrassed by their bold enterprise.

Worst 10 Seattle Owners

1. Clay Bennett, Sonics
2. Ken Behring, Seahawks
3. Dewey Soriano, Pilots
4. Max Soriano, Pilots
5. George Argyros, Mariners
6. Howard Schultz, Sonics
7. Jeff Smulyan, Mariners
8. Barry Ackerley, Sonics
9. Vince Abbey, NHL franchise
10. Gene Klein, Sonics

the team bought him a new suit. The unfinished outfield seating was just the first in a series of irreversible gaffes that gave this Seattle big-league franchise no chance at all.

On a nightly basis Dewey Soriano was left to wander the ballpark and its rows of now fully completed yet unoccupied seats, muttering to himself about the failure of others to give his Pilots a real chance to succeed. He knew right away that the baseball team he fought so hard to bring to Seattle was slipping away from him. Once others found this out, things got ugly

around the city for the Sorianos, especially Dewey. He was burned in effigy in Pioneer Square. He received threatening phone calls at home.

"It was really hard for him to see this shatter so quickly," said Cathi Soriano, Dewey's daughter. "It was the worst nightmare he could go through. He wanted it so badly for so long. I wouldn't go so far and say he was never the same after that, but it was a life-changing thing for him."

Dewey Soriano and his younger brother Max forever will be remembered as the men who first delivered big-league baseball to Seattle, becoming local heroes, and the ones who couldn't hang onto it, turning into civic pariahs. Their intentions for the city were admirable but their execution was woefully inept.

Seattle clearly was a desired big-league destination, with both the National League and American League fighting over it as an expansion franchise recipient, after the Cleveland Indians and Kansas City Athletics alternately mulled franchise moves to the city and passed.

In gaining league approval, the Sorianos sold themselves as homegrown ownership with a proven pro baseball track record — Dewey previously was the PCL president, Max the Triple-A league's legal counsel — and they teamed up with an experienced big-league insider in William Daley, a former Cleveland Indians owner.

Yet they couldn't make it work in that antiquated ballpark that was nearly doubled in size to 25,000 seats and leased from the city but still minor league in too many respects to overcome. They couldn't sell nearly enough tickets — a season total 677,944 — to help recoup their initial $5 million investment and meet operating costs. Typical of the inexcusable failures involved, the Sicks' Stadium bathrooms wouldn't flush if more than 10,000 people showed up, which happened 20 times, counting four doubleheaders. Makeshift

restroom alternatives were no better at building a loyal fan base.

"There were Port-O-Potties beyond the leftfield fence," Pilots publicist Bill Sears said, retelling a story that involved team executive Edo Vanni. "Edo was out back, checking things out, and hears a guy pounding on the door. He was locked all night in that Port-O-Potty."

The Sorianos also made a misguided and bigoted business decision that backfired on them: They chose to price Pilots tickets at the top of the A.L. scale to discourage Seattle's African-American community, which filled up the lower-income, south-end neighborhoods that surrounded the ballpark, from attending games, according to Sears. It was purely economics, they maintained, figuring too many blacks would hurt the overall attendance.

The brothers were self-made men from modest beginnings, Canadian natives and sons of a Spanish-born fisherman. Two of 10 siblings and three years apart, Dewey and Max grew up in Rainier Beach at 4836 S. Gazelle St. and shared a mutual love for baseball. They were all-city pitchers for Franklin High, with Dewey teaming with future big-league pitcher and manager Fred Hutchinson. Max later pitched for the University of Washington and rejected a pro contract offer from the PCL's San Francisco Seals in order to pursue law school.

Dewey played for four minor-league teams over 10 seasons, originally signing with the Seattle Rainiers and spending most of his pro career with the local Triple-A team. As a kid, he served as a peanut vendor for the Rainiers. As a young pitcher, he had a lot of people at home counting on his paycheck.

"They were really a poor family," Cathi Soriano said. "Their father would leave for months on end and there always was concern whether he would come back at all.

The family was saved by Dewey's arm, because Dewey could pitch."

Dewey Soriano's best chance of advancing to the big leagues came in 1947 when the Pittsburgh Pirates acquired the right-hander from the Rainiers for $30,000 and two players. He even roomed briefly with the great Pirates slugger Ralph Kiner. Yet a lingering knee injury ended his career and he turned his attention to baseball administration, first becoming the Rainiers general manager before heading up the PCL.

Dewey Soriano also was a Puget Sound ship pilot — hence the expansion baseball team's nickname — and engaged in two careers simultaneously. His saltwater pursuits sometimes mirrored his ballpark follies. In 1967, he ran a ship into a rock and lost his license, and then reclaimed his credentials with a lawsuit that pointed out that he had struck an uncharted rock. He also clipped another ship and a bridge near Tacoma in separate incidents, all of this leading to a local drink named after him: Dewey on the Rocks.

The Soriano brothers came up with $2 million of the required $5 million to fund the Pilots franchise, with two-thirds of their share put in Max's name because Dewey was going through a contentious divorce that didn't endear him to the sporting public.

His wife, Alice, was the daughter of influential Seattle *Post-Intelligencer* sports editor Royal Brougham, and it was widely known around the city that Dewey had left her for his secretary, Jean, who became his second wife. The marital split practically guaranteed there wouldn't be any extra support on the pages of the morning newspaper from Brougham for the new big-league baseball team and its most visible owner.

After that disastrous first season, the Sorianos were out of money. With their bank loans due, they traveled to the World Series in Baltimore and made a handshake deal with Bud Selig to move the team to Milwaukee.

"It was a comedy of errors," Sears said. "We had great characters in [Frank] Crosetti and [Sal] Maglie. It was a great organization. It just seemed like there was a kiss of death on it. If we could have had a couple of years, we could have got a new stadium and got momentum. Who knows?"

The brothers borrowed money to pay for 1970 spring training, stunningly announced the franchise was lost and overnight was transformed into the Brewers, and they slunk away from this mess financially intact but with their baseball reputations ruined for good. They declared bankruptcy and reclaimed their $2 million, and even came out $225,000 ahead.

"I think they'd do a lot of things different," said Larry Soriano, Max's son. "When things don't work out, you

Dewey and Max Soriano in 1967.

learn a lot. They would have had more of a connection to the establishment, better capitalization. Unfortunately, the city wasn't behind it."

Once the Pilots and Seattle split up, the Soriano siblings went in opposite directions. Baseball was only part of the reason. The brothers had personal differences that weren't readily resolved.

"They were really close up until my father married my stepmother," Cathi Soriano said. "Max couldn't stand her and they had very little contact after that. My father was a jerk a lot of the time. He could be delightful to others but he also could be really cruel, and perhaps we saw that more than anyone because we were his family. Max once said Dewey was wonderful to everyone except family. After his 1971 marriage, my dad and Max didn't speak for years. They got together again when my dad was sick."

Dewey Soriano suffered dementia and was no longer cognizant of his baseball failure when he died at age 78 on April 6, 1999. A family friend later dropped some of Dewey's ashes around home plate during midseason opening ceremonies for newly built Safeco Field, the second home for the Seattle Mariners, the Pilots' replacement team. This gesture brought the former baseball owner close to the big-league game one more time in Seattle. Luckily, the seats were fully installed for the first pitch that night.

Max Soriano outlived his brother, but he, too, was overcome by dementia, and the Pilots were wiped from his memory banks. The Sorianos' Seattle legacy was similar to a starting pitcher drawing a huge assignment but failing to get out of the first inning.

"We did not do a good job," Max Soriano said of the brothers' big-league baseball foray. "We started it but we didn't complete the deal." ❖

LOU PINIELLA
The Temper Tantrum

The Seattle Pilots needed 7½ hours to sift through the American League expansion pool and choose 30 worthy bodies from which to start a big-league baseball team. One turned out to be a noteworthy find.

Huddled in Boston on Oct. 15, 1968, and alternating draft picks with the Kansas City Royals, the Pilots made their 12th selection by staying true to a prearranged strategy of adding experienced but not necessarily older baseball talent to their roster: That player was identified in Seattle news accounts as Louis Piniella, picked up for the draft acquisition fee of $175,000.

Left unprotected by the Cleveland Indians, the 26-year-old Piniella drew no special mention while changing organizations nor was he listed among the Pilots' potential starting outfielders. He was no mystery to the people of the Northwest, though. He spent the three previous seasons with the Triple-A Portland Beavers, regularly facing the Seattle Angels as a Pacific Coast League rival, and he was a solid minor-league hitter, batting .289, .308 and .317.

Piniella, however, was underappreciated from the beginning of this expansion process, a situation that earmarked his brief five-and-a-half-month connection to the Pilots franchise and was totally reversed once he returned as a popular Mariners manager for a decade — making him the city's most ingeniously recycled sports figure.

Early on in Pilots spring training in Tempe, Ariz., Piniella proved to be a brash, outspoken player who complained loudly about his lack of playing time, which didn't endear him to the Seattle front office but landed him a prominent place in teammate Jim Bouton's best-selling book *Ball Four*. Piniella turned up repeatedly in the Bouton tell-all, generally described as unhappy each time. He was convinced Seattle didn't really want him and he promised right off to quit baseball rather than return to the minors.

When the Pilots' exhibition games began, Piniella was named as the first-game starter in left field but removed from the lineup at the last minute in favor of Jose Vidal, a former Portland teammate. Piniella didn't draw regular playing time until the second week of the spring schedule. He used a couple of 3-for-4 hitting performances to force Pilots manager Joe Schultz to give him a longer look.

"Truly, Lou was a shining example of management's problems," Bouton pointed out. "One of the things Joe Schultz didn't do well was know his personnel. With a guy like Lou Piniella, an outspoken guy in spring training, the thinking was he's going to be trouble so we're going to get rid of him. The idea was let's get rid

> Piniella, however, was underappreciated from the beginning of this expansion process, a situation that earmarked his brief five-and-a-half-month connection to the Pilots franchise.

of the weirdoes. But to be different means having a lot of character."

Piniella was batting a solid .378 when news accounts surfaced that the Pilots were entertaining trade talks for him. He was pulled from the lineup, played sparingly thereafter and quit hitting. He went through a 1-for-15 slump to end his Seattle spring-training stint.

On April 1, 1969, a week before the regular-season opener at California, Piniella was traded to the Royals for outfielder Steve Whitaker and minor-league pitcher John Gelnar. On April Fool's Day, the last laugh was on Seattle: Whitaker, a Tacoma native and previously an expansion-draft pick-up from the New York Yankees, was just as opinionated as Piniella only he didn't hit as well.

"When I got traded for him, it was one red ass for another," said Whitaker, who had reported late as a Royals' spring holdout, speeding his departure from Kansas City. "They wanted to get rid of both of us."

Piniella played in 16 spring-training games for Seattle, finishing with a .288 batting average in 52 at-bats. He rapped out three doubles, a triple and a home run, and collected seven RBI. Before packing up and leaving, he expressed great displeasure with the Pilots one last time.

"When Lou got the message, I was about six feet from him," said Max Soriano, a Pilots owner with his brother Dewey. "If he could have jumped through the roof, he would have. He said, 'What the hell is wrong with them? What do they want from me?' He was really playing well. If I would have called Dewey, it wouldn't have happened."

As the more cerebral of the two Sorianos explained it, Pilots general manager Marvin Milkes made up his mind to trade Piniella before spring training was complete, unimpressed with the young outfielder and his mood swings. When the Kansas City trade was put on the table, Milkes alerted only Max Soriano,

who knew the move wasn't right for the Pilots but did nothing to stop it.

Dewey Soriano, the far more powerful of the siblings and the franchise point man, was back in Seattle at the time, overseeing the difficult conversion of Sicks' Stadium from a minor-league ballpark into a makeshift big-league facility. The older brother wasn't informed of the transaction until it was too late and he was livid. He had every reason to be.

Piniella enjoyed a breakout season with Kansas City and was named A.L. Rookie of the Year after batting .282 with 11 home runs and 68 RBI. He went fairly easy on the Pilots, batting just .244 with a homer and six RBI in 16 games against them, but none of that was any consolation for Seattle.

This was a player with enough personality and pop to put more fans in the seats at Sicks' Stadium and he practically was given away. It was a major misstep among many for a doomed baseball franchise that would be one-and-done, uprooted to Milwaukee the following season after declaring bankruptcy — ironically joining Piniella in the Midwest.

"When he did find out about it, he was ready to fire Marvin Milkes," Max Soriano said of his brother. "Dewey got all the blame and didn't even know about the trade. I should have called Dewey on the phone. Milkes came to me and said, 'I'm going to send that player out.' I couldn't understand it. I should have said, 'Marvin, we should talk to Dewey first.' But I didn't want Marvin to think I was working behind his back. It was one of the biggest mistakes we made and I have to put big blame on myself."

It was 25 years before Seattle would get another shot at Piniella's services. The city's baseball leaders wouldn't blow the second opportunity. After the disastrous season for the Pilots and 16 fairly uneventful

Lou Piniella's temper was legendary.

ones turned in by the Mariners, Piniella was hired as Seattle's big-league manager in 1993 by the replacement franchise. He had the team in the playoffs for the first time and two victories shy of a World Series berth by his third season.

For all that crankiness and attitude that might have turned off Milkes, Piniella was revered for his unrefined ways as the Mariners field boss. His base-throwing and dirt-excavating tantrums ignited by questionable umpiring calls at the Kingdome and Safeco Field were unforgettable theater, if not ticket-selling magic, and he became one of Seattle's all-time favorite sporting personalities.

There were rough, lovable edges to the man. Before every game, Piniella entertained reporters casually in his office, whereas every other Mariners manager who succeeded him did this chore in a formal dugout setting. Piniella answered questions while pouring over stock tables, filling in crossword puzzles, eating large bags of potato chips, smoking nonstop and sitting in his baseball undergarments.

Occasionally, he offered some eye-opening revelation about someone in the game or himself, such as the time he admitted to illegally corking his bat briefly as a big-league player. He figured it was the only way to combat pitchers who slyly were doctoring the ball before finally concluding it made no difference at all in his performance.

What was great about Piniella was he was so honest in his personal interactions with everyone that even a newspaper beat writer could experience a similar relationship with him that a Mariners player might have: 1) Question him in a persistent manner, and die in the face of his explosive temper; 2) suffer unexpected misfortune, and watch him intervene on your behalf, and 3) get involved in an inadvisable dust-up in his presence, and have his admiration forever. One *Seattle Post-Intelligencer* reporter — yes, it was me — weathered each of these changing seasons..

In Chicago, I dared to ask the manager after a doubleheader about his use of a sore-kneed Mike Blowers in leftfield, leading to a couple of errors, and it brought Piniella out of his chair, firing off expletives right and left and circling the room like an extremely agitated lion, abruptly ending the question-and-answer session for everyone.

In New York, I was seriously ill with the flu while gamely trying to do my job in the visiting clubhouse before a game at old Yankee Stadium. Piniella spotted me, led me into the team training room (resolutely off-limits for media members), and instructed the team doctors to administer me. "I'm so sorry you feel this way, son," Piniella said gently.

Finally in Baltimore, I was elbow to elbow with journalists in a tiny manager's office when I implored a local TV crew not to run over me while I was still scribbling down a Piniella quote. I got hit in the head by a camera. Out of anger I slammed a burly cameraman into a wall with a reactive forearm. Sheepishly, I looked up to find the Mariners manager smiling and quite entertained by the unexpected blow-up in front of him, which he spoke about on his pre-game radio show in an amused fashion for the next couple of days. Our working relationship thereafter was never better.

Piniella lasted 10 seasons in Seattle the second time before deciding his work was done, especially after his next-to-last Mariners team and the final postseason qualifier of his four won a rousing 116 games in 2001. He got tossed from games, made young pitchers uncomfortable and turned the franchise into a winner. He was inducted into the Mariners' Hall of Fame on Aug. 9, 2014.

The manager also came up with one more memorable show of theatrics. After his virtually unbeatable 2001 team dropped its first two playoff games to New York at home, an emotional Piniella was walking through the concourse when he suddenly wheeled on a large collection of reporters gathered outside the clubhouse door and shouted out a surprising guarantee. He promised that his team wouldn't be intimidated in the upcoming games at Yankee Stadium and would bring the series back to Seattle again. It was a nice try, but it didn't work. The Mariners were ousted in New York, done in five games.

The Florida native resigned a year later, leaving town with an 840-711 Mariners record, and he took over as manager of his hometown Tampa Bay Devil Rays and later the Chicago Cubs. In 2003, Piniella made an emotional return to Seattle, the place that had rejected him before fully embracing him. He greeted Mariners employees in and around the clubhouse. In his aqua Devil Rays uniform, he walked into a room jammed full of reporters waiting on him and quipped, "Are we in the playoffs or what?"

To chants of "Lou, Lou, Lou," Piniella took a sweeping bow once on the field. He drew big laughs when he accepted gifts from Mariners front-office staff, foremost an autographed first-base bag. He surprisingly struggled to keep his composure, fighting back tears instead of his quick-trigger temper, while telling the large crowd in all sincerity, "You made it a pleasure for me to come to the ballpark every day. I love you all and I'll never forget you."

That Pilots snub was long forgotten. ❖

JIM BOUTON
Seattle's Best-Selling Author

Jim Bouton was as unpredictable as the knuckleball that came dancing out of his hand. Bouton was not like most big-league baseball players. He spoke his mind. He questioned authority. He scribbled down notes on everything. He wrote a controversial best-seller based largely on a hapless Seattle Pilots team that no longer existed, coming up with what was widely considered the best sports book ever published and one that has had an extraordinary four decades of staying power and counting.

Bouton turned up in the Northwest in the summer of 1968 as this New York Yankees castoff, once a hard-throwing pitcher and World Series hero and now-damaged goods and a Pilots reclamation project. He was roster insurance for the upcoming expansion big-league team, acquired for cash and sent to the city ahead of nearly everyone else who would join the new franchise.

Bouton was put in the rotation of the Pacific Coast League's Seattle Angels, given an audition with a Triple-A franchise ready to disappear at season's end, and was asked to show what he had left. He took the opportunity to develop his knuckleball pitch, plus a literary side unmatched by any other Seattle athlete.

Cognizant his baseball career might be nearing an involuntary end, Bouton started jotting down daily entries about his experiences with the Angels. The year before, he wrote a well-received article for *Sport* magazine detailing his fall from Yankees prominence to the minors with the Triple-A Syracuse Chiefs of the International League. He was thinking about writing a book now.

New York Post sportswriter Leonard Shecter encouraged the effort, offered to help and put the pitcher in touch with his agent. Bouton received a $5,000 advance from a publisher for words and direction relatively unknown.

"The agent asked what were the odds of me making it back to the Majors?" Bouton said. "Shecter said it would be an interesting book, even if it was about the minor leagues. I had no idea about anything. The agreement was it was going to be a book about the minor leagues. The title was *Baseball Diary*."

What emerged instead was *Ball Four*, a surprisingly revealing inside look at the Pilots and big-league baseball. Bouton's opus, originally 371 pages and updated several times through the years, sold 4 million copies. It made him known more as a bold if not turncoat messenger who turned over sacred ground, rather than an accomplished pitcher who won 21 games in a season, was an All-Star selection and enjoyed World Series success. Bouton transformed a bumbling and short-term Pilots baseball team into poetic and endearing folklore.

His writing also gave the Massachusetts native a permanent bond with the Northwest city that supplied him with opportunity similar to drawing a winning lottery ticket. "I knew once the book came out I'd always have a connection to Seattle," Bouton said.

Using the 1969 baseball season as his guide, Bouton exposed teammates and opponents as real people, warts and all. He wrote of players' drug use and pettiness. He wrote of their quirkiness and voyeurism. He described Yankees icons Mickey Mantle and Whitey

"I was as surprised as anyone when the book came out," Sears said. "It was a mixture of truth and fiction."

Ford as something less than the baseball gods they were perceived to be by everyone else.

In diary format, Bouton chronicled his stay with the Pilots, a brief demotion to Triple-A Vancouver, his return to Seattle and his late-summer trade to the Houston Astros, this after summing up his time in New York. Not all of his Pilots exploits made the book.

"Bouton was a piece of work, a free spirit and there have been a lot worse guys in baseball than him," Pilots publicist Bill Sears said. "I had a good-looking secretary named Sharon and I couldn't keep Bouton out of my office. He really hounded her."

The book was excerpted by *Look Magazine* prior to the following season in 1970, making baseball purists uncomfortable at every level, and it was released in its entirety at midseason, creating a full-blown backlash for the journeyman pitcher.

"There were three months of pent-up anger," Bouton said. "The people most angry were sportswriters. They weren't on the bus. They weren't in the clubhouse. They didn't have access. They were telling players they should be pissed off at me. There was a lot of anger from people who didn't read the book."

"I was as surprised as anyone when the book came out," Sears said. "It was a mixture of truth and fiction."

An amazing thing about the best-seller was that the most damaging information collected was omitted on purpose. Bouton submitted more than 1,500 manuscript pages, which were pared to nearly a third of that. Blatant racist and sexual material was withheld.

"We felt there was a lot of stuff we didn't use and couldn't use because we didn't want to embarrass anyone," said Bouton, who kept all of his original notes. "This was not a tell-all book; it's a part-tell-all book."

Still, baseball players shunned him. Baseball commissioner Bowie Kuhn criticized Bouton. *New York Daily News* columnist Dick Young repeatedly attacked him in print. A New York Mets crowd booed him unmercifully, bringing his mother to tears at the ballpark, which was the low point.

Typical of the *Ball Four* reaction was that supplied by Dooley Womack, a pitcher who teamed with Bouton on the Yankees and was traded to the Pilots from Houston for Bouton. The South Carolinian was mocked early and late in the book. In 1970, Womack was playing for Triple-A Des Moines when he spotted the new author, who had been demoted to Oklahoma City, on the field doing a TV interview about *Ball Four*.

"I walked by and told him as they were interviewing him, 'Jim, you can take that book and stick it up your ass, page by page,' " Womack recalled. "I didn't care what he said about me. It didn't matter. You just don't cut down Mantle and Ford."

Womack pointed out that Bouton was not always the open-minded, fun-loving guy as portrayed in the book. He referred to a Bouton run-in with Frank Crosetti in New York, of how the pitcher only casually referenced an argument he had with the Yankees coach after getting spotted in the stands in street clothes during a doubleheader and told to put his uniform back on.

"Did he write that he threw his watch and shattered it into a million pieces? Did he write that he ripped his clothes off and started screaming? Did he write that he put a chokehold on Frank and [Yankees manager] Ralph Houk saw it and had to pull him off?" Womack pointed out. "I don't think so."

Discarded by the Yankees after seven seasons, Bouton joined the final Seattle Angels team at midseason in 1968. He appeared in 27 games, making eight starts, and was 4-7 with a 4.00 earned run average. Arm trouble had robbed him of his trademark fastball, one that had made his hat fall off in mid-delivery and contributed to his nickname "Bulldog." That summer allowed Bouton to perfect a knuckleball and rescue his career.

"In 1968, I roomed with Jim Bouton on the road and I can remember coming back to the hotel and he was writing things down in a notebook," said Ed Sukla, a fellow Seattle Angels pitcher and former big leaguer. "I said, 'What are you doing?' He said, 'I'm thinking of writing a book about baseball.' Jim was a good guy, real liberal, a real bright guy. I liked rooming with him and picking his brain about things."

As a non-roster player, a persistent Bouton earned a bullpen spot with the Pilots in spring training. Back in the big leagues, he appeared in 57 games for Seattle's expansion team and had a 2-1 record and 3.91 ERA, making him trade bait. On Aug. 26, 1969, Bouton was shipped to the Astros for Womack and minor-league pitcher Roric Harrison once the Pilots bottomed out, with the expansion team losing 10 games in a row amid news reports that manager Joe Schultz would be fired.

"I had made the remark that I wouldn't mind if we lost a game or two so I could get a chance to pitch," Womack said of his image with the pennant-contending Astros. "On the Houston TV news that night they said, 'The controversial Dooley Womack has been traded for the more controversial Jim Bouton.' I thought that was funny."

Not long after the book was published, with positive reviews now obscuring the baseball fallout, Bouton retired and became a New York TV sportscaster at WABC and WCBS. He also was an actor in the 1973 film "The Long Goodbye," plus appeared in the lead role as "Jim Barton" in a short-lived 1976 TV series called "Ball Four" patterned after the book.

Eight years between big-league appearances, he made a much-publicized comeback and briefly rejoined the Atlanta Braves as a relief pitcher in 1978. *Ball Four* only seemed to grow in popularity, becoming timeless. Because of the book, the Pilots were immortalized rather than forgotten. Gradually, players who had turned their backs on Bouton forgave him.

"Most of us read it in self-defense," former Pilots pitcher Bob Locker said. "It was an exposure that was going to happen. Most of it was true because Jim never got sued."

The biggest peace offering came in 2009 when Bouton and 10 other Pilots returned for a 40-year reunion hosted by people making a documentary film about the team. The players gathered at a suburban Bellevue hotel. They were treated to a Mariners-Kansas City Royals game that night and the then-70-year-old Bouton threw out the ceremonial first pitch.

"I didn't know if this would ever happen," Bouton told a room full of loyal Pilots fans. "I'll try to keep from crying if I can. It's a family reunion. These guys have been part of my life every single day. I have come to love these guys. I don't know how they feel about me. The great thing about the Pilots is there were no egos on that team. We had egos when we got to the big leagues. But by 1969, the egos had been pounded out of us."

The former Pilots reminisced, recounting a fake paternity suit, fake telegrams and real kissing on the bus, among other mayhem. As the *Ball Four* stories came tumbling out once more and were still provocative and funny, Bouton sat at one end of the front table and Womack on the other. Asked if they finally had become friends, Womack was honest about it: "I can take or leave him."

More surprising was the revelation by the man who was seated next to Womack, outfielder Steve Whitaker, a Bouton teammate with the Yankees and Pilots as well as a Tacoma native. He was not able to quote liberally from *Ball Four* and for good reason.

"I didn't read it, I never did," Whitaker said. "I might now." ❖

Top 10 Seattle Sports Books

1. *Ball Four* by Jim Bouton
2. *Boys in the Boat* by Daniel James Brown
3. *The Dave Kopay Story* by Dave Kopay
4. *Out of Left Field* by Art Thiel
5. *Hard Knox* by Bill Plaschke
6. *Pitchers of Beer* by Dan Raley
7. *What's Happenin?* by Blaine Johnson
8. *Bitter Roses* by Sam Farmer
9. *James* by Don James
10. *Bow Down to Washington* by Dick Rockne

HARVEY BLANKS

The Black Revolutionary

Harvey Blanks could put on a masterful performance. Radically different from any other University of Washington running back before him, he had dazzling 9.6-second speed in the 100-yard dash and all the open-field moves, and in 1967 he was advertised as the next big thing for Husky football. A theater major from Chicago, he was always on stage, compelled to do almost anything to get a reaction out of people.

Returning to school during the summer from the Midwest, Blanks was with UW football teammates Bob Burmeister, Creed Hubbard and Dennis Hurley on a Yellowstone Park stopover when he snuck up on a little black bear and got in a wrestling position with the startled animal, leaving his traveling companions laughing hysterically.

"I liked Harvey," former Huskies defensive end Mark Hannah said. "He was a showman. He was at his best with an audience. He loved to get up and tell jokes and be the center of attention. He was fun to be around."

Yet these were turbulent times on college campuses, with Vietnam War protests and civil rights demonstrations leaving everyone in a dark mood; Blanks was caught up in that, too. He was brash, confrontational and not the least bit concerned what anyone thought of him. Blanks chose to push a lot of buttons.

One day he fought with equally extroverted UW basketball player Dave Willenborg in front of the Husky

Union Building – and the two athletes considered themselves friends. However, no one felt more threatened by Blanks and his impertinent ways than Jim Owens, the Washington's rigidly old-school football coach. Blanks tried to fight him, too.

From the beginning, Blanks loudly questioned things that other African-American players had only whispered. Joining the Huskies a year after stalwart running back Donnie Moore was thrown off the team in 1966 for a trivial training infraction, Blanks helped organize secret meetings for black players to air their complaints.

Blanks was much more visible in his dissident ways when his thoughts and a pensive photo of him wearing a UW letter sweater appeared in the March 15, 1968, issue of *Life Magazine* that examined the growing unrest of African-American athletes nationwide. Owens felt compromised by the running back's actions. Blanks had moved past the point of no return in his crusade against the coach and his staff, and his actions would forever cast him as Seattle's most rebellious athlete.

"I loved the man when I first met him, his bigness, the grandness of the guy, the whole thing about him walking on water to work every morning, that whole myth," Blanks told the *Seattle Times*. "I've never said this to him, but [with] everybody I know, he had that

> Blanks had moved past the point of no return in his crusade against the coach and his staff, and his actions would forever cast him as Seattle's most rebellious athlete.

effect on the team. But he was just a racist and, to me, that's the tragedy of it."

The Huskies discovered the outspoken Blanks, whose given first name was Havard, at the Farragut School in suburban Chicago, a notable place that later produced NFL running backs Otis Armstrong and Mack Herron, and NBA forward Kevin Garnett. Blanks was stashed at Shoreline Community College to improve his grades, playing just one season for the north Seattle school that counted Jim Lambright as its football coach.

Blanks showed early on he was a magnet for controversy; he was in the middle of a nasty on-field brawl during a game at Shoreline Stadium that required police intervention and sent people to the hospital.

As a touted sophomore transfer for the Huskies, Blanks was kept under wraps much of his first season because of injuries. The next season in 1968, however, he provided glimpses of what he could do: He rushed for 121 yards against Rice in the opener, snapped off a 62-yard touchdown run against Idaho, and streaked 66 yards on a punt return for a score and 83 yards on a kickoff return without scoring against Wisconsin.

Washington sports publicists made plans to promote Blanks as an All-America candidate for his senior season,

> Blanks showed early on he was a magnet for controversy; he was in the middle of a nasty on-field brawl during a game at Shoreline Stadium that required police intervention and sent people to the hospital.

and the shifty tailback developed a following as word of his improvisational skills spread across the city.

"Harvey could do phenomenal things on a football field," said Terry Metcalf, then a standout Franklin High runner and future NFL Pro Bowl selection. "He inspired me to be a better football player."

Blanks' reputation as a trouble-maker was in full throttle, too. After meeting with Harry Edwards, a San Jose State professor and highly visible black activist, the animated Huskies running back and other African-American athletes presented UW administrators with a list of demands: 1) They asked for the formation of a four-man black athletic commission to settle racial differences; 2) the hiring of a black assistant coach; 3) the requirement that the coaching staff take sensitivity training, and 4) the immediate dismissal of white athletic trainer Bob Peterson for regularly using the "N" word.

With certain provisions, the four edicts were accepted by the UW. Other requirements, such as Owens publicly endorsing Muhammad Ali and the black boxer's anti-war stance, were rejected.

Blanks, who lived at 2271 Boylston Ave. E., never really got a chance to flourish for Washington on the football field after battling so hard away from it. During 1969 spring practice before his senior season, he broke his ankle in a gruesome manner when he was tackled hard by linebacker Clyde Werner, a future NFL player. The mishap only served to heighten Blanks' growing unhappiness and send the football team into an unprecedented funk, with the Huskies suffering through a miserable 1-9 season without him. "The injury to Harvey was so devastating it could destroy his soul," said Lee Brock, a black defensive end and team captain who died in 2009. "He used to rub that ankle all the time. I think he could have been as good as

anybody out there who ran the ball, including [all-time UW rusher] Napoleon Kaufman. He was that good, but his ankle snapped and he tore tendons. I'm sure that was part of Harvey's frustration – he would never be the same again."

The racial situation surrounding the UW football program reached a boiling point on Oct. 30, 1969, when Owens handed out midseason suspensions to defensive back Gregg Alex, wide receiver Ralph Bayard, defensive back Lamar Mills and the idle Blanks. Their crime was a failure to offer "100-percent program commitment" in one-on-one meetings with the head coach on the field.

Players had questioned Owens' excessive punishment of fullback Landy Harrell for fumbling twice against Oregon. Harrell ran stadium stairs during practice well after everyone else went to the locker room, spurring him to quit the team that night and transfer to Montana State.

Before the week was out, all 13 of the team's African-American players stayed home voluntarily or involuntarily in protest for a game at UCLA, which the Huskies lost 57-14, Owens' most embarrassing defeat to that point.

The four suspended players' names and faces were plastered across the front pages of Seattle's newspapers and the fallout was unsettling. Hearings were held and lawyers hired. UW faculty members considered conducting their own protest. Carver Gayton, the Huskies' newly hired African-American student assistant coach, quit. Fights between black and white students broke out during the next two games at Husky Stadium. Owens' oldest daughter, Kathy, was stopped in her car in north Seattle by four men, two black and two white, and had her hair pulled and was slapped in the face.

"My parents got threatening phone calls that said, 'Your son will be killed if he steps back on the field,' " Alex recalled. "I got a postcard in the athletic department from a guy who said he had a high-powered rifle and if I stepped back into Husky Stadium he would blow my head off. I'm trying to remember how he signed it – maybe 'A loyal Husky fan?' "

It took more than five weeks, but Owens, under upper-campus and community pressure, reinstated Bayard, Mills and Alex. Yet the coach refused to allow the injured and outspoken Blanks back on the team. Owens said the running back's suspension was irrevocable. The specific reason wasn't made public, but UW players said an out-of-control Blanks had a meltdown during a meeting, first demanding an apology from the coach in front of the team, and, receiving none, committing unforgivable insubordination.

"Harvey came down and cussed him out in front of the team and challenged him to a fight," Brock said disapprovingly. "I told him I would never let him back on my team. Harvey knows me well. I wouldn't take that [bleep]. You don't cross the line. I wasn't raised like that. It's about respect. You can't take this man's job. He's in charge of the team. You don't have to like it."

Blanks later confided to his fellow players, "I would have kicked myself off the team, too." He never played college football again, though he ultimately made peace with Owens, shaking his hand and being permitted to play in the UW's 1974 Alumni-Varsity spring game. He briefly ran the ball for the Steve Spurrier-coached Chicago Fire of the WFL and was cut in an NFL tryout with the Denver Broncos.

The Huskies' suspended black players were no outlaws. Bayard was hired as a UW assistant athletic director before leaving to run a Seattle-based charity foundation. Alex emerged as a Seattle street minister,

overseeing a center for the homeless before serving as the Huskies football chaplain. Mills became a Seattle defense attorney and married a judge. Blanks transformed himself into a successful actor, director and producer.

The Washington program ultimately reached the point where race was no longer a contentious issue, but great damage was done. Talented black players went elsewhere, scared off by the negative publicity. Metcalf, an NFL star in the making, grew up as a kid who wanted to play for the Huskies but ended up going to Long Beach State.

"I used to think about Bobby Moore, or Ahmad Rashad, and he could have been there if I had come there," Metcalf said. "Harvey would have been finishing up. There was a lot of potential talent the University of Washington could have had. It could have been a powerhouse team."

While his methods might have been contrived and over the top at times, Blanks was the central figure responsible for bringing about social change for UW athletes. He put his football career on the line to get players to question racial injustice. The status quo with Owens' program was no longer acceptable.

A year later the Huskies had a Native American player, Sonny Sixkiller, starting at quarterback. Six years later, under new coach Don James, the UW had a starting black quarterback, Warren Moon, who later took it to the Rose Bowl.

"Harvey changed us all," Brock said. "He deserves credit for that." ❖

10 Suspensions/Expulsions

1. **Harvey Blanks**
   (insubordination)
2. **Donnie Moore**
   (training rules)
3. **Peller Phillips**
   (point-shaving charge)
4. **Billy Joe Hobert**
   (improper loan)
5. **Charlie Williams**
   (point-shaving charge)
6. **Ralph Bayard**
   (insubordination)
7. **L.J. Wheeler**
   (point-shaving charge)
8. **Gregg Alex**
   (insubordination)
9. **Jesus Montero**
   (performance-enhancing drugs)
10. **Lamar Mills**
    (insubordination)

Seductive Seventies

Seattle overcomes decade-long economic despair by welcoming the relocation of a little New Mexico start-up, a software company called Microsoft, and the emergence of another novel concept, a locally branded coffee company named Starbucks.

The city pushes aside the bitter disappointment of losing its big-league baseball franchise to Milwaukee by welcoming another in the Mariners, adding an NFL team in the Seahawks and a pro soccer club in the Sounders, building the Kingdome and sharing in the Sonics' NBA championship.

SONNY SIXKILLER

Seattle's Sixth Sense

John Goodwin counsels Sonny Sixkiller.

Chartered buses pulled up outside Husky Stadium, doors opened and Michigan State football players piled out. Arriving for their 1970 season opener, the Spartans felt a sense of superiority as they sized up the situation before them. The Big Ten team had legendary Duffy Daugherty as its coach and future NFL standouts Billy Joe Dupree, Joe DeLamiellure and Brad Van Pelt on its roster.

These guys had traveled to Seattle for a rematch against a University of Washington team coming off its worst season in school history to that point – a 1-9 disaster that began with a season-opening 27-11 loss to Daughterty's previous team in East Lansing, Mich., and ended after African-American players leveled charges of racism against Jim Owens' coaching staff and walked out.

There was no reason for the Spartans to think this outcome or the UW's program harmony would be any different. As these confident Michigan State players made their way through a Hec Edmundson Pavilion corridor to the visitors' locker room, they passed by the Huskies' dressing area.

That moment alone should have alerted them that things had changed in a year's time. It was raucous and pulsating. Daugherty's players peered inside and saw sophomore quarterback Alex "Sonny" Sixkiller and his Washington teammates getting ready for the game in a spirited manner.

"Our doors were open and I remember them walking by and we had Jimi Hendrix and 'Purple Haze' turned up to about 10 in the locker room," Sixkiller said, referring to the Seattle rock god's anthem. "Guys were singing. Guys were dancing around. We were having fun. We had 'Purple Haze' as loud as you could play it. Those guys just walked by with blank stares."

It didn't stop with the pre-game taping and head-banging. Sixkiller was the self-appointed leader of the mayhem, soon to become a rock star in his own right, so cocky and self-assured that he couldn't contain his brashness. The UW's new quarterback threw out his first challenge that day way before he threw his first pass. He wasn't afraid of insulting a college football icon either.

"I remember standing on the field, looking at the sunshine and the lake, and Duffy Daugherty ran by in warm-ups with all that gray hair," Sixkiller said. "I said,

Sixkiller, a full-blooded Cherokee from Ashland, Ore., with the great arm and even better surname, was at the forefront of the resurgence. With school officials recognizing the publicity potential, the quarterback was encouraged to switch from a forgettable double-digit number he wore as a freshman to the obvious No. 6.

'Duffy, you're going down today, we're going to kick your butt.' Then I thought, 'Wow, what did I just say?' But that was my attitude back then."

On his first collegiate play, Sixkiller dropped back and rifled a 12-yard completion to senior tight end Ace Bulger. On his fourth play, the nimble 5-foot-11 quarterback set up and hit fellow sophomore Ira Hammon in full stride with a 59-yard touchdown strike, sending his team on its way to a stunning 42-16 rout of Michigan State — officially unveiling the most swash-buckling, risk-taking and entertaining period of Husky football, with a dashing Native American and promoter's dream leading the way into the revolutionary 1970s.

Sixkiller, a full-blooded Cherokee from Ashland, Ore., with the great arm and even better surname, was at the forefront of the resurgence. With school officials recognizing the publicity potential, the quarterback was encouraged to switch from a forgettable double-digit number he wore as a freshman to the obvious No. 6. Purple T-shirts with that favored digit became a hot-selling item in Seattle. Sixkiller had a song written about him. He landed on the cover of *Sports Illustrated*, *Boy's Life* and every college-football preview magazine. Overnight Sixkiller became Seattle's most-publicized and marketed college athlete — and he hated all of the adoring attention that came with it. Worst of all, he couldn't even order his own hamburgers at fast-food staple Dick's Drive-In.

"I had to sit in the car and slump down, and my buddies would get food for me and bring it back," Sixkiller said. "I would go out to dinner with my family, there were 14 of us, and my brother-in-law used to get really pissed off with people. The fans would just be nonstop. He would finally say to them to just leave me the [bleep] alone. It got to the point we didn't go out to dinner after the game. We just stayed in."

Sixkiller's Washington teams were serious contenders for a Rose Bowl trip each of his three years, but couldn't make it happen. Jim Plunkett's presence, a last-second missed field goal at Oregon and a Sixkiller knee injury were the primary obstacles.

These Huskies never played in the postseason at all because Pacific-8 teams, by arcane rule, either qualified for the New Year's Day game in Pasadena or stayed home, a league edict that wouldn't change until four years after Sixkiller was gone. They still won plenty of games — finishing 6-4, 8-3 and 8-3 — and piled up points in electrifying fashion. Even their mistakes were over the top.

Sixkiller threw 36 scoring passes in his career but he had 50 intercepted, four returned for touchdowns. Always looking for the upper hand, the Huskies had him attempt 10 two-point conversions and he was successful five times. UW teams in the Sixkiller era won eight games by a touchdown or less, but agonizingly lost five games by a six-pointer or less.

Offensive coordinator Jerry Cheek pushed the limits with his playmaking quarterback whenever he could, making the Huskies gamble incessantly. "We took a lot of risks," Sixkiller said. "We threw inside the 10. We threw from our own 1. It didn't matter to Jerry Cheek. He had confidence we could do it. We threw a lot of low-percentage passes."

Sixkiller entered his first spring football practice as the fourth-string quarterback on the depth chart, not yet a big-name player. Owens preferred to call him Alex rather than by his more familiar childhood nickname, which originated as "Sonny Boy" and was given to him by his grandmother.

Sixkiller made his move once veteran Steve Hanzlick skipped spring drills and played UW baseball, returning starter and fellow Ashland product Gene Willis injured

a knee in practice, and fellow sophomore Greg Collins broke his collarbone early in the spring game. "Collins was considered the better recruit," Sixkiller said. "He was Owens' favorite when he got up here." Left with the Huskies spring game all to himself, the little-known Sixkiller completed 24 of 50 passes for 389 yards, and the job was his.

After reawakening the football program with his three-TD-pass, 276-yard showing against Michigan State, Sixkiller was named *Associated Press* National Back of the Week, setting his instant celebrity in motion. He unloaded three TD passes in a tough 31-28 loss to California, with a potential game-winner dropped in the end zone. Sixkiller set school records by completing 30 of 57 passes for 341 yards in a 28-25 near-miss loss at USC, with the quarterback intercepted on the Trojans' 30 in the closing minutes. He threw six interceptions against Oregon State but led the Huskies to a 29-20 victory. With the Rose Bowl on the line, Sixkiller locked in a duel with the Heisman Trophy-winning Plunkett before Stanford University pulled out a 29-22 victory in a nationally-televised game. Sixkiller threw for 277 yards and three more TDs in a 61-20 blitzing of UCLA.

Teammates loved Sixkiller for his ever-present swagger and toughness. He had nine senior offensive

Pass-happy Sonny Sixkiller occasionally ran the ball.

starters surrounding him, but wasn't afraid to get in the face of any of the older guys in the huddle. He threw a tight spiral that hummed loudly as it zipped through the air. He had long black hair flowing out the back of his helmet. Sixkiller even suffered a concussion, possibly against California, but never left the field.

"I remember I played one game and literally looked to the sideline and the whole thing was a collage," he said. "The play came in, we ran the play, we scored and we got off. I don't remember any of it. I literally didn't remember any of that drive. I think back and it was, 'How did I do that?'"

As a junior in 1971, Sixkiller's team was Rose Bowl-worthy but lost three games by 16 points, including 23-21 to Oregon and 13-12 to USC. The Huskies missed a potential game-winning, 22-yard field goal with 24 seconds left against the Ducks, and were beaten by the Trojans' 28-yard field goal with 2:12 remaining. The season also served up Sixkiller's favorite football game, a wildly entertaining 38-35 victory over Purdue at home that was nationally televised. The Boilermakers built leads of 14-7, 21-17, 28-24 and 35-31. Sixkiller pulled it out with a brilliant five-play, 71-yard drive, hitting Tom Scott with a 33-yard TD pass with 2:35 left.

Sixkiller's senior year in 1972 was extra painful as he missed four and a half games with ankle and knee injuries. The Huskies were pegged as a top-10 team but couldn't hold it together. At midseason, they started four different quarterbacks in as many games: Sixkiller, Dennis Fitzpatrick, Collins and Mark Backman. The Huskies were 5-0 when they went to Stanford and lost 24-0. In the first quarter, Sixkiller suffered strained left-knee ligaments and left the game after a blitzing safety hit him on a screen play. Sixkiller returned in the third quarter and a lineman dove and hit him in the same knee as he planted on a pass; he wouldn't play again for a month.

He considered his final game, a 27-10 defeat to Washington State in Spokane, the most disappointing. The UW blew a 10-3 halftime lead. Cougars linebacker Gary Larsen repeatedly did a sack dance that mocked Sixkiller's Indian heritage. The Huskies lost all motivation.

"Half of the team was, 'Whatever, we're not going to a bowl game,'" Sixkiller said. "It was just crazy that we didn't go. It would have been nice to play in a bowl game for three years, for what it would have done for the guys on our team, for what it would have done for recruiting. It really would have defined our class. [Assistant coach] Bob Schloredt said, 'What bowl wouldn't want us to come and play?'"

Sixkiller didn't make it in the NFL; the Los Angeles Rams cut him in favor of Ron Jaworski. The CFL cut him, too. He played two seasons for the WFL's Hawaii Hawaiians before the league folded and he gave up the game. He was considered too short for a pro quarterback. He also admitted to playing more hurt than anyone knew.

"To be honest with you, I was able to hide a torn rotator cuff for my last two years of college football," Sixkiller said. "That was a problem. I still have it today. It was from landing on it in practice. I never really lost total velocity on it, though."

While publicity-shy in college, Sixkiller grew to accept and capitalize on his fame. He appeared in the original version of the football film "The Longest Yard." He became a TV and radio broadcaster for Huskies games. Sixkiller turned up as a TV pitchman for the 7 Cedars Casino and the neighboring Cedars at Dungeness Golf Course, both Native American-owned.

He owned a Laurelhurst house just two miles from Husky Stadium and his former glory. He worked for and promoted his alma mater, largely using his unforgettable name. He grew comfortable with his celebrity.

"I didn't want to be on the cover of *Sports Illustrated* but ended up being there," Sixkiller said. "Looking back, it was pretty cool." ❖

LARRY OWINGS
The Giant Killer

On a snowy night outside Chicago, Dan Gable lost. This was a breaking news bulletin everywhere. College wrestling wasn't that big with the American sporting public, but Gable was. He was unbeatable, dominant, a perfect athletic metaphor for his country as it asserted itself as a global power. He was a man the Russians referred to reverently as "The Machine." And Gable lost. In arguably the most meaningful amateur wrestling match ever held in the U.S., the sport took on biblical proportions in the truest sense on March 28, 1970, when this Midwest Goliath, in a garish burgundy and gold uniform, was toppled by a David impersonator from Seattle who wore sleek, black tights.

In the 142-pound finals of the NCAA Championships at Northwestern University's McGaw Hall, Gable of Iowa State stepped onto the mat with a 181-0 career record and was beaten 13-11 by Larry Owings, an Oregon teen-ager bravely competing for Washington.

This happened after Gable taped a commercial spot for ABC-TV "Wide World of Sports" 30 minutes before the match, imploring viewers to tune to the replay a week later. "They had me say, 'Come watch me next week finish my career 182-0,' " Gable said. "Obviously they couldn't use it." Beating the great Gable was the most gargantuan upset in Seattle athletic history and

> Beating the great Gable was the most gargantuan upset in Seattle athletic history and in any sport, and it was made possible by Owings, still the city's most celebrated underdog.

in any sport, and it was made possible by Owings, still the city's most celebrated underdog.

Before a crowd of 8,500 in a darkened arena, outside of a spotlight that was focused on the wrestlers, Owings scored three takedowns and four escapes. He used a fireman's carry, getting a shoulder under Gable, and next a double-arm bar, letting his shoulder go limp to free himself from Gable. Owings was the aggressor and built a 7-2 lead.

The great Gable admittedly felt tired and sluggish during the match, which was unusual. He remembers the crowd making gestures and getting on him. He twice lost contact lenses. He was called for stalling, another first. Gable still led 11-9 with 25 seconds left when he tried to put Owings away. But Owings escaped twice and made wrestling history. The roar in Evanston, Ill., was heard all the way to the Northwest.

"I beat him mentally, not physically," said Owings, who finished with a 33-1 record that year, 87-4 for his Washington career. "I didn't take that approach, it just happened."

Ken Kraft, Northwestern's senior athletic director and former wrestling coach, was on the sideline, working as a broadcaster for ABC. He saw a mat classic. He didn't want the upset to end.

"I wish it would have kept going and going," Kraft said. "It was so exciting and had so much drama. I

wanted it to last another 10 minutes. I knew what it meant. I think it had more impact on amateur wrestling than any other match in history."

Gable was in shock, tears streaming down his cheeks during the awards ceremony. Still, he received a four-minute ovation. The enormity of what happened didn't sink in until Gable saw headlines in the Iowa newspapers the next day: Iowa State won the team title but his loss was bigger news.

Five hundred cheering students greeted ISU's team when it returned to campus; they went dead silent when Gable emerged from a car. His mother called him repeatedly and he choked up every time; finally she drove out to see him. It took a few months for him to regroup. "I wasn't really the same person for quite a while," Gable said. "I'm still not. He put a big mark on my life."

How it happened went like this: Owings — as shy and introverted as Gable was bombastic and intimidating — shrewdly calculated his moves leading up to the 1970 NCAAs. He lost to Gable 13-4 as a high school wrestler at the Olympic Trials two years earlier and compulsively wanted another shot at him.

Owings won the Pacific-8 championship at 158 pounds, but dropped two weight classes specifically to face Gable. Similar to Gable, Owings went overboard when it came to conditioning. He ran three miles every morning around Husky Stadium and wrestled for two hours each afternoon in Edmundson Pavilion. He made Gable a target, rather than a concern, and it was no secret.

"I was interviewed by *Sports Illustrated* before the meet and [the reporter] asked me why I would be so stupid to cut weight and come down and meet Gable," Owings said. "I looked him right in the eye and said, 'I'm going to beat him.' I remember the guy. His jaw fell open. He was speechless."

Gable was floored when he heard this and started obsessing about Owings, watching his matches, wondering who he was. Owings obviously wasn't the same guy he had wrestled earlier. "He basically said he was going to whip me," Gable said. "When somebody is direct and bold like that, it diverts your attention. Nobody had said that to me before."

Owings, in pulling his pre-tourney macho act, said this, "I always had this thing that if someone had beaten me, I wanted a second chance."

That night shaped their lives forever, but not as one might have assumed. The setback drove the maniacal Gable to greater heights, assuring him legendary status as both wrestler and wrestling coach. Owings, however, peaked at Northwestern. He never wrestled internationally, made it to the Olympics or won another NCAA title, even when Washington hosted the wrestling championships during his senior year. Owings made his mark in wrestling history only with his dramatic upset of Gable.

For the longest time in Stillwater, Okla., a taped replay of the 1970 Owings-Gable match was one of the more popular displays at the Wrestling Hall of Fame. People came to see the fall of Goliath.

Gable returned to the mat with a fury, eventually winning a gold medal at the 1972 Olympics in Munich. He was so good he didn't give up a point. He thanked Owings for that motivation. They even met again on the mat, though much later than Gable envisioned. Seven months after the NCAAs, Gable thought he had a rematch lined up with Owings in the Midlands Tournament, also at Northwestern. Gable wanted it bad. But Owings got upset in an early round and Gable was incredulous.

"I was wrestling someone else and watching him wrestle at the same time," Gable said. "I won 10-2, but I gave up a lot of points watching him."

Two years later, Gable finally wrestled Owings again and won a lopsided decision. Both wrestlers turned to college coaching but went their separate ways. Owings spent several years molding wrestlers at Oregon's Clackamas Community College, enjoying modest success before becoming facilities director for the Molalla School District. Gable became a coaching icon at Iowa, bringing the Hawkeyes 15 NCAA wrestling titles in 21 seasons.

In the decades that passed, Gable and Owings had only a solitary conversation, briefly discussing a college recruit but not their 1970 match. These two, once so closely intertwined, needed distance not just to show proper respect but to exist. As they became middle-aged men, the wrestlers saw each other as larger than life, almost as spiritual influences.

"If I ever did sit down and talk with him and become close with him, it would take the edge off my life that I want there," Gable said. "It's an edge that keeps me going every day."

Two lives changed immeasurably on that snowy 1970 night in Illinois. Owings, who lived at 10745 Bartlett Ave. N.E., won the big prize but lost a few things in the process. Six years after the Gable upset, the Washington wrestling program was discontinued, a casualty of federal requirements that forced schools to offer women's sports on an equal basis and eliminate some men's athletic activities.

As satisfying as the outcome was at the time, Owings wasn't even sure the Gable victory was worth it. Along the way, he lost his identity.

"If I had known what was going to come, I don't know if I would have beat him or not," Owings said. "It was a culture shock going from underdog to a person everybody is shooting for. I went from nobody to celebrity. It was very difficult for me to adjust to. I dealt with criticism better." ❖

Tom Gorman was a dashing, curly-haired newcomer from Seattle when he played Wimbledon for the first time and became a Centre Court sensation. On June 28, 1971, Gorman shocked the world tennis establishment when he scored a 9-7, 8-6, 6-3 victory over Rod Laver, the tournament favorite, four-time champion and widely acknowledged as the greatest player on Earth.

On a windy yet magical afternoon in London, Gorman beat the best and drew raves that went global as he advanced to the semifinals. He seized upon this moment to remind himself exactly how far he'd come in an elite athletic endeavor that didn't let just anyone have his or her way.

"He was the Arnold Palmer of his sport," Gorman said of Laver. "I was just this kid from University Playfield."

Circling the globe for the next decade, Gorman became a pro tennis circuit fixture, winning seven singles titles and nine more in doubles. He also was the longest-serving American Davis Cup coach, bringing home a couple of world championships. He remains Seattle's greatest tennis figure, man or woman. And University Playfield made all of his dreams come true.

The well-worn playground, tucked in the shadows of the University of Washington, was Gorman's original testing ground. He lived in three childhood homes that surrounded it, the last at 5011 8th Ave. N.E. His older twin sisters, Celia and Shaughn, first discovered

> Circling the globe for the next decade, Gorman became a pro tennis circuit fixture, winning seven singles titles and nine more in doubles.

TOM GORMAN
The Racquet Man

the sporting paradise, which offered a well-worn baseball diamond and two tennis courts, and he followed them there.

Soon, a young Gorman from University Playfield was playing in city championship matches against kids from other playfields, these modest beginnings eventually bringing him a Seattle Tennis Club junior membership, a Seattle University scholarship and All-America billing, and finally his greatest tennis day at Wimbledon.

At a time when there were no tennis academies, Gorman was an aspiring player with exceptional court speed who needed extra time to develop the necessary shots to utilize it. Graduating from University Playfield, he left home and rode the 22 Roosevelt bus, changed to the 11 Madison bus, and arrived daily at 10 a.m. to use his newfound privileges at the exclusive Seattle Tennis Club, staying until he was shooed away at 4 p.m. He was fascinated by Ed Myerson, the Seattle Tennis Club pro, who drove a convertible, wore a wide-brim hat and dressed in fancy clothes — an image that always stayed with him.

As a Seattle Prep student, Gorman was never ranked higher than 31st nationally as a junior, which ruled out any chance of him playing for collegiate tennis powers USC and UCLA, who typically had their pick of the top 10. He realized he was better off becoming Seattle U's No. 1 player for three seasons.

"If I had gone to USC or UCLA, I would have been No. 5 or No. 6," Gorman said. "I don't know if I would have progressed. My three years at Seattle U were the best thing that could have happened to me. I was always the No. 1 player playing against the No. 1 player. I noticed a huge improvement during my college days. Most guys improve during their high school years. It just took me longer."

Graduating from Seattle U in 1968, Gorman considered pursuing business school, but tennis at its highest level underwent a timely and welcome change: It started offering prize money. He still had to prove he belonged and was capable of earning a check. The first time he faced Laver, Gorman was so nervous he was shaking and sweating. Yet he won a set from the imposing Australian player that day before losing the match.

"That meant more to me than any confidence-booster in my entire career," Gorman said. "It allowed me to understand the axiom that every time you walk on the court you have to be ready to win. It was not that I was better than Rod Laver, but I now believed on any given day that I could beat him."

A month and a half later in the London Grass Courts Championships, Gorman had his first break-through moment, upsetting the great Laver 6-4, 4-6, 6-1. Two weeks later at his first Wimbledon, Gorman did it again in the quarterfinals at that tennis Mecca, though hurting his back in the process and limiting his chances of beating Stan Smith in the semis and possibly winning it all.

"It was the best singles match I ever played," Gorman said of his Laver conquest at Centre Court. "If I don't win that earlier set, I don't know if I do that."

Establishing himself among the world best, Gorman proved to be the third-fastest player on the circuit. Only Romanian Ilie Nastase and Dutchman Tom Okker were speedier from baseline to frontcourt, leading to memorable battles.

Gorman lost his first 12 matches to Nastase, including the semifinals of the 1972 U.S Open and 1973 French Open, before beating him in four of their next five meetings. Gorman won the 1973 Swedish Indoors, besting Bjorn Borg in the finals. He never lost to Arthur Ashe. He never beat John McEnroe. He enjoyed steady doubles success with the aforementioned Smith, Erik van Dillen and Marty Riessen as partners.

The end came quick. Gorman was 34 when he abruptly retired in 1980, as certain that his 12-year career was over as he had been of its promising beginning. He was mentally worn out.

> "How I knew was I didn't want to go out and practice anymore," Gorman recounted. "I never had that feeling before."

"How I knew was I didn't want to go out and practice anymore," Gorman recounted. "I never had that feeling before. I played through the summer and I had to gut out matches. I went to Australia and in the first match, for the first three or four games, it was revealed to me that this was it. The feeling was relaxed. It was the only match I lost where I wasn't really upset. I shook hands, got on the plane and went back to the U.S. There were no second thoughts."

Gorman's tennis stature, however, brought him greater opportunity in the game. From 1986 to '93, he was the longest-serving U.S. Davis Cup captain, guiding the likes of Andre Agassi, Michael Chang, Jim Courier, Pete Sampras and McEnroe. Bringing out their best, Gorman was responsible for world championships in 1990 and '92.

"We created a generation of great American players," Gorman said. "We dominated like no other country ever had. I was always challenged to pick two of the four singles players. I would have to call up Pete and say, 'I can't pick you this week. I don't think you're good enough. I'm playing Andre Agassi.' I had to be forthright and completely honest with them. Ultimately, the biggest challenge was keeping them all happy. They weren't always happy. I know that because neither was I."

Gorman was next asked to lead some of the nation's most revered private tennis resorts in Atlanta and Palm Springs, Calif., teaching tennis to the next generation. Similar to that Seattle Tennis Club pro, he now drove a Mustang convertible, wore a wide-brim hat and dressed immaculately.

He could tell the aspiring players he encountered about the determined kid from University Playfield who went to Wimbledon and beat Rod Laver, and did it not just once but twice within two weeks, and returned home as a tennis hero in 1971, changing his life for good.

"When I got back to Seattle, I was put in a whole different perspective: 'Tom had made it,' " Gorman said. ❖

BOONE KIRKMAN
Seattle's Rocky Balboa

Every Tuesday and Thursday night a bell sounded inside Renton's Melrose Tavern, signaling "Happy Hour" like none offered at any other local drinking establishment. Heavyweight boxer Daniel Vincent "Boone" Kirkman, who only minutes before was filling up pitchers of beer, wiping off the bar and ringing up sales, emerged from a back storeroom dressed in boxing trunks and a T-shirt.

He was taped up by longtime handler Mario Guiang. As the regulars yelled out encouragement, Kirkman pounded away at a punching bag hanging in the middle of the crowded room. These workouts south of Seattle, meant to stir up new tavern business, supplemented the boxer's more conventional trips to the gym and proved challenging only when dealing with the lingering second-hand smoke and unrecognizable late-night arrivals.

"It was fun until about 11:30 when all the weirdoes started coming in," said Kirkman, co-owner of the popular beer hall with friend Jim Baggett.

Boone remains Seattle's most popular boxer, the city's own version of Rocky Balboa albeit without a title. The real-life heavyweight and fictional character

> Boone remains Seattle's most popular boxer, the city's own version of Rocky Balboa albeit without a title. The real-life heavyweight and fictional character were contemporaries.

were contemporaries. Kirkman's pro career ended in 1978, two years after the infamous "Rocky" fight film featuring Sylvester Stallone turned up on the big screen and won an Oscar for best motion picture. Both the fictional fighter and the real thing had huge followings and great storylines. In Kirkman's case, he was a guy who didn't stray far from his working-class neighborhood, which was populated with Boeing jet machinists and home to the now-defunct Longacres horse-racing track.

The Melrose occupied a 100-year-old building at 819 Houser Way S. in downtown Renton, just a few blocks from the home of Kirkman's parents. Future NFL offensive lineman Jim Skaggs lived next door to Boone and offered to wrestle the boxer but not trade punches. Kirkman's father, brother and sister all worked at the tavern, which was purchased with fight earnings.

A likeable and ruggedly handsome man, Kirkman used to walk outside his home during the day and yell, "Popsicles!" and a dozen kids would come running to get a frozen treat and a chance to brush up against their hero. Adults were drawn to him, too. For more than a decade, he filled the Seattle Center Coliseum with fans, often outdrawing the NBA Sonics with his headline events.

The city produced accomplished professional boxers in Al Hostak, Larry "Pat" McMurtry, Harry "The Kid"

Boone Kirkman is declared the winner over Charles Atlas.

Matthews and Eddie Cotton, all guys who could throw a punch, draw headlines and get the town excited, and Kirkman was the last of this popular breed. But none of them had the overall drawing power of Boone, and none could consistently sell tickets like he could.

"When I was fighting, I felt that way," Kirkman said. "I don't know how I compared to those older fighters, but there I was striving for the heavyweight title of the world and people could feel that in their heart."

Kirkman was 14 when he took up boxing after a few street scrapes, encouraged by his father, Oehm, a former University of Washington rower, and the Paul

Newman film "Somebody Up There Likes Me." He rode a bus every day to train at the Cherry Street Gym in downtown Seattle. He captured local Golden Gloves events throughout the region.

When he was 20, Kirkman won the heavyweight title at the 1965 AAU boxing championships in Toledo, Ohio, and became an overnight sensation. Everything about his trip to the Midwest endeared him to fight fans. He easily knocked out all three opponents. Offered a victory sip of champagne by his father, he didn't like it and ordered a milkshake.

Always humble, Kirkman said and did all the right things. He mentioned how the AAU trip would have been a huge thrill even had he lost. He spoke respectfully of meeting former ring greats Tony Zale and Archie Moore, and how Moore wrote the following inscription on a program for him: "Boone, you sure lowered the boom." Kirkman already was known as Boone, so nicknamed by his dad, after lagging behind him on hunting trips and drawing the gentle reminder, "Come on, Dan'l Boone. Keep up with me."

Kirkman climbed into the ring for 36 professional fights and won 30, 24 by knockout. Managed by the crusty and manipulative Jack Hurley, the boxer proved a steady money-maker at the Coliseum. He pulled in four home crowds of 10,000 or more, topped by the 13,711 who showed up for his victorious rematch with Doug Jones, the first man to beat him.

He had one shot at making it big but it ended disastrously. On Nov. 18, 1970, he faced heavyweight contender George Foreman at New York's Madison Square Garden. With 18,036 at ringside and a nation-wide closed-circuit TV audience looking on, Kirkman was dropped to the canvas by a second-round knockout, an outcome eerily similar to Kid Matthews' defeat to Rocky Marciano 18 years earlier in the same city.

Kirkman was shoved hard on their first exchange and things got progressively worse. The nice kid from Seattle was taken out by a street brawler with a rough edge about him. "When I fought him, nobody liked him," Kirkman said of Foreman. "He was unlikable. He was a mean guy. With religion, he's now one of the nicest guys you'd ever want to meet."

Kirkman's career was stymied by a number of factors, though it was hard to tell which one affected him most. He broke his collarbone as a kid and fractured it at least four more times as a boxer. He was considered a "Great White Hope," joining an unofficial fraternity of fighters that included Jerry Quarry and Gerry Cooney, boxers who wore that politically incorrect label and never rose above challenger status.

It was no secret that Hurley and Kirkman were not an ideal pairing. They argued over training methods, sparring partners and money. Kirkman wanted to do three to six miles of roadwork; Hurley limited him to two. Kirkman was offered three different sparring partners in New York and his manager rejected each one. Hurley was a notoriously cheap man who once hired someone with bruised ribs for sparring purposes while instructing Kirkman to throw only high punches.

Then there was the matter of gate receipts. The aging Hurley demanded a 50-50 split, whereas most managers asked for 33 percent. Kirkman received far less than half of the $80,000 take from the Foreman fight and pocketed just $2,500 from the closed-circuit TV revenues. They parted ways after the New York fight, primarily over money, and never patched up their differences. Hurley died less than two years later in 1972.

"I forgave him," Kirkman said. "I think he ripped me off for a little money but it was just a sport. Money means nothing anymore. Health is more important to me. Hurley was one of the best promoters and he taught me a lot. He taught me how to punch harder."

Kirkman's ultimate dream was to fight Muhammad Ali, with Joe Frazier a close second. A Kirkman-Frazier bout briefly was a possibility. Frazier even walked into the Melrose Tavern one night for a friendly, unannounced visit. Kirkman had to settle for Ali-beater Ken Norton and lost to him in an eighth-round knockout in Seattle on June 25, 1974. If there was any consolation to the Norton defeat, Kirkman sensed a great uneasiness coming from his higher-ranked opponent early in that fight.

"He was scared of me, I swear to God," Kirkman said. "He looked over to his corner and didn't know what to do. But I over-trained for the Norton fight and I ran out of gas and he saw that. He hit me with a punch that, if normally in shape, I would have been able to take it. He was too cocky for me. His head blew up after he beat Ali."

Kirkman's highest ring ranking was seventh, achieved twice. He never got his title fight and never had his shot at Ali, but Kirkman did a smart thing: He got out of his sport intact. He retired in 1978, walking away after four consecutive victories with a good feeling. His time had come and gone.

"Boone just wasn't in the right place at the right time," said McMurtry, a former heavyweight who often refereed Kirkman's fights. "It's all politics. 'You have to have everything going for you. Boone was a crowd-pleaser and that's what they liked. He drew real well. He was good for boxing.' "

Outside of an aching collarbone, Kirkman left the fight game in fairly good condition. He lost hearing in his right ear but chalked that up to an acoustic tumor that wasn't boxing-related. He had cataract surgery but that was from the normal aging process. If there was fight residue, he tore an Achilles tendon in the ring and had surgery. Yet Kirkman stayed healthy enough to later climb each of the region's most prominent mountain peaks, including Mount Rainier several times.

To earn a living and land a second career, Kirkman became a Boeing truck driver, working side by side with several members of his once loyal constituency, delivering loads sometimes before the sun came up.

As for the Melrose Tavern, he sold it long ago. The place became a steakhouse, at one time employing Kirkman's niece as a waitress, though it wasn't nearly as fun and boisterous as it once was with a heavyweight fighter serving drinks one moment and pounding a punching bag the next. ❖

> Kirkman's ultimate dream was to fight Muhammad Ali, with Joe Frazier a close second. A Kirkman-Frazier bout briefly was a possibility.

Top 10 Seattle Boxers

1. Boone Kirkman
2. Al Hostak
3. Kid Matthews
4. Eddie Cotton
5. Greg Haugen
6. Ibar Arrington
7. Robert Shannon
8. Pat McMurtry
9. Pete Rademacher
10. Fraser Scott

SPENCER HAYWOOD

The Rulebook Exception

This new-age player was a pro-sports pioneer, the early-entry guy who challenged and successfully changed the hard-and-fast rules preventing college underclassmen from entering the NBA, and later the NFL, before four years of scholastic eligibility were used up.

Haywood confers with Bill Russell.

Spencer Haywood drove around Seattle in a Cadillac with a Rolls-Royce grille and leather top that caused him more grief than admiration. He wore outlandish clothes, his personal favorite a three-piece, powder-blue suit, leaving him with an image more Superfly than SuperSonic. On the way to the airport in those look-at-me wheels and threads, the flamboyant NBA player was pulled over by police and asked if he was a pimp — and detained long enough that he missed the team flight.

Seattle basketball fans knew Haywood as a man with extraordinary gifts, an All-Star Game selection multiple times, someone with style. He also was a reckless cocaine user, someone who stunted his NBA career with drugs after fighting so hard for it with a cauldron of attorneys, all of which he described in great detail in his authorized biography, *Spencer Haywood, the Rise, the Fall, the Recovery.*

What others or even his book failed to address in a profound manner was this: This new-age player was a pro-sports pioneer, the early-entry guy who challenged and successfully changed the hard-and-fast rules preventing college underclassmen from entering the NBA, and later the NFL, before four years of scholastic eligibility were used up. Haywood was Seattle's ultimate rule-breaker.

Haywood pulled on a Sonics uniform for the first time Dec. 30, 1970, though he was limited to warm-up shots for a game against the Chicago Bulls at the Seattle Center Coliseum. He received a thunderous ovation simply for taking a seat on the bench that night.

By conventional means, he should have been a senior at the University of Detroit or, had he not encountered trouble passing the school's entrance requirements, would have been in his final season at Tennessee as the Southeastern Conference's first black basketball player.

Haywood arrived in Seattle after spending a throwaway season at Colorado's Trinity State Junior College and coming up with a first-team *Associated Press* All-America season for Detroit. He jumped early to the ABA's Denver Rockets to dominate the new pro basketball league for a season.

Brazen Sonics owner Sam Schulman feverishly pursued Haywood, a sleek, high-scoring forward who refused to play a second year in the ABA and was a determined contract holdout. Schulman chose creative means to restock his Seattle roster after he lost fan favorite Bob Rule, his starting post player, to a career-changing Achilles heel injury just four games into the season and deemed Pete Cross, a veteran backup center, an inadequate full-time replacement.

Everyone in the league except the Phoenix Suns condemned the Sonics' pursuit of Haywood, though nine of the 17 NBA teams in operation tried to sign the player who could jump and touch the top of the backboard. Schulman got what the others wanted by promising to pay all of Haywood's legal bills and push the case all the way to the U.S. Supreme Court if necessary.

"I could have gone straight to the Lakers," Haywood said. "I could have signed with the Lakers, but I chose Seattle because of Sam Schulman and the sales pitch he gave me. Also, my brother Joe had come here to go to Vietnam. He said, 'If you ever want to go to a place with no racism, this is it.' I said there was no such place. He said Seattle was that place. He was right. Who wouldn't have wanted to come here?"

Haywood had done unconventional things before. While others such as UCLA's Lew Alcindor and Lucius Allen gave in to racial pressures and boycotted the 1968 Olympics in Mexico City, Haywood made himself a household basketball name by stepping up and leading the U.S. team to a gold medal. Just 19 and the youngest to make an American roster, he shot a record 71.9 percent from the field while averaging a team-best 16.1 points per game.

Coming off considerable Olympic momentum, Haywood played one season of Division I college basketball for hometown Detroit, averaging 32.1 ppg

Spencer Haywood powers his way to the basket.

and a nation-leading 21.5 rebounds. He was voted to an *AP* All-America team alongside LSU's Pete Maravich, Niagara's Calvin Murphy, Purdue's Rick Mount and Alcindor.

The NBA wouldn't welcome him until he was four years removed from high school, so Haywood signed a six-year, $1.9 million deal with the ABA's Rockets. The players in the fledgling league were no match. He averaged 30 points and 19.5 rebounds an outing and simultaneously was named Most Valuable Player and Rookie of the Year. There was only one place to go now.

To obtain Haywood's NBA rights, Schulman forked over $500,000 in legal fees and another $200,000 in league fines after signing the player to a six-year, $1.5 million contract. A federal case in Los Angeles challenged the league's antitrust protection and lasted three months before it was settled out of court after the season ended; the Supreme Court provided the Sonics and their forward a favorable ruling.

Another lawsuit, brought on by the renamed Denver Nuggets claiming breach of contract by Haywood, hung over his head. He played on and off between courtroom appearances. He was welcomed enthusiastically in Seattle but was scorned and mistreated everywhere else. Opposing crowds booed him. Opposing teams played against him under protest. Opposing players ignored or hurt him. Schulman reported receiving a death threat. Owners briefly hinted at expelling the Sonics from the league.

"I was tearing down a college bedrock rule," Haywood said "I was tearing up basketball as they knew it. I was the enemy of the state."

Fans who encountered him were equally hostile. Coming out of a Washington, D.C., hotel one night, Haywood was approached by a man requesting an autograph. After signing, Haywood was punched in the stomach by the stranger, called the N-word, and goaded to fight back, with another man holding up a camera, apparently ready to document this outlaw player involved in a scrape. Haywood wisely retreated. Veteran NBA players were no friendlier. They viewed Haywood and his radical youth movement as a threat to job security across the league when he joined the Sonics. They hit him every chance they could on the floor. They clothes-lined him coming off picks or shoved elbows into his midsection in the paint, letting him know he wasn't welcome. They knocked out his teeth. They were protected, too.

"They tried to break my spirit," Haywood said. "There were times I was brutally beaten. The referees didn't call the flagrant stuff on those players because they thought they were doing the league a favor."

Haywood played 21 games during the 1970-71 season for the Sonics after a Los Angeles district court judge in January issued a temporary restraining order. The forward sat down when a California appeals court in February overturned the ruling. The case next went to the Supreme Court and was overturned again when Justice William O. Douglas, a Yakima native, signed an order allowing Haywood to return to action. The NBA appealed Douglas's decision, which the Supreme Court denied.

Haywood won his case against the NBA when the courts determined that the four-year draft rule violated the Sherman Antitrust Act and players had the freedom to turn pro early. In 1971, the NBA instituted a hardship rule that allowed underclassmen who could "prove need" to become draft eligible. The NFL braced for the pro basketball fallout and, within three years, college football players started leaving school early, too.

"Do you know how many guys like myself capitalized on millions of dollars by him breaking that rule?" Sonics forward Shawn Kemp asked. "He created an opportunity for all of us in a lot of sports."

Haywood spent five years in Seattle and the points flowed freely as he averaged 20.6, 26.2, 29.2, 23.5 and 22.4 per game. On Jan. 4, 1973, he scored 51 points against the Kansas City-Omaha Kings, establishing a club record that later was surpassed. He was an All-Star selection four times for Seattle. He helped the Sonics secure their first playoff appearance in 1975. He made the Sonics the league's third-best attendance draw behind the Los Angeles Lakers and New York Knicks.

He was everything except the ultimate franchise savior. His one-on-one style was not conducive to championship chemistry. Haywood was at his best only for a couple of seasons. In 1972, he injured his right knee and suffered permanent damage when he slipped and fell on a wet floor in the 10-year-old Seattle Coliseum, ending his season. The roof leaked. During the game, five kids scurried around with towels and valiantly tried to keep the floor dry. Haywood sued the city of Seattle, NBA and league commissioner Walter Kennedy, and the Sonics also sued the city. Settlements were negotiated.

Adding to his discomfort, Haywood encountered someone with a bigger ego than him: Sonics coach Bill Russell. The forward no longer was the center of attention under the Hall of Fame player's direction, speeding his departure. Haywood became the first pro athlete in Seattle to build a house, a sprawling waterfront residence in Leschi at 830 Lakeside Ave. S., and soon he had to part with it. Haywood publicly blistered the Sonics, fans and media after his trade on the eve of the 1975-76 season to the New York Knicks for forward Eugene Short and a first-round draft pick.

"Russell called me in and spoke to me and asked me if I would let this trade take place," Haywood said. "My pride was hurt, that they would ever bring it up in the first place. Why would I want to leave Seattle? It was like my mother kicking me out of the house."

New York wasn't his best career move. He met supermodel Iman and married her, and Alcindor – now Kareem Abdul-Jabbar – served as his best man. He became a jet-setter and got involved in the fashion scene. He was introduced to cocaine, which was ingrained in the sports and fashion worlds that now claimed him. It took him three years to get clean again. He admitted his problem to the Lakers, who suspended him two games before entering the NBA Finals without him. "Eighty percent of the players in the league were users, not to indict anyone," Haywood said. "I was just made an example. I was guilty of it."

His game suffered as he became a journeyman, never again the explosive, dominant superstar he once was in Seattle. He retired in 1983 after being waived by the Washington Bullets. In 2007, Haywood made a triumphant return to Seattle after a long estrangement. His No. 24 was retired.

Haywood became a far less flamboyant middle-aged man, almost professorial in appearance with wire-rimmed glasses, a gentle nature and healthy habits. In assessing his basketball career, he came up with the following determination: He preferred to be known as an NBA pioneer, rather than the sometimes self-centered and drug-addled player that he had been labeled. He became the first player to buck an antiquated pro rule and he wanted to be recognized for it.

"I don't want people to think I went through it just to make money, for the teams to make money, for the owners to make money," Haywood said. "It was deeper than that. I was the guy who broke the four-year rule. It wasn't a joke what I did. I tell the young guys, 'I'm Spencer Haywood, I went to the Supreme Court.' " ❖

Billy North was a big-league baseball player raised in Seattle, not the heavyweight champion of the world. Yet this feisty centerfielder, a free-swinging member in more ways than one for the Oakland Athletics dynasty teams and others of the 1970s, somehow hit baseballs and punched people simultaneously, and turned it into a lasting career. For 11 seasons, he mixed innings and rounds together. He had backbone, a temper and a memory.

In 1973, North put all of those attributes on display when newly called-up Kansas City relief pitcher Doug Bird entered a game late at the Oakland Coliseum. After telling A's teammate Darold Knowles to "Watch this," North stepped in against Bird, took a slider down and in, and let go of his bat, sailing it out to the shortstop, and then he made his move.

"The bat was over there and I'm walking straight to the mound," North said. "I said, 'I remember you!' He started to open his mouth and I hit him above the eye, three punches in the head, before he hit the ground. Of course, I got thrown out of the game."

> North, who played for
> four big-league teams,
> appeared in two World Series
> and won a pair of
> American League stolen-base
> titles, ranks as Seattle's most
> hot-tempered, high-profile
> athlete, a label built on a
> half-dozen, big-league brawls.

North rather emphatically had settled a score from 1970, when, as a player for Single-A Quincy, he took a purpose pitch in the ear from Bird, landing him in a Waterloo, Iowa, hospital for three days. North's mistake was following two batters who had homered off Bird and he paid for their success.

By exacting revenge North drew an ejection, a three-game suspension and $100 fine. He also had to explain the situation to Dick Williams, Oakland's equally combative yet momentarily mystified manager.

"What was that all about?"

"Skip, he hit me in the head three years ago and I said when I saw him again I was going to beat him within an inch of his life."

"Don't ever do that again in one of my ball games; I'd rather you go to his room and beat him up."

"Skip, if I did that, it would be premeditated murder."

North, who played for four big-league teams, appeared in two World Series and won a pair of American League stolen-base titles, ranks as Seattle's most hot-tempered, high-profile athlete, a label built on a half-dozen, big-league brawls.

His most famous squabble came in 1974 when Reggie Jackson and North suddenly started fighting in the clubhouse in Detroit, were separated and fought some more. Both Oakland players could grate on each

North wanted to be a pro baseball player once he watched the Milwaukee Braves and New York Yankees split the 1957 and 1958 World Series on TV.

other's nerves and they had chirped at each other until punches were the last resort. Although neither player was ever willing to lay out the specifics for that particular outburst, Jackson previously dressed down North in front of the team for not running out a play; in return, North gave the slugger the silent treatment for weeks, even refusing to congratulate him after hitting home runs. Things seemed to escalate from there.

"You could say it was that, but there was more to it than that," North said, still unwilling to share the whole story.

North was declared a unanimous winner, mostly for fearlessly taking on one of baseball's biggest egos. The Royals' Amos Otis, John Mayberry and Hal McRae were among those who counted themselves among the judges for the heavyweight bout. They mischievously left a blown-up photo of George Foreman standing victorious over a fallen Joe Frazier in the visitors' clubhouse the next time the A's visited Kansas City, with North's name written over Foreman's image.

"To this day, I know Reggie and he's an acquired taste," North said of the Hall of Fame slugger known as "Mr. October." "I liked him. Reggie was an extremely intelligent person but insecure like the rest of us. Sometimes you wanted to deal with him and sometimes you didn't. There were things that happened and some things that needed to be straightened out. The guys on

my team didn't like him. It was the kind of thing where they wanted to see it happen. I won."

North grew up as an innocent kid at 811 13th Avenue, a block from the Seattle University campus. The Langendorf Bread bakery was across the street, the Coca-Cola and Canada Dry bottling plants nearby.

North wanted to be a pro baseball player once he watched the Milwaukee Braves and New York Yankees split the 1957 and 1958 World Series on TV; Hank Aaron and Mickey Mantle became his favorite players. North earned money picking beans in the morning in order to buy a ticket that night to the Triple-A Seattle Rainiers game and catch a glimpse of pro baseball up close. He also played for Broadway Kiwanis Little League teams that were coached by Booth Gardner, future Washington governor and an altruistic man. "He was always the third- or fourth- or fifth-best player, never the best," Gardner said of North. "I was really glad to see him make it to Oakland." Gardner drove the players to games in his yellow '57 Chevy Bel Air station wagon and took them out for hamburgers and milkshakes afterward at Gill's Drive-in in a post-game ritual. North considered Gov. Gardner a lifetime mentor. "What he did, he didn't have to do, and he did it all the way," North said. "I've still got a picture of our Little League team."

Gardner didn't teach him how to fight. North learned that from his two older step-brothers, Butch and Woodson Williams. They were tough guys. They took him around, matched him up against others in Seattle's Central District and goaded Billy into defending himself. When he followed his siblings to Garfield High, North still wasn't a polished baseball player but he had plenty of attitude thanks to his upbringing.

It took him to Central Washington State College, where North started out as a basketball player but

ended up as one of the top baseball prospects in the country, still abrasive yet now fully physically developed. He hit .476 as a junior and was drafted by the Chicago Cubs. He also pummeled a Gonzaga runner who purposely spiked one of his teammates. As for his ever-present anger, he always felt it was properly channeled.

"It wasn't so much rage as it was intensity," North said. "I didn't like to be beaten. Between me and the pitcher was always a fight. These kids today sometimes don't realize the opportunity they have. I still have dreams about baseball. The game was there before you got there and is going to be there when you're gone. Don't cheat yourself. And if you don't want a ring more than money you're not much of a player."

North came up to the majors with the Cubs, but he wasn't a good fit until he was traded to the A's for Bob Locker. North blended in well with Oakland's other tough guys, among them Sal Bando, Joe Rudi and Don Baylor. Williams loved North's surliness and stuck him in centerfield and encouraged him to run at will, and the Seattle speedster didn't stop until he had 395 career steals. North stole 45 bases or more five times, topped by 75 in 1976, which was the most in the A.L. since another testy player, Ty Cobb, had 96 in 1915. North understood what his presence meant to Oakland.

"When I was at first base, now you're in my ballpark," North said. "I can take two steps to second base and the pitcher ducks, the catcher comes out, the shortstop and the second baseman come across, and the centerfielder comes up. If I took two steps, all those things happened and they couldn't stop me anyway. Being a base-stealer, I likened the lineup to a car. Bando, Rudi and Reggie drove the car. The car wasn't going anywhere until I turned it on. That was my job."

North was always an agitator, if not the ignition, whether defending someone's honor or swiping bases, and it contributed to a lot of winning. He played in the World Series twice and it should have been three times. In 1973, he injured an ankle late that season that forced him to watch the A's beat the New York Mets in six games.

The following year, he shared in Oakland's five-game victory over the Los Angeles Dodgers. North was the last man stripped from the A's roster when owner Charlie O. Finley arbitrarily decided to discard his talent pool, and North's next World Series trip came in 1978 with the Dodgers, who lost in six games to the Yankees.

North, who retired and returned to his hometown as a financial advisor, wasn't sure that Seattle knew or appreciated what he did in his big-league career. It's possible he made his hometown squeamish. After all, who gets in Reggie Jackson's face? Who cold-cocks a rookie pitcher without any warning?

By his count, North was beaned six times as a pro player and he determined that only Doug Bird did it maliciously, and he got even — more than once actually. After decking the Kansas City relief pitcher, this baseball bad man from Seattle issued the following public edict: He would level Bird again if the right-hander threw inside on him in the future. Intimidation was a great tool for those who knew how to use it. North faced Bird eight more times that season, and came away with five hits and three walks.

"That's how crazy I was," North said. ❖

> North, who retired and returned to his hometown as a financial advisor, wasn't sure that Seattle knew or appreciated what he did in his big-league career.

10 GHS ALUMS TO PROS

1. Brandon Roy (NBA)
2. Bill North (MLB)
3. Jeff Heath (MLB)
4. Tony Wroten (NBA)
5. Charlie Mitchell (NFL)
6. Anthony Allen (NFL)
7. Eric Wilkins (MLB)
8. Johnny Taylor (NFL)
9. Will Conroy (NBA)
10. Joe Staton (MLB)

FRED BROWN
The Downtown Ordinance

For two NBA seasons he was just Fred Brown, nothing more. He had no urban-redevelopment label or lyrical basketball address, just a mesmerizing jump shot that hadn't been fully removed from its holster. He also carried a few too many pounds, which caused him to spend most of his rookie season watching from the bench when he joined the Seattle SuperSonics for the 1971-72 season.

Brown wasn't properly christened until a couple of kids approached him following a game at the Seattle Center Coliseum, after he had enjoyed a particularly hot shooting night from long range. They asked for his autograph, requesting a slight alteration to his signature in the process.

"They wanted me to sign it 'Downtown' and I asked them why?" Brown recounted. "They said I was shooting from downtown that night, not the Space Needle. The next thing I know when I was in a gym, when I hit a shot from afar, everyone said, 'Downtown.' It was a nickname that kind of became synonymous with what you do."

Downtown Freddie Brown was hatched. The new-found tag quickly grew legs because *Sports Illustrated's* Curry Kirkpatrick was present when Brown was approached by the creative autograph-seekers and later referenced it in his writings. Brent Musberger, calling NBA games for CBS-TV, soon used it on the air whenever he could and Sonics radio broadcaster Bob Blackburn

Brown, a Milwaukee native who played two seasons for the University of Iowa, previously was known as "Machine Gun" or "Freaky Freddie," hardly keepers. He joked that he was earlier identified as "Crosstown" or "Uptown," and just moved up to a better neighborhood.

eventually piped in, as well. It was now a permanent part of the NBA lexicon.

Brown, a Milwaukee native who played two seasons for the University of Iowa, previously was known as "Machine Gun" or "Freaky Freddie," hardly keepers. He joked that he was earlier identified as "Crosstown" or "Uptown," and just moved up to a better neighborhood.

"You had nicknames that were sort of catchy, like Dr. J and Ice, and so forth and so forth," Brown said, referring to labels fastened to NBA contemporaries Julius Erving and George Gervin, respectively. "'Downtown' had this beautiful ring to it. I never turned it away."

He never turned his back on an open shot either. In a 13-year career, spent exclusively in Seattle, he piled up 14,018 career points, second in franchise history only to Gary Payton (18,207). Brown scored a Sonics record 58 points against the Golden State Warriors in a 1974 road game, the same season he was christened.

Brown became arguably Seattle's greatest reserve player in any sport, coming off the bench for nine seasons. Starter or sub, he also was one of the NBA's finest shooters. His touch was comparable to that of Reggie Miller, Larry Bird, Chris Mullin, and onetime Sonic guard Ray Allen. Brown had a natural gift.

"His jump shot was so pure and he had great range," former Sonics general manager Bob Houbregs said of Brown. "Off the dribble he would get into you a little bit and not hit you, but go up and have great accuracy on the ball. When it went down, it went down fast."

Sonics center Jack Sikma noted that Brown's outside game helped make him far more effective inside, saying, "He was one of the best pure shooters the game has ever seen. With the balance and rotation of his shot, he could drain it any distance, use the backboard. It was unique."

Brown was the sixth player taken in the 1971 draft by Seattle on the advice of scout Henry Akin, a center who had played on the Sonics' expansion team, and at the insistence of Houbregs. They were enamored with Brown's passing and shooting, and envisioned him eventually replacing point guard Lenny Wilkens. However, Brown played in only 33 games that first season, sporting his puffy body and unable to entice the aging but stubborn Wilkens to give up any meaningful playing time.

An impatient Brown finally had his agent write a letter to the Sonics, voicing his displeasure over his lack of playing time. The front-office guys got the message: On the eve of the 1972-73 season, they traded Wilkens to the Cleveland Cavaliers, mainly to get Brown more involved on the floor. The young guard also slimmed down noticeably, finally embracing better conditioning.

"Somehow he realized the problem and lost a ton of weight, which made him quicker and much faster,"

said former Sonics forward Zaid Abdul-Aziz, a big influence in prodding Brown to become more fit.

With added game minutes, a deadly shot and a catchy nickname, Brown developed a huge Seattle fan following, which proved both flattering and embarrassing at times. The latter was true the night he sat on the bench during the 1973-74 season and the Coliseum crowd started to chant, "We want Fred! We want Fred!" and new Sonics coach Bill Russell called for him. Brown, expecting to enter the game, peeled off his warm-ups and stopped at the coach's feet for instructions.

"He was sitting down, in Bill Russell style, and he said, 'Hey Fred, see all those people saying we want Fred? Why don't you go up there and see what they want?' Then he started laughing," Brown said. "I was looking at him and I thought, 'This man is crazy.' "

Brown unloaded his 58 points on a Rick Barry-led Warriors team on March 23, 1974, in Oakland. There was more to it than a scoring outburst. At the buzzer, Brown sank a twisting, turnaround 20-foot bank shot for the deciding points in a 139-137 victory, a difficult offensive maneuver that left him seated on the floor. Brown drained 24 of 37 shots (with an NBA 3-point line still six seasons away) and 10 of 13 free throws to ring up his points, which were 20 more than his previous career high.

"I got to watch Freddie come off my picks and swish 45-foot jumpers, some leaning, others not," said former Sonics forward Vester Marshall, exaggerating the moment some.

Brown was an All-Star selection during the 1975-76 season, but the following year he was a reserve — at his request. The Sonics, with a surplus of young players and yet another new coach, got off to a horrible 5-17 start and fired Bob Hopkins, Russell's replacement.

Wilkens was brought in to clean up the mess and he overhauled the starting lineup that included Brown, leading to an incredible turnaround that landed the team in the NBA Finals that season against the Washington Bullets, one victory shy of a championship.

A year later, Brown was still a sub when he came off the bench and hit seven of 10 shots, four of five

Fred Brown's No. 32 was retired by the Sonics.

down the stretch, to sew up a 97-93 victory over the Bullets and the NBA title. He had embraced coming off the bench, something the ever-popular Slick Watts wouldn't consider the season before, making the little, bald guard expendable and miss out on the Sonics' championship.

"I was the guy who went to Lenny and I said the better thing for our team was to put young Dennis Johnson and Gus Williams in there and tire opponents out," Brown said. "When I got in there I would have a chance to have a major impact. It just worked. To this day, I still tell Lenny if Slick had maintained that mental attitude, we would really have been outstanding. He

was young and wanted to go to greener pastures. Everybody wanted to be a star. To me, it was never about being the star."

Brown played five more seasons and was done. He put his deadly shot away. The Sonics retired his No. 32 in 1986, at the time just the second for the team alongside Wilkens (19), his one-time teammate and coach.

Entrenched in the Northwest, Brown lived on Mercer Island and watched his sons become accomplished high school players and pursue college opportunities. He took a job as a Bank of America executive, working downtown, of course. He considered new arena possibilities with others once the Sonics left town and people started mulling ways to bring the NBA back to the city. He sold his league championship ring in a manner that became public, demonstrating his limitations on sentimentality.

As for his catchy basketball calling card, Brown happily hung onto it. Seven years after the sweet-shooting guard left the game, his Downtown Freddie Brown label popped up in a throwaway line quoted by one of the characters in the Denzel Washington film "Mississippi Masala," making Brown a lasting pop-culture figure. ❖

In the early hours
of Feb. 16, 1974,
Jugum was pulled
out of bed at his parents'
home at 4137 48th Ave. S.W.
by Seattle police
and arrested for
Backman's death,
creating nonstop headlines.

The hulking pro football player cornered the tall, skinny high school kid in the parking lot of a Herfy's hamburger joint in West Seattle, creating 10 minutes of unspeakable violence. George Jugum savagely delivered kick after kick to Eric Backman, leaving him crumpled on the wet pavement. There was no saving the teenager from being stomped to death.

In the early hours of Feb. 16, 1974, Jugum was pulled out of bed at his parents' home at 4137 48th Ave. S.W. by Seattle police and arrested for Backman's death, creating nonstop headlines. This marked the most brutal and gruesome crime committed by one of the city's high-profile athletes.

Once a much-decorated University of Washington linebacker who thrived on controlled mayhem, Jugum let his famous temper go unchecked – possibly heightened by performance-enhancing drugs – and he shocked his hometown with his ruthless actions. He drew a 30-year prison sentence for second-degree murder and was shipped off to Monroe Correctional Complex after going through a trial that drew full-bore media attention.

GEORGE JUGUM
Seattle's Biggest Bully

"There were reporters and TV cameras everywhere," Jugum said. "When all that started, I thought I was John Dillinger."

The tragic evening began with Jugum and a neighborhood friend, Michael Kirk, lifting weights together at a downtown gym. A fitness buff, Jugum was a three-year Huskies starter who played two seasons for the CFL's British Columbia Lions and another for the minor-league Seattle Ramblers. He was cut twice by the Los Angeles Rams, unable to make it in the NFL. With an opportunity to join another CFL team, the Winnipeg Blue Bombers, Jugum was on a concentrated conditioning regimen.

After completing their workout that night, Jugum and Kirk, both 27, visited three taverns on the way home. Leaving the last drinking establishment in West Seattle, they watched a red 1965 Ford Falcon speed past with teenagers Dave Rodal and Backman inside. The teens had been drinking at a nearby high school party. Backman, 17, flashed a mischievous middle finger at the strangers on the street. He paid for that gesture with his life.

Confronted several blocks away at the 5275 California Ave. S.W. burger outlet, Backman was knocked to the ground and kicked repeatedly. Jugum was 60 pounds heavier and egged on by Kirk to inflict serious damage. Backman was kicked from his head to his waist. He was injured so badly that Jugum had to get out of the car and move the legs of the immobile Backman so he and Kirk could drive off.

"I think about it," Jugum said. "I wasn't even that mad. It was confusing to me. I wasn't going to go out and harm someone. I was never a criminal. I was just an average, everyday guy. It was like going on a journey. I wish the thing had never happened. It was terrible. They say I killed the guy but he was alive when we left; if I'd done that, he wouldn't have had a head left. It was shock. If you could predict life, you wouldn't be in that situation. I never had any thoughts in my life of doing something like that."

Jugum claimed that Backman pulled a knife on him. Kirk testified he saw slashing motions but no knife. Police discovered a small pocket knife inside the dead teen's coat, but it was unopened and harmless in appearance. No one took the self-defense argument seriously. Jugum also claimed that Backman, an Eagle Scout and aspiring musician, threw beer bottles at him from the moving car. There was no evidence of that happening either.

"We probably weren't angels," Rodal said. "Eric flipped him off and I told him not to do it. We were crazy and we were kids. He was a good guy, a normal teenager like everybody else. When it's late and dark at night, who do you know you're messing with? It happened so fast. They kicked me in the head. I was kind of delirious or they would have done me in, too. We were just going to Herfy's. They followed us, came up in the car and grabbed us. It didn't give him the right to kill Eric."

Lonnie Saisslin, 25, stopped at Herfy's for a hamburger and was leaving in his van when he witnessed the deadly incident. He shielded his eyes after watching Jugum kick Backman six times. He saw two people attempt to pull Backman away, but Jugum kicked the downed teen three more times. Saisslin attempted to intervene, too, but he drew angry swings from an out-of-control Jugum. Saisslin was warned by Jugum that he hadn't seen anything and was ordered to leave the restaurant.

"The kid went airborne a few times," Saisslin said. "After about 12 kicks, Jugum started going after witnesses in the parking lot, me being one of them. George then started kicking on the kid again. It was pretty gruesome. George in those days was notorious for causing bodily harm to other people. His dad had a lot of influence. I saw George in fights at Alki Beach."

The jury decided the Herfy's encounter was the worst-case scenario of macho retribution gone horribly wrong for no acceptable reason. As the son of a longshoreman who was one of the waterfront's toughest labor leaders, Jugum grew up a bully and nonstop brawler.

On a break from Los Angeles Rams' training camp, defensive back Bob Burmeister and Jugum, former UW teammates and aspiring NFL players, were in a strip club in the San Fernando Valley when Jugum became annoyed with a man who stood up, tried to slip a dollar to a dancer and blocked his view. Jugum cracked the other guy over the head with a glass beer pitcher,

> Lonnie Saisslin,
> 25, stopped at Herfy's
> for a hamburger
> and was leaving in his van
> when he witnessed
> the deadly incident.

dropping the unsuspecting person to the ground. The football players went out the door in a hurry. "I scoured the papers for the next few days looking for a reported murder," Burmeister said. "I was stunned. George was a bit Neanderthal."

Jugum wandered through West Seattle bars with a friend obscenely named Dick Hard and asked people to guess the other's man name. If they laughed when it was revealed, Jugum pummeled them. Another man needed a steel plate inserted under his eye following a Jugum pounding seven years earlier at a party. There were countless other examples of Jugum brutality recounted during testimony in his murder trial.

"He toyed with his victim and it was not out of character for him," said Frank Eberharter, the King County Superior Court judge who presided over the murder case. "It was not the first time his boots had been applied to a downed man."

Yet Jugum had never killed another man before. He crossed an unconscionable line this time, even for his ruthless ways. It's possible something else might have set off his angry mood besides Backman.

Jugum was one of Seattle's first football players totally immersed in weight training and he changed his body size and strength dramatically, something even the linebacker proudly acknowledged. "When I got to the U-Dub in the spring of 1966, guys were lifting weights and struggling to do 325 pounds," Jugum said of his bench-press ability. "I could do it six or eight times."

Teammates were left to guess whether Jugum's strength was natural or chemically enhanced. Other Husky football players and track athletes from that era were the first at the school to experiment with PEDs. Jugum appeared to have all the telltale signs of a steroid user.

Top 10 Athletes in Prison

1. George Jugum (murder)
2. Reggie Rogers (negligent homicide)
3. Michael Green (murder)
4. Kyle Heinrich (negligent homicide)
5. Rick Fenney (fraud)
6. Dean Kirkland (fraud)
7. Doug Wrenn (assault)
8. Prentiss Perkins (drugs)
9. Matt Jones (fraud)
10. Terrence Powe (drugs)

"I don't know if 'roids were involved, but his skin was all waxy and pocky and he had this beefed-up frame," said Mark Hannah, a UW defensive end who played alongside Jugum. "He was a 235-pound guy with a 180-pound frame. He was very aggressive. It made a lot more sense if he had been using steroids where he got so angry that he wanted to hurt someone."

The popular belief was a steroid user would sooner admit to something like murder than artificially pumping up because body-building was such a macho thing. Jugum, a West Seattle High School alumnus and the state's first *Parade Magazine* All-America selection in 1963, was willing to discuss his heinous crime to a point, but denied any PED use.

"I never used steroids," Jugum insisted. "At the U-Dub, a shot putter I knew told me, 'Don't even play with those steroids. They make your nuts shrink up.' My biggest problem was booze."

Jugum was small and sturdy at best as a middle-age man compared to the oversized figure he resembled as a college and pro football player, caught up in a physical transformation that readily seemed to suggest chemical enhancement. Still others said it was entirely possible that the hot-tempered and ruthless Jugum could have been motivated only by anger and nothing more.

"George was from the other side of the tracks," said Dick Baird, a former Roosevelt High and Washington State linebacker who played against Jugum at both levels. "He grew up in a roughneck atmosphere. His whole attitude was he was one of the baddest asses in the city and he had to walk the walk."

Jugum thrived on being known as a fearless guy. He played inspired in two games against powerful USC teams that featured O.J. Simpson, the Heisman Trophy-winning running back. After a 14-7 slugfest won by the Trojans in Los Angeles in 1968, Simpson chatted up the UW linebacker as they walked off the field, telling Jugum that no one had ever hit him harder. Ironically, Simpson and Jugum were both accused of murder and went to prison, two decades apart.

Jugum served a minimum six and a half years before he was released from Monroe, married an inmate's sister, had two children and took a job at a Woodinville lumber yard in Seattle's suburbs. The man punished for totally losing it and killing a defenseless teenager was credited with defusing a couple of prison riots at Monroe and let out early. He had spent two years in maximum confinement, holed up in a single four-foot-by-eight-foot cell. He later pulled kitchen duty, took up a serious interest in prison politics and served most of his prison time on a nearby Monroe work farm, milking cows.

Outside of a man who made a foolhardy sexual advance on Jugum, and was badly beaten for it by the former football player, inmates were aware of his reputation and did not provoke him. Jugum was permitted to lift weights but not allowed to play for the prison football team.

"That was for his own protection," said Bob Kastama, former Monroe associate superintendent, of the football ban. "We thought that hair-trigger temper might be tempted and get him into further trouble. We watched the games together. I can't go along with what he did to go to prison, but I got along with the guy."

Jugum was given $100 when he was released in 1980 and walked out of the Monroe prison to an empty setting, wondering where all the TV cameras had gone. He eased back into the real world and stayed out of trouble. He watched his son play linebacker for Bothell High School. He reconnected with former teammates and attended Huskies football games and reunions. He settled into a quiet existence as an ex-convict on his best behavior.

Within a month of his Monroe prison release, Jugum was driving his car when an impatient driver flipped him off. Jugum kept going, looking the other way, showing no interest or reaction. It was something he should have done with the West Seattle teenager on that rainy night at the Herfy's restaurant and he knew it.

"You can give me the finger all day long if you want," Jugum said. ❖

VINCE ABBEY

Seattle's Empty Net

Vince Abbey kept well-worn hockey sticks, ice skates and the rest of the Seattle Totems equipment stored for decades. He had boxes and boxes of court papers stacked in the basement of his Olympic Manor house and at his daughter's suburban home. These were the scattered remnants of Seattle's most agonizing pursuit of a National Hockey League franchise.

On June 13, 1974, the banner headline across the top of the *Seattle Post-Intelligencer* sports section blared the following news, leaving the city giddy with anticipation: "Seattle Awarded NHL Franchise." Hockey at the highest level was coming to Seattle. Abbey, a local lawyer who held majority ownership in the Western Hockey League's Totems since 1958, had done it, securing one of two NHL expansion franchises available for 1976, with the other going to Denver.

He posed for photos and exchanged congratulatory handshakes with NHL president Clarence Campbell in Montreal. Seattle was overjoyed, long picturing itself as a serious hockey town. All Abbey had to do was pay for it. That would be a problem. After what happened next, someone deserved to sit in the penalty box for a long time. Eight months later, the franchise offer to Seattle was rescinded. The league explanation was this: Abbey failed to come up with a $1 million letter of credit by a prescribed deadline and lost his place in line to enter the NHL.

Abbey angrily countered that there was a well-orchestrated conspiracy in place to undermine expansion efforts because of a sudden change in the league's business plans. He claimed that the NHL secretly agreed to dissolve its competition with the upstart World Hockey Association and take on four of its teams, creating a merger that wouldn't happen for three more years. Seattle and Denver weren't needed now.

The hockey owner insisted he always had the necessary cash to enter the NHL when a lot of people said otherwise. Yet he wasn't blindly handing it over until he was supplied with the necessary paperwork, which he said the league strangely refused to provide. Abbey came away from the ordeal as possibly Seattle's most swindled pro sports owner, given an NHL franchise that never materialized, and he was left to explain all this to an incredulous city.

"It was never about money," Abbey said. "I had to pay $2 million for the franchise. That was never a problem. They said I didn't have the money, but I had the money from 10 different sources. I had money from Hong Kong, Vancouver, comedian Dick Cavett, sources up and down the coast. I never sent the money because

> Abbey came away from the ordeal as possibly Seattle's most swindled pro sports owner, given an NHL franchise that never materialized, and he was left to explain all this to an incredulous city.

I wasn't going to take money from people without documentation. The NHL was supposed to send the papers in 30 days. Nothing. Then it was 60 days. And 90 days. Still nothing."

The Totems owner was convinced it was the league's way of running him off and Denver — the Colorado city later obtained a WHA franchise and eventually entered the NHL — all orchestrated by a consortium of Yale-educated men, foremost William Jennings, who was the New York Rangers president and NHL expansion committee chairman. Abbey fought back by attempting to purchase the Pittsburgh Penguins and California Golden Seals franchises and move them to the Northwest, and then by suing the league for antitrust violations.

The conspiracy theory took a wide-ranging turn once Abbey entered the courtroom. Seeking a legal team, he found the NHL had hired the same Seattle lawyer, Bill Helsell, who was at the top of his list. Abbey also felt his hockey camp had been infiltrated, noting that Totems minority owner Irving Clark was a Yale man and one-time college roommate of Jennings.

Clark likewise was a business partner with U.S. District Court Judge Donald Voorhees, who requested that he preside over the hockey case. Voorhees seemed all too anxious to get involved. He pointedly told Abbey in chambers to settle his disagreement with the NHL out of court. Abbey refused and Voorhees promptly dismissed the complaint in 1983. At least that was Abbey's version.

"We had that case won," he said. "I had three NHL owners come in and testify to what they had done. I was so mad I wanted to climb over and hit Voorhees in the face."

Abbey appealed the decision and lost that court battle in 1986. He was sued by the Vancouver Canucks,

once an ally and business partner but now an aggrieved creditor. If there was any justice for Abbey, it was this: Within a few years, nearly every principal figure who had opposed him or whose loyalty he had questioned in his fight against the NHL — among them Jennings, Clark, Voorhees, a Canucks executive, a lead trial attorney — died suddenly of heart attacks, strokes, cancer and even a Hawaiian drowning.

"The people of the National Hockey League didn't know there was a curse," Abbey said smugly. "You don't mess with the Abbey curse."

A Seattle native and 1939 Lincoln High grad, Abbey had hockey blood running through his veins. He skated for the University of Michigan for a year, three years in a Seattle senior league and one season in the pros with Portland. In 1958, Abbey, by now a lawyer, was one of 12 men who purchased the Totems, eventually whittling the ownership to just him and his brother-in-law, Eldred Barnes.

With the NHL expanding throughout the 1960s and adding Vancouver in 1970, Abbey felt league membership was a logical next step for Seattle. Making the Totems fan-friendly, he had fielded the biggest line in professional hockey — including the NHL — with his 1967-68 Jolly Green Giants who featured Noel Picard and Pat Quinn, both 6-foot-4, and Don Ward, who was 6-3.

Six months before Abbey was awarded the NHL expansion franchise, his Totems upset the defending world-champion Russian national team 8-4 in an exhibition game in Seattle. His hockey teams often outdrew their fellow Seattle Center Coliseum tenants, the NBA's Sonics, four to one. His teams were competitive. The big leagues were beckoning, but an open net was missed.

Abbey held onto Seattle's territorial rights, hoping for an eventual NHL franchise. A team couldn't be

placed within 50 miles of the city unless he was paid a nominal fee. He instructed Bill McFarland, one of his former Totem coaches and players and a fellow attorney who once worked for him, to get the best deal he could if someone requested the rights.

Yet through the years the only people who wanted to see Abbey's mountain of basement paperwork, which required a certain amount of dexterity in climbing through the maze of boxes, was the occasional Canadian hockey reporter and an Alberta professor, all interested in writing hockey books, not pursuing an NHL team for Seattle.

In 2013, almost four full decades after Abbey's failed franchise pursuit, Seattle was poised to build an arena and obtain NBA and NHL franchises. Local investors pursued the league-owned Phoenix Coyotes before a deal was struck to keep that team in Arizona. High-level hockey hopes were rekindled after a long dormant period and then squashed again.

Abbey, who turned 90 that year and needed a walker to move around his longtime residence at 9005 21st Ave. N.W., still owned the territorial rights. He put it in his will that a grandson would acquire the rights in the event of his death. Abbey watched with increasing amusement as talk of securing the Phoenix franchise escalated, knowing it still wouldn't be easy to bring the NHL here. He shook his head over the fact that this city, after all these years, was still on the outside.

"A lot of people feel I'm the reason there is no NHL team in Seattle because I sued the NHL," Abbey said. "There's nothing I would ever do to stop someone sincere about obtaining a team but it's not something I'm living or dying for. There are very few people left who are connected to this.

"I don't think there will be a team in Seattle in my lifetime, but there should have been." ❖

DON CORYELL

The Coaching Genius

All Don Coryell did was hand off. He was a single wing-formation quarterback at Seattle's Lincoln High School, a team that ran the ball almost exclusively under the direction of Bill Nollan, a tough-minded, grind-it-out football coach. No team in the city threw it less.

With Coryell behind center for five games in wartime 1942, as a senior installed as a midseason starter and only after the team was left with a miserable 1-3 record, the Lynx averaged just seven attempts and one completion per game — and usually one of his backfield mates did all of the passing.

Coryell was so anonymous he didn't appear in the team photo in his Lincoln High yearbook. His chief responsibility was to run a huddle, take a snap and shove the ball into someone's midsection, though the Lynx seemed to respond well to his leadership, closing with a 4-0-1 finish with him at quarterback.

These were ultraconservative football beginnings for a man whose revolutionary offensive approach as a collegiate and NFL coach would be christened "Air Coryell" and become football legend. His high school games were played on Civic Stadium's dirt field, hardly a lasting inspiration for a yard-gobbling genius.

Yet Coryell, who was 85 when he died on July 1, 2010, emerged from Seattle's mud and the shadows to become one of football's greatest innovative minds anywhere and the most accomplished homegrown coach produced by the city for any big-league sport.

"Lincoln had some tough kids in those days and he was one of them," said Bob Jorgensen, a former Roosevelt High basketball and baseball player. "He was scrappy and that's why he became a good coach. Still, everybody was amazed when he started coaching around the country."

Coryell was one of four brothers who grew up in Green Lake at 5712 Ashworth Ave. N. and one of three who served in World War II. His grandfather, George, was a Seattle city councilman and city clerk. A sense of purpose was a family trait.

Coryell's college playing career offered no clues as to what was coming either. After a four-year wartime interruption as an Army paratrooper, he returned home and played football for the University of Washington — as a defensive back. He appeared in every game except one as a senior for the Huskies in 1949, starting just once against Oregon State. He usually shifted between the second and fourth units. He often got hurt, leaving a game against Notre Dame with a severe leg injury and one against UCLA with a concussion.

He played enough to earn a letter for a 3-7 team, but his stint with the Huskies was so forgettable that

> Coryell, who was 85 when he died on July 1, 2010, emerged from Seattle's mud and the shadows to become one of football's greatest innovative minds anywhere.

All-America fullback Hugh McElhenny, as a sophomore teammate, remembered him only as a UW graduate assistant coach for Howie Odell's staff the following season. Coryell was more tough than talented as an athlete to those who encountered him in Seattle. The sport he excelled at was boxing, and he won a Pacific Coast Conference championship for the Huskies.

Jorgensen, his high school contemporary, was an accomplished Huskies basketball and baseball player. He knew Coryell as a UW athlete but hardly in flattering terms: "I don't think he really was that good a football player. He couldn't crack it. When he came back from the war, I don't think he fit in."

Coryell used the next decade to find his place, to make people take him seriously. He spent a year each at two Hawaii high schools; two years as head coach at the University of British Columbia; a season as coach at two-year Wenatchee Valley College; another year coaching a Fort Ord military team in northern California; three years as coach at Whittier College in California, and as an assistant for John McKay's 1960 USC staff, the latter putting him on the receiving end of a 34-0 pounding from a Rose Bowl-bound Huskies team.

In 1961, Coryell took over at then-San Diego State College, which played at the Division II level. He stayed a dozen seasons, compiling a 104-19-2 record and making a firm commitment to the passing attack, something he had witnessed at the UW while trying to defend in practice against Huskies All-America quarterback Don Heinrich. "I decided, hell, you can't just go out and run the ball against better teams," Coryell told *Sports Illustrated* shortly before his death. "You've got to mix it up. So we started throwing the ball."

"Air Coryell" was born. It meant lots of points and yards were coming quickly. After playing in the considerable shadow of McElhenny and under wraps at Lincoln High, he moved to the football forefront. He used his pass-first offense and persistent attacking style to make himself the only man to win 100 games at both the pro (St. Louis Cardinals, San Diego Chargers) and college levels (San Diego State).

In 1972, his final season as a college coach, Coryell guided the Aztecs to a 10-1 record, which included a 14-0 victory on the road over a 9-2 Kent State team coached by Don James, who three years later took over at Washington. Along the way, Coryell turned down an opportunity to coach Arizona and his interest in Wisconsin was rebuffed.

Seattle didn't immediately recognize Coryell when he ran around the football field in a uniform, but it wanted to claim him later. UW football boosters repeatedly tossed his name around in private as the program sagged in the late 1960s, considering Coryell the perfect replacement candidate if and when they determined that Huskies coach Jim Owens needed to be removed.

"If people were saying that in those days, I never heard it," Coryell told the *Seattle Post-Intelligencer*. "I was content to stay at San Diego State. My goal was to see our school in the Coast Conference [PCAA] sometime before I retired. I was happy and I thought we were doing some good things for the school."

But it was time for Coryell to take his highly effective air show to the NFL, first with St. Louis for five years, leading the Cardinals into the playoffs twice, and then with the Chargers for nine seasons, four of which ended in the postseason.

While in St. Louis, Coryell turned to his hometown for offensive firepower, making fellow Seattle native Terry Metcalf from Long Beach State and Franklin High his go-to running back, a formidable receiving threat and one of the most feared players by NFL defenses in the mid-1970s.

"I got drafted because of Don Coryell, because I had played against him for two years in college and beat up on him," said Metcalf, who was first pegged as an NFL defensive back by a Cardinals assistant coach. "Coryell looked over and said, 'No, that's going to be my running back.' That gave me a great boost of confidence. I loved playing for that man."

At the same time, Coryell's hometown was making plans for him once more, again without his knowledge. McElhenny, bidding for an NFL franchise and working on behalf of prospective owner and Minnesota businessman Wayne Field, drew up plans for stocking an expansion team ultimately awarded in 1974 to Herman Sarkowsky and the Nordstrom family, an opposing faction that created the Seattle Seahawks.

Had he become the general manager, McElhenny envisioned Coryell as one of his coaching options. "He and Bill Walsh were my candidates to be head coach if we had got the franchise," McElhenny said. "I felt at that time that throwing the ball was the way the game was going. Don Coryell was just a great mind and would have been perfect."

While he never ended up in a Seattle coaching capacity again, Coryell welcomed the expansionist Seahawks into the NFL, though not quite as McElhenny envisioned. In 1976, Coryell brought Metcalf and the rest of the Cardinals to the newly opened Kingdome and beat the Seahawks 30-24 in the first regular-season game played in Seattle franchise history. Ironically, he chose to run the ball (281 yards) far more than pass it (175 yards) that day. Lincoln coach Bill Nollan would have been proud. ❖

TERRY METCALF

The Spectacular One

From his tearful youth-football beginnings, Metcalf toughened up and evolved into the first homegrown Seattle running back to make it big in the NFL.

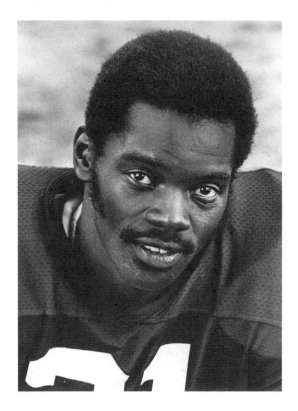

Terry Metcalf was hit hard in the helmet the first time he played football at Rainier Playfield in south Seattle, two stinging blows actually. It hurt and he cried. He was just 9 and at that tender age the running back in training wheels decided he would run away from people rather than into them, that he would use his nimble feet to shield himself from all that head-banging agony, and that he would be in total control in a breath-taking manner. His elusive, stutter-step style carried him from Franklin High stardom to NCAA record-holder to the most spectacular NFL player of his day. Metcalf supplied one breakaway run after another.

In 1974, he snapped off a 75-yard touchdown run against the Washington Redskins, the longest rushing play in the NFL that season, and came back the following week with a 94-yard kickoff return for a score against the Cleveland Browns. In 1975, Metcalf went the distance against the Redskins on a 93-yard kickoff return, broke a 69-yard punt return for a score against the New England Patriots and showed up Joe Namath and the New York Jets with a 52-yard scoring dash. And in 1977, he ran 62 yards for a touchdown against the Dallas Cowboys and followed that with a 68-yard scoring catch against the Redskins.

"It's not something I brag about but I did some things that nobody thought I could ever do," Metcalf said. "I knew I could play. As I got to each level, my confidence grew. When I got to the NFL and finally made it, I believed I was the best. I just figured if you gave me some space, I was going to make something happen."

From his tearful youth-football beginnings, Metcalf toughened up and evolved into the first homegrown Seattle running back to make it big in the NFL, something Corey Dillon duplicated two decades later. Both players were groomed for greatness at Rainier Playfield and Franklin High, but Dillon wore a uniform for the University of Washington, if only for a season, while Metcalf shunned the Huskies, convinced he had to leave the city to make his mark in football.

Metcalf, who grew up in Judkins Park at 2459 S. Irving St., rushed for 1,055 yards and scored 15 times and was selected as a first-team, All-Metro running back as a wildly elusive Franklin senior. He drew considerable recruiting interest from the UW, but poor grades made him detour to Everett Community College, where he had an incredible freshman season. He averaged 23 yards per carry, scoring 11 touchdowns in his first four games alone. He did everything at Everett: Offense, defense, punting and placekicking.

He was still just 30 miles away from Seattle. Yet while he prospered, the Huskies program disturbingly fell apart when Jim Owens and his assistant coaches were repeatedly accused of discriminatory practices.

"I wanted to go there but I didn't particularly care about the coaching staff at the time," Metcalf said. "I didn't want to be a part of that. I wanted to play and not have to worry about those things. I took my talents elsewhere. All I knew were the Huskies and that's all I had wanted to do. I played Little League championship games at the University of Washington. I remember Junior Coffey. I remember Dave Williams. I remember a lot of players and I wanted to be like them."

In a roundabout way, Metcalf wound up at Long Beach State. It wasn't the big time, but the Southern California climate was conducive to his running-back ambitions. After playing in the mud and rain in Seattle, he welcomed the chance to see what he could do in the sunshine. Metcalf originally signed a national letter of intent to play for Oklahoma State but second-guessed his decision to spend two years in secluded Stillwater, Okla., and backed out. Long Beach State ran the I formation with power sweeps, same as nearby USC, and he was perfectly suited for the style.

In his first season with the 49ers in 1971, Metcalf rushed for 1,673 yards and scored a then-NCAA record 29 touchdowns. He had kickoff returns for scores of 98 and 99 yards. An Achilles tendon injury limited him some as a senior, but he still managed 779 yards rushing and 16 TDs. He got out of school just in time: Long Beach State was slapped with three years of probation for NCAA rules violations, and some of them involved Metcalf.

According to published reports in *Sports Illustrated* and elsewhere, investigators determined the elusive running back from Seattle had received cash and

help in purchasing a car from booster Russell Guiver, and he and a girlfriend were housed in several local motels for a week at the school's expense.

"A couple of Oklahoma State recruiters were trying to steal him so we hid him," Long Beach State coach Jim Stangeland told reporters. "We moved him. We moved him again. All we were doing was playing hide-and-seek."

"They were crooks," Metcalf said of Long Beach State, conveniently excusing his own involvement. "The program could have really elevated itself but didn't take the proper procedures to do that. Jerry Tarkanian was there at the same time, and you know the trouble he got in [in basketball]."

Before joining the Cardinals as a third-round draft pick, Metcalf made the college all-star game rounds. In Lubbock, Texas, he was named the West team's Most Valuable Player after rushing for 135 yards in a 20-6 victory over the East. He showed up all of the college game's more publicized running backs, foremost Oklahoma's Greg Pruitt.

Metcalf was coached by USC's John McKay, who asked him rather pointedly why he hadn't become a Trojan.

> Metcalf was coached by USC's John McKay, who asked him rather pointedly why he hadn't become a Trojan. The tailback had a ready response: He told McKay that he had sent him a letter that went unanswered.

The tailback had a ready response: He told McKay that he had sent him a letter that went unanswered.

He wound up in the NFL with St. Louis because Cardinals coach Don Coryell, a fellow Seattle native, was there. Metcalf played sparingly as a rookie, later concluding he had put on too much weight and lost quickness. Dropping from 195 pounds to 175, he regained his speed and terrorized the league with all of those breakaway runs over the next four seasons.

In 1975, Metcalf gained 2,462 multi-purpose yards to set a league record and scored 13 touchdowns. That year, he was the runner-up to Minnesota Vikings quarterback Fran Tarkenton in voting for the NFL's Most Valuable Player. "I lost weight and ran more, and that's when I became a possessed runner," Metcalf said.

In 1976, he returned home to play in the Kingdome against the Seattle Seahawks in their first game in franchise history, and rushed for 113 yards in the Cardinals' 30-24 victory. He supplied tickets for 100 friends and family members who showed up in T-shirts that read, "Little man, big moves."

Teams resorted to squibbing kickoffs to avoid Metcalf, trying to limit the runback damage. The Cardinals often used him as a decoy to free up players such as wide receiver Mel Gray, or used him on the front end, with Metcalf throwing two touchdown passes to Gray.

Metcalf also lost the ball a lot, always holding it loosely with one hand, coughing it up 62 times and twice leading the league in fumbles. He was exciting and unpredictable, a Pro Bowl selection for three of his final four seasons in St. Louis, and sometimes a bothersome distraction away from the field.

Metcalf was flamboyant, an early-day Deion Sanders, and he played the role to the hilt. There was an arrest for cocaine possession and another for bringing firecrackers aboard a jetliner. "I wasn't quite so upstanding," Metcalf admitted. "We all went through phases. I did some foolish things, made some foolish decisions."

Radical financial decisions were made, too. Seeking a contract extension following the 1977 season, Metcalf was convinced he wasn't getting paid what he was worth, especially after learning at the Pro Bowl how a Washington Redskins special-teams player was earning more than him. Metcalf asked to attend a Cardinals negotiating session with his lawyer, Richard Bennett. He nearly went ballistic when Joe Sullivan, the St. Louis operating vice president, compared the running back to a Cadillac just leaving the lot, suggesting there was significant depreciation in value to consider. Metcalf was asked to accept $50,000 again for the upcoming season and forgo a $20,000 raise.

"I said to Bennett, 'You better get me out of here,' " Metcalf said. "I was a little wild when I was younger. I would have punched the guy. I would have gone over the desk. I said, 'You better get me out here now.' I was so mad we walked around Busch Stadium three times."

The Cardinals agreed to pay Metcalf his $70,000, but he was done with them. He became a free agent and shopped himself to the rest of the league, but $150,000 per season was the most anyone offered him and that still wasn't enough. Metcalf became the first star-quality NFL player to jump to the CFL, accepting $250,000 per season from the Toronto Argonauts for seven years.

He didn't dominate as expected. His performance fell off noticeably for a franchise that was in constant disarray. The Argonauts didn't do him any favors with the surrounding cast, running through 163 players in his first CFL season while trying to fill out a meager 33-man roster. He had four coaches in three years. He returned to the NFL, hoping to reclaim his football magic.

Metcalf spent the 1981 season with the Washington Redskins, mostly as a receiver, catching 48 passes. A fitness fanatic, he was working hard in the off-season to reclaim a running-back assignment when a freak accident ended his career. He got hit in the head while playing pick-up basketball, hard enough that he was temporarily paralyzed on his right side. Adding to his misery, the Redskins won the Super Bowl that season without him.

Metcalf, whose son Eric became an NFL player, wasn't physically right for five or six years because of the injury and even quit watching football. He returned home to Seattle and got back into the game, eventually becoming the head coach at Renton High School. He had a lot to share with his teenage players, with passion at the top of the list.

"I love the game," Metcalf said. "I wasn't just a football player, I was a professional competitor. That's different with the great athletes today. They might be athletic but they're not the greatest competitors. I did some pretty good things." ❖

10 FHS Alums To The Pros

1. Ron Santo (MLB)
2. Terry Metcalf (NFL)
3. Fred Hutchinson (MLB)
4. Jason Terry (NBA)
5. Corey Dillon (NFL)
6. Aaron Brooks (NBA)
7. Peyton Siva (NBA)
8. James Hasty (NFL)
9. Jesse Chatmon (NFL)
10. Bruce Jarvis (NFL)

University of Washington running back Dave Kopay had blood streaking down his cheek, a tired but satisfied look on the rest of his face and the arm of coach Jim Owens draped around his shoulder as he walked out of Husky Stadium following a 22-7 upset of USC in a game heavy with Rose Bowl implications. A *Seattle Post-Intelligencer* photographer snapped Kopay in this classic 1963 football pose.

Frozen in time was a tough guy from Los Angeles who had come to Seattle and proved himself once more on this day against the mighty Trojans, the marquee team from his California hometown. A Marquette transfer after that school discontinued its football program, Kopay resurfaced in the Northwest as a swift, solidly built athlete with Hollywood features and someone who didn't need a stunt double.

The two-way back could hit people or run over them and still look good doing it. His combination of grit and style landed him in the Rose Bowl as a co-captain against Illinois, and in the NFL as a journey-man ball carrier for the San Francisco 49ers, Detroit Lions, Washington Redskins, New Orleans Saints and Green Bay Packers. Surprisingly, there was much more to the man than a handsome face and competitive instincts.

> Two years after playing his final pro football game, Kopay became the first athlete from Major League Baseball, the NBA or NFL to reveal he was gay, uncovering Seattle's biggest sporting secret.

DAVE KOPAY
Seattle's Coming-Out Party

Kopay had the courage, or some say the fool-hardiness, to make himself the ultimate social pioneer in the ultraconservative world of professional sports with a startling newspaper headline on Dec. 11, 1975: Two years after playing his final pro football game, Kopay became the first athlete from Major League Baseball, the NBA or NFL to reveal he was gay, uncovering Seattle's biggest sporting secret.

Without reservation, the disclosure shook up an athletic establishment that didn't want to hear it. It temporarily broke down all sorts of longstanding stereotypes, overriding the notion that this particular segment of the population — those who scored touchdowns, hit home runs and slam-dunked basketballs at the highest level — couldn't possibly be as diverse as everyone else.

"I left people behind in my life who weren't going to get on with the program or get on with their own bigotry or see how hateful some of their decisions were," Kopay said. "You have to finally make a stand."

Kopay's news reverberated from the nation's capital city, where he impulsively and voluntarily outed himself in a *Washington Star* newspaper series about homosexuality in sports, compiled by Lynn Rosellini. He wrote a best-selling book, *The David Kopay Story*, offering detailed admissions of a lifestyle that he previously hid. He became estranged from his brother,

Dave Kopay, at right, looks for an opening behind the blocking of Junior Coffey.

Tony Kopay, who was a University of Washington football player and teammate, and an assistant coach for several college teams, including the Huskies, before they later settled their differences as best they could.

"I think he loves me as a brother but I think he really prefers that I would be straight," Kopay said. "That's the way it is. I have to give him that right. He's been distantly supportive. I made my brother Tony proud that I was the ballplayer that I was. It hurt him so much when I spoke out because it blew apart what he thought I was. I didn't want to hurt him, but I certainly had a right to my own life."

Kopay played two seasons for the Huskies, mostly punting in 1962 before becoming a full-time backfield starter as a senior. His career offensive statistics were modest, just 319 yards rushing on 75 carries and 175 yards receiving on 12 catches for a collective five touchdowns. One of his scores came on a 17-yard run in a 17-7 loss to Illinois and a future NFL Hall of Fame linebacker in the 1964 Rose Bowl. "I remember Dick Butkus lying on his ass before they came back and won the game," Kopay said.

He played nine NFL seasons and filled a utility role, rushing 236 times for 876 yards and catching 77 passes for 593 yards, and he scored eight times, once on a fumble recovery.

Briefly married to a woman he met in college and divorced, Kopay had his first gay encounter at the UW, ending up with a fraternity brother after a night of drinking at the Theta Chi house at 4535 17th Ave. N.E. He never publicly identified the other man, choosing to give him the fictitious name of "Ted Robinson" in his book, while later acknowledging the person was killed during fighting in the Vietnam War.

Playing for the Washington Redskins in 1969, Kopay became sexually and secretly involved with high-profile teammate Jerry Smith, an All-Pro tight end. They shared in a casual relationship that proved both exhilarating and discouraging. They went to dinner, discos and gay bars together, trying to stay underground but nonetheless taking big risks and never getting caught.

The thrill of tempting fate and being reckless with their public identities seemingly was the basis for the liaison. They had sex but no intimacy. That left Kopay feeling rejected for the first time.

In his tell-all book, Smith was identified by an alias, "Bill Stiles," because the Redskins tight end wasn't willing to go public with his personal life. Kopay revealed that Smith was gay after his teammate's death from AIDS on Oct. 15, 1986, making Smith the first pro athlete to succumb to the dreaded disease. Kopay outed his teammate when he got up and spoke at Smith's funeral.

"I was totally enthralled with Jerry, with the possibility that we could have a relationship," Kopay said. "He wasn't really interested in any kind of relationship with a teammate. I couldn't understand that at all. He was caring. But he had a whole lot more life experiences than I did. He'd been out a whole lot longer. He had money to travel and enjoy himself. He was a lot freer. I never experienced that. We kind of stayed in touch from a distance afterward. We

In his tell-all book, Smith was identified by an alias, "Bill Stiles," because the Redskins tight end wasn't willing to go public with his personal life.

were never really as close again as we were as teammates. We had a physical, not a fulfilling, relationship."

Kopay turned into a visible advocate for gay rights, making nonstop speaking appearances nationwide. He wrote newspaper pieces for the *New York Times* and *San Francisco Chronicle*. He counseled countless young men about publicly disclosing their sexuality. He appeared in an HBO special about homophobia in sports. He helped NBC News correspondent Pete Williams come out.

At the same time, Kopay was shunned by the sports world, given no consideration for coaching opportunities to stay in football. He moved home to Los Angeles and went to work in his family's linoleum business, dealing with all sorts of Hollywood types, entertainment figures and interior decorators, including gays.

Retiring once more, Kopay generously pledged $1 million to set up a University of Washington endowment fund for the Q Center, an organization that supported gay, lesbian, bisexual and transgender students.

It was assumed that Kopay's openness would make it easier for other gay athletes in the NFL, NBA and

big-league baseball to freely disclose their sexuality. That didn't happen for nearly four decades.

In 2013, Jason Collins, a free-agent NBA center at the time who later joined the Brooklyn Nets, became the first active pro athlete in any of the four major sports to acknowledge publicly that he was gay. Several months later, Michael Sam was the first openly gay person to be drafted by an NFL team. One by one, people felt empowered to be themselves with sports fans and fellow athletes.

Previously, NBA player John Amaechi had disclosed that he was gay in a book after retiring. Former major-league players Alan Wiggins and Glenn Burke acknowledged their sexuality before dying from AIDS in 1991 and 1995, respectively. Journeyman MLB player Billy Bean admitted as much after his career was over. Former NFL players Ron Simmons, Ray McDonald, and Esera Tuolo were outed, or outed themselves, and Kwame Harris was retired when an altercation with a former boyfriend became public.

"I think it's important for people to know we're everywhere," said Kopay, who remains a cultural pioneer. "If a superstar came out in any of the major sports, it would be 'so what' after that. As for me, I think I've learned to find peace where I can find it." ❖

HERMAN SARKOWSKY

The Top Negotiator

The Seattle Seahawks were always identified as the Nordstroms' team, owned and operated by the Northwest family that established the department-store chain emblazoned with its name across it. These were people known for providing a comfortable pair of shoes and a quality pro football team. But the most valuable player in the NFL franchise power structure was Seattle businessman Herman Sarkowsky, not the local retailers.

Sarkowsky was the one who decided that a local ownership group should bring the NFL to Seattle. He was the one who pulled everyone together. He was the managing partner, the owner most involved with the football minds. He walked away with an impressive return that far exceeded his investment when the team was sold to California businessman Ken Behring for $79 million in 1988.

"Herman Sarkowsky was a genius," said Dick Vertlieb, former Sonics and Mariners general manager, before his 2008 death. "The Nordstrom family had the 51-percent majority and Sarkowsky headed up the 49-percent minority, and Herman negotiated that the minority group had all the same rights as the majority group, and the Nordstroms bought it. The Nordstroms had to pay Herman a 15-percent bonus for the minority group to OK the sale. He was the greatest negotiator in history."

Sarkowsky at different times owned the Portland Trail Blazers and Seahawks, supplying financial backing for the Oregon NBA team on a whim and the local NFL franchise out of civic duty. While Paul Allen fulfilled this exact same roles decades later in becoming a Northwest sports philanthropist, Sarkowsky, one of Seattle's richest and most powerful men from his generation, drew up the blueprint. As pro sports franchises gravitated to his hometown, he became the city's most influential owner, outweighing the efforts of the Sonics' Sam Schulman, who came before him, and the Mariners' Hiroshi Yamauchi and Allen, who came after.

Sarkowsky, who was 89 when he died on Nov. 2, 2014, helped found the teams that Allen would diligently maintain. All that was necessary to get into the high-stakes game of professional sports ownership was equal amounts money and guile.

"I'm pretty much a people person and many of the things I became involved in were not planned," Sarkowsky said. "I was able to take advantage of opportunities as they came along. I could recognize opportunity. I'm a risk-taker by nature. The greater the risk, the better I liked it, really."

In 1973, Sarkowsky and fellow businessman Ned Skinner determined over lunch that they should bring the NFL to the city and do it only with local money. They convinced four others to join their core ownership group — and the Nordstroms initially were not involved. They lobbied hard for Seattle with NFL owner Lamar Hunt and the rest of the expansion committee. They met with NFL commissioner Pete Rozelle and attended league meetings.

In '74, they beat out a competing ownership bid presented by Pro Football Hall of Fame running back Hugh McElhenny, who represented Minnesota businessman Wayne Field, and another promoted half-heartedly by Schulman, a California native.

Lloyd Nordstrom was asked to join Sarkowsky's Seahawks inner circle only after Longacres owner Morrie Alhadeff withdrew, convinced the NFL would frown upon his involvement in the horse-racing business because of the betting involved. The retailer teamed up with fellow businessmen Howard Wright, Monty Bean, Lynn Himmelman, Skinner and Sarkowsky as the original owners.

This Nordstrom, however, never saw the Seahawks play a game. Lloyd Nordstrom died of a heart attack on Jan. 20, 1976, nine months before the franchise opener, while playing tennis in Mexico, leaving the family's pro football responsibilities to his brother Elmer and nephews John, Jim and Bruce Nordstrom. As majority owners, they became the media face of the franchise.

"The Nordstroms get a little too much credit, but that's OK; I've never been bothered by that fact," Sarkowsky said. "We had what we called a required 66-percent vote. The Nordstroms could not do anything unilaterally. They had to have the support of the minority partnership."

For a dozen years, Sarkowsky attended every Seahawks game. He expected to break even financially on pro football, but the league's TV contracts made it a surprisingly profitable venture. The NFL was fun for him yet he understood his limitations. He let his football people assess the talent.

"I never saw myself as one who had to go out and measure and judge guys," he said. "I was in the game for some time and could probably tell the difference between a mediocre player and a really good player, but I think anybody in between was still a mystery for me."

Sarkowsky's only regret was that he didn't stay with the franchise longer and prevent Behring, an outsider, from brazenly trying to uproot the team to the Los Angeles area. Twice Sarkowsky negotiated with the Nordstroms to obtain the Seahawks majority interest. However, Skinner died and another partner dropped out, ultimately discouraging these efforts. Sarkowsky also had concerns about the future viability of the Kingdome as a football stadium with no ready alternative. Behring was brought into the mix by Jim Nordstrom, which proved to be a near-disastrous move for Seattle.

"We reluctantly sold to him and he turned out to be a very bad owner," Sarkowsky said of Behring. "He had no idea of his responsibility to the community. He was going to pull an Al Davis, but we didn't let him do it. Letting it go then was probably one of the biggest mistakes I made."

Sarkowsky's first dalliance as a pro sports owner came from a plea for help in 1970. After creating his fortune in the home-building industry, developing Seattle's 62-floor Key Tower and holding ownership in the Frederick & Nelson department store chain, he was approached for an emergency loan when financing for the Trail Blazers' expansion franchise fell through at the last minute. A Portland basketball bailout didn't interest

Herman Sarkowsky, at left, watches scouts time prospects.

him. He wanted more than that. The negotiating was creative and hard-line.

Vertlieb, between pro sports management jobs, was working for Sarkowsky when he was told they were getting on a jet to Portland in 45 minutes. As they prepared to leave town, Sarkowsky mentioned how it always was his dream to own a sports franchise. He had been approached by Trail Blazers owner Harry Glickman for financial help. The Fred Meyer grocery chain had backed out of the ownership group and Glickman was having trouble raising more money.

Over lunch at a Portland club, Sarkowsky cut a deal, one far different than proposed when the soup, their main course, was served.

"Glickman said to Herman, 'If you give me money, I'll give you 50 percent of the team,' " Vertlieb recalled. "Herman, who was the best negotiator in the country, said, 'I'll give you the money, $2.2 million, but I'll own 100 percent of the team and you can have an option on 10 percent. Our plane is leaving in 25 minutes and we can still make it. Now make up your mind.' "

The return flight to Seattle left without them but the deal was completed. They headed to Glickman's attorney's office and signed the necessary paperwork. Money was due the next day. Sarkowsky put in a phone call to another Oregonian, Larry Weinberg, who was a successful builder like him and had created his wealth by putting up housing compounds and coming up with creative means to sell them.

"Herman calls Weinberg and asks him, 'How much cash do you have in the house?' " Vertlieb said. "Herman needed $500,000 for the first payment. It came in bearer bonds and you took the bonds and got the cash and delivered it to [NBA commissioner] Walter Kennedy. Herman said to Weinberg, 'I'll call you back and tell you what we bought.' He said to me, 'You always use other people's money.' "

As an NBA owner, Sarkowsky flew down and back to Portland on the same day for games or he drove to the highest point near his suburban Clyde Hill home and sat in his car and listened to a faint Blazers radio broadcast signal. He shared in an NBA championship with a team built around Bill Walton.

The German-born Sarkowsky was never an athlete but always counted himself as a huge sports follower.

At now-defunct Broadway High School, he was the sports editor of the student newspaper, patterning his column, "The Water Boy," after the work of the *Seattle Post-Intelligencer's* Royal Brougham. For a first date with his wife of six decades, Faye, Sarkowsky took her to a University of Washington basketball game at Edmundson Pavilion.

His legacy eventually became this: No owner became more involved in so many different ways with Seattle's pro teams and its sporting outlets. He owned a piece of the original Sounders soccer franchise, became a major investor in the building of Emerald Downs horseracing track and led a group formed to keep the Mariners from moving elsewhere.

In later years, Sarkowsky spent his winters in Rancho Mirage, Calif., and the rest of the time in Seattle. He was still an active businessman, always looking to make money. However, his sporting involvement became confined to owning and breeding four dozen thorough-breds, most kept in Kentucky. Sarkowsky, who lived in high-rise condo 1901 at 91 Union St., always looked for interesting ventures, at one time even considering backing a Broadway play. He had plenty of capital to do whatever he wanted.

"He was one of the first billionaires in Seattle," Vertlieb said.

In 2014, Sarkowsky watched his former team drub the Denver Broncos 43-8 in Super Bowl XLVIII. There was no big gathering, no raucous party, no time to take a bow for what he started. He and Faye simply sat alone in front of a TV set in their California desert home, far away from the big-game hype gripping the New York area and beckoning loyal Northwest fans there.

The former owner, who pulled on a Seahawks shirt for the special occasion, preferred his solitude. He wanted his privacy so he could yell and scream at the screen without any restrictions. He was under doctor's orders not to fly. He also was the only one of the six original owners still alive to see this crowning moment, something not lost on him. The entire afternoon carried his stamp of approval on it, as did his ownership successor.

"It was unbelievable," he said. "I don't think I've ever seen a team play as perfect as the Seahawks did, particularly on defense. I believe in [coach] Pete Carroll. I believe in the system. Paul Allen is a great owner." ❖

Top 10 Seattle Owners

1. **Herman Sarkowsky,** Seahawks

2. **Sam Schulman,** Sonics

3. **Paul Allen,** Seahawks

4. **John Nordstrom,** Seahawks

5. **Adrian Hanauer,** Sounders

6. **Hiroshi Yamauchi,** Mariners

7. **Walter Schoenfeld,** Sonics, Mariners

8. **Emil Sick,** Rainiers

9. **Danny Kaye,** Mariners

10. **Walt Daggatt,** Sounders

Steve Largent was a Pro Football Hall of Fame wide receiver in the making, but neither he nor the Houston Oilers knew this when he reported for training camp in 1976. A fourth-round draft pick from the University of Tulsa, he was mesmerized by the big-name players surrounding him, coach Bum Phillips' laissez-faire way of doing business and the NFL in general.

Largent tried to fit in. He ran across the street on beer runs for the veteran players. He ran pass routes alongside returning Oilers starters Billy "White Shoes" Johnson and Ken Burrough, plus future Hall of Fame inductee Otis Taylor, acquired in an off-season trade from the Kansas City Chiefs. Largent also ran out of chances.

Four games into the exhibition season, Largent got on the field for just six plays, catching two passes. It was a clear sign he wasn't long for the team. It was made official when Largent was summoned to Phillips' office and told to bring his playbook. The folksy coach explained to Largent that he was cutting him to give the receiver a chance to catch on with another team, which was just another way of saying, "We don't want you." The Oilers coach said some other stuff, too, but it was indecipherable. "He talked for five more minutes and I didn't hear a word," Largent said. "I'd heard basically, 'You're fired.' "

Largent and his wife, Terry, drove home to Oklahoma City. He wasn't totally unprepared for the moment after

STEVE LARGENT
The Fingertip Catch

making sure he left college with a biology degree and other options in place. He was interested in the oil and gas industry, specifically offshore drilling. He was going to become an Oiler or an oiler, one way or another.

Largent was home only for a day when the phone rang and his pro football career was restored. The Seattle Seahawks wanted him at their training camp and offered him a plane ticket. Still, he showed some hesitation in joining the expansion team. "I said, 'Let me think about it. I'll call you back,' " Largent said. "I can't believe I said that now."

He was acquired on waivers for a low draft pick, arrived on a Thursday and played Sunday against San Diego, entering the game in the second half and catching two passes for 36 yards. He was in a situation as comfortable and ideal as the Oilers experience was foreign and hopeless to him.

Jerry Rhome, Largent's Tulsa offensive coordinator, was the Seahawks quarterbacks and receivers coach now, and he had pressed for the Seattle team to pursue the young wide receiver. Not only that, Rhome was asked to install the passing game, and he had put in the entire Tulsa package. With the same formations, routes and labels in place, Largent hit the training camp lottery.

"I knew all the nomenclature," Largent said. "They could call Split-I 79 and I already knew what that

> Largent was a keeper.
> He became an
> immediate starter and
> had ample opportunity
> to catch the ball.

meant. It gave me a real leg up. I felt totally confident coming in from Houston. That was a huge advantage for me in making the team and making a good first impression."

Largent was a keeper. He became an immediate starter and had ample opportunity to catch the ball. The Seahawks weren't very good — it took them three seasons to post a winning record and eight to qualify for the playoffs — and they played from behind all the time, forcing quarterback Jim Zorn and Zorn's successor Dave Krieg to throw a lot.

Largent showed off great hands. He ran creative and disciplined routes. He just wasn't very big or fast, which made it all the more maddening for defensive backs when he beat them over and over with his resolute play. With only modest aspirations for his Seahawks career at the outset, Largent became the greatest comeback story in Seattle sports history after transforming himself from NFL reject to Pro Football Hall of Fame inductee.

"Sherman Smith and I used to talk that our goal was to play four years, to basically get our degree in the National Football League," Largent said, referring to the Seahawks' starting running back and fellow rookie and now assistant coach. "The average career was three and a half years in the NFL. We didn't have a lot of long-term goals."

Largent was as unique off the field as he was on. He publicly professed his Christian faith without hesitation, same as Zorn. He served as his own agent, negotiating his first Seahawks contract, which paid him $28,000, $32,000 and $40,000 per season, plus a $20,000 signing bonus, more than anyone in his family had made, and his last contract, which brought him $1.1 million plus incentives, more than any other Seattle teammate made. He sought outside representation just once, hiring Bob Walsh to renegotiate his contract for his

Largent became the greatest comeback story in Seattle sports history after transforming himself from NFL reject to Pro Football Hall of Fame inductee.

fourth season, before reconsidering. "It didn't work and it was my fault," Largent said. "I didn't feel comfortable having somebody talk for me. I relieved Bob."

During the 1987 players' strike, Largent was the most visible of five Seahawks regulars who crossed the picket line and played in the final replacement game, indicating he felt compelled to honor the contract he had signed.

Largent always delivered and sometimes celebrated. He caught a game-winning, 43-yard touchdown pass over cornerback Louis Wright with 1:40 remaining in a 28-23 victory over Denver in 1979 — Seattle's first win against the Broncos. It was such an emotional moment Largent uncharacteristically spiked the football in the end zone, which he said was right for the moment but wouldn't happen again.

In a 33-0 victory over Cleveland to open the 1984 season, Largent felt immense satisfaction even while catching just two passes for a middling 17 yards. Browns cornerbacks Hanford Dixon and Frank Minnifield, always extra-vocal adversaries, were left speechless by the outcome.

"They would talk the whole game, that we're going to shut you down, and I was so happy we beat those guys; I remember how good I felt beating those two loudmouths," he said. "You know as a receiver, you were

always winning the day when you were catching the ball and you heard a defensive back saying something, cussing, being frustrated. That was always my goal: To hear them say, 'That rotten SOB Steve Largent.' "

Largent could have pointed to any one of his record-breaking receptions but he singled out consecutive catches against Miami in the 1983 playoffs as the most memorable of his career: Double-teamed and shut out for three and a half quarters, he pulled in a 16-yard pass followed by a 40-yarder, both in single coverage, that put the ball on the Dolphins 2 and set up the game-winning score in a 27-20 victory in Miami.

"Those two passes I caught in that game were the most significant passes I caught in my Seahawks career because they put us in the AFC championship game," Largent said.

Largent played 14 seasons and led the Seahawks in receiving for the first 12. He established six NFL career records, all since broken: Most receptions (819), most receiving yards (13,089), most touchdown catches (100), most 50-catch seasons (10), most 1,000-yard seasons (eight) and longest regular-season streak for consecutive games with a reception (177). He was shut out on catches in just three NFL games of the 200 he played. He was a seven-time Pro Bowl selection. He was the first Seattle player selected to the Hall of Fame. He was the first Seahawk to have his jersey (80) retired.

Out of the game, Largent faked people out once more. After claiming he wouldn't run for office, he entered politics. He served as an Oklahoma congressman for six years before making an unsuccessful bid for governor, the popular Republican proving far too conservative for a conservative state.

Largent was still a Seahawks player when he first considered a life of policy-making. On team charter flights, he held long, thought-provoking discussions with quarterback Jeff Kemp, son of former Buffalo Bills quarterback Jack Kemp, the latter a congressman and presidential candidate.

Largent made his move after disagreeing with countless political decisions emanating out of Washington. In 1994, he declared his candidacy for a U.S. Representative seat. The nation's leader at the time was responsible for the former NFL player's leap into the political arena.

"It was probably Bill Clinton more than anything else – total frustration," Largent said. "Gays in the military, repealing abortion, tax increases, government health care, scandals; it was one thing after another. I've met him and he's a very personable guy. He's very likeable. I like him. I just didn't like the way he was doing things."

Largent proved to be a formidable legislator. He wasn't afraid to go across the middle and take a hit. Or give one out. In 1997, Largent and 10 other Republicans boldly derailed a GOP spending bill, infuriating Newt Gingrich. Zeroing in on the dissident 11, Gingrich asked why these individuals thought they were so much better than everyone else? He waited for a meek response. Largent stood up. "I told him I had been in a lot smaller rooms with a lot bigger men," Largent said.

Largent left politics once his gubernatorial bid failed and his health took a strange turn. He was four years out of office and working as a telecommunications lobbyist in Washington, D.C., when the rigors of his pro football career likely caught up with him. In 2005, Largent suffered a stroke that affected his memory.

It was a surprising setback for a 51-year-old man who was still devoted to fitness. He took anti-cholesterol medication to prevent a reoccurrence. He shrugged it off like some cloying cornerback. "It was more an anomaly than anything else," Largent said while admitting to short-term memory loss. However, others saw signs of greater damage.

Bob Houbregs, a former NBA player and general manager who was a regular tennis partner for the Seahawks legend and considered himself a good friend, called to say hello and was taken aback when Largent said he didn't know him.

Asked about his career, Largent couldn't recall Otis Taylor's or Bob Walsh's names without considerable help, or the names of the two Cleveland defensive backs who had bumped and baited him for several seasons, or his ongoing battles with Oakland's Lester Hayes.

Krieg encountered Largent at a Seahawks' charity golf tournament and noted an unmistakable change in his former teammate. The quarterback, in some ways, said he might have been responsible for Largent's stroke.

"Some of that could have been from the low passes I threw him and him getting hit from behind by guys like Mike Harden, and I'm really concerned for him," Krieg said, referring to Largent's battles with the Denver Broncos safety and others. "The brain is just jelly in the cranium. Steve used to be a quick-witted guy."

The NFL was tough on him, no doubt about it. Largent's introduction to the league, coming in his failed attempt with the Oilers, and his stroke following retirement, showed how fickle pro football could be.

Largent, who lived at 18604 N.W. Cervinia Court in Issaquah, ended up convincing everyone except himself that he was one of pro football's greatest players because he knew how close he had come to a life of offshore drilling.

"I think if I hadn't been in Seattle I probably wouldn't have made it in the National Football League," Largent said. "The difference in not making it in the league and being a great player is not much, maybe a second. I definitely came into the league not cocky or overconfident, for sure. I never saw myself as a Hall of Fame player. I'm not sure I believed it when I was inducted." ❖

Top 10 Seahawks
1. Walter Jones, OT
2. Richard Sherman, CB
3. Steve Largent, WR
4. Russell Wilson, QB
5. Cortez Kennedy, DT
6. Steve Hutchinson, OG
7. Marshawn Lynch, RB
8. Kenny Easley, SS
9. Earl Thomas, FS
10. Dave Krieg, QB

DON JAMES

The Dynasty Builder

The University of Washington, in need of a football coach for the first time in 18 years, wanted a big name to lead the program. Dan Devine met the qualifications. Yet he canceled his Tuesday job interview with the Huskies because he got a better offer, jumping from the Green Bay Packers to Notre Dame.

Attention shifted to Mike White, the first to interview on a Monday in Seattle. White met with UW athletic director Joe Kearney, school president John R. Hogness and the screening committee, but he chose to keep his job at Cal.

Now 0-for-2, the Huskies brought in an African-American candidate. Doug Porter, Howard coach and former Grambling assistant for the legendary Eddie Robinson, took part in a Wednesday interview, but he wasn't selected.

Darryl Rogers, an up-and-coming coach from San Jose State, was the frontrunner after sitting down on Friday with UW officials. At least the *Seattle Post-Intelligencer* thought so, offering the headline: "Rogers Top UW Candidate?"

There was one more applicant: Kent State's Don James. He drew the final interview slot on Saturday. Most people in Seattle didn't know him. After all, he was a Mid-American Conference coach just back from a Tangerine Bowl loss, both college football rungs well below the Pacific-8 Conference and Rose Bowl.

Washington's previous coach, Jim Owens, was this all-encompassing physical presence with the folksy Southern twang, whereas James was a short man with a receding hairline and stoic presence.

A day later, however, Washington named James as the next Husky football coach, creating an unlikely pairing because the Ohio native didn't know the West Coast any better than it knew him.

"It was an area I obviously had never been to," said James, who was confident he could do the job. "I just felt I had been in big stadiums as an assistant at Michigan, Colorado and Florida State. I wasn't overwhelmed. I had a good enough background to know if you didn't get good players in here you weren't going to last long."

James' hiring was seriously questioned after he lost four of his first six games in 1975, none more distressing than a 52-0 defeat to Alabama in Tuscaloosa. He slept in his office for four nights a week the rest of the season rather than make the 20-minute drive to his Bellevue home, as if to show people that no one was going to outwork him.

He calmed everyone by winning four of his final five games, a notable finish because he swept the Los Angeles schools, which Washington hadn't done in 11 seasons. He made significant recruiting inroads

After a solitary
losing season in 1976,
James became Seattle's
most consistently successful
modern-day coach and
an unmatched empire builder.

in Southern California, something the Huskies had never done before.

After a solitary losing season in 1976, James became Seattle's most consistently successful modern day coach and an unmatched empire builder. He came up with 16 consecutive winning seasons accompanied by 14 bowl trips, which included six Rose Bowls, beginning with a 27-20 upset of Michigan in 1978. At times, he even amazed himself with the direction his program took.

"It was hard to believe that we ever got to a place where we were physically better than SC and UCLA," James said. "It used to be win one out of three against them and consider it a victory. I was a little surprised that we could get that much ahead of some of the sun-belt coaches in our league."

James, who lived at 3325 N.E. 126th Ave. in Bellevue, pulled this off with organizational skills that were the envy of corporate America. He was a notorious note-taker at all times – games, practices, even in bed. More than once he woke up at 3 a.m. with an inspiration and immediately jotted something down.

He also coached the coaches, not necessarily the players, rightfully figuring this approach would generate more respect among those inside the program. To create a proper distance yet keep an eye on everything, James coached from a box-like tower.

"From what I learned at Florida State and Michigan, the one thing I knew was assistant coaches wanted to coach," James said. "You can't just turn them loose but you have to give them responsibility to coach. Some head coaches like to coordinate the defense or the offense but I didn't feel the need to do that. I couldn't stand on one end of the field not knowing what was going on at the other end. That's when I became a tower coach."

In compiling a 153-57-2 UW record, James made it clear at all times that he was in charge. Sometimes it was humorous, other times not. Before a 1988 game against USC, he told beat writers to hold off reporting a thumb injury suffered by starting quarterback Cary Conklin until the end of the week. James angrily put his practice sessions off-limits when his edict was disregarded and a couple of reports surfaced.

The Husky coach was genuinely offended when Conklin's thumb made front-page news and raged at anyone who dared mention it later, even though the quarterback eventually was cleared to play and had a career day against the Trojans. The coach's dark mood seemed so uncharacteristic, yet others said it was routine.

"When he believes in something, he's not going to back down," said Jim Mora Sr., James' original UW defensive coordinator. "He's a tough guy. We had disagreements. We battled. We had arguments."

There's a bus driver out there somewhere who went through all of that in one exchange. Chances are his ears haven't stopped ringing. It was 1979 when the infamous "Husky bus race" took place. Washington was en route to Oregon in a two-bus caravan to play the Ducks. James' bus was always the first one in line, except on that day.

As Husky fullback Toussaint Tyler recounted, "I was on the second bus and me and Curt Marsh, James Davis and Kyle Stevens were talking to the bus driver and we said, 'Pass the bus, pass the bus.' We were cheering this guy on. I was waving to Coach James and laughing, and he didn't like that as we went right by. We knew Coach James was going to be mad. You knew that with the look he had on his face. He hated it."

When the two buses finally rolled to a stop halfway to Eugene, James went after the other driver with a verbal blitz. The driver quit on the spot.

For James, things had to be just so. There could be no wavering. Former players can remember him stopping practice a half-hour into it and making everyone start from the top to get it right. What that meant was they had to run onto the field and do their calisthenics again.

Players preferred the James approach, especially after comparing him to their professional, and sometimes more legendary, football coaches.

"Don James was God," said Steve Emtman, a UW All-America defensive tackle and James' most decorated player. "I never saw a coach anywhere I played, and that includes Jimmy Johnson and Don Shula, who was as organized and had as much respect from his players as Don James did. I was scared to death to talk to him until I was done playing."

As the victories and bowls piled up, the recruits kept coming – better and better players. James' Huskies nearly won the 1984 national championship, capturing 11 of 12 games, which included a 28-17 victory over Oklahoma in the Orange Bowl. A late-season 16-7 loss to USC, however, left the UW second in the polls behind unbeaten BYU.

Seven years later, the Huskies ran the table with an overly dominant team, going 12-0 after beating Michigan 34-14 in the Rose Bowl, and shared the national title with fellow unbeaten Miami.

"I don't know if I was totally disappointed after the Oklahoma win, but to be that close a second time and not get it would have been a great disappointment," James said.

With all of that success came numerous job opportunities. James resisted serious overtures from Ohio State and the Seattle Seahawks. In 1982, speculation was rampant that James was bound for the local NFL team and it escalated to a fever pitch when the Seahawks fired original coach Jack Patera during the season. James, with an undefeated team at the time, called a news conference to clarify that he wasn't leaving the UW, at least not at that time.

"I knew them all and I talked to them," James said of the Seahawks owners. "I had a pretty good team in '82. I'd made up my mind to stay. I said maybe I'd talk to them again at the end of the season if they could wait. The bad thing was they fired Patera at midseason."

UW athletic director Mike Lude wouldn't give the Seahawks official permission to speak to James, but he came up with another candidate. Buffalo Bills coach Chuck Knox asked Lude who he should contact about the NFL job, and Lude called owner John Nordstrom on his behalf.

"The Seahawks and Ohio State would have taken him with the snap of their fingers," Lude said of his coach. "But he liked the fact we got it going at Washington. And Don James was not the kind of guy you could wave a million dollars in front of and he'd jump."

The good feelings, however, didn't last forever at the UW, bringing a premature end to a golden era. As was the case with many top college programs, success was followed by players feeling invincible and turning reckless, and scandal emerged.

Following the 1992 season and a third Rose Bowl appearance in as many years, the Huskies were found guilty of 15 charges of impropriety levied by the Pac-10 Conference. Violations involved quarterback Billy Joe Hobert's $50,000 in personal loans from an Idaho businessman, boosters providing free meals and excessive wages for summer jobs, and improper recruiting inducements.

At closed-door hearings in San Francisco, Pac-10 athletic directors were overheard sarcastically degrading James' program between sessions. *Seattle Times* reporter Tom Farrey and I snuck into an adjoining conference room, stretched out on the floor for a couple hours in the dark and listened to the proceedings in secret, chased out only when a clean-up crew came in and flipped on the lights. We heard enough to know the athletic directors were bent on handing out severe penalties to the UW no matter what was uncovered.

Receiving penalties more severe than any in Pac-10 history, the Huskies were stripped of two possible bowl appearances, $1.4 million in TV revenue for a year, and 20 scholarships and 65 recruiting visits for two years. When James stepped to the podium to address his football team on the day the penalties came down, solemn words were expected. James told his players he was quitting and started to cry. They stared in disbelief as he walked out the door.

He had planned to coach at least through the length of his contract, which ran for three more seasons through 1995, but he was a man of rigid principle.

"I made up my mind to quit the night before that if they didn't ratify," James said. "I had the sanctions in my pocket for a week. I didn't agree with everything. It was not a big deal; give us 11 games of penalties and it would have been over. I wanted to save the TV money. They weren't going to take us off TV, but they wanted to keep raping and pillaging us in what we were doing, and I wasn't going to do it."

Twenty years later, James would leave Seattle as suddenly as he embraced it. After attending the first game at remodeled Husky Stadium, he became terminally ill. On Oct. 20, 2013, the former coach was 80 when he died of pancreatic cancer, surrounded by family members, at his waterfront condominium in Kirkland, one looking across Lake Washington at the football facilities. A memorial service was held in Edmundson Pavilion and James' stark beginnings were referenced among the eulogies.

"Who in Seattle knew what you were getting?" asked Gary Pinkel, Missouri coach and former James assistant, at the ceremony. ❖

Top 10 Coaches & Managers

1. Don James, UW
2. Pete Carroll, Seahawks
3. Lenny Wilkens, Sonics
4. Lou Piniella, Mariners
5. Don Coryell, Chargers, Cardinals
6. Mike Holmgren, Seahawks
7. Jim Owens, UW
8. Marv Harshman, UW
9. George Karl, Sonics
10. Fred Hutchinson, Tigers, Reds, Cardinals

A talented junior-college quarterback was available in Los Angeles. Don James, the new University of Washington football coach, was on the job for just a few months in 1975 and on the verge of running his first spring practice when his defensive backs coach Chick Harris entered the room with this urgent news.

James wanted to know why the player wasn't already signed. Harris responded that the recruit had played only a year of JC ball. James started backpedaling after hearing this. He had been advised that if you took an underclassman early from a West Coast two-year school, you might get blackballed in future recruiting.

The situation surrounding Harold Warren Moon was different, a persistent Harris pointed out. Moon had played for West Los Angeles College with the understanding he would stay just one season and leave for a bigger school. James started to warm to the idea. "If you get an agreement with the coach, we just picked up a recruit," James told the assistant coach.

Putting the new quarterback on the field and keeping him there would be more difficult than signing

On Sept. 13, 1975,
Moon drew the opening start
against Arizona State on
the road, quietly breaking
a Seattle color line as the
Huskies' first starting
African-American quarterback
and becoming a landmark
player for the city.

WARREN MOON

Seattle's Black Magic

him: Moon was African-American. In a program fraught with racial strife over the previous decade, even in an enlightened city such as Seattle, a black starting quarterback was going to be a tough sell.

Yet for the 1975 Huskies and their new coach, this seemed an inevitable path. James chose his No. 1 quarterback from three candidates: Moon and a pair of inherited seniors, Chris Rowland and Cliff McBride. Rowland, who was white and a local favorite from Seattle, was the starter the previous season until he broke his ankle while running an option play with the Huskies running up the score in a 66-0 victory over Oregon. McBride, a New Yorker and a transfer, became the designated starter coming out of James' first spring drills. McBride also was black.

"The biggest thing we had to do is we wanted to be totally fair," James said. "We didn't want to bring Warren in and just give him the job. Somebody had to step up and win the job. The coach's responsibility is to be fair. With [quarterbacks coach] Ray Dorr, it was making him nuts. We logged every pass and competition, filmed every practice. We had Chris Rowland and we wanted to be fair to all the quarterbacks. It was close."

On Sept. 13, 1975, Moon drew the opening start against Arizona State on the road, quietly breaking a Seattle color line as the Huskies' first starting African-American quarterback and becoming a landmark player for the city. It was an otherwise forgettable experience. He fumbled the first snap and completed just 12 of 23 passes for 121 yards, and the offense stalled in a 35-12 defeat.

Moon came home and lost to Texas. Boos greeted him with every miscue. He lost at Alabama 52-0. After six games, four of which the Huskies lost, the newcomer from California had received far more backlash than backslaps, his confidence was shot and he was benched in favor of Rowland.

"Not to take anything away from Warren, but I don't think he was ready," said Rowland, remembering a young Moon as a road roommate who conscientiously put on his pajamas and said his prayers before he went to bed. "James wanted to play as many young guys as he could to help recruiting. Players see that and it's 'Where do I sign?' I think our team was sacrificed for the longer good of the program."

James tried to prepare his young quarterback for the obvious pratfalls that were sure to come for a UW team not only rebuilding under a first-year coach but relying on an untested junior-college transfer to run the new offense. The coach did his best to try and take the race card out of it, though it was clear that feelings bordering on bigotry were ever-present on game day at Husky Stadium.

"The thing we tried to emphasize with Warren is when we lose it's going to be the head coach and the quarterback," James said. "When we win, the coach is going to get too much credit. When they're booing, it's not going to be color; it's going to be us not being successful."

It didn't help the new quarterback's standing with the local fan base any that the Huskies won four of the five games that Rowland started, including a sweep of USC and UCLA. Moon stayed on the sideline until the

Apple Cup, when a combined hepatitis-mononucleosis virus knocked Rowland out of all but the opening series against Washington State.

Moon came off the bench and threw a twice-deflected, 78-yard touchdown pass to Spider Gaines inside the final two minutes for a stunning 28-27 victory.

People conveniently forgot about those heroics when Moon and the 1976 Huskies struggled to a 5-6 season – James' only losing record among his 18 years at Washington. The negative reaction to Moon cascaded throughout the cavernous stadium. It was never louder than after a fourth-and-1 play against California when he purposely threw the ball out of bounds near the end of the first half thinking he had another down to use. The Huskies lost the game 7-0.

Moon considered going home to Los Angeles. He thought about it a lot. He had to be talked out of it. "It hurt deep," Moon said, acknowledging the racial bias from his critics. "It was a big shock for me to go out at 19 years old and be booed by 60,000 people. I would talk to my mom and girlfriend about it. My mom would say, 'If you decide to leave and go to another school, it could happen again. Just stay and let things work out.' And that's what happened."

Moon and the Huskies lost three of their first four games in 1977 before all that patience and perseverance started paying off. This was a different Moon, even in appearance: He switched jersey numbers, from 12 to 1. He also settled down, helped his team win six of the final seven contests and ended up in the Rose Bowl.

One of his biggest moments came at home in a 28-10 victory over USC, when Moon threw for a touchdown and ran for two others, breaking free from the Trojans for a late 71-yard scoring dash. He heard

nothing but cheers and people chanting his first name in Husky Stadium that day. Yet he wasn't done.

In Pasadena, Moon was named Rose Bowl offensive MVP after he ran for two touchdowns and passed for another in a 27-20 upset of the University of Michigan. It was such a defining moment for the quarterback that he was still in uniform hours after the game wandering the locker area. He fielded so many questions and did so many interviews that the Rose Bowl was empty and the team buses were gone when he departed. Luckily, his family was waiting.

"It kind of started the whole James era off; it put Washington on the map and people knew us all over the country," Moon said. "That was basically the start of it all, for me, too. It got my name recognized."

The Huskies and Moon had plenty of motivation for beating the Big Ten team. Traditionally, the two Rose Bowl quarterbacks posed together for a photograph. Michigan's Rick Leach declined, sending over one of his linemen instead. Moon and his teammates were friendly to Wolverines players at Disneyland but were ignored. The Huskies, taking chances whenever they could, finally got a measure of respect by running out

"It kind of started the whole James era off; it put Washington on the map and people knew us all over the country," Moon said. "That was basically the start of it all, for me, too. It got my name recognized."

to a 24-0 lead before hanging on for the win. "It erased all the bad times," Moon said.

Turning to the pros, Moon enjoyed a Pro Football Hall of Fame career, but not before dealing with some of the same issues that he battled through with the Huskies. The NFL initially wasn't open to a black quarterback, forcing him to play six seasons in the CFL with the Edmonton Eskimos.

Five Grey Cup victories later, he chose the Houston Oilers over the Seattle Seahawks in a free-agent bidding war, persuaded by a $4.5 million signing bonus to play in Texas rather than his college town. Moon ran into similar impatience with the Oilers when he suffered through three consecutive losing seasons before leading them into the playoffs and engineering a 23-20 postseason victory over the Seahawks in 1987.

"Coming down to Houston, when things weren't going well in the beginning, I could reflect back to college and that made things easier," Moon said. "Eventually things turned around."

Moon played 23 pro seasons, joining the Minnesota Vikings and Kansas City Chiefs before coming back to Seattle for two years with the Seahawks. He was a nine-time Pro Bowl selection. He finished with combined NFL-CFL stats of 5,357 completions in 9,205 attempts for 70,553 yards (more than 40 miles) and 435 touchdowns.

In 2000, Moon retired from football, a quarter of a century after stepping into Husky Stadium for the first time, and turned to a Seahawks broadcasting career and wrote his autobiography. He moved to Seattle's northern suburbs to Duvall, now comfortable with the local landscape. His skin color was irrelevant now, the boos a faint memory. ❖

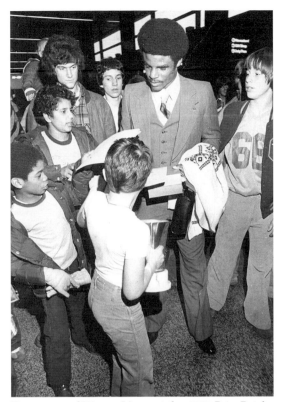

Fans surround Warren Moon at the 1978 Rose Bowl.

TOP 10 UW QUARTERBACKS

1. Warren Moon
2. Don Heinrich
3. Bob Schloredt
4. Sonny Sixkiller
5. Billy Joe Hobert
6. Mark Brunell
7. Marques Tuiasosopo
8. Chris Chandler
9. Steve Pelleur
10. Jake Locker

SPIDER GAINES

The Tangled Web

Robert "Spider" Gaines every so often called up a *Seattle Post-Intelligencer* sportswriter he knew and asked him to send the proof. The request directed to me was always the same and always urgent. The proof was a video copy of the NBC telecast of the 1978 Rose Bowl game between Gaines' Washington football team and the Michigan Wolverines, plus assorted newspaper clippings about him, in his full athletic glory.

Spider always needed to convince a newfound friend, a disbelieving neighbor, even his skeptical teenage daughter of who he once was.

At the height of his sporting prowess, Gaines was a gifted college football player and trackman whose next destination easily could have been the NFL or Olympic Games, and whose reward might have been a lifetime of riches and never-ending fame. Yet he was a street kid from Richmond, Calif., who couldn't shake his past, who allowed his misguided impulses to obscure and destroy ultimate dreams. He took unbelievable risks.

His reckless approach was never more apparent than when he ran onto the field on New Year's Day to share in the Huskies' memorable 27-20 upset victory over a powerful Michigan team. "I played 'high' in the Rose Bowl," said Gaines, admitting to heavy cocaine and marijuana use over several hours leading up to kickoff.

Under the influence or not, Gaines was a heroic figure in Pasadena that day, scoring on a 28-yard pass

from quarterback Warren Moon and having another touchdown on a 31-yard end-around play nullified by a clipping penalty.

Yet in a maddeningly short time, the fleet wide receiver went from postseason legend to Seattle's most renegade and irresponsible athlete, frittering away countless golden opportunities. His rap sheet, mixed with his medical chart, was painful to peruse. Twice in Seattle and once in Phoenix, Gaines was arrested and accused of sexual assault without facing conviction. He bore deep physical scars from being stabbed in the stomach and taking a liquor bottle to the side of the face, wounds received in fights in his hometown of Richmond.

He was deported from British Columbia after coming under surveillance as a pimp who made Canadian women readily available for sexual favors and subsequently refusing to turn informant on this clandestine trade.

In 2008, Gaines was publicly linked by Seattle's KIRO-TV to the shooting deaths 18 years earlier of a pair of South Park lawyers, his alleged involvement taken at the word of a woman informant. He was met by a news crew in an ambush interview on a Seattle street corner. He was never questioned, arrested,

> Yet in a maddeningly short time, the fleet wide receiver went from postseason legend to Seattle's most renegade and irresponsible athlete, frittering away countless golden opportunities.

charged or convicted of the crime, though King County Sheriff investigators privately still consider him a prime suspect.

"They said I executed two people but I didn't know them cats," Gaines said. "I said come talk to me when you have some damn proof."

Gaines was a product of northern California's East Bay mean streets, but he could be personable and charming. He also could be brutally honest in discussing his sins, so much so that one was left to wonder whether he didn't know any better or he was the ultimate con man. "That was my lifestyle," he said.

Gaines showed up at Washington as part of coach Don James' original recruiting class, as a tall, blazing receiver who couldn't wait to make things happen. He was nicknamed "Spider" as a young kid, by the father of Lance Theoudele, a high school and UW teammate, for the skittery way he ran around the bases.

As a Huskies freshman, he played just seven minutes during the season but was able to block five kicks and catch two TD passes, including a 78-yarder that led to an improbable 28-27 victory over Washington State in the 1975 Apple Cup.

His penchant for the heroic moment pulled fans from their Husky Stadium seats and had them cheering wildly at all times, especially in big games. He caught 74- and 58-yard scoring passes against Alabama and dropped a third deep toss. In his college career, he came up with 70 receptions for 1,651 yards and made 17 trips to the end zone.

Yet with success came temptation and submission. Gaines accepted cash loans from sports agent Mike Trope and assorted gifts from UW boosters, illegal inducements such as a free stereo system, stuff that he said were enjoyed by several of his Huskies teammates at the time. If so, everyone got away with it undetected.

> Gaines showed up at Washington as part of coach Don James' original recruiting class, as a tall, blazing receiver who couldn't wait to make things happen.

He temporarily quit the team at the outset of his senior season because Moon's quarterback replacement, Tom Porras, couldn't adequately deliver the ball to him. And he was that Rose Bowl headliner, even with his body compromised.

On New Year's Eve leading up to the 1978 Rose Bowl, Gaines complied with the 11 p.m. curfew put in place by the Huskies' coaching staff. In fact, he never left his Newport Beach hotel room that night. Instead, he waved four high school friends inside at 1 a.m., guys he identified as Mario, Antonio, Eric and Mickey, and they proceeded to party hard together until dawn. "We were smoking weed and we did cocaine," Gaines admitted. "I always had beer in my room."

Gaines got just two hours of sleep before the biggest game in his college football career. He was still feeling fairly buzzed for pre-game warm-ups. Not surprisingly, he dropped his first pass from Moon against the Wolverines. He was lethargic much of the opening quarter. He didn't feel in control of his football abilities until the second quarter. "I didn't come down from the cocaine until I started running and sweating," he said.

So big and fast, Gaines had the makings of a first-round NFL draft pick. But he wasn't always motivated and the scouts picked up on that; he wasn't selected

until the sixth round by the Kansas City Chiefs. He signed for $30,000 and it should have been 10 times that, but he dropped in value in a hurry by his own doing.

A few weeks before training camp, Gaines tore knee cartilage while playing catch with friends back home in Richmond and needed surgery. Sadly, he was never an explosive player again. He went to camp with the Chiefs, San Francisco 49ers, Green Bay Packers, Baltimore Colts, the USFL's Oklahoma Outlaws, and the CFL's British Columbia Lions and Montreal Alouettes. He played only a handful of games for Montreal and was released.

A world-class hurdler, Gaines also had his Olympic hopes dashed for good by that knee injury, though if healthy he would have shared in the disappointment of the American boycott of the 1980 Moscow Olympics.

"He had a lot of ability but he kind of piddled it away," said Mike Lude, former UW athletic director, who through the years received reports of the wide receiver's spiraling ways, including a family member's account. "He was panhandling in downtown Seattle, on the street with his hand out and begging, and he didn't know it was my son-in-law he stopped. He said he was a former Husky athlete, down on his luck. My son-in-law recognized him as Spider."

After exhausting his pro football opportunities, Gaines returned to Vancouver, the city that seemed the most vibrant and fun. He started hanging out in downtown clubs. He started working the streets. He called himself "Slam," rode around in limousines and made prostitutes available to an eager clientele.

"If you're a black guy up there you're either a ballplayer or pimpin', and I was out on the street all the time, doing anything to get a girl to put money in my pockets," Gaines said. "I don't know if it was my destiny, but it was just one of those things that fell into my lap and I went with it."

Spider Gaines was a risk-taker at the UW.

For 18 months, ending in 1985, Gaines made two different women available for sex. He earned $80,000 to $100,000 a year. He wandered through busy Vancouver nightclubs such as the Warehouse, Richard's and Desmond Inn to find paying customers. He had plenty of cash. He bought nice clothes. He didn't blink either when he ran into a pair of shocked UW teammates, former running back Ronnie Rowland and linebacker Antoine Richardson, who were visiting the city while working as musicians.

Gaines also encountered a guy who slapped one of his girls and a sailor who said he wouldn't pay for the services provided, and Gaines used his football size to persuade them to settle down and settle up.

What ultimately cooled this unsavory business venture was the day Gaines emerged from his downtown apartment, which was filled only with mattresses, and he was confronted by Canadian immigration agents. They were watching him. They knew what he was doing. They interviewed him a couple of times. They demanded that he become an informant and he refused. "I wasn't going to be a damn snitch," Gaines said.

An uncooperative Gaines was deported from Canada. He ended up living in Tacoma near then-McChord Air Base with a woman he met in Vancouver and they had a daughter together.

He had 27 job offers after a *Post-Intelligencer* story written by me detailed his down-and-out existence a decade after the Rose Bowl, and he accepted construction work from former UW and NFL player Rick Redman. He was allowed to re-enroll at the school and became a graduate assistant coach for James, only to lose it all when he made an unwanted advance on a woman in a University District tavern and was accused of fondling her.

Gaines returned to northern California and worked as a school playground monitor until he got into a fight, took a bottle to the head and nearly lost an eye. He took a job at a Walgreen's drugstore near his hometown, working the graveyard shift all alone as a security guard.

After wandering without direction, Gaines returned to Seattle. He had a lengthy stay at the Sea Mar Residential Alcohol and Drug Treatment Center at 24215 Pacific Highway S. in Des Moines, not far from Seattle-Tacoma International Airport. He reconnected with his daughter, who became a high school basketball star. He went back to class at the UW and finally obtained a college degree, an achievement he advertised on his cell phone with the following voice-mail message: "This is Robert Gaines, college graduate."

With rounder features and middle age taking over, Gaines found it tougher convincing people who he once was, that he formerly answered to this misguided character named Spider who was involved in all sorts of mayhem. Maybe that was a good thing. ❖

Jack Thompson was what was known as a "lay-down" recruit for the University of Washington football team. He was a quarterback for Evergreen High in south Seattle, someone with a big arm who didn't need a persuasive scholarship sales pitch or any prodding at all. He had made his college choice long ago and everyone involved knew it: He wanted to play for the Huskies, and they wanted him.

Thompson grew up with the hometown program and considered no one else. In terms of recruiting, this was a done deal. There was no conceivable way to screw this up.

The Thompson family got all excited on the day in 1974 when Huskies coach Jim Owens called and said he was in Issaquah with another recruit and wanted to stop by for a home visit that afternoon at 4 p.m. The quarterback woke up his father, a night-shift Boeing worker who got out of bed, shaved and put on a tie, eager to meet someone he deeply admired. Thompson's mother likewise turned giddy and got dressed up for the big moment.

Owens, however, never showed at the quarterback's residence at 10439 7th Ave. S.W. in White Center, and never explained himself. The Huskies coach made another appointment with the Thompsons. Owens stood up the family a second time, too.

Thompson took his indignation across the state and became an NCAA record-setter and a two-time all-conference quarterback for rival Washington State.

JACK THOMPSON
The Not-Goin' Samoan

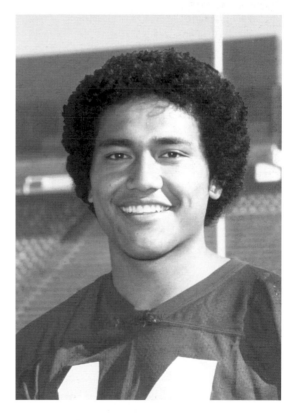

The UW coach still wanted the accomplished passer, even if he had a funny way of showing it. Owens must have really bought into the lay-down recruit stuff but it backfired. Thompson took his Huskies recruiting trip, only for a much different reason than was originally intended: He wanted to deliver a personal message to the leader who couldn't seem to follow a schedule and keep his word.

"I took it all in, and, boy oh boy, I was dreaming of being purple and gold," Thompson said. "I got to meet the coach at the end. Jim Owens called me in and he was an intimidating guy, and he said, 'Are you ready to wear No. 14 for us?' I said, 'No, I can't.' I said, 'You could do anything to me but what you did to my mom and dad, I just can't let you do that.' I cried in front of him. I was hurt. I really wanted to play there badly."

Thompson took his indignation across the state and became an NCAA record-setter and a two-time all-conference quarterback for rival Washington State. His No. 14 was the second of two jerseys retired by the Cougars, joining center Mel Hein (7), and those closely associated with the program have since considered the quarterback the most prominent player in school history. Thompson, of South Pacific heritage, came away from his college experience with the best nickname of any homegrown Seattle athlete when he was tagged "The Throwin' Samoan."

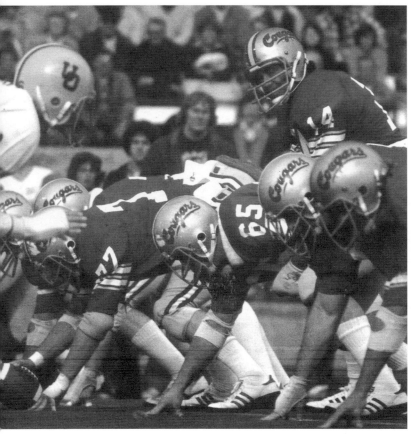

Jack Thompson calls the signals for WSU against Oregon.

As it turned out, some of those involved in the WSU recruiting process were no better at keeping appointments than Owens. Once he arrived in Pullman, Thompson was told by Cougars freshman quarterback John Hopkins, his player host, that he would be picked up at 7 p.m. and taken on a campus tour. Hopkins never showed. Luckily, Thompson's parents weren't disrespected this time. This slam had the reverse affect on him.

"What I did for my recruiting night was walk the campus," Thompson said. "It was a Thursday night and I talked to people who didn't know me from a hill of beans and I loved it. The next morning [assistant coach] Mike Price, who was the guy who was on me, asked me, 'How did Hollywood [Hopkins] treat you?' and I told Price that he never showed up. I said if anything, I wanted to come back and beat his brains out. I ended up at Washington State because the freshman quarterback who recruited me stiffed me."

Thompson didn't get his college career off the ground right away. In warm-ups for his first game in 1974 against Kansas, Thompson tore up his left knee in a gruesome manner, catching it on the Astroturf at Spokane's Joe Albi Stadium. After recovering, he played only sparingly in his second season.

In 1976, however, the third-year sophomore came off the bench for the first three games for coach Jackie Sherrill before becoming the Cougars starter and program fixture for good, Thompson threw for 2,762 yards and 20 touchdowns and was selected first-team All-Pacific-8 quarterback that year.

The nickname was slapped on him during his transition from back-up quarterback to starter and it was created in the Midwest. Before a Sept. 26, 1976, game at Wisconsin, an outing the Cougars lost 35-26, Thompson was described as "The Throwin' Samoan" in the *Wisconsin State Journal*. Harry Misseldine, the *Spokane Spokesman-Review* beat writer, used it so much thereafter the nickname stuck. The crusty, opportunistic Misseldine even took credit for it.

"I was still the second-string quarterback but, based on how I played the previous week against Minnesota, they somehow thought I was going to play a lot," Thompson said. "I woke up Saturday morning for the game and there on the front page was the headline, 'The Throwin' Samoan is in town,' and they had a picture of me. It was the darnedest thing. That's the first time I ever saw the nickname."

Thompson put it to better use in 1977, leading the now Warren Powers-coached Cougars to a 7-4 season, highlighted by a 19-10 victory over 15th-ranked Nebraska before a crowd of 75,922 in Lincoln. People still consider that game, with the raucous setting in mind, as the greatest victory in school history.

WSU was a 17-point underdog, but the Throwin' Samoan threw two touchdown passes and linebacker Don Nevels left a Cornhuskers quarterback knocked out cold on a goal-line plunge. Respect came well before the upset was complete, too.

"I got flushed out of the pocket and ran to the Nebraska sideline and realized I was too far away to run out of bounds, so I slid and the linebackers flew over me," Thompson said. "I got up and one of their coaches came over and ripped me and called me chicken [bleep] for not taking those guys on. I said, 'What, are you kidding?' Tom Osborne came over and pulled the assistant coach back, class man that he was. Osborne looked at me and said, 'You're playing a great game and you're smart.' "

Answering to four WSU head coaches in his five seasons, the Throwin' Samoan set an NCAA record with 7,818 career passing yards. As a senior, he was named the first-team All-Pacific-10 quarterback (the league had expanded by then), even while his team slipped to 3-7-1.

He considered leaving early for the NFL and was told he would be the 15th pick in the draft, but he waited another year and was taken No. 3 overall by the Cincinnati Bengals. He was the first quarterback selected in 1979, taken four slots higher than Phil Simms and 79 picks before Joe Montana.

Thompson lasted six years in the pro ranks, backing up Ken Anderson with the Bengals and getting a chance to start with the woebegone Tampa Bay Buccaneers. Draft analysts considered him a bust. Thompson had his moments, though, sharing in Cincinnati's 1981 Super Bowl appearance against the San Francisco 49ers, throwing four touchdown passes against the Houston Oilers, collecting 373 passing yards against the Detroit Lions, and coming off the bench to rescue a 30-28 victory over the Pittsburgh Steelers and his quarterback idol Terry Bradshaw.

"After the game Bradshaw came right up to me and said, 'Kid, helluva game,' " said Thompson, who wore No. 12 with the Bengals because it was Bradshaw's and 14 already belonged to Anderson. "I always liked him and he always treated me with kindness and respect. I called him Terry. I felt like a kid in the candy store every time I played against the Steelers. When I saw Mean Joe Greene, though, I could never get myself to call

him Joe. I always had to call him Mr. Greene. He found that amusing."

Thompson was traded to Tampa Bay after a falling-out with Bengals offensive coordinator Lindy Infante and mulling a jump to the USFL's Michigan Panthers. He later received an on-field apology from Cincinnati owner Paul Brown, who said he regretted making the deal, before Thompson played the game that day against the Bengals.

The quarterback was released after two seasons in Tampa Bay and, while making the free-agent rounds, was encouraged to retire by the Buffalo Bills' team physician because of his deteriorating left knee. The Throwin' Samoan moved back to Seattle, Husky country. The one-time lay-down recruit now felt wanted on multiple fronts in his hometown.

"The only redemption I got was from Don James," Thompson said of Owens' UW coaching successor. "He was forever gracious to me and my family. I saw him at dinners and events throughout my college career. He was very good to me. I liked Coach James a lot. He told my dad if he had been here one year earlier I would have never have been anything but a Husky. But I was very happy being a Cougar." ❖

Top 10 Seattle Nicknames

1. The Throwin' Samoan (Jack Thompson)
2. The Big Unit (Randy Johnson)
3. Downtown (Fred Brown)
4. King Felix (Felix Hernandez)
5. The King (Hugh McElhenny)
6. The Glove (Gary Payton)
7. Big Mama (JoAnne Carner)
8. The Reign Man (Shawn Kemp)
9. Spider (Robert Gaines)
10. Cuffs (Bill Caudill)

DAVE NIEHAUS

Special Delivery

Before the Seattle Mariners could settle on a voice, they first had to clear their throat. The job of play-by-play broadcaster for the 1977 American League expansion team was offered to Bill Schonely and he readily accepted. His rich, soothing tones behind a microphone were familiar to the city.

Schonely was the No. 2 man on the Seattle Pilots' KVI radio team, paired with Jimmy Dudley, during that ill-fated expansion franchise's solo season in 1969. Schonely previously called Seattle Totems minor-league hockey and Seattle Angels Triple-A baseball.

When the Pilots' venture fizzled, Schonely moved south and created a loyal basketball following bringing the NBA's Portland Trail Blazers to life on the Oregon airwaves. He was a proven Northwest talent and liked calling baseball best. Sought out by Mariners general manager Dick Vertlieb, Schonely agreed to return to a city that gave him his sports broadcasting start.

"I was going to be the guy," Schonely said. "I was going to get back into baseball. Dick Vertlieb offered me the job, but asked me to keep it quiet for 10 days. He then called me up and cried, and apologized, and said Danny Kaye wanted Niehaus."

"Niehaus" was Dave Niehaus, an Indiana native and the third wheel on the California Angels' KMPC broadcast team. He swung between radio and TV, working with lead announcer Buddy Blattner and former Los Angeles

Dodgers pitcher Don Drysdale. Earlier in his career Niehaus counted the highly accomplished Dick Enberg as an Angels' broadcast partner.

Niehaus was a rising star ready to move up. Kaye was a Hollywood icon, one of the Mariners' original owners and smitten with the Niehaus baseball sound that echoed throughout the Los Angeles area. The entertainer made it clear that this man was his choice.

"Danny Kaye was the most remarkable man God put on Earth," Vertlieb said. "There was nothing he couldn't do. He also was the most difficult man on Earth. Kaye got what he wanted."

Overruled on Schonely, Vertlieb began negotiations with Niehaus that were far harder than anticipated. Using his leverage and figuring he had nothing to lose, Niehaus boldly asked for a salary amount that unknowingly exceeded the general manager's. Vertlieb sputtered in return that there was no way the brash broadcaster was going to make more money than he did. Niehaus responded that he didn't care what the front-office executive was paid; that's what he wanted, take it or leave it. A perplexed Vertlieb said he had to think about it and would get back to him.

Niehaus' bold contract play left the radio man convinced he had pushed too hard and blown it. "I told my wife, 'There goes Seattle,' and then he called me back, blasted me and said, 'You've got what you want,'"

> Once behind the microphone, Niehaus became Seattle's most beloved and longest-serving broadcaster. He stayed 34 years.

Niehaus said of Vertlieb. "I didn't think I was coming after we first met. The only reason I came up here was the chance to be the No. 1 guy because I was a No. 3 guy. Obviously, the best thing happened for me."

Once behind the microphone, Niehaus become Seattle's most beloved and longest-serving broadcaster. He stayed 34 years. He provided drama for a franchise that otherwise had trouble generating any on its own when it opened with 15 consecutive losing seasons. He made ineptitude sound reverent and exciting. His ratings were often double those of his head-to-head competitors.

As the Mariners shuffled through players, managers, No. 2 broadcasters and even radio networks (KVI, KIRO, KOMO), Niehaus, with his voice reflections and pet phrases, was the only one at his best every night until his waning seasons in the booth, when his mistakes were still acceptable. His timing, emotional delivery and storytelling made Mariners outings memorable and it helped turn Seattle into a lasting baseball town.

Niehaus was the logical choice to throw out the ceremonial first pitch when Safeco Field opened in 1999. He was rewarded for all his hard work with a Frick Award selection during the 2008 Hall of Fame ceremonies in Cooperstown, N.Y. He showed up every year, just like spring training.

With a game hanging in the balance, Niehaus took his listening audience on a mesmerizing ride with each pitch, his descriptions rising and dipping like a Phil Niekro knuckleball. "Loooooooooooooow, and just outside, ball three," he cooed in a gravelly voice that was partly the function of 40 years of smoking Marlboros.

Home runs didn't come often enough for the earliest Mariners, but Niehaus' long-ball call was a thing of beauty, coming across with the pop of a Nolan Ryan fastball and the urgency of a major disaster: "Swung on

and belted! Deep to left! Smith looks up! It will fly, fly, awaaaaaay!" He had settled on "fly away" after hearing the phrase turned in an obscure rock 'n roll song on the car radio one day.

Niehaus later came up with a customized call for grand-slam homers that was corny in concept but an excitable delivery readily accepted by the Mariners faithful: "Get out the mustard and rye bread, grandma! It's grand salami time!"

From the beginning, however, Niehaus offered his

signature phrase during moments of wonderment, three words that Mariners fans loyally would mimic for more than three decades and plaster on their cars with bumper stickers: "My, oh, my." It was an admitted knockoff from Enberg, whose identifiable broadcasting exclamation was "Oh my." Acknowledged Niehaus, "I just put another 'my' on it."

Niehaus grew up listening to legendary baseball announcer Harry Caray's description of the St. Louis Cardinals, the nearest big-league team to his hometown of Princetown, Ind. Early on, Niehaus knew baseball was his passion, a fact to which his wife, Marilyn, could attest. "When Dave and I met at a party, the first thing he asked me was if I liked baseball? I said no," she said. "Then he asked me to dance. Then he asked me my name. Then he asked me out."

Niehaus was on hand to call Gaylord Perry's 300th victory, Randy Johnson's no-hitter and Ken Griffey Jr.'s endless heroics at the plate. In 1995, he made his most satisfying and emotional call for a Mariners team that advanced within two victories of the World Series. In a clinching, walk-off victory over the New York Yankees in the American League Division Series, Niehaus offered the following banter turned into high-pitched historic mayhem:

"Right now, the Mariners are looking for the tie. They would take a fly ball. They would love a base hit into the gap and they could win it with Junior's speed. The stretch, and the 0-1 pitch to Edgar Martinez. ... Swung on and lined down the left-field line for a base hit! Here comes Joey! Here's Junior to third base! They're going to wave him in! The throw to the plate will be late! The Mariners are going to the American League championship! I don't believe it! It just continues! My, oh, my!"

As he went back and forth from the clubhouse to

the broadcast booth, he had the respect of everyone — except when it came to his wardrobe. With a little ham in him, Niehaus wore garish sports coats every chance he could; a pink one was a personal favorite. For the Fourth of July, he pulled out a red, white and blue blazer. Everything was accented with a pair of white shoes that Griffey would ridicule, repeatedly reminding the broadcaster that his prom days were over. Niehaus' wardrobe improved markedly following his Hall of Fame selection; he wore a jet-black tuxedo to a Safeco Field ceremony honoring him for his proudest moment as a broadcaster.

If there was a weakness in his game, Niehaus had significant health problems that showed up early in his Mariners' broadcast career. He was on the job for just a few seasons when he became dizzy in the booth and learned from a medical check-up that he had diabetes and high blood pressure. He was forced to quit smoking and change his diet.

In 1996, Niehaus, then 61, left the team in Minnesota after experiencing dizziness and shortness of breath. He underwent two angioplasties to treat clogged heart arteries. Yet he was never gone from the game long. He always felt a sense of duty to be at the ballpark.

On Nov. 10, 2010, nine days after the World Series had ended, and 37 days after the Mariners lost 4-3 to the Oakland A's to close out a miserable 61-101 season, Niehaus suffered a fatal heart attack as he prepared a barbecue dinner on the back deck of his home at 13406 Montreux Dr. in Issaquah. He was 75. Baseball was rocked by his death. Seattle was left numb and the franchise went into deep mourning.

Major League baseball commissioner Bud Selig called Niehaus "one of the great broadcast voices of our generation." Griffey, in retirement for just six months, expressed his sadness by saying, "No one in the organization, or any of the fans, wanted this day to come."

Multiple public memorials for the beloved broad-caster were held in Seattle, a street outside Safeco Field later was renamed for him — Dave Niehaus Way — and a bronze statue with him seated behind a microphone was erected in a centerfield concourse.

And to think Niehaus might not have been heard across Seattle for all those summers and made such a lasting impression had Danny Kaye not interceded and strongly urged a change of course on the hiring of the Mariners' lead broadcaster. My, oh my, but Bill Schonely, not Niehaus, would have been the guy. ❖

Top 10 Broadcasters

1. Dave Niehaus, Mariners
2. Leo Lassen, Rainiers
3. Kevin Calabro, Sonics
4. Keith Jackson, UW, Rainiers
5. Bob Blackburn, Sonics
6. Bill Schonely, Pilots, Totems
7. Pete Gross, Seahawks, UW
8. Rod Belcher, UW, SU, Rainiers
9. Bob Rondeau, UW
10. Steve Raible, Seahawks

Lenny Wilkens was a contract holdout, as stubborn as any NBA player who wanted to improve his financial situation. Over eight seasons, he helped the St. Louis Hawks to the playoffs seven times and was selected to the All-Star Game on five occasions. He was one of pro basketball's elite talents and he wanted to be paid like it.

During the stalemate, the Hawks franchise relocated to Atlanta in the off-season, but Wilkens wouldn't budge from St. Louis. Training camp started without him, and it was nearly over when frustrated Hawks executives announced that the veteran point guard was unwilling to move to the South. For Wilkens, money, not location, was the only hold-up. His salary reportedly was $60,000 a season, he asked for $70,000, and Wilkens was willing to wait as long as necessary for an increase.

Four days before the 1968-69 season began, the Hawks ended the contentious standoff by trading Wilkens, seemingly enacting revenge in how they moved him out. They shipped him to the second-year Seattle SuperSonics, which was akin to NBA Siberia. The lefthander won all eight games he played against the hapless Sonics team the season before and now he was

> While Wilkens was the city's first pro athlete worthy of superstar status, earning three more All-Star Game selections (giving him eight, plus the 1971 All-Star MVP award), he left a bigger imprint as a coach.

LENNY WILKENS
The Championship Coach

the centerpiece of it. Wilkens was floored by how things turned out. "I couldn't believe it because I knew other teams were interested, teams that were contenders," Wilkens said, mentioning the Boston Celtics as one of the possibilities. "Seattle was an expansion franchise. I said, 'Oh, no.' "

Once he arrived in the Northwest, Wilkens was in for another surprise: He and his family liked the city a lot. He played four seasons for the SuperSonics, three as a player-coach, before the team traded him to the Cleveland Cavaliers, but part of him never left town.

Even while later coaching five other NBA teams, including those same Atlanta Hawks he had avoided, the Brooklyn native made Seattle his permanent home. He rejoined the Sonics organization twice more and handled a variety of positions — director of player personnel, head coach, general manager and president of basketball operations — before the franchise was uprooted to Oklahoma City in 2008.

While Wilkens was the city's first pro athlete worthy of superstar status, earning three more All-Star Game selections (giving him eight, plus the 1971 All-Star MVP award), he left a bigger imprint as a coach. He guided the SuperSonics to their greatest glory during the 1978-79 season and brought the city a crowning moment: An NBA title. Seattle, 11 years after installing the franchise and welcoming Wilkens, discarding him

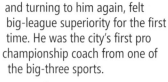

and turning to him again, felt big-league superiority for the first time. He was the city's first pro championship coach from one of the big-three sports.

Wilkens came to the Sonics in a straight trade for Walt Hazzard, orchestrated by general manager Dick Vertlieb. Hazzard was a productive player, averaging 24 points a game in Seattle's first season, but he didn't fit the image that Vertlieb wanted for the face of the franchise. The former UCLA guard was a brawler on the floor and had converted his well-known basketball name to Islam, to Mahdi Abdul-Rahman, something fans weren't totally sure about. Wilkens, however, came without a religious make-over and any conflict, outside of his extended Hawks contract negotiations. He presented a gentlemanly image.

"I traded for Lenny for his personality and character," Vertlieb said. "Lenny was well-educated, well-spoken and well-liked. He was everything I liked about a basketball player. He was a helluva basketball player, though he was getting a little old. But the referees used to give him a little room and he used that little left hand, and he would cheat over and get the right angle and take off."

As kids all over Seattle imitated his moves – with his left-handed runner in the key the patented shot – Wilkens scored a career-best 22.4 points a game during his first SuperSonics season and topped the NBA in assists during his second (683) and fourth years (766).

He was with the franchise only for a season when original coach Al Bianchi was pushed out and Wilkens was asked to become the Sonics player-coach, a dual role in vogue throughout the league. Bill Russell and Dave DeBusschere previously pulled the duty with Boston and Detroit, respectively, and Richie Guerin now wore both hats in Atlanta. Wilkens, with his calming presence during games, seemed like a natural leader.

"He felt like I was a coach on the floor," Wilkens said of Vertlieb. "When they let Al Bianchi go it was so close to training camp that Dick felt it would be tough to get someone in who knew the team. He was persistent with me. He just kept it up. It was so close to training camp I said, 'What the heck. I'll try it.'"

The Sonics showed progress under Wilkens' two-pronged guidance, compiling 36-46, 38-44, and 47-35 records, but they didn't make the playoffs. Owner Sam Schulman grew impatient, especially after taking on the NBA and paying exorbitant legal fees to secure the services of forward Spencer Haywood from the ABA.

With the 1971-72 season winding down, Wilkens was asked to choose between coaching and playing, and he opted to stay in uniform. His sacrifice proved moot. Four months later, he was traded with forward Barry Clemens to Cleveland for All-Star guard Butch Beard.

"We had drafted Fred Brown and we felt he wasn't progressing fast enough because he wasn't playing; Lenny wanted to play and he had that right," said Bob Houbregs, who replaced Vertlieb as Sonics GM. "We

also had a new coach [Tom Nissalke] coming in who didn't want the old coach around."

Wilkens publicly expressed his unhappiness in leaving the Sonics and hinted that he might not report to the Cavaliers. Sonics fans were so incensed they cheered Wilkens' every move in his first game back at the Coliseum and booed Beard throughout the season, turning Beard into damaged goods and forcing his trade to Golden State a year later.

"There was a lot of disappointment," Wilkens said. "I had heard rumors. I understood, because as a professional athlete you know it could happen. But I thought I had elicited a promise that I would be traded to a contender, because I thought I had a couple of years left that I could play, but no such luck."

Houbregs said it wasn't for lack of effort in attempting to place Wilkens with an NBA team on more solid footing. "We tried, and he may not believe that, but we tried," Houbregs said. "We called all around. There wasn't much interest in him with contending clubs, because they had players and didn't want to bring in an older player who controlled the ball."

Wilkens played two seasons in Cleveland and spent another in Portland as player-coach before retiring from the court and turning solely to coaching. The Trail Blazers, however, gave him just one season as a non-playing coach before pushing him out after the 1975-76 season.

Wilkens returned to the Sonics, who continued to churn out coaches, and became director of player personnel. Bill Russell was the Seattle coach but he grew weary of the job after four seasons, and the team was turned over to Bob Hopkins, Russell's assistant coach and cousin. Hopkins lasted just 22 games before he was fired early in the 1977-78 campaign. Six years after stepping down and getting traded, Wilkens was

Wilkens returned to the Sonics, who continued to churn out coaches, and became director of player personnel.

installed as the Sonics coach again by Schulman.

"There was a little panic on everybody's part," Wilkens said. "I kept telling the owner to be patient and give it a chance. They were 5-16 when they lost to New Jersey [the league's worst team]. I wasn't at the game because I had to go to a dinner. When I got home there were all kinds of messages on my phone. Sam was beside himself and wanted to make the change right then. I couldn't get to Denver the next night; I told them it would have to be in Kansas City."

After beating the Kings 86-84 with Hopkins' lineup still in place, Wilkens conducted his first practice in Boston and tinkered with the rotation. He replaced starters Marvin Webster, Paul Silas and Brown with, in order, Jack Sikma, John Johnson and Dennis Johnson.

The resulting chemistry was astounding. The Sonics were transformed from the league's second-worst team — the Nets were 3-19 at the time — into an instant contender, ultimately losing to the Washington Bullets in seven games in the NBA Finals. A year later they won the 1978-79 championship, beating the Bullets in five games in the finals, and Wilkens was considered a coaching genius.

With back-to-back finals appearances and a fairly young team, it was assumed the Sonics would rule the league for some time. The following season, however, they lost to the Los Angeles Lakers in five games in the Western Conference finals, forced to play the postseason series at the University of Washington's Edmundson Pavilion because their new court, the Kingdome, and their old one, the Coliseum, were booked for other events.

Things got worse when Schulman and his general manager Zollie Volchok tried to rein in salaries rather than reward the players with pay raises.

"I think we would have been pretty good, but they started to want to make changes," Wilkens said. "They didn't want to pay Fred Brown and I was a little upset with that. They traded Gus and I thought that was terrible. D.J. was unhappy because he wasn't getting paid like Fred and the rest of them, and D.J. was the MVP of the playoffs. Certainly there was chaos during that season."

Wilkens, a Hall of Fame inductee three times over (NBA coach, pro player, Olympics assistant coach), couldn't re-create another championship season in Seattle. He spent six seasons trying after the first title. Had the owners shown some foresight and a willingness to invest in the players, a mini Seattle pro basketball dynasty might have resulted.

"Ownership started to make moves not conducive to keeping the same level of players we were so used to," Brown said. "It was unlike what the Celtics did with the tutelage of [Red] Auerbach, where they were able to keep it going and win eight in a row. I think we were good for one more, possibly two more titles, very easily."

Wilkens, who lives in Medina, coached the Sonics through the 1984-85 season, stepping down when he became uncomfortable with the direction of the franchise. He served as Seattle GM for a season before he left that job, too. The talent falloff was fairly steady.

"At the end of the season, I didn't want to coach that team anymore," said Wilkens, whose franchise departure brought the championship era to a close.

More than two decades later, Wilkens returned to the Sonics for a third time, briefly serving another administrative stint before the franchise was uprooted to Oklahoma. He became a TV broadcaster. Pro basketball left the city, but Wilkens remained entrenched in Seattle. He could be stubborn that way. ❖

JACK SIKMA

Seattle's Big Mistake

Jack Sikma was an NAIA basketball player, small-time, unorthodox. He was a 6-foot-11 center from obscure Illinois Wesleyan University who was taken by the Seattle SuperSonics with the eighth pick of the 1977 NBA Draft, a choice that initially drew only stares and yawns from pro basketball fans.

He was so unfamiliar to outsiders during the draft proceedings that an *Associated Press* report misidentified him as "Jack Sikman." Within weeks, the rookie was privately labeled a bust by franchise owner Sam Schulman.

Bob Hopkins, the man who scouted, supported and selected him, is willing to take it to his grave that Sikma was the chief reason he was fired after just 22 games into the 1977-78 season as the new Sonics coach.

In the worst way, Schulman wanted to draft Tennessee swingman Ernie Grunfeld, who went two slots behind Sikma to the Milwaukee Bucks. Lenny Wilkens, the team's director of player personnel, was enamored with 6-10 North Carolina center Tom LaGarde, who was taken one spot following Sikma by the Denver Nuggets. Hopkins made the call for Sikma and heard nothing but criticism.

"When I brought Jack in they wanted to run me out of town," he said. "But Jack was a banger."

Sikma fully understood the unenthusiastic response that greeted him in Seattle on draft day. He didn't

take it personal. He was drafted higher than even he envisioned.

"I think it was a surprise to most that I went as high as I did," he said. "I think people thought I'd be taken 10 picks later. It took a while to get to know me."

Hopkins felt great pushback after Sonics front-office personnel showed up in Los Angeles for a summer league game, informing the coach that everyone would convene afterward at Schulman's Southern California home to discuss team matters. The meeting never happened. Houston Rockets center Moses Malone embarrassed Sikma by outscoring him 32-4 and out-rebounding him 15-3, leaving Seattle executives enraged in the stands and looking for the door.

"Everyone left before halftime," Hopkins said. "They never spoke to me again. I heard the owner say that I had screwed up the franchise. They talked about firing me in the middle of the summer."

The funny thing about all of that inner-organizational angst was this: Hopkins couldn't have been more right about Sikma. The big man with the Dutchboy haircut and catapult jump shot was the most productive player culled from the 1977 draft by any team and turned out to be a huge find for the Sonics at the eighth pick. The Illinois native became the most decorated and productive center in Seattle's four decades of pro basketball. Sikma was the final and most important

> The funny thing about all
> of that inner-organization
> angst was this:
> Hopkins couldn't have been
> more right about Sikma.

piece – a quality big man – necessary to lead the SuperSonics to their only NBA championship in 1979. Sikma was the best "mistake" Seattle ever made in acquiring one of its pro sporting heroes.

"Anybody playing against Moses Malone wouldn't look great," Wilkens said of Sikma's summer debut. "Sam was a little bit upset and said, 'Who is this guy?' People pointed to me and I said, '[Hopkins] drafted him.' But I said, 'Give Sikma a chance.' "

Hopkins' real mistake was he waited too long to insert the raw post player into Seattle's starting lineup, leading to a disastrous 5-17 start and his firing on Nov. 30, 1977. Hopkins tried to be patient with the big rookie and it cost him.

Wilkens, who succeeded Hopkins, warmed to the newcomer's ability while watching him play. As Hopkins' coaching replacement, Wilkens inserted guard Dennis Johnson, forward John Johnson and Sikma in the Sonics starting lineup two games after taking over, putting them alongside forward Lonnie Shelton and guard Gus Williams – and the results were stunning. The revamped Seattle team put together a six-game winning streak and captured 18 of the first 21 games following the coaching change.

The SuperSonics meshed together so well with the arrangement, particularly once Webster was yanked out as a starter in favor of Sikma, they advanced to the seventh and final game of the 1978 NBA Finals before losing to the Washington Bullets 105-99 at the Seattle Center Coliseum. The players fed off the adrenaline together and just missed making a complete turnaround.

"There wasn't a Larry Bird, Michael Jordan, Julius Erving or Magic Johnson on the team," Sikma said. "The uniqueness was how fast it came together and how the pieces really fit. There will never be another connection between a city and a team as there was then. The NBA

wasn't big-time yet, we had a relatively young franchise and it was a lot of new players coming together. It gives me goose bumps remembering how loud the Coliseum was. You did things you didn't think you could do because you were so pumped."

The Sonics made everything happen during the 1978-79 season, bringing the city its first big-league championship in any of the three primary sports. They finished first in the Pacific Division with a 52-30 record, beat the Los Angeles Lakers in five games in the Western Conference semifinals, outlasted the Phoenix Suns in seven games during the Western Conference finals and captured an NBA finals rematch against the Washington Bullets in five games.

The celebrating began on June 1, 1979, following a 97-93 victory over the Bullets, a road game that offered the typical Sikma stat line: 12 points and 17 rebounds. Everyone on this SuperSonics team brought something different to their championship pursuit.

It was a team in the truest sense, and Sikma, the closest thing to a superstar player, never lost sight of the unique qualities that each Sonics player provided to the title run. His personal breakdown of each of Seattle's starters went as follows:

(Shelton) – "Lonnie was a force, a power forward, and there always was lots of room to work underneath the hoop defensively. Lonnie controlled his man so well. His speed and power was so unique at that time. His soft touch was something. He was a quiet man until he got into the ballgame."

(John Johnson) – "Lenny, in trying to figure out how to mix and match everybody, realized with D.J. and Gus that neither one was strictly a point guard. Both could handle the ball well. Put that mix with J.J.'s ability to push it and it let those two guys run. J.J. would deliver the ball."

> It was a team in the truest sense, and Sikma, the closest thing to a superstar player, never lost sight of the unique qualities that each Sonics player provided to the title run.

(Dennis Johnson) – "D.J. was a graceful athlete, though not the greatest shooter, in a sense that people would play off him a little. If you left him alone late in the game, D.J. could knock it down. In those days, there were a lot of good two guards in the game, [George] Gervin, [David] Thompson. To have one go nose-to-nose and not break down defensively made D.J. very important to us."

(Williams) – "Gus was a wild card. He put a lot of pressure on the other team defensively. Even when they were on offense he would leak out and go. There were many photos where somebody was taking a jump shot and Gus would be heading out. Gus wasn't the greatest shooter in the world but he could knock down the shot. He was a lot of fun to be around. His speed got us going up and down the court. He was fun to play with."

(Sikma, about himself) – "I fit in with the defensive concept real well, which was bend but don't break, and make people beat you over the top. If you were positioned right defensively, you had a good chance of controlling the defensive board. That fit my skills. I could go after the ball. Offensively, I wasn't going to

Sikma played nine seasons in Seattle, seven as an All-Star selection, and was the last to leave the 1978-79 title team's roster. The center became a franchise untouchable, receiving elite status none of his teammates enjoyed because a great big man was so hard to find.

Dennis Johnson, unhappy because Schulman wouldn't pay him more, was traded after a third consecutive season of Sonics glory stopped just short of the NBA championship round in the 1980 Western Conference Finals. Williams sat out the entire 1980-81 season for similar reasons, a money dispute, and later was traded. Shelton was traded after five seasons. John Johnson retired in 1982.

Sikma wasn't going anywhere right away. He was so valuable to the franchise that general manager Bob Whitsitt called him "bigger than the Space Needle." Previous general manager Zollie Volchok was even more creative and emphatic in measuring the center's worth to the Sonics when he supplied this memorable line, "I wouldn't trade Jack Sikma for the resurrection of Marilyn Monroe in my bedroom."

Yet, in 1986, Sikma surprised the franchise and the city when he requested a trade, unwilling to take part in a Seattle rebuilding project while recognizing his career was winding down and his postseason chances were dwindling. The team obliged by shipping him to the Milwaukee Bucks for center Alton Lister, two first-round draft picks and two second-round selections.

Sikma didn't make a total break from Seattle, at least emotionally. Five years later, he held discussions with SuperSonics executives about a possible return to the franchise before all parties concluded that retirement was best for him. The team honored him by retiring his No. 43.

Sikma met his wife in Seattle and lived in Bellevue. Eighteen years following his trade, Sikma rejoined the Sonics as an assistant coach, a job he held for four seasons.

Once the franchise was transferred to Oklahoma City in 2008, Sikma resurfaced as an assistant coach with the Houston Rockets and Minnesota Timberwolves, still maintaining the Seattle area as a permanent address.

"I was chosen by Seattle and the day I was drafted here there was no way I could tell how it was going to affect me," Sikma said. "It was a big, wide door I opened and walked through, and it gave me lots of future choices that I otherwise wouldn't have had. Being tied to a part of the sports history of the city, that in itself added a lot to my life." ❖

go over the top or by you. I had an inside pivot move, which wasn't anything special, but when we got into a half-court game we needed an inside game."

Seated at courtside in Landover, Md., broadcaster Bob Blackburn started counting down the final seconds of the Seattle SuperSonics' 97-93 victory over the Washington Bullets in the deciding Game 5 of the 1979 NBA Finals, treating the moment as if it were a New Year's Eve celebration. As Blackburn brought the Sonics' glorious championship run to a close on KIRO radio, his words were neither flowery nor extra creative, just matter of fact, as was always the case with his on-air style.

"Rebound, John Johnson. The Sonics have it! Seven seconds, six, five, four. Pass to Gus Williams. Three, two, one. And the Sonics win their first-ever NBA championship! The ball sails high in the air! Les Habegger does the Habegger hop! The Sonics are ecstatic! The horns are honking around the Pacific Northwest! I'm sure there ... Here's a big round of applause by the Washington Bullets fans for both ball clubs, though mostly for the Bullets. The last two games of this series, simply outstanding ballgames. As we take time out for the hosts who brought you this ballgame, the final score, Seattle 97 and the Washington Bullets 93."

> Blackburn was Seattle's
> first big-league voice.
> For the 1967-68 season,
> the Sonics gave the city
> something it hadn't
> experienced before
> and brought the broadcaster
> along for the ride.

BOB BLACKBURN
The Victory Voice

Before there were Mariners or Seahawks, Blackburn's rich, authoritative narrative was everywhere describing the SuperSonics. It echoed through the convenience store near Nathan Eckstein Junior High School in north Seattle, coming from Philadelphia or New York. It radiated through the car full of teenage basketball players headed home from practice to Laurelhurst, this time transmitted from Boston or maybe Detroit. And it was faintly heard across the city from transistor radios hidden under the pillows of young boys who delayed sleep and defied their parents to follow the newly installed NBA activity coming from the Seattle Center Coliseum. I was part of each attentive audience.

Blackburn was Seattle's first big-league voice. For the 1967-68 season, the Sonics gave the city something it hadn't experienced before and brought the broadcaster along for the ride. It was his job to get everyone hooked on the expansion franchise. The words came tumbling out of Blackburn's mouth in a hurry, as if he were in the middle of a fast break racing down the floor, and not just describing one. The California native spoke eloquently as the Sonics squared off against Wilt Chamberlain and Oscar Robertson, and excitedly as the new team pulled the occasional upset. He was big on stats, rattling off numbers whenever he could. The fast-paced game suited him best as he spent 25 seasons wandering through NBA arenas with the Sonics.

Bob Blackburn interviews one of his favorite players, Wilt Chamberlain.

"Of all the sports broadcasting I'd done, basketball was probably best for me with the speed and style," Blackburn said. "I felt comfortable doing basketball."

Blackburn beat out 110 others in his SuperSonics audition. He came north after calling Triple-A Portland Beavers baseball games for 18 years, and Oregon State University and University of Oregon football and basketball games for a decade. He grew up in the Los Angeles area, listening to old Pacific Coast Conference football broadcasts as an 8-year-old boy bedridden with tuberculosis, imagining himself in the booth someday calling games. He later landed a series of jobs in California, playing music, reporting news, calling games and building a resume, before eventually moving to Portland.

Blackburn's Sonics job was a glamorous one, but hardly easy. For 16 seasons, he was the play-by-play announcer, color man and engineer, all wrapped into one, carting the heavy radio gear around by himself. For a Christmas game in Baltimore, he arrived in the arena to find the phone lines misrouted and he had to locate them because no one else was working the holiday. He had his broadcast up and running five minutes following the opening tip. "That was the only time we missed the start," he said.

In Chicago, he went off the air during a game when Bulls guard Norm Van Lier crashed hard into the broadcast table and tore out the lines. "He knocked me all to hell," Blackburn said. On another trip to the Windy City, some wise-guy fan climbed under the seats and purposely cut Blackburn's lines, forcing the broadcaster to rewire them out of necessity.

In Philadelphia, the broadcaster watched as Sonics forward Tom Meschery launched a shot and the lights went out all at once after lightning struck the building. Blackburn was forced to ad-lib in the dark for several minutes. Blackburn was rapid-fire but straightforward in his approach, big on detail but devoid of gimmicks. For that matter, he didn't use a signature call. Supplying the occasional nickname was as outlandish as he got. "He called me Woody," appreciative Sonics forward Spencer Haywood said.

Blackburn's most satisfying moment was that title-clinching Game 5 of the 1979 NBA Finals. He enjoyed the franchise's breakthrough, but made sure to maintain his composure on the air. He later shared in all of the Sonics' celebratory trappings, including a downtown parade that brought out thousands of fans. Same as the players, coaches and team executives, Blackburn received a championship ring that held a large diamond in the middle and his name engraved on the side, which he considered his most coveted keepsake. "I didn't make a basket or a steal, but the club gave me that diamond ring, and I cherish it and wear it," he said.

Blackburn, who resided at 12134 S.E. 16th Pl. in Bellevue, survived open-heart surgery during the 1983 season, returning to the air within three weeks after having three of his five major arteries unclogged. However, he didn't survive management's abrupt decision following the 1992 season to turn everything over to a younger and hipper Kevin Calabro, after the two briefly shared the Sonics broadcast duties. The team cut Blackburn loose like some aging veteran player who had hung around one season too long.

The Sonics chose to brusquely push the older man aside rather than salute his long service. Calabro was the new-age broadcaster, full of memorable catch phrases and energy, while Blackburn was old school, matter of fact and almost Walter Cronkite-like in his stoic delivery. It was a business decision devoid of any celebration. It was a generational changing of the guard. It stung.

Feeling unwanted by the Sonics, Blackburn became a professional auctioneer, led worldwide vacations tours and became a spokesman for an Issaquah retirement community. He was given a lifetime pass by the team, but didn't bother going to another NBA game for a decade.

The Sonics finally reached out to Blackburn in 2002, asking him to become part of a team legends program initiated by new owner Howard Schultz and club president Wally Walker in an effort to connect Sonics fans with former franchise mainstays. Previous owner Barry Ackerley wasn't big on sentiment. At a *P-I* Star of the Year banquet, I casually told Schultz about the ongoing disconnection between the pioneering Sonics broadcaster and the team and Schultz immediately did something about it. Blackburn was back, greeting fans coming in the door for games and signing autographs until the franchise was uprooted to Oklahoma City in 2008.

"I supposedly retired, but I think everybody knew it was a forced retirement," Blackburn said. "I have no hard feelings with Barry Ackerley."

Blackburn would outlive the Sonics by only 18 months. Shortly after the franchise was relocated to the Midwest, he suffered a bad fall and received a serious head injury that led to a series of health setbacks that he couldn't overcome. He was 85 when he died from pneumonia on Jan. 8, 2010.

This time, Blackburn exited with a proper and dignified farewell, with the broadcaster saluted in obituaries and newspaper stories and on sports radio talk shows for having a long and distinguished career, for being the first to man a big-league mike in Seattle. ❖

Lenny Wilkens and Kevin Calbro share a moment with Bob Blackburn.

Eighties and Nineties

Seattle revamps its port facilities and becomes a major player in international trade, and transforms itself into a musical hotbed with the advent of "grunge" and wildly successful bands such as Nirvana, Pearl Jam, Soundgarden, Alice in Chains and Queensryche.

The city deals with sporting temptation and redemption, suffering through Seattle University basketball and UW football scandals and Mariners and Seahawks relocation threats, which is countered by the Huskies sharing in a national championship, the Sonics appearing in the NBA finals again and the Mariners and Seahawks experiencing respective World Series and Super Bowl near-misses.

DAVID KRIEG

The Little Big Man

No Seattle football player, amateur or pro, has emerged from more obscure beginnings and enjoyed more high-level success than Krieg, who against all odds helped turn the 1980s into a decade of opportunity and a platform for the underdog.

Dave Krieg took the long way to reach the NFL. No college football team recruited him. No pro team drafted him. And to travel to a free-agent tryout in 1980 offered by the Seattle Seahawks, Krieg caught a flight out of Central Wisconsin Airport in the middle of his home state – noteworthy because it was the first time he had been on an airplane – and he made stops in Minneapolis and Kansas City before touching down in the Northwest.

Krieg, a quarterback from NAIA school Milton College and a somewhat closeted kid from Wisconsin, was wide-eyed once he arrived at Seahawks headquarters in suburban Kirkland. He grew up working on his grand-parents' 400-acre farm, milking cows and shoveling manure, and in college at a paper mill, pulling swing shifts and doing other dirty jobs, but he had never been anywhere else.

When he saw the expansive practice facilities for the first time, Krieg was dazzled. While many of the Seahawks' other seven quarterback candidates groused about the constant coaching critiques and the monotony of camp, he played loose and free. Incredibly, he made the roster on the final cut as the No. 3 guy at his position.

"It was shock, awe, surprise," said Krieg, who speaks with a trace of a Fargo accent. "The guys gave me a hard time, coming from a small college. They gave me a hard time for a year, but they accepted me."

No Seattle football player, amateur or pro, has emerged from more obscure beginnings and enjoyed more high-level success than Krieg, who against all odds helped turn the 1980s into a decade of opportunity and a platform for the underdog.

Krieg still had a lot of catching up to do. He had to learn the Seahawks offense and terminology, and it was hard for him. He had to quit gawking in practice at high-profile teammates such as running back Sherman Smith and wide receiver Steve Largent, and that was equally hard. The Kingdome, an indoor stadium, was such a different environment for him it made Krieg claustrophobic and prone to hyperventilating, and he had to overcome that, too. He also needed an immediate wardrobe adjustment.

"I didn't know how to tie a tie and on the first or second road trip I had a clip-on tie on and it was sticking out on the flight," Krieg said. "Largent pulled it off and held it up and said, 'Hey, he's got a clip-on tie,' and that was sort of embarrassing."

Yet Krieg had many more conquests than disasters. He settled in and enjoyed a resilient 19-year NFL career – a dozen seasons coming with the Seahawks, more than any other Seattle quarterback (Matt Hasselbeck was next with 10). Krieg was a three-time Pro Bowl selection for the Seahawks, unseated original quarterback starter and fan favorite Jim Zorn, and brought the franchise within a game of reaching Super Bowl XVIII in 1983.

Krieg was part of an unusual and unintentional Seahawks' quarterback troika: The franchise took unsung, small-college guys and turned them into established NFL players. Krieg followed Zorn, who emerged from NCAA Division II entry Cal Poly and was selected 1976 AFC offensive Rookie of the Year and played 11 NFL seasons; and Krieg preceded Jon Kitna, who went from Central Washington and an NAIA national championship to the NFL for 15 seasons and played for four teams, beginning with the Seahawks in 1997.

"Both have mentioned that to me, but their schools didn't have only 300 students," Krieg said, convinced his football journey was far more difficult than those of the other two. "Their stories aren't even close to mine. They went to small colleges, but not anything close to the smallness of Milton College. The people didn't even know me in Wisconsin."

Seattle got acquainted with Krieg in 1981 near the end of his second season, when he replaced an injured Zorn and led the Seahawks to two victories in the final three games. As a first-time starter Krieg threw for two touchdowns and ran for a third to lead his team to a 27-23 victory over the New York Jets and its vaunted "New York Sack Exchange" defense.

Krieg hooked up with Largent from 57 yards out for a late game-winner.

By 1983, Krieg was the midseason starter and relegated a healthy Zorn to a backup role, and he directed the Seahawks to a pair of electric playoff victories, beating the Denver Broncos 31-7 and Miami Dolphins 27-20 before losing to the Los Angeles Raiders 30-14 in the AFC Championship Game.

He was so gritty and resourceful his teammates nicknamed him "Mudbone," with Seahawks offensive guard Bryan Millard offering a simple explanation to reporters: "He's like an old bone that you find in the mud."

Yet breaking up the iconic Zorn-Largent passing combination was no easy task for Krieg, even with his other teammates rallying around him.

"Jim and Steve were the talk of Seattle, they did everything together and they were born-again Christians," Krieg said. "Now I'm throwing to Jim's best friend and that was a little awkward for awhile. It wasn't awkward for me. I know Jim was on the sideline, thinking, 'He's throwing to my receiver, he's throwing to my friend,' and there was a little animosity for awhile. When another starter takes over, I was aware that could happen. Sure, the fans wanted to see Jim Zorn play, and it was, 'Who's this? And will the Seahawks ever get a quarterback that they draft?' "

Krieg got wound so tight that he sometimes forgot the snap count and sheepishly had to ask Seahawks centers Blair Bush and Grant Feasel for immediate assistance as he stood clueless at the line of scrimmage.

The quarterback's youthful exuberance caught up with him in the 1983 AFC Championship Game, the biggest moment of his football career. Before leaving his Los Angeles hotel, he called his grandfather and a high school buddy back in Wisconsin to commiserate

Dave Krieg played a dozen seasons for the Seahawks.

because he wasn't sure how to handle the situation. The kid from the rural Midwest had no point of reference for a football game of this magnitude.

Before the opening kickoff that day, Raiders quarterback Jim Plunkett came up and congratulated Krieg on having a good season, which made his head spin more. Prior to the blowout defeat, Krieg admittedly allowed himself to think one game ahead and it backfired on him. "I daydreamed a little bit about being in the Super Bowl and lost some focus, and it cost us," he acknowledged.

In 1984, Krieg enjoyed his first Pro Bowl season by throwing for 3,617 yards and 32 touchdowns, both career highs.

In 1984, Krieg enjoyed his first Pro Bowl season by throwing for 3,617 yards and 32 touchdowns, both career highs. He led the Seahawks past the Raiders and lost to the Dolphins in the playoffs, enacting and receiving postseason payback from the previous year. It should have brought him job security.

Seahawks fans, however, became so impatient with Krieg in ensuing seasons, when expected playoff berths repeatedly eluded the team, they booed the quarterback to the point he ran onto the field during introductions when a teammate's name was called. The front office was just as restless, bringing in Gale Gilbert, Kelly Stouffer and Dan McGwire to challenge Krieg for the position.

Krieg managed to hold them off and enjoy Pro Bowl seasons in 1988 and 1989 before the inevitable change was made two years later. Typical of Krieg's hot-and-cold play was a 1990 game at Kansas City. He was sacked seven times by Derrick Thomas but then got out of Thomas' grasp on the final play of the game and heaved a 25-yard touchdown pass to Paul Skansi with no time on the clock, supplying the Seahawks with a stunning 17-16 victory – the franchise's first road win over the Chiefs in 10 years. "I threw the pass and didn't see him catch it," Krieg said. "All I heard was quiet and I thought that had to be pretty good."

Krieg was let go by Seattle after the 1991 season. He roamed the league and played for the Arizona Cardinals, Chicago Bears, Detroit Lions, Kansas City Chiefs and then-Tennessee Oilers. He kept coming back until he couldn't get another job, falling short of his goal of 20 NFL seasons.

He finished with career stats that ranked him among the top-15 quarterbacks all-time – 38,147 passing yards and 261 scoring passes among them – but figured a Hall of Fame selection was out of reach because he didn't appear in the Super Bowl.

Krieg never had a college scholarship offer, because all he did in high school was hand off, and Milton College abruptly closed on him in 1982, losing its accreditation because it lacked financial backing. His name wasn't called on draft day, because nobody knew him.

Yet the NFL made a place for him, which wasn't bad for a kid from Wisconsin who wore clip-on ties. He made the most of it with the Seahawks.

"It was big-time sad leaving Seattle," Krieg said. "They gave me my first opportunity. Even though the fans were down on me, Wisconsin was my first home and Seattle was my first city. They took me in and gave me an opportunity to play in the NFL. I had 12 great years there. The longer away it gets, the more appreciative they are of what I did." ❖

Marv Harshman's retirement party lasted the entire 1984-85 college basketball season. Touring the Pacific-10 Conference a final time, the veteran University of Washington coach was saluted at every stop. He was given a pickup truck, framed photos, lifetime passes and gag gifts that included a rocking chair.

The elongated ceremony presented one problem: Harshman, 68, wasn't ready to quit. He wasn't in a nostalgic mood at all. He was forced out of his job by UW president William Gerberding, wasn't coming back, and it wasn't a voluntary decision.

Watching on TV, Gerberding became angry when he saw Harshman argue vehemently and draw a pair of technical fouls at UCLA. He wanted him fired. Gerberding had to be talked out of the impulsive move by Huskies athletic director Mike Lude, who flew to Los Angeles to calm and warn his coach. The president, however, made it clear that change was forthcoming: Gerberding decided the UW basketball program would be turned over to a younger, more vibrant coach.

Harshman wanted to keep going. He was still a sturdy man. His coaching mind was sound. Entering his 14th season at the UW, and his 40th as a college basketball head coach counting stops at Washington State and Pacific Lutheran, he had program momentum. His removal would represent the worst coaching firing in Seattle history.

> Harshman wanted
> to keep going. He was
> still a sturdy man.
> His coaching mind
> was sound.

MARV HARSHMAN
Unwanted Early Retirement

The coach was in the process of guiding the Huskies to consecutive NCAA Tournament appearances for the first time in school history. His previous 1983-84 Huskies team landed in the Sweet 16 and just missed advancing to the next round. Harshman felt he had at least two more seasons in him, if not five or six.

"I thought probably in the back of my mind that I'll get to 70," Harshman said of his age. "I was never too concerned about it. I never expected to see 80 or 85. I would have liked to continue. We were on a par with most schools right then. UCLA was still having their problems. That was a good era for the league because more people had a chance."

Harshman was saddled with just one losing season in Seattle, 11-16 in 1978-79. Ironically, that happened with a team that featured future NBA players in Icelandic center Petur Gudmundsson and Los Angeles point guard Lorenzo Romar, the latter later becoming the Huskies coach.

Gerberding, not Lude, chose Harshman's replacement. The school president settled on Louisiana Tech's Andy Russo. Gerberding picked the Chicago-area native, just 36, to create college basketball excitement in Seattle and enliven a program that had experienced local recruiting failures, unable to land blue-chip recruits Quin Snyder and Joe Buchanan, who chose Duke and Notre Dame, respectively.

Marv Harshman, shown as a Tacoma Indians semipro player, concentrated on football before coaching basketball.

"It was not his fault," Harshman said. "He had one great player, Karl Malone, and he rode him to a job. He wasn't a teacher."

Once Welp used up his eligibility and turned to the NBA, Washington suffered through eight seasons without a winning record. Harshman's premature removal, when the program was on championship footing coupled with its resulting spiral, was a huge mistake.

In coaching exile, Harshman was offered a pair of jobs. Denver's Metro State asked him to coach for two or three seasons with a capable assistant coach in tow, with the idea he would groom this person as a ready replacement. He said no because of Colorado's wintry climate. Harshman was encouraged to take over at Hawaii, but he rejected that offer, too, though he was lobbied hard to take it by Joe Kearney, then Western Athletic Conference commissioner and previously the UW athletic director who had hired him.

"At one time I just thought I shouldn't coach anymore," Harshman said. "I had two job offers. I was burned out. Joe Kearney wanted me to go to Hawaii for three years. They were on probation. I really didn't want to move. Two years later, I wished I had taken the job. I missed the coaching part."

Harshman originally envisioned himself as a football coach, his primary sport as a college player. Yet when Pacific Lutheran, his alma mater, asked him to run its basketball program, he accepted and held the job for 13 seasons. He had two national title near-misses in the 32-team NAIA Tournament — guiding the Lutes to the semifinals in 1956 and the title game in 1957, losing 71-70 on Dick Barnett's last-second shot the first time, and 97-87 to the same Tennessee A&I State team and the NBA-bound Barnett again — and became a hot coaching commodity.

A concentrated advertising campaign was initiated, putting the new coach's face on bus placards and elsewhere. The handsome, personable Russo had become a hot-coaching property by directing Tech to its first NCAA Tournament appearance in 1983-84 and its finest season in school history (29-3) in 1984-85. What Gerberding failed to realize was that Russo had built his coaching credentials largely on the talents of one player, future NBA standout Karl "The Mailman" Malone.

The new UW coach took Harshman's talent, led by 7-foot center Christian Welp, and made one more NCAA trip before the program fell apart. Russo recruited questionable players, had two disastrous seasons while people challenged the depth of his coaching knowledge, and he was fired by Lude. Russo coached at lower-level Lynn and Florida Tech before he was fired again and, after being pushed out of the college game, bought and operated a Florida car wash.

> Allowed to view Bruins
> workouts as the WSU coach,
> Harshman watched with
> deep fascination in how
> Wooden ran things.
> He took notes.

Washington State pried Harshman away in 1958 and he spent 13 seasons with the Cougars. With limited resources, he made the Cougars competitive, guiding them to a second-place league finish behind UCLA and center Lew Alcindor during the 1967-68 season. Four years later, the Huskies and Kearney pursued him as a replacement for Fred "Tex" Winter, who left to coach the NBA's San Diego Rockets amid racial unrest at the school.

"We had a new president and Stan Bates, the athletic director who hired me, advised me I should listen to Kearney, because it wasn't going to be very good here, and I knew if I took the job at Washington it would be easier to get players," Harshman said.

Harshman was hired over Ohio State's Fred Taylor, Grambling's Fred Hodby and Central Washington's Dean Nicholson, but only after Seattle Pacific's Les Habbegger reportedly had been offered and turned down the job.

Moving across the state, Harshman became the first in conference history to coach at two member schools. He later shared the feat with his Cougars successor, George Raveling, who coached at WSU and USC; Kevin O'Neill, who coached at Arizona and USC; Mike Montgomery, who ended up at Stanford and California; and Ernie Kent, who directed Oregon and WSU.

Harshman, who lived at 19221 90th N.E. in suburban Bothell, was never a flamboyant coach but brought a sense of humor to the job. On his first trip back to Pullman, he pulled on a woman's wig and sat on the bench for warm-ups unnoticed for the longest time. Of course, these were long-haired times, giving him some camouflage. "A doctor friend walked right by me and asked 'Where's Marv?' and then saw me and said, 'You've got to be kidding,' " the coach recalled.

In 1976, to defuse the overly volatile atmosphere at Oregon's McArthur Court, Harshman and five of his Huskies players wore Groucho Marx glasses and mustaches onto the floor during pre-game warm-ups.

Set as the UW coach, Harshman never applied for a job, asked for a raise or clashed with an athletic director. He coached in 1,090 college games, which at the time ranked him third all-time behind North Carolina's Dean Smith (1,133) and Oklahoma A&M's Henry Iba (1,105). Among his Division I coaching peers, Harshman became good friends with UCLA's legendary John Wooden and bitter enemies with Nevada-Las Vegas's Jerry Tarkanian.

Allowed to view Bruins workouts as the WSU coach, Harshman watched with deep fascination in how Wooden ran things. He took notes. "I was in Los Angeles for something, maybe trying to find a player, and I was invited to come to practice," he said. "I was amazed. John was all demonstration. For two days, he didn't do anything with a basketball. They simulated everything. It was, 'Get in position, always.' There was a focus on basketball footwork. John made me realize how important the right footwork was. You could even put an average player in position and he could become a good player, though not a great player."

Footnoting his long and winding career, Harshman beat the unbeatable Wizard of Westwood in their first meeting (WSU 71, UCLA 54, 1959) and their last (UW 103, UCLA 81, 1975), the latter Wooden's final career loss to anyone.

The season-long retirement party for Harshman in 1984-85 was not a pleasant memory. It took its toll on his players as they slogged through a 22-10 season that should have been far better. The distraction presented by an outgoing coach sent emotions skyrocketing. For the lame-duck Harshman, it showed in his bark. He bickered with Schrempf, assistant coach Mike Frink and reporters, including me.

Harshman's coaching career ended in Salt Lake City at the NCAA Tournament with a 66-58 loss to Kentucky. Another victory would have paired the UW coach against Tarkanian, someone Harshman previously had accused of cheating.

"I don't know how he could have said those things. He's a lyin' SOB. If he ever took a lie-detector test, he'd be electrocuted," Tarkanian said excitedly in Salt Lake City, welcoming a grudge match that never came.

In forced retirement, Harshman and the UW basketball program were never far apart. The former coach attended most home games, often sitting with one of his sons, Dave, who briefly was the PLU coach. He watched Romar, one of his former players, try to hang onto the Huskies coaching job forever, same as him.

Four coaches and 28 years after he was forced out, Harshman died on April 12, 2013. He was 95. He was finally ready to retire. ❖

GEORGE IRVINE

The Reluctant Coach

George Irvine was in the shower when the phone rang. Late in the 1999-2000 NBA season, he had wrangled a few days free from his job as Detroit Pistons assistant coach to go home to California and throw his wife a surprise birthday party. Pistons general manager Rick Sund was on the line. Irvine told his wife he would call Sund back as soon as he got out, but Sund insisted on speaking with him right away.

Irvine knew what that urgent tone meant: Detroit head coach Alvin Gentry was fired. Irvine turned off the water, took the phone in his hand and didn't even bother to say hello to Sund when he started talking.

"Don't do it."

"Well, George, we've decided to let Alvin go and want to hire you as interim coach."

"No, don't let him go."

"We already let him go. We want to hire you to take over."

"No, I don't want to do it."

Irvine was an NBA coach before, twice called out of the Indiana Pacers front office to run young teams relying on tight budgets, hardly a blueprint for pro basketball success. He went from Indiana director of player personnel to a 1984-85 coaching replacement for the fired Jack McKinney, taking over for a man still suffering from memory loss stemming from a near-

fatal bicycle accident. Irvine stayed on for two unmemorable seasons before resigning for personal reasons, attempting to save a marriage that failed anyway. And with the 1988-89 season winding down, Irvine was a Pacers vice president when he was asked to take over as a temporary coaching fill-in for Jack Ramsay, who resigned unexpectedly.

Now, more than a decade later, with the season playing out poorly for the Pistons, Irvine stood there, dripping wet, trying to avoid more career calamity. It took another hour, plus phone calls from veteran Pistons guard Joe Dumars and even the fired Gentry, to convince Irvine to become an NBA head coach again.

Irvine accepted the job against his better judgment. He did it knowing the outside scrutiny would be brutal, with ESPN fully ensconced in its coverage and twice as much media covering the league than during his previous stint. He did this aware of the consequences.

"It was really a screwed-up team that I didn't think had any chance of making the playoffs and I thought, 'If I take over and take all the flak that goes with it and all the pressure, all they'll do is pay me $2,000 more and at the end of the year they'll fire me and get somebody new,'" Irvine said. "That was going through my head. It wasn't worth it."

As it turned out, Irvine guided the Grant Hill-led Pistons into the playoffs over the final 24 games and was hired full-time. He only succeeded in delaying the inevitable. He was fired the following season once the Pistons staggered to a 32-50 record after losing Hill to free agency.

Irvine dropped nearly twice as many games as he won as a pro basketball coach (100-190). He will never be confused with Red Auerbach, Phil Jackson or Gregg Popovich. Heading up three different teams from two sorry franchises over parts of five seasons, he was Seattle's only homegrown NBA coach until the Utah Jazz hired Quin Snyder in 2014.

Irvine, who grew up at 11240 Phinney Ave. N., was previously known as a superlative shooter who went from Ballard High School to the University of Washington to the ABA, as someone capable of going off offensively at any time with the flick of his wrist. He had a textbook jumper, squaring up to the rim with perfect form and launching the ball with a stroke as pleasing to watch as it was accurate.

The 6-foot-6 Irvine was an All-Pacific-8 forward who averaged 20 points a game as a senior for a 1969-70 Huskies team that opened 8-0 and was ranked ninth in the nation before 6-foot-9 post player Steve Hawes and playmaker Rafael Stone suffered broken legs in consecutive games and the season was ruined. In a 90-86 victory over a 12th-ranked USC team at the Far West Classic, Irvine scored 41 points, fourth highest in school history, connecting on 16 of 20 field-goal attempts.

"We were good, we were really good," Irvine said of a Huskies team that dropped to 17-9 once it became shorthanded. "Lose your point guard and center and it's going to hurt most teams. We couldn't get out and run as much. We struggled until they came back. It was disappointing."

Irvine drew coaching inspiration from Fred "Tex" Winter, his Washington coach. Winter previously had guided Kansas State to the Final Four and later became an NBA coach for the Houston Rockets. He was successful wherever he went and Irvine wanted to be just like him. Besides, Irvine wasn't sure his deft shooting touch was enough to make him a pro basketball player.

"I really liked Tex," Irvine said. "We became close. I liked the idea of coaching. I always wanted

to teach. I didn't think I would make it to the pros coming out of college. It was only a dream."

Irvine was drafted by the hometown Seattle SuperSonics, but saw more opportunity and money in the newly formed ABA. He played five seasons for the Virginia Squires, sharing the floor with a Who's Who list of teammates, among them Julius Erving, George Gervin, Charlie Scott, Swen Nater, Doug Moe and Larry Brown, and briefly with the Denver Nuggets before injuring a knee.

His shooting touch proved golden on the pro level, too, earning him the nickname "Hawkeye." He set a pro basketball record, since broken, by hitting 56 of 85 shots for the Squires in the 1972 ABA playoffs, a blistering 66 percent.

"That was playing with Julius," said Irvine, who spent two seasons alongside the player known as Dr. J. "They would double-team him and he would give up the ball. That would space the floor and I would get easy shots. Playing with Julius made life easier. I respected the hell out of him."

Irvine was in Denver when he became a basketball coach for the first time, more out of guilt than anything. Unable to play because of his knee injury, he was still drawing a paycheck for hanging around. He wanted to be useful. Larry Brown let him scout and then turned him into an assistant coach.

He followed the well-traveled Brown to Indiana and was his assistant there, too, before moving into the front office when Brown left for UCLA. Unexpectedly thrust into the Pacers head-coaching job twice, Irvine didn't try to be heavy-handed nor do anything fancy.

"I was basically me," Irvine said. "Players appreciated that. Players knew I was pretty easygoing but I could blow up once in a while. I was honest with the players. Sometimes that meant saying things that were tough. I

didn't play a role and I know sometimes guys do that. I was just me. I wasn't clever enough to play a role and fool them. With NBA players, if you don't know what you're doing, they will figure that out fairly quickly. You can try to fool them. But too many things happen too quickly in the NBA and you can't fool them long."

In Detroit, Irvine reluctantly took over for Gentry, feeling a sense of loyalty to his fired friend while expecting very little from the Pistons team he inherited. He was left with Hill and a bunch of support pieces, including some that didn't fit together at all.

Typical of the dysfunctional situation at hand, the Pistons, in the midst of a 4-1 West Coast road trip, beat the Sonics 100-90 in Seattle in front of Irvine's friends and family members, and the coach entered the locker room and found two of his players, whom he still won't name, fighting each other.

"It showed what kind of chemistry we had on that team," Irvine said. "I went off on those guys. Then I turned to the [rest of the] team and went off on them. I threatened all of them."

Irvine got that team into the playoffs, even with Hill getting hurt down the stretch, and then went three-and-out against the Miami Heat. Hill left as a free agent and the coach had no chance of returning to the postseason the following year.

Irvine was fired with four kids in college, two at Ivy League schools. He turned to scouting for the Orlando Magic and Utah Jazz before contracting an auto-immune disease, Lupus, and finally retiring to the Northwest.

"I was disappointed I never really got to coach a good team for a number of years, but the fact I was head coach in the NBA was significant," Irvine said. "Being the first guy from Seattle to achieve that says something." ❖

CURT MARSH

The Full Confession

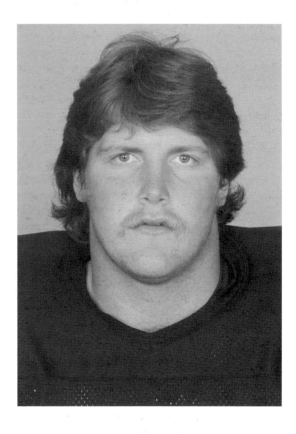

Curt Marsh said yes. He used anabolic steroids during his pro and college football careers, he wasn't proud of it, and he was willing to talk about it to the *Seattle Post-Intelligencer*. Yet full disclosure of the sensitive subject had to be done on his terms. Marsh stressed that he wanted to read whatever was written about him before the public did. The former University of Washington and NFL offensive lineman was given pre-publication access to the story, though he was never afforded the right to kill it.

It was 1988 and any steroids disclosure from the football world was shocking and rare and had to be negotiated. Tommy Chaikin, a former University of South Carolina defensive lineman, got everyone talking again after telling *Sports Illustrated* how using performance-enhancing drugs turned him suicidal, mean and anxiety-ridden.

Chaikin's story came three years after Steve Courson, a former Pittsburgh Steelers and Tampa Bay Buccaneers offensive guard and yet another South Carolina collegian, became the first NFL player to publicly acknowledge his steroid usage in elaborate detail in a *Sports Illustrated* story and told how it left him with heart problems.

Nearly 100 current and former college and pro football players were asked by the *Post-Intelligencer* about steroids. Just three people admitted to past usage for performance enhancement: 1) Smiley Creswell, a former

Marsh rightfully deserved to be castigated for giving into steroids, but he also had to be commended for providing the only honest portrayal by a Seattle athlete about a performance-enhancing drug that, still, nobody talks about openly.

Michigan State and Philadelphia Eagles defensive end and straightforward guy from Monroe; 2) a mysterious man, someone named Mike Davis; and, 3) Marsh.

Steroid conversations turned downright strange at times. Typical was Jeff Toews, a UW and NFL offensive lineman, who said, "No, no, no. ... I think we have a bad connection. ... [Click]." Dave Pear, a UW and NFL defensive lineman, said he never used steroids for football purposes but acknowledged the drug might have been among those prescribed to him for healing purposes following three back surgeries. Dean Kirkland, a Huskies offensive guard who didn't stick in the NFL and later went to prison for investment fraud, warned if he was asked about steroids again he would conduct no more football interviews with local media. A former UW lineman and Super Bowl participant said emphatically that he wouldn't discuss steroids and didn't want anyone to know he even had been approached about them.

The drug was an extremely touchy subject. None of the aforementioned former UW players admitted to steroid usage or tested positive for it. However,

Courson, a pro football contemporary, said in his *Sports Illustrated* account that he suspected 75 percent of all NFL linemen in that era regularly used the drugs and 95 percent had at least tried them.

Weirder yet was the man who called himself Davis and almost too easily volunteered his supposed steroids story. He submitted to an interview that seemed believable and even spoke about the clandestine nature of the different drugs used by teammates. "With cocaine, we all knew who was in trouble with it," he said. "That's all we talked about. Not steroids."

However, the information provided by this man, at the time a Bothell High School assistant football coach and Seattle warehouse worker, was tossed out once all of his football credentials turned up bogus. He said he had played for Kansas State and the Green Bay Packers. Representatives of those teams couldn't find any record of him after making thorough checks of past rosters and Davis couldn't explain the discrepancies when pressed. Soon he disappeared from the local coaching ranks.

Marsh had no problem verifying who he was or where he'd played. He went from Snohomish High School's 1976 state championship team to the Washington Huskies' 1978 and 1981 Rose Bowl entries to the Los Angeles Raiders' 1984 Super Bowl XVIII title team. He was a nimble 6-foot-5, 285-pound athlete with superstar written all over him. He had unlimited college scholarship offers. He was a first-round NFL draft pick, the 23rd player overall selected in 1981.

If only crippling injuries hadn't limited his success so severely, affecting his neck, back, knees, hips and ankles. He was a starter at offensive tackle in his senior season at the UW and a force in pro football at offensive guard as a rookie, opening big

holes for Marcus Allen, yet that was the extent of his success.

Marsh rightfully deserved to be castigated for giving into steroids, but he also had to be commended for providing the only honest portrayal by a Seattle athlete about a performance-enhancing drug that, still, nobody talks about openly. In 2003, Mariners outfielder/first baseman Mike Morse briefly discussed his steroids use as a minor-leaguer, but only after he had been caught and it brought him a big-league suspension and he had no recourse but to say something.

Although voluntary, it still was not an easy process for Marsh. After reading an unpublished *Post-Intelligencer* story written by me that detailed his steroid use, he wasn't happy. He said it was too harsh. He felt under attack by it. Marsh was encouraged to tell about his drug use in his own words. Efforts were made to mollify the former football player because, after all, he was the one sticking his neck out. Settling on a first-person account rather than an outsider's observations, Marsh was satisfied with that.

"I already was slated to start at left tackle for the Huskies in 1980 and had overcome back surgery to get there," Marsh said of his introduction to steroids. "While lifting weights a teammate and I noticed a player who had been fairly strong the year before but now was much bigger and stronger. Eager to learn his routine, we asked what he had done to make such an improvement. He finally told us he was seeing a doctor who was prescribing for him an anabolic steroid, namely Dianabol. In our youthful zeal to tap our full potential and then some, we decided to see the doctor ourselves.

"I certainly was doing fine without, but my 'win-at-all-costs' attitude kicked into gear. At the last minute, I backed out of seeing the doctor, fearing

what might happen if I took the pills and someone found out."

The doctor in question had an office on Seattle's Capitol Hill. Marsh and others described how the man routinely made his services available to any UW athlete who needed a performance boost, specifically those from the football and track and field teams. He never met the doctor in question, but he took advantage of him.

"My friend went to the doctor as planned and was on the program that week," Marsh said. "A couple weeks later he was lifting like mad and getting stronger fast. This coupled with the fact that he looked fine to me – I mean he hadn't grown a third eye or anything – forced me to reconsider my decision. I still didn't want to see the doctor but I did want to take the Dianabol. So my buddy simply said he had lost his prescription and gave me the refill."

After injuries and stiff competition previously kept him from making a breakthrough, Marsh became a Huskies starter for the first time for all 12 games during the 1980 season, which ended with a 23-6 loss to Michigan in the Rose Bowl. For the first time as a collegiate player, his health held up and he showed his potential. He wasn't an All-American or All-Pac-10 selection, but he played well enough to draw the attention of pro football scouts. He had used steroids for a month.

"The bottle contained a two-week supply and it said to take three of the five-milligram tablets a day," Marsh said. "To this day, I'm not sure which was really responsible for the improvement I made: The fact I was taking an anabolic steroid or the belief that taking them would surely make me stronger. In any case, my strength improvement was definitely accelerated. We repeated the lost prescription routine once more and

> Marsh progressed from
> steroid tablets to injections
> as a rookie with the Raiders,
> probably the last NFL team
> he needed to join.

then I quit using them altogether. As far as I know, the only people taking steroids at the University of Washington were the two people I mentioned and myself.

"Even if you suspected someone might be using them, you could never know for sure. It was something one kept strictly to oneself."

Marsh progressed from steroid tablets to injections as a rookie with the Raiders, probably the last NFL team he needed to join. The outlaw franchise was deeply immersed in drug use. Among Marsh's teammates were defensive linemen Lyle Alzado and John Matuszak, high-profile players who admitted to taking performance enhancements or were exposed, and died as young men from health issues likely related to steroids.

With the Raiders, Marsh dealt with chronic injuries and appeared in just 45 games over five seasons, playing what amounted to just under three full seasons. He was subjected to more than a dozen surgeries, and steroids were a way to heal quickly. "My use of steroids was limited to a couple of injuries, trying to play catch-up in the race to get to the top," Marsh said. "Sometime in late 1985, I began to come to my senses and realized what I must be doing to myself. Until that time, I had heard of some of the side-effects these muscle builders caused, but didn't see any occurring in me or in three or four other Raiders who sporadically used them."

Marsh later changed his mind on steroid drawbacks. During 1986 training camp, Marsh suspects he broke a bone in his right ankle. He claimed the injury was misdiagnosed by the team doctor and didn't receive proper treatment. He played in two Oakland games that season before the pain became too unbearable and he was done with pro football.

Marsh was so highly thought of he was drafted two rounds before the Raiders selected Hall of Fame defensive lineman Howie Long. But Marsh was labeled as one of the team's five biggest draft busts because of his abbreviated career.

Eight years after quitting the NFL – and six years after his steroids admission in the *Post-Intelligencer* – Marsh, then a motivational speaker, was still in extreme pain. The only solution was horrifying. He had his right leg amputated eight inches below his knee at Seattle's Harborview Medical Center. He was fitted for a prosthetic limb, learned how to cope with depression and returned to Snohomish to raise his family.

No medical malpractice suits were filed or threatened by Marsh. The Raiders no doubt were outwardly confident they would never be held responsible for the offensive lineman's health decline: Marsh, after all, had used steroids. ❖

JAMES EDWARDS

The NBA Houseguest

The NBA couldn't get rid of James Edwards. He was the guy who stayed way past last call, who wouldn't go home, who wouldn't take off his uniform. Edwards played in the league for 19 seasons, enjoying a career nearly four times longer than that of the average player and was historic for its staying power. He entered the NBA when disco was all the rage and left it with the grunge scene winding down.

Only four players – Kareem Abdul-Jabbar, Robert Parish, Kevin Willis and Kevin Garnett – hung around the big show longer than Edwards, each chalking up 20 seasons or more demonstrating the elite company the Seattle native kept.

Edwards' NBA fountain of youth was simple: He was used as a reserve early in his pro career, saving wear and tear on his 7-foot-1, 250-pound frame; even as a starter, he remained a specialist good for low-post points, and averaged just 24 minutes per game. And the well-traveled big man played for anyone who wanted him, suiting up for eight different teams. Edwards was 40 when he finally gave in and retired in 1996.

"I had a few injuries but nothing that beat me down," Edwards said. "I was able to come back for training camps. I was able to get my body ready and play. I was always called the old man on the team and I tried to help out the younger guys when they came into the league. I was definitely blessed to play that long. But after 19 years, I think you've had enough."

> Edwards became Seattle's longest-serving pro player, as well as the city's winningest big-league athlete.

Edwards became Seattle's longest-serving pro player, as well as the city's winningest big-league athlete – collecting NBA championship rings in 1989, 1990 and 1996. His longevity was a surprising development considering what happened to him when he first pursued the game. In 1969, as a ninth-grader at north Seattle's Nathan Eckstein Junior High School, he was all legs and no coordination, and was cut during basketball tryouts.

There were spots for 15 players at Eckstein – one went to me – but there wasn't room for the shy, gangly kid who was bused in each day from his Madrona family home at 302 30th Ave. E. Edwards was lopped for supposedly lacking the very quality that made him an NBA fixture for almost two full decades: Durability.

Robert Cutler, Paul Stone and John Noel were boys' physical education teachers at Eckstein back then and each had a hand in picking the basketball team. Cutler took over as head coach because no one else could make time for the job. Tryouts lasted a few days. A list was posted. Edwards was not on it.

"It's amazing how someone can have that ability later in life," Stone admitted. "You don't realize it. You don't see it. You wonder, did you do something wrong when you cut someone like that?"

James Edwards went from Roosevelt High to the UW to the NBA.

Edwards didn't argue with the verdict handed down. He was rightfully disappointed, but he shrugged it off and decided to find another sport. When he was a sophomore at Roosevelt High School, his friend

John Nelson convinced him to turn out for the cross-country team.

On the first day of school, Edwards was wandering through the Roughriders' athletic locker room when Larry Whitney, who doubled as varsity basketball assistant and sophomore team coaches, stopped him. Whitney looked the kid up and down and envisioned all sorts of possibilities.

"I saw this guy who was 6-5, legs split to his ears," Whitney said. "I asked him if he played basketball and he said, 'No, I got cut from my junior high team.' I said, 'No, this year you play.' He was a little reluctant. He was a little embarrassed. He said, 'I'm too awkward.' I said, 'Not this year.' He became kind of a crusade."

For the next three years Edwards was subjected to a daily regimen of agility drills by Roosevelt coach Ben Snowden and Whitney, regularly hopping over benches. Edwards was taught how to shoot. He was encouraged to attend the Al Bianchi summer basketball camp on Whidbey Island.

Edwards had painful setbacks, such as catching a ball in the face or tripping over his feet and falling down in practice, but he kept growing and progressing. It all came together for him as a senior in 1973 when he helped lead the Roughriders to a state championship.

Edwards was rewarded with a college scholarship for his rapid basketball ascent, choosing his hometown Washington over California. He was the central figure behind a Huskies' resurgence, none more pronounced than in his junior year in 1975-76 when his UW team started out 14-0 and was ranked sixth in the country before losing 72-70 to a Lonnie Shelton-led Oregon State team at home. Edwards helped the Huskies land an NCAA Tournament berth for the first time in 23 years, only to lose to Missouri 69-67 in the first round.

Edwards appeared to have pro potential but no one was sure how much, which might have been a blessing for his NBA career. In the 1977 draft, the Huskies big man was still available when the Los Angeles Lakers, with the second pick of the third round and 46th choice overall, took him even though they had Jabbar, the league's best center.

Edwards got a chance to study at the feet of the master and took full advantage. "Going to the Lakers, who's a better teacher than Kareem? I come in as a rookie and had to play against him every day in practice and he's telling you things. You have to guard Kareem as a nobody going against someone really good. He was my idol when I was growing up."

When Jabbar slugged the Milwaukee Bucks' Kent Benson and broke his hand in the opening game that season, the Lakers' drafting of the former Husky center appeared shrewd. In his first game as a replacement, Edwards scored 25 points in a 133-120 victory over the Indiana Pacers and thereafter helped keep the team together during Kareem's absence. The Pacers were so impressed they traded for him two months later, sending Adrian Dantley and Dave Robisch to Los Angeles for Earl Tatum and Edwards.

The big man's long-winding pro career took him from Los Angeles and Indiana to, in order, Cleveland, Phoenix, Detroit, back to Los Angeles to play for the Clippers and the Lakers, and Portland and Chicago.

"He could definitely score," said George Irvine, a former UW player and a Pacers assistant coach when Edwards arrived. "I don't know if he had the mentality to be a great scorer or the ability to be a great scorer but he could get shots, especially for a team like Detroit; he wouldn't get double-teamed because he had so many good players around him. He could get decent shots off against Jabbar or whoever the hell it was."

Edwards spent parts of six seasons in Phoenix, which was his longest stay anywhere in the NBA, but one that seriously threatened his basketball reputation. With drug use rampant throughout the league, the Suns' Walter Davis traded grand-jury testimony for immunity from his own cocaine charges and gave up the names of Edwards and other players who were recreational users. Wild drug and gambling claims also were made, seemingly tied together, and indictments were filed but later dismissed. Edwards was guilty of nothing more than being naïve and careless.

"A lot of that stuff was a lot of garbage," Edwards said. "Davis said me and Jay Humphries were gambling and I read in the paper where we made $800,000 gambling, betting on the game. I called Jay and said, 'Where's my money?' It was something where you just had to be strong at that point. I got a good lawyer that helped me out. With all that stuff with Walter Davis, and him getting busted three times and spilling beans on everybody, even people out of the league, it was a terrible situation. We went different ways."

Edwards bounced back nicely. He left his worst NBA experience for his best when he was traded to Detroit midway through the 1987-88 season. He shared in two NBA championships, the first as a reserve and the second as a starter and replacement for Rick Mahorn. Edwards expected to go to the Minnesota Timberwolves

> "To start my career playing with Kareem and end it with Michael Jordan, who could ask for more?" Edwards said.

in the expansion draft following the first title, but Mahorn was left unprotected instead and ended up in Minneapolis, making Edwards a Pistons starter.

Detroit typically threw the ball into Edwards the first few times down the floor, just to see how the defense would react. He was an integral part of a group nick-named "The Bad Boys" for its rough style of play, and personally christened "Buddha" by backup guard Vinnie Johnson and Mahorn for his Fu Manchu mustache and squinty eyes.

"I'm always going to be one of the 'Bad Boys,' " Edwards said. "We changed the way basketball was played."

Edwards closed out his career as a member of one of the greatest NBA teams, sharing in a third championship and a 72-10 season with the 1995-96 Chicago Bulls and Michael Jordan in his prime.

Bringing him full circle, Edwards and the Bulls were paired against his hometown SuperSonics in the finals. He went home after collecting his third ring, knowing he hadn't been shortchanged as a pro player.

He appeared in 1,168 games. He played for a 63-19 Pistons team in 1988-89 and that Bulls squad seven seasons later that were considered two of the 10 best NBA teams in history. He stayed relatively healthy, with a partial Achilles tendon tear and broken knuckle his worst setbacks. Edwards cashed in on his free-agent status to pull a four-year, $3.2 million contract out of Cleveland but suffered through a dismal 23-59 season and was shipped out.

In his 19 NBA seasons, he earned a small fortune, with his yearly contracts ranging from $50,000 to $1.4 million, but underhanded agent issues and his own financial ineptitude left him with far less money. Still, he walked away satisfied.

"To start my career playing with Kareem and end it with Michael Jordan, who could ask for more?" Edwards said. "To go 19 years and win championships, I think I had a great career. I played with one of the worst teams ever in the Cleveland Cavaliers. You would never think you would be on one of the best teams ever in the Detroit Pistons, and retire with one of the best teams ever in the Chicago Bulls. I saw it all." ❖

REGGIE ROGERS

The Failed Breathalyzer Test

Reggie Rogers sat down on a porch in Seattle's Central District and died. It was lunchtime. It was neither complicated nor unexpected. Rogers, 49, knew the end was near.

Four days before taking his final breath, the former University of Washington All-America defensive lineman and first-round NFL draft pick called an old teammate and asked for help in getting his personal affairs in order. He suffered from seizures. He had been hospitalized. He walked in fear of the immediate future.

"He basically knew he was going to die," said Brett Smith, a Seattle narcotics detective and one-time UW special-teams player. "He wanted me to put a will together for him to make sure his kids got his NFL money."

On Oct. 24, 2013, Rogers was found in a prone position outside a friend's home at 2761 E. Yesler Way. He was already deceased when police and fire units arrived just before 1 p.m. The coroner officially ruled Rogers' death accidental from alcohol and cocaine intoxication. There was more to it than that, though.

Rogers seemed to die in stages over 27 years, going from one of Seattle's most gifted and physically dominant athletes to its most publicly shamed. No high-profile sports figure from the city has been deeper immersed in substance abuse. Rogers was arrested eight times for alcohol-related driving offenses, convicted four times.

> Rogers seemed to die in stages over 27 years, going from one of Seattle's most gifted and physically dominant athletes to its most publicly shamed. No high-profile sports figure from the city has been deeper immersed in substance abuse.

In his ugliest moment, Rogers blindly plowed his vehicle into another and killed three teenagers outside of Detroit. He spent five years in Michigan and Washington correctional facilities. He became a rudderless and wandering soul. He couldn't stop drinking and driving.

"I'm not happy he's dead," said Bob Willett, whose son and two nephews died at the hands of Rogers. "I'm happy the world is a safer place because he's dead."

Rogers had his shining moments as an athlete, but they didn't last long. He came to the UW as a basketball player and started 28 of 31 games in his freshman season. He could dunk and block shots explosively but he couldn't shoot. As a sophomore, he was replaced in the lineup by 7-foot Christian Welp, who eventually became the school's all-time leading scorer, Pacific-10 Player of the Year and an NBA player. Rogers openly pouted about the demotion and claimed he didn't deserve it. He ultimately traded in basketball for football.

As a Sacramento high school football player, Rogers was a serious prospect until he got into a fight with opposing players that involved swinging a yard marker. Oklahoma and USC reportedly withdrew scholarship offers because of the violence, which left him injured. Don Rogers, his older brother, a UCLA All-America safety and Cleveland Browns standout, encouraged him to give the game another try at the UW. Reggie played both Huskies football and basketball for a year before walking away from the latter.

The 6-foot-7, 250-pound Rogers was an instant football sensation for Don James' Huskies, first playing linebacker before moving to defensive tackle. He used his raw strength and great speed to become the Pac-10 Defensive Player of the Year and a first-team *AP* All-America selection by his third and senior season in 1986.

He was fearsome on the pass rush, especially in national-TV victories over Big Ten powerhouses Ohio State and Michigan. Rogers played in the Orange, Freedom and Sun bowls. He was the seventh player taken in the NFL draft.

"Defensively, he was an absolute warrior," said Mike Lude, former UW athletic director. "He never was big trouble with us. He lived on the edge a little bit, though."

Rogers' ascension to college football stardom was dulled by his first alcohol-related misstep, followed by a crushing family tragedy involving drugs. On June 4, 1986, Rogers was pulled over on Lake City Way N.E., operating a 1983 black BMW, which was a gift from his brother. "Reggie" was scripted in gold lettering across the driver's side door. He was driving 60 miles per hour in a 35 zone and weaving, according to the police report. He blew 0.18 and 0.14 on a breathalyzer.

Three weeks later in California, as the Rogers family prepared for a big wedding, Don Rogers let out a scream and collapsed in the shower at home, dead in an instant from a cocaine overdose. He was to be

married the next day. His mother, Loretha Rogers, was so distraught she suffered a heart attack. Reggie Rogers' world was completely turned upside down.

"When I lost him, it was like losing a father, my best friend and my brother all at once," said Rogers, who later wore a black armband in games to honor his sibling.

Nine days later, Rogers had to answer for that DUI in Seattle. He got away with it. His lawyer said he deserved leniency because of his brother's death. Lude called the court and lobbied hard on Rogers' behalf. Judge George Holifield dismissed the DUI offense, upsetting others by only fining Rogers for speeding.

Steve Newman was a Seattle Municipal Court bailiff who took the insistent phone call from Lude and passed the information along to the judge. He came away convinced a double-standard was put in place for Rogers.

"I've thought about Mike Lude calling me at court and Judge Holifield letting him go on the first DUI," Newman said. "I won't say it has haunted me, but pretty close. Certainly it made me supremely cynical."

Rogers signed a four-year $1.7 million contract with the Detroit Lions, but his glory days were over. He appeared in only a handful of games as a backup player during the strike-interrupted 1987 rookie season. He suffered a nervous breakdown and went on the reserve

list. His second season lasted just a few games, too, before he went on the injured list. The fatal accident came next.

In the early morning hours of Oct. 20, 1988, Rogers blew through a red light traveling 60 mph in his Jeep Cherokee and plowed broadside into a Dodge Omni in Pontiac, Mich. His victims were Kenny Willett, 19, who lived six miles from the accident scene, and his cousins Kelly Ess, 18, and Dale Ess, 17, who had come from a small Missouri town to visit their dying grandmother. One cousin was ejected, his brain matter left splattered on the road. The other cousin was left trapped in the back seat, his body nearly cut in half. Willett was barely alive and recognizable to his parents at the hospital before dying.

Rogers had been drinking at Big Art's Paradise Lounge with Lions teammate Devon Mitchell. Rogers left his pregnant fiancée, Sheila Dorsey, sister of former UW basketball player Chester Dorsey, at home and he and Mitchell had picked up two girls at the bar. They made a couple of stops before Mitchell drove through an intersection as the light changed and Rogers tried to follow. Rogers had consumed seven drinks and purchased a 40-ounce beer at a store, court records showed. His alcohol level was 0.15.

The teens were on their way to Willett's home and had been drinking, too, but not heavily. Rogers, who broke his neck in the crash, tried to use this information to paint himself as a victim. When charged in the accident, he asked, "Why? What did I do wrong?" He was convicted of vehicular homicide and spent a year in prison.

The Lions released him and he played briefly for the Buffalo Bills, Tampa Bay Bucs and CFL's Hamilton Tiger-Cats before he was pushed out of football for good. He appeared in just 15 NFL games. He complained that he was treated like a monster.

"He tried to say he apologized to us, but that was a lie," Bob Willett said. "He never said one single word to the family. He never owned up to anything he did."

Rogers was married three times, fathered six children and worked a series of jobs in Seattle that included UPS, construction and even some electrical work at the *Seattle Post-Intelligencer*. He continued to drink and drive. In 1993, he was arrested for his third DUI-related offense in suburban Bellevue. Charges were dropped once he entered a treatment program for 23 months and completed probation.

In 1997, Rogers was stopped for erratic driving in the Central District. Open beer cans were found in his vehicle. He told officers he was a designated driver — but was riding alone. He blew 0.20 on a breathalyzer and was arrested a fourth time and convicted of DUI. He was sentenced to a year in jail. His attorney, David Kraft, told the court that Rogers struggled "with an incurable disease."

In 2004, he was arrested for a fifth time under the suspicion of drinking and driving, but was found guilty only of reckless driving and paid a $500 fine. In 2008, Rogers was arrested for the sixth and seventh times within 40 days. He was cited for DUI and hit-and-run after his 2002 Chevy Suburban collided with a van on Interstate 5 near Southcenter and was pulled over on Highway 99. He was belligerent and cursed at troopers. He called one of them "Coach James." He fell asleep in

the patrol car. He told an officer at the station that he wanted to "give him a hug and kiss him." His second arrest also involved I-5 and a minor collision.

The court heard how Rogers' latest marriage was failing and he was taking medications for clinical depression. Rogers stood up and made a bizarre statement, asking Judge Darrell Phillipson for leniency by declaring, "I carried this whole team, this whole state, on my back. I can do it again if given the chance. I do feel I could be a blessing on this community; people look up to me." To which an unimpressed Phillipson responded, "You're not the role model I want my kids to have." Rogers was sentenced to two years of jail time after pleading guilty to avoid an additional 12 months behind bars.

In 2010, Rogers, incredibly, was stopped in Tacoma and cited once more for DUI, his eighth alcohol-related arrest. He was on work-release at the time and hadn't completed his previous jail term. He was given another year of incarceration tacked onto his existing sentence.

Rogers claimed to have a football-related head injury that affected his judgment and was among those suing the NFL for damages, hence the urgent need to write a will for his heirs. But his actions always counteracted everything he said. It was that way until the day he slumped over, his body no longer able to withstand the substance-abuse overload. ❖

In a Snohomish High School football uniform, Rick Fenney resembled a big, red blur when he crashed through the line of scrimmage and sprinted 50 yards or more to the end zone, which was often. He was a heavily-muscled fullback with breakaway speed. He could bench press 500 pounds.

He was a true "Friday Night Lights" attraction for his rural hometown, regularly drawing overflow crowds and large numbers of college recruiters to his games. In 1982, in fact, a Notre Dame talent scout effusively labeled Fenney as the best running-back prospect in the nation without differentiating between tailbacks and fullbacks.

Fenney similarly was an intimidating presence when he graduated to the college and pro levels, and pulled on different shades of purple jerseys for the University of Washington and Minnesota Vikings. He appeared in four consecutive bowl games for the Huskies. He spent five productive seasons in the NFL until a dislocated hip sent him into retirement.

The 6-foot-3, 240-pounder was at his ball-carrying best in the fourth quarter of the 1985 Orange Bowl. He snapped off one punishing run after another and finally a clinching short touchdown blast against a

> Red, purple or orange,
> it all looked good on Fenney.
> The color he clashed with
> was green. He couldn't handle
> money. He didn't lose
> many yards, but he
> squandered $2.2 million.

RICK FENNEY
The Money Player

usually stout Oklahoma defense built around linebacker Brian Bosworth, helping his Huskies to a rousing 28-17 victory in Miami.

Red, purple or orange, it all looked good on Fenney. The color he clashed with was green. He couldn't handle money. He didn't lose many yards, but he squandered $2.2 million. He fumbled away the savings of 17 friends and relatives as a self-styled and poorly prepared investment broker and lied about it. Once the money was gone, Fenney solicited more investors to pay off his original clients, becoming a small-scale Bernie Madoff conducting a traditional Ponzi scheme. It landed him in a California jail and Oregon federal prison for nearly two years. He was guilty of the worst white-collar crime committed by a high-profile Seattle athlete.

"There was always something missing in my life so it was easier to give up my integrity and honesty because I didn't stand for anything," said Fenney, his once jet-black hair turning gray. "When I got in a real difficult situation it brought out the worst in me instead of the best."

From May 2006 to November 2007, Fenney was confined to FCI Sheridan, a red-and-white prison sprawled over the Oregon countryside, an hour's drive southwest of Portland. He lived in a minimum-security camp, next to the razor-wire-enclosed prison, and shared a dormitory wing with 31 other inmates.

He spent his days exercising, attending a drug and alcohol rehabilitation class, cleaning out a waiting room and wondering how he could have fallen so far. He wore a prison-issued jumpsuit – green, no less – and was identified by the white label that was stitched across the top: Fenney 94417-198.

Just as disturbing, Fenney could have started up his own prison football team if not his own "Longest Yard" sequel. Early in his FCI Sheridan stay, he encountered former UW teammate Dean Kirkland, an offensive guard serving time for a criminal offense similar to Fenney's. Kirkland was involved in a Ponzi scheme in Portland that bilked labor groups out of investment and pension money.

Matt Jones, a former running back from Portland who played for the Huskies after Fenney, was a Sheridan inmate prior to the fullback's arrival before his transfer to Lompoc FCC in California. Jones took part in an elaborate car-selling ruse that involved scamming 37 people out of $1.3 million.

Fenney, who had lived in condo unit 306 at 1805 186th Pl. S.E. in Bothell, felt invincible after conquering football at every level, especially the NFL. He received a game ball for his performance in a Monday Night Football victory over the Cincinnati Bengals that advanced the Vikings to the playoffs. Fenney memorably lowered his shoulder and knocked Hall of Fame safety Ronnie Lott on his back and kept on running. Fenney played in Seattle against his hometown Seahawks with friends and family members sharing in the moment. And then it was over.

"It's really difficult to give up a career in the NFL, the excitement, the benefits of it," Fenney said in 2007. "I found myself getting bored. There didn't seem to be a challenge. There was something missing. When I had it all, a good NFL career, marriage and family, I really didn't feel fulfilled like I thought I would."

He started an investment company, attracted a small clientele and had success for 18 months. He went bigger and bolder, with more investors getting involved by word of mouth. It backfired.

His solution was the world of finance. After drawing NFL salaries of $300,000 to $400,000, he turned an off-season job as a financial planner with Northwest Bank in Minneapolis into a full-time position.

Needing more than that, he moved home to Snohomish and started a construction company with a friend, financing projects while a buddy built them. He finally uprooted his family to San Diego, went to work as a Merrill Lynch broker and read a book entitled *Market Wizard*, which was a compilation of successful traders offering tips for success that inspired him to branch out on his own.

He started an investment company, attracted a small clientele and had success for 18 months. He went bigger and bolder, with more investors getting involved by word of mouth. It backfired.

"I've learned you can't obtain happiness by getting material things and money," Fenney said. "It's OK to have them but not to obsess over them and chase after them. That's what happened. I let greed dictate my decisions. I wanted those things but I also wanted to feed my ego – that I was this great success as a trader, making all this money. I wanted to prove to myself that I could be this huge success in something other than football."

Within the first two months of creating a hedge fund, Fenney started losing money, thought he could fix it and made things worse. For two years, he kept soliciting cash, telling investors through emails that profits were way up.

By 2004, Fenney was past the point of no return and finally admitted what he had done. Indicted on wire fraud for the misleading investor messages, he received a 37-month sentence with three years of probation and was ordered to pay restitution. As part of his penalty, he could never handle other people's money again for investment purposes.

"I was distinctly unimpressed by him," said Anne Perry, the assistant U.S. attorney in San Diego who prosecuted Fenney. "It was kind of like, 'Me, me, me. I tried. I failed.' They trusted him. His letter to the court in mitigation was all about him and I found that disturbing. Basically he was in over his head from the get-go."

Fenney's actions were revealed when people started asking for their supposed profits. They were shocked to learn there weren't any, especially after filing tax returns indicating there were. Angry and tearful investors spoke at Fenney's sentencing. Two elderly couples lost their retirement money. Fenney's letter to the judge was read aloud, requesting a reduced sentence, and it wasn't well received by his former clients.

Paul Smithers was a Poway, Calif., attorney who became friends with Fenney after representing him in a legal matter. He lost more than any other investor, $514,206. "He ruined a lot of lives," Smithers said. "He took some people's last dollar, and he did that knowingly. I have no sympathy for him."

Mark Berdan was Fenney's next-door neighbor. They became good friends and socialized together. Berdan lost $30,154. "I think his intentions were good; I think he just wasn't very good," Berdan said. "The problem is

Rick has a big ego, like most athletes."

Leaving prison, Fenney said he was a reformed man. He dropped from more than 300 pounds to 224, well under his playing weight. He went through prison drug and alcohol-abuse classes, which were largely responsible for his weight loss. Now divorced, he talked of reuniting with four teenaged daughters once he was released to a halfway house in Phoenix. He spoke about making restitution to the victims.

Considering his devious actions that landed him behind bars, it seemed only fair to ask Fenney, a spectacular athlete at times, whether he used steroids or any performance-enhancing drugs during his football career to get ahead. Fullbacks don't often run 4.5-second 40-yard dashes or bench press 500 pounds, plus he seemed injury-prone.

"I never in my life have taken steroids or supplements, period," Fenney insisted. "I know a lot of people think I did. I can honestly say I've never taken that stuff. I was never approached. I never saw anybody take them. First of all, I never had a need for it because I worked so hard at such a young age."

His truthfulness, however, was hard to measure. Several months after Fenney's release, Paul Goeke, a Phoenix-area resident who worked for a video surveillance company, encountered the former Huskies and NFL fullback at Harold's Cave Creek Corral, a local bar north of Scottsdale. Fenney casually mentioned to his new friend how he was a commodities trader and had proficient investment skills. Goeke, his surveillance background kicking in, went home and did an Internet search that brought up a *Seattle Post-Intelligencer* story written by me detailing Fenney's Oregon prison stay and corresponding missteps. The next time they met in the bar, Goeke informed Fenney of what he found online.

"I told him I had Googled him and his face turned white," Goeke said, referencing another color that Fenney didn't wear well. ❖

MIKE UTLEY

The Broken Man

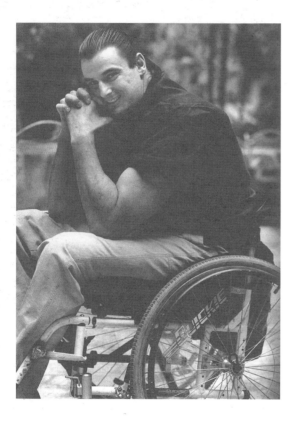

Mike Utley was pass-blocking, nothing more. The Detroit Lions offensive guard was trading shoves with Los Angeles Rams defensive lineman David Rocker, someone he would forever confuse with Tracy Rocker, when he was pulled to the ground and his spinal cord gave way. The Seattle native fractured three vertebrae and couldn't move. He wouldn't be celebrating the Lions' 21-10 victory in the Silverdome that day.

After a long delay in a stadium turned silent and apprehensive, Utley was gently lifted up and carried off the field on a stretcher, knowing it was bad but still flashing a thumbs-up sign to the crowd. On Nov. 17, 1991, his three-year NFL career was over in an instant. His life had changed forever. He was a quadriplegic.

Utley was the second of four high-profile Seattle collegiate or pro athletes left paralyzed by spinal cord injuries, three while engaged in athletic pursuits. The free-spirited Lions lineman became the most animated face of a luckless group that included the late Brian Sternberg, a record-setting University of Washington pole vaulter permanently injured during a 1963 trampoline accident on campus; Mike Frier, a Seattle Seahawks defensive end immobilized as a passenger in a 1994 single-car accident in suburban Kirkland, and the deceased Curtis Williams, a UW defensive back paralyzed on a goal-line hit in a 2000 football game at Stanford.

Utley was the victim of the brute strength of pro football, not some open-field collision or defenseless hit, such as the one that put the late New England Patriots wide receiver Darryl Stingley in a wheelchair for the rest of his life and led to an early death. It was a wonder more people in the league weren't hurt under the crush of all that humanity up front.

At 6-foot-6 and 288 pounds, the former Washington State University and Kennedy High School player was big enough and strong enough to control the line of scrimmage, but Utley landed awkwardly after interacting with a smaller and younger opponent. Rocker, a rookie, was two inches shorter and 21 pounds lighter.

"People ask if I remember, and I see it all the time," Utley said. "I was kicking the crap out of him. We were physically better than they were on that given Sunday. I got caught. He caught me and pulled me down. He was doing what he should have been doing. I would have done the same thing. I was focused. I was on my game. I had my man the right way, doing what I needed to do. It was 100-percent testosterone. I just got caught. That's it. I wish it was, 'Coach, I have a hangnail.' "

As the Lions advanced to the NFC Championship Game without him, Utley spent nine days in the intensive care unit at Detroit's Henry Ford Hospital, was transferred out and suffered two blood clots, and

> Utley was the second of four high-profile Seattle collegiate or pro athletes left paralyzed by spinal cord injuries, three while engaged in athletic pursuits.

returned to the ICU for another nine days. From there, he was moved to Denver's Craig Hospital, considered one of the nation's foremost spinal-cord rehabilitation centers.

While despair set in, Utley still had to be the carefree goofball he'd always been. Super Bowl Sunday, coming nine weeks after his crippling injury, was one of those moments. Preparing to watch the game on TV from his hospital room, Utley had a revelation. "I wanted something to drink," he said. "They didn't have one on tap." Utley snuck out of the hospital in a wheelchair, traveling four blocks to a Denver 7-Eleven store. He was wearing only shorts and a shirt in the brisk Colorado weather and his once-robust NFL frame was 105 pounds lighter, with his upper body resembling, in his words, "Pamela Anderson cleavage."

Crossing a street, he got the wheels stuck on a curb and stayed there until a passing motorist jumped out of his car and gave him a push. Once inside the convenience store, Utley had the clerk retrieve a 40-ounce beer and count out the money from his wallet in a backpack hanging behind him. Back in his hospital room, Utley needed an hour and half to get the beer open. His hands and wrists weren't strong enough to make it happen, forcing him to put the container up against his body and continually squeeze. He finally sipped that beer while watching quarterback Mark Rypien, a former Washington State teammate, lead the Washington Redskins to a 37-24 victory in Super Bowl XXVI over the Buffalo Bills and receive Most Valuable Player honors. Utley felt a sense of accomplishment that day, same as Rypien.

"Sure, I should have done it with permission and, sure, I should have done it with a therapist, but I wasn't going to be held back," the lineman said. "My goal was to be there in front of the football game with a cold one and I got it done."

Utley stayed in Colorado for six years learning how to become independent again before choosing to move home. He wanted a water view. He bought a rambler on 2½ acres in Orondo, an out-of-the-way community bordering the Columbia River, and he shared the three-bedroom waterfront home with his wife, Dani, a paramedic he met while working out. He had two docks, one equipped with a lift that allowed him to launch his 25-foot boat and race up and down the river.

Utley was resolute and hilarious, everything except hopeless. Days were spent working out at his residence or at Gold's Gym in nearby East Wenatchee, taking part in some unlikely new adventure such as fighter-plane combat re-enactment, and running his home-based Mike Utley Foundation dedicated to finding a cure for spinal cord injuries.

This wasn't exactly what Utley envisioned when he left Seattle's Kennedy High for WSU, became a first-team *Associated Press* All-America selection and headed for Detroit as a third-round draft choice banking on a 10-year NFL career. He helped lead the Cougars to an Aloha Bowl victory over Houston and posed for a memorable TV greeting aimed at his hometown rivals who were left out of the postseason. "Happy holidays, Huskies," he and his teammates teased into the camera. Utley was pegged for pro football greatness once he hit college. He was passed over by hometown Washington recruiters and those coaches later admitted they had made a mistake. Utley, who grew up in south Seattle at 10221 59th Ave. S., went from a tall, skinny kid with a mullet haircut to a behemoth on a weight-room and pizza diet. The Cougars found out fairly quickly that they had a big-time player.

"This is one of those rare kids who didn't get the notoriety and we got him," WSU coach Jim Walden said at the time. "He's as fine a lineman as I've seen come

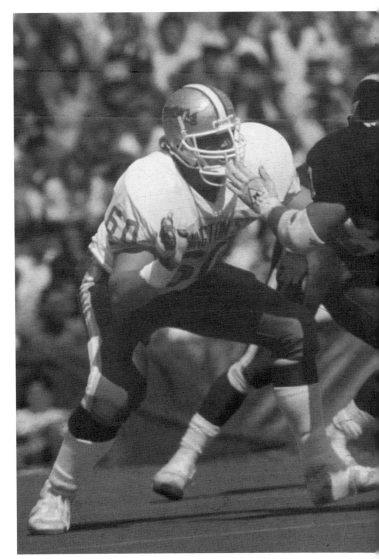

Mike Utley was a first-team All-America pick for WSU.

out of this state since I've been here. If he will go into the weight room and work just moderately, he can become one of the finest offensive linemen to ever play in the league, and not just at Washington State."

Once paralyzed, Utley was forced to fight and win insurance battles instead of those in the trenches. He raised millions for spinal cord injury research. He made himself available to counsel other quadriplegics and their families. He traveled and spoke to groups around the country, allowing people to follow him around and see how he lived.

In 1999, he stood up and moved his feet. He didn't exactly walk, but he showed what biofeedback and exercise could do, allowing him to rebuild neuro-signals and make his back and hips stronger to give him more functionality. His shoulders became NFL-sized again from working out. He pushed his weight back up to 245. He improved his nutritional intake. "As my wife says, I've got to cut out my girlfriend – Wendy's," he said.

To become mobile, Utley drove a Cadillac Escalade SUV with special hand controls. He used a wheelchair with mountain bike tires for more cushion. He had a lockdown seat in his boat. He skydived and skin-dived.

He was always up for an adventure, spending a wedding anniversary with his wife in California 5,000 feet in the air in separate mock warplanes shooting at each other. Utley pushed ahead, keeping a positive outlook even with the suicide of his older brother, Tom. As basketball players at Kennedy High, the siblings resembled the hockey-playing Hanson brothers of cinematic fame, barreling into opponents and causing all sorts of mayhem. Utley dealt with all setbacks, continuing to mix work and play in heavy doses. He never felt sorry for himself.

He never turned his back on football, never blamed the sport for his misfortune. In 2006, Utley attended Super Bowl XL between the Pittsburgh Steelers and his hometown Seattle Seahawks at Detroit's new Ford Field, invited back for the festivities because of his Lions connection. His dream was to someday return to the abandoned Silverdome, to the spot he was injured, and walk again. He never once wanted to turn his back on football, no matter what it did to his body.

"If I had a chance to go back and do it all over again, knowing I would break my neck, I would do it all over again," Utley said. ❖

STEVE EMTMAN

Intensity Overload

Steve Emtman stood at midfield at Husky Stadium for the opening coin toss, surrounded by other University of Washington game captains. The imposing defensive tackle shook hands with Arizona players across from him, making eye contact with Wildcats offensive guard Nick Fineanganofo, a stout Samoan player pushing 340 pounds and responsible for blocking Emtman that afternoon. The Huskies leader looked Fineanganofo up and down. Emtman was 50 pounds lighter but he seemed the much bigger man.

With kickoff nearing, his engine already revving, the Huskies' defensive leader couldn't help himself while mixing with the enemy: Emtman cracked a menacing smile, as if to signify he was going to swallow another canary whole. Fineanganofo wilted in the face of this guiltless gamesmanship. The Arizona lineman knew what was coming. Everyone in the stadium knew what was coming on that 1991 day.

"If he wasn't sweating, he was pissing down his leg; he was almost stuttering," said Huskies center Ed Cunningham, a witness to this territory-marking moment and later an ESPN broadcaster. "On the first play of the game, Emtman picked him up and threw him down. Emtman picked him up on the second play and threw him down again. It was sheer terror. If there's

> ### Emtman was the most imposing player on the most dominant team in Seattle sports history. No other athlete took over a game like he did, using brute force.

not humor in a 340-pound man in terror, I don't know what then."

Emtman was the most imposing player on the most dominant team in Seattle sports history. No other athlete took over a game like he did, using brute force. Largely because of him, the 1990s represented a sporting decade in the city's history known for its over-the-top physical prowess. Every Saturday, Emtman was a freight train barreling through the city, a boulder crashing downhill, a Pamplona bull careening through the streets of college football.

He marched the Huskies to 22 victories in 24 games in his final two seasons and back-to-back, lopsided Rose Bowl victories over Iowa and Michigan, and a share of a national championship in 1991 with Miami.

Individually, Emtman piled up a lot of hardware. He captured the Outland Trophy, was the Lombardi Award recipient and finished fourth in the Heisman Trophy voting that favored Michigan wide receiver Desmond Howard. The relentless defender was twice chosen Pacific-10 Defensive Player of the Year and a consensus 1991 first-team All-America selection on six different lists. Further validating his unique skill set, the Indianapolis Colts picked Emtman No. 1 overall in the 1992 NFL draft.

Emtman grew up on a farm outside of Cheney, a town of 6,000 in the shadows of Spokane not far from the Idaho border. He was raised on a 2,000-acre spread that was home to cattle, horses, elk and the occasional cougar, and annually produced wheat, barley, lentils and alfalfa. He wasn't widely recruited, pursued only by Washington State and Washington. At a time without pestering recruiting websites, he was an unknown talent to Seattle.

Emtman became an angry young man once at the UW when he asked to wear his high school number, 74, and was rebuffed. He was told a higher-regarded recruit, Mike Lustyk, who happened to play his position, had already claimed it. Emtman was not happy either when it was suggested that he consider converting to an offensive lineman. Transforming from a skinny, unsung freshman to a smoldering, intimidating presence, he turned No. 90 into one of the more unforgettable jerseys in Huskies football annals.

Even in practice, Emtman couldn't turn it off. He had to overpower everyone. He had to outwork everyone. He would get all amped up and let everything come pouring out, drill after drill.

"My first love will always be football," Emtman said. "Nothing else I do in life will give me the rush that football does. I'm always going to have that drive. It's basically an addiction."

Emtman demanded no less from his teammates. He often talked about playing the perfect game, of making every tackle in a game. He had little patience for any other approach. During a 1991 spring practice scrimmage, the second-team offense easily moved down the field on the No. 1 defense and scored, and vintage Emtman emerged. He walked to the bench outwardly perturbed. He took off his helmet, wound up and slammed it against a large equipment chest. The sound echoed loudly through Husky Stadium. Heads turned.

Emtman demanded no less from his teammates. He often talked about playing the perfect game, of making every tackle in a game.

Emtman screamed out, "Ones right here!" Teammates quickly surrounded him on all sides. For several minutes, Emtman talked heatedly, gesturing with his helmet for emphasis. Ears burned. The impromptu meeting ended and an agitated Emtman continued to stalk the sideline alone until his next series, unable to accept anything less than total control.

"He checked out as a recruit and we couldn't understand why more people weren't after him," Huskies coach Don James said. "When we got him, he had a pretty good motor. He got bigger, stronger and harder to block. The competitiveness was there from day one. I had to put the best against the best a little bit every week and the thing is we would say to him there would be no winners or losers in the drill, but that was hard for Steve to figure out. He would compete like gangbusters. We had to keep people healthy."

Still, there were massive casualties created by his scary aggressiveness. In spring practice, the 6-foot-4, 290-pound Emtman crashed into the backfield and spilled into Huskies quarterback Mark Brunell, who was coming off a Rose Bowl offensive MVP performance, and left Brunell with a torn-up knee. Emtman locked up in practice with fellow defensive lineman Tyrone Rodgers and the latter likewise was carried out with a blown knee. Emtman put Huskies linebacker Chico Fraley out

with a broken thumb. Emtman even rammed into one of his roommates, center David Ilsley, and left him crumpled with a broken leg in need of surgery. The opposing side wasn't any safer: Emtman put Nebraska fullback Omar Soto writhing on the ground with a broken leg.

"He's destruction and terror," Huskies defensive end Andy Mason summed up.

Emtman, who was so athletic he could windmill dunk a basketball and do back flips, was the point man in the Huskies' 12-0 season in 1991. Games were decided so early he played in the fourth quarter just two or three times. He overpowered nearly every player he faced that season, and he went up against the best from USC, Nebraska and Michigan. He conceded that California center Eric Mahlum gave him all he could handle, but added that Mahlum was the only one. He was such a disruptive force against Arizona and Fineanganofo, the Wildcats resorted to punting on third down in the second half.

Winding up a spectacular year, Emtman had the flu and a 103-degree temperature, missed nearly every practice in the last week leading up to the Rose Bowl against Michigan, and was taken to a Huntington Beach hospital for intravenous fluids, requiring five liters. Although not 100 percent, he still dominated the Wolverines in a 34-14 victory and was named Rose Bowl defensive MVP.

Taking his game to the NFL, Emtman was still capable of wondrous stuff; his heroics just didn't last long. In his seventh game with the Colts, he stepped in front of a Dan Marino pass on the last play of a 31-20 victory over the Miami Dolphins and lumbered 90 yards for a touchdown — still the longest interception return by a defensive lineman in pro football history. "That was the high point of my NFL career," he said.

In his eighth game against the Chargers, Emtman had a career-high 11 tackles. In his ninth game, however, he blew out his right knee and headed for surgery. It was the start of a rapid decline that would limit him to just six seasons and 51 games as a pro football player. He injured his other knee, had a herniated disc in his neck and shattered a finger, and never bounced back.

Emtman, who had a 550-pound bench press and 735-pound squat, played in the pros at 340 pounds, Fineanganofo size. He said the work ethic that made him a college stalwart had worked against him in the NFL, where he realized way too late that he needed to pace himself.

Skeptics quickly suggested that Emtman's rapid football ascent and descent could be attributed to only one thing: Steroids. People in Cheney, watching his body mushroom, kidded him incessantly about the use of performance-enhancing drugs, with wisecracking deli owner Tony Carpine making the player blush one day when he asked Emtman in front of others to show him his needle marks.

Emtman, however, never tested positive for any illegal substance. He never admitted to using anything improper. He was either clean or good at covering up. He admittedly understood why others might have pegged him as a user, but insisted people had overlooked his maniacal approach to the game.

"I actually love that question," Emtman said. "Anyone who wants to ask that question can come train with me. I over-trained, no question. It bothers me when people say it who know me. I never decreased in a single lift my whole career. Every max period, I took five- to 10-pound increases, never 30-pound increases, which anybody on juice would do. I kind of take that as a compliment when people say that. There's no reason for me to defend it or say anything about it.

"If I didn't know me, and I looked at this strong, powerful athlete and saw him get injured, I'd think the same thing."

Once the pros were over for him, Emtman joined the Huskies weight-training staff during the program's serious down years and lived in north Seattle at 4915 N.E. 85th St. Once he applied and failed to land the job as head weightlifting coach, a miffed Emtman went home to eastern Washington and started building houses.

He became a rich man for being the NFL's No. 1 draftee, banking an initial $13 million. Yet the pros weren't fun for him, with the added pressure of being that first overall draft choice. He started losing games, too. And the talent level was such that there were no more Fineanganofos cowering in his midst. It was fun, and annoying, while it lasted.

"I thought I was invincible until that first injury," Emtman conceded, though he was never one given to hyperbole. "I didn't think anything could touch me and that I could run through a wall. I was a good player, maybe a great player." ❖

Top 10 UW Football Players

1. Steve Emtman, DT
2. Hugh McElhenny, RB
3. George Wilson, RB
4. Don Heinrich, QB
5. Bob Schloredt, QB
6. Sonny Sixkiller, QB
7. Reggie Rogers, DT
8. George Fleming, RB
9. Corey Dillon, RB
10. Donnie Moore, RB

BILLY JOE HOBERT

The Loan Officer

Billy Joe Hobert was a character pulled straight from the *North Dallas Forty* and *Semi-Tough* novels and movies: He was a real-life version of the unrefined side of big-time football. He had that country name. He was a gifted quarterback. He was a major goofball.

At the University of Washington, Hobert helped steer a powerful Huskies team to a 12-0 record and co-national championship with Miami in 1991, and he was installed as Rose Bowl royalty, selected as the game's offensive MVP. And then, with barely enough time to adjust his crown, he shockingly brought down the entire UW program and was branded an outlaw.

Hobert, his personal life a constant roiling mess with an estranged wife and a disgruntled mistress, decided to cash in on his sudden fame. Prior to the 1992 season, he accepted a series of loans totaling $50,000 from benevolent Idaho businessman Charles Rice and the results were widespread and crippling — the money abruptly ended his collegiate career in midstream, destroyed another serious UW run at a national title, led to the exposure of other middling misdeeds and exorbitant NCAA penalties, and forced legendary coach Don James to quit.

Hobert's actions pulled the momentum out of a budding dynasty that had collected three consecutive Rose Bowl trips before a postseason ban was handed down. As Husky football crumbled around him, Hobert

> **Hobert's actions pulled the momentum out of a budding dynasty that had collected three consecutive Rose Bowl trips before a postseason ban was handed down.**

received or was offered death threats while overnight turning from one of Seattle's most revered athletes to its most reviled — a transformation unmatched in the city's sporting annals. He went from hero to outcast in a blink.

His fancy new car, a white Camaro purchased with the loan money, was stolen from him and left riddled with bullets. Things got so out of hand, a man even called up the banished quarterback and startled him with an offer to kill Tom Farrey, the *Seattle Times* reporter who first reported on the loans and sent the whole scandal in motion.

"The guy was a friend of a friend and he said, 'Now Billy Joe, you know what I do, and I usually charge nine or 10 grand to do it, but I'll do this one for free; if you want me to take out Tom Farrey, let me know,' " said Hobert, who was so unnerved he urgently passed along the contract hit information to the UW. "I went to [athletic director] Barbara Hedges' office. I said I wasn't going to take any responsibility for what happened to Tom. I haven't talked to that other guy since that day. I'm not going to drop any names either. I was scared to death, to be honest."

Farrey, who later joined ESPN and *ESPN the Magazine* as an investigative reporter, said he was never informed of any perceived threat against his life by university officials. "Hedges may have been afraid to tell us out of fear of a bad headline, who knows?" he said.

As for Hobert, it was just another part of his Husky football calamity. He had made people shuffle uncomfortably once he joined the program from Puyallup High School, where he won a state championship. He was a poor practice player. He wasn't a serious weight-room guy. He was crass and said outlandish things. Coaches tried to tone down his act. Teammates viewed him as a total bumpkin.

As a redshirt freshman at quarterback-rich UW, Hobert backed up sophomore Mark Brunell in 1990 when the Huskies went 10-2 and won the Rose Bowl, and Hobert was backed up by freshman Eric Bjornson. A year later, that trio was joined by Damon Huard, and all four eventually played in the NFL, though Bjornson as a receiver.

Hobert, who seriously considered changing positions to tight end to get on the field more, became the quarterback starter by default, promoted after the more polished Brunell suffered a debilitating knee injury during spring practice that required surgery. No one was comforted by the sudden change behind center.

"When Mark got hurt, we went home that evening and James [Clifford] and Brett [Collins] and me were sitting around, and we freaked out," said starting center Ed Cunningham, referencing a pair of Huskies linebackers and his housemates. "We thought we were going to be lucky to go 4-7 with that jackass at quarterback."

The joke was on them, though. Hobert was a far different player when the stakes were serious, almost frighteningly so in 1991. He was super competitive with everything on the line, demonstrating his strong will in

a stunning 36-21 win at Nebraska by bringing the Huskies back from a 21-9 third-quarter deficit.

The comeback in Lincoln, Neb., began with Hobert completing a risky fourth-and-eight pass to Orlando McKay deep in Cornhuskers territory to set up a score. It ended with Hobert scoring on a goal-line option run following an adrenaline-filled conversation with James. The coach told him to protect the ball, to which the brash young quarterback responded in his typical roughhewn manner, "No [bleeping bleep]!"

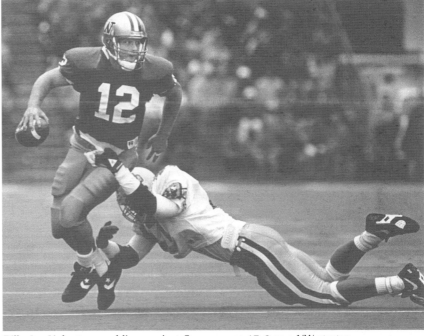

Billy Joe Hobert, scrambling against Oregon, was 17-0 as a UW starter.

Hobert readily acknowledged his practice habits were poor, that his mindset was different during the rest of the week compared to game day.

"That is absolutely the truth," he said. "That was my biggest downfall, even in the NFL. A lot of coaches didn't have faith I could get the job done because I was so crappy in practice. I knew in practice I would get a do-over or if I made the wrong read I could learn from it with no repercussion. But I treated every game like it was life or death for me."

Hobert was at his best when he put the finishing touches on that unbeaten season in a crushing 34-14

defeat of Michigan. He was superb for all 12 games, completing 191 of 319 passes for 2,463 yards and 24 touchdowns.

For the following season in 1992, Hobert and a healthier Brunell – also a Rose Bowl offensive MVP – shared the starting job as the Huskies opened 8-0 and the team alternated with Miami week by week for the top spot in the polls. Hobert, still a junior, was 17-0 as a UW starter when everything blew up.

His former mistress tipped off the *Seattle Times* about his loans from Rice, who had helped other students financially and was introduced to the quarterback by a relative. Hobert admitted to this financial arrangement when quizzed about it by Farrey, and that he had spent the cash on the Camaro, golf clubs, guns, stereo equipment and entertaining friends. He was done when the story broke.

His team lost on the road to Arizona that weekend, abruptly ending the Huskies' 22-game winning streak. Ten months of nonstop turmoil also uncovered recruiting and summer job improprieties by the UW, leading to stiff sanctions and James' bitter departure.

James was convinced Hobert did nothing wrong except blow through $50,000 haphazardly. The coach suggested a court battle would have exonerated Hobert, but conceded the process would have been too cumbersome for the quarterback to regain eligibility for his senior year.

"In my opinion, Billy Joe didn't have an NCAA violation," James said. "The only way there would have been one is if one of the coaches set up that loan. We couldn't have got him eligible again. He would have had to wait five or six months and I don't know if he would have wanted that. But the way he was spending money was borderline stupid."

Hobert said the UW actually gave him pre-approval to accept the loans from Rice and then distanced itself from him during the resulting fallout. Recruiting coordinator Dick Baird acknowledged meeting with Rice and, after hearing him out, determined the school was in compliance with NCAA rules because the man wasn't an alumnus, booster or connected to the UW in any manner. Baird blamed Hedges for caving in to league officials overeager to penalize the school. "I still believe if Mike Lude was athletic director a lot of the stuff would have blown over," he said.

Hobert pursued a baseball career in the Chicago White Sox organization for a summer and then turned to the NFL, with the Huskies controversy dogging him all along. Drafted by the Oakland Raiders, he received death threats on his first trip to Seattle to play against the Seahawks, prompting game-long security at the Kingdome. Four police officers shadowed him as he walked the Raiders sideline holding a clipboard.

He played parts of five pro football seasons for the Raiders, Buffalo Bills and New Orleans Saints, and was on the Indianapolis Colts and Oakland rosters for four seasons without getting on the field. He threw three touchdown passes for the Raiders in a game against Denver and John Elway. Hobert heaved a 90-yard touchdown pass to Saints wide receiver Eddie Kennison against Atlanta. He even went head to head with Brunell in a Saints' 41-23 loss to the Jacksonville Jaguars in one of his final NFL games in 1999.

He was an ordinary pro football player, starting just 17 games, while tossing 17 touchdown passes. Yet in typical fashion, he couldn't keep his mouth shut. In Buffalo in 1997, after a poor performance against the New England Patriots, Hobert said he hadn't read the Bills playbook, which wasn't true. The quarterback always seemed on a self-destructive path. He popped off, nothing more, because his home life was a mess. Buffalo released him two days later.

"I intentionally shot myself in the back," Hobert said.

"That probably was the most idiotic thing I could have done. I knew the playbook inside and out, though that didn't mean I could execute it. Quite frankly, I deserved to get fired by Buffalo. I was an absolute schmuck."

As for those loans that brought down the Huskies, Hobert paid Rice back with 10-percent interest. Finished with the NFL, Hobert had baseball tryouts with the San Diego Padres and Colorado Rockies that didn't go anywhere.

Hobert married again and relocated to California. He attended a few UW road games, but didn't really reconnect with the football program or his former teammates until the national championship team came together in 2011 to celebrate its 20th anniversary.

By now Hobert could walk around Husky Stadium virtually unrecognized, as a middle-aged man with thinning hair and a thicker, beaten-down frame. He suffered severe neck, hip and back injuries, and lived off NFL disability checks. All of that Seattle hatred aimed at him had dissipated. One thing hadn't changed, though: Hobert still had a cocky swagger about him, especially when considering his football legacy.

"People who know me, like me; I don't think they care about that situation too much," Hobert said. "I'm so far removed, geographically and chronologically, that I don't give it much thought anymore. I can't do anything about the past. I don't dwell on it.

"How people want to remember me is entirely up to them. How I'm remembered, I don't really care." ❖

Michelle Akers grew up in Lake Forest Park, across the street from Brookside Elementary School that counted her as a student, safely tucked away in a north Seattle suburb. Yet to pigeonhole this woman to any particular school, neighborhood, city, state or even country would be doing her a huge disservice.

Except for those who remain unwavering Mia Hamm or Julie Foudy supporters, Akers is widely considered the world's greatest female soccer player of all time. She belonged to the entire soccer universe. For a decade and a half, she ruled it.

It all began in Seattle, where Akers emerged as this tall, willowy player with mangy hair and plenty of attitude — to the point she could be downright annoying, transforming herself into a thunderous soccer presence from midfield to the front row in an international setting. She walked away from the game with her body broken and spent, yet holding up an athletic career as rich and complete as anyone's, man or woman.

If desire was the criteria for greatness, she was willing to embrace the suggestion that she had no soccer equal worldwide and take a sweeping bow.

"To be considered in that line of thought is pretty cool, though it was more about character to me and winning," Akers said. "When people say that, they still don't know what kind of person I am inside. And are you judging that on my accomplishments or skill? More people say it wasn't that, that it was more the grit, and I say, 'Thank you.'"

Akers' global soccer success makes her Seattle's most prominent female athlete in any sport.

MICHELLE AKERS
The World-Beater

Akers' global soccer success makes her Seattle's most prominent female athlete in any sport, overshadowing the exploits of locally produced Helene Madison and JoAnne Carner, who remain among the world's greatest female swimmers and golfers, respectively, from any era. With her 10 goals leading to a World Cup championship in 1991, followed by a gold-medal victory in the 1996 Summer Olympics and yet another World Cup breakthrough in 1999, Akers received much of the credit for establishing U.S. women's soccer as a major world player.

If further validation was needed, Akers was the first in her sport to receive a shoe-endorsement contract. "There is no one like her in the world," Hamm said at the time.

Akers set herself apart by leaving everything she had on grassy fields, courageously playing on despite chronic fatigue syndrome, major knee surgery and multiple concussions that tore apart her body. It was not surprising that this 5-foot-10, 150-pound soccer warrior took a special, final curtain call by walking away gingerly yet triumphantly in Pasadena.

"In the 1999 World Cup, when we beat China in overtime, it was my last game and I had gone out in the 90th minute," Akers said. "I was standing in the middle of the field with the team doctor and the whole stadium was chanting my name at the Rose Bowl — and it was like a dream."

Michelle Akers, shown against Canada in 1991, was tough to stop.

As a fourth-grader, Akers moved to Seattle from California's Bay Area when her parents divorced. She was a rowdy little girl in desperate need of an outlet to channel her pent-up emotions. She tried ballet, but the finesse wasn't for her. She signed up for Bluebirds and got kicked out of the girls' organization for acting up. She turned to Little League baseball and grew impatient with it. She even rejected soccer the first time she played it, crying whenever her team lost, though she actually was much tougher than that.

"I was like the only girl who played football and whatever else the guys were playing in the street," she said.

Early on in Seattle, Akers joined a team called the Shorelake Thunderbirds and made a permanent soccer connection. Her 19-year-old coach was passionate about playing and good at the game, and he made things fun for Akers and her teammates. "That's where I fell in love with playing and focused on one sport," she said.

Akers, who lived at 3340 N.E. 178th St. in Lake Forest Park, established her elite soccer credentials at Shorecrest High, a sports-minded Seattle school that supplied Mark McGrath, Mike O'Brien, Ray Pinney and Marc Wilson to the NFL, Glendon Rusch to big-league baseball, and Bill Sander to the PGA Tour.

She led the Highlanders girls' team to a state championship as a junior in 1983, but often practiced with the boys' team for more of a challenge. She played indoor soccer usually as the only girl involved in those arena games.

What Akers didn't do was play for a select soccer team because her father, Bob, who worked as a Safeway grocery store butcher before becoming a counselor, couldn't afford it. She was stuck at the club level. That still didn't hurt her college chances any. Everyone in soccer knew about Michelle anyway.

Typical of Akers, she did the unconventional when accepting a college scholarship offer, choosing unsung Central Florida instead of the consensus top pick for a women's soccer program, defending national champion North Carolina. She showed typical brashness in rejecting the Tar Heels and their coach, Anson Dorrance.

"I didn't like the coach so I didn't go there," said Akers, who was a four-time All-America selection. "I thought he was very conceited. Frankly, I thought my club team was better than his team. The way he pitched it, the package, the deal, the team, it just wasn't what I wanted to be part of. They were national champions and I didn't like his demeanor. Central Florida wasn't polished, the forerunner, the expected winner. They were like blue-collar workhorses and that's why I liked them."

Following her freshman year at UCF, Akers became a national team player, if not a true pioneer in the American women's soccer movement. On Aug. 18, 1985, she played in the first U.S. international match, a 1-0 loss to Italy, and three days later scored her country's first goal in a 2-2 tie with Denmark.

She scored 105 goals in 153 national team outings, including an amazing 10 over a six-game stretch en route to the 1991 World Cup. She had five goals in a quarterfinal victory over Taiwan and both goals in a 2-1 victory over Norway in the finals.

In 1988, Akers became the first woman to win the Hermann Trophy, annually awarded to the top male or female collegiate soccer player. She was the first American woman to play pro soccer, spending three seasons with Sweden's Tyresco Club. And she never hesitated in speaking her mind when it came to the actions of U.S. Soccer.

"What I did not like or appreciate was the lack of support from the federation on the initial movement of the World Cup and Olympics," Akers said. "We called ourselves the redheaded stepchild. They were pushing the men and that was their focus. We interrupted their plans by winning."

When soccer was over, Akers moved to central Florida and operated a 12-acre horse rescue shelter, which meant one beaten-down thoroughbred was looking out for others. She had a large image of a galloping stallion tattooed across her left shoulder blade.

She got married for a second time, fittingly to her personal-injury attorney Steve Eichenblatt, and they raised a son. She often pined for the Northwest, especially when hurricanes ravaged her home and horse barn.

Once Akers became a middle-aged woman, she had little to do with soccer, conceding she could no longer kick with her right leg and admitting she didn't even keep a soccer ball on her expansive Florida property. Yet soccer wouldn't let go of her. She was inducted into the National Soccer Hall of Fame. FIFA named Akers and the great Pele as soccer's players of the century.

Finally, in 2012, she moved to Atlanta and reconnected with her sport, opening up a youth-soccer training company in Georgia, perhaps in hopes of discovering and developing another player as gifted, motivated and confident as she was. Of course, that would be a challenge. There was no one else quite like her.

"I played with dogs," Akers said. "I broke windows with a soccer ball. I broke fences with it. I was so immersed in just playing. I just loved it. I loved training. I dominated games and practices, but I didn't realize until I got to college that, 'Gosh, I'm good.' " ❖

Top 10 Female Athletes

1. Michelle Akers, USA soccer
2. JoAnne Carner, LPGA
3. Helene Madison, Olympic swimmer
4. Sue Bird, Storm
5. Doris Heritage, Olympic runner
6. Lauren Jackson, Storm
7. Ruth Jessen, LPGA
8. Joyce Walker, Globetrotters
9. Janet Hopps, pro tennis
10. Hope Solo, USA soccer

FRED COUPLES

Seattle's Green Jacket

Fred Couples' Beacon Hill home was Rae's Creek and the front parking strip was the 12th green at Augusta National Golf Club, and he leisurely launched Wiffle balls from the backyard and over the roof to the narrow patch of grass. Growing up just a few blocks from south Seattle's Jefferson Park Municipal Golf Course, he used his imagination as a young boy to play the Masters over and over in total solitude outside his family's modest, white rambler at 4328 13th Ave. S. His birdie putt was good only if he bounced it off the curbside fire hydrant.

Playing for real in the 1992 Masters, Couples made all of his dreams come true, collecting a compelling two-stroke victory that solidified his stature as one of the PGA Tour's most talented and popular players, stamped him as Seattle's greatest golfer ever, and brought his hometown its most cherished golf moment.

Usually emotionless on the course to the point that the game's leading analysts and his fellow players sometimes accused him of not caring, Couples wore a smile that stretched from Georgia to his Northwest birthplace when he pulled on his green jacket with the help of Ian Woosnam, the previous winner. It was the ultimate reward for all of those pretend rounds at home.

"Fred predicted that very early the ultimate goal for him was to one day win the Masters," said Jim Nantz, the lead CBS-TV golf broadcaster and one of Couples'

college roommates and best friends. "That he was going to win the green jacket was very much in the air that week. Dream became reality."

A Masters triumph finally made sense of Couples' much-debated PGA Tour career. He was a hard guy to figure out. He was likeable yet perplexingly distant. He had an effortless swing envied by anyone who saw it. He also left those same people downright puzzled by his nomadic preferences, such as his abject reasoning for not picking up a ringing phone: "Because someone might be on the other end." With his good looks, Couples seemed like a natural golf pitchman, but for years he kept his distance from the companies that sought him out for endorsements, unwilling to share himself.

Couples grew up as the youngest of three children for a Seattle Parks and Recreation groundskeeper. Early on it was clear that he had a natural affinity for golf. He was short in stature but appreciably long off the tee. He never said much to anyone, though he once shocked an unsuspecting junior golf official as a hot-tempered teenager who slammed his bag to the ground and let go with an unapologetic string of obscenities while approaching a green.

Playing for real in the 1992 Masters, Couples made all of his dreams come true, collecting a compelling two-stroke victory that solidified his stature as one of the PGA Tour's most talented and popular players.

While golf came easy to him, other stuff was a struggle. He was cut from his O'Dea High School basketball team, forced to become an equipment manager, a caddie of sorts for the likes of future NBA player Clint Richardson. He didn't obtain his driver's license until he was 22, or two years into his PGA Tour career, leaving him legally able to operate a golf cart and nothing more well into adulthood. Golf provided him with an immediate identity, which proved both a blessing and a curse. "I got better fast, that's why I liked it," Couples said. "I just picked it up. I don't know how."

Couples couldn't leave the house and make the three-block walk to Jefferson Park until a bucket of weeds had been collected. Yet once at the tree-lined public course, he was genius with a golf club in his hands, entertaining groups of envious older players with a variety of wedge flicks on the driving range and natural power that soon had him banned from swinging a driver in the practice area.

He easily became bored as a member of O'Dea High's golf team; he played holes backward for sport, teeing off with a wedge and trying to land a second shot on the green with a driver. He had length off the tee to go with all that creativity, his extra-thick calves supplying an amazing power source. The 1977 O'Dea alumnus won a pair of high school state championships convincingly, the second by an ominous 14 shots.

Jefferson Park golf pro Steve Cole took an interest in Couples and soon had him on a barnstorming tour around the state, at the same time keeping other influences away. Cole resisted any impulses to tinker with that irresistible swing, deciding it was one of a kind.

"Mike Davis said, 'He'll never make it, his swing is too vertical,'" Cole said of a fellow Northwest pro. "I shielded Fred from that. We never talked about mechanics. I thought about it once and then I thought, 'No way.'

The rhythm is what ties his whole swing together in one motion. His tempo has always been the same. His rhythm has always been pleasing to look at. His club-head speed to the ball is uncanny, really."

Looking for a college golf program to embrace, Couples wasn't on anyone's recruiting lists because he couldn't afford to play in national junior golf events and gain widespread exposure. BYU and New Mexico rejected him. Arizona State showed only a passing interest.

Houston finally offered him a half-scholarship, with legendary Cougars coach Dave Williams taking him on the recommendation of others, trusting his previous luck in finding Seattle golfers who could play at a high level, such as Jim McLean (the elite instructor) and Kermit Zarley (the 1962 NCAA champion).

"I had a fellah from Seattle write me a letter and he said there was a boy up there that could get out of trouble better than anyone he had ever seen," Williams said. "As soon as he stepped on the first tee, I could tell he was going to be a player."

Couples spent three seasons at Houston, long enough to meet Deborah Morgan, a tennis player and California native who became his first real girlfriend and his wife. They were the oddest of odd couples as Mr. and Mrs. Couples: She was loud, the center of attention, dressed garishly and always wanted to go dancing; he preferred to stretch out on the couch, grab the remote control and leisurely watch TV. She needed lots of attention and he wanted none.

Returning for his senior year at Houston, Couples stopped off to visit Morgan in the Los Angeles area. Restless on the interlude, he tried to enter the 1980 Queen Mary Open in nearby Long Beach as an amateur. Told there were only pro spots available, Couples impulsively gave up his college eligibility and teed it up, finishing in sixth place. Three months later, he survived

tour qualifying school with a last-hole birdie and began his long-winding PGA Tour career.

Couples' first of 15 tour victories was both satisfying and unnerving. In 1983, he survived a five-man playoff at the Kemper Open, winning on the second extra hole at the stuffy Congressional Country Club in Bethesda, Md. He looked sheepish when Morgan ran across the 18th green in a cowboy hat, spiked heels and a skimpy blue mini-dress, and jumped into his arms.

Couples didn't care for his newfound celebrity. He made this clear by turning away all product endorsement opportunities that automatically came with it. His relationship with the national golf press corps was initially strained.

After twice blowing the 1984 Phoenix Open with 18th-hole water balls in regulation play and a playoff, and losing to Sandy Lyle, he hustled to his courtesy car to make a quick getaway and swore at several reporters who chased after him in the parking lot. He wouldn't speak to any media from his hometown either for a couple of years following a *Seattle Post-Intelligencer* story that I had written detailing his sometimes erratic behavior, referring to me "as that Riley guy."

Yet as the victories piled up, Couples made peace with everyone who wanted a piece of him, including me. Soon he was promoting luxury cars and golf equipment in network TV ads, and sharing himself more willingly in the interview room with national writers, and the people back home. Admittedly, it took some maturity and patience on his part.

"My first two or three years on the tour, I didn't have a gallery, nothing, and then you get paired with Greg Norman," Couples said in the Masters clubhouse, telling me to sit down so he could explain himself. "People catch you as an idiot. I would never yell at people, but you can say the wrong thing in front of everyone. I wouldn't want anyone to think I'm an idiot in the Northwest, especially the golf pros."

By 1992, Couples had it all figured out. He was the No. 1 player in the world, winning three events, with his Masters breakthrough serving as his crowning moment. He grabbed the lead for the first time at Augusta National as he headed for a final trip around extra-challenging Amen Corner.

In the most memorable and precarious moment of his golf career, Couples survived a tee shot that came up well short at the same par-3 12th hole he once emulated playing at his parents' Beacon Hill home. His drive somehow settled into the steep front bank and avoided the watery grave of Rae's Creek by a mere two feet, which was a lot like barely finding the parking strip at home and not hitting the street. "The biggest break, probably, in my life," he conceded.

On April 12, 1992, Couples finished two shots ahead of Raymond Floyd, cried as he pulled on his green jacket, which was three inches too short in the sleeves, and pocketed a check for $270,000. Couples had to conduct the prerequisite winner's TV interview with Nantz, his old college buddy, and that proved emotional, too.

"He spent most of that time in Butler's Cabin shielding his eyes; he wouldn't look at me," Nantz said. "I had to ask a couple questions and I saved the big one for last: 'Back in the dorm room, even I said one day you were going to win the green jacket and …' He shielded his eyes. He was laughing so he wouldn't cry."

Life didn't get any simpler for the player nicknamed "Boom Boom" once he conquered the Masters. Chronic back pain curtailed his PGA Tour career some, though he continued to stay as competitive as he could before turning 50 and joining the Champions Tour.

He had gone through a lot of life changes. His parents, Tom and Violet, died of cancer within months of each other shortly after his Masters conquest. His first wife, Deborah, committed suicide in an outlandish fashion, jumping off the ledge of a church in Los Angeles in 2001. His second wife, Thais Bren, died from breast cancer in 2009.

The Seattle golfer launched balls up the fairway as a middle-aged man in search of solitude and in need of back-pain relief. Everything was so much easier for Fred Couples when all he had to do was follow the flight of that Wiffle ball as it disappeared over his Beacon Hill rooftop. ❖

Top 10 Seattle Golfers
1. Fred Couples, PGA
2. JoAnne Carner, LPGA
3. Rick Fehr, PGA
4. Ruth Jessen, LPGA
5. Anne Sander, amateur
6. George Bayer, PGA
7. Kermit Zarley, PGA
8. Don Bies, PGA
9. Pat Lesser Harbottle, amateur
10. Jeff Gove, PGA

GRIFFEY, JOHNSON, RODRIQUEZ

Hall of Fame Clubhouse

Deep inside the Kingdome, the Seattle Mariners' clubhouse had a strong Cooperstown feel to it. The place was more Hall of Fame display than dressing area. Yet it offered living and breathing baseball legends to interact with rather than propped-up mannequins and memorabilia. Entry was free to anyone with a proper baseball press credential or a spot on the 25-man roster.

Walk in the first door, go through a long hallway and a second door, take a sharp right and a few cubicles over was Randy Johnson. The 6-foot-10 pitcher often was alone in his thoughts and wanted his privacy. He wore a set of headphones or had his long frame leaning forward into his locker to shield himself from the steady parade of roaming media inquisitors seeking pre-game interviews.

If Johnson wanted to share himself, he made small talk with fellow starting pitchers Jamie Moyer and Jeff Fassero, though he once angrily wrestled and fought with first baseman David Segui in front of everyone over a trivial matter: The volume on the clubhouse stereo was too loud. For an outsider, however, catch him right on certain days and he could be disarmingly thoughtful and charming. But on most, Johnson never seemed happy. He always was one of the game's most complicated souls.

Using a nearby corner area to conduct his personal business was Alex Rodriguez. The young shortstop usually stood in front of

Ken Griffey, Jr   Randy Johnson   Alex Rodriguez

his cubicle and pulled off some garish shirt and pant ensemble – a bright-green outfit was among his worst selections – that had teammates privately and not so privately ripping him while his eyes darted around the room to see who was looking at him.

He always seemed to be in a hurry. He always appeared to be a solitary figure in this exalted workplace. He was an innocent kid back then, slender and seemingly uncompromised by performance-enhancing drugs. He was years away from being accused of shacking up with Madonna while a married man, of being found guilty of drug use, lying about it and drawing an unprecedented year-long ban, and of dealing with an image that always seemed insincere and under attack.

Around the corner to the left was Ken Griffey Jr., a centerfielder widely considered the best player in the game at the time and the Mariners' undeniable center of attention. He often lounged in a recliner chair and clutched a bat in front of his corner dressing area that

> At no point in the history of Seattle sports was there a greater array of proven talent in one lineup. This trio was composed of two sluggers ... and a left-handed pitcher. They weren't particularly close friends; rather they merely tolerated and respected each other's talents.

Ken Griffey Jr., blowing a bubble between at-bats, was the Mariners centerpiece.

consisted of multiple cubicles. This particular sacred ground was located next to a doorway leading to the field and was closest to manager Lou Piniella's office.

Griffey tossed out rapid-fire wisecracks and insults to anyone who entered his pre-game airspace, whether that person wore a baseball uniform or not. He understood the power he wielded and used it. Once asked by a clubhouse attendant if he was privy to Rodriguez's whereabouts, Griffey from his perch first looked a beat writer in the eye, which was me, and then at the inquiring kid, as if searching for a punch line rather

than a response, and finally came up with the big finish: "I don't know where she is."

At no point in the history of Seattle sports was there a greater array of proven talent in one lineup. This trio was composed of two sluggers who in their composite big-league careers exceeded 600 career home runs (put a PED asterisk next to A-Rod's total) and each earned at least one A.L. MVP selection, and a left-handed pitcher who was so dominant he accepted five Cy Young awards and rang up 303 victories. They weren't particularly close friends; rather they merely tolerated and respected each other's talents.

The Mariners kept these guys together for parts of five seasons, beginning in 1994 with Rodriguez's first call-up from the minors, and ending in 1998 when a certifiably sullen Johnson was traded in midseason to the Houston Astros and a pennant race for shortstop Carlos Guillen and pitchers Freddy Garcia and John Halama. With the way everyone's Kingdome lockers were assigned at the time, the clubhouse configuration formed a triangle, a Cooperstown triangle.

"You have to give Seattle credit for bringing us together," Rodriguez said. "It was pretty unique."

While sharing in two playoff appearances and coming within two victories of a World Series appearance in 1995, these three players actually weren't all on the field that much for the Mariners. Injuries sidelined Griffey and Johnson for long stretches, and Rodriguez required two stops at Triple-A Tacoma before settling in with Seattle, plus Johnson pitched just every fifth day as a starter. They played just 63 games with all of them in the lineup at the same time, including postseason outings, leaving witnesses to those contests unknowingly something extra to savor. They won 40 times collectively, a modest .635 winning percentage considering the assembled manpower.

Still, there was an unmistakable confidence level they brought to the team that suggested winning was never out of the question when all or some of them were on the field.

"It was who was going to beat us today?" said Moyer, who was in Seattle alongside all three players in 1996-1998. "We never won a World Series but we were a pretty good ball club. It's an honor to say I played with those guys."

Griffey, baseball's No. 1 overall selection in 1987, was first on the scene in Seattle. He was a rookie who opened the 1989 season as the starting centerfielder, answered to "Junior" because he was the son of an established and active big-leaguer who had the same given name and became a Seattle teammate, and the younger Griffey was an instant Mariners success.

That same year, the pitcher later known as the "Big Unit" arrived in the city without fanfare in a midseason deal with pitchers Gene Harris and Brian Holman from the Expos for pitchers Mark Langston and Mike Campbell, with Seattle fans bemoaning the loss of Langston, the trade centerpiece.

Four years later, the Florida kid nicknamed "A-Rod" was baseball's No. 1 draftee and went through the usual protracted contract negotiations conducted by super-agent Scott Boras before he reported to the Seattle organization. He easily was on the fast track to the big leagues, playing for three minor-league baseball teams and the Mariners in his first pro season in 1994.

Griffey, Johnson and Rodriguez had three seasons together as full-time players before the inevitable break-up came, primarily based on baseball economics. A mid-level big-league team couldn't afford to keep all three.

Johnson was the first to go in 1998 after spending 10 seasons in Seattle, unable to get anywhere in contract-renewal negotiations with the Mariners and deeply offended by it. He was notified of the trade to his National League destination midway through a Kingdome game against the New York Yankees. With two protective sports agents escorting him out of the stadium, he climbed into a Suburban sports utility vehicle idling outside the clubhouse door and was whisked away to complete the nasty divorce.

Johnson later suggested the split from Seattle was unavoidable, noting the transient nature of modern-day baseball. "Keeping a team together is a challenge and, for whatever reason, we didn't do it," the pitcher said of the Mariners. "I know people expected more from me."

Johnson, who lived at 16100 Cougar Mountain Way in Bellevue, wasn't offered a new contract. Seattle ownership, losing money every year at the Kingdome and stuck with $98 million in cost overruns while building Safeco Field, couldn't afford to keep the three headliners together. The Mariners front office was convinced, too, that Johnson was resentful because his teammate in center field was the dominant face of the franchise and he wasn't.

"Randy Johnson was insanely jealous of Griffey and it was difficult," said Chuck Armstrong, who retired as Mariners president and chief operating officer in 2013.

Griffey, who kept his baseball-season home at 24606 S.E. Old Black Nugget Road in Issaquah, was the next to go in 1999. He requested a trade following 11 Mariners seasons for family reasons, publicly explaining his need to be within a short flight of his wife and kids in Florida. There was more to it than that. His parents were divorcing and his younger brother was struggling with alcohol abuse, and Griffey felt it necessary for him to go home and fix everything, according to Armstrong. Griffey seemed a little sur-

Ken Griffey Jr. played two Mariners seasons with his dad, Ken Sr.

prised when the Mariners accommodated his request without offering more resistance and begging him to stay. He was sent to the Cincinnati Reds in exchange for outfielder Mike Cameron, pitcher Brett Tomko and two players who never advanced to the big leagues, pitcher Jake Meyer and infielder Antonio Perez.

"If I was single, I would have had no problem staying here," Griffey said more than a decade later. "Having kids and trying to get them to live a normal life is a huge difference. People don't understand that. I do, because I grew up in the game."

For sure, Griffey made the Mariners locker room interesting. I learned this first-hand. No fan of my $10 drug-store sunglasses, he yanked them off my head one day and threw them to the ground. He came back with $150 Oakleys from his cubicle stash and made me put them on. When I tried to return the expensive eyewear, he sneered at me and told me he was improving my look.

On another occasion, Griffey called me onto the field before a game and said he was angry with the Mariners and wanted to be traded immediately. When I scoffed at this, he waved over the rest of the press corps and shared this tidbit, sending everyone scurrying for confirmation. A few minutes before the first pitch, Griffey slyly called me in the press box from the dugout and offered one word: "Gotcha." He wanted revenge for a story I had written the day before about his brother's release from the organization.

The Mariners let Griffey leave only to regain his services as a free agent 10 years later. He spent another season and a half in Seattle even though it was clear his skills had eroded significantly, and he abruptly retired at midseason in 2010, leaving without ceremony.

"We were certainly grateful he decided to come back home," Armstrong said. "I'm not sure we'd have baseball in Seattle today if not for Ken Griffey Jr."

In 2000, Rodriguez made it a clean break for the power trio. He signed as a free agent with the Texas Rangers for a staggering $252 million over 10 years that was orchestrated by the demanding Boras. In each of three consecutive seasons, the Mariners lost a high-profile hero, and not even to baseball's richest franchises in New York and Los Angeles, though Rodriguez and Johnson later joined the Yankees together.

Randy Johnson was the first of Seattle's three super-stars to leave.

"I think it was inevitable," Rodriguez said of the break-up. "Griffey wanted to go where he went. Randy wanted to go to Arizona. I wanted to go. We all kind of decided what we wanted to do."

The Mariners countered with an eight-year deal worth $160 million, but knew the chances of keeping A-Rod were not favorable at all. Money was the big reason, but not the only one.

"Both Alex and Scott Boras indicated that once we moved into Safeco Field, Alex would not be coming back," Armstrong said. "They said he would lose eight to 10 home runs per year at Safeco."

The return of each Mariners superstar in an opposing uniform meant a box-office bonanza in Seattle. On July 20, 1999, five days after Safeco Field opened and a year after he left, Johnson arrived with the Diamondbacks to face a Seattle lineup that still included Griffey and Rodriguez. He was greeted warmly by a sellout crowd of 44,884. He hit Griffey with a pitch and was touched for a double and a single by A-Rod. Otherwise he was at his flame-throwing best, beating the Mariners 6-0 with an eight-hit shutout.

"I imagined myself, like Junior and Jay [Buhner], finishing my career here," Johnson said the day before the game.

On April 16, 2001, Rodriguez was just 14 games into his Rangers career when the schedule called for his return to Seattle. He was not well received. A sellout crowd of 45,657 jeered his every move, held up signs and tossed fake or real money from the Safeco Field stands. An enterprising man seated in the front row used a fishing rod to dangle a dollar bill behind A-Rod in the on-deck circle and drew big laughs until his recreational equipment was confiscated by ushers. Rodriguez went 1-for-5 and the Rangers lost 9-7, pleasing the home fans no end.

"I don't think they were booing me really," the former Mariners shortstop naively said. "I think they were booing the uniform."

It wasn't the uniform. On a subsequent visit, Rodriguez turned up in the Seattle clubhouse and was no more welcome with his former teammates than he was with the fans. "Get that [bleep] out of here," Buhner growled out of A-Rod's earshot.

Griffey was the last to reconnect with the Mariners. On June 22, 2007, he returned to Safeco Field with the Reds for a much-anticipated baseball weekend. He was all quips and smiles as broadcaster Dave Niehaus, front-office executives and other team employees sought him out before the Friday night game outside of the visitors' clubhouse.

Yet he clearly was not looking forward to the main event. "They're going to boo me," Griffey said, changing into his uniform with teenage son Trey at his side. Griffey couldn't have been more wrong.

A sellout crowd of 46,340 — larger than Johnson and Rodriguez's homecoming gatherings — roared its appreciation throughout a pre-game ceremony that included speeches, former teammates Edgar Martinez and Buhner joining Griffey on the field, and the presentation of framed keepsakes of his career and the ballpark. "I didn't realize how much I missed being in Seattle," a touched Griffey told the crowd.

Tina Turner's song "Simply the Best" played overhead as he made his way to the dugout to start the game. Griffey drew a standing ovation with each at-bat and went 1-for-5 as the Reds won crushingly, 16-1. He received nonstop standing ovations over the next two games.

As if to reward everyone for their unmistakable loyalty, Griffey hit a pair of homers on Sunday in the final game of the series, one the Reds lost 3-2. He took his show of gratitude one step further by sitting down for a pre-game FOX Sports Northwest TV interview with broadcaster Angie Mentink and suggesting strongly that he wanted to finish his career with the Mariners.

Two years later, Griffey made good on those words, playing his final season and a third in Seattle. His baseball skills had fallen into great decline but no one seemed to initially care. On a sore knee, he upped his career home runs to 630, surpassed at the time only by Barry Bonds (762), Hank Aaron (755), Babe Ruth (714) and Willie Mays (660), until his long-ball power was sadly shut off.

Hard as it was for everyone to acknowledge, including himself, Griffey stayed a third of a season too long. He didn't hit, not one homer over two months in 2010, and his playing time diminished. He drove out of Seattle and across the country to Florida in his SUV, leaving only a statement in a stark news release to explain his decision to leave.

While part of the Mariners dream team was restored for nostalgic purposes with Griffey, one had to wonder what would have happened had it been completely reassembled or never dismantled in the first place. Johnson went on to win a World Series, picking up a 2001 championship ring with Arizona. Rodriguez had a few near-misses with the Yankees before receiving his World Series ring in 2009. Griffey never came close.

These guys needed each other. The threesome might have made the Mariners unbeatable, especially in the postseason, and showered Seattle with multiple World Series titles. It was enough to make the principle figures involved consider the possibilities well after the fact.

"If we had wanted to stay together and I continued to progress, and Junior and A-Rod signed back on, it would have been pretty special," Johnson acknowledged. "I know the fans had an appreciation of us."

Even the player forever branded a Mariners outcast for taking all that money and never looking back gave the Seattle dynasty idea some passing thought.

"You see what the Yankees did by keeping Derek Jeter and Mariano Rivera and some of their other legends, and it definitely makes it more fun for the fans," Rodriguez said. "It didn't quite work out for us in Seattle, but it was a good idea."

Martinez, after watching his high-powered Mariners team break up, saw only rings and glorious things had everyone stayed together. "I thought about what it would have been like if we had kept the team together," the Mariners designated hitter said. "It could have been real different for the team and Seattle. I believe we could have played in a couple of World Series."

Johnson was the first to retire from the game, going out as a member of the San Francisco Giants once the 2009 season ended. He made an immediate Seattle return, accepting an invitation to throw out the ceremonial first pitch at the Mariners' home opener the following season. Two months later, Griffey was done with baseball with his sudden in-season retirement. As for the Hall of Fame, Johnson was the first of the three to be inducted in 2015 as soon as he became eligible for enshrinement, though he chose to enter as a member of the Arizona Diamondbacks. Griffey was expected to join him the following year when he first went on the ballot. Rodriguez, however, was suspended from the game in PED disgrace in 2014, and his Hall of Fame inclusion seemed unlikely.

The Kingdome home clubhouse, which had housed more than its fair share of baseball legends, disappeared, reduced to rubble and baseball myth when the domed stadium was demolished. That old dressing area should have been preserved and sent directly to Cooperstown intact.

The Mariners could have been the Big Blue Machine when they entered the 21st century. With enhanced stadium revenues in place from the new ballpark, the ability to pay for high-priced baseball talent finally existed in Seattle.

"If we had this situation repeat itself at Safeco Field, that's a different situation," Armstrong said. "We could have kept all three." ❖

GARY PAYTON & SHAWN KEMP

The Dynamic Duo

Gary Payton, left, and Shawn Kemp spent seven seasons together in Seattle.

Gary Payton was the sassy point guard from Oregon State, a college basketball stop that was never a feeder school for the serious-minded NBA player. He wasn't a great shooter. He wasn't particularly speedy. His teams didn't get far in the NCAA Tournament. It seemed sneers and scowls were all he needed to become the second overall selection of the 1991 NBA Draft for the Seattle SuperSonics, taken behind Syracuse forward Derrick Coleman, who went to the New York Nets.

Skeptical people were ready to tear Payton apart at the first sign his game was built more on hype than substance at basketball's highest level.

Shawn Kemp was a somewhat shadowy figure who canceled out his collegiate career with his impulsiveness, exhibiting a trait that would follow him throughout much of his pro basketball existence. The power forward left Kentucky after he was accused of stealing and attempting to pawn two gold chains that belonged to teammate Sean Sutton, the coach's son. After an equally short stay, Kemp abandoned Trinity Valley Community College in Texas, failing to play a game for either college he attended.

Seattle basketball fans weren't sure what to make of this guy either, cautiously welcoming his questionable reputation and untapped potential.

Once all the rough edges were smoothed out, though, Payton and Kemp came together as Sonics

Once all the rough edges were smoothed out, though, Payton and Kemp came together as Sonics teammates for seven often electrifying and sometimes mystifying seasons.

teammates for seven often electrifying and sometimes mystifying seasons. They became "The Glove" and "The Reign Man," answering to nicknames that made them sound like superheroes, if not cartoon characters, and together they formed Seattle's most compatible and successful pro basketball tandem. They were self-centered players who didn't get along with everyone, but they appreciated each other's presence and flourished together.

From 1991 to 1997, they ran the floor in a fearless and intimidating fashion, propelling the Sonics to playoff appearances each year, resounding 63- and 64-victory seasons in 1994 and 1996, and an NBA Finals berth in 1996. They took turns leading the Sonics in scoring. They shared in multiple All-Star Game appearances. They just needed to get their bearings.

"My agent was telling me, 'You're going to go high and it looks like No. 2 to Seattle; they've got the balls to draft you,' " said Payton, acknowledging his uncertain status. "A lot of people hadn't heard of me until the last two years of college when I became an All-American. I thought being in the Northwest, where I had been there in college, would be a good opportunity for me. [Sonics coach] Bernie Bickerstaff gave me the opportunity to

play. He saw me and played me a lot, and he knew the kind of ability I had. I just came here and I had to prove myself. The first two years were kind of rough."

Payton's play was so spotty and uneven early on he was treated to continual boos and frequent trade speculation. Just when it appeared the Sonics might give up on him, he established himself in the league by using a street mentality gleaned from his in-your-face hometown of Oakland. He decided no player would be tougher than him in the NBA.

He fought in the locker room with teammates Vernon Maxwell and Ricky Pierce. He was suspended for a game after picking a fight with Nate McMillan only a week after his former teammate took over as the Sonics coach. He was restrained from throwing a punch at *Seattle Post-Intelligencer* Sonic beat writer Jim Moore, unimpressed with a guy who was as direct and flippant as he was. Payton was relentless in his disdain for oft-injured Sonics center Vin Baker, goading him nonstop with pointed insults of "softness" and "out-of-shape crybaby." All these people were supposed allies or neutral figures, too, not necessarily the enemy.

"I'm going to be a feisty guy," Payton said. "If I was a nice guy, you guys would ask, 'What are you doing?' "

By his third pro season, Payton settled in and became a double-figure scorer for the first time, averaging 13.5 points a game, while maintaining his potent playmaking ability, and he helped guide his Seattle team to 55 victories. In season four, he was an All-Star Game selection for the first time, an honor bestowed on him nine times in his career. In season five, he topped the Sonics in scoring for the first time, averaging 20.6 points a game to Kemp's 18.7.

However, Payton's true sign of NBA acceptance came from his heat-of-the-battle acquisition of a nickname created by a respected opponent who paid him a

postseason compliment. Payton received a custom label that identified him for the rest of his career.

"I was playing against Kevin Johnson in the Western Conference Finals in 1993 and he said I was 'guarding him like a ball in a glove,' " Payton said of the former NBA guard and Sacramento mayor. "The next season it started to stick. Signs were made up. Everybody had been calling me 'GP' but everybody liked 'The Glove,' and it stuck."

Sonics fans adored Payton. He won them over with his attitude, using that chip on his shoulder to challenge teammates and infuriate opponents. He wanted to play every minute of every game. A classic trash-talker, he told everyone exactly what he thought of them. He also knew how to work a crowd away from the court.

It wasn't unusual for Payton and his entourage of childhood friends to show up at a Seattle or Bellevue nightclub after Sonics games and stay long into the night, relaxing and having a beverage or two. He left the hard edge at the gym. Payton, who lived at 14003 S.E. 43rd St. in Bellevue, was approachable and engaging on his trips into the general public, chatting up people who encountered him and sometimes buying drinks for them.

His Sonics career peaked with a trip to the 1996 NBA Finals, the first for Seattle in 17 seasons, on the heels of a franchise-record 64-18 regular season. Unfortunately, Payton and his teammates had to contend with the Chicago Bulls and a Michael Jordan still in his prime. The series went six games before Seattle was eliminated.

Payton spent 13 of his 17 NBA seasons with the Sonics before he became expendable as an aging player on a rebuilding team and was traded in 2003 while he still held ample value — packaged with guard Desmond Mason to the Milwaukee Bucks for guards Ray Allen,

> Payton, with his fierce
> desire to win at all costs,
> his lengthy service to the
> city and impressive statistical
> outpour, is regarded
> by many fans as the
> greatest Sonics player in
> franchise history.

Kevin Ollie and Ronald Murray, plus a first-round draft pick. He later played for the Boston Celtics, Los Angeles Lakers and Miami Heat, capturing his elusive NBA championship in 2006 as a reserve for Miami. He finished his pro career with 21,813 points and 8,966 assists, appearing in 1,335 games.

Payton, with his fierce desire to win at all costs, his lengthy service to the city and impressive statistical outpour, is regarded by many fans as the greatest Sonics player in franchise history. Of course, he thought so, too. "I did a lot of good stuff," Payton said in his typical brash manner. "I came to Seattle and did what I had to do. This is where I created myself. It would be where I established something. I wouldn't argue it that I was the best ever. I'm not going to dispute that."

Kemp was just 19 when the Sonics brought him to town with the seventh pick in the 1990 NBA Draft, a year before Payton's arrival. The 6-foot-10 Kemp hadn't played in a regulation basketball game since high school in Elkhart, Ind., and he needed time to unwind. His stay in Seattle was marked by spectacular dunks and crass foolishness.

He was dubbed "The Reign Man" by animated Sonics broadcaster Kevin Calabro, caught up in the excitement of describing Kemp's raw athleticism night after night.

Kemp was called "Dad" by nine children he fathered with six women — nearly enough kids to fill two basketball teams. One of them, Shawn Kemp Jr., was talented enough to warrant a basketball scholarship that brought him to Seattle and the University of Washington.

The elder Kemp was fully unleashed by his fourth season with the Sonics, earning the first of his six All-Star Game selections, all but one coming with Seattle. He averaged a double-double for five consecutive seasons. Each dunk topped the previous one for style points. Yet Kemp couldn't allow himself to enjoy a good thing for long.

For every memorable play Kemp served up, he missed a practice, flight or charter-bus ride. He was moody, unpredictable and undependable. It got to the point he wouldn't speak to teammates or stay with them in the team hotels on the road.

Everything became a hot-button issue for Kemp in 1997, rapidly accelerating his departure from the franchise: 1) He reported late to the Sonics training camp, outwardly bitter over contract issues; 2) he had to

> Kemp was just 19 when the
> Sonics brought him to town
> with the seventh pick
> in the 1990 NBA Draft,
> a year before
> Payton's arrival.

answer for drinking heavily at a north Seattle restaurant in the early morning hours before a nationally televised game against Jordan and the Bulls at midseason; and 3) he used an ESPN interview as a platform to announce in an ugly manner that he would never wear a Sonics uniform again.

Keg Steakhouse and Bar employees were appalled at Kemp and his late-night drinking binge at their establishment. They called the *Post-Intelligencer* to voice their displeasure after the player sat with another man and two women and tossed back several Crown Royal whiskey shots and Corona beers until closing time.

He had a 12:30 p.m. tip-off the next day against Jordan. He looked extra sluggish against Chicago, going scoreless for the game's first 18 minutes and was described as a virtual no-show by broadcasters and columnists.

A female Keg employee, who asked not to be identified, listened to the game on the radio and at halftime heard one of the commentators wonder out loud, "Where's Kemp today?" She had a ready answer: "I felt like telling them, 'He has a hangover.' "

When pressed about his late-night drinking excursion before a big game, Kemp was hardly apologetic or remorseful. "You can't stop living your life because of other people," he said. "I'm always going to go out with my friends and hang out. I've done that my entire career. I'll continue to do that, no doubt about it."

Six months later, Kemp and the franchise parted ways. The big man forced an off-season trade to the Cleveland Cavaliers, with the Sonics receiving Baker, another guy with motivational problems, who came from Milwaukee as part of a three-team transaction.

Kemp found it unforgivable that Seattle backup center Jim McIlvaine was paid more than him, though

> Payton and Kemp,
> The Glove and The Reign Man,
> together were a good fit
> for the Sonics. They provided
> the city with an unforgettable
> era of basketball.

it was simply a matter of free-agent timing. Kemp received a $100 million contract from Cleveland and had every reason to flourish. However, his resulting decline was unsettling.

Kemp was an All-Star Game selection once more for Cleveland before his production fell off the charts. He became 50 pounds overweight and was no longer explosive. Cleveland gave up on him after three seasons. He was sent to rehabilitation for drug and alcohol abuse. The Portland Trail Blazers and Orlando Magic picked him up and let him go. By 2003, he was out of the league, ending a 14-year NBA career in which he collected 15,347 points and grabbed 8,834 rebounds.

Way too late, Kemp slimmed down and attempted a series of comebacks, never rising above minor-league

basketball. He had other problems, too. In 2005, he was arrested in Seattle for cocaine possession and a year later he got picked up in Houston for having marijuana.

Finally, Kemp moved back to Seattle and embraced middle age and a sedate lifestyle, residing at 18237 240th Ave. S.E. in Maple Valley and becoming part-owner of Oskar's Kitchen restaurant. In 2015, he was reunited with his former Sonics headliner in a quaint setting; he sat courtside with Payton as they watched their sons, Shawn Jr. and Gary II, play against each other for Washington and Oregon State, respectively.

Payton and Kemp, The Glove and The Reign Man, together were a good fit for the Sonics. They provided the city with an unforgettable era of basketball. Yet they were capable of doing so much more had they stayed longer, and the All-Star guard rued those possibilities in retirement. If only ego and substance abuse hadn't gotten in the way they might have brought a championship or two to Seattle.

"That was the great problem of the best of times," Payton said. "I had one of the best power forwards to ever play the game. We started a dynasty for ourselves. It was very discouraging to me when he left in '97. I thought we really had something going on. I thought we could win championships. I didn't want it to end." ❖

Top 10 Sonics
1. Jack Sikma, C
2. Gary Payton, PG
3. Spencer Haywood, F
4. Shawn Kemp, F
5. Lenny Wilkens, PG
6. Fred Brown, G
7. Dennis Johnson, G
8. Kevin Durant, F
9. Nate McMillan, PG
10. Bob Rule, C

DEMETRIUS DUBOSE
Life And Death

Demetrius DuBose, a Seattle kid with a big smile and cheery personality, was a success story. From humble beginnings, he was raised as an only child by his unwed mother at 3939 S. Lucille St. in Rainier Valley, supported by aunts, uncles and cousins while barely acquainted with his father, and he used football to escape his long-odds existence. He became Washington's top schoolboy player in 1989 as a linebacker for O'Dea High, traded in that reputation for an athletic scholarship to Notre Dame, and played four NFL seasons for the Tampa Bay Buccaneers.

Yet on the night of July 24, 1999, DuBose was just 28 when he was killed by police officers in San Diego. He was shot 12 times, five times in the back. In an incident never fully explained to everyone's satisfaction, he was accused of creating a public disturbance in a tony beach community and gunned down for resisting arrest. Three years out of pro football, he commandeered two officers' *nunchakus* – martial-arts weapons that consisted of two sticks tied together by a short chain, and swung them, causing police to fire.

For months afterward, community protests and court hearings were held to mollify outraged people. The FBI ruled that the shooting of DuBose was justified, but a police review commission criticized the need for deadly force in that situation and the department's general use of *nunchakus*.

DuBose's death stands as the most violent on record for any high-profile Seattle athlete, outweighing: 1) The mysterious 1978 disappearance and presumed demise of Seattle SuperSonics forward John Brisker on a trip to Africa; 2) the 2002 death of former Washington defensive back Anthony Vontoure during a struggle in police custody in Sacramento; 3) the 1970 shooting death of Seattle Pilots pitcher Miguel Fuentes outside a bar in Loiza Aldea, Puerto Rico, and 4) the 2011 stabbing death of Seattle Mariners outfielder Greg Halman in Rotterdam, the Netherlands, at the hands of his deranged brother.

Brisker was a hot-tempered man who may have been executed for his involvement with ruthless Uganda dictator Idi Amin. The NBA player's body was never found and he was declared legally dead by a Seattle judge in 1985. His exact fate likely will never be fully explained.

Vontoure, in a manic state and possibly suffering from bipolar disease, died during a physical exchange with two sheriff's deputies. His death came 25 days after former UW teammate Curtis Williams, a fellow defensive backfield starter, died from complications suffered as a quadriplegic from a football spinal-cord injury.

Fuentes, who pitched in just eight games for Seattle's first MLB team, was gunned down in his Caribbean hometown, shot three times after stepping outside and apparently urinating too close to a parked car.

Halman was killed during an argument with his knife-wielding sibling, Jason, who later was ruled temporarily insane and acquitted of any crime.

> ## DuBose's death stands as the most violent on record for any high-profile Seattle athlete.

San Diego police said DuBose was under the influence when they riddled him with bullets. Others believe he might have been guilty of nothing worse than a bad case of stubbornness, making his death all the more tragic. Regardless, his life ended abruptly and it didn't seem fair. "This might have been the case of a big black man who intimidated somebody," said Lou Hobson, DuBose's former O'Dea basketball coach.

San Diego citizens were so incensed by the shooting of the former pro football player in their backyard that they held an angry 90-minute protest march that was watched carefully by police. Protesters said officers were guilty of racism in attempting to detain DuBose. "They provoked a man to his death," Abdur-Rahim Hameed, president of a San Diego-based black contractors association, told the *Los Angeles Times*. "This was a callous, brutal murder."

DuBose's problems with San Diego police began when he was discovered in a neighbor's apartment uninvited, asleep on a bed, mirroring a recent Hollywood incident that had involved an inebriated actor Robert Downey Jr. in Los Angeles. DuBose was cooperative when awakened by the apartment tenant, even remarking that he found his landing place "comfortable."

A block from Mission Bay, DuBose still was cordial as officers ordered him and his roommate, Randy West, to sit on a curb and answer questions. West, a law school graduate who was trying to establish a new beach volleyball league, lived nearby with DuBose and had come to find his meandering roommate.

Everything was fine until officers ordered DuBose to stand and they tried to handcuff him. The former football player became agitated and decided he had been compliant enough. He mumbled something about police always stopping him and took off running down a courtyard. West said that DuBose blurted out, "Why is this happening?" A few minutes later, a few blocks away

and near a convenience store, the 30-minute ordeal was over. DuBose lay dead in the street.

Before the gunfire rang out, DuBose was maced, grabbed and struck by *nunchakus*. Nothing slowed him. The 6-foot-2, 237-pound athlete lifted an officer over his head and threw him into a planter. He disarmed both officers of their *nunchakus*. After wielding the weapons in a menacing fashion, ignoring commands to stop, DuBose was shot when he came within 10 feet of the officers. Officers said they felt no recourse but to open fire.

"We're always dismayed when someone acts in an erratic manner for any reason, whether it's a private citizen or a professional athlete," San Diego Police Lt. Glenn Breitenstein said. "It's an unfortunate incident."

After serving as a co-captain at Notre Dame, graduating with a pair of degrees in African-American and government and international studies, and playing four seasons on special teams in the NFL, DuBose was living the good life in California. He spent winters working at a ski resort and summers at the beach while mulling a future as a pro volleyball player.

In retracing his steps, however, there were signs that something was amiss. DuBose lived in the mountain community of Mammoth, working as a lift operator and member of the local ski patrol, once he was cut by the New York Jets in 1997, and the resort job ended with his dismissal. "He was an OK guy but he had a couple run-ins," said Bobby Hoyt, a ski patrol manager. "He harassed a bunch of women on patrol. We had to let him go."

Even without a job, DuBose stayed in the area and continued skiing. Apparently, there were no hard feelings between him and his former employer. "He had an edge to him but he was a likable guy," Hoyt said. "He wasn't the greatest skier, but he became a better skier because he always wanted to be on patrol."

Moving to the beach, DuBose was spotted working out, driving a Range Rover and pedaling an expensive mountain bike. He informed people that he had lost his California condominium. A former Notre Dame teammate, Aaron Taylor, who played for the San Diego Chargers, told reporters he had seen DuBose and remarked that "the guy looked like he was sleeping in his car or something."

DuBose last made contact with people in his hometown six months before his death. He had changed his appearance, from his trademark shaved head in favor of more contemporary dreadlocks. Yet he was the same upbeat youngster that Hobson remembered. "Off the court, he was a teddy bear," Hobson said. "I never saw him bully anybody. I never saw him use his size outside of the playing field to escalate anything. He was just a great kid."

Still, there was a downside to DuBose that permeated his success. He was arrested for underage drinking at a campus party in South Bend, suspended for two games at Notre Dame for accepting gifts and loans totaling $1,300 from a Bainbridge Island couple, which he repaid. He was linked to an overeager Washington football supporter, Jim Heckman, who was accused of attempting to coerce DuBose to leave Notre Dame and come home and play for the Huskies.

A year before he died, DuBose was arrested once more in South Bend for a nightclub disturbance involving an off-duty police officer. He was charged with battery, criminal mischief, resisting arrest, disorderly conduct and possession of marijuana. DuBose allegedly spat on the officer, unwilling to take orders and displaying a temper.

If there was a flaw to DuBose, he had an angry, uncooperative streak behind that big smile and shining personality and all that promise, and it might have cost him his life. ❖

EDGAR MARTINEZ

The Hit Broadway Play

Edgar Martinez stood coiled in the batter's box, wriggling his bat high over his head, holding it almost vertical. The Seattle Mariners' designated hitter dug in against Jack McDowell, a New York Yankees pitcher trying to preserve a 5-4 lead in the bottom of the 11th inning and sidestep big trouble.

The Mariners' Ken Griffey Jr. and Joey Cora hugged first and third bases with no outs. Cora cleverly dragged a lead-off bunt up the first-base line to get on. Griffey followed with a sharply hit single to right-centerfield, sending the sold-out Kingdome into a deafening din as the fifth and deciding game of the 1995 American League Division Series played out.

In his stiff and mechanical motion, McDowell delivered a 0-1 pitch belt-high and inside. Martinez chopped at it violently. The ball scooted into left field, skipped past Yankees replacement leftfielder Gerald Williams, and hit the padded wall on a bounce for a game-ending double, and 57,178 fans went berserk.

Cora and Griffey scored and disappeared under ecstatic, pile-diving teammates at home plate, creating a scene alertly photographed and later reproduced in framed images, on T-shirts and in artwork, representing the baseball franchise's defining moment. Out of still-camera range, Martinez was swallowed up by yet another mound of celebratory teammates just inside the second-base bag as fireworks crackled overhead.

Martinez's two-base hit settled one of the most entertaining games in MLB postseason history, making 6-5 winners and unlikely series victors out of the Mariners. People credited the clutch double with helping keep the beleaguered team from moving to Tampa and with building a glistening new ballpark across the street from the Kingdome.

Historical significance was attached to it. Martinez's double on Oct. 8, 1995, is widely hailed as the single greatest play in Seattle sports history, surpassing Griffey's 1990 homer that followed his father's in consecutive Mariners at-bats, supplying a true big-league family rarity in Anaheim; Elgin Baylor's 35-foot buzzer-beating jump shot, which won a 1958 NCAA Tournament game for Seattle University in San Francisco; Warren Moon's 1975 "Hail Mary" 78-yard touchdown pass to Spider Gaines, enabling Washington to pull out a last-minute Apple Cup victory at Husky Stadium, and Richard Sherman's game-saving deflection for the Seahawks in the 2014 NFC championship game, sending them to the Super Bowl.

For Martinez, it was a redemptive at-bat. In the bottom of the ninth, McDowell, normally a starter but pressed into postseason relief, struck out the Mariners DH with two runners on and two out in a 4-4 game, forcing extra innings. It was one of the few times Martinez, who hit .571 (12-for-21) in the series, was retired by the Yankees that week. The day before,

> Martinez's double
> on Oct. 8, 1995,
> was widely hailed as
> the single greatest play
> in Seattle sports history.

Seattle's clean-up hitter launched two homers and drove in seven runs to even the series. Mariners relief pitcher Norm Charlton told Martinez that he'd get another chance to end the game, and he was right.

"It was a splitter that stayed up in the strike zone; I remember everything," Martinez said. "In the previous at-bat McDowell struck me out with that pitch and I thought he would throw it again, and I was able to drive it."

Martinez, a New York native raised in Puerto Rico, was a fastidious man who played 18 seasons with the Mariners, more than anyone in club history. He weighed his bats, making sure they met his personal specifications and weren't an ounce more. He did eye exercises when his vision was threatened. Originally a third baseman, he was a great batsman with a mediocre glove who, out of necessity, was converted into a full-time designated hitter by his fourth season. He was a .300 hitter for 10 seasons, seven consecutive.

He won A.L. batting titles in 1992 (.343) and '95 (.356), and was the league runner-up in '97 (.330); he remains the only designated hitter to claim a big-league batting title. He was the A.L. doubles leader in 1992 with 46 and RBI leader in 2000 with 145. And he did all this in the considerable shadow of Mariners headliners Randy Johnson, Alex Rodriguez and Griffey.

"When you believe you can hit, you eventually hit," Martinez said. "When I was a little kid in Little League, I hit. In semipro, I hit. I hit in every league I played in. I won batting titles in every league I played in. I won a Triple-A batting title. I was always the best hitter. I believed I could hit. All those years, I had it inside me that I could hit and play well in the big leagues."

Unassuming by nature, Martinez could be surprisingly resourceful and combative when he needed to be. Deciding his personal life was lacking, he asked *Seattle*

Mariners Ken Griffey Jr. and Henry Cotto, from left, greet Edgar Martinez at home plate.

Post-Intelligencer beat writer Jim Street if he knew of any local women he could date. Street, after consulting with his wife, came back with a name and introductions were made. That's how Martinez met his wife, Holli. Martinez also had a temper that didn't need to be disturbed. In the visitors' clubhouse at Dodger Stadium, Martinez mentioned to me how he was suffering from assorted aches and pains. Trying to commiserate, and failing badly at it, I joked that soreness simply was part

of the aging process, which was a big mistake. "Did you call me old?!" Martinez, then 36, shot back indignantly to my great bewilderment. He cussed me out and stalked off muttering. Before I knew it, I was surrounded by Jay Buhner and Griffey, who quizzed me about insulting Martinez and then berated me for it. "I don't like you," Buhner said emphatically, "because you made Edgar mad."

A consistent hitting machine, Martinez had a routine and he didn't stray from it, at least until his 12th big-league season, when he showed up noticeably buff for spring training. He had a smaller waist and legs that year. His weight was the same but his body fat had dropped a full percentage point. He talked about lifting lighter weights and running more in the off-season. To curb his hunger, he downed a chocolate protein drink, a large can of which he kept in his clubhouse cubicle. Some of his Seattle teammates exhibited cut physiques and stat increases overnight that seemed to suggest something steroid-related. Martinez was never asked about performance-enhancing drugs.

"I noticed as you get older, you get out of shape sooner and it takes longer to get back into shape," Martinez said, considering his advancing years this time with no protests.

Martinez, who lived at 3 Diamond S. Ranch Road in Bellevue, stayed in the game until 2004, long enough to see Johnson, Griffey and Rodriguez depart Seattle in consecutive seasons and leave him behind. He stayed until his hits stopped coming.

Yet, on that rollicking night in 1995, Martinez had everyone feeling confident in the Seattle dugout when he stepped in against McDowell in the bottom of the 11th inning. "I knew Edgar was going to put the ball in play," Mariners manager Lou Piniella said. "He doesn't strike out in these types of situations." A fan held up a homemade sign that read, "It's Double Martinez Time," paying homage to Edgar and Mariners first baseman Tino Martinez, who were no relation.

With Edgar standing there, McDowell wheeled and threw to first base, moving Griffey back to the bag. Coming to the plate, the veteran pitcher got a called strike on the outside corner. Martinez didn't let another pitch get past him. He devoured it and made history.

Halfway through his big-league tour of duty, Martinez came up with the most memorable of his 2,247 hits. He delivered the most important of his 514 two-base hits, and it came against the Yankees. Martinez added "Mr. Double" to his list of nicknames, which included "Gar" and "Papi." The game-winning play became a steady YouTube video clicker on the Internet. His double played a part in a Seattle street in the stadium district – Edgar Martinez Drive South – being named after him.

"At the time, it was strange," Martinez said. "At the time, I felt it was an important at-bat but not so big. But now I know how big it was. It was a special moment. That hit defined my career." ❖

Top 10 Seattle Games

1. **Edgar Martinez,**
    game-winning ALDS 2B (1995)

2. **Felix Hernandez,**
    perfect game (2012)

3. **Ken Griffey Sr. and Jr.,**
    consecutive HRs (1990)

6. **John Tresvant,**
    40 rebounds (1963)

5. **Mike Cameron,**
    four HRs (2002)

6. **Warren Moon,**
    Hail Mary TD (1975)

7. **Randy Johnson,**
    no-hitter (1990)

8. **Elgin Baylor,**
    NCAA buzzer-beater (1958)

9. **Fred Brown,**
    58 points (1974)

10. **Corey Dillon,**
    222 yards in QT (1996)

The New Millennium

Seattle becomes a serious national economic force built around Boeing, Microsoft, Amazon, Costco, Starbucks, Nintendo and T-Mobile, which brings a significant population spurt followed by some of the nation's highest housing prices.

The city replaces or remodels all of its major athletic arenas, most notably blowing up the Kingdome in favor of Safeco Field and CenturyLink Field, and tearing down Husky Stadium for a new one. However, the results are mixed: The Sonics move to Oklahoma City while the Seahawks make three Super Bowl appearances, winning once.

JASON TERRY

The Popcorn Man

His hometown, however, wasn't very forgiving. Once he left, Terry was considered Seattle's ultimate sports traitor with local roots.

Jason Terry was as close as one could get to the University of Washington basketball program without pulling on a uniform and high-tops. Throughout high school, he worked as a concessionaire selling bags of popcorn during games at Hec Edmundson Pavilion.

On one wintry night, Terry set up his cart outside the visitors' locker room and turned around just in time to see someone walk by, brazenly reach in and snatch a handful of popcorn on the run, drawing an immediate Terry rebuke. The guilty party was Arizona basketball coach Lute Olson.

"A guy stuck his hand in there and grabbed some popcorn and I said, 'Hey, people have to eat that,' " Terry said. "Then I saw who it was and I said, 'That's OK, coach.' "

To the chagrin of Seattle basketball fans everywhere, Olson wanted more than popcorn. In 1995, he stole Terry, too.

The talented Franklin High School guard had made a non-binding commitment to play for Washington. He had appeared at a news conference called by Lake Washington High's Donald Watts, the son of former Sonics guard Slick Watts, and reaffirmed his college basketball intentions before a bank of TV cameras while Watts revealed a similar choice. The future looked promising for the Bob Bender-run UW program with two top-notch local guards delivered to the Huskies.

At the 11th hour, however, Terry received a better offer from Olson. Arizona had kept him on the back-burner during his recruitment, but when two guard prospects, Eddie Shannon (who went to Florida) and Kyle Cartmill (Stanford), reneged on commitments, the Wildcats backtracked to Terry.

The guard felt he had no choice but to accept, choosing the proverbial top-10 program over the always-rebuilding Huskies. Terry never forgot how nervous he was calling Bender on a Sunday night to tell the coach of his change in plans. Bender understood. As a player he had done something similar, leaving Indiana and coach Bobby Knight after one season for Duke and Mike Krzyzewski. Bender sounded shaken on the other end, but wished Terry well.

"It's how the program is set up, especially for a guard," Terry said of his Arizona defection. "It was a great place. You have a chance to showcase yourself at a national level. At Washington, I didn't see that. In a situation like that, you've got to be selfish. It's for you. You can't play for anybody else."

Terry followed his basketball dreams and they all came true. No Seattle-produced athlete has been a bigger winner at so many different levels: His 1993 and 1994 Franklin High clubs were Class AA state champions, his 1997 Arizona team captured the NCAA title and his 2011 Dallas Mavericks team secured the NBA title, creating a rare championship triple. In the process, Terry was an all-state prep selection, a 1999 first-team *Associated Press* All-America college choice, the 1999 Pacific-10 Player of the Year and 2009 NBA Sixth Man of the Year. He became just one of five homegrown players to share in an NBA championship, joining Brian Scalabrine (2008), James Edwards (1989, 1990, 1996), Clint Richardson (1983) and Jack Nichols (1957).

"I've won at every level," said Terry, who made a headband and knee socks his trademark look at each basketball rung. "How many players have won at the high school, college and NBA levels?"

His hometown, however, wasn't very forgiving. Once he left, Terry was considered Seattle's ultimate sports traitor with local roots. Others had fled the city to seek their athletic fortune elsewhere — point guard Quin Snyder to Duke before him and football safety Taylor Mays to USC after, among a wide array of defectors — but none had made such a demonstrative public commitment to stay and play, and then did a reversal.

A backlash was expected after Terry switched college destinations, and local fans didn't hold back. Terry, who grew up in South Seattle at 2428 S. Irving St. – unknowingly a few doors down from NFL

> "I've won at every level," said Terry, who made a headband and knee socks his trademark look at each basketball rung. "How many players have won at the high school, college and NBA levels?"

standout Terry Metcalf's childhood home – was jeered whenever he played against the Huskies at home. People were more than willing to shower him with the popcorn that he once sold. Taunts were nonstop. Wounds were left by the knee-jerk reactions he heard on a Seattle sports talk show. "One guy on the radio said I was never going to work in this town," Terry said. "I heard it. It hurt me."

While Terry chose Arizona, that didn't stop him from daydreaming about what might have been with the Huskies. During pre-game warm-ups at Edmundson Pavilion, he pictured himself running up and down the floor in a white UW uniform rather than the blue-and-red one he wore. Yet he had no regrets. Overnight, Arizona made Terry a can't-miss player. Growing up, he didn't always believe it. To his benefit, he did something about it and heading to the desert was a crucial step in making it all come together.

Terry, nicknamed "Jet" for his initials (Jason Eugene Terry), had quickness but initially couldn't hit a jumper. "It was a set shot from 3-point range or a lay-up, nothing in between," said Lou Hobson, former Franklin assistant coach. This one flaw in Terry's game got him cut from a Seattle AAU select team as an eighth-grader. It hurt, especially when all of his friends made it.

"He couldn't shoot but he was quick and nobody could stop him, even if they knew he could only go right," said Francis Vela, a Franklin High teammate who later played at Seattle University. "The difference with him and every other player in the city was his work ethic. He was making 600 jumpers a day. I know, because I was rebounding for him."

Terry patterned himself after Seattle SuperSonics guard Gary Payton, stressing defense first, convinced the offense would follow. Terry started hanging out at the suburban Bellevue Pro Club because Michael

> "That's the way I dedicated myself to the game and never disrespected it," Terry said. "You've got to love the game and the game will love you back."

Dickerson, a highly regarded Federal Way High player and another Arizona recruit, played there. Dickerson, a year older, helped persuade Terry to go to Tucson. It was then up to Terry to make himself a polished player through hard work.

"That's the way I dedicated myself to the game and never disrespected it," Terry said. "You've got to love the game and the game will love you back. Guys get all the stardom and they quit working. Then a guy like me comes up and I'm as good as them, if not a little better."

The condensed version of Terry's life was found tattooed on his body. Across his right arm was a headstone for an aunt and a nephew who died young, the latter in a drowning accident in Tacoma. The number 206, his hometown area code, was inscribed over his right pectoral muscle, a tattoo copied by other Seattle basketball players that came after him. He wore a soldier figure on his left arm, adorned with the word "captain" and digits 31 (his jersey number since high school) and 211, signifying him as the Arizona record-holder for steals in a most unique manner (the number, he pointed out, also is police code for armed robbery). The initials "JT" stood for him, of course. He had the cartoon figure, Underdog, for obvious reasons. "Every time I get on the court, that's how I feel," Terry said. And in 2011 he added a tattoo of the NBA championship trophy, well before the fact, promising to have it removed if the Mavericks didn't win, which wasn't necessary.

Terry went to the Atlanta Hawks with the 10th pick overall in the 1999 draft but his transition to the pros was bumpy at first. Two people from that Georgia city showed up at his news conference claiming to be long-lost relatives, insisting they were his cousins, which they weren't. Terry also was guilty of questionable behavior; he had an otherwise glossy basketball record tarnished when an Arizona investigation revealed that the guard had improperly taken $11,500 from two sports agents his senior year, forcing the school to vacate its 1999 NCAA appearance and return post-season revenues of $45,362, which the remorseful Terry paid off himself.

In Atlanta, Terry answered to Lenny Wilkens, the former SuperSonics coach and a fellow point guard. Later traded to Dallas, Terry teamed with German big man Dirk Nowitzki, giving the Mavericks two players capable of instant offense and championship possibilities. They twice made it to the NBA finals together with Dallas, losing to Miami before reversing the outcome against the Heat five years later and making Terry's basketball career complete with championships.

Amid all of his travels, Seattle remained important to him. Arizona was just a temporary stop, as was the NBA. Terry said as much as thunder and lightning crashed overhead on a stormy Northwest day as he sat inside his favorite gym at St. Joseph church on Capitol Hill.

Terry was an NBA success, making hard choices to get there, but making everything happen just the same. When people said he wouldn't work in his hometown again, they got it partly right as he piled up his basketball championships. His popcorn-selling days were over. ❖

ICHIRO
The Japanese Import

Ichiro Suzuki required a translator at his side when he joined the Seattle Mariners, beginning with his introductory Safeco Field news conference on Nov. 30, 2000. Practically every English word sent his direction had to pass through a human filter. The imported baseball player and his franchise-paid assistant would engage in lively Japanese banter amongst themselves, formulating an answer, before a much more condensed and stoic message was offered to inquisitors.

Even then, Ichiro's innermost thoughts always came off as overtly philosophical, if not comical. Nothing attributed to him was stranger than his 2006 All-Star Game explanation in Pittsburgh regarding the Mariners' first-half difficulties. Some swore it was a line stolen from a "Karate Kid" film, a knockoff of Mr. Myagi's sage wisdom passed down to a protégé.

"For example, if we're talking about a tree, and the tree has a problem, you need to look at the root," Ichiro prattled on to a cluster of baseball writers taken aback by the unexpected Zen moment. "But you cannot see the root. The mistake is to keep watering the fruit. That's not going to solve anything."

Similar to Shakira and Bono, the Mariners outfielder preferred to be identified only by his first name. He also

> Ichiro accomplished things never done in the history of the game, batting .300 and collecting 200 hits in each of his first 10 big-league seasons.

left the impression that he enjoyed fooling people, could comprehend and speak far more English than he let on, and that absolute control was of utmost importance to him. Ichiro held the same power whenever he stood in the batter's box, too. With a bat in his hands, he did whatever he wanted without plausible explanation. The difference was he needed no middle man to pull off the feat.

Ichiro accomplished things never done in the history of the game, batting .300 and collecting 200 hits in each of his first 10 big-league seasons, while capturing a pair of batting titles and becoming Seattle's most unusual baseball presence for 11-plus seasons before his 2012 midseason trade as a declining superstar to the New York Yankees.

There was no simple justification offered from the complicated batting maestro because he debated even the most obvious conclusions, such as his place in history as one of baseball's greatest hitters.

"I wonder why you asked that," Ichiro said impatiently through his translator before offering me a dismissive wave of the hand and turning his back. "I don't know who labeled me a star. I don't consider myself a star. Next question."

The aloof Ichiro turned up in Seattle as a replacement for Alex Rodriguez, who fled the franchise following the departures of fellow headliners Randy Johnson and Ken

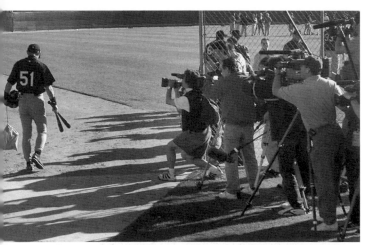

Cameras follow Ichiro everywhere, including at spring training.

Griffey Jr. Into the new century the baseball newcomer from the Far East transformed the city's baseball image from raw, unlimited ability to that of the cool and calculating.

Ichiro was a curiosity from the beginning with his moussed hair, contemporary stubble and regal persona. Accompanied by his wife to his introductory news conference, he stood at home plate like some visiting political dignitary and watched big-screen footage of himself as a Japanese player and an outfielder once on spring-training loan to the Mariners. By coincidence, he arrived at Safeco Field on the same day that Japanese schoolgirls were touring the facility. They screamed when they spotted him and he acknowledged them, such hero worship demonstrating his Elvis-like popularity back in his homeland.

Surrounded by enough media to cover a World Series game, a group that included four dozen Japanese reporters, Ichiro was his least guarded when the Mariners formally introduced him. Asked how much

the presence of Japanese ownership and relief pitcher Kazuhiro Sasaki affected his decision to join the Mariners, Suzuki delivered a rambling answer that drew laughs from his fellow countrymen in the media.

Translated, Suzuki said this of Sasaki: "He likes to drink. I hope I don't have to go out with him. I'm going to have a clause in my contract that says I don't have to go out and drink with him." While nearby Mariners' officials looked aghast, the translator quickly added, "That's a joke."

Asked about Safeco Field's large dimensions, the 5-foot-9, 156-pound newcomer said he wouldn't hit many home runs because he had "skinny arms," but he promised gap power. Quizzed about the abrupt exit of Griffey a year earlier, a player he deeply admired, Suzuki kidded that he would name his first son "Junior." Turning pensive, Ichiro called the moment the best day of his life.

Seattle saw high value in Ichiro, paying $13.1 million for the right to negotiate for him before signing him to a three-year, $15 million contract. "We probably have the best left-handed hitter we could find in the world," Mariners general manager Pat Gillick said.

While the Mariners trumpeted Ichiro's arrival, others needed a lot more convincing that this slender, reserved player would be successful at the big-league level. Japanese pitchers had fared well, but every-day players had struggled.

Rob Dibble, former reliever turned excitable baseball TV analyst, promised publicly that he would have Ichiro's name and No. 51 tattooed on his lower posterior, and run through New York's Times Square with little or no clothing if the Seattle player won the batting title or hit .300 in his first season.

Even the Mariners' Edgar Martinez, another two-time A.L. batting champion, initially was dubious about

his new teammate. "At the beginning of spring training, when I saw him, I had my doubts he'd be able to make the transition," Martinez confided. "But there was something about Ichiro and he showed confidence right away. He wasn't a player who had amazing talent like a five-tool player, but I respected how he got the best of everything he had with discipline and his ability."

For those who wanted to emulate him, it simply wasn't possible. Ichiro was a rigidly meticulous man with peculiar tastes. His wardrobe sometimes included shocking-pink underwear that he kept folded neatly on a hanger in his Safeco dressing area, a black T-shirt with a pink skull on it and rainbow-colored sneakers.

If that wasn't convoluted enough, his approach to hitting was a lot like watching a bird craft a nest, a bee create a hive and an ant build an anthill, all at once. The pre-at-bat monotony was enough to drive any pitcher crazy. The build-up on the way to home plate was an exhaustive series of stretches, squats and tugs that would have turned most aerobics instructors weary.

A typical Ichiro at-bat went something similar to this 2008 moment against the Boston Red Sox: He took two looping swings in the on-deck circle. He adjusted his right batting glove and then the protective shield covering his right elbow. He swung the bat with each hand. He tapped the ground with his bat. He pulled at the elbow pad again. He looked at his bat. He took two two-handed swings. He took two one-handed swings. He pulled at his pants. He readjusted both batting gloves. He readjusted the elbow pad. He tapped the top of his helmet with his right hand. He took two more swings. He strode to the plate. He stopped and swung twice more. He squatted. He dug his cleats into the dirt at home plate. He held his bat aloft with his right hand alone in his customary manner, aimed at the pitcher as if it were a cobra ready to strike. He was now ready to swing at the first pitch.

Standing in line at the Lakemont Starbucks coffee shop one day, Eric Sallee, a Bellevue accountant and former college pitcher, had to laugh when he turned to see Ichiro, dressed in metallic-colored warm-ups, go through his series of stretches while waiting to place his caffeine order.

More amazingly, Ichiro could hit. He hit from the beginning and he hit nonstop. He was the second coming of Rod Carew, another Tony Gwynn, a clever, bat-wielding genius. He made contact with everything thrown in his direction. In his first big-league season of 2001, he batted .350 to capture the American League batting title and send Dibble scurrying to a tattoo parlor, was easily selected A.L. Most Valuable Player and Rookie of the Year, and played an integral role for a playoff-bound Mariners team that won a record 116 games.

In 2004, Ichiro was even a more formidable presence at the plate. He put his name in the big-league record books with a season-long assault on a sacred record: Most hits in a season. He came up with 262, five more than Hall of Fame player George Sisler, whose standard stood for 84 seasons. Ichiro also won a second A.L. batting title that season with a robust .372 average.

All along people waited for a falloff that was certain to come, not just for a Japanese ballplayer but for any modern-day baseball player. Few could manage such a blistering batting pace at this level of play for so long. Gwynn posted nine consecutive .300 seasons before the hits stopped coming in big bunches. Pete Rose came up with 10 .300 seasons spread over 15 years before he tailed off.

Ichiro was left to defend himself while he surpassed different milestones, especially in 2008 when he approached his 3,000th hit with combined Japanese and American totals, the first 1,278 hits coming in his homeland.

"For me, I know it's tough to get hits in Japan and it's tough to get hits in the United States," Ichiro said, seated in a clubhouse cubicle, his legs crossed. "It's real tough, because I've experienced it. Some people in the United States think Japanese players play with metal bats and that's disappointing."

The often standoffish Ichiro, who kept a waterfront home at 4101 185th Place S.E. in Issaquah, finally let his guard down some. Normally a stoic clubhouse presence, the Japanese player was tackled, tickled and insulted by Griffey, who returned to Seattle in 2009 to finish off his certain Hall of Fame career and do his best to keep the clubhouse loose. Ichiro laughed uncontrollably when under assault.

In 2011, Ichiro finally showed the first substantial evidence of a drop-off, a development that proved surprising in another way: People actually had come to believe that he was immune to such things. His amazing streak of .300 seasons ended at 10, leaving him tied with Rose for the most in big-league history, when he slipped to .272 and didn't top 200 hits for the first time, settling for 184.

On July 23, 2012, after demonstrating more slippage, he was traded to the Yankees. His first game in his new uniform came at Safeco Field. After receiving a long ovation from Mariners fans, Ichiro bowed twice in appreciation and then singled to center.

Ichiro usually had that team interpreter stationed at his side and communicated in Japanese whenever he was quizzed about something, but not always. Once when asked in a Safeco dugout what he thought about his bobblehead doll that was to be given out that night, he smirked and in perfect English wise-cracked, "Ugly." ❖

Top 10 Mariners

1. Ken Griffey Jr., CF
2. Randy Johnson, P
3. Felix Hernandez, P
4. Ichiro Suzuki, RF
5. Alex Rodriguez, SS
6. Robinson Cano, 2B
7. Edgar Martinez, DH
8. Jamie Moyer, P
9. Mark Langston, P
10. Jay Buhner, RF

RICK NEUHEISEL

The Pool Shark

In hindsight, someone more conservative than the risk-taking Neuheisel would have been a safer choice.

Gary Pinkel called Chris Tormey to congratulate him, and Tormey tried to return the favor. The former University of Washington assistant football coaches had been publicly identified as the leading candidates to become the next Huskies head coach in 1999, replacing the fired Jim Lambright, their former colleague from Don James' UW staff. Word was out that the coveted job had been filled.

Pinkel and Tormey, Toledo and Idaho head coaches, respectively, were dumbfounded when they learned that someone else had been hired: Rick Neuheisel. The Colorado head coach, former UCLA quarterback, Rose Bowl hero and program outsider was an 11th-hour selection after Huskies athletic director Barbara Hedges and her 10-person search committee concluded that someone far more dynamic was needed for the position.

"It was a high-profile job and I wasn't a high-profile guy," Tormey said.

In hindsight, someone more conservative than the risk-taking Neuheisel would have been a safer choice. As the new millennium kicked in, no coach or manager would be held responsible for more collateral damage to a Seattle athletic program or franchise with his off-field actions than the man whom Huskies fans derisively dubbed "Slick Rick" before settling on the even more unflattering "New-weasel."

"I was one of 10 people on the selection committee for Neuheisel and I can tell you the vote was 10-0; we were enthused about him," said Ron Crockett, Emerald Down horse race track owner and leading UW alumni booster. "It's an inexact science sometimes."

Neuheisel's unexpected appointment brought a high-water moment for the UW in his second season with a 2001 Rose Bowl victory over Purdue and Drew Brees. However, the coach's abrupt firing two years later for his involvement in a basketball betting pool sent the once-proud program into absolute ruin for seven dreary non-winning seasons, creating the darkest period in Husky football history.

Neuheisel, now a CBS-TV broadcaster, lasted just long enough to see one recruiting class graduate. In 2008, he even turned up in Husky Stadium as the UCLA coach with a ready apology and left town with a 27-7 victory over a UW team headed for the worst record (0-12) in the program's 119 seasons to that point. Not far behind this uncomfortable reunion was the firing of Tyrone Willingham, joining the earlier removal of Keith Gilbertson as coach. Fans blamed all of the nasty fallout on Neuheisel.

Neuheisel originally rode into Seattle on a wave of youthful enthusiasm and bold boasts, winning over a big segment of fans, alumni, returning players and recruits with his charm. He was 37, cocky, pass-happy, a skilled golfer and a man with a $1.1 million contract, leading to an easy comparison. "I'd call him a young Steve Spurrier," said David Norrie, FOX TV college football analyst, another former UCLA quarterback and one-time Neuheisel teammate.

Yet the flashy Neuheisel, who often rode to work in a powerboat across Lake Washington from his waterfront home at 226 E. Overlake Dr. in Medina, was never accepted by the UW's football old guard, which considered him more used-car salesman than football coach. There was the feeling that the Huskies would try and finesse teams rather than beat up on them. And the fact that Hedges, a former USC assistant athletic director, put a former UCLA quarterback in charge of the local football program seemed blasphemous and way too Hollywood for the skeptics.

"Her hiring of Neuheisel was demeaning to me," said Lincoln Kennedy, an All-America offensive tackle in the James era. "It wasn't a true Northwest attitude. It wasn't a true Husky attitude to me."

Jim Cope, a big-play wide receiver for tough-minded Husky coach Jim Owens, was equally put off by the New Age leader, saying, "I felt out of touch with Neuheisel. I never met him but I could never get over his pretty-boy UCLA look."

Washington State football coach Mike Price was hardly a big fan either. "I'm going to go sit on my Neuheisel," he wisecracked before heading to his office and a bathroom break.

Neuheisel's Washington teams went 7-5, 11-1, 8-4 and 7-6. He supplied bowl-game appearances each year, though he won just one of them. He also was responsible for minor NCAA infractions for excessive recruiting contacts early on and had to answer for a series of serious off-field indiscretions that landed players in prison or jail.

He secretly interviewed for the San Francisco 49ers coaching job, denied it initially and came clean after *Seattle Post-Intelligencer* columnist John Levesque overheard Neuheisel talking with his mother on a not-so-private cell phone call in the San Francisco airport and wrote about it.

Neuheisel was brought down by his involvement in a seemingly innocent NCAA Tournament betting pool that served more as a social gathering than ripe gambling outlet for a collection of businessmen, Husky football followers and athletic notables such as former Seattle Sonics center Jack Sikma and former WSU quarterback Clete Casper.

Over two years Neuheisel invested $5,000 and won $20,000. He denied everything when first quizzed about his participation by the NCAA. The beleaguered Huskies coach did all he could to keep his job, even producing an internal athletic department memo from the UW rules compliance officer which stated that comparable betting pools were permissible. Hedges still fired him on June 12, 2003.

Neuheisel, who later won a $4.7 million settlement from the UW in a wrongful-termination lawsuit, likely will never know who brought him down in such calculated fashion. That person went to great lengths to hide his or her identity and disappear into cyber-space. The Neuheisel case documents, unsealed at the request of the *Post-Intelligencer*, showed an elaborate ruse: A persistent whistle-blower claimed to be a former pool participant and exposed the coach for gambling with friends on NCAA Tournament games while revealing precious little else about himself.

"I never found out who it was," Neuheisel said. "It's one of those things I'll never know. It's a great mystery."

The NCAA fought release of the documents. Among the reasons cited was the need to protect the confidentiality of its Neuheisel source, when in reality all the collegiate governing body was doing was shielding an alias. The person behind the pointed emails referred to himself as "Peter Wright."

There were two-dozen Peter Wrights living within the Greater Seattle area. There was no Peter Wright involved at any time in a Bellevue based betting pool that was in operation for 15 years and disbanded after Neuheisel was fired, according to its participants. As messages were traded with the NCAA over the next three months, this supposed Peter Wright presented a scolding tone, a righteous tone, a taunting tone.

"The guy is dirty and I personally feel that gambling on NCAA-sanctioned events when you are a coach in the NCAA is a travesty," the tipster wrote in an email.

"He has shown his colors in his recruiting style and who knows whatever else goes on. Rick must not know how good he has it to risk losing his job over such a silly thing."

Once Neuheisel was pilloried publicly, Peter Wright's email account – peterwright70@ yahoo. com – was quickly shut down. No one disputed the accuracy of the information provided. The intrigue came in the motivation for someone to create an apparent fictitious persona to turn in Neuheisel. The pool had 20 core members and up to 40 participants at the end. Involvement was by invitation only. Pool organizers examined past brackets and found no evidence of a Peter Wright. This person insisted he was a pool participant eight years earlier and got out of the pool because the betting had become too rich for him. It was all a lie.

People had all sorts of theories about who the person was, including one that suggested the tipster was a former Neuheisel neighbor and WSU supporter who became wealthy in the Internet world, making him savvy and sophisticated enough to pull off the scam, and that person was identified to me.

"That would not surprise me," said Neuheisel of that possibility. "I never had any problem with him. We didn't hang out a lot. But he was a different sort of guy."

Bob Williams, NCAA managing director of public and media affairs, said his organization never determined the tipster's identity and probably never would. Neuheisel's admission was enough to corroborate things for the investigators.

Once the coach's misstep was made public, the tipster emailed NCAA investigator Bill Saum as if seeking validation for his actions: "See, I told you I wasn't making it up. At least Rick had the guts to tell you the truth when confronted. Part of me feels bad for coming

forward, but at the same time Rick did this to himself. When will guys in his position learn that they're not invincible?"

In the fallout from Neuheisel's ouster, Tormey was hired by Nevada and fired four seasons later in 2003, even after upsetting a Gilbertson-coached Huskies team in Seattle. Tormey later returned to the UW as an assistant coach for a third time, working for both Gilbertson and Willingham, before relocating to Hawaii, WSU and Wyoming.

Pinkel was hired by Missouri in 2001 and became the kind of football coach the Huskies' faithful wanted all along, diligently transforming the Tigers into a tough-minded Big 12 Conference powerhouse. Pinkel's rise to coaching prominence was solidified by a 12-2 season and national Coach of the Year honors in 2007, and his success brought the Tigers membership in the prestigious SEC. The Huskies could have hired him on numerous occasions, but bungled the pursuit with three different athletic directors.

Neuheisel lasted just four seasons at UCLA. He stayed out of off-field trouble but became boring and predictable as a coach. He guided the Bruins into the inaugural Pac-12 championship game but only because USC was on probation. He did everything right – except win sufficiently.

With his program underperforming and his fan base eroding, Neuheisel was fired in 2011 by his alma mater, the dismissal coming eight and a half years after his bitter Seattle disengagement. As the end became clear, no doubt there was an office pool somewhere taking wagers on his departure date. ❖

Corey Dillon asked to meet with a *Seattle Post-Intelligencer* sportswriter through an intermediary – and then he didn't want anything to do with me. The gathering was set up for self-serving publicity interests, but initially it was a public-relations disaster.

For 10, maybe 15, long minutes, I watched as Dillon bounded down a stairway and nervously wandered through his two-story apartment at 34C1 on 952 S.W. Campus Drive in Federal Way like a big cat. The then-Cincinnati Bengals running back wouldn't look at me, speak to me or acknowledge my presence.

Finally, I interrupted Dillon's hypnotic trance and let him know I was still there, at his request, and casually suggested in the next breath that I wouldn't stick around much longer if this visit made the NFL player so uncomfortable.

For the next hour and a half, Dillon, who called the meeting to promote a summer youth football camp that he was sponsoring in his hometown, bared his soul. The edge was still there but words became part of his complicated makeup, too. They came tumbling out. Trust was a major issue with him. Strangers were like aliens to him. He said people wouldn't accept him for who he had become as an adult.

The overt suggestion that he was once a teenage criminal before he became a highly successful college and pro football player was a major sticking point, one that he wanted to disappear from his resúmé. Let him

> ## Dillon, always playing in a full-blown rage, was more successful in the NFL than any other homegrown Seattle player.

COREY DILLON
The Angry Man

move on without further interruption to his reputation, he said pointedly.

"That ain't me," Dillon said in a raised voice of a youth interspersed with arrests and court dates. "I admit I had issues growing up in Seattle, but I'm at peace with myself. People don't want to forget, but I've moved on. I'm not saying I'm an angel. I had my share of problems. I thought I was at least better than Bill Clinton."

Dillon, always playing in a full-blown rage, was more successful in the NFL than any other homegrown Seattle player. In 2005, he shared in a Super Bowl XXXIX victory with his second pro team, the New England Patriots, doing his part with 75 yards rushing, another 31 receiving and a short fourth-quarter touchdown run that proved the difference in a 24-21 victory over the Philadelphia Eagles in Jacksonville, Fla. This was after he became a multiple record-setter.

With the Bengals, Dillon established the NFL single-game rushing mark of 278 yards on 22 carries against the Denver Broncos (since broken by Jamal Lewis' 295 for Baltimore in 2003 and Adrian Peterson's 296 for Minnesota in 2007). He also set the single-game rushing record for a rookie running back with 246 yards on 39 carries against the Tennessee Titans in 1997 (later broken by Peterson's 296).

"I was shocked," he said. "It was like, man, did I do that? I know I was capable of doing good things. I had

Corey Dillon (2) teamed with Ed Raiford (20) at Franklin High School before taking a winding path to the NFL.

good games. At the time it happened, I had to let it go quick. I had another game to get ready for."

His hard shell, perpetual smolder and piercing stare made Dillon an exceptional pro player for a decade, if not someone extremely difficult to bring down. He retired following the 2006 season with career totals of 11,241 yards rushing, 89 touchdowns and four Pro Bowl selections (1999, 2000, 2001 and 2004).

He ran with a manic purpose, pointing out while he was still an active player that only he and Jim Brown at that juncture had their rookie jerseys hanging in the Pro Football Hall of Fame. Dillon's shirt was retrieved after his rookie rushing record. Brazenly making plans for the future, Dillon said he wanted a bigger display area if or when he was inducted.

"When I'm done, I will take my kids to Canton, Ohio," he said at the time. "I think that's everybody's dream, when they leave the game, is to be the best if not be one of the best. I'd be lying if I didn't say it was a goal of mine. I want be recognized as one of the best in my era."

Dillon began his march to football immortality at Seattle's Franklin High, a place well known for producing NFL talent: Running backs Terry Metcalf and Jesse Chatman, defensive backs James Hasty and Tony Zackery, linebacker Fritz Greenlee, tight end Aaron Pierce and center Bruce Jarvis were others who made the jump. The multi-talented Dillon also was drafted as an outfielder by the San Diego Padres, but turned down a pro baseball contract. Instead, he took a most unusual path to reach the NFL.

Questionable grades and behavior sent him on an extensive tour of junior colleges — Edmonds, North Seattle, Garden City in Kansas and Dixie State in Utah — where he experienced the occasional scrape along the way, before he spent one season, and just one academic quarter, at the University of Washington.

"I went the back route," Dillon said. "I took a couple of alleys but it worked for me. It made me tougher."

He passed on offers from Arkansas, Tennessee and Washington State to come home and pull on a purple uniform. Dillon was always one step from trouble; on his Cougars recruiting trip, he picked up a potted plant at a house party and randomly threw it through a large window on his way out.

In 1996, Dillon was so magical and mysterious in his limited stay with the Huskies that people couldn't help but dig through his background, wondering if he had some sort of Cinderella wish rewarding him handsomely at the time and requiring a harsh toll later. He scored five touchdowns against UCLA. He rushed for 222 yards against San Jose State — in a single quarter. He ran for 259 yards against Oregon, second-most in school history. Weekend after weekend, he did something bordering on fantastic.

Dillon quickly learned the price of fame. He was subjected to a background check by the *P-I* and seven alleged crimes over five years, five resulting in convictions, were pulled from his King County juvenile files and made public. The most serious was his 1989 arrest and ensuing punishment for selling crack cocaine to three undercover police officers in downtown Seattle.

Court records showed that a 15-year-old Dillon and two others were detained and drugs were found stuffed in the underwear of one of his friends. Dillon spent 10 days in the county juvenile detention center, received nine months of probation, was handed 40 hours of community service, told to enter an anger-management program and ordered to start attending school on a regular basis. On other occasions, he was convicted of assault, criminal trespass, malicious mischief and twice for obstructing a police officer.

As an adult, any mention of the drug bust outraged Dillon. He admitted to getting into fights, a volcanic temper and teenage angst. But cocaine dispersal, no way. He protested that this particular arrest came from guilt by association with no questions asked. He claimed he was hanging out with friends, not engaged in the illegal activity taking place around him. He insisted he didn't abuse any illegal substances either.

"I invite anybody to open the file and show me where it says I sold drugs to a police officer; I'll give them a million bucks if they can," he said. "I come from a decent family. I know better. I've taken a long time to really shake it. I don't use drugs. They stop you from performing. Everything I got, God gave it to me."

No matter how it was interpreted, this past criminal revelation did a lot to spoil his triumphant return to Seattle. Some suggested that was his primary reason for abandoning his UW career after just three months, though others were quick to point out he rarely attended class and would have had major eligibility issues had he tried to stay in school.

His juvenile record hurt him in the NFL draft, too. He was projected as a high first-round pick, but slid to the 13th selection of the second round and the 43rd player taken overall by the Bengals, because of widespread concerns over his behavior as a teenager.

Dillon was a hard guy to know and often surly until the end of his NFL career, but 10 highly productive pro seasons supplied him with an enhanced image and made him richer beyond his wildest dreams, obscuring his childhood missteps.

"I basically came from nothing," he said. "I know how it is not having something to eat or begging for rides, riding the bus, riding a bike."

In pro football retirement, he moved to Los Angeles and resurfaced in the news only when something

No matter how it was interpreted, this past criminal revelation did a lot to spoil his triumphant return to Seattle.

unpleasant happened. Dillon was accused of domestic assault and driving while intoxicated, and twice presented with divorce proceedings by his wife. His anger still complicated things.

If there was a comfortable moment for Dillon, in becoming an ex-football player in the public eye, his hometown provided it. In 2009, the retired running back was asked to attend a UW-LSU game in Seattle and take a bow between the third and fourth quarters as a legendary player. He was cheered loudly by the Husky Stadium crowd. There was no nervous pacing this time. There was no bitterness.

"I was only out there for a hot flash, but I'm considered a Washington Husky," Dillon said, feeling accepted and respected in his hometown. ❖

QUIN SNYDER

The Golden Boy

Seattle couldn't keep him. Quin Snyder was the city's first can't-miss high school basketball player to bolt for a glamour college program. He was a clever, rubber-legged point guard from suburban Mercer Island High School who people immediately knew was better than anyone else in the Northwest. For a college destination, he chose Duke over Arizona, Kansas, Stanford, Virginia and his hometown Washington. Who could blame him for leaving? Snyder played in three Final Fours for the always-successful Blue Devils, the last one in Seattle in 1989.

Snyder was the city's gifted one, someone capable of doing great things in practically any profession. He earned MBA and law degrees from Duke. He voluntarily walked away from an Indiana Pacers' training camp, convinced he was NBA material but turned off by the individualistic style of play in the pros and minimum salary scale. He considered a Wall Street career. He settled on coaching, taking over at Missouri when he was 32 and making more than $1 million a season.

"I expected him probably to be president," Mercer Island High coach Ed Pepple said. "Either that or chairman of the board of NASDAQ."

Running counter to his national aspirations, Snyder found he should have come home and accepted an offer to become the UW coach. The Northwest understood and coveted him, and would have been more patient with him, which wasn't the case in the Midwest. His hometown school vigorously pursued him to run its basketball program, even after the failed attempt to land him as a player, and he said no again. Had he become the Huskies coach, it might have kept his glowing basketball reputation intact and avoided scandal. It might have preserved his marriage. It might have kept him from briefly considering something drastic.

No Seattle sports figure has suffered more for rejecting his roots than Snyder. On Feb. 9, 2006, he was fired after seven seasons at Missouri for a combination of things, a somewhat shocking development considering his potential and grooming. Seventeen NCAA violations were uncovered. He had consecutive losing seasons and went three years without an NCAA Tournament berth. And those demanding Missouri basketball fans never grew fond of his hair, long and slicked back, or his flashy designer suits, which ran counter to the look and feel of his conservative predecessor and the program's iconic Norm Stewart.

Snyder was three years into his Tigers tenure, coming off the third of four consecutive NCAA appearances, when the Huskies pursued him after firing Bob Bender as coach. Although it was his hometown beckoning, Snyder found the situation uncomfortable. Bender had been one of his Duke assistant coaches and a mentor,

> No Seattle sports figure
> has suffered more
> for rejecting his roots
> than Snyder. On Feb. 9, 2006,
> he was fired after
> seven seasons at Missouri.

and Snyder felt an obvious reluctance to succeed him at the UW.

Similar to Minnesota's Dan Monson and Gonzaga's Mark Few, Snyder said no thanks to UW athletic director Barbara Hedges, who ultimately hired Lorenzo Romar, the Saint Louis coach, a former Huskies point guard and someone who flourished his second time in Seattle. Snyder regretted his decision.

"I was trying to please the whole state of Missouri and it couldn't be done," Snyder said at the time. "I didn't know what it was like to follow Norm Stewart. At Washington I knew how many great players were there, but I felt loyal to Missouri. What if I had come home? I think I still would be coaching there."

The Missouri job fell apart for Snyder after he brought an outlaw player named Ricky Clemons into the program. Clemons assaulted a girlfriend, crashed an all-terrain vehicle onto the lawn of the school president's home, and alleged he received improper payments from an assistant coach and basketball clothing from Snyder. NCAA penalties were instituted and scholarship limitations put into place. Three-fourths of the way through the 2005-06 season, Snyder was forced out by Tigers athletic director Mike Alden.

The firing sent Snyder into a downward spiral for a year. It led to his divorce from basketball coach Larry Brown's daughter, Helen. It sent Snyder into seclusion in Wilmington, N.C. It was responsible for alcohol abuse, he insisted, not heavy drug involvement as was rumored in Missouri. It put him into rehab. It put him on antidepressants. It forced him to seek therapy for possible bipolar disorder. It made him unstable.

"Frankly, I didn't have an interest in living," Snyder said. "In Seattle a couple of buddies sat me down and said, 'Dude, what's going on?' I was suicidal, in a room for three days. I went away and

"I was trying to please the whole state of Missouri and it couldn't be done," Snyder said at the time. "I didn't know what it was like to follow Norm Stewart."

got better. But I felt like, over time, I lost myself, and not just in coaching."

Twenty years earlier, Snyder could do no wrong. The 6-foot-3 guard won a state championship during a 28-1 run with Mercer Island High. Residing at 8838 S.E. 72nd Place on the island, he was a two-time Washington Basketball Player of the Year, clearly a cut above anyone else, and the state's second McDonald's All-America selection and first in more than a decade. Snyder had unlimited college choices. These were fun times.

"I remember seeing my brother Matt and Jon Barry with big 'Qs' on their chests," Snyder said, with Barry briefly a Mercer Island classmate well before embarking on a 14-year NBA career with nine teams.

As a Duke freshman, the graceful Snyder appeared in 32 games as a reserve for a 37-3 team that advanced to the 1986 Final Four in Dallas, where the Blue Devils lost 72-69 to Louisville in the championship game. As a sophomore, he started 14 of 33 games for a 24-9 Duke team that didn't make it out of the NCAA Midwest Regional. As a junior, he became a full-time player for the first time, drawing starting assignments in 34 of 35 games for a 28-7 Blue Devils team that qualified for the 1988 Final Four in Kansas City but lost to Kansas 66-59 in the semifinals.

Quin Snyder went from Mercer Island to Duke.

And as a senior, he was a team captain and 36-game starter, averaging 7.2 points and 6.5 assists per game, for a 28-8 Duke team that earned a trip to the 1989 Final Four at Seattle's Kingdome, losing 95-78 to Seton Hall in the semis. Earlier that year, Snyder and the Blue Devils played at Washington and won 87-61 in a midseason game scheduled specifically to give him a chance to play at home.

Considering options after his playing career ended, Snyder became a Los Angeles Clippers assistant coach for Brown for a year before spending six seasons as a Duke assistant for Mike Krzyzewski. Once Stewart retired at Missouri, Snyder was a hot coaching property and an easy choice as the successor. He had no idea how bad of a coaching fit this was for him.

The Mizzou Arena opened while he was there, ratcheting up expectations. Snyder clashed with Alden, especially after the UW beckoned and Snyder came off a 25-11 season, forcing the athletic director to give his young basketball coach more money. Stewart never warmed to Snyder. Stan Kroenke, owner of the Denver Nuggets, St. Louis Rams and Colorado Avalanche, husband of an heir to the Walmart fortune and father of a Missouri player, also was a distraction.

With frustrations mounting, Snyder had popcorn thrown on his head at the arena. Alden brought in a team of lawyers to sort through the potential NCAA violations, keeping the coach on edge. Snyder's final Missouri team in 2005-06 had a 10-11 record coming down the stretch when, with seven games left, Alden sent broadcaster and special assistant Gary Link to tell Snyder to resign immediately or be fired when the season ended. Snyder, as it turned out, was terminated right away.

"Stan Kroenke's wife wouldn't talk to my wife and he was yelling, 'Payback is going to be unreal,' " Snyder said. "It was [bleep] what I went through. I'm not filled with this great load of shame. I was taught to fight. I should have resigned."

Snyder once was considered a likely candidate to become the next Duke basketball coach whenever Krzyzewski retired. At the very least, Snyder could

> "I couldn't walk away,
> I couldn't do it," Snyder said.
> "When it was stripped away,
> Missouri was the stuff
> that would define me
> for the rest of my life."

have settled in at the UW, where people didn't care how long he wore his hair or how expensive his suits were, and he could have flourished under far less pressure with an abundance of local talent. Instead, he was banished and scorned.

"I couldn't walk away, I couldn't do it," Snyder said. "When it was stripped away, Missouri was the stuff that would define me for the rest of my life."

Collecting himself from his negative thoughts and lingering alcohol abuse, Snyder got back into coaching when the NBDL's Austin Toros hired him as coach after Dennis Johnson, the former Seattle Sonics and Boston Celtics guard, died of a heart attack in 2007. Snyder coached the minor-league team for three seasons and returned to the NBA with the Philadelphia 76ers, Los Angeles Lakers and Atlanta Hawks as an assistant coach. He was back on the basketball fast track.

On June 6, 2014, the Utah Jazz hired Snyder as head coach, fully restoring his basketball reputation after nearly a decade in X's and O's purgatory. It wasn't Seattle, but it wasn't Missouri either. He was halfway home. ❖

Lorenzo Romar wasn't confident he could play basketball in the Pacific-10 Conference. In his Compton, Calif., living room, he said as much to University of Washington coach Marv Harshman, who had come to offer him a scholarship.

Up to that point, Romar had a checkered career. He was cut in multiple tryouts at powerful Verbum Dei High School. After transferring, he was briefly a starter at Pius X Matthias High before drawing a team suspension for an eat-and-run restaurant incident and finishing as a reserve player. At Cerritos College, he was ineligible for half a season at the two-year school because of a failing grade before making his basketball breakthrough.

An astute judge of talent and character, Harshman wasn't put off by Romar's reticence. The veteran Huskies coach had big plans for the left-handed point guard.

"I said, 'We don't have anybody to get people excited and when they announce Lo-Ren-Zoooooo! Ro-Maaaaaaar! it will get the student body excited, and I'm going to offer you a scholarship anyway,' " Harshman recalled.

Romar not only showed he could handle the Pac-10 level, he took his game to the NBA. And not only could he play for the Huskies, Romar came back and coached

LORENZO ROMAR
A Proper Introduction

them at a high level. Returning to the school 23 years after he last pulled on a uniform, he was named Washington's 18th basketball coach for the 2002-03 season, promising to stay on the job as long as his alma mater would have him.

While he was an adequate player, Romar engineered a Huskies basketball renaissance as the head coach, directing his teams to six NCAA Tournament berths in his first nine seasons, including three trips to the Sweet 16 round. And while his game-day tactical skills were maligned at times, Romar became the city's most successful early 21st century coach, exhibiting rare staying power during an extended downturn for most Seattle sports.

The California native built coaching momentum by taking advantage of a surprisingly deep local talent pool, one that provided him with future pro players in Brandon Roy and Nate Robinson without much effort. He kept everything moving by promoting an up-tempo style of play and establishing a solid track record for putting players in the NBA.

Romar, who accepted the job only after it was offered to three others who turned it down, saw something people didn't readily envision: Basketball success for a program with a history of decided mediocrity. "If I didn't think we could win a national championship, I wouldn't have come," Romar said.

> While he was an
> adequate player,
> Romar engineered
> a Huskies basketball
> renaissance as
> the head coach.

To find his way to the Northwest, however, Romar had to negotiate Compton's mean streets. His family moved from one side of the tension-filled Los Angeles suburb to the other to own a bigger home. Different agendas came with the different neighborhoods, though. The Crips gang claimed one area, Piru Bloods the other. Romar lived on the same street with gang members, rode city buses with these gangsters and learned how to co-exist with them without handing over his soul. But there were moments not easily dismissed or forgotten.

When he was 14, Romar had a handgun pressed against his head by another kid, 16. "He joked, 'If this goes off, you know what could happen,' " Romar said. "I said, 'Take the gun away.' "

There was a trip to the market where Romar was shoved to the ground and a bunch of street toughs started walking away with his bicycle, only to have an older, more intimidating guy named Greg Bell intercede and reclaim it for him.

Scarier yet were the whistles at night. This meant trouble was cutting through the darkness and just around the corner. The whistles could start hearts racing. Anthony Collins tried to ignore those shrill sounds after a dance and turned down a ride home from Romar; he got his front teeth knocked out with a pipe and didn't return to school for a week. Another friend, Anthony Jenkins, was shot in the head and murdered. So was Timothy Blunt.

"We despised those guys, they were losers to us," Romar said of the ever-present Compton gang members. "As soon as they rode up, we ran into the house. We were playing touch football once, there were four of us, and gang members drove up and said they wanted us to go around the corner and join up. I said, 'Bro, I'm not going to do it.' My brother [Wayne] and I held each

> "We despised those guys, they were losers to us," Romar said of the ever-present Compton gang members. "As soon as they rode up, we ran into the house."

other accountable. I didn't want to let him down by joining a gang or using drugs. He didn't want to let me down."

Romar learned to negotiate this urban obstacle course much like a full-court press. He never panicked or took undue chances. He figured out a mode of survival. He used his basketball skills to sell himself to the neighborhood, to obtain unobstructed passage, to clear a safe path for others.

He befriended Michael Cunningham, an independent gangster from Atlantic Avenue who was feared by everyone else in Compton but played basketball with the Romar brothers and had their backs. Years later, when Romar was an NBA guard in town to play against the Lakers or the Clippers, Cunningham always had a seat directly behind the visitors' bench at the Forum. He cussed out everyone. He shared in Romar's good fortune. The gangster was still watching Romar's back.

Basketball was a struggle at first. Romar boldly enrolled at one of L.A.'s midtown high school hoop havens, Verbum Dei, and was cut from the varsity and junior varsity as a sophomore. That was only part of his misery. Roy Hamilton, who later played at UCLA and briefly in the NBA, made fun of Romar when he showed up wearing his oversized kneepads, telling him that no one would ever recruit someone dressed like that.

A disheartened Romar transferred to Pius X Matthias, closer to Compton. His senior season started promisingly enough. The guard dropped in 27 points for the Victorians in a Christmas tournament game and he made the all-tourney team. A few weeks later, he was suspended. Romar's team always gathered for pre-game meals at Chris and Pits Bar-B-Q restaurant. On this particular occasion, several teammates grabbed the cheapest dinner bills on the table and ran out, sticking Romar and two others with inflated charges. Romar wasn't going to pay for his wise-guy friends and stuff he didn't eat. Figuring his meal had been covered, he left without paying.

Pius X coach Bob Burns, a self-styled disciplinarian, didn't see it that way. He suspended Romar for two games. Once the senior returned, the coach decided he would go with younger players, making Romar a sub for the rest of the season and devastating him.

Without impressive credentials to offer, Romar scrapped his way onto the Cerritos College roster. He outplayed guys who had been high school opponents and all-league selections. However, just when everything started to fall into place he became ineligible for the second half of his freshman season.

"I had a history class: Pass it and I'm eligible, and I failed it," Romar said. "I had done what I had done in the past: I realized at the last minute that I was in trouble. I messed up and it was too late to cram, which is why I'm such a stickler for academics now. I saw what happened to me."

As a sophomore, Romar averaged 14.1 points and 6.8 assists for a 23-8 Cerritos team and set a school record with an 18-assist game. Scholarship offers started rolling in. Nevada-Las Vegas coach Jerry Tarkanian was there the night Romar scored 24 points and led his team to a 116-106 victory over Saddleback College, the state's No. 1 JC team. The two left the floor together, the bald-headed coach putting the promising guard in a headlock, seemingly unwilling to let go.

Romar considered San Diego State but he didn't want to play behind a guard named Tony Gwynn, who proved to be more adept with a bat in his hands. Romar also was pursued by Utah, Idaho State and Montana before turning to Washington.

Harshman was recruiting junior-college point guard Dean Jones, who ended up at USC, when he spotted Romar in the preliminary game and decided he had to have him instead.

"He was not a great athlete but he was a good athlete," the Huskies coach said of Romar. "He played the way the game should be played. He got the ball to the others."

For an 11-16 Washington team in 1978-79, Romar, stylish in a big Afro, was a part-time starter who funneled the ball to NBA-bound center Petur Gudmundsson, a 7-foot-2 player from Iceland. As a senior, Romar was part of a three-guard offense that relegated Gudmundsson to sixth-man status and led to an 18-10 season and NIT berth.

The Golden State Warriors drafted Romar in the seventh round, as the 141st player taken, and the rookie guard from Compton by way of Seattle surprised everyone by making the roster. "Every day I would cut him and every night Lorenzo would do something to make me keep him," Warriors coach Al Attles said.

Romar won over the coach as a poor man's Nate Archibald with his no-look passes and unselfish play. "I stayed up all night when I made it and called everyone I knew," Romar said. "I said, 'I might be there for only a week, but I had made it.' "

He played parts of six NBA seasons, becoming a 64-game starter for the Warriors in his third year, appearing in 13 playoff games for the Milwaukee Bucks his fourth year and finishing up with the Detroit Pistons. He was released three times, the last cut coming at camp with the Indiana Pacers.

Romar became a player-coach for the Christian based Athletes in Action, joined UCLA as an assistant coach and held coaching jobs at Pepperdine and Saint Louis before re-emerging in Seattle with the Huskies.

His UW scholarship allowance was replaced by $1 million salaries. The Afro was replaced by a shaved head. Where he once slept in his car at times as a college kid, he now had a handsome suburban home in Bellevue.

He ran into some turbulent times when his teams failed to make the NCAAs, but far longer than Harshman predicted, Romar's rhythmic name came over the public-address system in a drawn-out and teasing fashion, followed by prolonged cheering. ❖

NATE & JACQUE ROBINSON
Seattle's DNA Test

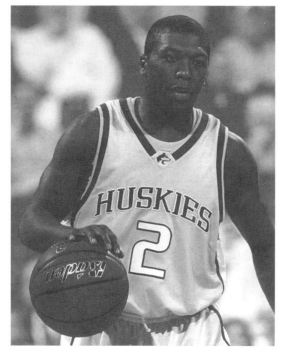

Nate Robinson, left, and his dad, Jacque, were Huskies standouts.

Nate Robinson was an explosive figure, a tiny yet supremely gifted basketball player who at any moment might streak down the middle of the key, tip-jam on anyone and send a ripple of electricity shooting through a packed Seattle high school gym. If that wasn't unsettling enough, Jacque Robinson often sat just a few rows up from the court, a thick man dressed all in black like some shadowy character, offering in a low but audible growl a running commentary of insults and challenges directed at anyone who attempted to get in his son's way.

When you went up against the Robinson family, you always had to be ready for the unexpected and deal with plenty of attitude.

From Seattle's most fertile athletic gene pool, Jacque turned up first as a 1982 Rose Bowl hero in the unlikeliest fashion. He was 18, a freshman running back from San Jose, Calif., and largely an unknown player for the University of Washington when he came off the bench well into the New Year's Day game. He didn't sit down again until he had rushed 20 times for 142 yards and two touchdowns, playing a little more than two quarters.

After his sterling role in the Huskies' 28-0 victory over Iowa, Jacque was named the game's offensive MVP, becoming the first freshman to receive the post-game honor. Robinson was such a surprise in front of the crowd of 105,611, a reporter asked Huskies coach Don James, "Who is Jacque Robinson?" To which James replied, "I don't know. I just introduced myself to him. I do know he's a freshman. I checked the program."

While his football career floundered at times because he was maddeningly overweight, Jacque went out in the same glorious manner as he came in for the Huskies. He was awarded 1985 Orange Bowl offensive MVP honors as a senior in his final collegiate game after running 28 times for 135 yards and a score in a 28-17 upset victory over Oklahoma.

Seven months before that final bowl game in Miami, however, Jacque and his UW girlfriend, Renee Hollingsworth, gave birth in Seattle to a son they named Nathaniel Cornelius Robinson. The newborn took only the best traits from each parent. He acquired his father's scary athleticism and ever-present cockiness. From his mother, a former high school dance-team member, he embodied her lean physique and nimble feet.

A college romance that didn't last was responsible for Nate, who became an even bigger sporting presence than his father, though at 5-foot-7¾ he was more than three inches shorter. The younger Robinson was 18 when he played a single season of Washington football as a starting cornerback in homage to his dad, even appearing in the Sun Bowl — without MVP honors — before switching to Husky basketball to satisfy his athletic desires.

"I wanted to play football one time," Nate said. "I wanted to run down the tunnel like my dad. I tried to get his number, 28, but [junior Chris Massey] wouldn't trade it. I got 13 instead, my number in my junior year of high school. I could have played football at the U-Dub for all three years but I wanted to better myself. I had to leave it alone."

The Robinsons are Seattle's most accomplished father-son combination, with both performing at high levels when connected to the city.

Football sentiment was one thing, but round-ball had a deep hold on Nate. "I just love to play the game of basketball," he said. "It makes me extremely happy. I can't describe it. It just makes me feel great. I play it how I think it should be played — with energy, to feed the crowd, for my family and friends."

The Robinsons are Seattle's most accomplished father-son combination, with both performing at high levels when connected to the city. The Griffeys (Ken Sr., Ken Jr.) pulled off the most unique and historic family stuff, playing in 51 games together for the Seattle Mariners in 1990-91 while hitting back-to-back homers in a memorable '90 game, but the elder Griffey was well past his prime when in the city. Other notable father-son athletic couplings for Seattle came from families named Averill (Earl and Earl Jr.), Borchardt (Jon and Curtis), Burleson (Al and Al Jr., Nate, Lyndale), Heinrich (Don, Kyle), Evans (Norm and Ron), Kemp (Shawn and Shawn Jr.), Metcalf (Terry and Eric), Miles (Eddie and Troy), Murrey (Dorie and Dorie Jr.), Mays (Stafford and Taylor), O'Brien (Eddie and Eddie Jr.) Olerud (John and John Jr.), Tuiasosopo (Manu and Zach, Marques, Matt), Ulbrickson (Al and Al Jr.), and Watts (Slick and Donald).

The big-league level was where the Robinsons went different directions. Jacque was an eighth-round NFL draft pick for the Buffalo Bills in 1985 and not much more than a pro football afterthought. He failed to stick in training camps with the Bills and Miami Dolphins before he appeared in three games and carried the ball 24 times for 114 yards as a replacement player for the 1987 Philadelphia Eagles strike team.

Bypassing his senior UW basketball season for early pro entry, Nate emerged as a first-round selection of the Phoenix Suns in the 2005 NBA draft and was part of a prearranged, four-player trade that sent him to the New York Knicks. A natural showman, this Robinson used the bright lights to sell himself as one of the NBA's more entertaining players for the Knicks, Celtics, Thunder, Warriors, Bulls and Nuggets.

It didn't take long for NBA fans to embrace the magnetic player. He was the shortest guy in the league, consequently forced to become more of a playmaker than shooting guard. Nate still was capable of filling up the hoop at any time. He dropped 45 points on the Trail Blazers in his third season, 41 against the Pacers in his fourth season and 41 against the Hawks in his fifth. Perhaps his most amazing NBA game came in 2013 when he was summoned off the bench and supplied 34 points — 23 in the fourth quarter — to propel the Bulls from a 14-point deficit to a three-overtime 142-134 playoff victory over the Nets.

"He might be the best under-6-foot player ever," Bulls teammate Joakim Noah said admiringly.

Robinson showed his fun and creative sides when he became the first player to win three All-Star Game dunk contests. Picking up his second dunk title, he pulled on an all-green "Krypto-Nate" uniform to fend off Magic center Dwight Howard, who advertised himself as "Superman," and he used Howard as a stationary prop and leaped over him for the decisive dunk. Nate networked during his New York games, fist-bumping with actor Will Ferrell on his way up the court and trading nonstop banter with film director Spike Lee.

Multiple choice was always a family option when it came to sports. Jacque settled on a UW football scholarship when he left San Jose High School, but he also was a top-50 national basketball recruit and had plenty of suitors for that wintertime sport, including the Huskies. A 5-11 shooting guard, the older Robinson averaged 22 points a game as a senior and attended elite summer basketball camps in Atlanta and San Diego.

"If I was going to play basketball it would have been at Michigan State," said Jacque, pursued by the Big Ten school two years after Earvin Johnson led the Spartans to an NCAA championship. "Magic would have been a big factor."

Jacque considered playing both Husky football and basketball as a freshman, similar to his son two

Nate Robinson, left, and Brandon Roy were UW teammates and NBA opponents.

In hindsight, Jacque might have stayed fit and avoided football weight issues had he played Husky basketball.

decades later. The UW's Marv Harshman was the first basketball coach to recruit him. However, Robinson's Rose Bowl trip cut into too much of the basketball season, plus the Huskies' conservative approach to hoops was a turn-off, so he passed.

In hindsight, Jacque might have stayed fit and avoided football weight issues had he played Husky basketball. Ballooning up in the off-season, a pudgy Robinson was in and out of the lineup throughout his UW football career, starting just 17 of 48 games. James had little patience for out-of-shape players and publicly chastised him, especially after the tailback's weight closed in on 250 pounds, 30 more than his Rose Bowl physique.

Jacque still built up a formidable resume by rushing more than 2,300 yards for the Huskies. He came up with a 203-yard game against Texas Tech as a sophomore. He had a powerful, slashing style that was copied by one of his biggest admirers.

"I'd go to Oakland and ask my grandmother, Where's Dad's tapes?' " Nate said. "I used to watch how he moved and how he played. I used to go out and emulate that out in the street. I used to do everything my dad used to do."

Out of allegiance to his father, Nate gave football equal time. He was a 1,200-yard rusher as a Rainier Beach High senior. The Robinsons shared the same athletic explosiveness: Nate had a top vertical leap of 41 inches; Jacque's best was 37.

"He had the ability to make people miss and that was my best attribute," Jacque said. "He was probably a little quicker than I was."

Football recruiters took note of the bloodlines and natural gifts and pressed hard for Nate, who lived in Seattle at 10063 62nd Ave. S. He took recruiting trips to Arizona State, USC and UW, informing coaches that he intended to play two sports. USC's Pete Carroll told Robinson that he was Heisman Trophy material. Nate eliminated the Sun Devils and Trojans, not convinced they would fully endorse his two-sport plans. UW coach Rick Neuheisel said all the right things.

"I wanted to be a Husky," Nate said. "My dad was a Husky. I didn't go on a recruiting visit until I had committed. Coach Neuheisel said, 'I like you a lot,' and I said, 'I'm coming.' Coach Neuheisel said I could play basketball. I met with coach [Lorenzo] Romar. He said he had one rule for me, 'You have to cut your hair off,' because I had braids."

Nate was a six-game starter for the Huskies as a freshman football player; Jacque didn't start at the UW until he was a sophomore. Holding his arms out like Popeye, thumping his chest and skating along the playing surface after making a huge play, the smaller Robinson gave off energy as if it were heat, and this, too, was different from his dad. Jacque was less demonstrative, a laidback personality.

"I wanted to be a Husky," Nate said. "My dad was a Husky. I didn't go on a recruiting visit until I had committed."

Top 10 Father-Son Combos

1. Jacque & Nate Robinson
   (UW, NBA)

2. Ken Sr. & Ken Griffey Jr.
   (MLB, MLB)

3. Slick & Donald Watts
   (NBA, UW)

4. Terry & Eric Metcalf
   (NFL, NFL)

5. Don & Kyle Heinrich
   (NFL, UW)

6. Manu & Marques,
   Matt & Zach Tuiasosopo
   (NFL, NFL, MLB, UW)

7. Stafford & Taylor Mays
   (NFL, NFL)

8. Shawn & Shawn Kemp Jr.
   (NBA, UW)

9. Jon & Curtis Borchardt
   (NFL, NBA)

10. Al Sr. & Al, Nate & Lyndale
    Burleson (UW, UW, NFL, Nev.)

By his second collegiate basketball season, Nate was dunking on everyone and packing arenas with curious fans. His personal favorite was a back-door dunk in his sophomore year against Arizona. It came off a lob pass that appeared well over his head and out of reach. He caught the ball and slammed it through with two hands; he was caught in a *Seattle Post-Intelligencer* photo hovering in the air like a UFO. Jacque was there to witness the signature moment, exploding out of his seat and high-fiving everyone around him as the arena roared.

Jacque moved back to his native California and, amazingly, lost all of that extra weight he had carried around for so long, likely at the insistence of his NBA son. Nate wouldn't let go of the place in which he and his father had established a unique sporting legacy. Hometown acceptance remained important to the younger Robinson and he made sure everyone knew it.

"I hope they love me in Seattle," Nate said. "This is where I started. For all the hard work and everything I put into it, in representing my city, I want to be loved the way I love them." ❖

BRANDON ROY
The Short-Term Superstar

Once in the pros, Roy put his exceptional talent on full display. Creative and deliberate with the ball in his hands, he was a perfect fit for the NBA.

Brandon Roy possessed rare basketball skills, offering glimpses of greatness at every level of the game, but he never had the whole stage to himself. He played in his older brother Ed's shadow at Seattle's Garfield High School. He deferred to teammate Nate Robinson at the University of Washington. He was drafted behind LaMarcus Aldridge by the Portland Trail Blazers.

Roy's sporting anonymity was such that Huskies coach Lorenzo Romar, standing at a podium at the Pacific-10 Conference basketball media day in early November 2005, made this observation about his senior guard to a room full of yawning newspaper writers and TV reporters at the Los Angeles Airport Hilton Hotel: "People don't understand how good Brandon Roy is."

Even with Romar's preseason pleadings, it took another five months before everyone finally caught on. They started to come around once Roy was named Pac-10 Player of the Year, played sensationally during the NCAA Tournament and nearly led the Huskies to the Final Four.

That didn't prevent a couple of organizations promoting All-America teams from completely omitting Roy from consideration before they owned up to their mistakes and offered hasty public corrections, making him a consensus selection — just the Huskies' third behind Depression-era guard Hal Lee and post-World

War II-era center Bob Houbregs. Roy was deceptively good and the secret was out.

Once in the pros, Roy put his exceptional talent on full display. Creative and deliberate with the ball in his hands, he was a perfect fit for the NBA. For the Blazers, he was a near-unanimous choice as the 2007 Rookie of the Year and a logical pick for the All-Star Game for each of the following three seasons. This was individual stuff no other player from his city had accomplished — Jason Terry and Jamal Crawford were NBA Sixth Man of the Year recipients, but never All-Stars — and it made Roy far and away Seattle's most accomplished home-grown pro basketball player.

The unselfish Roy became the Blazers' leading scorer, supplied a memorable 52-point game before a national audience and led the team back to the playoffs. He was singled out as the player largely responsible for restoring a wholesome image and filling the seats again for a Portland franchise that had alienated its devoted fan base with numerous arrests accompanied by poor play. Roy was so proficient he developed a huge following among his NBA peers.

"He's amazing," veteran Dallas Mavericks forward Dirk Nowitzki said of Roy, speaking without any prodding while seated, tired and sweaty, after a 2010 game. "He's got pull-up. He's got post-up. He's a big shot-maker. He is one of the superstars in the league."

Oklahoma City Thunder forward Kevin Durant, while much flashier when attacking the rim and serving up high-wire shots, admitted a deep admiration for Roy's unique and customized playing style. In 2010, the Thunder player even suggested that the NBA's highest individual honor was well within reach of the Trail Blazers' leader if not justifiably overdue.

"A lot of people see LeBron James, Kobe Bryant, Carmelo Anthony and Dwyane Wade as the MVP, and I think it should be Brandon," Durant insisted at the time. "What he does for his team is unreal because his team is always shorthanded. He's been overshadowed by a lot of people."

Roy was so important to the Trail Blazers' newfound success and image restoration that he was rewarded with a five-year, $83 million contract extension entering the 2009-10 season, seemingly a guarantee that he would remain a long-term Portland sporting fixture.

Financially, Roy was now light years from his modest West Seattle upbringing, which included living in an apartment at 4137 Delridge Way S.W. and a humbling stint working for a waterfront company that cleaned and repaired shipping containers. The versatile back-court player was a fan favorite in Portland because he had made such a deep-rooted connection with the city and continually let everyone know how he felt. He even allowed himself a moment to consider a gilded future.

"I've got too much at stake to walk away, not just for my family, but for the fans," Roy said of Portland. "And it's not just the feeling between me and the fans. I care about this team. I have a legacy to uphold. I have a chance to be in the Hall of Fame."

Unfortunately for Roy, he became as cursed as he was blessed as a pro basketball player. His knees gave out on him during his fifth year in the league, erasing those dreams and forcing him into temporary retirement

on the eve of the 2011-12 season. He returned a year later with the Minnesota Timberwolves, the team that drafted him and traded him to Portland, and lasted five games before re-injuring himself and submitting to a seventh knee surgery, and finally limping away from the game.

He turned into a most unwanted NBA footnote: Roy had one of the shortest careers among all pro players branded with superstar status. His abrupt departure was exceeded only by that of Maurice Stokes, a Cincinnati Royals forward who, likewise, was a Rookie of the Year recipient and three-time All-Star selection before he was pushed out of the league by a game-inflicted head injury and ensuing stroke after just three seasons (1956-58). Roy admittedly had never heard of the incapacitated Stokes, who was 36 when he died in 1970.

Roy's health started to desert him just as he elevated himself to the highest level as an NBA player. The website SI.com, in releasing its 2010 midseason report, listed the following as the league's top five players: Cleveland's LeBron James and Dallas's Nowitzki at forwards, Orlando's Dwight Howard at center, and the Lakers' Kobe Bryant and Roy in the backcourt. People in a far wider spectrum had caught on to Roy's endless basketball possibilities.

Then-Charlotte Bobcats coach Larry Brown, cognizant of the deception surrounding and sometimes lack of appreciation for Roy's all-around game, had no problem stumping and standing up for him either.

"He's one of the most underrated players in our league from a public perception, but not from a league standpoint," Brown said, standing casually in an arena hallway before

a late-season 2010 game and clearly an interested participant in the conversation involving Roy. "He's an underrated playmaker. He's an underrated defender. He doesn't take a lot of shots to get his points. He seems like the ultimate teammate."

Roy, who had experienced knee trouble since he was in middle school, tried to go to the NBA straight from Garfield High before getting a tryout with Portland and realizing he wasn't physically strong enough. He envisioned leaving the UW for the pros following his junior year, but knee surgery made him stay and play his senior year for the Huskies.

The 2009-10 season offered Roy plenty of sentiment to help ease the increasing knee pain. A man all about relationships and friends, Roy often found himself on the floor with a player, sometimes two, even as many as three, who hailed from Seattle's neighborhoods or college courts. It was no wonder he felt comfortable in the NBA. Every game that season was practically old home week.

At one point, Roy was one of 13 people raised in some fashion in or around his hometown who were playing at basketball's top level. According to *Sports Illustrated*, Seattle had supplied the NBA with the fifth-largest number

Brandon Roy has his own team: Son, Brandon Jr., wife, Tiana, and daughter, Mariah.

of participants of any American metropolitan area, while ranking just 15th in population. The Northwest city was an unexpected basketball gold mine, and Roy was its biggest discovery.

The roll call of players with a Seattle-area pedigree went like this: forward Jon Brockman (Snohomish HS) and center Spencer Hawes (Seattle Prep) of the Sacramento Kings; forward Marvin Williams (Bremerton) and Jamal Crawford (Rainier Beach) of the Atlanta Hawks; guards Will Conroy (Rainier Beach, Garfield) and Aaron Brooks (Franklin) of the Houston Rockets; forward Brian Scalabrine (Enumclaw) and guard Nate Robinson (Rainier Beach) of the Boston Celtics; Jason Terry (Franklin) of the Dallas Mavericks; guard Rodney Stuckey (Kentwood) of the Detroit Pistons; forward Terrence Williams (Garfield, Rainier Beach) of the New Jersey Nets; forward Martell Webster (Seattle Prep) of Portland, and Roy. Add to that fellow Washington-bred players in forward Adam Morrison (Spokane's Mead) of

the Los Angeles Lakers and guard Luke Ridnour (Blaine) of the Milwaukee Bucks.

The latest generation of players pushed each other to achieve basketball greatness. They hung out together. They worked out together all over Seattle. Many of them wore matching "206" area-code tattoos. They shared in a midsummer basketball tournament, the Adonai Hood Classic at Garfield, which at times turned into a mini NBA All-Star Game. The older, established players shared their expensive vehicles and fancy apartments with the college players coming up, encouraging the younger guys to join them as pros.

Roy transformed himself into the best player of this illustrious hometown bunch, past and present. He joined Crawford as the only players from Seattle to average 20 points or more per game during an NBA season, with Roy pulling the feat twice (22.6, 21.5) to Crawford's once (20.6).

Seattle's influence over the NBA during the 2009-10 season was comprehensive and impressive: Roy gained All-Star status for a third time, Crawford earned his Sixth Man of the Year award, and Brooks accepted the newly created Most Improved Player honor.

Roy remained atop this elite Northwest group by developing his basketball gifts to the fullest, while borrowing little nuances when he could from the others to supplement his skills.

"I would come home in the summer and he worked out at one end of the gym and I worked out at the other end," Terry said of Roy. "He would be watching. He would see the drills I was using and he would use them."

Roy, as everyone found out, learned how to play in the shadows while casting a sizeable one of his own. ❖

TIM LINCECUM
The Big-League Arm

Tim Lincecum was this skinny pitcher with a powerful right arm. He was an intriguing if not unconventional big-league prospect from the University of Washington. Entering the Amateur Baseball Draft, scouts informed Lincecum that he was likely a top-five pick, possibly the first guy to go.

On June 6, 2006, however, team after team retreated from Lincecum in the first round, unwilling to invest in quirky. While he played a golf round at Redmond's Willows Run Golf Course with a cell phone tucked in his pocket, the Kansas City Royals, Colorado Rockies, Tampa Bay Rays, Pittsburgh Pirates, his hometown Seattle Mariners, Detroit Tigers, Los Angeles Dodgers, Cincinnati Reds and Baltimore Orioles passed on him in favor of others. Lincecum didn't find a pro baseball home until the San Francisco Giants, sensing a bargain pick-up, took him with the 10th selection.

Lincecum's lowered draft position cost him anywhere from $1 million to $4 million in a signing bonus, but everything else worked in his favor. The return on him was immediate and huge for the Giants. All torque and supreme confidence, he advanced to the big leagues within 11 months of his draft selection, pitching in just 13 minor-league games for Single-A Salem-Keizer (Oregon), Single-A San Jose and Triple-A Fresno.

Lincecum received the National League Cy Young Award in his second and third seasons. He earned four consecutive All-Star Game selections. He helped pitch

> ## No other Seattle-raised baseball player experienced as much immediate success as the limber 5-foot-11, 174-pound Lincecum.

San Francisco to three World Series championships. He threw no-hitters in his fifth and sixth seasons. While others weren't sure about him at first, he never doubted his big-league ability.

"You have to have arrogance on the mound," Lincecum said. "I'm pretty cocky, though it's more confidence than anything."

No other Seattle-raised baseball player — Floyd Bannister, Jeff Heath, Fred Hutchinson, Bill North, John Olerud or Ron Santo — experienced as much immediate success as the limber 5-foot-11, 174-pound Lincecum. Others received All-Star Game selections (all of the above except North), two won World Series titles (North, Olerud), another captured an American League batting title (Olerud) and one landed in the Hall of Fame (Santo). But none had as many overall accolades as Lincecum, making him the city's greatest homegrown big-leaguer.

"It's pretty impressive for a guy his size to be so over-powering," Bannister said. "He definitely throws hard and impressed me with how good his breaking ball was."

Some scouts had registered concern over Lincecum's slight stature, his unconventional whip-like delivery and his dependence on the breaking ball. Others were put off by his propensity to play up his skater-boy and stoner image, which was further validated by his shoulder-length hair with the Giants early on — longest

> ## Lincecum was the seventh pitcher selected in the draft and five of the six taken ahead of him were each at least four inches taller and 15-20 pounds heavier.

in the Majors — and his 2009 citation for misdemeanor marijuana possession during an Interstate 5 traffic stop in Vancouver, Wash.

Owning the top pick, the Royals had veteran scout and former big-league pitcher Greg Smith sit in the stands and chart pitches at nearly every 2006 UW game that involved Lincecum. For a game at USC, Kansas City brought in a large collection of front-office executives and scouts to look over the Huskies standout. A Royals assistant general manager stood in the shadows and watched Lincecum throw at Oregon State.

Kansas City did intense homework and still passed. The once pitching-rich franchise previously relied on Bret Saberhagen, a player with a slight build and big arm similar to Lincecum's, to take them to the World Series a couple of times. Yet like everyone else holding an elite pick that summer, Kansas City turned to a pitcher with a bigger physique, in this case 6-foot-5, 220-pound Luke Hochevar from Tennessee. Lincecum was the seventh pitcher selected in the draft and five of the six taken ahead of him were each at least four inches taller and 15-20 pounds heavier.

After passing on Lincecum, it wasn't surprising that the Mariners, in the midst of making several personnel gaffes, overhauled their front-office staff and scouting department. They had a potential Cy Young Award winner and World Series hero in their own backyard, and didn't recognize it. Lincecum was cognizant that Seattle's big-league franchise wasn't interested in him, but he was amenable to playing for the local team.

"It would be really nice, close to home, convenient for my dad, to be a local kid who made it," Lincecum said.

On June 16, 2012, six years after he was drafted, Lincecum pitched in his hometown for the first time as a big-leaguer. It wasn't a glorious return. His velocity was down and his pinpoint control was missing, and his big-league career had tailed off some. On a cold, damp night at Safeco before a crowd of 30,589, he lasted just five-plus innings and took the loss in a 7-4 decision to the Mariners. Lincecum, however, went to the bullpen for the postseason that year, righted himself and helped bring the Giants a second World Series championship in three years, beating the Detroit Tigers.

Coming to the UW from Renton's Liberty High School, Lincecum was the first player named Pacific-10 Pitcher of the Year and Freshman of the Year in the same season. He led the NCAA in strikeouts with 199 in his final season as a junior and finished as the Pac-10's all-time strikeout leader with 491.

At the original Tubby Graves Field, a Spartan-like ballpark with scenic views of Lake Washington yet utilizing primitive bleacher seats and Sani-Can restrooms, the pitcher's outings often were treated like rock concerts. Warming up, Lincecum had nearly 100 people milling around him, with curious fans snapping off distracting flashbulb photos, multiple TV camera crews trying to shoot him and diligent big-league scouts watching each delivery.

Lincecum was blessed with a fastball that ran in the low to mid-90s and he developed a wicked change-up once in the majors, but his pitching approach at the UW was to use his breaking ball almost exclusively. "I love the curveball so much, it's my bread and butter," Lincecum said at the time. "I'd throw it every pitch if I could."

Scouts admittedly were put off by this preference, looking at potential arm problems. "He dominates but there is concern that he uses his curve a lot and he could break down later," a San Diego Padres scout warned.

What those guys didn't factor in enough was Lincecum's uncanny physical and mental composition. His arm was so resilient it didn't require ice after games, rare for any pitcher at any level of baseball. Lincecum was so strong he regularly walked on his hands, entertaining college teammates. If pushed, he could do more pushups than any of them. Then there was his zany side. If pitching hadn't worked out, Lincecum could have turned to the comedy club circuit. A master impersonator, he did computer voices, mimicked "Lord of the Rings" characters and did physical routines reminiscent of Jim Carrey.

Huskies teammates called him "Seabiscuit" or just "Biscuit" before they settled on "The Freak." Of his ability to entertain others, Lincecum said, "I have a weird talent for that. I just don't care what people think. It makes them laugh. Most people call me a freak of nature."

Lincecum had a college ride to match his offbeat nicknames. He drove a 1990 Ford Ranger XLT, nick-named "the Silver Bullet." It had a silver shell casing protruding from the license plate. The rig should have been taken out and shot. It had dents, scrapes and rust all around, a broken front parking light, damaged grille and busted-out keyhole. The brakes locked on him on a slick Renton road one night and the pitcher drove into a fence and a stump. The well-worn Ford was broken into three times and three compact-disc players and a backpack were stolen.

Of his ability to entertain others, Lincecum said, "I have a weird talent for that. I just don't care what people think. It makes them laugh. Most people call me a freak of nature."

Well aware of his impending resources, Lincecum parked the truck wherever he wanted at the UW and kept the campus cops busy. At $55 a pop, he ran up more than $3,500 in university parking tickets, more than the vehicle's Blue Book value. Yet the truck stayed in the minors. Lincecum soon was driving a Mercedes CLK55 purchased from Giants teammate Dave Roberts.

Lincecum was drafted twice previously — in the 48th round by the Cubs out of high school and 42nd by the Indians in 2005 and offered a reported $700,000 by Cleveland — but he wisely waited. He excelled against top-level amateur competition in the Cape Cod League.

He also got a headache and a scare on the East Coast. In his third start for a Massachusetts team, Lincecum took a liner off the side of his head. He lost consciousness for a second but not his sense of humor. He was taken off the field on a stretcher, carted off to a hospital for a CAT-scan examination. Borrowing a line from the film Any Given Sunday, the dazed Lincecum wisecracked, "Don't drop me, guys, I'm worth a million bucks."

It was way more than that. Once he was carried off the field on the shoulders of his Giants teammates after the 2010 World Series, Lincecum, who lived for a time in a downtown Seattle condo in unit 2806 at 1920 4th Ave., signed a two-year, $23 million contract extension, followed by another two-year, $40 million deal in 2012, and yet another two-year $35 million package for 2014.

Lincecum, who cut his hair and grew a wispy mustache as he became an older and more conservative player, is not only Seattle's most successful homegrown big-leaguer, he is by far its richest. Any draft-day slight has long been forgotten. ❖

WALTER JONES
The Building Block

Walter Jones typically broke from the Seattle Seahawks huddle without clapping, did a little hop to get into rhythm and plopped into a football stance, using his left hand to steady himself. And then the fun began as the offensive tackle, with a perfect blend of mobility, strength and balance, slammed into defensive players like a souped-up bulldozer, shoving people eight to 10 yards off the ball and opening gaping holes.

"It was like wrestling a bear for three hours," defensive end Patrick Kerney, both an opponent and teammate for Jones, memorably told reporters.

With his streamlined 6-foot-5, 315-pound physique, Jones was so proficient at left tackle he graded out with a perfect game against the Oakland Raiders in 2001, an incredible feat for such a demanding position. He permitted just 23 career sacks during 5,703 passing plays, or fewer than two per year. He was called for only nine career holding penalties, obviously going some seasons without one.

He was selected to the Pro Bowl on nine occasions, more than any other Seahawks player (defensive tackle Cortez Kennedy is next with eight). He was the most dominant player on Seattle's first Super Bowl team that met the Pittsburgh Steelers in Detroit in 2006. And eight years later, to no one's surprise, he was a first-ballot Pro Football Hall of Fame selection.

As the sixth overall pick of the 1997 draft, Jones spent a dozen NFL seasons with the Seahawks and remains the most physically overwhelming pro football player to come though the city. He was a true superstar for Seattle, someone who had an impact on pro football similar to that of George Wilson, Hugh McElhenny, Steve Largent and Richard Sherman, yet without their finesse, bold headlines or the ball in his hands. When he ended his career, officially walking away on April 29, 2010, Jones was labeled by John Madden and others throughout the league as the best of his NFL generation. Becoming the greatest left tackle anywhere was something Jones strived for in Seattle.

"It just depends on who you talk to, but I know I went out there and gave my best," Jones said. "It felt good. Sometimes I dominated, and that happened more as the years went on. It just took a couple of years to learn the game of football and what was going on around me. Sometimes I felt I could just overpower a guy."

Jones took a circuitous route to NFL superiority, both in geography and concept. He initially was a tight end from tiny Aliceville, Ala., a country town of 2,500

> As the sixth overall pick of the 1997 draft, Jones spent a dozen NFL seasons with the Seahawks and remains the most physically overwhelming pro football player to come though the city.

located near the Mississippi state line. Running drag routes over the middle, he caught the occasional pass for the Aliceville High School Yellow Jackets, none more important than his scoring grab that won a 1992 playoff game. College recruiters throughout the South knew all about this hulking guy, including those from nearby Alabama, just 45 miles away.

Jones was content with his pass-catching existence. However, Aliceville High coach Pierce McIntosh, who once played in the CFL, saw something else as he watched the oversized kid grow and mature. He pulled Jones aside and told him that he should strongly consider playing left tackle in college because it was a glorified and well-compensated NFL position.

McIntosh handed him an instructional tape featuring Anthony Munoz, recently retired from the Cincinnati Bengals and widely considered the most accomplished offensive lineman in pro football history. Jones soon was imitating Munoz's every move.

"Coach said, 'You could be a tight end, but you've got the feet to be a left tackle,' " Jones said with his soft Southern accent. "Coach said, 'With those feet you're a millionaire walking around broke.' I didn't know what that meant. Coach said, 'You could be one of the best ever at left tackle.' He gave me an Anthony Munoz tape, an offensive lineman tape, and I watched it every day. It showed how to get into a stance. I just did what Anthony Munoz said. I figured if I'm going to do this, I'm going to be the best at it."

Jones had stops at Holmes Community College (Miss.) and Florida State, choosing the latter over Alabama because: 1) It was more of a passing team, important for showcasing his blocking potential; 2) he wanted to get away from home and not be constantly pestered for game tickets from everyone in Aliceville, and 3) as he said jokingly, "The Florida State check was bigger."

He became an Anthony Munoz clone. He alternately lined up at tight end and left tackle for Holmes. He concentrated on the interior-line position only for a single, Sugar Bowl-bound season with the Seminoles, enough to become a coveted pro prospect.

Ten years later, Jones was a highly polished player who found himself in Super Bowl XL, which was a total blur to him. He was surprised how quickly the week, and the game itself, came and went. He was sequestered from all the outside hoopla in Detroit and later wished he had caught glimpses of it. On Feb. 5, 2006, Jones remembered the Seahawks making things happen in the third quarter before the game got out away from them in the fourth and they lost 21-10.

His most vivid recollection of the biggest football outing of his career was an expletive-laced exchange in the second half between Seattle quarterback Matt Hasselbeck and Pittsburgh linebacker Joey Porter. This came after Seahawks tight end Jerramy Stevens and Porter publicly denigrated each other's abilities at mid-week.

"In the third quarter, Hasselbeck had to say something," Jones said. "Jerramy blocked

Walter Jones was a nine-time Pro Bowl selection.

down on Porter on a play and Hasselbeck said, 'Good block, Jerramy!' All of a sudden, Porter went into a rage. He went off on Hasselbeck. Porter wouldn't stop. Hasselbeck was talking back to him. I said to Hasselbeck, 'You can't win that battle.' It went on for three more plays, with Porter talking and saying all kinds of things. I can't tell you what they said. Hasselbeck finally came up to me and said, 'You're right, I can't win this battle.'"

A lot of overmatched NFL defensive linemen felt the same way when meeting Jones in the trenches. The Seahawks player was vulnerable only during his first three seasons while learning the trade. He experienced early difficulty against Kansas City defensive end Derrick Thomas, not an unusual occurrence for anyone dealing with the now-deceased Pro Bowl player. Jones had what he considered his worst pro performance against a journeyman player, San Diego Chargers defensive end Raylee Johnson, blaming his own casual mindset.

"I kept watching him on film and I said, 'He's not all that,' " Jones said. "He kicked my butt. He gave me all types of moves. I learned that day that I wasn't going to disrespect any guy in the league again."

Even as a high first-rounder, Jones was overshadowed in the NFL draft. He wasn't the first offensive lineman selected; that was Orlando Pace, who went to the St. Louis Rams with the No. 1 overall pick. Jones wasn't even the first Seahawks draftee that year; that was cornerback Shawn Springs, who was taken by Seattle with the third overall choice.

"I wasn't a household name," Jones said. "Orlando Pace had all the accolades. I was a no-name. Some coaches knew who I was. I just wanted to get in the door."

Once he walked through it, Jones was so good he missed three consecutive Seahawks training camps as

a contract holdout and each time he showed up right before or after the opener and turned in a Pro Bowl season. Jones stayed in shape with customized personal workouts that went against convention, something his high school coach introduced to him. Jones stood in a park not far from his off-season home near Huntsville, Ala., and pushed his brother-in-law's Cadillac Escalade 20 to 25 yards, doing this 10 times, to build up his lower-body strength.

"I had to be ready because they were going to put me out there anyway," Jones said of the regular season while dismissing camp participation. "At the middle of the season my body felt good. I didn't go through that banging in camp."

Jones, who met Munoz just once at a Super Bowl awards ceremony, was a fairly stoic player in the heat of the battle. He dominated guys without a word. He was no trash-talker, no Hasselbeck on the field. Jones didn't feel the need to harangue opponents. Yet on the way to the Super Bowl, he let loose with a rare angry outburst in the middle of the NFC Championship Game, feeling wronged and blistering defensive end Mike Rucker of the Carolina Panthers for his actions.

"I blocked him and had my hands inside him and he tried to drive me down," Jones said. "He had my arms and I was falling and he was trying to collapse on me, so his body would fall on my wrist. He was trying to break my wrist. I got upset. I swore and cussed at him. He said he wasn't trying to break my wrist. But he knew what he was doing."

Jones stayed relatively healthy, missing only four games for medical reasons as a rookie because of a high-ankle sprain until his luck ran out. Late in a 2008 game against the Washington Redskins, during a lost season, he came off the field after the Seahawks used the two-minute drill to move the ball down the field, turned

to fellow offensive tackle Sean Locklear and told him his left knee felt funny. It was the beginning of the end.

Jones played one more game, against the Dallas Cowboys four days later on Thanksgiving, giving up a couple of rare sacks in a 34-9 blowout loss and he was done. Trying to overcompensate for his damaged knee, he felt pain shoot through his hip. He had micro-fracture surgery and follow-up arthroscopic surgery, and sat out the 2009 season with hopes of playing again before giving into retirement.

Jones, who kept an apartment two and a half miles from the Seahawks training headquarters at E215 1131 Lake Washington Blvd. N. in Renton, left a huge hole to fill. Seahawks coach Mike Holmgren called him the greatest offensive player he had coached. Hasselbeck's quarterback numbers fell noticeably without his left tackle. Running back Shaun Alexander, the 2005 NFL Most Valuable Player, was let go, deemed a byproduct of Jones' blocking rather than a singular force. The Seahawks ran four guys through the left-tackle position that first season without Jones, unable to find an adequate replacement.

Jones was so good
he missed three consecutive
Seahawks training camps
as a contract holdout
and each time he showed up
right before or after
the opener and turned in
a Pro Bowl season.

The franchise retired Jones' No. 71, the third of four jerseys pulled from service by the Seahawks, which included Largent's (80), Cortez Kennedy (96) and the loyal fan base (12). Gov. Christine Gregoire declared "Walter Jones Day" across the state. An eight-foot-high bronze statue of Jones was unveiled outside a Seahawks-styled restaurant at Sea Tac Airport.

In 2014, he was nominated for the Pro Football Hall of Fame on the first ballot. Jones embraced the moment, even after largely avoiding media contact and public interaction during his Seahawks career. He didn't have to open any more holes now, just his mouth.

"I think a lot of guys in Seattle just wanted to see if Walt could talk that long, if he could give a 17-minute speech," said Jones, notoriously media-shy as a player. "I didn't do it before because of my mentality: I had work to do."

Jones walked away from his sport just 35 days before Mariners slugger Ken Griffey Jr. gave up on his, forcing Seattle to scramble to find another superstar to call its own and begin another era of sporting enlightenment. Whoever came next needed to be all in on the big tackle's approach to greatness.

"I just wanted to play and be the best ever," Jones said. ❖

Top 10 Seattle Hall of Famers

1. Walter Jones, Seahawks
2. Lenny Wilkens, Sonics (player, coach)
3. Steve Largent, Seahawks
4. Hugh McElhenny, 49ers, Giants, Lions
5. Randy Johnson, Mariners
6. Ron Santo, Cubs, White Sox
7. Cortez Kennedy, Seahawks
8. Don James, UW
9. JoAnne Carner, LPGA
10. Al Hostak, boxing

ALAN HINTON

Seattle's Mr. Soccer

A white-haired Alan Hinton, 40 years removed from his English playing days and 20 years past his final Sounders coaching job, emerged from a suburban Seattle coffee shop. A young couple stopped him and swooned.

Even as time banished him to old age, Hinton remained soccer royalty, forever revered by the masses. He's the one who legitimized the game in Seattle, held it together when others tried to ruin it and helped turn the city into the American beacon for this wildly popular global sporting pursuit.

Hinton brought a first-division presence to the Northwest that has never wavered. He remains Seattle's most influential soccer figure, with his stature exceeding that of Adrian Hanauer, the current Sounders general manager and part-owner responsible for infusing Hollywood money into the franchise; John Best, the Sounders' original English import and first coach; and Clint Dempsey, a forward and transplanted Texan who supplies the Sounders with lofty World Cup credentials.

"Right from the start, I thought Seattle was the model franchise," Hinton said. "The uniforms looked so luxurious, with those white with aqua shirts and aqua shorts. I thought the Kingdome was unreal. I really thought this was the place to be — and it proved to be right."

Hinton intended to come to the U.S. for only six months. He was huge in his English homeland, but heartbroken over the death of his soccer-playing, nine-year-old son Matthew from cancer. He needed a temporary refuge. He discovered a permanent home.

After beating the Sounders at the Kingdome as a Dallas player, Vancouver player/assistant coach and Tulsa coach, Hinton was rightfully hired to coach them. He brought the 10-year North American Soccer League franchise some of its greatest glories in his three seasons in charge, among them a 25-7 record and average attendance of 24,247 in 1980 and a Soccer Bowl appearance against the New York Cosmos in 1982.

Hinton brought in European players still in their prime, such as Roger Davies, Alan Hudson and Tommy Hutchinson, as opposed to marquee names well past it, among them English World Cup legends Geoff Hurst and Bobby Moore, who filled out the earliest Sounders lineups.

He spoke with surprisingly more candor than Seattle's other top sports personalities. He was the one leading the Sounders into the bar on the road for a few beers to steady their nerves after a long flight. And, when combining his high-spirited nature with misguided ownership, he turned up at the center of one of the city's most bizarre athletic moments.

> Hinton brought a first-division presence to the Northwest that has never wavered. He remains Seattle's most influential soccer figure.

Hinton was fired for no good reason. His previous game was the Soccer Bowl. He was hugely popular with the fan base. In 1983, the franchise was sold to former NFL player Bruce Anderson, whose first order of business was to get rid of his highly visible coach at a bar in downtown Seattle and second was to ridicule the game at his ensuing press conference.

From the podium, Anderson told everyone that "lad" was what he called his dog and "pitch" was what came off of his Christmas tree, and those words were off-limits now as he Americanized the game locally. Hinton's ouster was part of the cultural restructuring. The coach's wife, Joy, wasn't informed of his firing until sitting and hearing it at the news conference, which Hinton didn't attend. It was all very strange and destructive.

"The day he fired me, Anderson, all 6-foot-5 of him, was standing against a wall in the bar, crying like a baby," Hinton said. "I went up to him and said, 'Come on Bruce, you've got a press conference to go to.' I was consoling him. That's the God's honest truth."

Anderson was gone seven months later, the once-proud Seattle franchise a few months after that. As everything crumbled, Hinton was even asked back as coach. The Sounders died for many reasons: A crippling recession, a deteriorating relationship with the local soccer community and, above all, the owner's buffoonery, which included Hinton's nonsensical firing.

After coaching the Vancouver Whitecaps and watching the rest of the NASL disappear in 1984, Hinton arrived at a soccer crossroads. He was offered the Aston Villa coaching job in the English Premier League. He had been a prominent first-division player for 13 years for Wolverhampton, Nottingham Forest and Derby County, plus a national-team player during that time, making him a natural candidate for the position. He could have made a heroic return home, but he couldn't pull himself away from the Seattle area. He said no.

"I know I was ready," Hinton said of joining Aston Villa. "I thought about it. I'd learned how to handle the media. I would have been accepted as the local boy. That's been my only regret."

Instead, Hinton went about restoring pro soccer in the Northwest. He coached the Tacoma Stars of the Major Indoor Soccer League for six seasons until 1990, reaching the championship game once.

He was brought in by Best, the first Sounders coach, then the Stars general manager and formerly a third-division English player, to help establish the indoor franchise and fired when those two butted heads over team control.

"I was always my own man," Hinton said. "I didn't tolerate fools. I didn't care for big shots. I like regular folks."

All along, Hinton kept an eye on a Sounders reincarnation, even purchasing the trademark rights to the name. He paid $1,000 in legal fees to procure it and sold it eight years later in 1994 to former Microsoft executive Scott Oki for $20,000 when a Seattle A-League team bearing that name was established, playing second-division soccer as a placeholder for something better.

"I didn't do it for profit," said Hinton, who became the new Sounders president and appointed himself as coach for one season. "I protected the name. I knew it had a value to the community."

Hinton and other former Sounders coaches and players also immersed themselves for several years as leaders in the mammoth Lake Washington Youth Soccer Association, rekindling lost relationships and developing local players. These were crucial steps in making pro soccer relevant in the city again.

The Sounders resumed playing as a Major League Soccer team in 2009 — 26 years after the previous big-league version folded. They were backed by an ownership consortium that involved movie producer Joe Roth, comedian/actor Drew Carey, Microsoft co-founder Paul Allen and Hanauer. The team was more popular than ever, drawing 43,734 on average to home games by its sixth season, while using quaint traditions such as the March to the Match and the chanting, bellowing, end-zone-based Emerald City Supporters to build a loyal following.

Hinton's time had come and gone as a pro soccer coach, but he still had a hand in just about everything else related to the newest version of Sounders. He turned up in the team radio booth, saying outlandish things until he made one undiplomatic comment too many and wasn't rehired. He still was asked to be a regular commentator on local TV and national radio, offering his colorful expertise and analysis. He remained a regular visitor to practice, welcomed by the coaches and players alike who valued his unfiltered input.

Hinton also could be found mixing with those adoring Seattle soccer followers at all times. Even now, he enters local bars and other business establishments as an official Sounders goodwill ambassador, which is a title he's always held whether asked or not. Fans similar to that coffee-shop couple instantly recognize him and want to rub up against the affable Englishman they call Mr. Soccer, the Grandfather of Soccer or the Crazy Old Fox, and he always wants to return the favor. This is where he belongs and these are his people and this is his team.

"Every time I go to a game, I look at the crowd behind the goal and I'm so proud," Hinton said of the ECS. "Sometimes I go sing with them." ❖

RON CROCKETT

The Man Who Saved Horse Racing

Ron Crockett set a white, three-ring binder on the table, one filled three inches thick with newspaper and magazine articles, editorials and cartoons. Among them were biting criticisms and lampoons of Crockett's efforts to build a new horse-racing facility for the Seattle area in the 1990s.

Two decades after first reading it, Crockett thumbed through the unflattering paperwork again with a sneer. He clearly was irritated one more time. Yet all of those dissenting opinions, even if inaccurate, served an important purpose: They made Crockett mad enough to become the man who saved horse racing in Seattle.

When race tracks were shutting down one after another around the country, the strong-willed Crockett came up with a new one a half-hour south of Seattle, Auburn's glistening Emerald Downs, which served as a replacement for one of the notable casualties, suburban Renton's 59-year-old Longacres. All people had to do was ridicule or doubt him, or both.

"I just got more and more determined," Crockett said of his critics. "It pissed me off, to be honest. It spurred me on."

Crockett, for his sport-saving heroics, remains one of Seattle's most influential horse-racing figures, joining Joseph Gottstein, who built and opened Longacres in 1933; Morrie Alhadeff, Gottstein's son-in-law who operated the Renton track for two decades until he closed it in 1992 after selling the property to the Boeing Company; Gary Stevens, a Hall of Fame jockey who won more than 500 times at Longacres; and Gary Baze, a Northwest rider who finished first more than 3,500 times in his career, which included lengthy runs at both Emerald Downs and Longacres.

Crockett rode Emerald Downs to the finish line like a jockey flailing away on a thoroughbred with a riding crop. He saw himself as the only solution, putting up $10 million of his own money while collecting $12 million from fellow track investors and arranging for loans to cover the remaining $60 million. He had no use for anyone who opposed him, permanently banning horseman Joel McCann from the new track for doing just that.

"What my baseline is, is everything is black and white to me; there is no gray," Crockett said. "I either like something or I don't. I'm not on middle ground on anything. People like me or they don't because of that. That's fine with me."

Emerald Downs began racing on June 20, 1996, following 80 site considerations, 40 court hearings and a couple of pestering lawsuits. The new track went into operation as tribal casinos and the newly introduced state lottery took an increasingly larger chunk of the annual gambling profits each year.

Crockett was a logical choice to lead this modern-day horse-racing rescue. Not only was he one of Longacres'

> ## Crockett, for his sport-saving heroics, remains Seattle's most influential horse-racing figure.

leading owners with 63 horses in his stables at the time, Crockett made his fortune by founding and selling off Tramco, which he built into the nation's leading aviation repair and maintenance company, giving him endless financial resources.

Steady cash flow, however, was never part of Crockett's Renton upbringing. His father was a service station mechanic and his mother a Boeing riveter who together made ends meet, but not much more. They lived in a tiny house not far from Longacres. At 12, Crockett worked for Pacific Auto Supply, grinding head gaskets in the back room. Two years later, he made deliveries for the same business, which was noteworthy because this happened two years before he was old enough to apply for a driver's license. Crockett was motivated to improve his economic standing and gain people's respect at all times.

"I really, really enjoyed coming from nothing," he said.

At Renton High School, Crockett was a visible, confident figure. He was class president for each of his junior and senior years. He started for two seasons at guard on the basketball team, playing alongside George Reed, who would become the Canadian Football League's all-time leading rusher, and he appeared in the state tournament during his final year. He was a decent student with big dreams.

Crockett still didn't have enough money to attend college, but he found a way. He received a University of Washington academic scholarship from former Huskies football player Jim McCurdy after spotting the opportunity posted on a bulletin board. Crockett took advantage to earn an engineering degree, land a job at Boeing and repeatedly show how smart he was.

"He was a mathematical genius," said Boone Kirkman, the former heavyweight boxer who graduated from Renton High six years after Crockett in 1963.

Crockett was first introduced to the horses as a high school senior while visiting a friend who worked at Longacres. He won $17 on his first wager, betting on a horse named Stuck Up, and was hooked. Several years later he claimed his first thoroughbred for $4,000, Tapper Blue, and became a notable national horse player, eventually entering one of his impressive animals in the Breeders' Cup and winning with another at Arlington Park near Chicago.

Professionally, Crockett was a risk-taker. After hearing someone say he needed to have a row of airline seats refurbished, Crockett, still employed by Boeing, volunteered his own company. Just one problem: He didn't have a company. Crockett soon had five employees and eventually 2,500. He mixed and matched replacement parts. He increased the instant maintenance operation from one hangar to three at Mukilteo's Paine Field. After 18 years in 1988, he sold Tramco for around $50 million to B.F. Goodrich, while making other outside investments to generate even greater wealth, and turned his full attention to horse racing and its changing landscape.

"Nothing has seemed hard or difficult for me," he claimed.

Emerald Downs was guided by someone who did things his own way. Crockett, who was 75 in 2014, maintains his health by performing 1,200 sit-ups and lifting light weights twice daily. Even as a senior citizen, he takes no medication. He quit drinking alcohol for good on May 11, 1978, coming to this steadfast decision after taking Frontier Airlines clients out to dinner, downing one too many J&B scotches and becoming violently ill at home.

For the longest time, Crockett was content to live, even as a rich man, in a plain 1,800-square-foot house at 413 N. Weller St. in Renton before he and his wife,

Emerald Downs, with Longacres Mile entries shown here rounding the first turn, opened in 1996.

Wanda, moved to a spacious Capitol Hill mansion. He still drives a Toyota 4Runner with 320,000 miles to and from the track with no immediate plans to part with it.

Others outside of the racing world have experienced the benevolent side of Crockett, too. He annually donates to two or three dozen different causes, everything from police funds to his former high school. Overall, he has given nearly $8 million to all departments at the UW,

Emerald Downs founder Ron Crockett surrounds himself with family members.

track and written by someone else – because he didn't personally know the author. He never took a salary.

Finally, in late 2014, Crockett announced he was backing away and selling track operations to the Muckleshoot Tribe, which a dozen years earlier had purchased the property. While others were concerned about Emerald Downs' staying power under new leadership in a seemingly stagnant racing climate, Crockett insisted the track was in good hands. He was confident it would remain one of those that, as a stable regional facility, would always be in business, following the racing heavyweights, such as Churchill Downs and Belmont, and the popular boutique tracks at Saratoga and Del Mar.

including $2 million for the new Husky Stadium, and has funneled more than $2 million to Seattle Children's Hospital.

Crockett built Emerald Downs into a new-age track that was family-friendly and did its best to survive the teetering gambling climate, briefly making it profitable 10 years after the facility opened before the economic downturn of the 2000s slowed momentum considerably. Even while losing money, Crockett remained loyal to his workforce, refusing to lay anyone off or diminish race-day track services. His temper could be fearsome if things weren't done properly, with his over-the-top anger once directed at me for a *P-I* story critical of the

Crockett said the infusion of Muckleshoot money would elevate Emerald Downs to a more competitive level. He envisioned purses increasing from $98,000 on the daily average to $120,000 and eventually bringing more people back to the sport. He also said negotiations of the sale would be fairly simple if certain provisions were met.

"I would take zero [money] if they would pick up the debt and keep it going in the future," he said then.

To the end of his long ride down the suburban backstretch, Crockett was still in the saddle, trying to save horse racing in Seattle. No one was making fun or doubting him this time. Or betting against him. ❖

FELIX HERNANDEZ

The Perfect Pitcher

Felix Hernandez was a Venezuelan kid with a powerful right arm that was no secret. Just 16, he was a Latin American prodigy, faced with determining his pro baseball future. His final choices were the New York Yankees, Atlanta Braves and Seattle Mariners, which was a lot like deciding among a fastball, a curveball and a changeup.

Hernandez went with the off-speed stuff. He turned down the more glamorous pinstripes and tomahawks in favor of a mid-market franchise fresh out of proven superstars following the exodus of Randy Johnson, Ken Griffey Jr. and Alex Rodriguez. In 2002, the baseball organization that waved the more attractive minor-league itinerary at him won his services.

"I didn't want to go to New York; I wasn't going to play there," Hernandez explained. "The Mariners said I was going to the United States right away. New York said I was going to go to the Dominican Republic. I thought Seattle would give me more opportunity."

A dozen years later, Hernandez is a sporting institution in his adopted American League home-town, pledging abject loyalty to it like no other Seattle superstar before him. He signed a pair of contract extensions with the Mariners even though the franchise was struggling to win and he easily could have gone

> A dozen years later, Hernandez is a sporting institution in his adopted American League hometown, pledging abject loyalty to it like no other Seattle superstar before him.

elsewhere, the latter deal worth $175 million and locking him up through 2019. He cried telling fans and his bosses how much he cared about the place. He couldn't fathom playing anywhere else.

"The general manager [Jack Zduriencik] and I, we can talk about a lot of things," Hernandez said. "The fans, they are the greatest fans in baseball. In this city, people are not going to walk all over you. They're going to say hi. Lots of respect. If you're happy in a job, why leave it?"

Oh yeah, Hernandez has been every bit as good as people predicted. He got on the Hall of Fame fast track early and stayed there, becoming arguably the greatest pitcher in the American League. He has five All-Star selections. He has a Cy Young Award with the promise of more. He pitched baseball's 23rd and most recent perfect game in history.

He has become Seattle sporting royalty, earning the nickname "King Felix" from the USSMariner.com website as a minor-leaguer and watching it evolve into a cult following when he reached the majors. Beginning in 2011, the Mariners started selling $30 King's Court tickets for each of his Safeco Field starts, supplying fans with a seat at the end of the left-field foul line in Section 150, a bright-yellow T-shirt that now has a silhouetted image of Hernandez celebrating the final out of his perfect game and an equally bright yellow

Felix Hernandez, right, greets former Mariners teammate Adrian Beltre in 2013.

"I kind of like it," Hernandez said. "King's Court is the best place. It's unbelievable. You hear it everywhere. They yell 'K, K, K' and I hear it, and I try to do it."

That Hernandez and Seattle would end up together was destined all along. As a young teen, he didn't have a favorite team, but his first pair of Nike baseball shoes was a signature Ken Griffey Jr. model. He watched just about anyone play on TV, but he was totally enamored with Mariners pitching ace and fellow Venezuelan Freddy Garcia, someone who came to Seattle as the centerpiece of the Mariners' 1998 Randy Johnson trade. "Freddy was my favorite pitcher, my idol," Hernandez pointed out.

After signing for $710,000 on July 4, 2002, Hernandez was brought to Safeco Field for three days. He threw a bullpen pitching session. He watched games from the stands. He met Garcia for the first time on the trip, plus Venezuelan shortstop Carlos Guillen. He would follow Garcia around during the next two Mariners spring trainings, sharing meals with him and soaking up everything.

By the time Hernandez reached the majors in 2005, Garcia had been traded away but the new Mariners pitcher wouldn't let anyone in Seattle forget him. Hernandez wore Garcia's No. 34 after briefly pulling on 59, first calling Freddy to ask his permission to use it. He wore a baggy uniform shirt and pants, same as Garcia. He later won an AL earned-run-average championship, same as Garcia.

Hernandez drew 34,213 curious fans to his Safeco Field debut, throwing five-hit ball over eight innings and beating Minnesota 1-0 while leading Twins manager Ron Gardenhire to remark, "I don't think we're talking about poise here. I think we're talking about a 97 mile-an-hour fastball with a curveball from hell."

placard with the letter "K" plastered across it. Up to 1,000 people fill up this designated rooting section. Some wear foam crowns and garish robes. All get on their feet whenever their favorite pitcher has two strikes on an opponent and loudly plead for the strikeout, furiously waving those neon signs.

One month into his big-league career, the now 19-year-old Hernandez went head to head with the legendary Johnson, who was two weeks shy of his 42nd birthday and pitching for the Yankees, coaxing a nostalgic sellout crowd of 46,240 to Safeco. The Big Unit came away with a 2-0 victory, but everyone was impressed with the youngster's sizzling performance in a pressurized atmosphere. "Doc Gooden was like that at a young age," New York manager Joe Torre noted.

If there was a harsh learning curve for Hernandez, it involved his eating habits. He let his weight get away from him during his second Mariners season. He was supposed to play at 230 pounds but acknowledged he had ballooned to 246. With a David Wells type gut hanging out, Hernandez actually was closer to 260. The added bulk was a big reason he struggled through 2006 with a 12-14 record. He dropped to 226 in the off-season. "I'm not 19 anymore, so I've got to be in shape," he said. "I was a little heavy. You learn."

Hernandez still was a big box-office draw throughout his pudginess. Across town, Tim Lincecum was a University of Washington pitching sensation as a senior preparing for his own brilliant big-league career. He didn't have a lot of time to be a spectator back then, but he had to see what all the excitement was at Safeco. "I went to one Mariners game," Lincecum said. "I went to see Felix."

In 2009, Hernandez won 19 of 24 decisions and made his first All-Star appearance. A year later, he captured the Cy Young Award with a pedestrian 13-12 record, the voters noting his abundance of quality starts and lack of run support, an ongoing dilemma. The Mariners posted seven losing seasons during Hernandez's first nine in Seattle, wasting his genius over and over. Baseball analysts everywhere suggested it was time for him to bolt, likely to the Yankees, when scheduled contract negotiations twice came up. Hernandez never flinched or started packing either time.

"It was hard a little bit, but you've got to deal with it," said Hernandez, whose unselfishness with his teammates, the fans, Mariners' staff and media members has made him exceedingly popular. "You have to be a man. You have to do your job."

In his eighth season, Hernandez treated Seattle to a glorious baseball moment, further establishing himself as an elite talent, and encountered an old friend between the lines, immersing himself in sentiment.

On June 15, 2012, in an afternoon game played in bright sunshine at Safeco, he was as overpowering as ever, methodically retiring all 27 Tampa Bay batters he faced for a 1-0 victory and rare perfect game. He struck out 12 batters. He was never in danger of giving up a hit. He went to a three-ball count just three times. He flung his arms into the air when it was all over. He addressed the crowd of 21,889 and told them he had done it for them.

"When I got home that night, I laid on my bed and thought, 'I just pitched a perfect game,' " he said. "I still remember all the pitches and all the counts. I try to do it every game."

On July 24, 2012, Hernandez faced Garcia on the mound for the first time, meeting in New York. It was the King against the Chief. It was one Mariner great against another. It was a 26-year-old pitcher on the rise against a 35-year-old winding down. At Yankee Stadium, they mirrored each other's efforts, both pitching seven-plus innings. Hernandez gave up four hits and two runs, Garcia five hits and three runs. Garcia struck out eight to Hernandez's four, but he was upstaged by the pitching protégé, who walked away with a 4-2 victory.

New York has had its designs on Hernandez, but he firmly belongs to the Northwest. He lived in a house at 9530 NE 1st St. in Bellevue before building another in Clyde Hill; he put his kids in local schools and lives in the area year-round, visiting Venezuela only for a month each year to spend the holidays with his relatives. The Northwest has a firm hold on him.

"He came up here and the fans just love him," said second baseman Robinson Cano, another player who has forsaken New York for Seattle. "How are you supposed to leave when you feel so confident here? I love it here. The fans make you feel so good. They make you feel like you're part of the family."

When asked if he wanted to be known as the best pitcher in baseball, Hernandez cautiously says he wants only to stay healthy. He's been on the disabled list only for a bout with elbow tightness and a sprained ankle. With a sound body, he says good things will come.

He's done everything for the Mariners except win championships, but he's confident that will change soon, especially after the franchise's notable roster upgrades in Cano and others. Seattle has a firm hold on him.

"Who wouldn't want to be here?" Hernandez asked pointedly. ❖

RICHARD SHERMAN

The Street Corner

The first time Seattle encountered him, Richard Sherman was this waifish 18-year-old kid who played for one of the worst college football teams in America, lined up at wide receiver and chose his words carefully. Hey, a guy can change his major, can't he?

Reaffirming that a Stanford education opens a lot of doors, Sherman went for a complete makeover, transforming his football world in almost fairy-tale fashion: Returning to the Northwest for an extended stay, he became a centerpiece for the best team in the NFL in 2013, knocked down passes rather than caught them, and, in building his own brand, engaged people in a running conversation that could veer off in any direction at any time.

With his dynamic play and explosive mouth, Sherman helped lead the Seahawks to a one-sided Super Bowl XLVIII victory over Denver and overnight become one of the most famous people on the planet, offering brashness unmatched by any other Seattle athlete before him, greater than that of the impetuous Gary Payton, Billy Joe Hobert, Jay Buhner and Jeff Heath.

Sherman was admired and scorned for telling everyone exactly what was on his mind, especially the part about him being the greatest cornerback in the game. He did what legendary self-promoters Muhammad Ali and Joe Namath once did. He did what people secretly wished the supremely talented and

maddeningly reticent Ken Griffey Jr. had done. Sherman shared himself almost on cue and became the face of the Seahawks, if not the voice of the NFL.

"I don't mind it," Sherman said of his widespread fame. "It's an honor that people think that way. I don't know if I speak for the entire NFL. Everybody has their voice. But I like giving my opinion. I don't mind being criticized either."

Sherman drew attention to himself by mocking acerbic ESPN-TV personality Skip Bayless to his face on the air; taunting New England Patriots quarterback Tom Brady to his face on the field resulting in the classic Twitter photo "U Mad Bro?" in response to earlier Brady digs and T-shirts made up featuring the quote; rhythmically dancing on the sideline with the team's Sea Gals cheerleaders during a game, and trading take-no-prisoners Twitter barbs with opposing players such as DeAngelo Hall and Patrick Peterson.

Nothing short of sensational since entering the league, Sherman added household name to his resumé following the 2014 NFC title game against San Francisco at Qwest Field. After swatting away a potential game-winning pass in electric fashion, a play later dubbed the "Immaculate Deflection," he let loose in a post-game rant with FOX Sports reporter Erin Andrews, slamming 49ers receiver Michael Crabtree — the intended end-zone target — for previously disrespecting

> With his dynamic play and explosive mouth, Sherman helped lead the Seahawks to a one-sided Super Bowl XLVIII victory over Denver.

him. In the same breath, Sherman offered that exalted assessment of his own football talents, all within earshot of every TV set tuned to the game nationwide. At the team's urging, he later apologized for being so honest. But Sherman had made himself an unforgettable character and there was no turning back.

His lip was set up by the tip, which was somewhat overshadowed by his hyperventilating discourse. Considering what was riding on it, Sherman's game-saver is widely considered the greatest play in Seahawks history, exceeding Marshawn Lynch's Beast Quake playoff run against New Orleans, Jermaine Kearse's game-winning playoff catch against Green Bay, the early-day Jim Zorn and Efren Herrera trickery and Steve Largent's various record-setting and playoff catches.

"Athletically, I've made better plays, but I don't think I've made a bigger play – it got us to the Super Bowl," Sherman said. "I had a feeling I'd get a chance. It was the final drive, cover three, the strong safety was leaned over. I thought I'd get a shot at it. It's where you go with it in that situation."

Sherman's clutch performance was endlessly praised and the ensuing bravado furiously debated over the next two weeks leading up to the Super Bowl, often bringing a discourse about racism and culture. It later landed Sherman, among other places, on the "Jimmy Kimmel Show," on a Harvard panel discussion, at the White House Correspondents dinner and at the ESPY Awards.

Opportunistic President Barack Obama mimicked Sherman's post-game tirade and got a lot of laughs when he told a star-studded crowd, "I'm the best president in the game! Don't you ever talk about me like that!"

No one poked fun at Sherman's football talents. He backed up everything he said by collecting a Super Bowl ring, earning a Pro Bowl selection, leading the NFL in interceptions with eight and receiving a four-year, $57 million contract extension. By 2014, he was the best cornerback in the game, and the most compensated. The only question now was would this sudden fame and fortune change him and his approach. He swatted that suggestion away, too.

"I never expected to be thrown into the spotlight like this," Sherman said of his newfound fame. "I take it for what it is. I try to stay the same person. I know who I am. I don't worry about it changing me too much. I'm pretty set in my ways. I just want to get better and be different."

While he was the breakout star of that NFC championship matchup with his deflection, Sherman curiously was a mere spectator for much of the biggest game of his life, Super Bowl XLVIII. On Feb. 2, 2014, Broncos quarterback Peyton Manning rarely tested him, plus Sherman suffered a high-ankle sprain and missed nearly all the fourth quarter. He was carted off the field and returned to watch the final five minutes while leaning on crutches, preventing him from taking a victory lap. The Super Bowl victory was satisfying for him, just not that memorable.

"I don't remember half of it truthfully," he said. "When I watch film, I realize I have forgotten a lot of what we did."

While he considers himself the best cornerback in today's NFL, it's only fair to ask Sherman if he thinks some day he could be hailed as the greatest of all time. Respectfully, he puts that label on legends Mel Blount and Deion Sanders for now. In his mind, he needs a lot more interceptions to surpass them in mystique. Each playing for 14 seasons, Blount finished with 61 pass thefts and Sanders had 58, counting the postseason. Sherman, with 26 interceptions in four years, has considerable catching up to do. Of course, he doesn't dismiss his chances.

"I'll figure it out soon enough," Sherman promised. "Anything is possible."

Sherman grew up in unforgiving Compton, Calif., originally a Los Angeles Raiders fan, with everyone in his family pulling on that NFL team's black and silver gear. He was a wide receiver first, counting himself as a devoted follower of Terrell Owens and Randy Moss and patterning himself after Jerry Rice. He was the first athlete from his high school to attend Stanford, finding classes such as Greek mythology and sign language extra enlightening.

He easily mixed his street background with higher education, becoming a man for all seasons. He developed a steely attitude about life knowing that his father, a garbage-truck operator, had been shot and survived along the way, and that his best friend was gunned down and killed while Sherman was in college. "Your life is always in danger there," he said of Compton.

Sherman still was a much more subdued personality when he showed up at Husky Stadium in 2006. His Stanford team was 0-9 entering the game. He was a freshman wide receiver. He was a far different player with one notable exception – a great play was always within his reach. Against Washington, he broke open a close game early in the fourth quarter when he caught a 74-yard touchdown pass from T.C. Ostrander, solidifying a 20-3 upset and the Cardinal's first victory of the season.

Meeting with the media in Seattle afterward, Sherman was notably bland when he described his game-breaking moment similarly to this: I caught the ball, I got a block, I broke a tackle, I scored. That would change with time. He was a receiver for two seasons at Stanford before switching to cornerback because he preferred defense and the Cardinal had a pressing need for it. It was unclear whether his quotes became livelier once he started hitting people, but he doesn't disappoint anyone with his observations now.

Asked if he would have been an NFL honors candidate had he stayed at receiver, Sherman responds confidently, "I think I'd be pretty good."

A fifth-round draft selection in 2011, Sherman was mad at everyone for this perceived slight, including the Seahawks. Twenty-three other cornerbacks were taken before he was, and he can still name each and every one. The Seahawks said they had him pegged as a third-round pick, but waited longer to take him because they had other needs and felt confident he would still be available.

Sherman needed just seven games to become a starter, three seasons to achieve NFL stardom. He also warmed to his Northwest pro football home fairly quickly, acquiring an oversized suburban residence at 1765 Monroe Ave. N.E. in Renton, not far from Seahawks headquarters, before he received his contract extension and purchased NBA player Jamal Crawford's Maple Valley house, and he settled in for a long stay. Sherman and the Seattle area were a good fit: It was different, just like him.

"It surprised me," he said of his new surroundings. "I was incredibly happy with it. With its greenery and outdoor stuff, with everyone out boating, it's unique from every place I've ever been."

The city, as it reached for more Super Bowls and entered one of its more enlightened sporting eras, as it spawned a host of Seahawks heroes in Russell Wilson, Earl Thomas, Marshawn Lynch and Pete Carroll, and as it commanded respect as an enthusiastic pro football outpost, had its own version of unique: Seattle discovered the second coming of Richard Sherman. Nearly a century later, the Seahawks cornerback is a radical departure from the pioneering George Wilson, the UW and NFL running back who brought Seattle its first national spotlight but didn't know how to make it pay off. With Sherman, more championships, more interceptions and a lot more words are practically guaranteed. ❖

Top 10 Seattle Teams

1. 2014 Seahawks Super Bowl champs
2. 1979 Sonics NBA champs
3. 1991 UW football national co-champs
4. 1936 UW rowing gold medalist
5. 1995 Mariners ALDS champs
6. 2006 Seahawks Super Bowl runners-up
7. 2001 Mariners 116-game winners
8. 1958 Seattle U Final Four runners-up
9. 2015 Seahawks Super Bowl runners-up
10. 1917 Metropolitans Stanley Cup champs

Without being asked, Seattle Seahawks coach Pete Carroll informed team beat writers on a Sunday night conference call that rookie Russell Wilson was his starting quarterback.

The reaction: Silence.

The pro football journalists on the other end were expecting quarterback news, only something entirely different. Incumbent starter Tavaris Jackson had been traded to Buffalo earlier in the day. Everyone needed a moment to comprehend Wilson's promotion.

While sensational throughout the 2012 preseason, Wilson was still a rookie, and a 5-foot-10½ rookie at that. The Seahawks had never started someone so short at quarterback. In fact, the average height for Seattle's 21 previous starting signal-callers was four inches taller. Plus the team had invested in a three-year, $19 million deal for the services of free-agent quarterback Matt Flynn, who was a strapping 6-foot-2. Wilson was young, undersized and a gamble.

Yet after winning the job, Wilson made the unexpected commonplace: He became a Pro Bowl selection in his first season and won a playoff game. He was a Pro Bowl choice again and a central figure in the Seahawks' pinnacle franchise moment to cap his second year — a crushing 43-8 victory over the Denver Broncos in Super Bowl XLVIII. And in his third season, Wilson helped pull out a miraculous 28-22 overtime victory over the Green Bay Packers to reach Super

Lacking only physical stature, Wilson has established himself as Seattle's greatest pro quarterback

RUSSELL WILSON

Seattle's Best Short Story

Bowl XLIX, only to have the repeat appearance end with a resounding thud, his last-second, goal-line interception leading to a 28-24 loss to the New England Patriots. Give him this: Win or lose, Wilson keeps things interesting.

Lacking only physical stature, Wilson has established himself as Seattle's greatest pro quarterback, surpassing Matt Hasselbeck, a three-time Pro Bowl player who guided the Seahawks to a Super Bowl XL loss; Dave Krieg, a three-time Pro Bowl selection and a Seahawks starter for parts of 11 seasons; Warren Moon, a Pro Bowl choice in one of his two Seattle seasons and a Pro Football Hall of Fame inductee, and Jim Zorn, the Seahawks' original starter behind center and a NFC Offensive Rookie of the Year selection.

If his story wasn't fairy tale enough, Wilson likes to tell how he and the Seahawks were meant to be together, how he was given a telltale sign prior to the draft that Seattle would be his pro football destination.

"I put all 32 teams in a hat and I said whatever team I pull out of the hat would be the team that picked me, and sure enough that's what happened," Wilson said of his third-round Seahawks draft selection. "I just believe in certain things. It's worked out for me in that way."

Wilson's ascension shouldn't be a huge surprise to anyone familiar with Seattle's franchise history: The Seahawks often go with quirky at quarterback.

Russell Wilson has defenses backpedaling when he leaves the pocket.

They've started six undrafted players (Zorn, Krieg, Gale Gilbert, Jeff Kemp, Moon and Jon Kitna); three first-round draft picks who were certifiable busts (Kelly Stouffer, Dan McGwire and Rick Mirer), three obscure players who were never heard from again after drawing first-unit assignments in Seattle (Bruce Mathison, Stan Gelbaugh and Glenn Foley), and two players who were much better suited for ESPN broadcasting careers (Trent Dilfer and Brock Huard).

Wilson is unconventional in ways other than size. He's a branding machine, appearing in more TV commercials than any other Seattle pro athlete, including the once highly marketable Ken Griffey Jr. The current Seahawks quarterback exhaustively sells himself on the screen, though he goes to great lengths to control and protect his image in distinctively corporate fashion. Wilson prefers to keep everyone guessing about his innermost thoughts. For that matter, he announced his divorce in a brief statement released through the team, leaving the Internet to wildly speculate about what might have gone wrong.

Teammates admit they don't really know Wilson all that well, other than the obvious: That he's a highly competitive person who doesn't stray from his strident beliefs. He offers no displays of excessive celebration or outward frustration, though tears of raw emotion poured out of him after the improbable NFC Championship victory over Green Bay. He's always businesslike to a fault. He prefers the old-fashioned handshake over the more spontaneous high-five. He's constantly reminding everyone to focus, even when it requires simply taking a game-ending knee, which might prove annoying to others. Wilson is a throwback. It's not something new either.

Seahawks offensive guard J.R. Sweezy and Wilson played together at North Carolina State and lived near each other. According to the lineman, his college quarterback was never the guy throwing the campus keggers. Wilson was far too polished for that.

"We were all kind of taken aback because he was so put together and we were just kids," Sweezy said.

Seahawks cornerback Richard Sherman, the polar opposite of Wilson with his inclination to say whatever is on his mind without any fear of consequences, didn't know the quarterback at all until he saw him play for Wisconsin in the 2012 Rose Bowl against Stanford, his alma mater. As a teammate, Sherman noticed Wilson's buttoned-down manner right away. He's seen it in every setting they've shared thereafter, too.

"You could tell from his demeanor that he was going to be a different guy," Sherman said. "He's even-keel. Whether it's the preseason, regular season or a championship game, that's the way he is. I've been out with him for a beer [though Russell doesn't drink] and that's the way he is. He rarely lets his hair down."

Even following the great Super Bowl letdown against New England, Wilson was resolute that he and the Seahawks would bounce back fairly quickly, that one disastrous play wouldn't dictate his career, that he was disappointed but unshaken by the game-deciding interception.

"When I threw it, it was like, 'Touchdown, second Super Bowl ring, here we go,' and it didn't happen," Wilson said. "You learn from experience. That's why you play the great game, because you look forward to the next opportunity; win, lose, no matter what the circumstances are."

Wilson remains a defensive coordinator's nightmare with his brains, feet and arm. He is a master scrambler on the same order as Fran Tarkenton. Super Bowl interception aside, he's got the uncanny accuracy of Joe Montana when throwing into a tight space with a lot on the line. He's a master ball-faker, an attribute that makes Moon envious. Wilson's presence keeps the Seahawks in every game; they've lost by no more than nine points since he joined the team. Wilson creates an offensive overload.

"What he can do with his legs is he can extend plays, and the best way to describe it is that he's an extra player on offense," St. Louis Rams coach Jeff Fisher said. "They're playing with 12 and that's very hard to defend."

"I'd put 13 men on the field," Sherman wisecracked.

Wilson still hasn't won over everyone. Detractors look at his height and quietly consider him no more than an opportunist. They suggest that he has ridden the shirttails of a great running back in Marshawn Lynch and an even greater defense to be successful.

Supporters counter strongly that Wilson is very much his own man and makes better decisions to protect the football and his body than most NFL starting quarterbacks. Robert Griffin III and Cam Newton are notable examples of talented signal-callers whose careers have regressed in recent seasons because they weren't able to stay out of harm's way.

While Wilson is as productive as any NFL quarterback, he doesn't get enough credit mainly because he doesn't throw as much as the elite players, according to Moon, his mentor. That should change in time.

"Everything gets measured by what Aaron [Rodgers], Peyton [Manning] and Tom [Brady] do," Moon said. "Russell's numbers come differently. At some point in his career he won't be the runner that he is now. He'll be older and have to throw the ball more, and he'll show that he can do that, too."

Seattle will take Wilson any way it can. He's an important reason why the city celebrated a Super Bowl victory and experienced a near-miss in sport's biggest spectacle. He's as responsible as anyone for pulling the Puget Sound seaport out of its lengthy and depressing sporting funk that affected every local team across the board. He's done his bit to help fill CenturyLink Field to the brim with deafening sellout crowds, with more people wearing his No. 3 jersey than any other Seahawks number.

Wilson is just what the city needed, even if his promotion to starting quarterback caught people a little off-guard and left everyone momentarily speechless. There's a connection there that works both ways.

"I obviously want to play in Seattle forever, that's my goal," Wilson said. ❖

TOP 10 WILSONS

1. Russell Wilson, Seahawks
2. George Wilson, UW football
3. Dan Wilson, Mariners
4. Luke Willson, Seahawks
5. George Wilson, Sonics
6. Marc Wilson, Raiders, Patriots
7. Josh Wilson, Mariners
8. Josh Wilson, Seahawks
9. Steve Wilson, UW basketball
10. Jim Wilson, Rainiers

Seattle's Best Of The Rest

*Birth and death years inside bold parentheses; Seattle connections (dates in light parentheses)

A

Zaid Abdul-Aziz — forward for Sonics (1971-1972, 1976) and Royals, Bucks, Rockets, Braves and Celtics; was Don Smith before Islamic conversion.

Barry Ackerley (1934-2011) — owner for Sonics (1983-2001); bought franchise from California businessman Sam Schulman for $21 million and sold it to Starbucks founder Howard Schultz for $200 million.

Rick Acton (1945-2000) — PGA Tour player for five seasons before auto accident curtailed career; PGA Tour Senior player; UW baseball player; Lake Washington HS.

Joe Adcock (1927-1999) — manager for Triple-A Seattle Angels (1968); manager for Cleveland Indians; former big-league player.

Shaun Alexander — running back for Seahawks (2000-07) and Redskins; Super Bowl XL starter (2006); rushed for career-best 1,880 yards and scored NFL-record 28 touchdowns (2005); Associated Press NFL Offensive Player of the Year (2005); Seahawks Pro Bowl selections (2003, 2004, 2005).

Anthony Allen — wide receiver for Falcons, Chargers and Redskins; Super Bowl XXII; University of Washington (1979-1982); Rose Bowls (1981, 1982); Garfield High School.

Chuck Allen — linebacker for Chargers; UW (1958-1960); Rose Bowls (1960, 1961); 1963 AFL Championship Game.

Keith Allen — player-coach for Seattle Americans (1957) and coach for Americans and Seattle Totems (1958-65); first coach for Philadelphia Flyers and general manager for Flyers; Hockey Hall of Fame inductee.

Paul Allen — owner for Seahawks (1997-to date) and Trail Blazers; built Seahawks Stadium (2002); Super Bowl XL (2006), Super Bowl XLVIII (2014), Super Bowl XLIX (2015); Microsoft co-founder.

Ray Allen — shooting guard for Sonics (2003-07), Celtics, Bucks and Heat; Sonics All-Star selections (2004, 2005, 2006, 2007); averaged 25.1 (2006) and 26.4 ppg (2007) for Sonics.

Larry Andersen — relief pitcher for Mariners (1981-82), Red Sox, Indians, Astros, Phillies and Padres; Interlake HS.

Steve Anderson — silver medalist in the 100-meter high hurdles in 1928 Amsterdam Olympics. UW (1928-30); Queen Anne HS.

George Argyros — owner for Mariners (1981-89); bought team for $13.1 million and sold it to Indianapolis TV and radio station owner Jeff Smulyan for $76 million.

Chuck Armstrong — president for Mariners (1981-89, 1993-2013); interim athletic director for UW (1991).

Debbie Armstrong — gold medalist in giant ski slalom in 1984 Sarajevo Olympics; raced in 1988 Calgary Olympics but didn't medal;

U.S. Ski Team member; Garfield HS.

Debbie Armstrong

Dale "Ibar" Arrington — heavyweight boxer fought out of Seattle (1974-82); compiled 27-7-2 record, with 20 knockouts; lost by TKO in 1977 to Larry Holmes at Caesar's Palace in Las Vegas.

Steve August — offensive tackle for Seahawks (1977-84) and Steelers; one of three draft picks obtained from Cowboys in exchange for Seahawks' No. 2 overall pick used to draft Tony Dorsett.

Earl Douglas Averill (1931-2015) — infielder and catcher for Triple-A Seattle Rainiers (1964) and Angels (1965); son of Hall of Famer Earl Averill; infielder and catcher for Indians, Cubs, White Sox, Angels and Phillies..

Howard Earl Averill (1902-1983) — outfielder for Rainiers (1941); nicknamed "Earl of Snohomish"; outfielder for Braves, Indians and Tigers; six-time All-Star selection; Baseball Hall of Fame inductee.

Bobby Ayala — relief pitcher for Mariners (1994-98), Cubs, Reds and Expos; one of most-booed Seattle athletes.

B

Enoch Bagshaw (1894-1930) — football coach for UW (1921-29); coached Huskies to first two Rose Bowls (1924, 1926); played for UW (1903-07).

Mario Bailey — wide receiver for UW (1989-91); first-team *AP* All-America selection (1991); school-record 18 TD catches (1991); Rose Bowls (1991, 1992); Franklin HS.

Vin Baker — forward for Sonics (1998-2002), Celtics, Rockets, Clippers, Bucks and Knicks; Sonics All-Star selection (1998).

Bobby Balcena (1925-1990) — outfielder for

Floyd Bannister

Rainiers (1955-58); first Filipino player in the major leagues with Reds.

Floyd Bannister – pitcher for Mariners (1979-82), Angels, White Sox, Astros, Royals and Rangers; Mariners All-Star selection (1982); No. 1 amateur baseball draft pick (1976); Arizona State University; Kennedy HS.

Dick Barrett (1906-1966) – pitcher for Double-A Seattle Indians (1935-37) and Rainiers (1938-42, 1947-49); *Sporting News* Minor League Player of the Year (1942); pitched for Braves, Cubs, A's and Phillies.

Bill Bavasi – general manager for Mariners (2003-08) and Angels; son of Dodgers general manager Buzzie Bavasi; brother Peter Bavasi was Padres general manager; brother Bob Bavasi owned Single-A Everett AquaSox.

Butch Beard – point guard for Sonics (1973), Hawks, Cavaliers, Warriors and Knicks; part

of one of Seattle's most unpopular trades, shipped from Cavs for Lenny Wilkens and Barry Clemens (1972).

Ken Behring – owner for Seahawks (1988-97); purchased team from Nordstrom family for $79 million and moved franchise temporarily to Anaheim before selling to Paul Allen for $200 million.

Rod Belcher (1920-2014) – KING-TV and radio sportscaster (1960-81); play-by-play broadcaster for UW football and basketball, Seattle University basketball, Rainiers and San Francisco 49ers.

Bob Bender – basketball coach for UW (1994-2002) and Illinois State; NCAA Tournaments (1998, 1999); fired after three consecutive losing seasons.

Clay Bennett – Oklahoma businessman bought Sonics for $350 million in 2006; moved franchise to Oklahoma City in 2008, ending Seattle's four-decade association with NBA.

John Best – first soccer coach for NASL's Sounders (1974-1976); NASL and English professional player.

Don Bies – golfer won PGA Tour's 1975 Sammy Davis Jr.-Greater Hartford Open in playoff over Hubert Green; won seven times on Champions Tour; Ballard HS.

Sue Bird – point guard for Storm (2002-2012); won WNBA championships (2004, 2010); Storm All-Star selections (2002, 2007, 2009, 2010, 2012); won Olympic gold medal, NCAA title and WNBA title.

Ralph Bishop (1915-1974) – center for UW (1934-1936); starter for 25-7 national championship team (1936); Huskies third in Olympic trials (1936); played for gold-medalist Universal AAU basketball team at 1936 Berlin Olympics.

Eric Bjornson – wide receiver for Cowboys

and Patriots; Super Bowl XXX; UW (1991-94); Rose Bowls (1992, 1993).

Bud Black – pitcher for Mariners (1981), Indians, Royals, Padres, Giants and Jays; manager for Padres.

George Black – all-conference receiver for UW and top target for two-time All-America quarterback Don Heinrich (1951-53); became dentist..

Brian Blades – wide receiver for Seahawks (1988-98); Seahawks Pro Bowl selection (1989); 581 career receptions for 7,620 yards and 34 touchdowns.

Mike Blatt – interim general manager for Seahawks (1989); accused and acquitted of hiring murder of former California real-estate colleague.

Mike Blowers – third baseman for Mariners (1992-95, 1997, 1999), Dodgers, Yankees and A's; Mariners TV analyst (2007-to date); UW (1986).

Sylvester Blye – basketball forward for Seattle U (1960) for one game, scoring 23 points against Memphis; forfeited eligibility after it was determined he played four games for the Harlem Clowns pro team.

Bruce Bochte – outfielder and first baseman for Mariners (1978-82), Angels, Indians and A's; Mariners All-Star selection (1979).

Ken Bone – basketball coach for Washington State University, Portland State and Seattle Pacific (1990-2002); assistant coach for UW (2003-05); forward for SPU (1980-82), Edmonds CC and Shoreline CC; Shorecrest HS.

Bret Boone – second baseman for Mariners (1992-93, 2001-05), Braves, Reds, Twins and Padres; Mariners All-Star selections (2001, 2003); 37 home runs and 141 RBI for Mariners (2001).

Bob Boozer (1937-2012) – forward for Sonics (1970), Bulls, Royals, Bucks and Knicks; played for Kansas State against Seattle U in 1958 Final Four.

Chris Bosio – pitcher for Mariners (1993-96) and Brewers; threw no-hitter against Red Sox (1993).

Trish Bostrom – tennis player for Sea-Port Cascades (1978), Boston Lobsters, Indiana Loves and New Orleans Nets in World Team Tennis; UW (1971-73); Chief Sealth HS.

Brian Bosworth – linebacker for Seahawks (1987-89); signed richest NFL rookie contract at time, 10 years for $11 million; shoulder injury ended career; "B movie" actor.

Bob Boyd (1930-2015) – basketball coach for Seattle U (1964-65), USC and Mississippi State; NCAA Tournament (1964); left SU following point-shaving scandal.

Gene Brabender (1941-1996) – pitcher for Seattle Pilots (1969), Orioles and Brewers.

George Briggs – athletic director for UW (1956-61); hired following slush-fund scandal; hired Darrell Royal and Jim Owens as Huskies football coaches.

Al Brightman (1923-1992) – basketball coach for Seattle U (1948-56); NCAA Tournaments (1953, 1954, 1955, 1956); fired for incident at NCAA Tournament game involving UCLA's John Wooden; coached ABA's Anaheim Amigos.

John Brisker (1947-1985) – forward for Sonics (1973-75) and ABA's Pipers and Condors; scored NBA-high 47 points against Kings (1973); disappeared on Uganda 1978 trip, possibly executed for his involvement with dictator Idi Amin; declared legally dead in Seattle in 1985.

Herman Brix (1906-2007) – offensive tackle for UW (1925-27); Rose Bowl (1926); silver medalist shot putter in 1928 Amsterdam Olympics; actor, notably Tarzan, appearing in 113 films; later known as Bruce Bennett.

Jon Brockman – forward for Bucks and Kings; UW (2006-09); Huskies all-time leading rebounder with 1,283 (2006-09); NCAA Tournament (2006, 2009).

Aaron Brooks – point guard for Rockets, Suns, Kings and Bulls; University of Oregon; Franklin HS.

Chad Brown – linebacker for Seahawks (1998-2005), Patriots and Steelers; Super Bowl XL (2006); Seahawks Pro Bowl selections (1998, 1999).

Charlie Brown – point guard for Seattle U (1958-1959); starter in Final Four championship game (1958); NCAA Tournament (1958); Indiana transfer.

Dave Brown (1953-2006) – defensive back for Seahawks (1976-86), Packers and Steelers; Seahawks Pro Bowl selection (1984); Seahawks Ring of Honor inductee (1992).

Dennis Brown – defensive lineman for 49ers; Super Bowl XXIX starter; UW (1988-89).

Dave Browning – defensive lineman for Patriots and Raiders, and USFL's Oakland Invaders; Super Bowl XV starter; 1985 USFL championship game; UW defensive tackle (1976-77); Rose Bowl (1978).

Mark Bruener – tight end for Texans and Steelers; Super Bowl XXX starter; UW (1991-94); Rose Bowls (1992, 1993).

Mark Brunell – quarterback for Packers, Jaguars, Saints and Redskins; Super Bowl XLIV; set NFL record with 22 consecutive pass completions; UW (1989-92); Rose Bowls (1991, 1992, 1993); Rose Bowl Offensive MVP (1991).

Bill Buchan – gold medalist in Star sailing class in 1984 Los Angeles Olympics; three-time world champion; UW (1954-57); Garfield HS; son Carl Buchan also was 1984 sailing gold medalist.

Jay Buhner – outfielder for Mariners (1988-2001) and Yankees; Mariners All-Star selection (1996); hit 40, 44 and 40 home runs (1995-1997).

Nate Burleson – wide receiver for Seahawks (2006-09), Lions and Vikings; Nevada; O'Dea HS.

Kayla Burt – guard for UW women's basketball team (2002-03, 2005); had heart attack on New Year's Eve 2002 and survived; sat out season and played 16 more games before cardiac complications ended career.

Blair Bush – center for Seahawks (1983-88), Bengals, Packers and Rams; Super Bowl XVI starter; UW (1975-77); Rose Bowl (1978).

C

Bill Cahill – punt returner for Bills; NFL teammate of O.J. Simpson; returned punt 51 yards for TD against Jets; UW (1970-72); Bellevue HS.

Kevin Calabro – TV and radio broadcaster for Sonics (1988-2008); ESPN-TV and Pac-12 broadcaster; ESPN Seattle radio sports talk show host; made cameo appearance in Prefontaine film.

Michael Callahan – coach for UW men's rowing team (2008 to date); IRA national championships (2009, 2011, 2012, 2013, 2014); UW rower (1994-96).

Mike Cameron – outfielder for Mariners (2000-03), Red Sox, White Sox, Reds, Marlins, Brewers, Mets and Padres; Mariners All-Star selection (2001); 30th big-league player to

hit four homers in a game (2002); traded to Seattle with three players for Ken Griffey Jr.

Mike Campbell – pitcher for Mariners (1987-89), Cubs, Padres and Rangers; player to be named later in Mariners trade for Randy Johnson; West Seattle and Newport HS.

Robinson Cano – second baseman for Mariners (2014 to date) and Yankees; signed to $240 million contract, richest in franchise history.

David Carr – forward for UW (1966-68); averaged 20 ppg (1968); brothers Luther and Gary played Husky football.

Charles Carroll (1906-2003) – running back for UW (1926-28); first-team *AP* All-America selection (1928); Rose Bowl (1926); scored school-record 15 TDs in season (1927) and six TDs in game (1928); No. 2 retired by school; College Football Hall of Fame inductee; King County prosecutor; Garfield HS.

Pete Carroll – football coach for Seahawks (2010-to date), Patriots and Jets; Super Bowl XLVIII (2014), Super Bowl XLIX (2015); coach for USC.

Harvey Cassill (1900-1979) – athletic director for UW (1946-56); had south upper deck of Husky Stadium built; fired after alumni slush fund revealed.

Bill Caudill – relief pitcher for Mariners (1982-83), Cubs, A's and Blue Jays; earned "Inspector" and "Cuffs" nicknames; first client for "super" sports agent Scott Boras.

Vince Cazzetta (1925-2005) – basketball coach for Seattle U (1959-63); NCAA Tournament (1961, 1962, 1963); fired by Chieftains at midseason after run-in with athletic director Eddie O'Brien; coached Pipers to 1968 ABA championship.

Tom Chambers – forward for Sonics (1984-88), Hornets, 76ers, Suns, Clippers and Jazz;

Sonics All-Star selection (1987); All-Star Game MVP (1987); averaged 21.5, 23.3, and 20.4 ppg for Sonics (1985, 1987, 1988).

Kam Chancellor – safety for Seahawks (2010-to date); Seahawks Pro Bowls (2011, 2013, 2014); Super Bowl XLVIII starter (2014), Super Bowl XLIX starter (2015).

Chris Chandler – quarterback starter for record eight NFL teams: Falcons, Bears, Oilers, Colts, Rams, Cardinals, Rams and Buccaneers; Super Bowl XXXIII starter; two-time Pro Bowl selection; UW (1983-87); Orange Bowl (1985).

Jesse Chatman – running back for Dolphins, Saints, Jets and Chargers; Eastern Washington University; Franklin HS.

George Chemeres (1916-2002) – boxing manager in Seattle who handled heavyweight Pete Rademacher, light heavyweight Eddie Cotton and light welterweight Greg Haugen; nicknamed "The Greek."

Doug Christie – shooting guard for Mavericks, Clippers, Lakers, Knicks, Magic, Kings and Raptors; Pepperdine; Rainier Beach HS.

Joe Cipriano (1931-1980) – point guard for UW (1951-53); starter for Huskies' Final Four team (1953); NCAA Tournament (1951, 1953); coach for Idaho and Nebraska.

Archie Clark – guard for Sonics (1975), Bullets, Pistons, Lakers and 76ers.

John Clayton – ESPN-TV and ESPN radio analyst, KJR radio broadcaster, and Tacoma *Morning News Tribune* sports writer.

Wayne Cody (1936-2002) – KIRO-TV and KIRO radio sports broadcaster (1975-1996); Seattle sports talk show; Seahawks sideline reporter.

Linda Cohn – ESPN-TV SportsCenter broadcaster; KIRO-TV broadcaster (1989-92).

Lynn Colella – silver medalist swimmer in 200-meter butterfly in 1972 Munich Olympics; UW; sister of Olympian Rick Colella; Nathan Hale HS.

Rick Colella – bronze medalist swimmer in 200-meter breaststroke in 1976 Montreal Olympics; UW; Nathan Hale HS.

Will Conroy – point guard for Rockets, Clippers, Grizzlies and Timberwolves; UW (2002-05); NCAA Tournament (2004, 2005); Rainier Beach and Garfield HS.

Ernie Conwell – tight end for Saints and Rams; Super Bowl XXXIV, Super Bowl XXXVI starter; UW (1992-95); Rose Bowl (1993).

Mike Cordova – quarterback for Stanford; Seattle Prep HS; *Parade Magazine* All-America selection (1972).

Robert "Bo" Cornell – linebacker for Bills and Browns; UW fullback (1968-70); Roosevelt HS.

Eddie Cotton (1927-1990) – light-heavyweight boxer fought out of Seattle (1947-67); compiled 56-23-2 career record; owned Capitol Hill restaurant that bore his name.

Al Cowlings – defensive lineman for Seahawks (1976), Bills, Oilers, Rams and 49ers; O.J. Simpson's driver in the white Bronco police chase.

Bobby Cox (1935-2003) – quarterback for UW (1954); transferred to Minnesota with greater offer of improper benefits; All-Big-Ten selection; played for AFL's Patriots.

Jamal Crawford – point guard for Hawks, Bulls, Warriors, Clippers, Knicks and Trail Blazers; two-time NBA Sixth Man of the Year; scored 52 points for Knicks, 50 for Bulls, and 50 for Warriors; Michigan; Rainier Beach HS.

Ed Cunningham – offensive lineman for Seahawks (1996) and Cardinals; UW (1988-91); starter on Huskies' national championship team (1991); Rose Bowls (1991, 1992); football broadcaster for ESPN-TV and ABC-TV.

Mike Curtis – linebacker for Seahawks (1976) and Colts; two-time Super Bowl starter.

D

Paul Dade – third baseman for Angels, Indians and Padres; 10th overall pick in amateur baseball draft (1970); Nathan Hale HS.

Roger Davies – striker for Sounders (1980-82); NASL MVP (1980); former English First Division player.

Alvin Davis – first baseman for Mariners (1984-91) and Angels; AL Rookie of the Year (1984); Mariners All-Star selection (1984); nicknamed "Mr. Mariner."

Clint Dempsey – midfielder for Sounders (2013-to date); US World Cup captain and two-time player; English player for Fulham.

Dean Derby – defensive back for Vikings and Steelers; one-time Pro Bowl selection; UW (1954-56).

Rod Derline – shooting guard for Sonics guard (1975-76); pro career curtailed by knee injury; Seattle U (1971-74); nicknamed "Rod the Rifle."

Dan Dickau – shooting guard for Hawks, Celtics, Mavericks, Clippers, Hornets and Trail Blazers; UW (1997) and Gonzaga; first-team *AP* All-America selection for Zags.

Gil Dobie (1879-1948) – football coach for UW (1908-16), Boston College, Cornell, Navy and North Dakota State; 58-0-3 record, including 39-game win streak for Huskies; College Football Hall of Fame inductee.

James Donaldson – center for SuperSonics (1980-83), Mavericks, Clippers, Knicks, Clippers and Jazz; unsuccessful Seattle mayoral candidate.

Nanci Donnellan – radio talk-show host for KJR 950 AM (1991-94); one of nation's first female sports radio personalities; known as "the Fabulous Sports Babe."

Dan Doornink – running back for the Seahawks (1979-85) and Giants; WSU; Yakima physician.

Charles Dudley – point guard for Sonics (1973), Bulls and Warriors; UW (1971-72).

Dan Dugdale (1864-1934) – built Yesler Way Park (1907) and Dugdale Park (1914); owned several Seattle minor-league baseball teams; killed in Seattle traffic accident in Seattle's SoDo District.

Dave Dupree – *USA Today* NBA writer; defensive back for UW (1966-67); Franklin HS.

Kevin Durant – forward for Sonics (2008) and Thunder; NBA Rookie of the Year (2008); averaged 20.3 ppg (2008); second overall NBA draft selection (2007) behind Greg Oden.

E

Kenny Easley – safety for Seahawks (1981-87); Pro Bowl selections (1982, 1983, 1984, 1985, 1987); NFL Defensive Player of the Year (1984); Seahawks Ring of Honor inductee (2002); career cut short by kidney disease from excessive medication.

Clarence "Hec" Edmundson (1886-1964) – basketball coach for UW (1920-47) and Idaho; NCAA Tournament (1943); Huskies' basketball arena christened Edmundson Pavilion (1948); middle-distance runner in 1908 London Olympics and 1912 Stockholm Olympics.

Carl Eller – defensive end for Seahawks (2004) and Vikings; started eight games for Seahawks in final season of career; four-time Super Bowl starter; Pro Football Hall of Fame inductee.

Dale Ellis – shooting guard for Sonics (1987-91, 1998-99), Hornets, Nuggets, Bucks and Spurs; Sonics All-Star selection (1989); wife Monique got into fight outside Sonics locker room with teammate Alton Lister's wife, Bobbi Jo.

Bobby Engram – wide receiver for Seahawks (2001-08), Bears and Chiefs; Super Bowl XL starter (2006).

Dennis Erickson – football coach for Seahawks (1995-98) and 49ers; coach for Arizona State, Idaho, Miami, Oregon State, WSU and Wyoming; won two national championships at Miami.

Dick Erickson (1935-2001) – men's crew coach for UW (1968-87); IRA national championship (1970) and CNCR national championship (1984); Huskies rower (1956-58); varsity-eight crew member that upset Leningrad Trud in Moscow (1958); U.S. National Rowing Hall of Fame inductee; cousin of former Seahawks coach Dennis Erickson.

Bob Ernst – women's or men's crew coach for UW (1974-to date); women's NCRC national championships (1981, 1982, 1983, 1984, 1985, 1987) and men's IRA national championships (1997, 2007); U.S. National Rowing Hall of Fame inductee (1994); coach of gold-medalist women's eight in 1984 Los Angeles Olympics.

Norm Evans – offensive tackle for Seahawks (1976-78), Oilers and Dolphins; three-time Super Bowl starter; published *Norm Evans' Seahawks Report* (1979-82).

Patrick Ewing – center for Sonics (2001),

Knicks and Magic; Basketball Hall of Fame inductee; won 1984 NCAA championship with Georgetown at Kingdome.

Sam Farmer — sportswriter for *Bellevue Journal American* (1990-91), *Kent's Valley Journal* (1991-95), *San Jose Mercury News* and *Los Angeles Times;* wrote *Bitter Roses,* book about University of Washington football scandal.

D'Marco Farr — defensive tackle for Rams; Super Bowl XXXIV starter; UW (1991-1993); Rose Bowls (1991, 1992, 1993).

Tom Farrey — sportswriter for *Seattle Times* (1988-1996); sports reporter for ESPN-TV and *ESPN the Magazine*; reporting led to UW football scandal and two-year bowl ban.

Rick Fehr — golfer won PGA Tour events in 1986 B.C. Open and 1994 Walt Disney World/ Oldsmobile Classic; BYU; Nathan Hale HS.

Duke Fergerson — wide receiver for Seahawks (1977-79) and Bills; WSU and San Diego State; created Harlem Hellfighters high school team; received acquittal and dismissal in two Seattle rape trials.

Jaime Fields (1970-1999) — linebacker for Chiefs; UW (1989-92); Huskies' national championship team starter (1991); Rose Bowls (1991, 1992, 1993); killed in Compton, Calif., hit-and-run traffic accident.

Tom Flores — football coach for Seahawks (1992-94) and Raiders; quarterback for Bills, Chiefs and Raiders.

Lee Folkins — tight end for Cowboys, Packers and Steelers; one-time Pro Bowl selection; UW (1958-60); Rose Bowls (1960, 1961); Roosevelt HS; survived construction accident electrocution.

Paul Fortier — forward for UW (1983-1986); NCAA Tournaments (1984, 1985, 1986); UW assistant coach (2005-2013).

Frank Foyston (1891-1966) — hockey forward led Seattle Metropolitans to Stanley Cup victory (1917); first Cup victory for an American team; one of 10 players to win Stanley Cup with three different teams; coached PCHL's Seattle Eskimos; nicknamed "The Flash"; Hockey Hall of Fame inductee.

Ray Frankowski (1919-2001) — offensive guard for Packers and Los Angeles Dons; UW (1939-41); first-team *AP* All-America selection (1941).

Michelle French — soccer defender for WUSA's San Jose Cyber Rays and Washington Freedom; U.S. National Team member; competed in 2000 Sydney Olympics; Portland; Kennedy HS; cancer survivor.

Mike Frier — defensive lineman for Seahawks (1992-94); left quadriplegic in 1994 from single-car accident involving teammates Lamar Smith and Chris Warren.

Jerry Frizzell — forward for Seattle U basketball team (1956, 1958-59); Final Four championship game starter (1958); NCAA Tournament (1958).

Chance Fry — soccer forward for NASL's Sounders (1983), WSA's Seattle Storm (1987-90), APSL's Sounders (1994-97) and NASL's Fort Wayne Flames, New York Cosmos, San Francisco Bay Blackhawks and Tulsa Roughnecks; U.S. National Team; Sammamish HS.

Jimmy Gabriel — soccer coach for Sounders (1977-79); midfielder for Sounders (1974-79); Scottish national team member.

Bob Galer (1913-2005) — shooting guard for

UW (1933-35); Helms All-America selection (1935); World War II war hero as brigadier general; Queen Anne HS.

Freddy Garcia — pitcher for Mariners (1999-2004), White Sox, Tigers, Yankees and Phillies; Mariners All-Star selections (2001, 2002); obtained with two other players in Randy Johnson trade.

Ted Garhart (1920-2000) — rower for UW (1939-42); stroked eight-man IRA championship shells (1940, 1941); U.S. National Rowing Hall of Fame inductee; Garfield HS.

Keith Gilbertson — football coach for UW (2003-2004), California and Idaho; assistant coach for Huskies (1989-91, 1999-2002); assistant coach for Seahawks (1996-98, 2005-08).

Mike Gilleran — WCC commissioner for 25 years; forward for Seattle U (1969-71); NCAA Tournament (1969); Seattle Prep HS.

Pat Gillick — general manager for Mariners (1999-2003), Orioles, Phillies and Blue Jays.

Chris Gobrecht — women's basketball coach for UW (1985-96), Cal State Fullerton, Florida State, USC and Yale; UW NCAA Tournaments (1986, 1987, 1988, 1989, 1990, 1991, 1993, 1994, 1995).

Kevin Gogan — offensive guard for Cowboys, Raiders, Dolphins, and Chargers; Super Bowl XXVII, Super Bowl XXVIII starter; three-time Pro Bowl selection; UW (1984-86); Orange Bowl (1985).

Eric Goodwin — NBA agent who shares management firm with twin brother Aaron; Jamal Crawford, Kevin Durant, LeBron James and Nate Robinson were clients; UPS; Garfield HS.

Rich "Goose" Gossage — reliever for Mariners (1994), Cubs, White Sox, Yankees, A's, Pirates, Padres, Giants and Rangers; Baseball Hall of Fame inductee.

Joel Gottstein (1891-1971) — Seattle businessman and horseman who led the push to operate legalized horse racing in Washington State and built Longacres race track (1933).

Jeff Gove — PGA Tour player; Pepperdine; Inglemoor HS, nephew of PGA Tour player Mike Gove.

Mike Gove — PGA Tour player for seven seasons; first-team NCAA All-American for Weber State; Walker Cup player; golf pro at Inglewood; Nathan Hale HS.

Horace Grant — forward for Sonics (2000), Bulls, Lakers and Magic.

Chris Gray — offensive lineman for Seahawks (1998-2007), Bears and Dolphins; Super Bowl XL starter (2006); played all five offensive-line positions for Seattle.

Jacob Green — defensive tackle for Seahawks (1980-91) and 49ers; Seahawks Pro Bowl selections (1986, 1987); Seahawks Ring of Honor inductee (1995).

John Grieg — forward for Sonics (1983); NBA agent who represented several players, including DeMarcus Cousins.

Marv Grissom (1918-2005) — pitcher for Rainiers (1951); compiled 20-11 record for Seattle (1951); pitched for Red Sox, White Sox, Tigers, Giants and Cardinals.

Dave Grosby — sports radio talk-show host for ESPN Seattle; city's longest running sports broadcaster for KJR (1991-93), KIRO (1993-96), KJR (1996-2010) and ESPN Seattle (2010-to date); Seattle U basketball broadcaster; known on the air as "the Groz."

Pete Gross (1937-1992) — radio broadcaster for Seahawks (1976-92); died from cancer three days after attending Seahawks Ring of Honor induction at Kingdome (1992); called Sonics and UW basketball games.

Petur Gudmundsson – Icelandic center and first European to play in the NBA; played for Lakers, Trail Blazers and Spurs; UW (1978-80); Mercer Island HS.

Les Habegger – Sonics general manager (1985-87); Sonics assistant coach (1976-84); NBA championship team (1979); basketball coach for SPU (1957-77); compiled 267-170 SPU record.

Brian Habib – offensive guard for Seahawks (1998-99), Broncos and Vikings; Super Bowl XXXII starter; UW (1986-87).

Ila Ray Hadley (1942-61) – pairs skater died with U.S. figure skating team in 1961 jet crash in Brussels, Belgium; brother and skating partner Ray also killed in crash; competed in 1960 Squaw Valley Olympics; Roosevelt HS.

Ray Hadley Jr. (1943-1961) – pairs skater died with U.S. figure skating team in 1961 jet crash in Brussels, Belgium; competed in 1960 Squaw Valley Olympics; Alan Graves School.

Dave Hamilton – pitcher for White Sox, A's, Pirates and Cardinals; 1972 World Series championship team; Edmonds HS.

Adrian Hanauer – owner and general manager for Seattle Sounders (2002 to date); obtained MSL franchise for Seattle (2007); brought in film producer Joe Roth, comedian Drew Carey and Seahawks owner Paul Allen as investors; UW; Mercer Island HS.

Chip Hanauer – unlimited hydroplane driver won APBA Gold Cup record 12 times while driving *Miss Budweiser* (1976-90); International Motorsports Hall of Fame inductee; Newport HS.

Rich Hand – pitcher for Angels, Indians and Rangers; career curtailed by arm injuries; basketball and baseball player UPS; Lincoln HS.

Lars Hansen – forward for Sonics (1979); Sonics NBA championship team reserve (1979); UW (1973-76); NCAA Tournament (1975).

Tom Hansen – Pac-10 commissioner for 26 years; NCAA administrator; UW student (1959-60).

Mike Hargrove – manager for Mariners (2005-07), Orioles and Indians; first baseman for Indians, Padres and Rangers.

Jim Harney – point guard for Seattle U (1956-58); Final Four championship game starter (1958); NCAA Tournament (1956, 1958); Seattle Prep and North Kitsap HS basketball coach; Seattle Prep HS.

Tommy Harper – infielder for Pilots (1969), Orioles, Red Sox, Angels, Reds, Indians, and A's; A.L. stolen-base leader for Pilots with 73 (1969).

Bruce Harrell – linebacker for UW (1976-79); Rose Bowl (1978); cousin of deceased Seattle U basketball player Keith Harrell; Garfield HS; Seattle city councilman; Seattle mayoral candidate.

Keith Harrell (1956-2010) – forward for Seattle U (1975-78); nationally recognized motivational speaker; Garfield HS; top player for "Super Dogs," state's greatest high school team; died of cancer.

Franco Harris – running back for Seahawks (1984) and Steelers; rushed for 170 yards in eight games for Seattle, retiring at midseason; four-time Super Bowl starter; Pro Football Hall of Fame inductee.

Homer Harris (1916-2007) – two-way end and first black captain for Big Ten football team in 1938; University of Iowa; Garfield HS.

Jan Harville – coach for UW women's crew (1987-2003); NCAA national championships (1997, 1998, 2001); National Rowing Coach of the Year (2002); rowed for UW (1970-73); Roosevelt HS.

Harald Hasselbach – defensive end for Broncos; Super Bowl XXXII, Super Bowl XXXIII starter; UW (1986-89); never started game for Huskies.

Matt Hasselbeck – quarterback for Seahawks (2001-2010), Packers, Titans and Colts; Seahawks Pro Bowl selections (2003, 2005, 2007); Super Bowl XL starter (2006).

James Hasty – defensive back for Chiefs, Jets and Raiders; two-time Pro Bowl selection; Central Washington University, WSU; Franklin HS.

Greg "Mutt" Haugen – boxer compiled 43-10-3 record fighting out of Seattle; IBF lightweight champ and WBO light welterweight champ; fought and lost to Julio Cesar Chavez in Mexico City before largest crowd to see boxing match: 132,243; World Boxing Hall of Fame inductee.

Spencer Hawes – center for Kings, 76ers and Cavaliers; UW (2007); nephew of former NBA player Steve Hawes; Seattle Prep HS.

Steve Hawes – forward for Sonics (1983-84), Hawks, Rockets and Blazers; UW (1970-72); averaged 20.2, 20.3, and 21.7 ppg for Huskies; Mercer Island HS.

Walt Hazzard (1942-2011) – shooting guard for Sonics (1968, 1974), Hawks, Braves, Warriors and Lakers; Sonics All-Star selection (1968); traded for Lenny Wilkens; became Mahdi Abdul-Rahman after Islamic conversion.

Garfield Heard – forward for Sonics (1971-72), Braves, Bulls, Suns and Clippers.

Barbara Hedges – athletic director for UW (1991-2004); provided Title IX advances and facilities expansion; resigned following Rick Neuheisel betting scandal.

Dave Henderson – centerfielder for Mariners (1981-86), Red Sox, Athletics, Giants and Royals; one-time All-Star Game selection; traded with Spike Owen to Red Sox for Rey Quinones, Mike Brown, John Christenson and Mike Trujillo.

Rickey Henderson – outfielder for Mariners (2000), Angels, Red Sox, Dodgers, Mets, Yankees, A's and Padres; 31 of record 1,406 stolen bases came with Mariners; Baseball Hall of Fame inductee.

Efren Herrera – placekicker for Seahawks (1978-81), Bills and Cowboys.

Dave Hoffmann – linebacker for Bears; UW (1989-92); Rose Bowls (1991, 1992, 1993); starter for Huskies' national championship team (1991); became Secret Service agent.

Ron Holmes (1963-2011) – defensive end for Broncos and Buccaneers; Super Bowl XXIV starter; UW (1982-1984); Orange Bowl (1985).

Mike Holmgren – football coach for Seahawks (1999-2008) and Packers; general manager for Seahawks (1999-2002); coached in Super Bowl XXXI, Super Bowl XXXII and Super Bowl XL (2006).

Rick Honeycutt – pitcher for Mariners (1977-80), Dodgers, Yankees, A's, Cardinals and Rangers; Mariners All-Star selection (1980).

Janet Hopps – tennis player who advanced to Wimbledon semifinals and French Open quarterfinals; played No. 1 on Seattle U men's team (1954-56); SU men's and women's tennis coach; Women's Collegiate Tennis Hall of Fame inductee.

Rogers Hornsby (1896-1963) – manager for Rainiers (1951); PCL championship (1951);

managed Braves, Cubs, Reds, Giants, Browns and Cardinals. Baseball Hall of Fame inductee.

Rogers Hornsby, right, confers with Benny Huffman.

Jack Horsley – swimmer won bronze medal in 200-meter backstroke in 1968 Mexico City Olympics; swam for NCAA championship team at Indiana with Mark Spitz; Highline HS.

Ray Horton – defensive back for Bengals and Cowboys; Super Bowl XXIII, Super Bowl XXVII; scored five NFL TDs as defender and punt returner; UW (1979-82); Rose Bowls (1981, 1982).

Willie Horton – outfielder for Mariners (1979-80) and Tigers; had 29 homers and 106 RBI for Mariners (1979).

Ron Howard – tight end for Seahawks (1976-78), Bills, and Cowboys; Super Bowl X; basketball forward for Seattle U (1971-1974).

Brock Huard – quarterback for Seahawks (2000-01) and Colts; UW (1996-98); ESPN-TV broadcaster; brother Damon Huard was UW and NFL quarterback; brother Luke Huard was North Carolina quarterback.

Damon Huard – quarterback for Chiefs, Dolphins and Patriots; Super Bowl XXXVI,

Super Bowl XXXVII; UW (1992-94); Rose Bowl (1993).

Jack Hurley (1897-1972) – boxing manager and promoter worked in Seattle, Chicago and Fargo, N.D.; managed Seattle heavyweights Boone Kirkman and Harry "Kid" Matthews; nicknamed "Deacon."

Steve Hutchinson – offensive guard for Seahawks (2001-05), Vikings and Titans; Super Bowl XL starter (2006); Seahawks Pro Bowl selections (2003, 2004, 2005).

Raul Ibanez – outfielder for Mariners (1996-2000, 2004-08, 2013), Angels, Royals, Phillies and Yankees; had 33 home runs and 123 RBI for Mariners (2006).

Darrell Jackson – wide receiver for Seahawks (2000-06), Broncos and 49ers; Super Bowl XL starter (2006).

Lauren Jackson – center for Storm (2001-2012); WNBA championships (2004, 2010); WNBA Most Valuable Player (2003, 2007, 2010); Storm All-Star selections (2001, 2002, 2003, 2005, 2006, 2007, 2009, 2010); competed in 2000 Sydney Olympics, 2004 Athens Olympics, 2008 Beijing Olympics and 2012 London Olympics.

Michael Jackson – linebacker for Seahawks (1979-86); UW (1975-78); Rose Bowl (1978); actor appeared in TV shows "21 Jump Street," "MacGyver," "The Commish" and "Wiseguy" and movie "Look Who's Talking, Too."

Jeff Jaeger – placekicker for Bears, Browns and Raiders; one-time Pro Bowl selection; UW (1983-86); first-team *AP* All-America selection (1986); NCAA record 80 field goals;

Orange Bowl (1985); Kent-Meridian HS.

Bruce Jarvis – center for Bills; member of "Electric Company" offensive line that blocked for O.J. Simpson's record 2,003-yard rushing season in 1973; knee injury ended pro career; UW (1968-70); Franklin HS.

Avery Johnson – guard for Sonics (1989-90); Mavericks, Nuggets, Rockets and Spurs; coach for Mavericks and Nets.

Dennis Johnson (1954-2007) – guard for Sonics (1977-80), Celtics and Suns; Sonics All-Star selections (1979, 1980); Sonics NBA championship team starter (1979); Sonics NBA finals MVP (1979); Basketball Hall of Fame inductee.

Earl Johnson (1919-94) – pitcher for Rainiers (1951-52); pitched for Sox and Tigers; Ballard HS.

Eddie Johnson – forward for Sonics (1991-93), Hornets, Rockets, Pacers, Suns and Kings.

John Johnson – forward for Sonics (1978-82), Cavaliers, Rockets and Trail Blazers; Sonics NBA championship team starter (1979).

Terry "Tank" Johnson – defensive tackle for Bears, Bengals and Cowboys; Super Bowl XLI starter; UW (2001-03); Rose Bowl (2001).

Trent Johnson – basketball coach for LSU, Nevada, Stanford and TCU; assistant coach for UW (1990-92); Boise State University; Franklin High.

Vinnie Johnson – guard for Sonics (1980-82), Pistons and Spurs; nicknamed "Microwave."

Jay Johnstone – outfielder for Seattle Angels (1966-68); batted .340 for Seattle (1966); played for Angels, Cubs, White Sox, Dodgers, Yankees, A's, Phillies and Padres.

Bobby Jones – forward for Nuggets, Rockets, Grizzlies, Heat, 76ers and Spurs; UW (2003-

06); NCAA Tournament (2004, 2005, 2006).

Calvin Jones – defensive back for Broncos; UW (1970-72); first-team *AP* All-America selection (1972); became San Francisco minister.

K.C. Jones – basketball coach for Sonics (1991-92), Celtics and Bullets, and ABA's San Diego Conquistadors; guard played for Celtics; Basketball Hall of Fame inductee.

Ruppert Jones – outfielder for Mariners (1977-79), Angels, Tigers, Royals, Yankees and Padres; Mariners All-Star selection (1977).

Ted Jones (1909-2000) – hydroplane builder who designed and constructed *Slo Mo Shun IV*, won the Gold Cup in Detroit and helped steer the race to his hometown (1951); son Ron and grandson Ron Jr. were hydro builders; Motorsports Hall of Fame inductee.

Regina Joyce – long-distance runner for UW (1981-1983); NCAA champion in 3,000 meters (1981); NCAA cross-country champion (1982); ran marathon for Ireland in 1984 Los Angeles Olympics but didn't medal.

Jimin Kang – LPGA Tour golfer won 2005 LPGA Corning Classic and 2010 Sime Darby LPGA Malaysia; Arizona State; King's HS.

George Karl – basketball coach for Sonics (1992-98), Bucks, Cavaliers, Nuggets and Warriors; led Sonics to three 60-win seasons, including all-time best 64-18 (1996).

Napoleon Kaufman – running back for Raiders; UW (1991-94); school's all-time leading rusher with 4,104 yards; rushed four times for 200 or more in game; Rose Bowls (1992, 1993); became Dublin, Calif., minister.

Danny Kaye (1913-1987) – one of six original owners for Mariners (1977-81); partnered with Seattle radio station owner

Les Smith and Seattle businessmen Walter Schoenfeld, Jim Walsh, Jim Stillwell and Stan Golub, before selling to George Argyros; film star and entertainer.

Joe Kearney (1927-2010) – athletic director for UW (1969-76); WAC commissioner for 15 years; athletic director for Michigan State and Arizona State; SPU.

Les Keiter (1919-2009) – national radio broadcaster in Philadelphia and New York; called 12 heavyweight fights for ABC and Mutual radio, including 1964 Ali-Liston bout; play-by-play broadcaster for New York Knicks and Giants and Rangers and Philadelphia 76ers; appeared in 14 episodes of original "Hawaii Five-0"; inducted into Baseball hall of fame; UW; Broadway HS.

Mick Kelleher – infielder for Angels, Cubs, Lions, Astros and Cardinals; UPS; Shoreline HS

Kasey Keller – goalie for Sounders (2009-11); U.S. national team player..

Steve Kelley – columnist and reporter for *Seattle Times* (1982-2013) and *Portland Oregonian*; made cameo appearance in Prefontaine film.

Joe Kelly – linebacker for Bengals; Super Bowl XXIII starter; UW (1982-85); Orange Bowl (1985).

Cortez Kennedy – defensive tackle for Seahawks (1990-2000); Pro Bowl selections (1991, 1992, 1993, 1994, 1995, 1996, 1998, 1999); *AP* NFL Defensive Player of the Year (1992); Seahawks Ring of Honor inductee (2006); Pro Football Hall of Fame inductee (2012); jersey No. 96 retired.

Karol Kennedy (1932-2004) – pairs skater who, with twin brother Peter, won a world championship (1950); five-time U.S. champion; silver medalist at 1952 Oslo Olympics; Colorado College; UW; St. Nicholas School.

Peter Kennedy – pairs skater won a world championship (1950); five-time U.S. champion; silver medalist at 1952 Oslo Olympics; Colorado College; UW; Queen Anne HS.

Tamerlane "Lincoln" Kennedy – offensive lineman for Falcons and Raiders; three-time Pro Bowl selection; Super Bowl XXXVII starter; UW (1989-92); Rose Bowls (1991, 1992, 1993); first-team *AP* All-America selection (1992); Morris Trophy winner (1991-92).

Patrick Kerney – defensive end for Seahawks (2007-09) and Falcons; Seahawks Pro Bowl (2007); married KING-TV sportscaster Lisa Gangel.

Ed Kirkpatrick (1944-2010) – utility player for Seattle Angels (1965, 1967); played for Angels, Royals, Brewers, Pirates and Rangers; 1981 auto accident left him partially paralyzed and wheelchair-bound; nicknamed "Spanky."

Jon Kitna – quarterback for Seahawks (1997-2000), Bengals, Lions and Cowboys; threw for 3,346 yards and 23 touchdowns for Seahawks (1999); Central Washington; 1995 NAIA national championship; became teacher and coach at alma mater Lincoln High (Tacoma).

Bill Knight – columnist, sports editor and sportswriter for the *Seattle Post-Intelligencer* (1961-98); UW; Queen Anne HS; high school basketball teammate of UW's Bob Houbregs.

Dick Knight – pro tennis player; played longest tournament match in U.S. history in Southhampton, N.Y., needing 5½ hours and 107 games to beat Mike Sprengelmeyer 32-30, 3-6, 18-17; UW (1968-70); All-American selection (1970); Shoreline HS.

Chuck Knox – football coach for Seahawks (1983-91), Bills and Rams; AFC championship game (1983); Seahawks Ring of Honor inductee (2005).

Charlie Koon (1931-2002) – guard for UW (1952-53); Final Four team starter (1953); NCAA Tournament (1953).

Olin Kreutz – center for Chicago Bears and New Orleans Saints; Super Bowl XLI starter; six-time Pro Bowl selection; UW (1995-97); punched and broke jaws of teammates Sekou Wiggs with Huskies and Fred Miller of Bears.

Jake Kupp – offensive guard for Falcons, Cowboys, Saints and Redskins; one-time Pro Bowl selection; UW (1961-63); Rose Bowl (1964); son Craig Kupp was Cowboys and Cardinals quarterback.

Tom Lampkin – catcher for Mariners (1999-2001), Indians, Brewers, Cardinals, Padres and Giants; Mariners clubhouse boy; Portland; Edmonds CC; Blanchet HS.

Mark Langston – pitcher for Mariners (1984-89), Angels, Indians, Expos and Padres; Mariners All-Star selection (1987); centerpiece of Randy Johnson trade.

Zach LaVine -- guard for Timberwolves; 2015 NBA slam-dunk champ; father Paul LaVine played linebacker for Seahawks' 1987 replacement team; UCLA; Bothell HS.

Danielle Lawrie – softball pitcher for UW (2006-07, 2009-10); NCAA championship (2009); College Softball Player of the Year (2009); first-team All-America selection (2009, 2010); had pitching records of 42-8 (2009) and 40-5 (2010); played in 2008 Beijing Olympics for Canada.

Jim Lea (1932-2010) – Sprinter who ran in 1956 Melbourne Olympics, failing to reach finals in 400-meter dash; set world record in 440-yard dash in 45.8 seconds in 1956

Modesto Relays; USC; Roosevelt HS.

Hal Lee (1910-1977) – point guard for UW (1932-34); first-team Helms Foundation All-America selection (1934); basketball referee.

Mark Lee – defensive back for Packers, Saints, and 49ers; UW (1977-79); Rose Bowl (1978); returned three punts for touchdowns (1979).

Jack Lelivelt (1885-1941) – manager for Rainiers (1938-40); PCL championships (1939, 1940); outfielder for Senators, New York Highlanders, Yankees and Cleveland Naps; died from heart attack suffered at Harlem Globetrotters game in Seattle.

Bob Lemon (1920-2000) – manager for Angels (1965-66); PCL championship (1966); big-league manager for Royals, White Sox and Yankees; pitcher for Indians; Baseball Hall of Fame inductee.

Mike Lentz – baseball's No. 2 overall draft pick by Padres (1975); played four seasons in minor leagues, reaching Double-A Amarillo; arm trouble curtailed career; Juanita HS.

Jeff Leonard – outfielder for Mariners (1989-90), Astros, Dodgers, Brewers and Giants; Mariners All-Star selection (1989).

Pat Lesser (Harbottle) – amateur golfer won 1951 U.S. Junior Girls and 1955 U.S. Women's Amateur; Seattle U men's team (1953-56); Holy Names Academy.

Mitch Levy – sports radio talk-show host for KJR 950 AM (1994-to date); city's most listened to sports broadcaster.

D.D. Lewis – linebacker for Seahawks (2002-06, 2008-09) and Broncos; Super Bowl XL starter (2006).

Greg Lewis – running back for Broncos; UW (1987-90); original Doak Walker Award recipient (1991); Rose Bowl (1991); Pac-10 Offensive Player of Year (1990); Ingraham HS.

Rashard Lewis – forward for Sonics (1999-2007), Magic and Wizards; Sonics All-Star selection (2005).

Jake Locker – quarterback for Titans; UW (2007-10); drafted and signed as outfielder by Los Angeles Angels.

Sean Locklear – offensive tackle for Seahawks (2004-10) and Redskins; Super Bowl XL starter (2006).

Jim Lonborg – pitcher for Rainiers (1964); pitched for Red Sox, Brewers and Phillies; became a dentist.

Plummer Lott – guard for Sonics (1968-69); Seattle U (1965-67); NCAA Tournament (1967); New York Supreme Court judge.

Bob Love – forward for Sonics (1977), Royals, Bulls, Bucks and Nets; nicknamed "Butterbean."

Maurice Lucas (1952-2010) – forward for Sonics (1987), Lakers, Knicks, Nets, Suns, Trail Blazers and ABA's Kentucky Colonels and Spirit of St. Louis.

Mike Lude – athletic director for UW (1976-91) and Kent State; football coach for Colorado State; had Husky Stadium north stands built.

Marshawn Lynch – running back for Seahawks (2010-to date) and Bills; Seahawks Pro Bowl selections (2011, 2012, 2013, 2014); one-time Pro Bowler with Bills; Super Bowl XLVIII starter (2014), Super Bowl starter XLIX (2015); nicknamed "Beast Mode."

M

Todd MacCulloch – center for Nets and 76ers; UW (1996-99); NCAA Tournaments (1998, 1999); played in 2000 Sydney Olympics for Canada.

Bill MacFarland (1932-2011) hockey player for Americans and Totems (1955-66); Totems coach (1967-70); WHL president; WHA president; UW law school graduate.

Dave Mahler – sports radio talk-show host for KJR (1994 - to date); known on the air as "Softy;" Bellevue Community College; Bellevue HS.

Rick Mallory – offensive lineman for Buccaneers; tight end and offensive guard for UW (1980-83); Rose Bowls (1981, 1982); UW (1993-98) assistant coach; Lindbergh HS.

Rex Manchester (1927-1966) – hydroplane driver for *U-7 Notre Dame* from Seattle and one of three killed during 1966 President's Cup Regatta on Potomac River in Washington, D.C.; Florida's Don Wilson in *Miss Budweiser* and Manchester died in final heat, and Seattle's Ron Musson in *Miss Bardahl* was killed in earlier heat.

Ray Mansfield (1941-1996) – center for Eagles and Steelers; Super Bowl IX starter, Super Bowl X starter; UW (1960-62); Rose Bowl (1961); died of heart attack while hiking in Grand Canyon.

Vic Markov (1915-1998) – two-way tackle for Rams; UW (1934-37); Rose Bowl (1937); College Football Hall of Fame inductee.

Dennis Martinez – pitcher for Mariners (1997), Braves, Orioles, Indians and Expos.

Tino Martinez – first baseman for Mariners (1990-95), Yankees, Cardinals and Devil Rays; Mariners All-Star selection (1995).

Kevin Mawae – offensive lineman for Seahawks (1994-97), Jets and Titans; NFL players' union president.

Kenny Mayne – ESPN-TV SportsCenter broadcaster; KSTW-TV broadcaster; reserve quarterback for Nevada-Las Vegas; Wenatchee Valley College; Jefferson HS.

Stafford Mays – defensive lineman for Vikings and Cardinals; UW (1978-79); Rose Bowl (1978); father of NFL safety Taylor Mays.

Taylor Mays – safety for Bengals and 49ers; four-year USC starter; first-team *AP* All-America selection; 2006, 2007, 2008 Rose Bowl; O'Dea HS.

Doug McClary (1932-1982) – forward for UW (1951-53); starter for Final Four team (1953); NCAA Tournament (1951, 1953).

Mike McCormack (1930-2013) – football coach for Seahawks (1982), Colts and Eagles; president and general manager for Seahawks (1982-89); played offensive tackle for Browns and New York Yanks; Pro Football Hall of Fame inductee.

Mike McCutchen – forward for UW (1951-53); Final Four team starter (1953); NCAA Tournament (1951, 1953); Garfield HS.

Xavier McDaniel – forward for Sonics (1986-91), Celtics, Nets and Knicks; Sonics All-Star selection (1988); averaged 23 ppg (1987).

Jim McDaniels – center for Sonics (1972-74), Braves, Lakers and ABA's Carolina Cougars and Kentucky Colonels.

Steve McDaniels – defensive tackle for Notre Dame; Cotton Bowl; 1977 natioal championship; Renton HS; *Parade* All-America selection (1973).

Jim McGlothlin (1943-1975) – pitcher for Seattle Angels (1965-66); pitched for Angels, Reds and White Sox; died of leukemia.

Cliff McGrath – soccer coach for SPU (1970-2007); NCAA Division II national championships (1978, 1983, 1985, 1986, 1993); overall coaching record 597-233-95.

Joel McHale – comedian and host of Comedy Central's "Talk Soup;" walk-on tight end for UW (1992-93); Rose Bowl (1993); Mercer Island HS.

Jim McLean – golf instructor for PGA and LPGA Tour players; owner and CEO of Jim McLean Golf School at Doral in Miami, Fla.; PGA Tour player; Houston; Highline HS.

Nate McMillan – point guard for Sonics (1987-98); coach for Sonics (2001-05) and Trail Blazers; club-record 25 assists against Clippers (1987); No. 10 retired by Sonics.

Pat McMurtry (1932-2011) – heavyweight boxer fought out of Seattle (1954-59); compiled 33-4-1 record with 25 knockouts; defeated Ezzard Charles and George Chuvalo; boxing referee.

Herb Mead – leading alumni donor for UW football program; disassociated by school in 1993 with fellow boosters Jim Heckman, Jim Kenyon and Roy Moore following Huskies scandal.

Jack Medica (1914-1985) – swimmer won gold medal in 400-meter freestyle and silver medals in 1,500-meter freestyle and 4x200-meter freestyle in 1936 Berlin Olympics; International Swimming Hall of Fame inductee; UW; Lincoln HS.

Ron Medved – defensive back for Eagles; UW (1963-65); Rose Bowl (1964).

Mario Mendoza – shortstop for Mariners (1979-80), Pirates and Rangers; batted .198 (1979), inspiring the "Mendoza Line" reference for anyone near the .200 level.

Tom Meschery – forward for Sonics (1968-71) and Warriors; Sonics assistant coach; poet; born Tomislav Nikolayevich Meshcheryakov.

Andy Messersmith – pitcher for Seattle Angels (1966, 1968); pitched for Braves, Angels, Dodgers and Yankees; one of the players responsible for removal of baseball's reserve clause.

Charlie Metro (1918-2011) – outfielder for Rainiers (1946); manager for Cubs and Royals.

Georg N. Meyers (1915-2007) – columnist and sports editor for *Seattle Times* (1949-1984); received chapter in football coach John McKay's autobiography as chief antagonist.

John Meyers (1940-1998) – defensive tackle for Cowboys and Eagles; UW tight end (1959-61) and basketball player (1960); Rose Bowls (1960, 1961).

Anna Mickelson – rower for UW women's team (1999-2002); won silver medal in women's eight 2004 Athens Olympics; won gold medal in women's eight in 2008 Beijing Olympics; women's eight NCAA championships (2001, 2002), women's four NCAA championship (1999); Newport HS.

Marvin Milkes (1923-1982) – general manager for Pilots (1969) and Brewers; responsible for trading Lou Piniella in training camp; general manager for WHA's New York Raiders and NASL's Los Angeles Aztecs.

Hugh Millen – quarterback for Falcons, Broncos, Rams and Patriots; UW (1984-86); Orange Bowl (1985); Roosevelt HS.

Lawyer Milloy – safety for Seahawks (2009-10), Falcons, Bills and Patriots; Super Bowl XXXI and Super Bowl XXXVI starter; four-time Pro Bowl selection; UW (1992-95); Rose Bowl (1993); first-team *AP* All-America selection (1995).

Don Mincher (1938-2012) – first baseman

for Pilots (1969), Angels, Twins, A's, Rangers and Senators; Pilots All-Star selection (1969).

Charlie Mitchell – running back and defensive back for Bills and Broncos; UW (1960-62); Rose Bowl (1961); Garfield HS.

Bobby Moore – defender for Sounders (1978); former English First Division player; led England to 1966 World Cup victory over West Germany.

Jim Moore – sports radio talk-show host for ESPN Seattle (2010-to date): columnist and editor for *Seattle Post-Intelligencer* (1983-2009); known as "the Go-2-Guy"; WSU, Redmond HS.

Jimmy Moore – fast-pitch softball pitcher for Seattle's Peterbilt Western (1981-92); ASA national championships (1982, 1985, 1986); compiled 54-5 record (1985); ASA Hall of Fame inductee.

Jim Mora Jr. – football coach for Seahawks (2009) and Falcons; 5-11 season was shortest tenure for any Seahawks coach; Seahawks assistant coach (2007-08); football coach for UCLA; linebacker for UW (1981-83); Rose Bowl (1982); son of Jim Mora Sr.; Interlake HS.

Jim Mora Sr. – football coach for Colts, Saints and USFL's Philadelphia Stars and Baltimore Stars; assistant coach for Seahawks (1978-81); assistant coach for UW (1975-77); Rose Bowl (1978).

Bill Morris (1920-1995) – shooting guard for UW (1941-44); NCAA Tournament (1943); UW assistant coach (1947-59).

Chrystal Morrison – volleyball player for UW (2004-07); first-team AVCA All-America selection (2006, 2007); NCAA championship (2005); NCAA Most Outstanding Player (2005).

Jamie Moyer – pitcher for Mariners (1996-2006), Orioles, Cubs, Rockies, Phillies, Cardinals and Rangers; pitched with

Mariners until 43, in majors until 49; Mariners All-Star selection (2003); compiled 269-209 career record; 20-6 and 21-7 for Mariners (2001, 2003).

Rudy Mucha (1918-1982) -- offensive guard for Bears and Rams; UW (1938-40); first-team *AP* All-American selection (1940).

Ron Musson (1927-1966) – hydroplane driver from Seattle was one of three racers killed during 1966 President's Cup Regatta on Potomac River in Washington, D.C.; Musson died when boat went airborne in heat 2B and disintegrated, ejecting the driver; Seattle's Rex Manchester and Don Wilson from Florida were killed in final heat.

Lynn Nance – basketball coach for UW (1990-93), Central Missouri State, Iowa State, Southwest Baptist and St. Mary's; fired by Huskies; assistant coach for Huskies (1967-69); forward for UW (1964-65); FBI agent.

Joe Nash – defensive tackle who played entire NFL career for Seahawks (1982-96); Seahawks Pro Bowl (1984); played 218 games, more than any other player in franchise history.

Petr Nedved – hockey winger for Seattle Thunderbirds (1990); played for Oilers, Flyers, Coyotes, Penguins, Rangers, Blues and Canucks.

Chuck Nelson – placekicker for Bills, Rams and Vikings; UW (1979-82); Rose Bowls (1981, 1982); first-team *AP* All-America selection (1982).

Louie Nelson – shooting guard for Bullets, Kings, Nets, Jazz and Spurs; UW (1971-73); averaged 23 ppg for Huskies (1973).

Blaine Newnham – columnist for *Seattle*

Times (1982-2005), *Eugene Register-Guard*; author of *America's St. Andrews*.

Jack Nichols (1926-1992) – center for Celtics, Hawks, Tri-Cities Blackhawks and Washington Capitals; 1957 NBA championship; UW (1944, 1947-48); five-time all-conference selection for UW and USC; NCAA Tournament (1948).

John Nordstrom – owner of Seahawks (1976-88); sold franchise to California real-estate developer Ken Behring for $79 million; uncle Lloyd Nordstrom was fellow owner who died of heart attack in 1976 while playing tennis in Mexico before Seahawks' first season.

Don Ogorek (1939-2007) – forward for Seattle U (1958-1960); Final Four championship game starter (1958); NCAA Tournament (1958); fifth-round Cincinnati Royals draft choice.

Apolo Anton Ohno – eight-time speed-skating medalist won gold medal in 1,500-meter race and silver medal in 1,000 in 2002 Salt Lake City Olympics; won gold medal in 500, bronze medal in 1,000, and bronze medal in 5,000 relay in 2006 Turin Olympics; won silver medal in 1,500, bronze medal in 5,000 relay, and bronze medal in 1,000 in 2010 Vancouver Olympics; Decatur HS.

Russell Okung – offensive tackle for Seahawks (2010-to date); Seahawks Pro Bowl (2012); Super Bowl XLVIII starter (2014), Super Bowl XLIX starter (2015).

Jawaan Oldham – center for Bulls, Nuggets, Rockets, Pacers, Lakers, Knicks, Magic and Kings; Seattle U (1977-80); Cleveland HS.

John Olerud – first baseman for Mariners

Jawaan Oldham

(2000-04), Sox, Mets, Yankees and Blue Jays; 1993 AL batting champion for Blue Jays; 1992 and 1993 World Series champions; Mariners All-Star selection (2001), one-time Blue Jays All-Star; recovered from brain aneurysm to resume baseball career; son of John Olerud Sr., former Seattle Angels catcher; WSU; Interlake HS.

Frank Oleynick – shooting guard for Sonics (1976-77); Seattle U (1973-75); averaged 25.1 (1974) and 27.3 points per game (1975) for Chieftains; WCAC MVP (1974); nicknamed "Magic."

Benji Olson – offensive guard for Titans; started 140 of 152 NFL games; Super Bowl XXXIV starter; UW (1995-97).

Claude Osteen – pitcher for Rainiers (1958-59); pitched for White Sox, Reds, Astros, Dodgers, Cardinals and Senators.

John Owen (1929-2014) – sports columnist and sports editor for *Seattle Post-Intelligencer* (1957-94).

Ray Oyler (1929 - 2014)– shortstop for Pilots (1969), Angels and Tigers; batted .165 for Pilots; "Ray Oyler Fan Club" created in attempt to help him hit.

P

Tom Pacioerk – first baseman and outfielder for Mariners (1978-81), Braves, White Sox, Dodgers, Mets and Rangers; Mariners All-Star selection (1981).

Mike Parrott – pitcher for Mariners (1978-81) and Orioles; went from 14-12 pitching record (1979) to 1-16 (1980) for Mariners.

Jack Patera – first football coach for Seahawks (1976-82); NFL Coach of Year (1978); compiled 35-59 record; fired in 1982 and never coached again; offensive guard for Colts, Cardinals and Cowboys.

Marty Pattin – pitcher for Pilots (1969), Red Sox, Angels, Royals and Brewers; pitcher for Seattle Angels (1966-68).

Dave Pear – defensive lineman for Colts, Raiders and Bucs; Super Bowl XV; one-time Pro Bowl selection; UW (1972-74).

Scott Pelleur – linebacker for Saints; UW assistant coach (1996-98, 2003-04); WSU; Interlake HS.

Steve Pelleur – quarterback for Cowboys, Bronco, and Chiefs; UW (1980-83); Rose Bowls (1981, 1982); Interlake HS.

Prentiss Perkins – guard for UW basketball team (1993); sentenced to four years in prison for cocaine dealing.

Gaylord Perry – pitcher for Mariners (1983), Braves, Indians, Royals, Yankees, Padres, Giants and Rangers; earned 300th victory for Mariners (1983), beating New York Yankees 7-3; 314 career wins; Baseball Hall of Fame inductee.

Johnny Pesky (1919-2012) – manager for Rainiers (1961-62); manager for Red Sox; infielder for Red Sox, Tigers and Senators.

Rico Petrocelli – shortstop for Rainiers (1964); played for Red Sox.

Jeremiah Pharms – linebacker for UW (1997-2000); Rose Bowl (2001); linebacker for Arena League's New York Dragons; sentenced to 41 months in prison for robbery.

Jimmy Phelan (1892-1974) – football coach for UW (1930-41), Missouri, Purdue and St. Mary's; coached NFL's Dallas Texans; Rose Bowl (1937); College Football Hall of Fame inductee.

Ken Phelps – utility player for Mariners (1983-88), Indians, Royals, Expos, Yankees and Athletics; ASU and WSU; Ingraham HS.

Gary Pinkel – football coach for Toledo and Missouri; offensive coordinator and assistant coach for UW (1976, 1979-90); Rose Bowls (1981, 1982); unsuccessful UW head-coaching candidate.

Ray Pinney – offensive lineman for Steelers and USFL's Michigan Panthers and Oakland Invaders; Super Bowl XIII starter, Super Bowl XIV; 1983 USFL championship; caught four pro TD passes, two in NFL; UW (1972-75); Shorecrest HS.

Vada Pinson (1938-1996) – outfielder for Rainiers (1958); Mariners coach (1977-80, 1982-83); played for Angels, Reds, Indians, Royals and Cardinals.

Bill Plaschke – sportswriter for the *Seattle Post-Intelligencer* (1981-1987); replaced legendary Jim Murray as lead columnist for *Los Angeles Times*; ESPN's Around the Horn panelist; authored books on Seahawks coach Chuck Knox and Mariners manager Dick Williams.

Quincy Pondexter – forward for Pelicans and Grizzlies; UW (2007-10); NCAA Tournament (2009, 2010); fourth-leading Huskies

scorer (1,786 points).

Mark Pope – forward for Nuggets, Pacers and Bucks; UW (1992-93); Pac-10 Freshman of the Year (1992); transferred to Kentucky; 1996 NCAA championship; Newport HS.

Craig Puki – linebacker for 49ers and Cardinals; Super Bowl XVI; Tennessee; Glacier HS.

Q

Pat Quinn – defenseman for Totems (1967); played for Flames, Maple Leafs and Canucks; coach for Oilers, Kings, Flyers, Maple Leafs and Canucks.

R

Dick Radatz (1937-2005) – relief pitcher for Rainiers (1961); pitched for Red Sox, Cubs, Indians and Expos.

Pete Rademacher – heavyweight boxer lost by sixth-round knockout to Floyd Patterson at Sicks' Stadium (1957); only boxer to fight for world heavyweight championship in first pro bout; gold medalist in 1956 Melbourne Olympics; Seattle Golden Gloves champion (1949, 1951-53).

Steve Raible – wide receiver for Seahawks (1976-81); KIRO-TV news and sports anchor; Seahawks play-by-play and color broadcaster for KIRO radio (1981-to date).

Dan Raley – sportswriter for *Seattle Post-Intelligencer* (1980-2009); author of *Pitchers of Beer* and *Brandon Roy Story*; Roosevelt HS.

Nancy Ramey – swimmer won silver medal in 100-meter butterfly in 1956 Melbourne Olympics; six-time national championship; UW; Mercer Island HS.

Clarence Ramsey – shooting guard for UW (1974-76); NCAA Tournament (1975); worked as Sea-Tac Airport skycap.

John Randle – defensive lineman for Seahawks (2001-03) and Vikings; Seahawks Pro Bowl selection (2001); Pro Football Hall of Fame inductee.

Merritt Ranew (1938-2011) – catcher for Pilots (1969), Angels, Sox, Astros and Braves; played for Seattle Angels (1965-67); hit in the head with a bat by Vancouver Mounties outfielder Santiago Rosario (1966).

Eldridge Recasner – shooting guard for Hawks, Hornets, Nuggets, Rockets and Clippers; UW (1986-89); NCAA Tournament (1986).

Rick Redman – linebacker for Chargers; UW offensive guard and linebacker (1962-64);

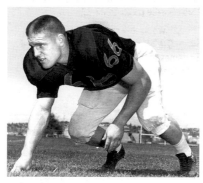

Rick Redman

Rose Bowl (1964); College Football Hall of Fame inductee; Blanchet HS.

George Reed – running back for CFL's Saskatchewan Roughriders; rushed for career 16,116 yards and scored 137 touchdowns; No. 34 retired by Roughriders; WSU; Renton HS.

Rick Reichardt – outfielder for Seattle

Angels (1965); played for Angels, White Sox, Royals and Senators; player who forced introduction of amateur baseball draft.

Bob Reynolds – relief pitcher for Orioles, Indians, Tigers, Brewers, Expos and Cardinals; nicknamed "Bullet Bob"; Ingraham HS.

Craig Reynolds – shortstop for Mariners (1977-78), Astros and Pirates; Mariners All-Star selection (1978).

Harold Reynolds – second baseman for Mariners (1983-92), Orioles and Angels; Mariners All-Star selections (1987, 1988); ESPN and MLB Network broadcaster.

Jerry Rice – wide receiver for Seahawks (2004), Raiders and 49ers; two-time Super Bowl starter; Pro Football Hall of Fame inductee.

Paul Richards (1908-1986) – manager for Rainiers (1950); manager for Orioles and White Sox.

Clint Richardson – shooting guard for Pacers and 76ers; 1983 NBA championship with 76ers; Seattle U (1976-79); all-time leading scorer with 1,823 points for Chieftains; totaled 8,028 points on prep, college and pro basketball levels; O'Dea HS.

David Riske – relief pitcher for Red Sox, White Sox, Indians, Royals and Brewers; Green River CC; Lindbergh HS.

Rick Rizzs – broadcaster for Seattle Mariners (1983-1991, 1995-to date); lead voice for Detroit Tigers.

Eugene Robinson – safety for Seahawks (1985-95), Falcons, Panthers and Packers; Seahawks Pro Bowl selections (1992, 1993).

Aurelio Rodriguez (1947-2000) – third baseman for Seattle Angels (1966-68); played for Orioles, Angels, White Sox, Tigers, Yankees, Padres and Senators; killed walking in Detroit by driver whose car jumped a curb.

Rich Rollins – third baseman for Seattle Pilots (1969), Indians, Brewers and Twins.

Darrell Royal (1924-2012) – football coach for UW (1956), Mississippi State and Texas; College Football Hall of Fame inductee.

Bob Rule – center for Sonics (1968-72), Cavaliers and 76ers; Sonics All-Star selection (1970); averaged 24 and 24.6 ppg (1969-70); career curtailed by Achilles' heel injury.

Glendon Rusch – pitched for Cubs, Rockies, Royals, Brewers, Mets and Padres; Shorecrest HS.

Bill Russell – basketball coach for Sonics (1974-77), Celtics and Kings; led Sonics to franchise's first playoff appearances (1975, 1976); compiled 162-166 record for Sonics; center for Celtics; Basketball Hall of Fame inductee.

Andy Russo – basketball coach for UW (1986-89), Louisiana Tech, Florida Tech, and Lynn; NCAA Tournament (1986).

S

Bill Sander – golfer won 1976 U.S. Amateur; played PGA Tour in 1977-93 and went winless; BYU; Shorecrest HS.

Casey Sander – character actor in more than 200 feature films, TV shows, movies and commercials; outfielder for Class A independent Seattle Rainiers (1975); UPS football; Nathan Hale HS.

Bob Sapp – pro wrestler in Japan; kick boxer and mixed martial arts competitor; UW offensive guard (1993-96); played one game for NFL's Minnesota Vikings in 1997.

Steve Sarkisian – football coach for UW (2009-13); left for USC, becoming first coach

in 57 years to voluntarily leave Huskies for another program.

Adam Schefter – sportswriter for *Seattle Post-Intelligencer* (1989), *Rocky Mountain News* and *Denver Post;* NFL reporter for NFL Network and ESPN.

John Schneider – general manager for Seahawks (2010-to date); Seahawks director of player personnel (2000); Super Bowl XLVIII (2014), Super bowl XLIX (2015).

Bill Schonely – radio play-by-play broadcaster for Pilots (1969), Angels (1965-68) and Totems hockey team (1958-69); Portland Trail Blazers broadcaster.

Detlef Schrempf – swingman for Sonics (1994-99), Mavericks, Pacers and Trail Blazers; Sonics All-Star selections (1995, 1997); UW (1982-85); NCAA Tournament (1984, 1985); played in 1984 Los Angeles Olympics and 1992 Barcelona Olympics for Germany.

Detlef Schrempf

Sam Schulman (1910-2003) – original owner for Sonics (1968-83); signed Spencer Haywood from ABA to break early-entry rule; sold franchise to Barry Ackerley for $21 million; owned NFL's Chargers.

Howard Schultz – owner for Sonics (2001-06); bought franchise from Barry Ackerley for $200 million and sold to group headed by Clay Bennett for $350 million; Starbucks CEO and founder.

Joe Schultz (1918-1996) – manager for Pilots (1969); compiled 64-98 record; fired after Pilots' only season; interim manager for Tigers.

Paul Schwegler (1907-1980) – defensive tackle for UW (1929-31); first-team *AP* All-America selection (1930, 1931); College Football Hall of Fame inductee; actor who appeared in several films.

Fraser Scott – middleweight boxer fought out of Seattle (1968-72); compiled 22-7-1 record, with nine knockouts; admitted to fight-fixing.

Diego Segui – pitcher for Pilots (1969), Mariners (1977), Red Sox, A's and Senators; pitched in first game for each Seattle franchise; nicknamed the "Ancient Mariner"; son David Segui played first base for Mariners (1998-99).

Aaron Sele – pitcher for Mariners (2000-01, 2005), Angels, Red Sox, Dodgers, Mets and Rangers; Mariners All-Star selection (2000).

Richie Sexson – first baseman for Mariners (2005-08), Diamondbacks, Indians, Brewers and Yankees; hit 39 and 34 homers for Mariners (2005-06).

Robert Shannon – super-bantamweight boxer fought out of Seattle (1984-90); had 18-6-2 pro record, 124-27 as amateur; competed in 1984 Los Angeles Olympics.

Jeff Shelley – editorial director of Cybergolf.com from 2000 to date; co-founder of Northwest Golf Media Association (1995);

author of three editions of *Golf Courses of the Pacific Northwest* and co-author/publisher of *Championships & Friendships: The First 100 Years of the Pacific Northwest Golf Association.*

Lonnie Shelton – forward for Sonics (1979-83), Cavaliers and Knicks; NBA championship team starter (1979); Sonics All-Star selection (1982).

Emil Sick (1894-1964) – owner for Rainiers (1938-60); built Sicks' Stadium; PCL championships (1939, 1940, 1941, 1951, 1955); Rainier brewery owner.

Sigurd "Sig" Sigurdson (1918-2006) – offensive end for original Baltimore Colts in 1947 in All-America Football Conference, which merged with NFL; PLU; Ballard HS.

Paul Silas – forward for Sonics (1978-80), Hawks, Celtics, Nuggets, Suns and Hawks; NBA championship team reserve (1979); coach for Bobcats, Hornets and Clippers.

Paul Silvi – sports broadcaster for KING-TV (1993 to date); all-conference placekicker for Bowling Green.

Ed Simmons – offensive lineman for Redskins; Super Bowl XXVI; EWU; Nathan Hale HS.

Jim Skaggs – offensive guard for Eagles; UW (1960-62); Rose Bowl (1961).

Paul Skansi – wide receiver for Seahawks (1984-91) and Steelers; UW (1979-82); Rose Bowls (1981, 1982).

Doug Smart – forward for UW (1956-59); Huskies' all-time leading rebounder with 1,051 until passed by Jon Brockman in 2009; Garfield HS.

Malcolm Smith – linebacker Seahawks (2011-2014); Super Bowl XLVIII starter, Super Bowl XLIX reserve; Super Bowl XLVIII MVP (2014).

Sherman Smith – running back for Seahawks (1976-82) and Chargers; scored 15 TDs for Seahawks (1979).

Hope Solo – goalie for U.S. women's national team in 2008 Beijing Olympics and 2012 London Olympics, and 2011 World Cup; UW (1999-2002); married former UW and NFL player Jerramy Stevens.

Dan Spillner – pitcher for White Sox, Indians and Padres; one of baseball's first designated long relievers; Federal Way HS.

Max Starcevich (1911-1990) – offensive lineman for UW (1934-36); first-team *AP* All-America selection (1936); Rose Bowl (1937); College Football Hall of Fame inductee.

Joe Steele – running back for UW (1976-79); set school career rushing record with 3,091 yards; Rose Bowl (1978); career-ending knee injury as senior prevented NFL career; Blanchet HS; *Parade Magazine* All-America selection (1975).

Gary Stevens – jockey won Longacres riding titles (1983, 1984); captured 1988, 1995 and 1997 Kentucky Derby; won 1994, 1998 and 2001 Belmont Stakes; captured 1997 and 2001 Preakness stakes; won eight Breeder's Cup races; appeared in Seabiscuit film; Hall of Fame inductee.

Jerramy Stevens – tight end for Seahawks (2002-06) and Buccaneers; Super Bowl XL starter (2006); Washington (1999-2001); Rose Bowl (2001); alcohol and drug abuse curtailed career; married soccer player Hope Solo.

Wes Stock – pitching coach for Mariners (1977-81), Athletics, Brewers; Mariners TV broadcaster; pitcher for Orioles and Athletics.

Alfred Strauss (1881-1971) – notable alumni donor for UW; Chicago surgeon recruited and funded Midwest players to join program; UW running back (1902-03).

Mack Strong – fullback for Seahawks (1994-2007); Super Bowl XL starter (2006); Seahawks Pro Bowl selections (2005, 2006).

George Strugar (1934-1997) – defensive lineman for Rams, Jets, Steelers, New York Titans; UW football and basketball player (1955-56); lost season of eligibility facing rape charge; Renton HS.

Rosalynn Sumners – silver-medalist singles figure skater Sarajevo Olympics (1984), second to German Katarina Witt; U.S. National champion (1982, 1983, 1984) and world champion (1983); Meadowdale HS.

Rick Sund – general manager for Sonics (2002-07) Hawks and Pistons.

Bill Swartz – radio talk-show host for CBS 1090 the Fan (2013-to date) and KIRO and ESPN Seattle radio (2002-12).

Sheryl Swoopes – shooting guard for Storm (2008) and Houston Comets; played 29 games for Storm in final WNBA season; Basketball Hall of Fame inductee.

Cedric Tallis (1914-1991) – general manager for Rainiers (1960); general manager for Royals and Yankees.

Chuck Tanner (1929-2011) – manager for Seattle Angels (1967); managed Braves, White Sox, A's and Pirates.

Cheryl Taplin – sprinter for U.S. National Team; three-time NCAA champion in 400-meter relay; LSU; Cleveland HS.

Lofa Tatupu – linebacker for Seahawks (2005-10); Seahawks Pro Bowl selections (2005, 2006, 2007); Super Bowl XL starter (2006).

Brice Taylor (1902-1974) – offensive guard for USC; Trojans' first football All-America selection in 1925; born without right hand; Franklin HS.

Art Thiel – columnist for the *Seattle Post-Intelligncer* (1980-2009) and founder of city's first sports website sportspressnw.com (2010-to date); PLU basketball player.

Earl Thomas – free safety for Seahawks (2010-to date); Seahawks Pro Bowls (2011, 2012, 2013, 2014); Super Bowl XLVIII starter (2014), Super Bowl XLIX starter (2015).

Courtney Thompson – volleyball setter for UW (2003-06); first-team AVCA All-America selection (2004, 2005, 2006); NCAA championship (2005).

David Thompson – shooting guard for Sonics (1983-84) and Nuggets, and ABA's Nuggets; career curtailed by cocaine abuse and knee injury; Hall of Fame inductee; nicknamed "Skywalker."

John Thompson – first general manager of the Seahawks (1976-82); NFL management council executive director; UW.

Steve Thompson – defensive lineman for Jets; UW (1965-67); Super Bowl III; minister in Marysville.

Rod Thorn – guard for Sonics (1968-71), Bullets, Pistons and Hawks; assistant coach for Sonics (1972); coached Bulls and ABA's Spirit; general manager for Bulls; NBA president of basketball operations.

Mike Tice – tight end for Seahawks (1981-88, 1990-91), Vikings and Redskins; coach for Vikings.

Bill Tindall – PGA Tour player for two seasons; U.S. Junior Amateur golf champion (1960); 10 USGA championship appearances; head pro at Broadmoor, Aldarra and Tumble Creek; UW golf coach; UW golfer; Lincoln HS.

Robbie Tobeck – center for Seahawks (2000-06) and Falcons; Super Bowl XL starter (2006), Super Bowl XXXIII starter; Seahawks Pro Bowl selection (2005).

Jeff Toews – offensive guard for Dolphins; Super Bowl XVII starter, Super Bowl XIX; UW (1975-78); Rose Bowl (1978).

Earl Torgeson (1924-1990) – first baseman for Rainiers (1941-42, 1946); played for Braves, White Sox, Tigers, Yankees and Phillies; Snohomish County commissioner.

Roscoe "Torchy" Torrance (1899-1990) – alumni booster who operated improper slush fund for UW; Huskies baseball player (1918-21); executive vice president for Seattle Rainiers.

Marcus Trufant – cornerback for Seahawks (2003-12); Super Bowl XL starter (2006); Seahawks Pro Bowl selection (2007).

Manu Tuiasosopo – defensive lineman for Seahawks (1979-83) and San Francisco 49ers; Super Bowl XIX starter; father of former Mariners infielder-outfielder Matt Tuiasosopo, former NFL and UW quarterback Marques Tuiasosopo, former UW fullback Zach Tuiasosopo, and former UW volleyball player Leslie Tuiasosopo.

Marques Tuiasosopo – quarterback for Raiders and Jets; Super Bowl XXXVII; UW (1997-2000); Rose Bowl offensive MVP (2001); only player in NCAA history to rush for 200 yards and pass for 300 in a game (against Stanford 1999).

Tom Turnure – offensive lineman for Lions; UW (1976-79); Rose Bowl (1978); Roosevelt HS.

Rebecca Twigg – silver-medalist cyclist in road race in 1984 Los Angeles Olympics and bronze medalist in pursuit in 1992 Barcelona Olympics; Garfield HS.

Rebecca Twigg

Al Ulbrickson Sr. (1903-1980) – rowing coach for UW (1927-58); IRA national championships (1936, 1937, 1940, 1941, 1948, 1950); varsity eight won gold medal in 1936 Berlin Olympics; varsity four won gold medal in 1948 London Olympics; upset Trud Rowing Club of Leningrad in 1958; rowed for UW (1923-26); stroke for UW varsity eight IRA championship shell (1924, 1926); U.S. National Rowing Hall of Fame inductee; son Al Ulbrickson Jr. rowed for UW and won bronze medal in 1952 Helsinki Olympics; Franklin HS.

Max Unger – center for Seahawks (2009-2014); Seahawks Pro Bowls (2012, 2013); Super Bowl XLVIII starter (2014), Super Bowl XLIX starter (2015).

Patty Van Wolvelaere (Johnson) – hurdler in 1968 Mexico City Olympics and 1972 Munich Olympics; held four world records in hurdles; received first USC women's scholarship in any sport; won two hurdles national championships for Trojans; Renton HS.

Edo Vanni (1919-2007) – outfielder, coach, and general manager for Rainiers and Angels (1938-41, 1946-48, 1950, 1964); season-ticket sales manager for Pilots (1969); UW freshman football player (1938); Queen Anne HS.

Krista Vansant – volleyball player for UW (2011-2014); AVCA National Player of the Year (2013, 2014); Honda National Player of the Year (2013, 2014); AVCA first-team All-America selection (2013, 2014); Pac-12 Player of the Year (2013, 2014).

George Varnell (1882-1967) – sports editor and sports columnist for *Seattle Times* (1925-67); sportswriter for *Spokane Chronicle*; college football official; basketball coach for Gonzaga; competed in 200- and 400-meter hurdles in 1904 St. Louis Olympics; played football for University of Chicago and coach Amos Alonzo Stagg.

Ed Viesturs – mountain climber reached summit of Mount Everest seven times from 1990 to 2009; first American climber to summit all 14 world mountains of 8,000 meters or more, and one of five without oxygen; UW.

Omar Vizquel – shortstop for Mariners (1989-93), White Sox, Indians, Giants and Rangers.

Zollie Volchok (1916-2012) – general

manager and president of Sonics (1977-83) and vice president (1969-77); NBA championship (1979); NBA Executive of the Year (1983).

W

Bobby Wagner – linebacker for Seattle Seahawks (2012-to date); Seahawks Pro Bowl (2014); Super Bowl XLVIII starter (2014), Super Bowl XLIX starter (2015).

Tom Wagner – manager for Pay'n Pak and Peterbilt Western fast-pitch softball teams (1979-88); managed five national championship teams (1980, 1982, 1985, 1986, 1987); ASA Hall of Fame inductee.

Joyce Walker – shooting guard played for Harlem Globetrotters; two-time All-America selection and all-time leading scorer with 2,906 points at LSU; Garfield HS coach and player.

Wally Walker – forward for Sonics (1978-82), Rockets and Trail Blazers; Sonics NBA championship team reserve (1978); president and general manager for Sonics (1994-2005).

Bob Walsh – sports promoter brought Goodwill Games (1990) and Final Four (1984, 1989, 1995) to Seattle; assistant general manager for Sonics; sports agent.

Curt Warner – running back for Seahawks (1983, 1985-89); Pro Bowl selections (1983, 1986, 1987); Ring of Honor inductee (1994); knee injury curtailed career; owned Vancouver, Wash., car dealership.

Chris Warren – running back for Seahawks (1990-97), Cowboys and Eagles; Seahawks Pro Bowl selections (1993, 1994, 1995).

Emmett Watson (1918-2001) – columnist for *Seattle Post-Intelligencer* (1956-82) and *Seattle Times* (1982-2001); UW; Franklin HS;

catcher for Rainiers (1943).

Donald "Slick" Watts – point guard for Sonics (1974-78), Rockets and Jazz; known for catchy nickname and trademark shaved pate and headband.

Mary Wayte – swimmer won gold medals in 200-meter freestyle and 4x100 meter freestyle relay in 1984 Los Angeles Olympics; won silver in 4x100-meter medley relay and bronze in 4x100-meter freestyle relay in 1988 Seoul Olympics; University of Florida; Mercer Island HS.

Martell Webster – swingman for Trail Blazers, Timberwolves and Wizards; among last class of high school players to go directly to pros; Seattle Prep HS.

Marvin Webster (1952-2009) – forward and center for Sonics (1978), Nuggets, Bucks, Knicks and ABA's Nuggets; nicknamed "the Human Eraser."

Arnie Weinmeister

Arnie Weinmeister (1923-2000) – lineman for NFL's New York Yankees and New York Giants; Pro Football Hall of Fame inductee; four-time Pro Bowl selection; UW (1942, 1946-47); player-coach for CFL's B.C. Lions; served as International Brotherhood of Teamsters president.

Bob Weiss – guard for Sonics (1968), Braves, Bulls, Bucks, 76ers and Bullets; coach for Sonics (2006), Hawks, Clippers and Spurs.

Rob Weller – yell leader at UW (1970-72); credited with creating "the Wave" at Husky Stadium (1981); original host of "Entertainment Tonight."

Christian Welp (1964-2015) – center for Warriors, 76ers and Spurs; UW (1984-87); NCAA Tournament (1984, 1985, 1986); all-time leading scorer with 2,073 points for Huskies; Pac-10 Player of the Year (1987); competed in 1984 Los Angeles Olympics for Germany.

Rick Welts – president and CEO for Warriors and Suns; Sonics ball boy and public relations director; publicly revealed he was gay; UW; Queen Anne HS.

Paul Westphal – guard for Sonics (1981), Celtics, Knicks and Suns; Sonics All-Star selection (1981); coach for Sonics (1999-2001), Suns and Kings.

Sammy White (1928-1991) – catcher for Red Sox, Braves and Phillies; one-time All-Star selection; played for Rainiers (1949); UW basketball and baseball player (1947-49); NCAA Tournament (1948); rejected contract offers from NBA's Minneapolis Lakers and Washington Capitols; Lincoln HS.

Bob Whitsitt – general manager of Sonics (1986-94) and Trail Blazers; president and general manager for Seahawks (1997-2005); NBA Executive of the Year (1994).

Charlie Williams – guard for ABA's Pittsburgh Pipers, Pittsburgh Condors, Minnesota Pipers, Memphis Tams and Utah Stars; 1968 ABA championship; two-time ABA All-Star selection; Seattle U (1963-65); NCAA Tournaments (1963, 1964); involved in 1965 point-shaving scandal and banned from NBA.

Clancy Williams (1942-1986) – defensive back for Rams; WSU; first-team *AP* All-America selection; Renton HS; died from cancer.

Curtis Williams (1978-2002) – defensive back for UW (1998-2000); left paralyzed after helmet-to-helmet hit in game at Stanford (2000); died from complications 20 months later.

Dave Williams – wide receiver and original player signed by Seahawks (1976) but released because of knee injury; played for Steelers, Cardinals and Chargers; UW (1964-66).

Dick Williams (1929-2011) – manager for Mariners (1986-88), Red Sox, Angels, Expos, A's and Padres; Baseball Hall of Fame inductee.

Greg Williams – forward for Seattle U (1971-73); scored 52 points in final college game against UNLV (1973).

Gus Williams – shooting guard for Sonics (1978-80, 1982-84), Hawks, Warriors and Bullets; Sonics NBA championship team starter (1979); Sonics All-Star selections (1982, 1983); jersey No. 1 retired by Sonics; nicknamed "The Wizard."

John L. Williams – fullback for Seahawks (1986-93) and Steelers; Seahawks Pro Bowl selections (1990, 1991).

Reggie Williams – wide receiver for Jaguars; drug arrests curtailed pro career; UW (2001-03); first-team *AP* All-America selection

(2002); Huskies' all-time leading receiver with 243 catches.

Tyrone Willingham – football coach for UW (2005-08), Stanford and Notre Dame; fired by Huskies after 0-12 season (2008), worst in school history;

Maury Wills – manager for Mariners manager (1981); unsuccessful managerial candidate for Pilots (1969); second baseman and shortstop for Rainiers (1957); infielder for Dodgers, Pirates and Expos.

Dan Wilson – catcher for Mariners (1994-2005) and Reds; Mariners All-Star selection (1996).

Marc Wilson – quarterback for Patriots and Raiders; Super Bowl XV, Super Bowl XVII, BYU; first-team *AP* All-America; threw seven touchdown passes in game; Shorecrest HS.

Fred "Tex" Winter – basketball coach for UW (1968-71), Kansas State, Long Beach State, Marquette and Northwestern; coach for NBA's Houston Rockets.

Grant Wistrom – defensive lineman for Seahawks (2004-06) and Rams; Super Bowl XL starter (2006).

Bud Withers – sportswriter for *Seattle Times* (1999-2015), *Seattle Post-Intelligencer,* (1987-1999); *Eugene Register-Guard*; author of *Bravehearts: The Against-All-Odds Rise of Gonzaga Basketball.*

Al Worley – defensive back for UW (1966-68); first-team *AP* All-America selection (1968); intercepted NCAA record 14 passes in season (1968).

Bill Wright – first African-American golfer to win USGA championship – U.S. Amateur Public Links (1959); WWU; 1960 NAIA national champion; Franklin HS.

Clyde Wright – pitcher for Seattle Angels (1967); pitched for Angels, Brewers and Rangers.

Y

Charle Young – tight end for Seahawks (1983-85), Rams, Eagles and 49ers.

Fredd Young – linebacker for Seahawks (1984-87) and Colts; Seahawks Pro Bowl selections (1984, 1985, 1986, 1987).

Matt Young – pitcher for Mariners (1983-86, 1990), Red Sox, Indians, Dodgers and A's; Mariners All-Star selection (1983).

Z

Kermit Zarley – pro golfer won PGA Tour's 1968 Kaiser International Open and 1970 Canadian Open; won once on Champions Tour; 1962 NCAA champion for Houston; West Seattle HS.

Phil Zevenbergen – forward for Spurs; UW (1986-87); NCAA Tournament (1986); SPU (1984); Edmonds CC; Woodway HS.

Hy Zimmerman (1914-1989) – sportswriter for *Seattle Times* (1953-82); specifically covered baseball for two decades, including Seattle Rainiers, Seattle Angels, Seattle Pilots and Seattle Mariners.

Richie Zisk – outfielder for Mariners (1981-83), White Sox, Pirates and Rangers.

Jim Zorn – quarterback for Seahawks (1976-84), Packers and Buccaneers; AFC Offensive Rookie of the Year (1976); Seahawks Pro Bowl selection (1978); assistant coach for Seahawks (1997-1998, 2001-2007); Ring of Honor inductee (2001); coach for Washington Redskins.

Photo Credits

Introduction

Dan Raley with the Sonics, Don James and Bob Houbregs, all courtesy of Dan Raley.

Roaring Twenties to World War II

Page 1: Dugdale Park, Dave Eskenazi collection; 2, 3: George Wilson, Eskenazi collection; 5, 6: Helene Madison, Eskenazi collection; 8, 9: Royal Brougham, Eskenazi collection; 11, 12, 12, 13: UW crew, Adolf Hitler, crew race, National Archives photo and courtesy of Dan Raley; 15, 16: Al Hostak, Eskenazi collection; 18, 19: Jeff Heath, Eskenazi collection; 21, 22: Ernie Steele, Pacific Trading Card Co. and Eskenazi collection; 24: Chuck Gilmur, Eskenazi collection.

Fabulous Fifties

Page 27: Sicks' Stadium, Eskenazi collection; 28, 29: Hugh McElhenny, courtesy of Seattle Post-Intelligencer and Eskenazi collection; 32, 33: Don Heinrich, Eskenazi collection; 35, 36, 37: Fred Hutchinson, Eskenazi collection; 38, 39, 40: Kid Matthews, Eskenazi collection and courtesy of P-I; 41, 42: Tippy Dye, Eskenazi collection; 43, 44, 45: Bob Houbregs, Eskenazi collection; 46, 47: Johnny and Eddie O'Brien, Eskenazi collection; 49, 50: Guyle Fielder, Eskenazi collection; 52, 53, 54: Keith

Jackson, courtesy of P-I and courtesy of KOMO-TV; 55: George Bayer, courtesy of P-I; 57: John Cherberg, courtesy of P-I; 60, 61: Bill Muncey, Eskenazi collection and courtesy of P-I; 63, 64: Ruth Jessen, courtesy of PNGA and P-I; 66, 67: Elgin Baylor, Eskenazi collection and courtesy of P-I; 69, 70, 71: John Castellani, courtesy P-I, P-I and Seattle University; 72, 73: Jim Owens, Eskenazi collection; 75, 76: Ron Santo, Eskenazi collection; 78, 79, 80, Anne Quast, Sports Illustrated and courtesy of PNGA; 81, 82: JoAnne Carner, courtesy of PNGA.

A Sixties Upgrade

Page 85: Husky Stadium, Eskenazi collection; 86, 87, 88: Bob Schloredt, Eskenazi collection; 89, 90: George Fleming, Eskenazi collection and courtesy of P-I; 92, 93: Ben Davidson, Eskenazi collection; 95, 96: Eddie Miles, Eskenazi collection; 98, 99: John Tresvant, Eskenazi collection; 101, 103: Jim Whittaker, courtesy of P-I; 104: Phil Shinnick, courtesy of P-I; Brian Sternberg, Eskenazi collection; 107, 108: Junior Coffey, Eskenazi collection and courtesy of P-I; 110: Peller Phillips, Eskenazi collection; 113, 114: Tom Workman, Eskenazi collection; 116, 117: Donnie Moore, Eskenazi collection and courtesy of P-I; 119, 120: Charlie Greene, Eskenazi collection and courtesy of P-I; 121, 122: Doris Heritage, courtesy of P-I; 123, 125: Dick Vertlieb,

Eskenazi collection; 126, 127: J Michael Kenyon, photo courtesy of Kenyon and P-I; 129, Walter Schoenfeld, courtesy of P-I; 131, 132: Max and Dewey Soriano, Eskenazi collection and courtesy of P-I; 134, 135: Lou Piniella, Eskenazi collection and courtesy of P-I; 137: Jim Bouton, Eskenazi collection; 140: Harvey Blanks, Eskenazi collection.

Seductive Seventies

Page 143: Seattle Center Coliseum, Eskenazi collection; 144, 146: Sonny Sixkiller, courtesy of P-I and Eskenazi collection; 147: Larry Owings, Eskenazi collection; 149: Tom Gorman, courtesy of P-I; 151, 152: Boone Kirkman, Eskenazi collection and courtesy of P-I; 154, 155: Spencer Haywood, courtesy of P-I; 157: Billy North, Eskenazi collection; 160, 161, 162: Fred Brown, Eskenazi collection; 163: George Jugum, courtesy of P-I; 166: Vince Abbey, Eskenazi collection; 168, 169: Don Coryell, courtesy of San Diego Chargers; 170: Terry Metcalf, Eskenazi collection; 173, 174: Dave Kopay, Eskenazi collection and courtesy of P-I; 176, 177: Herman Sarkowsky, courtesy of P-I; 179: Steve Largent, courtesy of P-I; 182: Don James, courtesy of P-I; 185, 187: Warren Moon, Eskenazi collection and courtesy of P-I; 188, 189: Spider Gaines, Eskenazi collection; 191, 192, 192: Jack Thompson, courtesy of Washington State University; 194, 195: Dave Niehaus, Eskenazi

collection; 197, 198: Lenny Wilkens, Eskenazi collection and courtesy of P-I; 200, 202: Jack Sikma, courtesy of P-I and Eskenazi collection; 203, 204, 205: Bob Blackburn, courtesy of Bob Blackburn Jr.

Eighties and Nineties

Page 207: Safeco Field, Anni Shelley photo; 208, 209: Dave Krieg, courtesy of Seattle Seahawks; 211, 212: Marv Harshman, courtesy of P-I and Eskenazi collection; 214: George Irvine, courtesy of Detroit Pistons; 216: Curt Marsh, courtesy of Oakland Raiders; 219, 220: James Edwards, courtesy of P-I; 222: Reggie Rogers, courtesy of MOHAI; 225: Rick Fenney, courtesy of Minnesota Vikings; 238,239: Mike Utley, courtesy of P-I and WSU athletics; 231: Steve Emtman, courtesy of P-I; 234, 235: Billy Joe Hobert, courtesy of P-I; 237, 238: Michelle Akers, U.S. Soccer; 240, 241: Fred Couples, courtesy of PGA Tour, Couples event; 243, 243, 243, 244, 245, 246, Ken Griffey Jr., Randy Johnson, Alex Rodriguez, courtesy of P-I; 248: Gary Payton, courtesy of P-I, and Shawn Kemp, Eskenazi collection; 252: Demetrius DuBose, courtesy of Tampa Bay Buccaneers; 254, 255: Edgar Martinez, courtesy of P-I.

The New Millennium

Page 257: CenturyLink Field, courtesy of Corky Trewin and the Seattle Seahawks; 258: Jason Terry, courtesy of San Antonio Spurs; 261, 262: Ichiro, courtesy of sportspressnw. com; 264, 265: Rick Neuheisel, UW trading card and MOHAI; 267, 268: Corey Dillon, courtesy of New England Patriots and *P-I*; 270, 271: Quin Snyder, courtesy of Utah Jazz and Bob Burmeister; 273: Lorenzo Romar, courtesy of *P-I*; 276: Nate and Jacque Robinson, UW schedule card and courtesy of Brian Blaisdell; 278: Robinson, courtesy of dawgman.com; 280, 281, 282: Brandon Roy, Greg Wahl-Stephens photos and courtesy of Roy family; 283: Tim Lincecum, courtesy of San Francisco Giants; 286, 287: Walter Jones, courtesy of Seattle Seahawks; 290: Alan Hinton, courtesy of Frank McDonald; 292, 293, 294: Ron Crockett, courtesy of Emerald Downs; 295, 296: Felix Hernandez, courtesy of sportspressnw.com; 298: Richard Sherman, courtesy of Seattle Seahawks; 301, 302, 303: Russell Wilson, courtesy of sportspressnw. com.

Best of the Rest

Page 305: Debbie Armstrong, courtesy of *P-I*; 306: Floyd Bannister, Eskenazi collection; 311: Rogers Hornsby, courtesy of *P-I*; 315: Jawaan Oldham, courtesy of *P-I*; 316: Rick Redman, Eskenazi collection; 316: Detlef Schrempf, courtesy of *P-I*; 318: Rebecca Twigg, courtesy of *P-I*; 319: Arnie Weinmeister, Eskenazi collection.

TOP 10 SEATTLE SPORTS MOMENTS

1. 2014 Super Bowl
   (Seahawks 43, Broncos 8)

2. 1979 NBA Championship
   (Game 5: Sonics 97, Bullets 93)

3. 1992 Rose Bowl
   (UW 34, Michigan 14)

4. 1995 ALDS Championship
   (Game 5: Mariners 6, Yankees 5)

5. 1936 Olympics rowing
   championship (UW, gold medal)

6. 1992 Masters
   (Fred Couples, green jacket)

7. 1960 Rose Bowl
   (UW 44, Wisconsin 8)

8. 2015 NFC Championship
   (Seahawks 28, Packers 22)

9. 2015 Super Bowl
   (Patriots 28, Seahawks 24)

10. 2006 Super Bowl
    (Steelers 21, Seahawks 10)

Seattle sports fans will never completely recover from "The Call." The Seahawks' ill-fated decision on Feb. 1, 2015, to throw the ball rather than run it from the 1-yard line at the end of Super Bowl XLIX in Glendale, Ariz., won't easily be dismissed or understood. It brought a shocking conclusion to a wildly played game, resulting in a goal-line interception, a 28-24 defeat to New England and bitter disappointment back home.

However, nearly a century of playing with the big boys, of reaching for ultimate sporting glory, of being put under a national and sometimes international microscope, has taught the people of Seattle to be patient and resilient. It's all part of our continual growing pains in being a big-league city. Nothing ever gets handed to us.

Yet we are well-prepared for extraordinary success now. We have some of the finest athletic facilities anywhere in the world in architecturally advanced CenturyLink Field, Safeco Field and Husky Stadium, with land set aside for a new-age pro basketball and ice arena when needed.

We have some of the most prideful fans in existence, namely those who have the No. 12 firmly attached to their businesses, homes, vehicles and wardrobes, and yet others who treat pro soccer as religion, by enthusiastically marching, standing and singing at the Sounder games. And we have some of the finest pitchers, defensive backs and midfielders who now wear a uniform.

Well into the new millennium, Seattle's sporting track record is this: We are 1-for-3 in Super Bowls, 1-for-3 in the NBA Finals, 1-for-3 in securing college football national championships, 0-for-2 in Final Fours and still waiting for a World Series, which might not take long now.

We can handle defeat because major victory has been so rare and unique and meaningful. As a sports city, we remain the perpetual underdog. But Seattle is now an established big-league town — and we have the documented history right here to prove it. ❖